The **Rough Guide** to

Southwest USA

written and researched by

Greg Ward

www.roughguides.com

Contents

Pueblo peoples color
section following p.216

Camera! Drive! Action!
color section following
p.440

◀◀ Monument Valley ◀ South Kaibab Trail, Grand Canyon

Introduction to

Southwest USA

The Southwest is the most extraordinary and spectacular region of the United States. The splendor and scale of its scenery consistently defies belief – a glorious panoply of cliffs and canyons, buttes and mesas, carved from rocks of every imaginable color, and enriched here by groves of shimmering cottonwoods and aspens, there by cactuses and agaves. In addition, the Southwest is unique in being the only part of the United States whose original inhabitants remain in residence. Though century after century has brought fresh waves of intruders, somehow none has entirely succeeded in displacing its predecessors, leaving the various groups to coexist in an intriguing blend of cultures and traditions.

 The area covered by this book roughly corresponds to the former Spanish colony of **New Mexico**, which has belonged to the US for little more than 160 years, and is now divided between the modern states of New Mexico, Arizona, Utah, Colorado, and Nevada. Though rainfall is scarce everywhere, it's not all **desert**; indeed, the popular image of the Southwest as consisting of scrubby hillsides studded with many-armed saguaro cactuses is true only of the Sonoran Desert of southern Arizona. Towering snowcapped **mountains** rise not only in southern Colorado and northern New Mexico, at the tail-end of the Rockies, but are scattered across Utah and Arizona as well, while dense **pine forests** cloak much of northern Arizona.

Where to go

The most dramatic landscapes lie on the **Colorado Plateau**, an arid mile-high tableland, roughly the size of California, which extends across the **Four Corners** region of Arizona, Utah, Colorado, and New Mexico. Atop the main body of the plateau, further layers of rock are piled level upon level, creating a "**Grand Staircase**" of successive cliffs and plateaus. During the last dozen or so million years, the entire complex has been pushed steadily upwards by subterranean forces. As it has risen, the earth has cracked, warped, buckled, and split, and endless quantities of crumbling sandstone have been washed away by the Colorado River and its tributaries. The **Grand Canyon** is simply the most famous

Fact file

• **New Mexico** – the fifth largest state – covers 121,355 square miles and holds a population of 1,954,599, just under ten percent of whom are of Native American descent. The state has 22 reservations, comprising 19 separate pueblos plus the Jicarilla and Mescalero Apache lands and part of the Navajo Nation. New Mexico became the 47th state on January 6, 1912; its capital is Santa Fe.

• **Arizona**, with an area of 113,635 square miles, is the sixth largest state. Around five percent of its 6,166,318 population are of native American descent; its 21 Indian reservations include the homelands of the Navajo, the Hopi, the Havasupai, the Hualapai, the 'O'odham, and the San Carlos, Tonto, and White Mountain Apache. With Phoenix as its capital, it achieved statehood in 1912, as the last of the "lower 48."

• Although **Utah** as a whole comprises 82,144 square miles – 65 percent of which is owned by the federal government – and has a population of 2,550,063, this book only covers the desert areas in the south of the state, where around 170,000 people are spread across 27,000 square miles. It became the 45th state in 1896; over 60 percent of Utahns are Mormons.

• The portion of southwest **Colorado** described in this book represents about 5000 of the state's 103,730 square miles, and holds about 126,000 of its total population of 4,753,377. Colorado was the 38th state to join the Union in 1876.

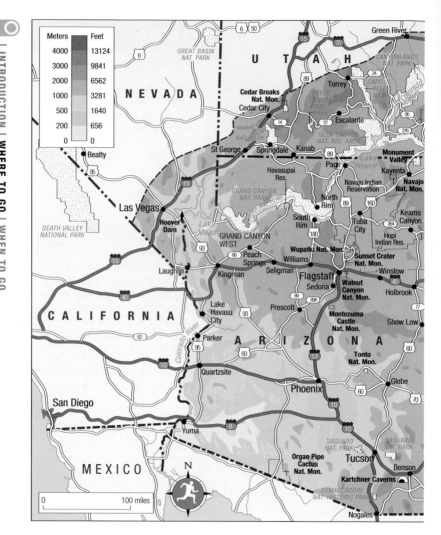

of hundreds of dramatic **canyons**, and can seem too vast for the human mind to comprehend. No one, however, could fail to be overwhelmed by the sheer weirdness of **southern Utah** – the red rocks of **Monument Valley**, the fiery sandstone pinnacles of **Bryce Canyon**, the endless expanses of **Canyonlands**.

Reminders of the Southwest's remarkable **history** are everywhere you look. Ancient archeological sites abound, ranging from the free-standing pueblos of Chaco Canyon and the cliff dwellings of Mesa Verde to the artificial caves of Bandelier and the haunting rock art of Horseshoe Canyon,

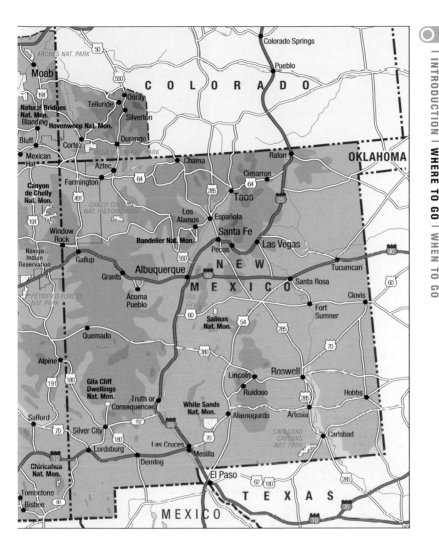

while the flourishing **Navajo** and **Apache** lands are merely the largest of around fifty modern-day Indian reservations. The **Spanish** too have been here for almost five hundred years; exquisite eighteenth-century missions survive at San Xavier and Tumacácori in southern Arizona, while northern New Mexico holds stunning adobe churches such as San Francisco de Asis at Taos, and the humbler but still ravishing shrine at Chimayó. Next to arrive after the Spaniards were the **Mormons**, who through utter determination and communal effort colonized Utah in the nineteenth century. **American** settlers arrived soon after, and swiftly outnumbered everyone else.

In the early years of US rule, the Southwest was very much the **Wild West**. A sense of that era survives in towns like **Lincoln**, New Mexico, where Billy the Kid blazed his way out of jail, and **Tombstone**, Arizona, where the Earps and the Clantons fought it out at the OK Corral. The century since Utah, Arizona, and New Mexico achieved statehood has seen the landscape transformed on an unprecedented – not to say unnatural, let alone unsustainable – scale. Monumental **water** projects, including the construction of the **Hoover Dam**, the damming of Utah's Glen Canyon to form **Lake**

◀ Antelope Canyon

Powell, and the creation of a network of canals across hundreds of miles of the Arizona desert, have brought the region prosperity as the **Sunbelt**.

While the wilderness remains the supreme attraction for most visitors, certain Southwestern **cities** make worthwhile destinations. **Santa Fe** is the best example, with its four-hundred-year history, top-quality museums and galleries, and superb hotels and restaurants; **Tucson** holds an enjoyable combination of desert parks, Hispanic history, restaurants, and ranch resorts; and **Las Vegas**, entirely and quintessentially a product of the modern era – it was only founded in 1905 – is far too amazing to miss. **Phoenix**, on the

▲ Chile peppers, Santa Fe

Route 66

If you do ever plan to motor west, there's still one definitive highway that's the best. Eighty years since it was first completed, seventy since John Steinbeck called it **"the mother road, the road of flight"** in *The Grapes of Wrath*, and sixty since songwriter

▲ Wigwam Motel, Holbrook, Arizona

Bobby Troup set it all down in rhyme, what better reason to visit the Southwest could there be than to get hip to this timely tip, and get your kicks on **Route 66**?

The heyday of Route 66 as the nation's premier cross-country route – winding from Chicago to LA – lasted barely twenty years, from its being paved in 1937 until it began to be superseded by freeways in 1957. It was officially rendered defunct in 1984, when Williams, Arizona, became the last town to be bypassed. Nonetheless, substantial stretches of the original Route 66 survive, complete with the motels and drive-ins that became icons of vernacular American architecture. Restored 1950s roadsters and the latest Harley Davisons alike flock to cruise along the atmospheric, neon-lit frontages of towns such as Albuquerque and Flagstaff, or through such empty desertscapes as those between Grants and Gallup in New Mexico, or Seligman and Kingman in Arizona.

other hand, is one to avoid; it's possible to have a good time there, but you'd have to have a *very* long vacation before there'd be much point including it on your itinerary.

Though most of the region's **smaller towns** are best treated as overnight pit-stops, some have blossomed into appealing bases for a few days' stay. **Moab** and **Springdale** make welcome exceptions to the typical monotony of southern Utah farming communities; the college town of **Flagstaff** is a lively enclave within easy reach of the Grand Canyon; and **Taos** still has the feel of the artists' colony that attracted Georgia O'Keeffe and D.H. Lawrence.

The only practicable way to explore the Southwest in any detail is to **drive** yourself around; the very limited public transport options are outlined on p.31. However long your vacation may be, aim to spend most of your time on the Colorado Plateau, seeing as much as possible of the Four Corners region and southern Utah.

Native Americans

Although the terrain may appear inhospitable in the extreme, the Southwest has been home to **Native Americans** for over ten thousand years. The fifty distinct reservations in the region today range from tiny **pueblo** villages in New Mexico to the huge "**Navajo Nation**," the largest in the US, which covers 27,000 square miles and takes up much of the Colorado Plateau. Most tribes continue to occupy the homelands of their ancestors, as opposed to the pattern elsewhere in the US, where Native Americans were forcibly displaced onto poorer lands with which they lack any spiritual connection.

Nonetheless, considerable bitterness still surrounds the allocation of reservations. The Navajo themselves only arrived in the Southwest shortly before the Spaniards, for example, and encroached upon the Hopi, so the fact that their reservation now surrounds and constricts that of the Hopi remains a source of ongoing contention. What's more, US law dictates that reservations can only consist of lands where a single tribe can prove it had exclusive use, so traditionally shared hunting grounds were excluded from the reservations and left open to exploitation by Anglo settlers.

▼ The dome of City Hall, Tucson

Your exact itinerary will depend largely on which city serves as your starting point. In **one week**, you could fly into **Las Vegas**, and loop around the Colorado River to Grand Canyon, Zion, and possibly Bryce Canyon national parks; into **Phoenix**, to reach Canyon de Chelly, Monument Valley, and the Grand Canyon; into **Albuquerque**, and see Santa Fe, Taos, and Ácoma Pueblo; or into **Salt Lake City**, and make a lightning tour of all southern Utah's national parks.

With **two weeks**, you can extend any of the above itineraries to cover most of the Colorado Plateau, making sure you get to Canyon de Chelly, Monument Valley, and Mesa Verde. Only if you have **three weeks** or more are you likely to detour south into southern New Mexico or southern Arizona, while adding any large-scale backpacking expeditions – for example into the stunning Havasupai Indian Reservation, or down to Phantom Ranch in the Grand Canyon – will curtail the amount of ground you can cover overall.

When to go

Summer is the peak tourist season for most of the Southwest, even though temperatures in excess of 100°F render cities such as Phoenix and Tucson all but unbearable, and make it an ordeal even to get out of your car in many of the national parks. Hikers, bikers, and rafters do better to come either between mid-September and late October, when the crowds are gone and dazzling fall colors brighten the canyons, or in April and May, when wildflowers bloom in the desert.

▲ Muley Point, Utah

◄ Skulls for sale, Santa Fe

If your timings aren't flexible, however, don't worry. It's always possible to escape the heat – the thermometer drops by 3°F for every thousand feet above sea level, so Santa Fe, for example, is always relatively cool – and the summer is also peak period for the region's festivals, as detailed on p.40.

Winters can be seriously cold, and snowfalls close down certain areas altogether – don't reckon on seeing Mesa Verde, or the North Rim of the Grand Canyon, between October and April. Those parks that remain open are often at their most beautiful when frosted with snow, however – Bryce

◄ Fall, the San Juan highway

Canyon is quite magical – while ski resorts like Telluride and Taos are in full swing, and Tucson and Phoenix fill up with sun-seeking "snowbirds" from colder states. The major disadvantage of visiting in winter is that with significantly fewer hours of daylight, it's much harder for example to drive from your overnight base into a national park, do any great amount of touring or hiking, and then drive on to your next stop.

Average temperature and rainfall

	Jan	Feb	Mar	Apr	May	Jun	Jul	Aug	Sep	Oct	Nov	Dec
Grand Canyon (South Rim)												
Av high °F	41	45	51	60	70	81	84	82	76	65	52	43
Av low °F	18	21	25	32	39	47	54	53	47	36	27	20
Rainfall (in)	1.3	1.5	1.4	0.9	0.7	0.4	1.8	2.3	1.6	1.1	0.9	1.6
Las Vegas, NV												
Av high °F	56	67	68	77	87	98	104	101	94	81	66	57
Av low °F	33	37	42	49	59	68	75	73	65	53	41	33
Rainfall (in)	0.5	0.5	0.4	0.2	0.2	0.1	0.5	0.5	0.3	0.3	0.4	0.3
Phoenix, AZ												
Av high °F	65	69	75	84	93	102	105	102	98	88	75	66
Av low °F	38	41	45	52	60	68	78	76	69	57	45	39
Rainfall (in)	0.8	0.8	0.8	0.5	0.3	0.3	0.7	0.9	0.6	0.6	0.6	0.8
Salt Lake City, UT												
Av high °F	37	43	51	61	72	83	93	90	80	66	50	38
Av low °F	20	27	30	37	45	53	62	60	50	39	29	22
Rainfall (in)	1.4	1.3	1.7	2.2	1.5	1.0	0.7	0.9	0.9	1.1	1.2	1.4
Santa Fe, NM												
Av high °F	40	44	51	60	69	79	82	80	74	63	50	41
Av low °F	19	22	28	35	43	52	57	56	49	38	27	20
Rainfall (in)	0.6	0.8	0.8	0.9	1.2	1.1	2.4	2.3	1.7	1.1	0.7	0.7
Tucson, AZ												
Av high °F	64	67	71	80	89	99	99	96	94	84	72	65
Av low °F	38	40	44	50	58	67	74	72	67	57	45	39
Rainfall (in)	0.8	0.8	0.7	0.3	0.1	0.2	2.4	2.1	1.3	0.9	0.6	0.9
Zion National Park, UT												
Av high °F	52	57	63	73	83	93	100	97	91	78	63	53
Av low °F	20	01	30	43	52	60	68	66	60	49	37	30
Rainfall (in)	1.6	1.6	1.7	1.3	0.7	0.6	0.8	1.6	0.8	1.0	1.2	1.5

29

things not to miss

It's not possible to see everything that the Southwest has to offer in one trip – and we don't suggest you try. What follows is a selective taste of the region's highlights: spectacular national parks, unforgettable outdoor activities, Wild West towns, and Las Vegas glitz. They're arranged in five color-coded categories to help you find the very best things to see, do, and experience. All entries have a page reference to take you straight into the guide, where you can find out more.

01 Monument Valley Page **65** • You may have seen them a thousand times in the movies, but your first real-life glimpse of the silhouetted buttes of Monument Valley is a guaranteed heart-stopping moment.

02 **Rafting in Canyonlands** Page **458** • Whether you choose a gentle float or a multi-day whitewater epic, Canyonlands National Park makes a fabulous destination for a raft trip.

03 **The Great Gallery** Page **441** • The most fascinating and mysterious ancient rock art in the Southwest, only accessible via a long desert hike into a remote region of Utah's Canyonlands.

04 **The buffets of Las Vegas** Page **485** • Las Vegas' all you-can-eat buffets have long been a byword for value; these days the food itself can be great too.

05 **Lincoln** Page **196** • The town that witnessed some of Billy the Kid's most legendary exploits still feels like a lonesome frontier outpost.

06 **Albuquerque International Balloon Festival** Page **185** •
The early-morning mass ascents of hundreds of colorful hot-air balloons during Albuquerque's October showcase are an utterly breathtaking sight.

07 **Zion Canyon** Page **373** • Carved by the Virgin River into the red-rock hills of southern Utah, Zion makes a lovely escape from the mayhem of Las Vegas.

08 **Las Vegas at night** Page **478** • The blazing neon along the Strip, with its volcanoes and pyramids, is an all-out assault on the senses.

09 **La Fonda de Santa Fe** Page **121** • Historic Western hotels don't come any more atmospheric than this beauty at the end of the Santa Fe Trail.

10 **Hiking in the Grand Canyon** Page **359** • Explore the innermost secrets of the Grand Canyon on one of its many superb hiking trails.

11 **Calf Creek Falls** Page **411** • Not far off the highway in the heart of southern Utah, this glorious waterfall is the highlight of Grand Staircase-Escalante National Monument.

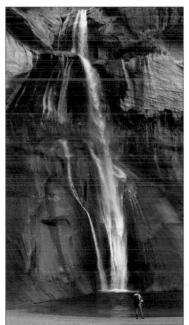

12 **Toroweap Point** Page **361** • At times the Grand Canyon can seem too vast to comprehend, but this unique canyon overlook, above a 3000-foot drop to the river, has an immediate visceral impact.

13 **Ácoma Pueblo** Page **110** • The Acomans defied the Spaniards from this stunning cliff-top village five centuries ago, and they're still here.

15 **Havasu Falls** Page **348** • These lush turquoise waterfalls turn the Havasupai Reservation into an amazing Grand Canyon oasis.

14 **The Inter-Tribal Indian Ceremonial** Page **105** • The classic Route 66 town of Gallup, New Mexico, comes alive in August for this annual Navajo fair.

16 **White Sands National Monument** Page **202** • This dazzling sandscape of knife-edge snow-white dunes amply rewards the long drive across southern New Mexico.

17 **Tombstone** Page **260** • With hourly Wild West shoot-outs on the streets outside the OK Corral, Tombstone loves to ham up its past, but it's great fun to visit.

18 **Saguaro National Park** Page **248** • The saguaro cactuses, spreading in majestic abundance through the deserts of southern Arizona, are one of the quintessential symbols of the Southwest.

19 Ride the Durango & Silverton Railroad Page **92** • Taking a steam train up to the old Colorado mining town of Silverton is the perfect way to spend a day in the Rockies.

20 Mesa Verde Page **86** • If you've never understood all the fuss about "cliff dwellings," the ancient remains hidden in these Colorado canyons should make their appeal abundantly clear.

21 **Bryce Canyon** Page **393** • An utterly unforgettable landscape, where the earth peels back to reveal a rainbow-hued forest of towering sandstone pinnacles.

22 **Taos Pueblo** Page **167** • The most famous of the modern pueblos still makes a dramatic sight at the foot of the Sangre de Cristo mountains.

23 **A mule ride to Phantom Ranch** Page **326** • Generations of Grand Canyon visitors have entrusted their lives to these sure-footed beasts; the reward, a night beside the river at historic Phantom Ranch.

25 **La Posada** Page **283** • This enormous, rambling and irresistible former railroad hotel, now lovingly restored, is an unexpected gem in the Route 66 outpost of Winslow.

24 **Native American crafts** Page **44** • From silver and turquoise jewelry to Hopi kachinas or fine Pueblo ceramics, the Southwest is renowned for its locally produced craft works and souvenirs.

26 **San Xavier del Bac Mission** Page **252** • Churches throughout the Southwest bear witness to the region's Hispanic heritage, but none is more exquisite than the "White Dove of the Desert" outside Tucson.

27 Canyon de Chelly Page **68** • Perhaps the most beautiful canyon in the Southwest, rendered all the more magical by its magnificent Ancestral Puebloan ruins.

28 Cirque de Soleil
Page **489** • Staging several of the finest shows the city has to offer, the Canadian circus troupe has transformed Las Vegas' entertainment scene.

29 Delicate Arch Page **450** • The trail up to the state symbol, an extraordinary free-standing natural arch, epitomizes the wonder of Utah's wilderness parks.

Basics

Basics

Getting there

For US and Canadian travelers who live too far from the Southwest simply to drive there, and for international travelers, the most cost-effective way to visit Southwest USA is to fly to one of three major cities covered in this book, rent a car, make a loop tour, and fly home from the same airport.

Las Vegas, Nevada, is probably the best bet, as it offers low air fares and rental-car rates, welcomes more direct flights from overseas than its rivals, and makes an exhilarating starting point for tours to the Grand Canyon and the national parks of southern Utah. Phoenix, Arizona, is equally well served by the major domestic carriers, and although Phoenix itself is a less appealing destination it's convenient for both the Grand Canyon and the deserts of southern Arizona. New Mexico's principal airport, in Albuquerque, receives fewer long-distance flights, but it's the obvious point of arrival if you want to see Santa Fe and Taos, and it's also the closest airport to the Four Corners region.

If Utah is your prime destination, you could also fly to Salt Lake City. Although the state capital lies in Utah's mountainous northwest corner, outside the area covered in this guide, it's little more than half a day's drive from lively Moab and national parks such as Canyonlands and Arches.

Flights from North America

Flights to the Southwest are at their most expensive in summer, which despite soaring temperatures is the peak season for travel. Prices drop from September to shortly before Christmas, and from March through May, and are cheapest from January to February. Flying on weekends, to Las Vegas in particular, can add a hefty premium to fares; price ranges quoted below assume midweek travel.

In general, the best bargains tend to be on flights to Las Vegas. It's usually possible to find round-trip fares to Las Vegas for little more than $100 from Los Angeles, $250 from Seattle, $350 from New York, and and

CAN$350 from Toronto. A round-trip from New York to Phoenix should also cost from $350; equivalent figures for Chicago might be $250–300, and for Los Angeles, less than $150. Sample fares from Montréal to Phoenix start from CAN$600, and from Vancouver CAN$350. Fares to Albuquerque are similar, with a round-trip from New York or Chicago costing upwards from $250; a round-trip between New York and Salt Lake City can also cost from $250, or again from CAN$500 from Toronto. A good first call is to contact Southwest Airlines, which travels to Phoenix, Las Vegas, Tucson, Salt Lake City, and Albuquerque from around fifty other US cities.

Commuter airlines like Skywest, Mesa Air, and Great Lakes Aviation connect the Southwest's major airports with smaller communities in the region. Thus several airlines link Phoenix with towns such as Durango, Flagstaff, Lake Havasu City, Telluride, Tucson, and Yuma; Albuquerque has connections to Carlsbad, Durango, Farmington, Roswell, and Silver City; and Salt Lake City is connected with airports in southern Utah such as St George. Las Vegas also has good connections, including direct flights to (and over) the Grand Canyon; operators are detailed on p.325.

Few of these flights are particularly suited to the needs of tourists, however. The cheapest fares tend to be on the scale of $75–150 for a one-way trip, and it's far easier to drive from place to place than to have to rent another car every few days. If you need to get somewhere that only has a minor airport, your best bet is to fly to the Southwest with a specialist regional carrier that will also provide a connecting service to your ultimate destination for a small additional cost.

Flights from the UK and Ireland

There are only two direct, nonstop flights from Britain or Ireland to any of the cities covered in this book: British Airways flies from London Heathrow to Phoenix daily except Wednesdays (all year) and Mondays (in winter), while Virgin Atlantic flies daily from London Gatwick to Las Vegas. Typical round-trip fares range from around £365 in winter up to more like £600 in summer.

Most other transatlantic carriers can get you to Phoenix, Las Vegas, or Albuquerque for similar or slightly lower fares, but all require at least one stop en route. From the UK, you can either fly nonstop to the West Coast and then double back toward the Southwest, or touch down on the East Coast and then fly west; time-wise, it makes little difference. If you'd rather keep your flying time to a minimum, it's also worth considering flying nonstop to California and driving to the Southwest from there, taking advantage of the state's low rental-car rates.

From Ireland, Aer Lingus flies from Dublin or Shannon to Boston, Chicago, New York, Orlando, and Washington, and Delta from Dublin and Shannon to Atlanta and New York. Alternatively, you can fly to London and take your pick of transatlantic routes.

Packages

Packages can work out cheaper than arranging the same trip yourself, especially for a short-term stay. **Fly-drive** deals, which give cut-rate (sometimes free) car rental when buying a transatlantic ticket from an airline or tour operator, are always cheaper than renting on the spot and give great value if you intend to do a lot of driving. On the other hand, you'll probably have to pay more for the flight than if you booked it yourself.

Several operators go one stage further and book accommodation for **self-drive tours**; some travelers consider having their itineraries planned and booked by experts to be a real boon. Schemes under which you buy pre-paid hotel vouchers in advance, and then have to seek out hotels that will accept them, tend to be more bother than they're worth, and seldom save any money.

Companies such as TrekAmerica organize **camping tours** of the Southwest, usually starting in California or Las Vegas and circling through Utah's national parks and the Grand Canyon. Typical trips range in price – excluding flights – range from £580 for a week in low season up to around £850 in mid-summer. TrekAmerica also offer some trips that use hotel accommodation, like the six-night "Footloose Canyons & Indian Lands" tours, which starts at £657.

Flights from Australia, New Zealand, and South Africa

There are no direct flights from Australia or New Zealand or South Africa to any of the Southwestern cities, so you'll have to fly to one of the main US gateway airports and pick up onward connections – or a rental car – from there.

The cheapest route, and the one with the most frequent services from Australia and New Zealand, is to Los Angeles, which also has plenty of onward flights to Albuquerque, Las Vegas, and Phoenix. Air New Zealand and Qantas/American fly to LA at least twice daily, while United flies once a day; other airlines that serve LA include Japan Airlines and Singapore Airlines. From South Africa, by far the cheapest route is usually to fly with Virgin from Johannesburg to London, and then from London to Las Vegas, which costs in the region of 10,000SAR.

Packages and tours

Package deals available to travelers in Australia and New Zealand range from fly-drive deals to fully escorted bus tours and camping treks, and can work out significantly cheaper than making the same arrangements yourself; some of the no-frills flight and car-rental packages, for example, can cost less than a flight alone. You can also add on whatever extra tours you choose; by way of example, Adventure World offer trips from LA like the ten-day "Western Highlights" that starts at A$1684, or a seven-day jaunt to the Grand Canyon, Zion, and Las Vegas for A$1042.

Trains

Amtrak rail service to and within the Southwest is restricted to three completely

Six steps to a better kind of travel

At Rough Guides we are passionately committed to travel. We feel strongly that only through travelling do we truly come to understand the world we live in and the people we share it with – plus tourism has brought a great deal of **benefit** to developing economies around the world over the last few decades. But the extraordinary growth in tourism has also damaged some places irreparably, and of course **climate change** is exacerbated by most forms of transport, especially flying. This means that now more than ever it's important to **travel thoughtfully** and **responsibly**, with respect for the cultures you're visiting – not only to derive the most benefit from your trip but also to preserve the best bits of the planet for everyone to enjoy. At Rough Guides we feel there are six main areas in which you can make a difference:

- Consider what you're contributing to the **local economy**, and how much the services you use do the same, whether it's through employing local workers and guides or sourcing locally grown produce and local services.
- Consider the **environment** on holiday as well as at home. Water is scarce in many developing destinations, and the biodiversity of local flora and fauna can be adversely affected by tourism. Try to patronize businesses that take account of this.
- Travel with a purpose, not just to tick off experiences. Consider **spending longer** in a place, and getting to know it and its people.
- Give thought to how often you **fly**. Try to avoid short hops by air and more harmful night flights.
- Consider **alternatives to flying**, travelling instead by bus, train, boat and even by bike or on foot where possible.
- Make your trips "**climate neutral**" via a reputable carbon offset scheme. All Rough Guide flights are offset, and every year we donate money to a variety of charities devoted to combating the effects of climate change.

separate east–west routes, two of which pass through Arizona and New Mexico on the way to and from Los Angeles, while the other crosses northern Utah.

The daily **Southwest Chief** originates in Chicago and crosses from Colorado into northern New Mexico near Raton, passing close to Santa Fe (connected by a bus service from tiny Lamy) and through Albuquerque before heading west via Gallup, Flagstaff – where connecting buses run north to the Grand Canyon – and Williams, the home of the entirely distinct Grand Canyon Railway (see p.325). The thrice-weekly **Sunset Limited** from New Orleans reaches southern New Mexico via El Paso, Texas, then calls at Deming, Lordsburg, before hitting Arizona towns Benson, Tucson, and Yuma. En route between Chicago and San Francisco, the daily **California Zephyr** calls at Green River in Utah, as well as Denver and Salt Lake City.

There is no rail service to Phoenix, or to Las Vegas, which is linked by bus with Barstow, California, on the Southwest Chief route.

For fares and schedules, visit @www .amtrak.com; do not contact individual stations.

Bus

If you're happy to sit on a bus for days on end, you can reach the Southwest using Greyhound, though these days it's no cheaper than flying. A one-way trip to Albuquerque from Los Angeles takes around nineteen hours and costs $69 if booked a week in advance, or $87 on the day of travel; the ride from Milwaukee takes a day and a half and costs $134 or $167, respectively; and the two-day cross-country trek from New York costs $147 or $183.

For full details of routes and fares, and to make reservations, visit @www .greyhound.com.

Online booking agents and general travel sites

Ⓦ www.ebookers.com
Ⓦ www.expedia.com
Ⓦ www.lastminute.com
Ⓦ www.opodo.com
Ⓦ www.orbitz.com
Ⓦ www.travelocity.com
Ⓦ www.travelonline.co.za
Ⓦ www.zuji.com.au

Airlines

Aer Lingus Ⓦ www.aerlingus.com
Air Canada Ⓦ www.aircanada.com
Air New Zealand Ⓦ www.airnewzealand.com
Alaska Airlines Ⓦ www.alaskaair.com
America West Ⓦ www.usairways.com
American Airlines Ⓦ www.aa.com
British Airways Ⓦ www.britishairways.com
Continental Airlines Ⓦ www.continental.com
Delta Airlines Ⓦ www.delta.com
Frontier Airlines Ⓦ www.frontierairlines.com
Great Lakes Airlines Ⓦ www.greatlakesav.com
Hawaiian Airlines Ⓦ www.hawaiianair.com
Horizon Airlines Ⓦ www.horizonair.com
JAL (Japan Airlines) Ⓦ www.jal.com
JetBlue Ⓦ www.jetblue.com

KLM Ⓦ www.klm.com
Mesa Airlines Ⓦ www.mesa-air.com
Northwest Ⓦ www.nwa.com
Qantas Ⓦ www.qantas.com.au
Scenic Airlines Ⓦ www.scenic.com
Singapore Airlines Ⓦ www.singaporeair.com
Skywest Ⓦ www.skywest.com
Southwest Ⓦ www.southwest.com
United Airlines Ⓦ www.united.com
US Airways Ⓦ www.usairways.com
Virgin Atlantic Ⓦ www.virgin-atlantic.com
Westjet Ⓦ www.westjet.com

Agents and operators

North South Travel UK ☎ 01245/608 291, Ⓦ www.northsouthtravel.co.uk. Friendly, competitive travel agency, offering discounted fares worldwide. Profits are used to support projects in the developing world, especially the promotion of sustainable tourism.
STA Travel US ☎ 1-800/781-4040, UK ☎ 0871/2300 040, Australia ☎ 134 782, New Zealand ☎ 0800/474 400, South Africa ☎ 0861/781 781; Ⓦ www.statravel.com. Worldwide specialists in independent travel; also student IDs, travel insurance, car rental, rail passes, and more. Good discounts for students and under-26s.
Trailfinders UK ☎ 0845/058 5858, Republic of Ireland ☎ 01/677 7888, Australia ☎ 1300/780 212; Ⓦ www.trailfinders.com. One of the best-informed and most efficient agents for independent travelers.

Southwest USA tour operators

Backroads, Inc ☎ 1-800/462-2848, Ⓦ www.backroads.com. Hiking and/or biking tours covering New Mexico, Arizona, and southern Utah; a week-long trip to Zion, the Grand Canyon, and Bryce costs around $2000 if you're camping, $3000 if you stay in hotels.
Canyonlands Field Institute ☎ 435/259-7750 or 1-800/860-5262, Ⓦ www.canyonlandsfieldinst.org. NPS-authorized adult and family wilderness expeditions, not exclusively in Canyonlands; from around $1250 for a five-night hike to remote Rainbow Bridge, $1000 for a six-day canoeing and hiking trip along the Green River.
Delta Vacations Ⓦ www.deltavacations.com. Flight and hotel packages, especially to Las Vegas.
GORP Ⓦ www.gorptravel.com. The Great Outdoors Recreation Pages website carries a tantalizing collection of energetic Southwest expeditions, like a week's backpacking along Utah's Escalante River or in northern Arizona, or a week-long biking and rafting jaunt in Canyonlands, all priced at around $1800.
Grand Canyon Field Institute ☎ 928/638-2485 or 1-866/471-4435, Ⓦ www.grandcanyon.org/fieldinstitute. Park-sponsored program of hikes and

educational expeditions in the Grand Canyon; typical prices range from around $450 for a three-night hike down into the canyon to $600 for a four-night rim-to-rim backpacking trip.

Green Tortoise ☏1-800/867-8647, ⓦwww.greentortoise.com. California-based, youth-oriented bus tours; the nine-day "Canyons of the West" tour from San Francisco costs around $700 including food kitty.

Museum of Northern Arizona ☏928/774-5213, ⓦwww.mnaventures.org. The prestigious Flagstaff museum runs an extensive program of tours and excursions in the Four Corners region.

REI Adventures ☏1-800/622-2236, ⓦwww.rei.com/travel. Small-group hiking trips in Utah and Arizona; a six-night trip, with accommodation, typically costs around $1700.

Sierra Club Outings ⓦwww.sierraclub.org/outings. The environmental group offers some fabulous opportunities to come to grips with the landscapes and resources of the Southwest, such as a week in Utah's Dark Canyon or Arizona's Rainbow Plateau for $795.

Smithsonian Journeys ☏1-800/258-5885, ⓦwww.smithsonianjourneys.org. Southwest tours, using upscale hotel accommodation, such as a four-night trip to Albuquerque's Balloon Fiesta for $2595.

Southwest Ed-ventures ☏1-800/525-4456, ⓦwww.sw-adventures.org. Hiking, backpacking and rafting trips for all ages on the Colorado Plateau, with a strong educational element; five days rafting on the San Juan costs $698, five days with archeologists in Chaco Canyon $847.

Suntrek ☏1-800/786-8735, ⓦwww.suntrek.com. Three-week camping adventure tour of the Southwest, starting from San Francisco; $1600–1800.

TrekAmerica/Footloose ☏1-800/221-0596, ⓦwww.trekamerica.com or www.footloose.com. Active tours and treks for 18- to 38-year-olds, including transportation by small van, guide services, and park and attraction entrance fees. Some, like the ten-day "National Parks Walk" tour, are predominantly camping; others, such as the seven-day, "Canyons and Indian Lands" trip, use motels and lodges.

Getting around

Attempting to tour the Southwest by public transport is an extremely bad idea. While buses and planes – and trains to a much lesser extent – connect the major urban areas, the national parks and wide-open landscapes that are the region's greatest attractions simply cannot be explored without your own vehicle. Even public transport within the cities is minimal. Unless you're an *extremely* energetic cyclist, therefore, you'll need a motorbike or car.

If you can't drive, the only itinerary that makes much sense is to cross northern Arizona and northern New Mexico by bus or train, flying in or out of Albuquerque in the east or Las Vegas in the west. Obvious stops would include Flagstaff, with a side-trip by bus to the Grand Canyon, and Santa Fe, the only city small enough to be seen on foot. Phoenix and Tucson are no fun at all without a car, while what little public transport exists in southern Utah is no use for seeing the parks. Hitch-hiking is not recommended under any circumstances.

By car

To rent a car, you need to have held your license for at least one year; drivers under 25 may encounter problems and have to pay higher than normal insurance premiums.

All the major rental companies have outlets at the main regional airports. Reservations are handled centrally rather than locally, so the best way to shop around for rates is either online, or by calling their national toll-free numbers. Potential variations are endless; certain cities and states are consistently cheaper than others, while individual travelers may be eligible for corporate, frequent-flier, or

AAA discounts. In low season, you might find a tiny car (a "subcompact") for as little as $120 per week, but a typical budget rate would be more like $40 per day, and $175 per week. A car rented in Las Vegas can easily cost $100 less per week than one rented in Colorado, and prices in Arizona, New Mexico, and Utah range between the two.

Don't automatically go for the cheapest rate. Little-known local rental companies may offer appealing prices, but if you break down several hundred miles from their offices it may be hard to get assistance. Even between the major operators, there can be a big difference in the quality of cars. Always be sure to get free unlimited mileage, and remember that leaving the car in a different city from the one where you rent it can incur a drop-off charge of as much as $200.

When you rent a car, read the small print carefully for details on Collision Damage Waiver (CDW), sometimes called Liability Damage Waiver (LDW), a form of insurance that often isn't included in the initial rental charge but is well worth considering. This specifically covers the car that you are driving yourself; you are in any case insured for damage to other vehicles. At $12–20 a day, it can add substantially to the total cost, but without it you're liable for every scratch to the car – even those that aren't your fault. Some credit card companies offer automatic CDW coverage to anyone using their card; contact your issuing company for details. Your rental papers should include an emergency number to call in case of breakdown or accident; contact the rental company before you arrange, or pay, for any repairs.

The American Automobile Association, or AAA (☎1-800/222-4357, ⓦwww.aaa.com), provides free maps and assistance to its members and to members of affiliated associations overseas, such as the British AA and RAC.

Car rental companies

Alamo ⓦwww.alamo.com
Avis ⓦwww.avis.com
Budget ⓦwww.budget.com
Dollar ⓦwww.dollar.com
Enterprise ⓦwww.enterprise.com
Hertz ⓦwww.hertz.com
Holiday Autos ⓦwww.holidayautos.com
National ⓦwww.nationalcar.com
Thrifty ⓦwww.thrifty.com

Renting an RV

Recreational vehicles – RVs – can be rented at prices starting at around $600 per week (plus mileage charges) for a basic camper on the back of a pickup truck, with sleeping room for two adults. If you're looking for one of those huge juggernauts that rumble down the highway complete with multiple bedrooms, bathrooms, and kitchens, you'll have to pay significantly more. Though good for groups or families traveling together, RVs can be unwieldy on the road, and as people tend to own their own, rental outlets are not as common as you might expect. On top of rental fees, you'll also have to take into account the cost of gas (some RVs do twelve miles to the gallon or less) and any drop-off charges. It's rarely legal simply to pull up in an RV and spend the night at the roadside; you are expected to stay in designated parks that cost $20–30 per night.

The Recreational Vehicle Rental Association (☎703/591-7130, ⓦwww.rvra.org) maintains a searchable online directory of rental firms. Among the larger companies offering RV rentals are Cruise America (☎1-800/671-8042, ⓦwww.cruiseamerica.com) and Moturis (☎1-800/559-8228, ⓦwww.moturis.com).

Driving for foreigners

Foreign nationals from English-speaking countries can drive in the US using their full domestic driving licenses. (International Driving Permits are not always regarded as sufficient.) Not having your license with you while driving is an arrestable offense.

Fly-drive deals are good value if you want to rent a car, though you can save up to sixty

For up-to-date information on current road conditions on major highways – which is essential if you're driving in the Four Corners region in winter – call the following numbers:

Arizona ☎1-888/411-7623
Colorado ☎1-877/315-7623
New Mexico ☎1-800/432-4269
Utah ☎1-866/511-8824

percent simply by booking in advance with a major firm. If you choose not to pay until you arrive, be sure you take a written confirmation of the price with you. Remember that most standard rental cars have automatic transmissions, and that it's safer not to drive immediately after a long transatlantic flight.

It's easier and cheaper to book RVs in advance from Britain. Most travel agents who specialize in the US can arrange RV rental, and usually do it cheaper if you book a flight through them as well. A price of £500 for a five-berth van for two weeks is fairly typical.

Desert driving

Whenever you drive in the desert, be sure to have two gallons of water per person in the car. You should also carry flares, matches, a first-aid kit, and a compass, plus a shovel, air pump, and extra gas. If the car's engine overheats, don't turn it off; instead, try to cool the engine quickly by turning the front end toward the wind. Carefully pour some water on the front of the radiator, and turn the air-conditioning off and heating up full blast. In an emergency, never panic and leave the car; you'll be harder to find wandering around alone.

By bus

Greyhound buses link all major cities and many smaller towns in the Southwest; for fares, schedules, and reservations, visit Ⓦwww.greyhound.com. Routes that are particularly useful for tourists – as well as services offered by other operators – are detailed at the relevant points in this book.

While scheduled buses can get you from city to city, they're of no use when it comes to enjoying the great outdoors. Tour buses, however, do set off into the wilderness from most major towns; they, too, are detailed throughout this book.

By train

Details of the very limited Amtrak rail service to and across the Southwest appear on p.28. The region also holds a number of historic and scenic railroads – some steam-powered or running along narrow-gauge mining tracks – including the Cumbres & Toltec line in northern New Mexico (see p.173); the Grand

Canyon Railway between Williams and the Grand Canyon in northern Arizona (see p.325); the Verde Canyon Railroad in northern Arizona (see p.301); and the Durango & Silverton Narrow Gauge Railroad in Colorado (see p.92).

By bike

Although cycling in the Southwest can be absolutely exhilarating, long-distance riders face a fearsome challenge, above all in the heat of summer. Neighboring towns can be as much as a hundred miles apart, along desert highways that offer no food, water, or shade. Quite apart from the high mountains and deep canyons, most areas covered in this book are a mile or more above sea level, so the altitude alone can be a real problem. The only road from A to B may well turn out to be a major interstate; when there's no alternative, cyclists are generally allowed to ride on interstate shoulders, but they have to battle the slipstream of mighty trucks.

If you have a good bike and know how to maintain it, however, and time your trip for the cooler months, it is feasible to explore the Southwest by bike. Specific regions that lend themselves to cycle touring are north-central New Mexico, where countless routes radiate from Santa Fe; the vicinity of Flagstaff and Sedona in Arizona; and southwest Utah, around Zion National Park. Areas hugely popular with mountain-bikers include Moab, Utah – home of the grueling Slickrock Bike Trail (see p.458) – and Durango, Colorado.

For general information and advice, contact the New Mexico Touring Society (☎505/237-9700, Ⓦwww.nmts.org), the Arizona Bicycle Club (☎602/264-5478, Ⓦwww.azbikeclub .com), or Bicycle Utah (Ⓦwww.bicycleutah .com). The national, nonprofit Adventure Cycling Association (formerly Bikecentennial; ☎1-800/755-2453, Ⓦwww.adventurecycling .org) publishes maps ($12.75 each) of several 400-mile routes, including the *Grand Canyon Connector*, detailing campgrounds, motels, restaurants, bike shops, and sites of interest. Backroads Bicycle Tours (☎1-800/462-2848, Ⓦwww.backroads.com) arranges group tours.

Greyhound, Amtrak, and major airlines all carry passengers' bicycles – dismantled and packed into a box – for a small additional fee.

Health and insurance

The major health and safety issues facing Southwest travelers are coping with desert conditions. For anyone unused to dealing with extremes of heat and cold and the sheer inhospitality of this kind of terrain, it's essential to take precautions. In addition, you may remember reports of the "mystery illness" that killed around fifty people in the Four Corners region in 1993. It was eventually traced to a hantavirus spread by the droppings of deer mice. Such viruses remain present in the region, so backpackers should take care to avoid camping near rodent nests.

Desert survival

If you plan to go hiking in the desert, it's crucial to plan ahead. Don't expect cellphones to provide coverage in all the remote regions described in this book; tell somebody where you are going and write down all pertinent information, including your expected time of return. Carry an extra two days' food and water and never go anywhere without a map. Try to cover most of your ground in early morning: the midday heat is too debilitating.

Stick to official trails in the national parks and you shouldn't face any serious technical difficulties. Many trails are marked only by occasional stone cairns, however, and if your concentration starts to wander your feet may do so too. If you do get lost, try your utmost to retrace your steps; if that fails, find some shade and wait. As long as you've registered, the rangers will eventually come and fetch you. There are two more good reasons not to try to blaze your own trail. The first is the risk of becoming rim-rocked; picking your way across even a shallow gully, it's much easier to climb up than down, and you may well find yourself stuck above a drop you're unable to negotiate. The other is the **cryptobiotic crust** – what looks like a faint coating of dead moss on the sand is the building block on which all desert life depends, and merely treading on it has serious ecological consequences.

Whatever experience you may have had anywhere else, hiking in **canyons** is different. Most hikers are far more familiar with walking up hills and mountains, where it's the initial climb that's most demanding, and when your energy levels flag you can simply turn around and walk back to base. Canyon hiking is deceptively seductive. The descent seems easy, and your progress quick. Eventually, however, you have to pay: start the climb back out when you're already tired and the midday heat has set in, and you're in for a murderously long haul. Turn back after a third of your allotted time; if you plan a six-hour hike, reckon on two hours hiking down and four hours to hike up.

To stay cool during the day, wear full-length sleeves and trousers. Shorts and a T-shirt will expose you to far too much sun – something you won't be aware of until it's too late. A wide-brimmed hat and good sunglasses will spare you the blinding headaches that can result from the desert light.

You may also have to contend with **flash floods**, which can appear from nowhere. One innocent-looking dark cloud can turn a dry wash into a raging river, and rain elsewhere can cause a flood even when the sky above is clear. Never camp in a dry wash, and don't attempt to cross flooded areas until the water has receded.

Much of the Southwest is more than a mile above sea level, and the **altitude** alone can impose severe demands on even the fittest of athletes. Be prepared for below-freezing temperatures at high elevations at night.

Water

It's essential to carry – and **drink** – large quantities of liquid in the desert. An eight-hour hike in typical summer temperatures of more than 100°F would require you to drink a phenomenal **thirty pints** of water. Loss of appetite and thirst are early symptoms of heat exhaustion, so it's possible to become seriously dehydrated without feeling thirsty. Watch out for dizziness or nausea, and if you feel weak and stop sweating, it's time to get to the doctor. You should always know whether water will be available on your chosen trail – ask park rangers – and carry at least two pints per person even if you expect to be able to pick up more en route. Just to confuse things, there's also the risk of **hyponatremia**, or water intoxication, which in its first stages closely resembles heat exhaustion, and happens if you drink too much without eating. As hikers can burn up to a thousand calories per hour, expect to eat at least twice as much **food** as normal, both during your hike and also, ideally, before it. Salty snacks such as cookies, crackers, and trail mix are recommended, as well as jerky or salami and dried ready made meals. Finally, it's easy to forget that at the end of a long hike there may be no facilities at the trailhead. Don't forget to leave some food and water in your vehicle as well.

Backpackers should never drink from rivers and streams, however clear and inviting they may look; you never know what unspeakable acts people – or animals – have performed further upstream. **Giardia** – a water-borne bacteria that causes an intestinal disease, characterized by chronic diarrhea, abdominal cramps, fatigue, and weight loss – is a serious problem. Water that doesn't come from a faucet should be boiled for at least five minutes or cleansed with an iodine-based purifier, or a giardia-rated filter, available from any outdoor store.

Insects and allergies

Mosquitoes and biting insects are rarely a problem in the Southwest, though in springtime you may encounter them near rivers in parks such as Zion. Anything containing DEET is a fairly reliable repellent. **Ticks** – tiny beetles that plunge their heads into your skin and swell up with your blood – can be a hazard. If you pluck them off you can sometimes leave their heads inside, causing blood clots or infections, so get advice from a park ranger if you've been bitten.

Beware, too, of **poison oak**, an allergenic shrub that grows all over the western states, usually among oak trees. Its leaves come in groups of three and are distinguished by prominent veins and shiny surfaces. If you come into contact, wash your skin (with soap and cold water) and clothes as soon as possible – and don't scratch. In serious cases, hospital emergency rooms can give antihistamine or adrenaline jabs.

Snakes and creepy-crawlies

Though the Southwestern deserts are home to an assortment of **poisonous creatures**, including snakes, scorpions, and spiders, but these are rarely aggressive toward humans. By observing obvious precautions, you should be able to avoid trouble. Don't attempt to handle wildlife; keep your eyes open as you walk, and watch where you put your hands when scrambling over obstacles; shake out shoes, clothing, and bedding before use; and back off if you do spot a creature, to give it room to escape.

If you are **bitten** or stung, current medical thinking rejects the concept of cutting yourself open and attempting to suck out the venom; whatever creature is responsible, apply a cold compress to the wound, constrict the area with a tourniquet to prevent the spread of venom, drink lots of water, and bring your temperature down by resting in a shady area. Stay as calm as possible and seek medical help immediately.

Medical resources for travelers

CDC ☎1-800/311-3435, ⊛wwww.cdc.gov/travel. Official US government travel health site.
International Society for Travel Medicine ☎1-770/736-7060, ⊛www.istm.org. Has a full

Rough Guides travel insurance

Rough Guides has teamed up with Columbus Direct to offer you tailor-made travel insurance. Products include a low-cost backpacker option for long stays; a short break option for city getaways; a typical holiday package option; and others. There are also annual multi-trip policies for those who travel regularly. Different sports and activities (trekking, skiing, etc) can usually be included.

See our website (🕸www.roughguides.com/shop) or call UK ☎0870/033 9988, Australia ☎1300/669 999, New Zealand ☎0800/559 911, or worldwide ☎+44 870/890 2843.

list of international travel health clinics, including an extensive list for the Southwest region.

Insurance

Because medical care in the US is expensive, all travelers visiting from overseas should be sure to buy some form of travel insurance.

American and Canadian citizens should check they're not already covered by their homeowners, renters, or – in some cases – credit card policies. Most Canadians are covered for medical mishaps overseas by their provincial health plans.

Accommodation

Accommodation in the Southwest is relatively inexpensive. Most travelers simply want a bed for the night before moving on the next day, so motels everywhere provide clean, no-frills places to sleep without bothering to offer additional amenities. Basic room rates in rural areas start as low as $40 per night, while prices along the principal highways and interstates tend to start at $60. Only in the most popular summer destinations – cities such as Santa Fe, or "gateway" towns near the major national parks – will you find it hard to get a room for under $80. If you prefer a bit more comfort, it's almost always available; in most areas covered by this book you can get a room in a top-class hotel for under $125.

Many motel rooms hold two double beds and will accommodate three or four guests for slightly over the normal two-person rate. On the other hand, the lone traveler has a hard time of it: a "single" room is just a double at a fractionally reduced rate.

Wherever you stay, you'll be expected to pay in advance, at least for the first night and perhaps for further nights too. Most places ask for a credit card imprint when you arrive, but they'll also accept cash or dollar travelers' checks. Reservations –

essential in busy areas in summer – are only held until 5pm or 6pm unless you've warned the hotel you'll be arriving late.

For advice on camping, see the "Outdoors" section beginning on p.41.

Hotels and motels

It's easy to find a basic **motel room** in the Southwest. Drivers approaching any significant town pass lines of motels along the highway, while the choice along major cross-country routes is phenomenal. Most of the towns mentioned in this book hold more motels than there's room to review; the very few that have none at all are clearly indicated.

Hotels and **motels** are essentially the same thing, although motels tend to be located beside main roads away from city centers, and thus are much more accessible to drivers. The budget ones are pretty basic affairs, but in general there's a uniform standard of comfort everywhere – each room comes with a double bed, a TV, a phone, and an attached bathroom – and you don't get a much better deal by paying, say, $80 instead of $60. Over $80 or so, the room and its fittings simply get bigger and more luxurious, and there'll probably be a swimming pool which guests can use for free. The great majority of hotels and motels offer **wi-fi** facilities, and many also offer lobby computer terminals for guests to use.

The cheapest properties tend to be family-run, independent motels, but there's a lot to be said for paying a few dollars more to stay in motels belonging to the national **chains**. Most travelers swiftly find that a particular chain consistently suits their requirements and budget. Not many budget hotels or motels bother to compete with the ubiquitous diners and offer breakfast, although many provide free self-service coffee and sticky buns.

During off-peak periods many motels and hotels struggle to fill their rooms, so it's worth haggling to get a few dollars off the asking price. Travelers who belong to the AAA can usually get a discount of around ten percent, as can members of equivalent foreign organizations such as Britain's AA. Staying in the same place for more than one night may

bring further reductions. Additionally, look out for **discount coupons**, especially in the free magazines distributed by local visitor centers and interstate welcome centers. These can offer amazing value – $40 for a double room in a comfortable mid-range chain – but read the small print, as rates are often limited to midweek.

Many towns throughout the Southwest still hold **historic hotels**, whether dating from the arrival of the railroads a century ago or from the heyday of Route 66 in the 1940s and 1950s. Not all will have up-to-date facilities to match their period charm, but they can make wonderfully characterful places to spend a night or two. Those that are exceptionally well preserved or restored may charge $200 or more per room, but a more typical rate for a not overly luxurious but atmospheric, antique-furnished room would be more like $120. Prime examples include *La Fonda* in Santa Fe (see p.121); the *Historic Taos Inn* in Taos (p.164); the *Strater Hotel* in Durango (p.94); *Andaluz* in Albuquerque (p.185); and the fabulous *La Posada* in Winslow (p.283). Occasionally, venerable Western hotels have been refitted to serve as budget-oriented accommodation options, as with Tucson's *Hotel Congress* (p.244) and Flagstaff's *Monte Vista* and *Weatherford* (p.287).

Several **national parks** feature long-established and architecturally distinguished hotels, traditionally known as **lodges**, that can be real bargains thanks to their federally controlled rates. The only drawback is that all rooms tend to be reserved far in advance. Among the best are *El Tovar* and *Grand Canyon Lodge* on the south and north rims,

Accommodation price codes

Throughout this book, **room rates** in hotels, motels, and B&Bs are indicated with the symbols below, according to the cost of their least expensive double rooms, **excluding taxes**, which can add between five and fifteen percent. Significant seasonal variations are indicated as appropriate, as are establishments that hold rooms at widely differing prices. The cheapest price code, ❶, is also used to indicate hostels which offer individual dorm beds, in which cases specific rates are also included.

❶ $35 and under	❹ $76–100	❼ $161–200
❷ $36–50	❺ $101–130	❽ $201–250
❸ $51–75	❻ $131–160	❾ $251 and above

respectively, of the Grand Canyon, and *Zion Lodge* in Zion Canyon.

Bed and breakfasts

Bed and breakfast has become an ever more popular option, often as a luxurious – if not necessarily any more expensive – alternative to conventional hotels.

The price you pay for a B&B – which typically varies from around $80 to $160 – always includes a huge and wholesome breakfast. The crucial determining factor is whether each room has an en-suite bathroom; providing private bath facilities can damage the authenticity of a fine old house.

In many areas, B&Bs have grouped together to form central booking agencies, making it much easier to find a room at short notice; we've given addresses and numbers for these where appropriate. Statewide organizations include the Arizona Association of B&B Inns (Ⓦwww.arizona-bed -breakfast.com); B&B Inns of Utah (Ⓦwww .bbiu.org); B&B Innkeepers of Colorado (Ⓣ1-877/770-4438, Ⓦwww.innsofcolorado .org); and the New Mexico B&B Association (Ⓣ1-800/661-6649, Ⓦwww.nmbba.org).

Southwest youth hostels	
Albuquerque, NM	p.186
Cedar Crest, NM	p.141
Cloudcroft, NM	p.199
Cuba, NM	p.148
Flagstaff, AZ	p.287
Las Vegas, NV	p.478
Moab, UT	p.456
Phoenix, AZ	p.228
Santa Fe, NM	p.122
Silverton, CO	p.95
Taos, NM	p.163
Tucson, AZ	p.244

Almost every B&B has its own website; simple searches will usually throw up myriad possibilities.

Hostels

Around a dozen **hostels** provide accommodation for backpackers and budget travelers in the Southwest. Most work out little cheaper than motels for two people traveling together, so there's not much point staying in hostels unless you prefer their youthful ambience and sociability. Many are not accessible on public transport, or particularly convenient for sightseeing in the towns and cities, let alone in rural areas.

These days, most hostels are independent, with no affiliation to HI-AYH (Hosteling International–American Youth Hostels) network. Many are no more than converted motels, where the "dorms" consist of a couple of sets of bunkbeds in a musty room, which is also let out as a private unit on demand; others may be purpose-built rural properties, or at least converted and modernized to a high standard. Most expect guests to bring sheets or sleeping bags. Rates range from $15 to about $24 for a dorm bed, from perhaps $35 for a double room. Those few hostels that do belong to HI-AYH tend to impose curfews and limit daytime access hours, and segregate dormitories by sex.

Especially in high season, it's advisable to reserve ahead, by phone or email. The maximum stay is often restricted to three days, though this rule tends to be ignored if there's space. Few hostels provide meals but most have cooking facilities.

Hostels can often be shoestring organizations, prone to changing address or closing down altogether. Similarly, new ones appear each year; check the notice boards of other hostels for news.

Food and drink

The short-lived international craze for contemporary Southwestern cuisine did little to turn the Southwest itself into a gourmet's paradise. However, in Santa Fe, dozens of top-class restaurants have followed in the footsteps of Mark Miller's trail-blazing *Coyote Café*, while the upscale resorts of Phoenix, Tucson, Taos, and Sedona – as well of course as Las Vegas – all offer opportunities for fine dining.

Out there on the road, the great American diner still holds sway. Southern Utah, for example, is the last place to go if lingering over an exquisite meal in atmospheric surroundings ranks high on your vacation wish list. With typical prices for a diner meal starting below $10, however, travelers happy to eat the same old steak or chicken, with baked potato and salad bar, can get excellent value for money.

The Hispanic regions of New Mexico and southern Arizona have their own indigenous cuisine, broadly similar to Mexican food but influenced by the Pueblo Indians. The essential ingredient is the chile, technically the "fruit" of the pepper plant. (New Mexicans insist it should never be spelled *chili* or *chilli*, which indicates the Texas-style stew made with ground beef and tomato sauce.) You'll soon become familiar with the bright-red *ristras* – strings of dried peppers that adorn the region's doorways and restaurant entrances, celebrating the fiery delights that lie within. In principle the red pepper is the mature version of the green, but confronted with a plateful there's no guarantee which will be hotter. Both are used to make spicy salsa, which at its most basic is simply dried peppers mixed with water, but more usually contains tomato and onion, cilantro (coriander) and other herbs, oil and lemon juice, plus other secret ingredients. If it's too hot for you, the best remedy is to drink milk.

A basic meal in a New Mexican café or diner is broadly similar to what you'd eat south of the border, though it may make more use of fresh meats and vegetables. The essentials are: lots of rice and pinto beans, often served refried as *frijoles* (ie boiled, mashed, and fried), with variations on the tortilla, a very thin cornmeal or flour pancake

that can be wrapped around the food and eaten by hand (a *burrito*); folded, fried, and filled (a *taco*); rolled, filled, and baked in sauce (an *enchilada*); or fried flat and topped with a stack of filling (a *tostada*). Meals are usually served with complimentary *nachos* (chips) and salsa dip, or with *sopaipillas*, deep-fried air-filled pastry "pillows," often sweetened with honey. The *chile relleno* is a good vegetarian option – a green pepper stuffed with cheese, dipped in egg batter and fried.

You'll also find Native American restaurants, both on and off the reservations. The most ubiquitous dish, generally known as a Navajo taco, consists of a piece of fry-bread – a puffy deep-fried slab of bread – smothered with beans, lettuce, and cheese. A Hopi taco, an Apache taco, and a Pueblo taco are all surprisingly similar. Corn or maize, the first crop cultivated in the Americas, comes in some amazing multicolored varieties. Blue corn chips have spread beyond the Southwest, but you may also encounter blue cornflakes and wafer-thin *piki* or *piiki* bread made with blue cornflour.

Drinking

In general, to buy and consume alcohol in the US, you must be aged 21 or over; you may be asked for ID even if you look much older. In New Mexico and Arizona, most restaurants have liquor licenses, and it's always easy to find a drink. In Mormon-dominated Utah things are a bit more complicated, though it's not quite the "dry" state of popular legend. Most small towns have at least one restaurant licensed to sell beer or wine to diners. On Indian reservations, however, alcohol is prohibited altogether; you can't have beer in your car, let alone in your motel room.

Festivals

The Southwest's major annual festivals are listed below. Specific annual events are described in the relevant town accounts, and you'll also find a full calendar of events in the pueblos of New Mexico on p.153. In addition, tourist offices for each state (see p.51) can provide full lists, or you can call local visitor centers ahead of your arrival and ask what's coming up. As a rule, only the Indian Market in Santa Fe and the Balloon Festival in Albuquerque attract large enough crowds to place a serious strain on accommodation and other facilities.

Annual festivals and events

Jan–Feb Gem & Mineral Show, Quartzsite, AZ
Early Feb Festival of the Arts, Tubac, AZ
Late May Waila ("chicken scratch") Festival, Tucson, AZ
Late May Iron Horse Bicycle Classic, Durango, CO
Late May Zuni Marketplace, Flagstaff, AZ
Late May to mid-July World Series of Poker, Las Vegas, NV
Early June Jazz Celebration, Telluride, CO
Mid-June Bluegrass Festival, Telluride, CO
Late June New Mexico Arts & Crafts Fair, Albuquerque, NM
Late June to Oct Utah Shakespeare Festival, Cedar City, UT
Late June to Aug Santa Fe Opera, Santa Fe, NM
Early July Hopi Marketplace, Flagstaff, AZ
July 4 Nambe Falls Celebration, Nambe Pueblo, NM
July (second week) Taos Pueblo Powwow, Taos Pueblo, NM
July (last week) Spanish Market, Santa Fe, NM
Early Aug Navajo Marketplace, Flagstaff, AZ

Aug (first week) Old Lincoln Days, Lincoln, NM
Aug (second week) Inter-Tribal Indian Ceremonial, Gallup, NM
Aug (third week) Indian Market, Santa Fe, NM
Aug (third week) Zuni Fair, Zuni Pueblo, NM
Late Aug Central Navajo Fair, Chinle, AZ
Sept 2 San Esteban Feast Day, Ácoma Pueblo, NM
Labor Day (first Mon in Sept) All-American Futurity (horse race), Ruidoso, NM
Early Sept Hatch Chile Festival, Hatch, NM
Early Sept Film Festival, Telluride, CO
Early Sept Fiestas de Santa Fe, Santa Fe, NM
Sept (second week) Navajo Nation Fair, Window Rock, AZ
Mid-Sept New Mexico State Fair, Albuquerque, NM
Early Oct International Balloon Fiesta, Albuquerque, NM
Early Oct Northern Navajo Fair, Shiprock, NM
Mid-Oct Western Navajo Fair, Tuba City, AZ
Late Oct Arizona State Fair, Phoenix, AZ
Oct (third week) Helldorado Days, Tombstone, AZ
Early Dec National Finals Rodeo, Las Vegas, NV
Early Dec Shalako ceremony, Zuni Pueblo, NM

The great outdoors

Cut by deep canyons, coated by dense forests, and capped by great mountains, the Southwest glories in some of the most fabulous wilderness areas in the United States.

The easiest way for visitors to enjoy this natural wonderland is to plot an itinerary that samples the countless national, state, and county parks. Although these are not invariably the most beautiful places of all – after all, some are simply lands that pioneer farmers, Indian tribes, and mining corporations never bothered or managed to grab – they do offer the campgrounds and hiking trails that make backcountry exploration possible even for the least experienced tourists.

National parks and monuments

The National Park Service administers both national parks and national monuments. It's sadly underfunded, however: the NPS doesn't even automatically get to keep park entrance fees, which are absorbed into the general Federal treasury. In style and design, many of its visitor centers and other facilities still date conspicuously from the 1950s. Nonetheless, park rangers do a superb job of providing information and advice to visitors, maintaining trails, and organizing such activities as free guided hikes and campfire talks.

In principle, a **national park** preserves an area of outstanding natural beauty, encompassing a wide range of terrain as well as sites of historic interest, while a **national monument** is much smaller, focusing perhaps on just one archeological site or geological phenomenon and thus holding a narrower appeal for tourists. In practice, however, that distinction is somewhat blurred in the Southwest. Most **parks** cover desert regions that have barely known human occupation, and thus boast little historic significance, and while the **Grand Canyon** and **Zion** are huge and very varied, parks such as **Bryce Canyon** and **Carlsbad Caverns** are essentially one-trick wonders.

And while many **monuments** do consist of a single Indian ruin or nineteenth-century fort, several more are as diverse and spectacular as the parks – Arizona's **Canyon de Chelly**, for example, would surely be a national park were it not on the Navajo reservation. In addition, vast national monuments have recently been created in areas that need extra federal protection but are not intended to become major tourist destinations. **Grand Staircase-Escalante** monument in Utah, the best-known example, is larger than any of the national parks covered in this book; others include the even newer **Grand Canyon-Parashant** and **Vermilion Cliffs** national monuments.

Fees and passes

Most national parks and monuments charge an admission fee of between $5 and $25, which covers a vehicle and all its occupants for up to a week. For anyone on a touring vacation, it will almost certainly make more sense to buy one of various **passes**. The annual **National Parks Pass**, officially known as the "America the Beautiful – National Parks and Federal Recreational Lands Pass – Annual Pass", costs $80, and can be bought at all federal parks and monuments, or online at ⓦ store.usgs.gov/pass. It grants unrestricted access for a year from the date of purchase to the bearer, and any accompanying passengers, to all national parks and monuments, as well as sites managed by such agencies as the US Fish and Wildlife Service, the Forest Service, and the Bureau of Land Management. It does not however cover or reduce additional park fees like charges for camping in official park campgrounds, or permits for backcountry hiking or rafting.

Two further passes, obtainable at any park but not online, grant **free access** for life to

Adventure travel

The opportunities for active traveling in the Southwest are vast. In the last twenty years, the former uranium mining town of **Moab**, Utah, has grown to become the region's major base for adventure travel of all kinds. Mountain biking is its specialty, with rafting and four-wheel-driving (universally abbreviated to 4WD) as close rivals; full listings can be found on p.458. Other towns popular with energetic visitors include **Durango**, Colorado (see p.91), and **Sedona**, Arizona (see p.295); guides, outfitters, and local tour operators are recommended throughout this book.

all national parks and monuments, again to the holder and any accompanying passengers, and also provide a fifty percent discount on camping fees. The **Senior Pass** is available to any US citizen or permanent resident aged 62 or older for a one-time fee of $10, while the **Access Pass** is issued free to blind or permanently disabled US citizens or permanent residents.

Other public lands

National parks and monuments are often surrounded by tracts of **national forest**, which are also federally administered but are much less protected. While these too tend to hold appealing rural campgrounds, each is, in the words of the slogan, a "Land of Many Uses," and usually allows some limited logging and other land-based industry – ski resorts more often than strip mines, fortunately.

Further government departments administer a whole range of wildlife refuges, national scenic rivers, recreation areas, and the like – such administration consisting basically of leaving the natural landscape alone. The **Bureau of Land Management** (BLM) has the largest holdings of all, most of it open rangeland, such as in Utah, but also including some enticingly out-of-the-way reaches.

State parks and state monuments are a mirror-image of the national system, preserving sites of more limited, local significance. Many are explicitly designed for recreational use and thus hold better campgrounds than their federal equivalents.

Information resources

For up-to-the-minute information on the National Park Service, access the official website at Ⓦwww.nps.gov.

Websites for individual parks are given throughout this book. For more general

maps, and information on camping on public lands, access the **Public Lands Information Center** website, Ⓦwww.publiclands.org, which contains information on both BLM and forest-service lands, or the **state parks** office for **Arizona** (Ⓦwww.pr.state.az.us); Colorado (Ⓦwww.coloradoparks.org); **New Mexico** (Ⓦwww.emnrd.state.nm.us); or **Utah** (Ⓦwww .stateparks.utah.gov).

Camping and backpacking

The ideal way to see the Southwest – especially if you're on a low budget – is to tour the region by car and **camp** at night in state and federal campgrounds. These may lack the amenities of the commercially run campgrounds, found in abundance near the larger towns, but they tend to be far more peaceful, scenic, and better positioned for days of hiking and canyoneering. Typical public campgrounds range in price from free (usually when there's no water available, which may be seasonal) to around $15 per night; commercial fees are more like $15–25, for sites that can be more like open-air hotels, with shops, restaurants, and washing facilities.

There may be plenty of campgrounds, but there are also plenty of people who want to use them: If you're camping during public holidays or the high season, either reserve in advance or avoid the most popular areas. By contrast, basic campgrounds in isolated areas may well be completely empty

---

For detailed advice on hiking in the desert, see p.34.

A list of the **top ten trails** in the Southwest appears in the *Camera! Drive! Action!* color section.

whatever time you go, and if there's any charge at all you'll be expected to pay by leaving the money in the bin provided.

Backcountry camping in the national parks is usually by permit and may be free or cost a few dollars per night. Before you set off on anything more than a half-day hike, and whenever you're headed for anywhere at all isolated, be sure to inform a ranger of your plans and ask about weather conditions and specific local tips. Carry sufficient food and drink to cover emergencies, as well as all the necessary equipment and maps. In summer in the national parks, you have to carry so much water – see below – that you'll need to lighten your load as much as possible, perhaps by sleeping in a light-weight sack rather than a sleeping bag.

When camping rough, check that **fires** are permitted before you start one; even if they are, try to use a camp stove instead of local materials – in some places firewood is scarce, although you may be allowed to use deadwood. In wilderness areas, try to camp on previously used sites. Where there are no toilets, bury human waste at least six inches into the ground and a hundred feet from the nearest water supply and campground. Burn what trash you can and take the rest away.

Flora and fauna

Though the Southwest is commonly imagined as an arid wasteland, it holds a broad spectrum of plant and animal life. Scientists divide the earth, according to climate and distance from the equator, into "**life zones**" that hold different assortments of species. In the Southwest, altitude substitutes for latitude; the higher the elevation, the cooler the temperature. Within the Grand Canyon alone, the range of habitat is equivalent to that experienced in a trip from the deserts of Mexico to the forests of the Canadian mountains.

It's the lowest, hottest level, the **Lower Sonoran** zone, that's home to the rattlesnakes and cactuses you're probably expecting. Southern Arizona is the obvious example, with its dramatic saguaro and organ-pipe cactuses, but a similar ecosystem can be found in the depths of the Grand Canyon.

By the time you reach a mile above sea level – the height of most of Utah's national parks – you're in the **Upper Sonoran** zone. This is characterized by smaller prickly pear cactuses and sagebrush, animals such as rabbits and prairie dogs, and predators like coyotes and mountain lions (not that tourists are at all likely to encounter lions). Low rainfall results in a "pygmy forest" where gnarled, long-lived trees such as the piñon (also spelled pinyon) pine and Utah juniper grow to a maximum height of little more than twenty feet.

Around ten thousand feet up in the mountains of southern Colorado, northern New Mexico, and central-southern Utah, the **Canadian** zone is even more densely forested, with Douglas firs joining the aspen and ponderosa, and bighorn sheep making an appearance in remoter areas. The Colorado Rockies and Utah's Henry and La Sal ranges rise higher still into the **Hudsonian** zone, between eleven and twelve thousand feet. Before the tree cover gives out altogether, ultra-resilient species such as the bristlecone pine, which can live for literally thousands of years, cling to the slopes.

The highest summits in the Southwest – places like the San Francisco Peaks (12,633ft) near Flagstaff, Arizona, Wheeler Peak (13,161ft) near Taos, New Mexico, and Uncompahgro Peak (14,309ft) near Ouray, Colorado – belong to the **Arctic** or **Alpine** zone, where the occasional tiny mammal scuttles through the tundra-like grasses and mosses.

Wherever and whenever **water** is abundant, however, the picture changes. Southwestern riverbeds are lined with magnificent **cottonwood** and **aspen** trees, so many a canyon buried deep in the desert still manages a superb display of fall colors, while spring snowmelts help bring the mountain hillsides and the meadows of Zion alive with wild flowers.

Traveling in Indian country

The Southwest holds around fifty separate Indian reservations, ranging in size from the vast Navajo reservation (or "Navajo Nation"), which extends across three states in the Four Corners region, to the nineteen autonomous pueblos of New Mexico, many of which consist of one single village.

Some reservations make no effort to attract or inform visitors; some do the bare minimum to sate tourists' curiosity; some eagerly encourage paying guests to stay in tribal-run motels and campgrounds. Among the most compelling attractions on Native American soil are **Monument Valley**, and Canyon de Chelly and Navajo national monuments, all on the Navajo reservation; the stupendous waterfalls of the **Havasupai reservation**, deep in the Grand Canyon; the **Skywalk** on the Hualapai reservation, in the so-called "Grand Canyon West" area; and the adobe pueblos of **Taos** and **Ácoma** ("Sky City") in New Mexico.

Many outsiders – Americans and non-Americans alike – feel uncomfortable about entering Native American land, but so long as you behave with due **cultural sensitivity** you will almost always be made to feel welcome. In particular, travelers in "Indian Country" should respect the laws that bar the sale, possession, and consumption of **alcohol** on the reservations. Always request permission before **photographing** (or even drawing) people or personal property, and accept that you may be asked for a fee. As well as obeying explicit signs that ask you not to enter specific areas, such as shrines or *kivas*, you should also be aware that off-road driving and off-trail hiking or climbing is forbidden. If you have to drive up to someone's home or *hogan* stay in your car and wait to be approached, rather than blundering in.

On a more general note, attempts to make friends may run contrary to what Native Americans regard as **good manners**. In the words of a leaflet issued by the Navajo, "the general exuberance many cultures define as friendliness is not considered such by the American Indians." Most Southwestern Indians regard **eye contact** as rude and will

avoid meeting your eye; they may also prefer not to shake hands. Your clothing may also be an issue; the Hopi, for example, request that visitors not wear shorts or hats, or use umbrellas. Persistent, intrusive questioning is obviously liable to offend. In Pueblo communities especially, don't ask about religious matters when children are present, as children are only initiated into religious secrets at the appropriate age.

Buying Indian crafts

For many tourists, the quest to buy **Indian crafts** becomes a major focus of their visit to the Southwest. Museums and galleries throughout the region display beautiful Pueblo pots, Navajo rugs, Apache baskets, and silver and turquoise jewelry of all kinds, stimulating a desire for affordable gifts and souvenirs with which stores everywhere can barely keep up.

Much of what's widely seen as traditional Indian craftwork has in fact only developed in the last hundred or so years. The collapse of traditional tribal economies coincided with the nineteenth-century arrival of the railroads, and with them the Southwest's first wave of tourists. Enterprising traders encouraged Indians to adapt or learn craft techniques to make souvenirs; as one anthropologist put it, the resultant hybrid was "the Indian's idea of the trader's idea of what the white man thought was Indian design."

To ensure good prices and good quality, you should ideally buy specific Indian crafts as near as possible to where they're made. On the Navajo reservation, head for the **Hubbell Trading Post** (see p.75); on the Hopi reservation, try the **Hopi Cultural Center** and the nearby stores; Ácoma, Taos, and San Ildefonso pueblos are also good bets. More accessibly, the Indian traders in front of the Palace of the Governors in **Santa Fe** are a reliable source, while that city's summer **Indian Market** is a showcase for the entire region. In addition, the Museum of Northern Arizona in Flagstaff, the Heard museum in Phoenix, and the Millicent Rogers museum in Taos all have excellent stores.

If you want to be sure that whatever you're buying was individually crafted by a South-western Indian, you're entitled to ask the vendor for a written certificate of authenticity. Only the phrase "Authentic Indian handmade" has any legal force. "Indian handmade" means that the object was designed and assembled by American Indians; "Indian crafted" means that American Indians had a hand in the process; and words such as "real" and "genuine" mean nothing. The **Indian Arts & Crafts Association** (℡505/265-9149, ⓦwww.iaca .com) can provide further detailed advice, and publishes lists of recommended crafts workers and retail outlets on its website.

Jewelry

Jewelry is perhaps the oldest Southwestern craft of all. The Ancestral Puebloans made necklaces of disks cut from seashells; a single specimen unearthed near Kayenta was 36 feet long and held over fifteen thousand beads. Such necklaces are now known as *heishi* and are the specialty of New Mexico's Santo Domingo Pueblo.

Turquoise has always been prized by Southwestern Indians; the prehistoric city at Chaco Canyon was probably founded on the proceeds of the turquoise trade, while to this day the Navajo see the greenish-blue, semiprecious stone as symbolizing the state of harmony and beauty known as *hozho*. Necklaces of raw and polished turquoise beads are widely available; the stone also adds color and character to the **silver** jewelry made by the Hopi, Zuni, and Navajo in particular.

Silversmithing is a relatively recent tradition, probably introduced from Mexico in the mid-nineteenth century. For many years,

acquiring chunky silver bracelets or belts studded with solid-silver conches was the standard Navajo way of accumulating wealth. Such items could be pawned for cash at trading posts on the reservation and then redeemed when times got easier; now known as pawn jewelry, they count as valuable collectors' pieces. Casual buyers tend to prefer – and to be more able to afford – the more delicate **overlay** style, in which a stenciled design is cut from a thin sheet of silver then soldered onto a solid backing sheet. This technique originated in 1947, when returning Hopi servicemen were trained in the technique as a means of earning a living, and the Hopi remain its finest exponents. Overlay designs can be seen on earrings, belt buckles, rings, and, especially, the clasps of *bola*, or bootlace, ties.

Weaving

The best **weavers** in the Southwest are generally acknowledged to be the Navajo. In legend, they acquired the craft from Spider Woman, who lives atop Spider Rock in the Canyon de Chelly; in fact, they were probably taught by the Pueblo peoples after the Pueblo Revolt of 1680. That was also when they began to raise sheep, which had been introduced by the Spanish a century earlier.

Originally, the Navajo wove blankets and clothing; **Navajo rugs** were the brainchild of nineteenth-century traders, who also suggested that using "earth" colors such as brown would appeal to tourists expecting a "natural" look. Many individual Navajo communities or families weave designs named for their own area, such as Teec Nos Pos, Ganado, or Two Gray Hills. As a rule, the patterns have no religious signifi-cance, but most include an "escape route" or "spirit line," a line that runs to the very edge of the rug and ensures that the weaver's spirit is not trapped within it. Tradi-tional rugs also have a hole in the center, as in a spider's web.

Authentic Navajo rugs take months to create and sell for thousands of dollars; anything you see cheaper is probably a mass-produced Mexican imitation. The monthly Navajo Rug Auction at Crownpoint in New Mexico (see p.105) is the best oppor-tunity to pick up a genuine bargain.

> Another Hopi specialty, the carving of the wooden statuettes known as *kachina* dolls, is described on pp.78–79.

Pottery

Spanish explorers in 1540 spoke of Pueblo women as making "jars of extraordinary labor and workmanship, which were worth seeing." The ceramic tradition of northern New Mexico's pueblos remains as strong as ever, having been revitalized in the twentieth century by the San Ildefonso potter Maria Martinez. Although she consciously modeled her earlier work on designs found in ancient archeological sites, the black-on-black museum pieces for which she became famous are a far cry from the popular conception of Native American crafts. Many tourists prefer either the straightforward pots and jars, painted with rectilinear "pueblo motifs," created at Ácoma Pueblo, or the ubiquitous "story-teller" figures, showing a mother surrounded by children, that were first created at Cochiti Pueblo. A representative cross-section of styles can be seen at the roadside store run by Pojoaque Pueblo, twelve miles north of Santa Fe (see p.149).

Travel essentials

Costs and money

This book contains detailed price information for lodging and eating throughout the Southwest. Accommodation rates are coded according to the system explained on p.37, which excludes any local taxes that may apply, while restaurant prices include food only and not drinks or tip. For museums and similar attractions, the entrance fees quoted are for adults; unless specified otherwise, assume that children get in half-price.

North American travelers find prices in the Southwest broadly similar to the rest of the US, with food and lodging generally cheaper than in major US cities and tourist regions, and gas and groceries, especially in out-of-the-way places, a little more expensive. Most visitors from Europe and Australasia feel that their money goes further in the US than it does at home. However, if you're used to traveling in the less expensive countries of Europe, let alone in the rest of the world, you can't expect to scrape by on the same minuscule budget in the US.

As explained on p.31, the only way to reach most of the places described in this book is to drive. If you can't bring your own vehicle, your least avoidable major expense will be **car rental**, at around $150 per week. What you spend on **accommodation** is more flexible. For most of the year, in most places, you should have no problem getting a motel room for under $70, though even the cheapest peak-season rates in or near certain national parks, or in downtown Santa Fe, are more like $90. Although **hostels** offering dorm beds – usually for $15 to $25 – are reasonably common, they're by no means everywhere, and in any case they save little money for two or more people traveling together. **Camping** is not only cheap, with federal and state park campgrounds ranging from free to perhaps $18 per night, but in many wilderness areas it's the only option.

As for food, $25 per day is enough to get an adequate life-support diet, consisting of perhaps one full-scale meal in a local diner supplemented by a stash of groceries, while for a daily total of around $35 you can eat pretty well. If you're visiting a significant number of national parks and monuments, buy a National Parks pass (see p.41); the $80 fee covers all passengers in your vehicle. You'll probably also spend another $5 to $12 a day on admissions to state parks, museums, and the like.

The most economical possible vacation, therefore, with two people sharing a rental car, camping in state and federal parks most

Tipping

You shouldn't depart a bar or restaurant without leaving a **tip** of at least 15–20 percent (unless the service is utterly disgusting). About the same amount should be added to taxi fares – and round them up to the nearest 50¢ or dollar. Tip hotel porters roughly $1 per item for carrying your baggage to your room. When paying by credit or charge card, you're expected to add the tip to the total bill before filling in the amount and signing.

nights, and eating one restaurant meal per day, will work out at a minimum of $350 per person per week.

Sales tax is added to virtually everything you buy in a shop, but isn't included in the marked price. The actual rate varies from place to place, but in the states covered in this book it ranges between around five and seven percent – except on Indian reservations, which do not levy sales tax. Most towns also charge lodging taxes of between five and fifteen percent.

Expect to pay most of your major expenses by **credit** or **debit card**; hotels and car rental agencies usually demand a credit card imprint as security, even if you intend to settle the bill in cash, and you'll be at a serious disadvantage if you don't have one. Visa, Mastercard, Diners Club, American Express, and Discover are the most widely used.

You'll also need to carry a certain amount of **cash**. If you have a Mastercard or Visa, or a cash-dispensing card linked to an international network such as Cirrus or Plus – check with your home bank before you set off – you can withdraw cash from appropriate automatic teller machines (ATMs). Also consider carrying US dollar **travelers' checks**, which offer the security of knowing that lost or stolen checks will be replaced. Checks issued by American Express, Visa, and Thomas Cook are universally accepted as cash in shops, restaurants, and gas stations, and change from your transactions will be rendered in hard currency. Foreign travelers should *not* bring travelers' checks issued in their own currencies; it can be hard to find a bank prepared to change them, and no other business is likely to accept them.

Crime and personal safety

No one could pretend that America is crime-free, although away from the urban centers crime is often remarkably low. All the major tourist areas and the main nightlife zones in cities are invariably brightly lit and well policed. By planning carefully and taking good care of your possessions, you should, generally speaking, have few problems.

When parking in the wilderness, in national or state parks for example, leave your belongings out of sight, and carry any valuables with you.

Electricity

Electricity The US electricity supply is 110 volts AC. Plugs are standard two-pins – foreign visitors will need an adapter and voltage converter for their own electrical appliances.

Entry requirements

Under the **visa waiver scheme**, passport holders from Britain, Ireland, Australia, New Zealand, and most European countries do not require visas for trips to the US, so long as they stay less than ninety days, and have an onward or return ticket. Instead you simply fill in the visa waiver form handed out on incoming planes. Immigration control takes place at your point of arrival on US soil.

As of January 2009, everyone planning to visit the US using the visa waiver scheme is required to apply for travel authorization in advance, online. It's a very quick and straightforward process, via the website Ⓦ www.cbp.gov/xp/cgov/travel/. Fail to do so, however, and you may well be denied entry. In addition, your passport must be machine-readable, with a barcode-style number. All children need to have their own individual passports. Holders of older nonreadable passports should either obtain new ones or apply for visas prior to travel.

Prospective visitors from parts of the world not mentioned above need a valid passport and a nonimmigrant visitor's visa. How you'll obtain a visa depends on what country you're in and your status when you apply, so call the nearest US embassy or consulate (see below). For full details visit ⓦhttp ://travel.state.gov.

US embassies and consulates abroad

Australia MLC Centre, Level 59, 19–29 Martin Place, Sydney ☎02/9373 9200, ⓦusembassy -australia.state.gov.
Ireland 42 Elgin Rd, Ballsbridge, Dublin ☎01/668 8777, ⓦdublin.usembassy.gov.
New Zealand 29 Fitzherbert Terrace, Thorndon, Wellington ☎04/462 6000, ⓦnewzealand .usembassy.gov.
South Africa 877 Pretorius St, Arcadia, Pretoria ☎12/431-4000, ⓦsouthafrica.usembassy.gov.
UK 24 Grosvenor Square, London W1A 1AE ☎020/7499 9000, ⓦwww.usembassy.org.uk; 3 Regent Terrace, Edinburgh EH7 5BW ☎0131/556 8315, ⓦwww.usembassy.org.uk/scotland; Danesfort House, 223 Stranmillis Rd, Belfast BT9 5GR ☎028/9038 6100, ⓦwww.usembassy.org .uk/nireland.

Government websites

Australian Department of Foreign Affairs ⓦwww.dfat.gov.au, ⓦwww.smartraveller.gov.au.
British Foreign & Commonwealth Office ⓦwww.fco.gov.uk.
Canadian Department of Foreign Affairs ⓦwww.international.gc.ca.
Irish Department of Foreign Affairs ⓦwww .foreignaffairs.gov.ie.
New Zealand Ministry of Foreign Affairs ⓦwww.mft.govt.nz.
US State Department ⓦwww.travel.state.gov.
South African Department of Foreign Affairs ⓦwww.dfa.gov.za.

Gay and lesbian travelers

Resources for gay and lesbian travelers in the Southwest include ABQ*MPower in Albuquerque (☎505/232-2990, ⓦwww .myspace.com/abqmpower); Prescott Pride Center (☎928/445-8800, ⓦwww.prescott pridecenter.com); Wingspan in Tucson (☎520/624-1779, ⓦwww.wingspan.org); and the Gay and Lesbian Community Center of Southern Nevada, at 953 E Sahara Ave, Las Vegas (☎702/733-9800, ⓦwww .thecenter-lasvegas.com). Websites catering

to visitors to, and residents of, Arizona include ⓦwww.visitgayarizona.com, run by the Greater Phoenix Gay and Lesbian Chamber of Commerce, while ⓦwww .abqpride.com is an equivalent for New Mexico. The Gay Las Vegas website, ⓦwww.gayvegas.com, can tell you all you need to know about Sin City.

Internet access

Almost every hostel, motel and hotel listed in this book, as well as most cafés, offers free wi-fi access; if you're not traveling with a laptop, you'll also have the option of using a computer in the lobby area of many hotels. On the streets, however, public internet access is not as widely available as you might expect; public and university libraries, and internet cafés in larger towns, are your best bet.

Mail

Post offices in the Southwest are usually open Monday to Friday from 9am until 5pm, and Saturday from 9am to noon, and there are blue mailboxes on many street corners. Ordinary mail within the US costs 42¢ for a letter weighing up to an ounce. Airmail between the US and Europe or Australia costs 94¢ for postcards or aerograms, or letters weighing up to one ounce (two single thin sheets), and generally takes about a week.

Maps

The best general-purpose **road map** for the principal areas covered in this book is the *Indian Country Guide Map*, available free to members of the AAA and sold throughout the Southwest for $4.95. It focuses on the Four Corners region, however, and does not extend into southern Arizona, southern New Mexico, or Nevada, and furthermore it's not reliable for dirt roads and backcountry routes. Each individual state also issues a free **highway map**, which is fine for general driving and route planning and can be obtained either direct from the tourist office or from local visitor centers. In addition, Rand McNally produces good regional maps – bound together in their *Rand McNally Road Atlas*, or printed separately for each state – while free town maps are generally available at local visitor centers.

All national parks, and most state parks, national forests, and the like provide reasonable maps to visitors. Both these, and the maps throughout this book, are adequate for day-hikes on the most popular trails. Serious hikers and backpackers, however, should equip themselves with detailed **topographical maps**. Among the best are the waterproof and tearproof maps of individual national parks published by National Geographic–Trails Illustrated (ⓦshop.nationalgeographic.com), which also produces state maps of Colorado, New Mexico, and Utah.

Measurements and sizes

US measurements are Imperial, though American pints and gallons are about four-fifths of Imperial ones. Clothing sizes are two figures less than in the UK – a British women's size 12 is a US size 10 – while British shoe sizes are half below American ones for women, and one size below for men.

Opening hours and public holidays

On national public holidays listed below, shops, banks, and offices are liable to be closed all day. The traditional summer season for tourism runs from Memorial Day, in late May, to Labor Day, in early September; some tourist attractions are only open during that period. Normal banking hours are from 9am or 10am until 3pm or 4pm Monday to Thursday, and slightly longer on Friday.

Jan 1 New Year's Day
Jan 15 Martin Luther King Jr's Birthday
3rd Mon in Feb Presidents' Day
Last Mon in May Memorial Day
July 4 Independence Day
1st Mon in Sept Labor Day
2nd Mon in Oct Columbus Day
Nov 11 Veterans' Day
Last Thurs in Nov Thanksgiving Day
Dec 25 Christmas Day

Phones

If you want to use your **cellphone** (mobile phone) in the Southwest, you'll need to check with your phone provider whether it will work there, and what the call charges are.

Unless you have a tri-band or a 4-band phone, a mobile bought for use outside the US may not work inside the States (and vice

Clothing and shoe sizes

Women's clothing

American	4	6	8	10	12	14	16	18
British	6	8	10	12	14	16	18	20
Continental	34	36	38	40	42	44	46	48

Women's shoes

American	5	6	7	8	9	10	11
British	3	4	5	6	7	8	9
Continental	36	37	38	39	40	41	42

Men's shirts

American	14	15	15.5	16	16.5	17	17.5	18
British	14	15	15.5	16	16.5	17	17.5	18
Continental	36	38	39	41	42	43	44	45

Men's shoes

American	7	7.5	8	8.5	9.5	10	10.5	11	11.5
British	6	7	7.5	8	9	9.5	10	11	12
Continental	39	40	41	42	43	44	44	45	46

Men's suits

American	34	36	38	40	42	44	46	48
British	34	36	38	40	42	44	46	48
Continental	44	46	48	50	52	54	56	58

versa), while many US phones only work within their local area code.

Otherwise, it's usually easy to find a public payphone. As a rule, local calls cost 50¢, but you may have to feed in a dozen quarters just to call the next town down the highway, and long-distance calls can cost far more. Some budget motels offer guests free local calls, but in general calls from motel rooms are even more expensive.

To save money on calls when you're on the road, it's well worth buying a **prepaid phone card**, available in various denominations from gas stations, supermarkets, and other outlets. These offer sizable savings on conventional phone rates – not least because they're normally accessed via a toll-free number that incurs no additional charge when called from a motel room.

Senior travelers

For older travelers, the Southwest makes a wonderful vacation destination. So long as you're driving rather than using public transport, everywhere is easily accessible, with motels and hotels of a high standard available almost everywhere. All the national parks hold overlooks and short trails suitable for older travelers.

Anyone over the age of 62, who can produce suitable ID, can enjoy certain discounts. Amtrak and Greyhound, for example, offer (smallish) percentage reductions on fares to older passengers. US residents aged 50 or over can join the American Association of Retired Persons, 601 E St NW, Washington DC 20049 (☎1-888/687-2277, ⓦwww.aarp.org), which organizes group travel for senior citizens and can provide discounts on accommodation

and vehicle rental. Elderhostel, 75 Federal St, Boston, MA 02110 (☎1-800/454-5768, ⓦwww.elderhostel.org) runs educational and activity programs in the Southwest for persons aged 60 and over and their companions. For details of Senior Passes, which allow free admission to national parks for US citizens or residents aged 62 or older, see p.141.

Spectator sports

The most popular spectator sports in the Southwest are baseball and football. Phoenix is home to renowned pro and college teams; for details, see p.234.

Study and work programs

AFS Intercultural Programs US ☎1-800/AFS-INFO, Canada ☎1-800/361-7248, UK ☎0113/242 6136, Australia ☎1300/131 736, NZ ☎0800/600 300, SA ☎11/447 2673; ⓦwww.afs.org. Intercultural exchange organization with programs in over 50 countries.
American Institute for Foreign Study US ☎1-866/906-2437, UK ☎020/7581 7300, Australia ☎02/8235 7000, South Africa ☎21/419 5740; ⓦwww.aifs.com. Language study and cultural immersion, as well as au pair and Camp America programs.
BTCV (British Trust for Conservation Volunteers) UK ☎01302/388 883, ⓦwww.btcv.org.uk. One of the largest environmental charities in Britain. Offers working holidays (as a paying volunteer) in Nevada.
BUNAC US ☎1-800/GO-BUNAC, UK ☎020/7251 3472, Australia ☎01/9329 3866, South Africa ☎021/418 3794; ⓦwww.bunac.org. Organizes working holidays in a range of destinations for students.
Camp America US ☎1-866/222-2074, Canada ☎902/422 1455, UK ☎020/7581 7373, Northern Ireland ☎028/9067 1929, Australia ☎02/8235 7000, New Zealand ☎09/416 5337;

Calling home from abroad

Note that the initial zero is omitted from the area code when dialling the UK, Ireland, Australia and New Zealand from abroad.
Australia international access code + 61
New Zealand international access code + 64
UK international access code + 44
US and Canada international access code + 1
Republic of Ireland international access code + 353
South Africa international access code + 27

@www.campamerica.co.uk. Organizes cultural exchange programs all over the world.

Time

New Mexico, Utah, Colorado, and Arizona all operate on Mountain Standard Time, which is two hours behind Eastern Standard Time, and seven hours behind Greenwich Mean Time, so 2pm in Santa Fe is 4pm in New York City and 9pm in London. Nevada and California are on Pacific Standard Time, another hour behind. Between the second Sunday in March and the first Sunday in November, New Mexico, Utah, Colorado, and Nevada adopt Daylight Savings Time and advance their clocks by one hour. Arizona, however, does not, so in summer it joins Nevada in being an hour behind New Mexico and Utah. That said, confusingly, the Navajo Nation in northeast Arizona does shift to Daylight Savings Time, making it one hour later than the rest of Arizona in summer, while the Hopi reservation, entirely surrounded by the Navajo Nation, stays put. The time in the part-Navajo, part-Hopi town of Tuba City, Arizona – see p.61 – varies from street to street.

Tourist information

There's no single perfect source for information on the entire Southwest; that's the point of this book, after all. Each of the states covered here has its own tourist office, accessible online or by phone. In addition, the region includes ten national parks, as well as dozens of other federally managed national monuments, national forests and the like, and fifty or so Indian reservations, each of which attempts to meet the needs of visitors in its own way.

Local information

Visitor centers in most towns – often known as the "Convention and Visitors Bureau," or CVB – provide details on the area. All also have **websites**, usually with extensive links to local businesses and attractions. In cities such as Las Vegas, Phoenix, and Santa Fe, **free newspapers** carry dining and entertainment listings. In addition, you're likely to come across the useful **Welcome Centers** along the interstates close to the state borders, which dispense maps and information on the entire state. For details on national and state parks, and other public lands, see p.41.

State tourist offices

Arizona Office of Tourism ☎1-866/275-5816, @www.arizonaguide.com.
Colorado Tourism Office ☎1-800/265-6723, @www.colorado.com.
Nevada Commission on Tourism ☎702/687-4322 or 1-800/638-2328, @travelnevada.com.
New Mexico Tourism Department ☎505/827-4000, @www.newmexico.org.
Utah Travel Industry ☎1-800/200-1160, @www.utah.com.

Useful Southwest websites

Websites for regional and local tourism information, activity operators, hotels and accommodation options, parklands, and other attractions are listed throughout this book. In addition, the following more general sites may be of interest.
Americansouthwest.net @www .americansouthwest.net. Private fan site devoted to the national parks and wilderness areas of the desert Southwest, featuring great photos, masses of links, and a copious section on slot canyons.
Discover Navajo @www.discovernavajo.com. The official tourism website of the Navajo Nation is packed with useful information for Four Corners travelers.
GORP @www.gorp.com. The Great Outdoors Recreation Pages website offers step-by-step practical guides to all the major national parks and wilderness areas as well as selling its own program of adventurous tours.
High Country News @www.hcn.org. Biweekly newspaper devoted to environmental issues in the West as a whole, with special reference to national parks and public lands, and a useful online archive.
Inside Outside Southwest @www .insideoutsidemag.com. The online version of this Durango-based magazine, offering in-depth coverage of all aspects of Southwest life, holds a useful archive of every edition ever published.
Las Vegas Review-Journal @www.lvrj.com. The online version of Las Vegas's daily newspaper provides news on the West as well as up-to-date listings of what's happening in the city.
National Park Service @www.nps.gov. This invaluable website covers every component of the national park system, with full practical details for the whole gamut of monuments and recreation areas

as well as for the parks themselves. For big names, such as the Grand Canyon, the range of information is breathtaking, covering camping, hiking, wildlife, and lodging, with links to accommodation options and activity operators in the vicinity.

National Scenic Byways Online ⓦwww .byways.org. Sponsored by the Federal Highway Administration, this luscious site honors America's most beautiful driving routes.

Sierra Club ⓦwww.sierraclub.org. The veteran environmental organization uses its website to promote awareness of issues and events throughout the US, with links to "chapters" in each individual state for coverage of local activities. For travelers, however, its most useful feature is the "Outings" section, which details not only fully-fledged adventure-travel expeditions, but also weekly activities for local volunteers.

Travelers with disabilities

For information on specific states, contact the tourism departments listed above. Useful independent sources of information include SATH (☏212/447-7284, ⓦwww.sath .org), Mobility International USA (☏541/343-1284, ⓦwww.miusa.org), and MossRehab Resource Net (ⓦwww.mossresourcenet.org). The Access Pass, issued without charge to permanently disabled US citizens, gives free lifetime admission to all national parks. *Easy Access to National Parks*, published by the Sierra Club, details access facilities in every national park for people with disabilities, senior citizens, and families with children.

Traveling with children

Although children traveling in the Southwest are likely to be enthralled by the spectacular Western-movie landscapes and the cowboys-and-Indians atmosphere of many

frontier towns, parent traveling a road trip in the region need to be very aware of quite how much time they'll have to spend in the car. If your kids don't like hours of driving, you're potentially letting yourself in for a miserable time.

Youth and student discounts

Full-time students are eligible for the **International Student ID Card** (ISIC, ⓦwww .isiccard.com in the UK, or go to ⓦwww .istc.org for more information), which entitles the bearer to special air, rail, and bus fares, and discounts at museums, theaters, and other attractions. The card costs $22 for Americans; Can$16 for Canadians; Aus$18 for Australians; NZ$20 for New Zealanders; £9 in the UK; and €13 in the Republic of Ireland.

For non-students, two other cards are available at the same prices as the ISIC card and offering the same benefits: you only have to be 26 or younger to qualify for the **International Youth Travel Card**, while teachers are eligible for the **International Teacher Card**. All these cards are available from student-oriented travel agents in North America, Europe, Australia, and New Zealand. Several other organizations and accommodation groups also sell their own cards, good for various discounts.

A university photo ID might open some doors, but is not as easily recognizable as the ISIC card; note that the latter is often not accepted as valid proof of age – in bars or liquor stores, for example. To prove your age, carry some form of government ID, such as a passport or driving license.

Guide

Guide

The Four Corners

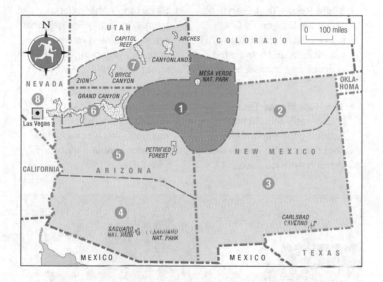

CHAPTER 1 # Highlights

* **Hiking to Betatakin** Beautiful ranger-led hike to one of the Southwest's most spectacular ancient ruins, in Navajo National Monument. See p.62

* **Monument Valley** Where the West was won, in the movies at any rate; nowhere in the world can match it. See p.65

* **White House Trail** Everything about the Canyon de Chelly is magnificent, but the one free-access trail down into it is absolutely unmissable. See p.73

* **The Hopi Mesas** These unbelievably remote and isolated desert fastnesses hold the oldest communities in North America. See p.77

* **Mesa Verde** Perhaps the most photogenic of all the Southwest's ancient cliff dwellings, tucked into the hillsides of southwestern Colorado. See p.86

* **Durango & Silverton Railroad** Ride a steam train through the majestic Colorado Rockies. See p.92

* **Silverton** Former mining town, high in the Rockies, that oozes Wild West romance from its every dirt-packed street. See p.94

* **Ácoma Pueblo** With the most dramatic setting of any Pueblo community, "Sky City" has occupied a sheer-sided butte for almost a thousand years. See p.110

▲ Monument Valley

The Four Corners

The **Four Corners** region is the heartland of the Southwest, not because the states of Arizona, Utah, Colorado, and New Mexico happen to meet here, but because it remains dominated by **Native American** cultures to an extent that's unique in the modern United States. The region centers on the **Colorado Plateau**, said to be the highest inhabited plateau in the world, bar Tibet. These dramatic and hauntingly beautiful uplands may have held a larger population a thousand years ago, when the people now known as the **Ancestral Puebloans** occupied settlements scattered throughout the deserts. Although they're chiefly remembered for their fabulous "**cliff dwellings**," which cling like eagle nests to the walls of soaring red-rock canyons, in fact they lived everywhere, from the valley floors to the mesa tops. Seven centuries ago, the Ancestral Puebloans left the plateau, to be replaced at some point thereafter by the nomadic **Navajo**. Now over 300,000 strong, the Navajo are the largest single Native American group in the United States, and their reservation occupies the bulk of the Four Corners area. Contrary to popular legend, however, the Ancestral Puebloans did not vanish completely. Some of their descendants still live nearby, in the **Hopi** villages of Arizona and the pueblos of **Zuni** and **Ácoma**, across the border in New Mexico. Still more migrated further west, to the valley of the Rio Grande.

The ruins left by the Ancestral Puebloans have become the Four Corners' prime tourist destinations. Among the most significant are those at **Mesa Verde National Park** in southwest Colorado, where dozens of graceful pueblo complexes are tucked into high rocky alcoves, and the fully fledged cities of New Mexico's remote **Chaco Canyon**, where Ancestral Puebloan civilization reached its peak. For sheer beauty, however, **Canyon de Chelly National Monument** in Arizona, where Navajo farmers live alongside the ancient remains, far surpasses both. Elsewhere, the main appeal is the scenery, which ranges from the Western-movie deserts epitomized by **Monument Valley**, via lone outcrops such as **Shiprock**, to the snowcapped peaks of southwest Colorado.

Planning a Four Corners itinerary can be hard work. The major attractions tend to be widely separated, while the towns in between are nothing special. Apart from a handful of expensive motels near Canyon de Chelly and Monument Valley, **accommodation** tends to be concentrated around the fringes. "Edge-of-the-res" towns like Gallup and Farmington may no longer be the alcohol-fueled hell-holes of yesteryear, but they're basically character-less concrete conglomerations, and you'd do better to stay slightly further afield, in places like **Durango**, Colorado, or **Flagstaff**, Arizona (covered in Chapter 5).

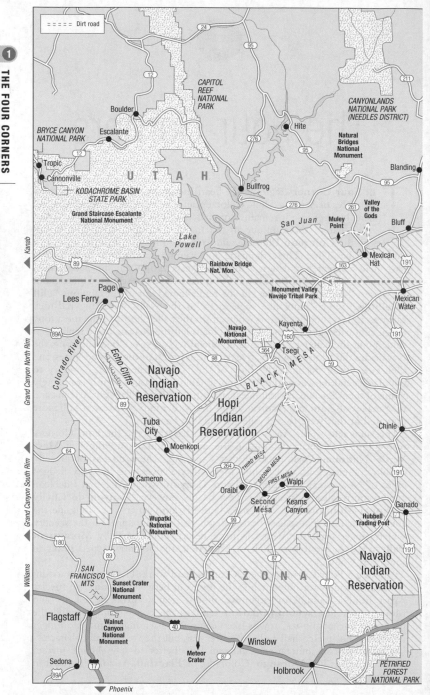

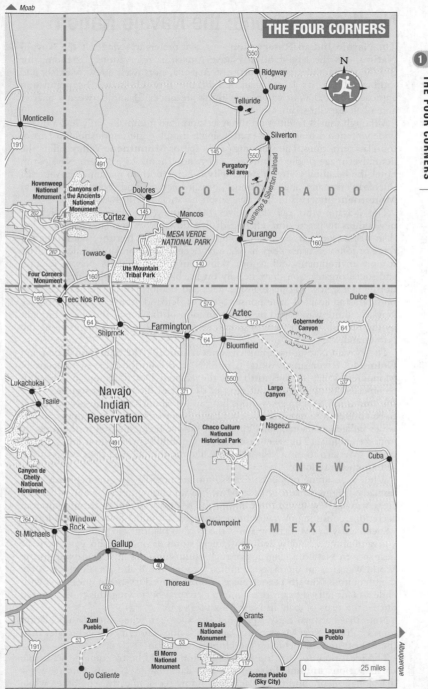

THE FOUR CORNERS

▲ Moab

N

Monticello

Ridgway
Ouray
Telluride
Silverton
Purgatory
Ski area
Durango & Silverton Railroad

Hovenweep
National
Monument
Canyons of
the Ancients
National
Monument
Dolores
C O L O R A D O
Cortez
Mancos
Durango

MESA VERDE
NATIONAL PARK

Towaoc
Ute Mountain
Tribal Park

Four Corners
Monument
Teec Nos Pos

Dulce

Aztec
Gobernador
Canyon

Shiprock
Farmington
Bloomfield

Lukachukai
Tsaile

Navajo
Indian
Reservation

Largo
Canyon

Chaco Culture
National
Historical Park
Nageezi

Cuba

Canyon de
Chelly
National
Monument

N E W

Window
Rock
Crownpoint

M E X I C O

St Michaels

Gallup

Thoreau

Grants

Zuni
Pueblo

El Malpais
National
Monument
Laguna
Pueblo

El Morro
National
Monument
Ojo Caliente
Ácoma Pueblo
(Sky City)

0   25 miles

▶ Albuquerque

Northeast Arizona: the Navajo Nation

The **Navajo Indian Reservation** – or, as it prefers to style itself, the **Navajo Nation** – is the largest of all Native American reservations. Extending for 27,000 square miles across northeast Arizona, northwest New Mexico, and southern Utah, it's larger than ten of the fifty US states. Its population approaches 350,000, of whom two-thirds are under 21 and between a quarter and a half are Christians.

Although tourist facilities on the reservation are minimal – only half a dozen widely scattered towns offer even a single motel – the region holds a trio of top-class attractions. The stunning sandscape of **Monument Valley** offers the definitive image of the Southwest, and is now home to a superb Navajo-run hotel; the beautiful **Canyon de Chelly** is home both to magnificent Ancestral Puebloan remains and traditional Navajo *hogans*; and **Navajo National Monument** preserves further awe-inspiring ancient cliff dwellings.

The Navajo, who call themselves the **Diné** ("the People"), are relative newcomers to the region. Having drifted down from the far Northwest less than a thousand years ago, they occupied their present territory within the last three or four centuries. They have always been great assimilators, quick to adapt to new environments and acquire skills from their neighbors. Navajo religion and social organization draw heavily on Pueblo examples, while many "traditional" crafts, now sold in roadside stalls and trading posts, were learned from outsiders and adapted in response to tourist demand. Above all, contemporary Navajo culture was shaped by the acquisition of the horses and sheep brought by the Spanish, which were originally seized in raids on settlements along the Rio Grande.

The Navajo Nation has minimal water resources – the **San Juan River** and **Colorado River** simply skirt its borders to the north and west respectively. Monument Valley in the north and the Painted Desert region in the south technically count as desert, but most of the rest of the terrain is **steppe**, where the land is too poor to grow crops but can just about support livestock. It used to be covered with native grasses, but having evolved in tandem with the Southwest's indigenous fauna, these could not survive being gnawed to the roots by imported animals. The sagebrush that now dominates the region looks appropriately Western to most visitors, but is, like the tumbleweed or Russian thistle, just another interloper.

While a declining proportion of Navajo are now farmers or shepherds, their nomadic origins remain evident. Most Navajo choose not to live in urbanized areas, so what few towns there are on the reservation tend to be ugly modern accretions, consisting of trailer homes gathered around a few disheveled lots.

Spend a day or two driving across the Navajo Nation, and you'll swiftly sense you're in another land. Whether in diners, stores or on the radio, you're sure to hear spoken Navajo, a language of such complexity that it was adapted during World War II as an uncrackable military code. You'll also get a chance to try the ubiquitous **Navajo taco**, a piece of open-topped fry-bread smothered with chile and/or refried beans that's another cultural borrowing, this time acquired during the years of exile in New Mexico.

Note that between early April and late October, when the Navajo Nation joins Utah and New Mexico on Daylight Savings Time, it's one hour later than the rest of Arizona, including the Hopi Reservation.

The ideal time to visit the Navajo Nation would be to coincide with one of its various **annual fairs** – the five-day Navajo Nation Fair (Ⓦwww.navajonationfair.com) takes place in Window Rock in early September, while the Central Navajo Fair is in Chinle in late August, and Tuba City welcomes the Western Navajo Fair in mid-October. Largely secular occasions, characterized much like county or state fairs throughout the West by country music, rodeos and other livestock-related events, these also double as pow-wows, and attract Native Americans from far and wide. For more information on the nation as a whole, check out the official websites ⓦwww.discovernavajo.com, ⓦwww.explorenavajo.com, and ⓦwww.navajo.org.

Tuba City

Though it's the largest community on the western side of the Navajo Nation, there's no great reason to stop at **TUBA CITY**. It stands on US-160 ten miles northeast of US-89, just under eighty miles north of Flagstaff and as far east of the Grand Canyon's South Rim; if you're feeling weary, spare a thought for the Hopi runner reported as having *run* to Flagstaff and back from Tuba City in under 24 hours. The town owes its unusual name to "Tuuvi," a Hopi from nearby Moenkopi who converted to Mormonism in 1877 and invited a group of Mormon families to settle here. Soon, however, the Mormons were monopolizing the site's precious springs, fed by an aquifer that reaches to Monument Valley. They were forced to move out when the area was added to Navajo lands in 1903.

Tuba City has two unusual claims to fame. The first is a set of petrified **dinosaur tracks**, near the highway five miles southwest of town. These widely spaced 65-million-year-old sandstone imprints were left by a ten-foot creature known as a Dilophosaurus. It's hard to spot the tracks on your own – in truth, they're not all that riveting – but waiting Navajo guides can lead you to them for a small donation. Secondly, Tuba City straddles two separate **time zones**. Most businesses along the highway, such as *Basha's* supermarket, operate on Mountain Standard Time, while clocks in the town proper, a block or two uphill to the north, are set in summer to Daylight Savings Time, an hour later.

Practicalities

In the center of Tuba City, a mile north from the US-160/Hwy-264 intersection, a complex of buildings around the *hogan*-shaped *Tuba City Trading Post* services most visitor needs. The large, attractively maintained *Quality Inn* here (☏928/283-4545 or 1-800/644-8383, ⓦwww.qualityinntubacity.com; ❺) has pricey but acceptable rooms, with RV spaces also available. Alongside, the *Hogan Restaurant* (☏928/283-5260) features a long, inexpensive Mexican–American menu; the lunch buffet is atrocious, but if you order from the menu the food is OK.

Tuba City holds two further very basic accommodation options: the *Diné Inn Motel*, on US-160 to the east (☏928/283-6107; ❹), and the *Grey Hills Inn*, left off US-160, half a mile northeast of town, which is more of a hostel attached to the high school, and only offers shared bathrooms (☏928/283-6271; ❸).

Navajo National Monument

Despite its name, **NAVAJO NATIONAL MONUMENT** has little to do with the Navajo. Instead, it's among the most beautiful Ancestral Puebloan sites in the Southwest. It's reached via a ten-mile spur road that runs north from US-160 fifty miles northeast of Tuba City and twenty miles southwest of Kayenta.

The monument's three separate parcels each preserve a long-lost Ancestral Puebloan **cliff dwelling**, a ravishing, centuries-old pueblo of interlocking, adobe-walled homes, plazas, and kivas. Set in an enormous rocky alcove, **Betatakin** can be admired from an overlook near the visitor center, or accessed via a six-hour, ranger-led hike. The even larger **Keet Seel** is a seventeen-mile round-trip hike from the road, and so is only seen by a dedicated few. Finally, fragile **Inscription House** has been closed to visitors for fifty years.

Archeologists divide the Ancestral Puebloans of the Four Corners into three subgroups. One centered on Mesa Verde (see p.86) and another on Chaco Canyon (see p.102); the focus here, **Tsegi Canyon**, is the definitive **Kayenta** site. Though its inhabitants were still living in pithouses long after the people of Chaco and Mesa Verde were constructing sophisticated pueblos, they were fine potters, and Kayenta ceramics are now much-prized museum pieces. Tree-ring dating pinpoints their move into the alcoves of Tsegi Canyon to around 1250 AD. Within fifty years, intensive irrigation had lowered the water table and rendered farming impossible, and the canyon had been abandoned.

What became of the Kayenta people is no mystery. According to the Navajo, Keet Seel was built by settlers from Navajo Mountain, and Betatakin by a group from Chaco. That dovetails with the **Hopi** legend that eight of their clans lived here shortly before their migrations ended at the Hopi Mesas, fifty miles south. A pictograph at Betatakin – a bird-like figure within a large white circle – shows Masaw, the symbol of the Hopi Fire Clan, and Hopis regularly return for ceremonies.

Navajo National Monument was established in 1909, after Navajo guides led members of the Wetherill family (of Mesa Verde fame; see p.88) to Keet Seel. Betatakin was "discovered" a year or two later, by chance already within the monument boundaries.

Practicalities

The paved section of Hwy-564 ends ten miles north of US-160, at the monument's **visitor center** (daily 8am–5pm; ☎928/672-2700, ⓦwww.nps .gov/nava; no admission charge). Ordinary vehicles should not continue any further along Hwy-564's unpaved extension. You can't see the ruins from the visitor center, but it holds some interesting displays, including a mock-up of three rooms from Betatakin.

The lovely little **campground** nearby is open year-round, and all its first-come first-served sites are free; there are no hook-ups for RVs. In summer, visitors who arrive after the campground is full are accommodated in a more primitive campground a mile north. The closest **motel** is the turquoise-roofed, 57-room *Anasazi Inn*, in **TSEGI** ten miles northeast on US-160 towards Kayenta (☎928/697-3793, ⓦwww.anasaziinn.com; ❹), which has a small restaurant.

The Sandal Trail

If you only have time for a brief visit, all you can do is gaze across the canyon to **Betatakin** from the end of the **Sandal Trail**, an easy, paved one-mile round-trip hike from the visitor center. The view at the end, where a sumptuous orange recess in the canyon wall arches above the 135-room cluster of dwellings, is especially amazing in late afternoon, when direct sunlight penetrates the alcove. Their straight walls rise in tiers from a ledge above the canyon floor; hence the Navajo name Betatakin, or "house on ledges." It's all in such good condition – everything you see is original, except for the ladders and a few of the roof beams – that it's hard to believe the 120 or so inhabitants left not seven years but seven centuries ago.

Hiking to Betatakin

While it's worth visiting the monument for the long-distance view alone, to get any closer to Betatakin you have to join a free, ranger-guided **hike**, which is

▲ The hike to Betatakin

also a great opportunity to learn more about the land and its history. Though schedules vary, typically two hikes depart daily in summer, between Memorial Day and Labor Day, at 8.15am and 10am, and one daily otherwise, at 10am. Numbers are limited, so call a day or two in advance to reserve a place. Remember the time difference if you're hurrying here from beyond the Navajo Nation; the monument is an hour ahead of other Arizona locations, like the Grand Canyon or Flagstaff, during Daylight Savings Time.

All hikers must bring enough food and water (at least half a gallon) to last the five-hour round-trip. Although you rendezvous for a briefing at the visitor center, the hike starts a mile or two's drive away, along a trail that drops steeply into spectacular **Tsegi Canyon** from the top of Skeleton Mesa. Betatakin itself only comes into sight right at the end, as you head up a steadily narrowing side canyon, filled with delicate aspens that turn a gorgeous yellow in the fall. The closer you approach, the more overwhelming the awesome dimensions of the alcove become; it's 452ft high, 370ft wide, and 135ft deep. Rangers normally lead visitors right into the ruin itself; you can't enter individual dwellings, but sitting in the plaza of the ancient pueblo is an extraordinarily evocative experience. Its remarkable echo was no doubt exploited to the full in ceremonies.

Keet Seel

Getting all the way to **Keet Seel** – Arizona's largest cliff dwelling – is a major undertaking. The grueling seventeen-mile, self-guided round-trip **hike**, which branches into Tsegi Canyon off the Betatakin trail, is generally considered too much to attempt in a single day, so most hikers spend the night at the primitive campground near the ruin. There's no drinkable water en route.

All hikers *must* make reservations through the visitor center, anywhere from one day to five months in advance. The trail is only open in summer, when up to twenty (free) permits per day are issued, on condition that you attend a briefing session, held daily at 8.15am and 4pm. You won't have time to do it as a day-hike unless you attend the briefing the day before.

Visitors to Keet Seel can only enter the ruins with the ranger stationed nearby. The village reaches deep back into the hillside, so well sheltered that its 150-plus rooms have barely deteriorated. No more than half a dozen are *kivas* – the Kayenta were not such relentless builders of these ceremonial chambers as their neighbors at Mesa Verde. Keet Seel was a longer-lasting and more dynamic settlement than Betatakin; its cliff dwellings date from the same era, but people lived in the vicinity from around 950 AD, and migrating groups came and went for the next few hundred years. Little now survives of the large free-standing pueblo that stood on the valley floor not far away.

Kayenta

KAYENTA, where US-160 meets US-163 twenty miles northeast of Navajo National Monument, is not in any sense an historic town. Having begun life in the 1950s as a dormitory community for workers in the uranium mines to the north, it later became the main base for the miners of Black Mesa. Just twenty

Hard times at Black Mesa

Immediately opposite the Navajo National Monument turn-off, a broad but poorly surfaced road sets off south to climb **Black Mesa**. Only 4WD vehicles can get more than a mile or two along here, so few tourists see the gaping **strip mines** where the Peabody Western Coal Company has long extracted the prodigious coal deposits for which the mesa is named.

The future of these mines is uncertain and surrounded by controversy. **Black Mesa Mine** itself, which supplied coal to the Mohave Power Plant in Laughlin, Nevada, closed down at the start of 2006. Amazingly enough, the coal was transported on its 265-mile, three-day trip around the Grand Canyon by pipeline, crushed and slurried using an extravagant 1.3 billion gallons of pure water per year. When springs and water sources, many of which were considered sacred, started to run dry across the Hopi and Navajo reservations, many tribal members called for Peabody's leases to be discontinued, or at least renegotiated. Black Mesa Mine closed not because of local activism, however, but because the Mohave Power Plant could not afford to reduce its sulfur dioxide emissions to meet air pollution standards. Recent reports have suggested that Black Mesa Mine may reopen in conjunction with the still-operational **Kayenta Mine** nearby, with the coal from both being carried by train up to the Navajo Generating Station at Page (see p.422).

miles south of Monument Valley, it now also caters to ever-increasing numbers of tourists, but remains little more than a conglomeration of trailer homes, with barely a two-story building to its name.

Practicalities

As well as some unenthralling diners, Kayenta is home to three upscale **motels**. The smartest and best-value is the *Hampton Inn–Navajo Nation*, on US-160 just west of the central intersection (⚒ ☎928/697-3170 or 1-800/426-7866, ⓦwww.hamptoninn.com; ❻), which has a pool and the surprisingly good *Reuben Heflin* **restaurant**, serving tasty $15 dinner specials such as lamb shanks or beef chimichangas in an appealing environment. Immediately south of the junction, facing drivers arriving from Monument Valley, the large *Holiday Inn–Kayenta* (☎928/697-3221 or 1-800/465-4329, ⓦwww.ichotelsgroup.com; ❻) also has a reasonable restaurant, as does the less fancy *Best Western Wetherill Inn*, a mile north on US-163 (☎928/697-3231 or 1-800/528-1234, ⓦwww.bestwestern.com; ❺).

Monument Valley

The classic Wild West landscape of stark sandstone buttes and forbidding pinnacles of rock, poking from an endless expanse of drifting red sands, has become an archetypal image. Only when you arrive at **MONUMENT VALLEY** do you realize how much your perception of the West has in fact been shaped by this one spot. Such scenery does exist elsewhere, but nowhere is it so perfectly concentrated and distilled. While movie-makers have flocked here since the early days of Hollywood, the sheer majesty of the place still takes your breath away. Add the fact that it remains a stronghold of **Navajo** culture, and Monument Valley may well prove to be the absolute highlight of your trip to the Southwest.

Monument Valley Navajo Tribal Park straddles the Arizona–Utah state line, 24 miles north of Kayenta and 25 miles southwest of Mexican Hat. Although you can see the buttes for free – silhouetted on the skyline from anything up to fifty miles away, and towering alongside US-163 – the four-mile detour to enter the park is rewarded with much closer views, while the tours beyond the end of the road are unforgettable.

A history of Monument Valley

Monument Valley is not really a valley. There's no permanent stream, nor higher ground to either side, and no valley has buttes along its floor. This whole region was once a flat plain, concealing the top of what are now the tallest "monuments." In the past ten million years, the Monument Uplift – part of the general upthrust of the Colorado Plateau – has pushed that plain up from below, bulging to create cracks that have since eroded to leave only isolated nuggets of harder rock.

On the surface, thanks to annual rainfall of under ten inches, this looks like an unpromising region in which to live. However, sand dunes are surprisingly efficient at conserving moisture, and a huge aquifer deeper down stretches all the way to Tuba City. Beneath the small **cliff dwellings** that burrow into the rocks, the slopes are littered with ancient potsherds; the Ancestral Puebloans were here until around 1300 AD. After that, the area may have remained unoccupied until a band of Navajo retreated here to avoid Kit Carson's round-up in 1864 (see p.71). Their leader, **Hoskinnini**, discovered silver nearby. Two white prospectors sneaked some of the metal away in 1880, but were killed when they returned, at the bases of **Mitchell Mesa** and **Merrick Butte** respectively.

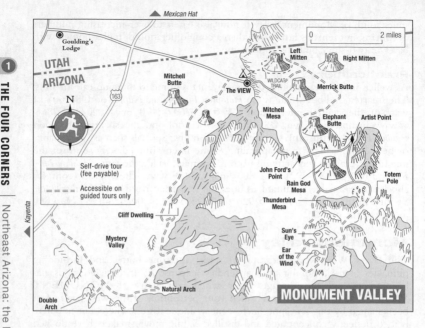

The Navajo, who named Monument Valley *Tse 'bii'ndisgaii'*, or "there is a treeless area amid the rocks," see the whole place as a *hogan*, with its "door" facing east from the visitor center, and the butte behind *Goulding's Lodge* (see opposite) its central hearth.

Park practicalities

The approach road to the tribal park ends four miles east of US-163, at a large raised parking lot where a booth collects the **admission fee** of $5. A stunning new Navajo-owned **hotel** alongside commands a magnificent panorama of Monument Valley; casual visitors can enjoy the same view from the adjoining terrace. Appropriately named *The VIEW* (☂ ☎928/727-3470, ⓦwww .monumentvalleyview.com; ⑨), the hotel offers luxurious rooms with unparalleled views, plus a reasonable **restaurant**. The attached **visitor center** holds displays on Navajo culture and history, including the story of the wartime Code Talkers, as well as on the valley itself (daily: hours are 6am–8pm in summer and 8am–5pm in winter; ☎435/727-5870, ⓦwww.navajonationparks.org). Nearby, the exposed *Mitten View* **campground** is first-come, first-served, with water available in summer only (summer $10, winter $5).

Seeing the valley

The most prominent buttes visible from the viewpoint are the pair known as **The Mittens**, which consist logically enough of the Left or West Mitten and the Right or East Mitten. Rising a thousand feet from the desert floor, each has a distinct "thumb" that splinters off from its bulkier central section. Alongside them stands **Merrick Butte**, completing a trio that's illuminated a glowing red at sunset.

A rough, **unpaved road** drops from the western end of the parking lot to run through Monument Valley. Taking a guided tour is preferable, but the

17-mile loop marked as the **self-drive** route (daily: summer 8am–6pm; winter 8am–4.30pm) makes a bearable if bumpy, hour-plus ride in an ordinary vehicle. You're allowed to stop en route to stretch your legs, but not to hike for any distance. At the main halt, **John Ford's Point**, you can enjoy the classic wide-screen valley panorama and also browse a few jewelry stalls. A Navajo man normally poses on horseback at the tip of the nearby promontory, while closer at hand, children in traditional dress invite you to photograph them for a dollar or two. The road goes on to pass near the **Totem Pole** before heading back via **Artist Point** to the visitor center.

Guided tours follow the same route, but they also take visitors "behind the scenes" beyond the main road and offer a fascinating Navajo perspective. Likely stops on longer tours include the **Sun's Eye** – a high natural arch, with petroglyphs of bighorn sheep at its base – and the similar, even more dramatic **Ear of the Wind**, as well as an obligatory visit to a *hogan* for a weaving demonstration. The most striking **Ancestral Puebloan remains** are in adjacent **Mystery Valley**, which you'll probably only visit if you take a full-day tour.

It's also possible to **hike** into the valley without a guide, so long as you stick to the 3.3-mile loop of the **Wildcat Trail**. Starting from a primitive campground just under half a mile down from the visitor center, this circles the Left Mitten butte. Assorted plants used by the Navajo are labeled along the way, but the real glory of the hike is the chance to be alone in such an overwhelming landscape, dwarfed beneath the mighty rock formations. Expect to take over two hours to complete the circuit. Wear sunscreen, carry plenty of water, and be prepared for a tiring climb back up at the end.

Goulding's Lodge

Two miles west of US-163, across from the park approach road, *Goulding's Monument Valley Lodge* began life as a 1920s trading post (☎435/727-3231,

---

Valley Tours

Taking a guided tour in and around Monument Valley is very highly recommended, though prices have risen considerably in recent years.

Both *The VIEW hotel* and *Gouldings Lodge* offer extensive programs of jeep tours, detailed on their websites. Broadly speaking prices range from around $40 for 1 hour, and $55 for 2 hour 30 minutes, up to $75 for a half-day and $110 for a full day. In addition, several Navajo-run outfits operate from kiosks in the parking lot, among the crafts stalls; all can be booked in advance, but it's usually easy to turn up and get on a tour straight away. Shop around, as prices can vary enormously for substantially the same experience. Most operators also offer **guided hikes** at slightly more expensive rates. Look for listings on ⓦwww.navajonationparks.org, or contact Roy Black (☎928/429-0637, ⓦwww.blacksmonumentvalleytours.com); Keya-Hozhoni Tours (☎928/674-1960, ⓦwww.monumentvalley.com); Monument Valley Tours (☎435/727-3313, ⓦwww.totempoletour.com); Simpson's Trailhandler Tours (☎702/476-5500, ⓦwww.trailhandlertours.com); or Sacred Monument Tours (☎435/727-3218, ⓦwww.monumentvalley.net).

Horseback tours generally work out cheaper if you book in advance rather than arranging them with the outfitters waiting in the parking lot. Typical prices range from $68 for 1 hour up to $146 for a half-day. Operators include Roy Black's and Sacred Monument, both listed above. In addition, if you drive down to the stables at John Ford's Point on the valley floor, it's often possible to saddle up on the spur of the moment for a good price, and you don't have to pay for the extra riding time to and from the valley proper.

Monument Valley and the Mythic West

The real star of my Westerns has always been the land ... My favorite location is Monument Valley. It has rivers, mountains, plains, desert, everything that land can offer ... I consider this the most complete, beautiful, and peaceful place on earth.

John Ford, *Cosmopolitan*, March 1964

In 1937, Harry Goulding, of *Goulding's Lodge*, heard that Hollywood producers were planning to shoot Western-themed movies in the Southwest. Although Monument Valley had featured in a 1925 silent, *The Vanishing American*, its splendors remained largely unknown. Goulding set off for California with a portfolio of photographs. Within a year, **John Ford** brought a crew to Goulding's remote desert outpost and was filming *Stagecoach*.

From their first moment on screen, Monument Valley's emblematic buttes served as a visual shorthand for the Wild West. The geographical reality was irrelevant. While *Stagecoach* supposedly followed a coach through Apache territory from Tonto in southern Arizona to Lordsburg in New Mexico, it did no more than duck in and out of Monument Valley; as John Wayne put it, "there's some things a man just can't run away from." Similarly, in *The Searchers* (1956), Wayne spent five years scouring Texas for Scar's band of Comanche, although in reality both he and they remained within the same five-mile radius of the Mittens. In *My Darling Clementine* (1946), Henry Fonda as Wyatt Earp drove his cattle across Monument Valley and into Tombstone, somehow transplanted from southern Arizona complete with saguaro cactuses; the OK Corral perched on a mesa nearby. Monument Valley consistently symbolized the untamed wilderness that lay beyond the ramshackle towns, beleaguered forts, isolated cabins, or crude fences of the West's earliest white pioneers.

In total, John Ford made seven movies in Monument Valley, including his "cavalry trilogy" of *Fort Apache* (1948), *She Wore A Yellow Ribbon* (1949), and *Rio Grande* (1950). Ford worked closely with the Navajo, who featured as all-purpose Indians, camping out in wigwams in *The Searchers*, for example, at what's now known as John Ford's Point. Medicine man Hosteen Tso, kept on hand to control the weather, is credited with producing a snowstorm and a sandstorm to order for *Stagecoach*. The construction of Monument Valley's first road, in the 1950s, spoiled Ford's hitherto pristine landscape, but he carried on filming here until *Cheyenne Autumn* (1963). He died shortly after announcing plans to make *Appointment at Precedence* in the valley, in 1972.

The spectacle of Henry Fonda's son smoking marijuana in Monument Valley, in *Easy Rider* (1969), may have marked an end to the days of the classic Western, but the valley itself has remained in demand. Clint Eastwood had some perilous moments atop the Totem Pole in *The Eiger Sanction* (1975), and Michael J. Fox's souped-up DeLorean outgunned pursuing Indian warriors in *Back to the Future III* (1989). Other visitors have included Tom Hanks in *Forrest Gump* (1994), while in Mario van Peebles' hip-hop *Western Posse* (1993), Monument Valley was bursting with Sioux Indians, gold mines, railroads, and buffalo soldiers.

Monument Valley's starring role as the setting for many Roadrunner cartoons probably stems from its appearances in the popular Krazy Kat comic strip of the 1920s and 1930s. Learned critics such as E E Cummings who referred to the strip's "strictly irrational landscape," and Umberto Eco, who spoke of "surrealistic inventions, especially in the improbable lunar landscapes," were clearly oblivious that artist **George Herriman** was a regular visitor to Goulding's Lodge. The adventures of Krazy Kat and Ignatz Mouse – set in Coconino County – were played out against realistic depictions of Monument Valley formations.

ⓦ www.gouldings.com; mid-March to April and first 2 weeks of Nov ❻, May–Oct ❼, mid-Nov to mid-March ❹). It now incorporates an upscale motel with great valley views, an indoor pool, a general store, a gas station, a museum of movie memorabilia, and a **campground** ($24). The adequate but unexceptional dinners at the *Stagecoach Dining Room* (daily 6.30–9pm) will set you back up to $20. As always on the reservation, no alcohol is served.

From Monument Valley to Canyon de Chelly

The most direct – and most scenic – route between the Navajo Nation's two major tourist attractions, Monument Valley and Canyon de Chelly, is **Arrowhead Hwy-59**. This gorgeous drive heads south off US-160 eight miles east of Kayenta, and then spends almost fifty miles skirting the northern flanks of Black Mesa.

For most of the way, it runs across flat desert grasslands, like a slightly more fertile version of Monument Valley, with cracks in the plains to either side hinting at unfathomable canyons. Occasionally, off to the south, villages such as **Chilchinbito** and **Rough Rock** nestle against the mesa, but the road ignores them. When it finally drops down **Carson Mesa** to reach Chinle Valley, you're confronted by the unlikely waters of **Many Farms Lake**. The road meets US-191 at the community of **Many Rivers**, fourteen miles north of Chinle.

Canyon de Chelly

A short way east of **Chinle**, twin sandstone walls emerge abruptly from the desert floor, then climb with phenomenal speed to become the thousand-foot cliffs of **CANYON DE CHELLY NATIONAL MONUMENT**. Between these sheer sides, the cottonwood-fringed Chinle Wash meanders through an idyllic oasis of meadows and planted fields. Here and there, a *hogan* stands in a grove of fruit trees, a straggle of sheep is penned in by a crude wooden fence, or ponies drink at the water's edge. And everywhere, perched above the valley on ledges in the canyon walls and dwarfed by the towering cliffs, are the long-abandoned dwellings left by the **Ancestral Puebloans**.

The monument in fact holds two main canyons, which branch apart a few miles upstream: **Canyon de Chelly** to the south and **Canyon del Muerto** to the north. Each twists and turns in all directions, scattered with immense rock monoliths, while several smaller canyons break away. The whole labyrinth threads its way upwards for thirty miles into the Chuska Mountains.

Canyon de Chelly is a magnificent place, easily on a par with any of the Southwest's national parks. Its relative lack of fame owes much to the presence of the **Navajo**, for whom the canyon retains enormous symbolic significance, despite the fact that they did not themselves construct its cliff dwellings. Casual visitors are restricted to peering into the canyon from above, from overlooks along the two "**rim drives**." There's no road in, and apart from one short but superb hike, you can only enter the canyons with a Navajo guide. Incidentally, "de Chelly" is pronounced "de shay;" it's a corruption of the Navajo *tségi*, meaning "rock canyon."

A history of Canyon de Chelly

Ancestral Puebloan Basketmakers first occupied Canyon de Chelly around 200 AD, digging primitive pithouses into the valley floor. Over the next thousand years, their descendants moved first into free-standing "pueblo" apartment-style blocks, and then into elegant cliff dwellings. Virtually all these

▲ Mummy Cave Ruin, Canyon de Chelly

canyon-wall complexes face south to catch the sun, with cooler storage chambers set in deep recesses. Many now look more inaccessible than they actually were, thanks to rock falls and the erosion of toe- and hand-holds in the soft sandstone. The valley's population peaked at roughly one thousand, shortly before drought drove the Ancestral Puebloans out around 1300 AD.

For the next few centuries, **Hopis** from the west farmed the canyon floor in summer, but no permanent inhabitants returned before the Pueblo Revolt of 1680 (see p.502). As the Spanish reasserted control over New Mexico, the first **Navajo** arrived in the region, quite possibly accompanied by Pueblo refugees. From then on, the Navajo and Spanish were locked in a bloody cycle of armed clashes and slave raids. As the "stronghold of the Navajo," Canyon de Chelly became the target of punitive Spanish expeditions. In 1805, Lieutenant Narbona's party gunned down over a hundred Navajo in the Canyon del Muerto.

After the Yankees took over in Santa Fe, the US Army in turn set about dislodging the Navajo. The process culminated in 1864, when General

Carleton's men despatched all the Navajo they could round up on the "**Long Walk**" to Fort Sumner (see p.193). In Canyon de Chelly, **Kit Carson** starved the last Navajo warriors down from the natural Navajo Fortress and destroyed their homes, livestock, and beloved peach orchards. Within a few years, however, Congress allowed the Navajo to return from their barbaric imprisonment. To this day, 25 Navajo families still farm the Canyon de Chelly in summer, the land having passed down from mother to daughter from the women between whom it was reapportioned in the 1870s.

Arrival and information

No entrance fee is charged at Canyon de Chelly. The monument's **visitor center** is a little over two miles east of Chinle and US-191 (daily 8am–5pm; ☎928/674-5500, ⓦwww.nps.gov/cach). Set on the mound where Kit Carson signed the "treaty" that ended his siege of the canyon in 1864, it holds useful displays and is the place to arrange hiking or motorized expeditions (see opposite). No **public transport** runs nearby.

Accommodation and eating

Although Canyon de Chelly remains remarkably unspoiled, nearby facilities are overstretched in summer, so it's essential to book **accommodation** well in advance. None of the three options could be considered cheap. The closest to the canyon is *Thunderbird Lodge*, reached by turning right just past the visitor

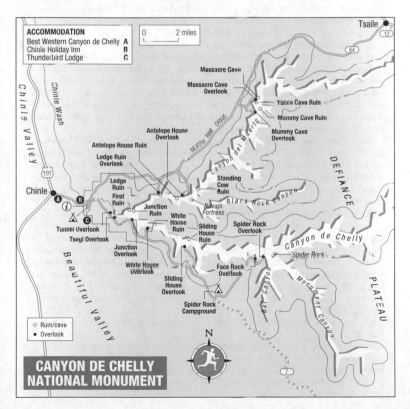

center (☎928/674-5841 or 1-800/679-2473, ⓦwww.tbirdlodge.com; ⑤). Its conventional motel rooms surround a century-old trading post, which houses a large and reasonably priced self-service **cafeteria** (daily 6.30am–9pm) that most visitors find interesting only because it's often busy with Navajo from surrounding communities. The consistently boring food is made no better by the prohibition of alcohol. The dining room is festooned with rugs from the **giftshop** next door (daily 7.30am–9pm). If you take a *Thunderbird* sightseeing tour on the day you leave, check out of your room first; they charge you for another day after 11am.

The former **Garcia Trading Post**, half a mile short of the monument entrance, holds the somewhat fancier, adobe-fied *Chinle Holiday Inn* (☎928/674-5000, ⓦwww.holiday-inn.com/chinle-garcia; ⑤). This comfortable hundred-room complex adjoins *Garcia's Restaurant*, which serves a breakfast buffet, full lunches (Mon–Fri only), and good-quality dinners. The *Best Western Canyon de Chelly*, just east of the US-191 intersection in Chinle (☎928/674-5875 or 1-800/327-0354, ⓦwww.canyondechelly.com; ⑤), is an adequate but somewhat characterless alternative, again with its own restaurant. There are also a handful

Canyon de Chelly tours

With the exception of the White House Trail (see opposite), the only way to get a close-up view of Canyon de Chelly's amazing Ancestral Puebloan remains, or to see the rock art that lines its walls, is to take a **guided tour** with a Navajo guide. That's also unforgettable for the scenery alone, with the glorious, glowing cliffs towering far above you, and tranquil Navajo farms to either side.

The most popular are the **4WD** trips organized by *Thunderbird Lodge* (see opposite). For most of the year, these "shake'n'bake" tours zigzag into either or both canyons in open-top flatbed trucks, lurching over the rutted riverbed, and the heat can be incredible; in winter they carry on in glass-roofed army vehicles with cater-pillar tracks. A **half-day** trip (daily: summer 9am & 2pm, winter 9am & 1pm; adults $46, under-13s $34.50) enables you to see a wide variety of sites and terrain, but to reach as far as Spider Rock, you have to take the **full-day** tour (late spring to early fall only, daily 9am; $74, no reductions).

Other companies offering **jeep tours**, with Navajo guides, include Canyon de Chelly Tours (☎928/674-5433, ⓦwww.canyondechellytours.com), who charge around $175 for two to three passengers for a three-hour jaunt, and $60 for each additional hour, and offer scheduled three-hour tours to White House Ruin from the *Chinle Holiday Inn* (March–Oct daily 9am, 1pm & 4pm; $60, under-13s $40). If you have your own 4WD vehicle, you can also hire a Navajo guide at the visitor center to accompany you for around $15 per hour.

In addition, the visitor center arranges highly recommended 4.5-mile, four-hour, Navajo-led **group hikes** into the canyon ($15). The precise schedule varies, but for most of the year a morning hike heads down the White House Trail at 9am and returns to Tunnel Overlook, and an afternoon trip goes into the Canyon del Muerto at 1pm. Separate **night hikes** last just two hours but cost slightly more. A fuller but much more expensive hiking experience of the canyon is offered by Footpath Journeys (☎928/724-3366, ⓦwww.footpathjourneys.com). They arrange five-day, four-night trips, usually to coincide with the full moon, during which you camp on family land close to the canyon at night and take different hikes each day, starting from $700.

Totsonii Ranch, located a mile along a dirt road from the end of the paved South Rim Drive (☎928/755-2037, ⓦwww.totsoniiranch.com), organizes **horseback** trips into remote parts of the Canyon de Chelly, including Spider Rock, for $15 per person per hour, plus $15 an hour for a guide. They too also offer multi-day trips.

of fast-food **restaurants** in **Chinle** itself, which is otherwise a brief nondescript straggle on the highway.

No **camping** is permitted in the canyons. However, the first-come first-served *Cottonwood Campground* spreads among the trees beside *Thunderbird Lodge*. All sites are free, with a five-day maximum stay, and RVs are welcome, but there are no showers, and when the water is cut off, as it often is between November and March, no restrooms either. The equally primitive and much less convenient Navajo-owned *Spider Rock RV & Campground* (☎928/674-8261, ⓦwww.spiderrockcampground.com; $10–15, cash only) is near the end of South Rim Drive. It also holds a couple of traditional *hogans* that can be rented at $29 per night and upwards.

The view from above: the rim drives

The monument's two rim drives are equally superb. The dead-end **South Rim Drive** traces the south rim of the Canyon de Chelly, while the **North Rim Drive** follows the north rim of the Canyon del Muerto and then heads off to the northeast. Each involves a round-trip drive of roughly forty miles from the visitor center, punctuated by overlooks where short walks across the mesa-top lead to views of natural or archeological wonders. Even if you don't stop at every overlook, each drive takes around half a day; for the best **photographs**, tour the North Rim in the morning and the South Rim in the afternoon. Thefts from cars are a major problem, so be careful.

The South Rim Drive

The first stop along the South Rim Drive – **Tunnel Overlook**, two miles from the visitor center – is a trailhead for guided hikes; unaccompanied travelers have no reason to stop. **Tsegi Overlook**, just beyond, stands high above a sweeping curve in the canyon. Though the wash itself is seldom more than a trickle, its broad sandy floor clears a wide gap between the fringe of cottonwoods. Behind the *hogan* near the stream, fields and paddocks reach to the cliffs.

Two miles further, **Junction Overlook** marks the meeting of the two main canyons. Canyon de Chelly narrows off to the right, behind a large monolith, while Canyon del Muerto to the left is much less conspicuous. Two tiny ruins indent the base of the canyon walls opposite.

By **White House Overlook**, six miles from the visitor center, Canyon de Chelly is 550ft deep, its rim topped by strange whorls of slickrock. Pale and majestic, the cliff that drops on the far side of the wash forms a stupendous backdrop for the photogenic **White House Ruin**. Squeezed into a tiny recess, well above the fields, this cluster of rooms originally stood above a larger pueblo on the valley floor, half of which has now eroded away; it was probably reached by ladders on the roofs of the topmost towers.

The **White House Trail**, to the right of the viewing area, offers the sole opportunity for visitors to hike alone into the canyon and is a major highlight of any Southwest itinerary. A beautiful if slightly precarious walk – some of it along ledges chiseled into the rock – it reaches the canyon floor through a tunnel that perfectly frames a Navajo *hogan* and its glowing attendant cottonwood. Thus far the ruin has been hidden from view, but once across the wooden footbridge that spans the wash you can admire it close up, separated only by a fence. Sixty feet above you, the ancient dwelling seems in almost perfect condition, still with the dazzling coat of plaster that gave it its name. Navajo traders nearby sell sodas and trinkets and ensure hikers wander no further than the permitted hundred yards in either direction. Allow at least two hours for the 2.5-mile round-trip hike back up to the overlook: 30 to 45 minutes to get down, and a good hour to climb up again.

From **Sliding House Overlook** – separated from the road by a couple of hundred yards of cairned slickrock, twelve miles along – the **Sliding House Ruin** appears to be tucked into the slenderest of crevices in the cliff face. It's now steadily slipping down toward the ploughed Navajo fields below.

South Rim Drive ends after twenty miles at the astonishing double monolith of **Spider Rock**, where Monument and Bat canyons split away from Canyon de Chelly. Soaring to within two hundred feet of the canyon rim, these eight-hundred-foot twin pinnacles of rock are said by the Navajo to be home to Spider Woman. She taught them the art of weaving, but also steals misbehaving children; their bleached, gnawed bones lie strewn across the top.

The North Rim Drive

Although you'll miss little by skipping the **Ledge Ruin Overlook**, five miles along the North Rim Drive, both the viewpoints at **Antelope House Overlook**, five miles beyond that, are well worth seeing. The first faces across to **Navajo Fortress**, at the tip of the mesa that divides Canyon del Muerto from Black Rock Canyon. It took Kit Carson's besieging forces three months, from December 1863 onwards, to starve down defiant Navajo warriors who reached the summit of this solitary tower of rock using ladders that they drew up behind them.

The other viewpoint looks down on **Antelope House Ruin**, at the base of a huge white overhang in a separate twist of Canyon del Muerto. This site was first occupied in 693 AD, and grew to comprise two square towers to the rear, plus a central plaza that held half a dozen dwellings. It's named after an antelope pictograph painted by the Navajo artist Dibé Yazhi, or Little Sheep, in the 1830s. He was also responsible for the "Spanish Mural" a little further along, which shows a Spanish lieutenant, priest, and troops advancing through the canyon.

The Navajo *hogan*

The traditional dwelling known as a *hogan* (pronounced *ho-wun*), as seen throughout Canyon de Chelly, is the focus of Navajo life and the venue for all sacred ceremonies. Few Navajo now live in a *hogan* year-round, but every family owns at least one, and those who still farm and raise sheep in the backcountry often have several.

The earliest *hogans*, first described in the sixteenth century and still widely used until the 1940s, were **"male"** *hogans*. They consisted of three vertical forked sticks propped against each other, aligned to the north, south, and west, covered with logs, brush, and mud, and with a door that faced east to greet the rising sun.

Virtually all *hogans* today are **"female,"** larger six- or eight-sided structures made of cribbed horizontal logs and once again covered with mud. These became more popular at the end of the nineteenth century, with the advent of steel saws to cut the timber and wagons to haul it; in fact many were made from salvaged railroad ties. The doorway still faces east, with a floor of hard-packed dirt to provide contact with the earth and a smoke hole in the domed roof for access to the sky. Each area of the *hogan* has a particular significance; the south side "belongs" to the women and the north to the men, while the male head of the household sits to the west. Food is prepared and stored on the northeast side; the southwest is the sleeping area.

Since the 1970s, more and more Navajo have chosen to live in trailers rather than face the labor of constantly renewing a *hogan*'s protective mud coating. *Navajo* custom dictates that a dwelling place in which a death has occurred must be abandoned.

Across the wash, in the **Tomb of the Weaver**, the embalmed body of an old man was found wrapped in golden eagle feathers.

The next, final spur road off the North Rim Drive splits to reach two separate overlooks. To the south, **Mummy Cave Overlook** offers a clear view of the single most striking ruin in the monument – **Mummy Cave Ruin**, which the Navajo call **House Under The Rock**. Inhabited for over a thousand years, it consists of two pueblo complexes deep in the shade of adjacent alcoves, with a prominent **Central Tower** on the spur in between. The sophisticated masonry of the tower has been dated to 1284, so archeologists speculate it was built by migrants from Mesa Verde.

In the "cave" visible from **Massacre Cave Overlook**, to the north, Narbona's expeditionary forces killed more than a hundred Navajo in 1805 (see p.516). It's less of a cave than a pitifully exposed ledge, far above the canyon floor, on which the huddled group were easily picked off by the Spanish, using ricochets off the overhang above. A short walk away – there's no sign, just look for the protective wall around the tip of the outcrop, lower down to your right – you can also see **Yucca Cave Ruin**, which is unusually close to the mesa-top. It's an amazing location, set in a hollow in the rock above a sheer drop, with no conceivable way down to the valley floor, but almost none of the buildings survive.

As Hwy-64, the North Rim Drive continues for fifteen miles to meet Arrowhead Hwy-12 in little **TSAILE**. The upper floors of Diné College here hold the stimulating **Ned Hatathli Museum** of Navajo history (Mon–Fri 8.30am–4.30pm; free), which also sells craft items. It's possible to hike into Canyon del Muerto from this end, with a guide hired in Chinle.

Ganado and the Hubbell Trading Post

The village of **GANADO**, halfway between Chinle and I-40 to the south and thirty miles west of Window Rock, was named after Chief Ganado Mucho ("Won a lot"), a signatory of the 1868 treaty that ended the Navajo's imprisonment at Fort Sumner.

After the Navajo returned from New Mexico, white entrepreneurs set up trading posts at the edge of the reservation, supplying goods from the world beyond in return for craft items such as blankets and jewelry. One such merchant, John Hubbell (1853–1930), established more than thirty trading posts during his long career. His original base, founded a mile west of Ganado in the early 1870s, is now run by the Park Service as the **Hubbell Trading Post** (daily: summer 8am–6pm; winter 8am–5pm; ☎928/755-3475, ⓦwww.nps.gov/hutr). At the end of a tree-lined avenue beside the Pueblo Colorado Wash, it's a fascinating living museum, where you can watch Navajo weavers at work and wander out to the old stables, piled with hay and filled with venerable wooden wagons. Serious collectors pay premium prices for the best rugs and silverwork, but the groceries in the general store – pretty historic themselves – make less expensive souvenirs. There's no admission charge, but it costs $2 to join the regular tours of the fascinating Hubbell family home, behind the store.

Ganado has no **motels**, but the *Cafe Sage* (☎928/755-3411) makes a good lunchtime stop. To the east, Hwy-264 climbs onto the thickly wooded Defiance Plateau and heads for Window Rock, while US-191 undulates for forty miles due south, through more forests, to Chambers on I-40.

Window Rock

The capital of the Navajo Nation, **WINDOW ROCK**, sits on the Arizona–New Mexico border 25 miles northwest of Gallup. An administrative headquarters rather than a lively town, it only became capital in the 1930s. Technically, if you simply pass through on Hwy-264 like most casual visitors, you're not in Window Rock at all; you also won't see the rock itself.

Both "town" and rock are a mile or two north on Arrowhead Hwy-12. The **Window Rock**, an impressive, almost circular hole in a golden sandstone cliff, used to surmount a spring where water was collected for the Water Way ceremony. With the spring now dry, it's the focus of a picnic area, dedicated as the Navajo Nation Veterans Memorial in 1995. A statue of a crouching Navajo soldier, complete with walkie-talkie, commemorates the work of the Code Talkers during World War II. Nearby, the **Navajo Tribal Council** meets at least four times yearly in the octagonal **Council Chamber**.

Back on Hwy-264, the large **Navajo Nation Museum and Visitor Center** (summer Mon & Sat 8am–5pm, Tues–Fri 8am–8pm; winter Mon–Fri 8am–5pm; donation; ☎928/871-7941) is a good spot to pick up tourist information and ask questions, but, surprisingly, doesn't hold permanent displays covering Navajo history and culture. Tucked among the rocky outcrops across the parking lot, a small **zoo** (daily 8am–5pm; free) holds specimens of local wildlife, including a bald eagle and a growling cougar that endlessly eyes the neighboring elk. The captions are in Navajo, so visits double as language lessons.

Window Rock also hosts the annual five-day **Navajo Nation Fair** (ⓦwww.navajonationfair.com), which starts on the Wednesday after Labor Day.

Practicalities

The **Navajoland Tourism** office, in the Economic Development Building on Hwy-264 a couple of miles west of town, can supply general information (Mon–Fri 8am–5pm; ☎928/810-8501, ⓦwww.discovernavajo.com).

Much of the Navajo's day-to-day business is conducted in the **restaurant** and coffee shop of the showpiece *Quality Inn Navajo Nation Capital*, at 48 W Hwy-264 (☎928/871-4108 or 1-800/662-6189, ⓦwww.qualityinnwindowrock.com; ④), which is open for all meals daily. Ask for details of their local **tours**, which can

▲ Navajo Code Talkers, Window Rock

incorporate pretty much anything you're interested in doing, but start at an expensive $100 per day. The rooms are good value, although they can be hard to come by in summer; if you're stuck, continue two miles west to the *Navajoland Inn* in St Michaels (☎928/871-5690, ⓦwww.navajoland-innsuites.com; ❸), which is, if anything, a bit smarter and has an indoor pool.

The Hopi Indian reservation

The ten thousand inhabitants of the **Hopi Indian reservation** can trace their ancestry back well over a thousand years, to the **Ancestral Puebloan** people who formerly dominated the entire Four Corners region. What's more, almost uniquely in the United States, the Hopi have occupied the same spot for at least eight hundred years. A detailed history of the Hopi appears in Contexts, on p.511.

To outsiders, it's not obvious why, with the whole Southwest to pick from, the Hopi chose to live on three barren and unprepossessing fingers of rock, poking from the southern flanks of **Black Mesa** in the depths of northeast Arizona. The answer lies within the mesa itself: although it has no perennial streams, its subterranean rocks are tilted at just the correct angle to deliver a tiny but dependable trickle of water, while the "black" in its name comes from the coal that gives the Hopi limitless reserves of fuel. In addition, the Hopi used to farm and hunt across a much wider area, only to be restricted to their mesa-top villages by the steady encroachment of their Navajo neighbors. Although the Hopi are celebrated for their skill at "**dry farming**," preserving enough precious liquid to grow corn, beans, and squash on hand-tilled terraces laid out beneath the villages, this precarious way of life was nonetheless forced upon them.

The Hopi **language**, Hopic, belongs to the Uto-Aztecan group of languages, and is spoken in different dialects on each of the three mesas. Although it bears similarities to Ute and Paiute, the Hopi have little in common with either tribe. Their culture and beliefs are instead closely related to those of the Pueblo peoples of New Mexico, to the east. Until the 1920s, the Hopi were generally known by a name coined by the people of Ácoma; **Moki**, or Moqui. Because that sounded too much like a Hopic word meaning "to have died," they then changed to *Hopi*, which means "well-behaved."

The Hopi are a matriarchal society, with homes, land, and clan affiliation passing down the female line. They are not a united people; each of the thirteen villages or settlements, is an independent entity. The Hopi Tribal Council is currently recognized by the religious leaders of only two villages.

By their very survival, and the persistence of their ancient beliefs and ceremonies, the Hopi have long fascinated outsiders. Visitors are welcomed, but the Hopi have no desire to turn themselves into a tourist attraction. A motel makes it possible to stay on the reservation, and stores and galleries make it easy to buy prized Hopi **crafts** such as pottery, basketwork, silver overlay jewelry, and hand-carved **kachina dolls**. However, tourists who arrive in the hope of extensive sightseeing – let alone spiritual revelations – are likely to leave disappointed and quite possibly dismayed by what they perceive as conspicuous poverty.

Since 1986, when increased mining revenues finally placed the tribal economy on a relatively secure footing, non-Indians have been barred from almost all Hopi ceremonies. These days, the easiest way for visitors to get a sense of traditional Hopi life is to take a guided tour of the magnificently situated village of **Walpi**, on First Mesa.

Arrival and information

The Hopi mesas – three distinct spurs along a 25-mile stretch of Black Mesa, numbered from east to west as **First**, **Second**, and **Third** mesas – are roughly fifty miles north of I-40, fifty miles east of Tuba City, and ninety miles southwest of Canyon de Chelly.

Hopi religion: The *Kachinas*

The Hopi feel neither the urge nor the obligation to divulge details of their **religious beliefs** and practices to outsiders. They have resisted attempts to make Hopic a written language, or to expose it to scrutiny by teaching it in schools. Missionaries and anthropologists have gleaned what they can, but well-known accounts of Hopi spirituality, such as Frank Waters' *Book of the Hopi*, are based on the reports of informants not initiated into the innermost secrets of the *kiva*. Inevitably, Hopi spirituality has been repeatedly misrepresented, whether as barbarous devil-worship or New Age guff.

There is in any case no single unified Hopi religion; ceremonials vary from clan to clan and village to village. The basic common element is the role of the *kachina* (often spelled *katsina*, with the plural *katsinum*). These "spirit messengers," which may represent the spirits of the dead, live in the San Francisco peaks north of Flagstaff, and return to the Hopi mesas in the form of rain-bearing clouds.

There are over three hundred different *kachinas*. At one time, they visited the mesas in person; now they come in the form of masked dancers. Not every village follows the same **ceremonial calendar**, but in general the *kachinas* arrive in early February for the *Powamuya* ceremony, or **Bean Dance**. Each matriarch receives fresh bean sprouts to plant for the coming year, and the *so'so'yoktu* ogres that threaten to eat disobedient (*ka-hopi*) children are placated by gifts of food. The *kachinas* continue to visit throughout the growing season, before returning home after the *Niman* ceremony or **Home Dance** in July.

The Hopi do not worship the *kachinas*; they are primarily examples and allegories for children. All Hopi babies receive a *tihu* – what outsiders know as a *kachina* **doll** – at their first *Niman* ceremony, and the girls receive further dolls at each *Powamuya* and *Niman* ceremony thereafter. Most boys and girls alike are initiated into a *kachina* **society** at around the age of 10, when they discover that the *kachina* dancers are their own relatives, and begin to participate themselves.

All the Southwestern pueblos had some form of *kachina* cult. Anthropologists suggest that it developed in **Mexico**, spreading north to the Hopi mesas and Zuni Pueblo via the **Mimbres** culture to the south, and then east to the Rio Grande. Its subsequent virtual disappearance along the Rio Grande was probably due to vigorous Spanish attempts to stamp it out.

The role and iconography of specific Hopi *kachinas* strongly echo **Aztec** deities such as **Tlaloc**, the god of rain, and **Quetzalcoatl**, the plumed serpent, who was also the bringer of rain and corn. For the Aztec preoccupation with death, blood, and human sacrifice, however, the Hopi and other Southwestern people substituted an obsessive focus on **rain**.

Attending Hopi ceremonies

The Hopi used to promote their ceremonies as tourist attractions. Even after cameras were banned in 1916, occasions such as the **Snake Dance**, when members of the Snake clan dance with live snakes between their teeth, drew as many as 2500 observers. More recently, however, the Hopi have **excluded** non-Indians. By 1989, Second Mesa had closed all its ceremonies to outsiders, and it was joined by all the First Mesa villages in 1992 after the publication of a *Marvel* comic that characterized the *kachinas* as violent avengers.

THE FOUR CORNERS | The Hopi Indian reservation

Both roads from the interstate up to the mesas, **Hwy-87** from Winslow and **Hwy-77** from Holbrook, run through a superbly desolate butte-studded segment of the Navajo reservation, on the western fringes of the Painted Desert. If you're coming from the Grand Canyon, take **Hwy-264** east from US-160. Once beyond the Hopi outpost of **Moenkopi**, just outside Tuba City (see p.61), this traverses rugged canyonlands before climbing onto Third Mesa after fifty miles.

While spectators are now very unlikely to be allowed at any *kachina* dances, some **social dances**, held between August and January when the *kachinas* are away from the mesas, may still be "open." Held in the village plazas, these usually take place at the weekend, so that Hopi who live off the reservation can return. Specific timings tend not to be announced until a few days in advance; for information, ask at the Cultural Center (see p.80) or call ☏928/734-2244. If you do get the chance to attend a ceremony, wear clothing that fully covers your body, keep your distance, and do not photograph, sketch, or question either dancers or audience.

Kachina dolls
Kachina **masks**, as worn by ceremonial dancers, are sacred objects; the Hopi have successfully petitioned to remove them from museum displays. However, a "*kachina* doll" or *tihu* (the plural is *ti'tihu*) is simply an instructional tool, and can therefore be sold to outsiders as a collector's item.

The *ti'tihu* given to Hopi children were originally flat dolls to be hung within the home. Made from kaolin clay, and thus white in color, the basic shape was painted to show a head, plus a pair of arms folded over a kilt that represented rain. Trading posts stocked these simple dolls in the 1890s, and by 1900 they were being made specifically for sale.

Since then, they have become much more complex in form and color, and acquired feet. Most are carved from cottonwood roots; the carving is seen as a prayer for water, symbolizing the root's own search for water. The artists themselves – who thanks to the art market's desire for signed pieces are no longer anonymous – became more interested in representing human anatomy, and also began to tailor their designs to suit the tastes of white collectors. Strictly speaking, only men should carve *ti'tihu*, but some women make them now as well.

Not all *ti'tihu* represent *kachinas*. Some popular designs depict the clowns who also appear during ceremonies, such as the black-and-white-striped *koshares*, and the knobbed "mudheads" or *koyemsi*. Just as the clowns may devise costumes to mock tourists, for example, certain *ti'tihu* are caricatures of figures like basketball players or anthropologists.

The Hopi do, however, draw the line at attempts by others to cash in on the commercial success of the *kachina*-doll business, though the tribal council has been unable to copyright the word "*kachina*" to stop Navajo and other non-Indian copyists using the name. Genuine hand-carved dolls are both exquisite and expensive, and a top-class carver will produce fewer than fifty per year, while fake *kachinas* are mass-produced in New Mexico. Good places to buy a *kachina* doll include the Hopi Cultural Center on Second Mesa, the Museum of Northern Arizona in Flagstaff, and Albuquerque's Indian Pueblo Cultural Center, though it's hard to find a reasonable-sized piece for under $300. The best bet of all is to come to the reservation, and either call in at stores like Tsakurshovi on Second Mesa (☏928/734-2478) or the Monongya Gallery at Oraibi (☏928/734-2344), or simply take a tour of Walpi and see what you're offered.

The first essential stop when you arrive is the roadside **Hopi Cultural Center**, below Second Mesa, which serves as motel and restaurant – see opposite – as well as gift store and information center. If any forthcoming events are open to tourists, the friendly staff should be able to tell you about them. Otherwise, check out the wide-ranging historical exhibits and the choice displays of Hopi arts and crafts, in the adjoining **museum** (summer Mon–Sat 8am–5pm, Sun 9am–4pm; winter Mon–Fri 8am–5pm; $3; ☏928/734-6650). The shop next door is particularly good for silver.

Touring the Hopi mesas

Each of the mesa-top Hopi villages centers around a **plaza**, where successive generations have built new houses on top of the old ones as they crumble into sand. Often the main entrance is via the roof, itself reached by a wooden ladder. Though a few buildings are now constructed of gray concrete blocks, they still blend almost imperceptibly into the ruins that trail away down the slopes. Several villages stand on open seams of coal, and large chunks of coal lie scattered around. Outhouses are dotted across the hillsides; all waste was traditionally thrown over the edge of the mesa to tumble down and fertilize the terraces, a policy that works less well now that refrigerators and old bedsteads are thrown over too.

The only village to offer **guided tours** is the most impressive, **WALPI** (daily: summer 9.30am–6pm; winter 10am–4pm; adults $8, ages 5–17 $5; ☏928/737-2262). By Hopi standards, Walpi is not that old; it was hastily thrown together in the aftermath of the Pueblo Revolt of 1680, when the people of First Mesa decided to move to a more secure site in the face of possible Spanish or Navajo attack (see p.512). The spot they chose is absolutely stunning, standing alone at the narrow southernmost tip of the mesa, and connected to the other First Mesa villages by the merest slender neck of stone, with a drop of three hundred feet to either side. It now serves as a permanent home to just three people, who live without electricity or running water. Others return to their family homes for special events, or come up each day to sell crafts.

To see Walpi, take Hwy-264 to modern **POLACCA**, at the foot of First Mesa, then drive a mile up the twisting paved road until it ends in **SICHOMOVI**. Although you can't tell where one village stops and the next begins, you've just passed through **HANO**. Its inhabitants arrived during the Pueblo Revolt to offer their services as the defenders of First Mesa, and still speak the Tewa language.

Tours assemble in Sichomovi's small Ponsi Hall Community Center, setting off at regular intervals for a half-hour walk to and around Walpi. Depending on the season, you may be in a group of twenty or so, or on your own, but either way there's plenty of opportunity to ask questions and to buy pottery, *kachina* dolls, and fresh-baked *piiki*, a flatbread made with blue cornflour.

Elsewhere on the reservation, signs beside the highway point out shops and stalls selling Hopi handicrafts. At some point down any side road you choose to follow, as you approach a village, a large notice will forbid you to drive any further, but may allow you to walk within a specified area. Once you've seen Walpi, the most intriguing destination on the other mesas is **ORAIBI** on Third Mesa, regarded as the oldest Hopi settlement of all. No scheduled tours can guide you around, but one or two stores are normally open and eager for your business.

Joining a Hopi guide for your own private **tour** will show you far more of the reservation than you can see alone. Both Gary Tso of the Left-Handed Tour Co (☏928/734-2567, ✉lhhunter58@hotmail.com) and Bertram Tsavadawa of Ancient Pathways Tours (☏928/306-7849) take visitors around Old Oraibi and to little-known petroglyph sites, as well as to craftspeople and galleries. Rates depend on how many of you there are; with just two, expect to pay from $75 per person for a three-hour tour, up to $175 per person for a full day.

Accommodation and eating

The only place to **stay** on the Hopi reservation is below Second Mesa, in the modern, mock-Pueblo *Hopi Cultural Center Motel* (☎928/734-2401, ⓦwww .hopiculturalcenter.com; ❹); in summer, its plain but acceptable rooms are usually booked solid a week or more in advance. The cafeteria serves good, substantial meals, including local delicacy *noqkwivi*, lamb stewed with hominy, but be warned that there's precious little to do between the time it closes, at 9pm (or 8pm in winter), and 7am the next morning, when you can indulge your curiosity by having blue cornflakes for breakfast.

Southwest Colorado

In ancient times, of course, the straight-line boundaries that divide the states of Arizona, New Mexico, Utah, and Colorado – and mark the northeastern limits of the Navajo Nation – did not exist. As a result, although Colorado might not spring to mind as a "Southwestern" state, its far southwest corner holds some fascinating archeological sites. **Mesa Verde National Park** is absolutely unmissable, while the ancient ruins in **Ute Mountain Tribal Park**, which lies well off the beaten track and can only be accessed with a Ute guide, offer adventurous travelers an even more exhilarating sense of discovery.

Once you've crossed the border into Colorado, it's hard to resist the lure of the Rockies, looming along the skyline to the north. There's no scope in this book to do more than sketch out a brief tour , looping up the **San Juan Skyway** from lively **Durango** to historic mining towns such as **Silverton** and **Ouray**.

Four Corners Monument Navajo Tribal Park

The **Four Corners Monument Navajo Tribal Park** (daily: June–Sept 7am–8pm; Oct–May 8am–5pm; $3), reached by a short spur road half a mile northeast of US-160, is the only place in the United States where four states meet at a single point. However exciting you may find the concept, the reality is bleak and dull. A steady stream of visitors mooch around the pivotal brass plaque, contorting a limb into each state for novelty photographs. Navajo stalls on all sides sell crafts, T-shirts, and fry-bread.

Ute Mountain Tribal Park

For a couple of centuries after **Ute Indians** acquired horses from the Spanish, their hunting territory extended east from Utah as far as Nebraska. As miners pushed the Victorian-era frontier westwards, however, the Ute were confined to poorer land. The creation of reservations split them into three separate groups: the **Northern Utes**, who now live in the mountains near Utah's border with Wyoming; the **Southern Utes**, who occupy a strip of southern Colorado south of Durango; and the **Ute Mountain Utes**.

The two-thousand-strong band of Ute Mountain Utes take their name from a long, low mountain ridge in Colorado's far southwestern corner, known to outsiders as **Sleeping Ute Mountain** because of its uncanny resemblance, when seen from the east, to a slumbering warrior. Also known as the Weeminuche, they long ranked among the Southwest's poorest peoples, and draw their income these days from mineral leases and a large **casino** near the main settlement of **Towaoc**, which offers hotel accommodation and a cheap restaurant (℡970/565-8800 or 1-800/258-8007, Ⓦwww.utemountaincasino.com; ➌).

The Ute Mountain Utes also run the inaccessible but utterly enthralling **Ute Mountain Tribal Park**, which abuts against Mesa Verde National Park and preserves an equally extraordinary but far less visited assortment of ancient **Ancestral Puebloan** remains. The only way to see the park is on a **Ute-guided tour**. In principle, these leave at 9am daily from a **visitor center**-cum-museum (April–Oct daily 8am–3pm, but hours subject to fluctuation; ℡970/749-1452), housed in a former gas station at the intersection of US-160 and US-491, twenty miles up from the Four Corners Monument. That schedule varies according to demand, however, and while in season it's usually possible to take the tour by turning up at around 8.30am, it's much safer to arrange things in advance (℡970/565-4653 or 1-800/847-5485, Ⓦwww.utemountainute.com).

If you don't have the time to take a full-day tour, which costs $45 and gets you back to the highway around 5pm, the half-day tour at $27 makes a very poor alternative. On the half-day trip, you simply leave the group at the end of the morning, having seen a couple of potsherd-scattered mounds, concealing ancient surface-level pueblos, at the foot of the cliffs. On the full-day tour, you continue along a remote and circuitous dirt road to the top of the mesa, and then inch down ladders onto a three-mile ledge skirting **Lion Canyon**. This leads to three beautifully preserved **cliff dwellings**, built at the same time as those on Mesa Verde: Tree House Ruin, the eighty-room Lion House, and the precarious Eagle's Nest, perched in a colossal natural alcove. The whole expedition demands a fair amount of walking and something of a head for heights, but only the final ascent to Eagle's Nest is difficult for vertigo sufferers – you can admire it from below if you prefer.

Visitors are expected to drive their own sturdy vehicles on the tour and to bring food and drink. However, the tour leader's van will accommodate half a dozen passengers; if there's room, you can pay an extra $10 to ride along, and thus get much more informed commentary on what you're seeing. For $12 per vehicle, you can stay overnight at a primitive **campground** close to the main highway.

It's also possible to arrange trips to more remote areas of the park, which involve significantly more **hiking**; groups must consist of four or more members, each of whom pays $60.

Hovenweep National Monument

Hidden in the fifty-mile-wide swathe of no-man's-land that straddles the Utah–Colorado border, the Ancestral Puebloan ruins at **HOVENWEEP NATIONAL MONUMENT** lack the scale and setting of the Mesa Verde cliff dwellings or similar Four Corners sites. Instead, sprouting from the rims of shallow desert canyons and dwarfed by the distant mountains, they offer a haunting sense of timeless isolation. They also have one unique feature: the tall **towers** that many archeologists regard as astronomical observatories.

Whatever most tourist maps may suggest, almost all the roads to Hovenweep have now been paved, thanks largely to companies drilling for oil and gas around Aneth. The monument is best reached by driving 35 miles **due west** from Cortez along County Road G, which leaves US-160 near the air strip at the south end of town, or 25 miles east from US-191 via Hwy-262, which branches off halfway between Bluff and Blanding in Utah; when conditions are dry, it's also possible to follow a dirt road southwest from Pleasant View in Colorado through Canyons of the Ancients National Monument.

▲ Hovenweep National Monument

The monument includes five abandoned villages – its name comes from a Ute word meaning "deserted valley" – a few miles apart, in four distinct parcels. Easy access, however, is restricted to **Little Ruin Canyon**, which lies behind the smart **visitor center** (daily: April–Sept 8am–6pm; Oct–May 8am–5pm; $6 per vehicle, or $3 per person; ☎970/562-4282, Ⓦwww.nps.gov/hove). It's no longer possible to walk among or into the structures ranged above and below the rim of this shallow cleft, known collectively as the **Square Tower Unit**; instead, a single trail loops around the edge, keeping visitors at a safe distance.

A complete circuit of the trail, which is open daily from sunrise until sunset, takes just under an hour. After meeting the canyon near the fortress-like **Stronghold House**, the trail heads right, past the prosaically named **Unit-type House**, where niches in the walls appear to line up with the angle of the sun at the summer and winter solstices. **Hovenweep Castle**, a four-square building five minutes' walk farther on at the head of the canyon, was constructed around 1200 AD. It may have stood guard over a much larger pueblo complex that nestled on the sandy canyon floor a mere thirty feet below, clustered around the perennial spring that was the site's only source of water. Of that whole complex, only **Square Tower Ruin** can still be discerned, while up above Hovenweep Castle has endured, a perfect illustration of the Biblical admonition that only a house built on rock shall stand. It takes another ten minutes to reach the final significant ruin, the **Twin Towers**. Doubling back on yourself at that point, rather than completing the loop, will spare you the final steep dip and climb through the middle of the canyon, but saves no time overall.

No accommodation, gasoline, or food is available at or anywhere near Hovenweep, but a 31-site **campground** near the visitor center remains open all year ($10; no reservations).

Cortez

The town of **CORTEZ**, twenty miles north of the US-160/US-491 intersection, consists of little more than a long curve of over-developed highway. Were it not so close to Mesa Verde National Park, there would be no reason to visit; as it is, Cortez offers a large, if not exactly broad, selection of roadside motels and diners.

Cortez's well-stocked **visitor center**, on the edge of City Park at 928 E Main St (daily: summer 8am–6pm; winter 8am–5pm; ☎970/565-3414, ⓦwww.swcolo.org), doubles as a Colorado Welcome Center, with information on the entire state.

Accommodation

A couple of dozen **motels** line Cortez's main strip, with a few of the big-name chains scattered among the local operators.

Aneth Lodge, 645 E Main St ☎970/565-3453 or 1-877/263-8454, ⓔanethlodge@hubwest.com. The good-sized rooms her are more kitsch than fancy, but they're clean, cheap, and close to Cortez's pulsating heart. Winter ❷, summer ❹

Best Western Turquoise Inn & Suites 535 E Main St ☎970/565-3778 or 1-800/547-3376, ⓦwww.bestwesternmesaverde.com. Smart, central two-story motel, with a small outdoor pool open in summer only and an indoor one for the winter. Winter ❸, summer ❻

Budget Host Inn, Bel Rau Lodge 2040 E Main St ☎970/565-3738 or 1-888/677-3738, ⓦwww .budgethostmesaverde.com. The "budget" tag doesn't quite do justice to this comfortable and nicely presented motel, with pool and hot tub, a short way out toward Mesa Verde. Winter ❷, summer ❸

Kelly Place 14663 County Rd G ☎970/565-3125 or 1-800/745-4885, ⓦwww.kellyplace.com. Truly exceptional B&B ranch, tucked amid the peach orchards of McElmo Canyon, ten miles west of Cortez towards Hovenweep. Accommodation, all en suite, is in seven comfortable lodge rooms or three cabins, and meals are served in the central dining room. Staff-led hikes to Ancestral Puebloan ruins – several are on site – cost $125 for a group of up to four for half a day, or $195 for a full day; it's also possible to ride horses or to take an overnight covered-wagon trip. Rooms ❹, cabins ❼

Super 8 505 E Main St ☎970/565-8888 or 1-800/800-8000, ⓦwww.super8.com. Comfortable, inexpensive three-story motel next to the *Turquoise Inn* in central Cortez, with a good free breakfast bar. Winter ❷, summer ❹

Eating

Cortez is bursting with **restaurants**, including all the usual fast-food options as well as the home-grown alternatives listed below.

Dry Dock 200 W Main St ☎970/564-9404. Unquestionably the best restaurant in town, serving delicious seafood specialties – they even have fresh oysters – in a garden decorated with underwater-themed murals. There's also steaks, fajitas, and burritos. Typical entrees cost $13–18. Daily 5–10pm.

Homesteaders 45 E Main St ☎970/565-6253. Old-time Western diner, piling plates high with deep-fried fish and chicken, as well as barbecued meats and big steaks – and don't imagine that the Mexican platters are any lighter. Mon–Sat 11am–9.30pm; summer also Sun 5–10pm.

Main Book Co 34 W Main St ☎970/565-8158. Part café, part book and antiques store, part wine

bar, housed in a former post office. Coffee and pastries for breakfast, sandwiches and salads for lunch, but just snacks in the evening. Daily 8.30am–8pm.

Main Street Brewery 21 E Main St ☎970/564-9112. Colorful central brewpub with a pressed tin ceiling, a wide range of microbrews, a lengthy wine list, and a full menu of pizzas, burgers, snacks, and steaks. Daily 3.30pm–midnight.

Silver Bean 410 W Main St ☎970/946-4404. This eye-catching, old-fashioned silver trailer just west of downtown serves espresso coffees, chais, and smoothies as well as burritos and pastries; drive-through customers welcome. Mon–Fri 6.30am–3pm, Sat 7.30am–1pm.

Canyons of the Ancients National Monument

Cortez is very much the largest town in **Montezuma Valley** these days, but a thousand years ago the entire valley was densely populated. In fact, it's said to contain the highest density of archeological sites in the United States, which explains why much of it was designated in 2000 as the **Canyons of the Ancients National Monument**. For the moment, however, the monument largely consists of several pre-existing small museums and lesser-known sites dotted around the valley. Its creation attracted considerable local opposition, because the economy here has long depended on extracting gas, oil, and minerals from the canyons all around. As 85 percent of the monument is already covered by leases that will still be exploited, fears that livelihoods are in danger seem somewhat misplaced.

Incidentally, romantic notions that Montezuma Valley was a peaceful agricultural community have been dashed by archeological research that as well as uncovering evidence of warfare and wholesale slaughter has even provided conclusive proof of ancient **cannibalism**. Human excrement discovered alongside the butchered remains of 23 Ancestral Puebloans in Cowboy Wash contained proteins that could only have come from eating their flesh.

Dolores

The national monument headquarters is located in the **Anasazi Heritage Center**, three miles west of **DOLORES** and six miles north of Cortez (daily: March–Oct 9am–5pm, $3; Nov–Feb 9am–4pm, free; ☎970/882-5600, ⓦwww .co.blm.gov/canm). This centers on a couple of twelfth-century pueblos, excavated during the construction of nearby McPhee Dam, responsible for turning the Dolores River into a broad lake at this point. The pueblos were named after the eighteenth-century Spanish friars Domínguez and Escalante, who first noted the traces of prehistoric Indians in the area. A trail leads around the ruins themselves, and there's to well-equipped **museum** of Pueblo life.

In Dolores, the *Rio Grande Southern Hotel*, 101 S Fifth St (☎970/882-2125 or 1-866/822-3026, ⓦwww.rgshotel.com; closed Dec–Feb; ➍), is an inexpensive, charming **B&B**, with period furnishings, while *Dolores Mountain Inn*, 701 Railroad Ave (☎970/882-7203 or 1-800/842-8113, ⓦwww.dminn.com; ➍), offers decent **motel** rooms. For **guided tours** to archeological sites in the vicinity, contact Talking Stones Tours (☎970/799-8066 or 1-866/634-4280, ⓦwww.talkingstonestours.com).

Lowry Pueblo

From **Pleasant View**, fourteen miles northwest of Dolores on US-491, the undulating but straight County Road CC leads a further nine miles west to **Lowry Pueblo Ruins** (no fixed hours; free). There's not a tremendous amount to see at this free-standing pueblo, but in summer, it's noteworthy as one of the few sites where at least part of an **Ancestral Puebloan mural** remains in place on the walls of a "Great Kiva" (see p.527). In winter, the mural is taken away for preservation, and the gravel surface of the approach road's last four miles is often impassable to vehicles.

Crow Canyon Archeological Center and Sand Canyon

Each summer, **Crow Canyon Archeological Center**, five miles northwest of Cortez at 23390 County Rd K (☎970/565-8975 or 1-800/422-8975, ⓦwww .crowcanyon.org), runs day programs for amateur archeologists (June–Aug Wed & Thurs 8.30am; $50) and week-long residential courses for more serious students of Southwestern prehistory ($1275). Both provide the chance to assist on digs at Ancestral Puebloan sites in the valley, such as the 1800-room **Yellow Jacket**, and **Sand Canyon Pueblo**, a walled city that once covered the clifftops at Crow Canyon, further south.

It's also possible to make your own free, unguided visit to Sand Canyon Pueblo at any time. Signs on the spot explain how the 420-room pueblo may once have looked, but there are no facilities. Either drive straight there along county roads P and N, which leave US-491 northwest of Cortez, or take County Road G off US-491 south of Cortez, which is also the main route to Hovenweep, and **hike** to the pueblo along the rough, six-mile **Sand Canyon Trail**.

Mancos

Fourteen miles east of Cortez, and seven miles east of the foot of the approach road that climbs into Mesa Verde, compact and attractive little **MANCOS** caters almost exclusively to visitors to the national park. **Accommodation** options include the comfortable *Mesa Verde Motel*, 191 Railroad Ave (℡970/533-7741 or 1-800/825-6372, Ⓦwww.mesaverdemotel.com; ❹), which has its own restaurant. The *Absolute Bakery & Cafe*, 110 S Main St (℡970/533-1200), serves coffees and fresh breads plus breakfast and lunch daily; it also doubles as a bookstore.

Mesa Verde National Park

MESA VERDE NATIONAL PARK, the only US national park exclusively devoted to archeological remains, is set high in the plateaus of southwest Colorado, off US-160 halfway between Cortez and Mancos. It's an astonishing place, so far off the beaten track that its extensive **Ancestral Puebloan ruins** remained unseen by outsiders until late in the nineteenth century.

Mesa Verde itself – the "green table" – is a densely wooded sandstone plateau, cut at its southern edge by sheer canyons that divide the land into narrow fingers. Hundreds of natural alcoves, eaten high into the canyon walls by seeping water, served as homes for over seven hundred years; by the time they were abandoned, around 1300, several held multistory **cliff dwellings** that have remained virtually intact to this day.

By Southwestern standards, the mesa is not especially pretty, and it doesn't offer the same **hiking** opportunities as the region's other national parks. Its compelling relics, however, make Mesa Verde an essential stop on any Four Corners itinerary; readers of *Condé Nast Traveler* even voted it the world's top tourist attraction. As things can get very crowded in summer, the **best months** to visit are May, September, and October. The 8000ft elevation means that most of the sights become inaccessible in **winter**, though the park itself, its main museum, and one ruin – Spruce Tree House – remain open year round. **Concessions** such as gas, food, and lodging only operate between late March and early November.

A history of Mesa Verde

Although Archaic sites in Montezuma Valley below date back to 5500 BC, the earliest trace of humans found on Mesa Verde is a 550 AD Ancestral Puebloan Modified Basketmaker pithouse. People first moved to the mesa, therefore, at around the time they acquired the skill of pottery. Not so much farmers as gardeners, they continued to gather wild plants and hunt deer and rabbits as well as grow small fields of corn and own domesticated dogs and turkeys. For five hundred years, they lived in pithouses dug into the floors of sheltered caves; then, around 1100, they congregated in walled villages up on the mesa tops. A century later, they returned to the canyon-side alcoves to build the "palaces" for which Mesa Verde is now famous. No one has lived here since the end of the thirteenth century.

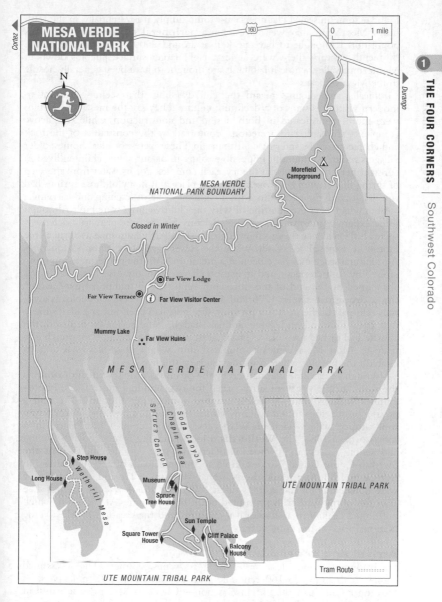

MESA VERDE
NATIONAL PARK

160

0   1 mile

Cortez

Durango

Morefield
Campground

MESA VERDE
NATIONAL PARK BOUNDARY

Closed in Winter

Far View Lodge

Far View Terrace   Far View Visitor Center

Mummy Lake   Far View Ruins

M E S A   V E R D E   N A T I O N A L   P A R K

Spruce Canyon

Soda Canyon

Chapin Mesa

Step House

Long House

Wetherill Mesa

Museum

Spruce
Tree House

Sun Temple

Square Tower
House

Cliff Palace

Balcony
House

UTE MOUNTAIN TRIBAL PARK

Tram Route

UTE MOUNTAIN TRIBAL PARK

Archeologists believe that each settlement held significantly fewer people than it did rooms, as many rooms were exclusively used for storage. They suggest the largest, Cliff Palace, housed a population of around 120. Two or three people may have slept in a typical living room, measuring six feet by eight feet, while each family had its own *kiva* – see p.527 – which when not in ceremonial use was used for weaving and domestic activities. No rigid social hierarchy is indicated either in the architecture, or the relatively few burials to have been found – some in sealed chambers, and some simply, if reverentially, in the trash heaps. Mesa Verde may well have been a **peripheral community**. While its population is thought to have peaked at around 2500, in the middle of the thirteenth century, there were at least eight larger surface pueblos down in Montezuma Valley, whose inhabitants are thought to have been generally hostile to the Mesa Verdeans.

Ironically, archeologists regard the cliff dwellings that seem so elegant to modern visitors as signs of a declining culture. They say the mesa-top pueblos were more sophisticated in both design and construction, while the alcove complexes are haphazard accretions, contorted by the constraints of the rock and characterized by inferior craftsmanship. These were not ideal homes; older villagers must have found it impossible to get in or out, while children lived in constant peril of fatal falls. In theory, each complex got its water from the seep or spring that created its alcove in the first place, but many of those springs had run dry, leaving the occupants with a constant cycle of fetching and carrying.

All of which begs the question of **why** the cliff dwellings were built. Although some experts argue that sites such as Balcony House were primarily defensive, there's little evidence they were ever attacked, and dwellings such as Spruce Tree House lie exposed to assault, while the towers are of little use as lookouts. Agricultural space may have been at a premium, with the entire mesa top criss-crossed by dams, terraces, and irrigation channels. In any case, Mesa Verde was abandoned by the end of the thirteenth century. The traditional explanation, that a **drought** between 1276 and 1299 drove the Ancestral Puebloans away, only tells part of the story; six previous droughts had been just as bad. It's likely that both firewood and game animals had become seriously depleted, the climate had turned too cold to grow crops, and survival became too much of a struggle. Most Mesa Verdeans migrated into what's now New Mexico, to establish the pueblos where their descendants still live.

Although Mesa Verde was named by the Spanish in the seventeenth century, the ruins themselves went unrecorded for two hundred more years. Photographer William Henry Jackson snapped some lesser sites in 1874, and a passing prospector spotted Balcony House in 1884, but the outside world first took notice when Richard Wetherill stumbled upon Cliff Palace in a snowstorm in 1888. The **Wetherills**, a local ranching family, took to finding and selling Ancestral Puebloan artifacts as a way of life, and helped the Swedish Count Gustaf Nordenskïold to ship caseloads of ancient pottery to Europe in 1891. As a result, the National Museum of Finland, to which they were donated, holds the world's finest collection of Mesa Verde artifacts. The activities of the Wetherills prompted both the Antiquities Act of 1906, which prohibited dealing in archeological treasures, and the creation of Mesa Verde National Park in the same year.

Arrival and information

For **information** on Mesa Verde, visit Ⓦwww.nps.gov/meve. The access road climbs south from US-160 ten miles east of **Cortez** and 35 miles west of **Durango**. Once past the entrance station – where the seven-day **admission charge** of $15 per vehicle, $8 for motorcyclists, cyclists, and pedestrians, reduced to $10 and $5 respectively between late September and late May, is payable – it twists and turns for fifteen miles to the parking lot for **Far View visitor center** (early April to mid-Oct daily 8am–5pm; ☏970/529-5036). Designed to resemble an Ancestral Puebloan tower, this impressive structure is reached via a tunnel and then a spiral walkway. Exhibits focus on Pueblo pottery and the story of Count Nordenskïold rather than the history of the site.

Mesa Verde tours and tickets

The three major ruins in Mesa Verde National Park can only be visited on guided tours, though it is possible to see Cliff Palace and Long House from nearby overlooks. To take a tour, you must first buy tickets at the visitor center. The exact seasons and times of the tours vary according to both funding and climate – the specific times given below are for general guidance only – each costs $3, with tickets valid for one specific time only. Allow several hours between tours on Chapin and Wetherill mesas. After the visitor center closes in late fall, tour tickets are sold at the museum on Chapin Mesa (see opposite).

On Chapin Mesa, during the busiest months, you will probably not be allowed to tour Balcony House and Cliff Palace on the same day (though many couples circumvent the regulations by queuing separately for tickets). If you're forced to choose, Cliff Palace can at least be seen from a distance without joining a tour, but on the other hand, touring Cliff Palace is much less strenuous than Balcony House. On days when they let you tour both, photographers should visit Balcony House first, for the best light. For most other ruins, the best time for photography is late afternoon.

daily hours	tour times	
Cliff Palace on Chapin Mesa		
early April to mid-May	9am–5pm	hourly
2nd two weeks of May	9am–5pm	half-hourly
late May to early Sept	9am–6pm	half-hourly
early Sept to mid-Oct	9am–5pm	half-hourly
mid-Oct to early Nov	9am–4pm	hourly
Balcony House on Chapin Mesa		
late April to early May	9am–5pm	9.30am, noon, 2pm, 3.30pm
early May to late May	9am–5pm	hourly
late May to early Sept	9am–5pm	half-hourly
early Sept to mid-Oct	9am–5pm	hourly
Long House on Wetherill Mesa		
late May to early Sept	10am–5pm	hourly
early Sept to late Sept	9.45am–4.30pm	hours vary

Half-day **bus tours** of the park start from the nearby *Far View Terrace* restaurant at 8am and 1pm daily between late April and late October, costing $42 for adults and $32 for ages 5–17; contact ☎1-800/449-2288 or ⊛www.visitmesaverde .com for reservations. Taking a tour can ease the laborious business of driving around Mesa Verde, and of queuing for tickets, but the sheer cost makes it hard to recommend them for family groups. Day-trips to Mesa Verde starting from **Durango** are listed on p.82.

Immediately beyond the visitor center, the road divides to the two main constellations of remains: Chapin Mesa to the south, and Wetherill Mesa to the west.

Accommodation and eating

The only **rooms** at Mesa Verde are in the summer-only *Far View Motor Lodge*, near the visitor center (☎970/564-4300 or 1-888/896-3831, ⊛www.visit mesaverde.com; closed late Oct to late April; ❺). It's a peaceful place, away from the bustle of the park; guestrooms, which lack phones or TVs, are in two-story units dotted around the mesa-top. Cellphones won't work, but there's wi-fi in the lobby. Though the sweeping views reach into the Rockies to the north, no archeological sites are visible. The *Metate Room*, in the mock-adobe main lodge, is a pretty good restaurant that's open daily for dinner only; entrees such as elk tenderloin are priced at up to $30.

The park's official **campground** – the very large and almost never full *Morefield Campground* (early May to early Oct; ☎970/564-4300 or 1-888/896-3831, ⓦwww.visitmesaverde.com) – is four miles up from the entrance, and thus a long way from the ruins. No reservations are necessary; a site for one or two vehicles costs $20, or $25 with hook-ups.

Food is also available in season at the *Far View Terrace* (early May to mid-Oct daily 7am–8pm), across from the visitor center – which serves espresso coffees and has a gas station – and all year round at *Spruce Tree Terrace* (daily: summer 10am–7pm; winter 10am–5pm), near the Chapin Mesa museum, which has a pleasant shaded terrace. Light snacks are sold at the end of the road on Wetherill Mesa.

Chapin Mesa

A couple of miles toward **Chapin Mesa** from the visitor center, **Far View** itself is a mesa-top pueblo abandoned in the thirteenth century. Thanks to the coal-burning power plants that stand in the middle distance, it seldom lives up to its name. Archeologists speculate that a large open area nearby, which has been dubbed **Mummy Lake**, doubled as both an open-air plaza and a reservoir which could hold half a million gallons. Some suggest that the rhythmic shuffling feet of ceremonial dancers were deliberately choreographed to wear grooves in the rock along which rainwater would flow to be collected.

Another four miles on, **Chapin Mesa Museum** (daily: early April to mid-Oct 8am–6.30pm; mid-Oct to early April 8am–5pm) contains the park's best displays on the Ancestral Puebloans, including several 1930s dioramas. It's also the starting point for the short, steep hike down to **Spruce Tree House**, the only ruin that can be seen in winter. Consisting of several well-preserved three-story structures, snugly molded into the recesses of a rocky alcove and fronted by open plazas, the neat little village was occupied from 1200 AD until 1276 AD. One *kiva* has been re-roofed, and visitors can enter the dusty, unadorned interior by way of a ladder. Between early November and early March, Spruce Tree House can only be seen on free guided tours, which set off from the museum daily at 10am, 1pm, and 3.30pm. For the rest of the year, the trail is open for free self-guided visits.

Ruins Road, beyond the museum area, is only open between April and late October, from 8am until sunset daily, and has two one-way, six-mile loops. At the **western** loop's first stop, **Square Tower House**, a 500-foot stroll is rewarded by views of an eighty-room alcove complex, focused around the four-story Square Tower – at 26 feet, the park's tallest tower. **Sun Point Overlook** looks across Spruce Canyon to as many as twelve distinct cliff dwellings, including Cliff Palace, making it clear just how crowded the canyon was in its heyday. Unlike the alcove sites, the mesa-top **Sun Temple**, next, was built to a premeditated design, and may have been a ceremonial center for the whole community. It was never finished, however, and its shape and function can only really be appreciated from aerial photos.

The first stop on the **eastern** portion of Ruins Road, **Cliff Palace**, is the largest Ancestral Puebloan cliff dwelling to survive anywhere. Tucked a hundred feet below an overhanging ledge of pale rock, it holds 217 rooms and 23 *kivas*, each thought to have belonged to a separate family or clan. It's thought this was a ceremonial or storage center rather than simply a communal habitation, and may have been home to around 120 people.

If you haven't managed to get a ticket to tour Cliff Palace (see opposite), you can still get a great view from the promontory where the tour groups gather, just below the parking lot. However, walking through the empty plazas and peering down into the mysterious *kivas*, especially on a quieter day, provides a haunting evocation of a lost and little-known world. Fading murals can still be discerned inside some of the structures. As you leave, climbing an unalarming metal stairway through a narrow crevice, you may spot the original toe- and footholds used by the Ancestral Puebloans.

Technically, Ruins Road passes out of the national park just beyond Cliff Palace and briefly enters **Ute Mountain Tribal Park**, where you can pick up information on tours (see p.81). It then arrives at **Balcony House**, one of the few Mesa Verde complexes that was clearly geared toward defense. Built around 1240, it was remodeled during the 1270s to make it even more impregnable; access is very difficult, and it's not visible from above. Guided tours involve scrambling up three hair-raising ladders and crawling through a narrow tunnel, above a steep drop into Soda Canyon. It's a spectacular site, with two circular *kivas* standing side by side in a commanding central position, but those who don't share the fearless Ancestral Puebloan attitude to heights should give it a miss.

Distant views of Balcony House can be had from three quarters of a mile along the forested **Soda Canyon Overlook Trail**, which starts a short way further around Ruins Road.

Wetherill Mesa

The tortuous twelve-mile drive onto **Wetherill Mesa** from the visitor center is usually open from late May until late September. Access is then permitted between 9.15am and 4.30pm daily, though cycles and large vehicles such as RVs are always banned. In recent years the road has been open from Tuesday to Saturday only for much of September.

From the parking lot at the far end of the road, where there's a ranger station and snack kiosk, a free **miniature train** loops around the tip of the mesa. Priority is given to visitors with tickets for the timed Long House tours (see p.89). Any time spent waiting can be occupied by walking down to nearby **Step House**, where a single alcove contains a restored pithouse, dating to 626, as well as a pueblo from 1226.

The mini-train stops at various trailheads from which hikers can walk to early mesa-top sites or alcove overlooks, but its principal destination is the **Long House**. The park's second largest ruin is set in its largest cave; hour-long tours descend sixty or so steps to reach its central plaza, then scramble around its 150 rooms and 21 *kivas*. These ruins are said to be especially authentic, having been "restabilized" in recent years, rather than subjected to the same extensive rebuilding as the better-known sites were earlier last century. Excavations here uncovered a number of unburied bodies, some of whom had clearly met violent deaths.

Durango

Named after Durango, Mexico, with which it's also twinned, **DURANGO** was founded in 1880 as a rail junction for the Gold Rush community of Silverton, 45 miles further north. **Steam trains** still run the same high-mountain route, through the Animas Valley, and thanks to their superb close-up views of the mountains are its main tourist attraction. In addition, Durango has become a new-style Wild West boomtown, attracting a large influx of computerized teleworkers. Combine them with outdoors enthusiasts, who come to ride their **mountain bikes** on the grueling local back roads, and in the morning at least

The Durango & Silverton Railroad

Between May and October, the steam trains of the **Durango & Silverton Narrow Gauge Railroad** make up to three daily return trips along a spectacular route through the mountains that parallels the gorgeous San Juan Skyway. Opened in 1882, the track took just nine months to construct. The most memorable of the train's many movie appearances was being blown up in *Butch Cassidy and the Sundance Kid* in 1969.

Precise schedules vary, but all trains leave **Durango** in the morning, with the first at 8.15am, departing from the depot at 479 Main Ave at the south end of town, and allowing time for lunch in **Silverton** at the far end. The journey takes 3 hour 30 minutes in each direction, at a maximum speed of 18mph.

No trains run for most of November, but between late November and April, when the higher mountain reaches are closed by snow, shorter excursions operate on the most scenic section only, as far as Cascade Canyon, departing at 10am daily, and only running from Thursday to Sunday in January and February. In the weeks leading up to Christmas, the Polar Express service offers hour-long trips to the "North Pole."

Reservations should be made at least two weeks in advance, via ℡970/247-2733, 1-877/872-4607, or ⓦwww.durangotrain.com. Summer fares are $79 for adults, $49 for ages 5–11; in winter they drop to $49 and $29 respectively. First and Premium Class service is also available.

the place has a youthful, energetic buzz. By the evening, most people seem too wiped out to do anything much.

Downtown Durango, located along Main Avenue between 7th and 11th streets, remains the liveliest urban area in the Four Corners, and is worth an hour or two of anyone's time. As well as the outdoors outfitters you might expect, it's packed with funky and upscale fashion and home furnishing stores. That said, in terms of any kind of formal tourist attraction, there's precious little to see. Like, say, Moab, Durango is very much a place where visitors come to do stuff, not see stuff.

Arrival and information

Durango's **visitor center**, south of downtown, at 111 S. Camino del Rio on the main highway near the train station, offers a reservations service (June–Sept Mon–Fri 8am–6pm, Sat 9am–5pm, Sun 11am–4pm; Oct–May Mon–Fri 8am–5pm; ℡970/247-0312 or 1-800/463-8726, ⓦwww.durango.org). Greyhound (TMN & O) **buses** call in at 275 E Eighth Ave (℡970/259-2755).

Mountain bikes can be rented for around $45 per day from Hassle Free Sports, 2615 Main Ave (℡970/259-3874, ⓦwww.hasslefreesports.com), while Southwest Adventures, 12th St and Camino del Rio (℡970/259-0370 or 1-800/642-5389, ⓦwww.mtnguide.net), runs guided biking tours for $60–125 per day. Mesa Verde Tours (℡970/247-8533, ⓦwww.mesaverdetours.net) picks up from local motels at around 8am daily for $75 **national park tours**.

Several operators run **river-rafting** excursions on the Animas River. Full-day expeditions with Mild to Wild Rafting (℡970/247-4789 or 1-800/567-6745, ⓦwww.mild2wildrafting.com), for example, cost from $75 upwards. If you just want a taster, brief float trips with Flexible Flyers (℡970/247-4628 or 1-800/346-7741, ⓦwww.flexibleflyersrafting.com) cost from as little as $18.

Accommodation

Downtown Durango only holds a handful of **accommodation** options, including a couple of fancy but expensive historic hotels. Most of the **motels**,

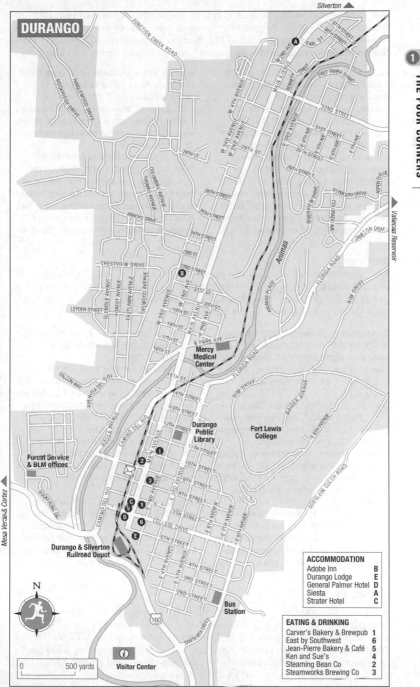

DURANGO

Silverton

THE FOUR CORNERS

Valiecias Reservoir

Airport & Pagosa Springs

Mesa Verde & Cortez

ACCOMMODATION
Adobe Inn   B
Durango Lodge   E
General Palmer Hotel   D
Siesta   A
Strater Hotel   C

EATING & DRINKING
Carver's Bakery & Brewpub   1
East by Southwest   6
Jean-Pierre Bakery & Café   5
Ken and Sue's   4
Steaming Bean Co   2
Steamworks Brewing Co   3

Durango & Silverton
Railroad Depot

Mercy
Medical
Center

Durango
Public
Library

Fort Lewis
College

Forest Service
& BLM offices

Bus
Station

Visitor Center

0   500 yards

N

including all the budget ones, are well to the north, on the farther reaches of the forty-block Main Avenue. At the best place to **camp** near town, the riverside United Campground, 1322 Animas View Drive (☎970/247-3853, ⓦwww.unitedcampgrounddurango.com), the well-shaded tent sites cost $26.

Adobe Inn 2178 Main Ave ☎970/247-2743 or 1-800/251-8733, ⓦwww.durangolodging.com. Reasonable cheap motel, not too far north of downtown, with a hot tub and coffee bar. ❹
Durango Lodge 150 East Fifth St ☎970/247-0955 or 1-888/440-4489, ⓦwww.durangolodge.com. Small, not particularly attractive but very convenient central motel, close to the railroad station. Spacious rooms plus a pool. ❺
General Palmer Hotel 567 Main Ave ☎970/247-4747 or 1-800/523-3358, ⓦwww.generalpalmerhotel.com. Very smart, old historic hotel, close to the railroad depot, that's slightly chintzier than the similar *Strater* nearby, but still provides an

enjoyable taste of old-Western style. Lower-priced rooms face inward, not out on the street. ❺
Siesta 3475 Main Ave ☎970/247-0741 or 1-877/314-0741, ⓦwww.durangosiestamotel.com. Very inexpensive motel, at the curve in the highway well north of the center; all rooms have phone and TV, but little more. ❸
🏃 **Strater Hotel** 699 Main Ave ☎970/247-4431 or 1-800/247-4431, ⓦwww.strater.com. Major downtown landmark that's bursting with frontier elegance and offers almost a hundred mostly small but appealingly antique-furnished rooms. Great buffet breakfasts, a reasonable restaurant, and frequent performances of theatrical melodramas. ❼

Eating

Main Avenue downtown, and the streets to either side, are filled with places to **eat** and **drink**; some set their sights on affluent train passengers, others aim at young mountain bikers. There's at least one **espresso bar** on every block; they even hold a coffee festival on the first weekend of September.

Carver's Bakery & Brewpub 1022 Main Ave ☎970/259-2545. Bustling brewpub, with a good menu of big breakfasts and grilled specials like bison bratwurst for $15 during the day and beer at night. Mon–Sat 6.30am–10pm, Sun 6.30am–1pm.
🏃 **East by Southwest** 160 E College Drive ☎970/247-5533. Ravishing "pan-Asian bistro" a block up from Main Avenue downtown, serving a wide array of delicious Thai, Vietnamese, Indonesian, and above all, Japanese dishes. Typical Thai entrees cost $12–16, while sushi or sashimi platters for two are around $30. Mon–Fri 11am–3pm & 5–10pm, Sat & Sun 5–10pm.
🏃 **Jean-Pierre Bakery & Cafe** 601 Main Ave ☎970/385-0122. It may be a little incongruous in this historic Wild-West building, but this classic French bakery/restaurant offers exquisite breads and pastries, plus sandwiches,

salads, and quiches for $8–10, and full meals like mussels or beef with crab for up to $30. Daily 7am–9.30pm.
Ken and Sue's 636 Main Ave ☎970/385-1810. Hip, stylish little downtown restaurant specializing in Southwestern cooking with a slight but definite Asian twist; cilantro-crusted halibut, for example, costs $19. Mon–Fri 11am–2.30pm & 5pm until late, Sat & Sun 5pm until late.
Steaming Bean Co 915 Main Ave ☎970/385-7901. Early-morning espressos and pastries, as well as specialty drinks, sandwiches, wi-fi, and live music later on. Mon–Sat 6.30am–9pm, Sun 7am–8pm.
Steamworks Brewing Co 801 E Second Ave ☎970/259-9200. Large brewpub just off Main Avenue, where in summer you can enjoy wood-fired pizzas served on a sunny open-air patio and in winter you can drink vast quantities of home-brewed beer. Daily 11am until late.

Silverton

North of Durango, the **San Juan Skyway** loops over two hundred miles through the Rockies, up US-550 and then back via Hwy-145 and US-160. Its first stretch, across invigorating high passes, is known as the **Million Dollar Highway**, for the amount of gold in the ore-bearing gravel used in its construction. As you skirt around the bald, red-striped **Engineer Mountain**, just beyond the Purgatory Ski Area, the views are spectacular.

The first town along the way, **SILVERTON**, spreads across a small flat valley 9318ft up in the mountains fifty miles along, and marks journey's end for the narrow-gauge railroad from Durango. It's one of Colorado's most atmospheric mountain towns, with wide dirt-packed streets leading off toward the hills to either side of the one main road, where the snow lingers year-round. Silverton's zinc- and copper-mining days only came to an end in 1991, leaving it dependent on tourism. The false-front stores along "Notorious Blair Street," paralleling the main drag, recall the days when legendary gunslinger Bat Masterson was the city marshal, and are the scene of frequent staged shoot-outs. Silverton is geared much more toward day-trippers than overnight guests, so even in summer it gets very sleepy at night, with just a handful of Western saloons and steakhouses providing the only sign of life.

Without a 4WD vehicle, it's hard to explore the mountains, but if instead of returning to the main highway you simply keep going beyond the end of Silverton's main street, you can continue for several miles in an ordinary car. The dirt road usually starts to get difficult around the ruins of **EUREKA**, seven miles along the Animas River, which make a good starting point for hikes to nearby waterfalls. The crest of the mountain ridge to the east marks the Continental Divide, with the source of the Rio Grande on the far side.

Practicalities

Silverton's helpful **visitor center** is close to the highway at the southern edge of town (daily: May–June & Oct 9am–5pm; July–Sept 9am–6pm; Nov–April 9am–4pm; ☎970/387-5654 or 1-800/752-4494, Ⓦwww .silvertoncolorado.com).

The cheapest **accommodation** is in the tin-walled *Silverton Hostel*, 1025 Blair St (check-in daily 8–10am & 4–10pm; ☎970/387-0015; ❶–❷), which offers $22 dorm beds as well as a few plain, private doubles, or at the ugly but well-maintained *Triangle Motel*, 848 Greene St (☎970/387-5780, Ⓦwww .trianglemotel.com; ❸), at the south end of town, which also offers good-value two-room suites and jeep rental. The central *Grand Imperial Hotel*, 1219 Greene St (☎970/387-5527 or 1-800/341-3340, Ⓦwww.grandimperialhotel .com; ❹), has far more historic ambience without being much more expensive, though its old-style rooms are not exactly opulent; it also has a **restaurant**, *Grumpy's*. You can get a bit more comfort at the *Teller House Hotel*, across the road at 1250 Greene St (☎970/387-5423 or 1-800/342-4338, Ⓦwww .tellerhousehotel.com; ❹), where some rooms share bathrooms. In addition to the Western-style steakhouses in the heart of downtown, *Romero's*, at 1151 Greene St (☎970/387-5501), is an enjoyable Mexican *cantina*, while *Avalanche Coffee House*, 1067 Blair St (☎970/387-5282; closed Wed), is a friendly hangout offering fresh coffee, pastries, and snacks.

Ouray

The equally attractive mining community of **OURAY** lies 23 miles north of Silverton, on the far side of 11,018-foot **Red Mountain Pass**, where the bare rock beneath the snow really is red, thanks to mineral deposits. The Million Dollar Highway twists and turns, passing abandoned mine workings and rusting machinery in the most unlikely and inaccessible spots. The best spot for an overview is the Red Mountain Overlook, where the relics of the Idarado Mine lie scattered below a magnificent red peak; tunnels once connected it with Telluride, little more than five miles west but sixty miles by road. Back roads into the mountains hereabouts offer rich pickings for hikers or 4WD drivers.

Ouray itself squeezes into an impossibly slender verdant valley at the head of the Uncompahgre River, with the **Ouray Hot Springs** ranged alongside the river at the north end of town. A mile or so south, a one-way loop dirt road leads to **Box Cañon Falls Park** (daily 8am–dusk; $3), where a straightforward 500-foot trail, partly along a swaying wooden parapet, leads into the dark, narrow Box Cañon. At the far end, the falls thunder through a tiny cleft in the mountain.

Practicalities

Ouray's **visitor center** is outside the hot springs (mid-June to Aug Mon–Wed 9am–5pm, Thurs–Sat 9am–7pm, Sun 10am–4pm; Sept to mid-June Mon–Sat 10am–5pm, Sun 10am–3pm; ☏970/325-4746 or 1-800/228-1876, ⓦwww .ouraycolorado.com). Switzerland of America, 226 Seventh Ave (☏970/325-4484 or 1-800/432-5337, ⓦwww.soajeep.com) and rents out **4WD vehicles** and also offers guided jeep tours.

All rooms at the upscale new *Hot Springs Inn*, at 1400 Main St at the north end of town (☏970/325-7277 or 1-800/706-7790, ⓦwww.hotspringsinn .com; ❻), have balconies facing the river. At *Box Canyon Lodge*, an old-style timber **motel** below the park at 45 Third Ave (☏970/325-4981 or 1-800/327-5080, ⓦwww.boxcanyonouray.com; ❺), you can bathe in natural hot tubs. The luxurious, brick *St Elmo Hotel* **B&B**, 426 Main St (☏970/325-4951 or 1-866/243-1502, ⓦwww.stelmohotel.com; ❺), adjoins the good *Bon Ton* **restaurant**, where Italian entrees cost $17–37. The central *Backstreet Bagel & Deli*, 524 Main St (☏970/325-0550), serves sandwiches and smoothies.

Ridgway

North of Ouray, the scenery changes abruptly, with the canyon of the Uncompahgre characterized by red rocks and sparse sagebrush. To complete the San Juan Skyway loop, turn west on Hwy-62 after eight miles at **RIDGWAY**, where the northern limits of the San Juan Mountains stand as a serrated ridge along the southern skyline. Ridgway was a pivotal location for the 1968 movie *True Grit*. The 62-year-old **John Wayne**, who won his first Oscar as one-eyed Marshall Rooster Cogburn, met his young sidekick outside the town courthouse, while their subsequent adventures were played out against the magnificent backdrop of the **Wilson Peaks**, which you'll see if you continue west on the San Juan Skyway.

Telluride

As Hwy-62, the San Juan Skyway meets Hwy-145 23 miles southwest of Ridgway, and then turns sharply back eastward on Hwy-145 along the pretty, well-wooded valley of the San Miguel River. The former mining village of **TELLURIDE** is a 74-mile drive from Silverton, even though as the crow flies, across the mountains, the towns are barely ten miles apart.

Telluride was briefly home to the young Butch Cassidy, who robbed his first bank here in 1889. It's now a **ski resort**, rivaling Aspen and Vail as a winter destination for the stars. Telluride has, however, achieved this status without losing its character – the wide main street, a National Historic District with low-slung buildings on either side, still heads directly up toward one of the most stupendous mountain views in the Rockies. Healthy young bohemians with few visible means of support but top-notch ski equipment form the bulk of the 2200 citizens, while most of the glitzy visitors hang out two miles above the town in **Mountain Village**, reached by a free year-round gondola service (daily 7am–midnight).

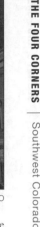

▲ Telluride, CO

Telluride's winter season, which starts as the fall colors fade, usually in late November, continues until early April. Prospective **skiers** should contact the Telluride Reservations Center (☎970/728-3041 or 1-888/339-2664, ⓦ www .telluride.com), which coordinates lodging and package deals, with discounted lift tickets for guests in certain lodges; otherwise a full-price lift ticket costs $92 per day.

The town also hosts US and world **snowboarding** championships, with many former ski trails now reserved for snowboarders, and expert instruction available from the Telluride Ski and Snowboard School (☎970/728-6900 or 1-800/778-8581, ⓦ www.tellurideskiresort.com). Several operators rent out ski and snowboarding equipment, including Telluride Sports (☎970/728-3134, ⓦwww.rentskis.com).

In summer, the **hiking** opportunities are excellent. One three-mile round-trip walk, which also makes a great if grueling bike ride, switchbacks up a bumpy 4WD road from the head of the valley to reach Colorado's highest waterfalls, the 365-foot **Bridal Veil Falls**. To join it, follow the main highway all the way through town, park where it ends at Pioneer Mill, and set off uphill. Don't expect to be able to cool off with a swim in the falls, however; it's far too perilous for that.

Practicalities

Telluride's extremely helpful **visitor center** is on the edge of downtown at 630 W Colorado Ave (Mon–Fri 8am–8pm, Sat & Sun 10am–8pm; ☎970/728-3401 or 1-888/355-8743, ⓦwww.visittelluride.com). **Accommodation** is less expensive in summer than during ski season, though prices do go up for the Jazz Celebration in early June (ⓦwww.telluridejazz.org), the Bluegrass Festival in mid-June (ⓦwww.bluegrass.com), and the Film Festival at the start of September (ⓦwww.telluridefilmfestival.org).

Of places to **stay**, the restored 1895 *New Sheridan Hotel*, 231 W Colorado Ave (☎970/728-4351 or 1-800/200-1891, ⓦwww.newsheridan.com; winter ❽, summer ❻), offers very luxurious rooms, while the *Victorian Inn*, 401 W Pacific

Ave (☎970/728-6601 or 1-800/611-9893, ⓦwww.tellurideinn.com; winter ❼, summer ❺), is a smart motel with its own sauna.

At the dinner-only *Cosmopolitan*, 300 W San Juan Ave (☎970/728-1292; closed Sun), the fanciest **restaurant** in town, the contemporary Southwestern entrees are priced at $20 and up, while *Smugglers Brewpub and Grille*, at San Juan and Pine (☎970/728-0919), is a lively evening hangout with a wide-ranging menu. *Baked in Telluride*, 127 S Fir St (☎970/728-4705), is a take-out deli that's good for morning espressos and pastries, and has a nice little terrace where you can enjoy soup, sandwiches, or pizza. *Between The Covers*, a bookstore at 224 W Colorado Ave (☎970/728-4504), also holds a coffee bar.

Northwest New Mexico

Although **northwest New Mexico** formed the heart of the Dinetah, the Navajo's original homeland in the Southwest, the Navajo territories here are now less visited than their more scenic equivalents in Arizona. Archeology buffs are drawn to **Chaco Canyon** and **Aztec Ruins**, which may rank among the most significant Ancestral Puebloan sites anywhere, but are less photogenic than their better-known rivals. None of the towns nearby, whether on or off the reservation, holds any lasting interest.

Instead the region is notorious as the home of the **Four Corners Power Plant**, near Farmington. After this coal-fired generating station opened in the 1960s, it was said to be the single greatest source of pollution in the United States, emitting more noxious gases than either New York City or Los Angeles. Regulations have been tightened since then, but with the **Navajo Mine**, the largest open-pit coal mine in the West, just a mile away, and several other generating plants in the immediate neighborhood, there's no incentive for outsiders to linger. For the Navajo, of course, who provide much of the industry's workforce, it's a different story.

Shiprock

By far the most striking landmark in the dusty red plains of New Mexico's far northwestern corner is the craggy monolith known as **Shiprock**. In Navajo legend, as *Tsé bit'a'i* or "Rock Wing," this awesome 1500-foot peak was home to one or two monstrous birds, which were either killed by the hero Monster Slayer or turned into an eagle and an owl. To Anglo eyes, it resembled instead a mighty ocean-going ship. Navajo medicine men continued to use it in sacred ceremonies until 1939, when Sierra Club members including David Brower – the "Arch-Druid" who later founded Friends of the Earth (see p.422) – defiled Shiprock by climbing it.

US-491 runs within a few miles of Shiprock's vast, eerie bulk; roadside signs explain that the mountain is a volcanic plug, the hard central core of a volcano that has itself eroded away. There's no point trying to approach it any closer; you can't even walk up to the base, let alone climb it. Neither is it worth stopping at the sprawling mining town six miles north, also known as **SHIPROCK**, other than in early October, when it hosts the **Northern Navajo Fair**.

Farmington

FARMINGTON, the largest town in northwestern New Mexico, lies fifty miles east of the Four Corners Monument; fifty miles southwest of Durango, Colorado;

The Beast Is Dead

Here is wisdom. Let him who has understanding calculate the Number of the Beast, for it is the number of a man: His number is 666.

Revelation 13·18

Until 2003, 666 was not merely the Number of the Beast, and the number of a man; it was also the number of the main highway north through the Navajo Nation from Gallup to Shiprock. **US-666** was assigned the dreaded "666" in 1942, as the sixth major road to branch off Route 66, and swiftly acquired such nicknames as the "Devil's Highway" and the "Highway to Hell." Despite being largely straight, and doubtless paved with good intentions, it became renowned for an appalling accident record. *USA Today* rated it as the most dangerous highway in the country, while in 1995 the *Wall Street Journal* ran an article headlined "Beast of a Highway: Does Asphalt Stretch Have Biblical Curse?".

Prompted by state governor Bill Richardson, New Mexico's House and Senate passed a Joint Resolution in 2003 that declared:

WHEREAS, people living near the road already live under the cloud of opprobrium created by having a road that many believe is cursed running near their homes and through their homeland; and

WHEREAS, the number 666 carries the stigma of being the mark of the beast, the mark of the devil, which was described in the book of Revelation in the Bible; and

WHEREAS, there are people who refuse to travel the road, not because of the issue of safety, but because of the fear that the devil controls events along United States route 666; and

WHEREAS, the economy in the area is greatly depressed when compared with many parts of the United States, and the infamy brought by the inopportune naming of the road will only make development in the area more difficult.

... the number of the road should be changed as soon as possible. A state highway official was reported as having no preference concerning the new designation: "As long as it's not 666 and it's nothing satanic, that's OK." The former US-666 therefore duly became US-491 on May 31, 2003.

and, more to the point, a mere ten miles west of both the Navajo Mine and the Four Corners Power Plant. Formerly renowned as a definitive "edge-of-the-res" community, rife with racism and violence, Farmington has cleaned itself up and prospered accordingly. Developments like the **Animas Valley Mall**, 4601 E Main St, make it the principal business center of a wide area.

Farmington's principal concession to tourism is its **museum**, in the Gateway Park on the northeast edge of town at 3041 E Main St (Mon–Sat 8am–5pm; free), which traces town history from the geological "New Mexico Seacoast" up to trading-post times; it also has extensive displays on mining and refining.

Practicalities

The local **visitor center** is in the museum (same hours; ☎505/326-7602 or 1-800/448-1240, ⓦwww.farmingtonnm.org). TNM&O Coaches, 101 E Animas St (☎505/325-1009), runs regular **buses** to Durango, Denver, and Albuquerque, while the Four Corners Airport, west of town, has commuter **flights** to Albuquerque, Denver, and Phoenix.

Of Farmington's twenty-plus **motels**, the best budget choice is the *Super 8*, southeast on US-64 at 4751 Cortez Way (☎505/325-1813 or 1-800/800-8000; ❷). Slightly smarter options include the *La Quinta*, 675 Scott Ave (☎505/327-4706 or 1-800/531-5900; ❹). There's a quite extraordinary alternative three miles out of town at 3204 Crestridge Drive: *Kokopelli's Cave*, a genuine **cave dwelling** hollowed out in 1980, 75 feet below ground level but opening onto a cliff-face balcony hundreds of feet above the La Plata River. It's rented out as a B&B apartment to groups of up to four people (T505/326-2461, Wwww.bbonline.com/nm/kokopelli; ⑧).

Back in town, the best **food** around is at the *Three Rivers Eatery and Brewhouse*, 101 E Main St (T505/324-2187).

Aztec

Fourteen miles northeast of Farmington, the lower-key and more enjoyable town of **AZTEC**, is the county seat of San Juan County. On its leafy central thoroughfare, the quaint **Aztec Museum**, 125 N Main Ave (summer Mon–Sat 9am–5pm; winter Mon–Sat 10am–4pm; $3), incorporates a pioneer village peopled by life-size mannequins, who hang out in frontier-style buildings like a schoolhouse, a jail, and a bank.

The main reason anyone comes to Aztec, however, is **Aztec Ruins National Monument**, across the Animas River a mile north of town (daily: summer 8am–6pm; winter 8am–5pm; $5 per person; T505/334-6174, Wwww.nps .gov/azru). This preserves an **Ancestral Puebloan pueblo** erroneously attributed by early Anglo settlers to ancient Mexicans. In fact, it's a large "outlier" settlement, built from 1111 onwards by people from the Chaco culture (see p.102), and connected with Chaco Canyon, 64 miles south, by a die-straight road now only visible from the air. Aztec stands halfway between Chaco and Mesa Verde, and is thought to have been remodeled by a new wave of settlers from Mesa Verde around 1225.

From the visitor center, which holds some interesting ancient artifacts, a short trail leads around and through the **West Ruin**, the only part of the site to have been excavated. This 500-room E-shaped structure held only one entrance and was entirely walled. The trail leads through room after room (you'll have to stoop to get through the low doorways) before culminating in the awesome **Great Kiva** – the term for a *kiva* used by an entire community rather than an individual clan or family. Reconstructed in 1934, this is the only Great Kiva in the Southwest that can be seen in anything approaching its original state. Aspects of the restoration remain conjectural, but there's no disputing the circular chamber's sheer size, which measured fifty feet across. Its 95-ton roof was supported by four pillars that rested on four 375-pound limestone disks, carried here from forty miles away. Archeologists say that the *kiva* may have been in use when the *kachina* religion was first being developed, and that its fifteen side rooms may have been changing rooms from which masked figures would emerge during ceremonies. An informative trail guide, written by an Indian from Santa Clara Pueblo quite possibly descended from the site's original inhabitants, explains much of what you see. A corresponding **East Ruin** lurks mysteriously beneath shapeless hillocks.

Practicalities

Aztec's **visitor center** is east of the river at 110 N Ash St (Mon–Fri 9am–noon & 1–5pm; T505/334-9951 or 1-888/838-9551, Wwww.aztecnm.com). Only two local **motels** are worth considering. Despite external appearances, the shiny modern *Step Back Inn*, where US-550 meets Main Avenue at 103 W Aztec Blvd (T505/334-1200 or 1-800/334-1255; ③), has rooms furnished with Victorian antiques. The smaller *Enchantment Lodge*, 1800 W Aztec Blvd (T505/334-6143 or 1-800/847-2194, Wwww.enchantmentlodge.com; ②), is an old-fashioned, no-frills alternative. There's also a tiny and slightly twee **B&B**, *Miss Gail's Inn*, 300 S Main Ave (T505/334-3452).

The Pueblitos of Dinétah

Although they now lie beyond the boundaries of the Navajo Nation, remote Largo and Gobernador canyons to the southeast of Farmington and Aztec were the original cradles of the **Dinétah**, the traditional Navajo homeland. The earliest known trace of a Navajo presence is a *hogan* in Gobernador Canyon, tree-ring dated to 1541, but the most significant era in its history followed the Pueblo Revolt of 1680. Refugees from the Rio Grande pueblos fled west during the aftermath of the revolt, to be joined by further waves of migrants when the Spaniards re-conquered New Mexico from 1692 onwards.

Between 1680 and 1750, Navajo and Pueblo Indians combined to build around 130 stone fortresses in the region, known as the **Pueblitos of Dinétah**. Perched on high eminences close to the canyon rims, or tucked into alcoves just below, these "little pueblos" are reminiscent of Ancestral Puebloan sites like those at Hovenweep (see p.82). Most were too small to house an entire community for any length of time; instead they were intended as lookouts, retreats for elders and religious leaders, and, above all, as shelters during raids. The Spaniards sent punitive expeditions into the area every summer between 1705 and 1716, while from the 1720s Ute war parties threatened Navajo and Spaniard alike.

The pueblitos played a crucial role in forging a new synthesis of Navajo and Pueblo cultures. Many of the modern hallmarks of Navajo identity, both in terms of skills such as rug-weaving and sheep-herding, and of religious beliefs, were acquired during this period. The driving force seems to have been the inter-marriage of Navajo men with women from the pueblo of Jemez. Their union created the **Coyote Pass People**, still a prominent Navajo clan. Influences were also absorbed from further afield. Not only were Spanish metal-working techniques introduced, but in Three Corn Pueblito, which was abandoned in the 1750s, archeologists have even unearthed a Qing dynasty plate from China.

While you can drive into both Largo and Gobernador canyons, along good-quality dirt roads used by gas-drilling companies, without expert assistance you won't be able to reach or even spot the pueblitos themselves. The Bureau of Land Management office at 1235 La Plata Hwy in Farmington (T505/599-8900) can provide detailed directions to sites located on BLM lands. A better idea is to join an **organized tour** with either the archeologists at Salmon Ruins (T505/632-2013, Wwww.salmonruins.com), who charge around $300 for an all-day 4WD trip for up to four people, or Aztec Archaeological Consultants (T505/334-6675, Wwww.aztecarcheology.com), which offers half-day trips for one or two people for $110 and full-day trips for $230.

Facing the museum, the *Main Street Bistro*, 122 N Main St (T505/334-0109; breakfast and lunch only, closed Sun), offers good coffee and pastries and has an outdoor patio, while the *Aztec Restaurant*, opposite the *Step Back* at 107 W Aztec Blvd (T505/334-9586), is a venerable steak-and-pancake **diner**.

Bloomfield

BLOOMFIELD, eight miles south of Aztec or twelve miles east of Farmington, is an unattractive little desert crossroads notable only for its **Salmon Ruins**, two miles west (Mon–Fri 8am–5pm, Sat & Sun 9am–5pm; Nov–April Sun noon–5pm; $3; T505/632-2013, Wwww.salmonruins.com). This outlying Chacoan pueblo was constructed between 1088 and 1094, twenty years before its neighbor at Aztec. Salmon Ruins may mark the first attempt to build a "new Chaco," which failed when the San Juan River proved too unruly to tame at this point, whereupon Aztec was built as a replacement.

Practicalities

If you find yourself in Bloomfield for the night, the best of its few **motels** is the *Super 8*, at 505 W Broadway (☎505/632-8886 or 1-800/800-8000, ⓦwww .super8.com; ❸). The *Triangle Cafe*, across the highway at 506 W Broadway (☎505/632-9918), is a traditional, friendly **diner**.

Chaco Canyon

Although the **Ancestral Puebloan ruins** of **CHACO CANYON** form the **largest pre–Columbian city** in North America, for sheer beauty and drama they can't compete with lesser settlements such as Canyon de Chelly. The low-walled canyon itself, now protected as **Chaco Culture National Historical Park**, is a mere scratch in the scrubby high-desert plains, and the Chaco Wash that runs through it is often completely dry. Add the fact that the site is a long, bumpy, twenty-mile ride off the nearest paved road, and more than double that

---

The Chaco phenomenon

To archeologists, Chaco Canyon represents the apogee of Ancestral Puebloan achievement. However, what they call the **Chaco phenomenon** remains one of the Southwest's greatest puzzles. How can the canyon's apparent unsuitability for large-scale occupation – if anything, it was slightly drier in Ancestral Puebloan times than it is today – be reconciled with its massive structures and demonstrable influence over an "empire" that covered at least 25,000 square miles?

Although pithouses built by early Ancestral Puebloan Basketmakers are scattered around the canyon, Chaco's first surface pueblo appeared during the ninth century. Around 1000, sophisticated masonry techniques, developed or introduced by migrants from the Mesa Verde region, enabled the construction of larger multistory apartments. The canyon's heyday came between 1050 and 1125; its last definite tree-ring date is 1132, and by 1200 it was abandoned. Prodigious work went into its construction. Upwards of 200,000 tree trunks, mostly ponderosa pines and corkbark fir, were carried here from hillsides fifty or more miles away, without the use of animals or the wheel.

Since Chaco became a national monument in 1907, archeologists have repeatedly revised their estimates of its ancient population downwards. As few burials have been found, there's little sign that the upper floors were ever inhabited, and the canyon's soil is so poor, it's now believed that Chaco never held more than two thousand inhabitants.

Thus Chaco was not a residential community so much as a **ceremonial center**, and the Great Houses were not homes, but some combination of warehouses, temples, and palaces. Huge quantities of **turquoise** have been discovered – harvester ants, who collect blue and green turquoise to adorn their nests, scavenged fifty thousand pieces in Pueblo Bonito alone. Still precious to contemporary Indian cultures, turquoise was the most valuable trading commodity in the ancient Southwest. The Chacoans acquired it raw from distant mines – mostly to the east, in the Cerrillos region (see p.140) – and crafted it into sacred and ornamental objects, which passed from hand to hand down trading networks into the heart of Mexico. It's said ninety percent of the turquoise found in the Aztec capital of Tenochtitlan was of Southwestern origin. Similarly, the parrots and scarlet macaws whose skeletons have been found here must have come from southern Mexico or beyond.

Chaco's primary significance, however, was much more local. Having started as a small trading settlement, it probably became a place of a pilgrimage, where individuals came, with appropriate rituals, to obtain sacred turquoise. From there, it's a small step to picture regional **festivals**, held at regular intervals, when large crowds would

from any significant town or facilities, and it's no wonder that visitors on tight itineraries often decide it's more bother than it's worth.

Once you accept that you won't have amazing photos to show the folks back home, however, there's still plenty about Chaco to take your breath away. Over 3600 separate sites have been logged in the canyon, of which the thirteen principal ones are open to visitors. Six of these, arrayed along the canyon's north wall, are what's known as **Great Houses** – self-contained pueblos, three or four stories high, whose fortress-like walls concealed up to eight hundred rooms. The largest, **Pueblo Bonito**, is claimed to have been the largest single building in America until structural steel was developed in 1898.

Arrival and information

Both **routes to Chaco Canyon** entail driving twenty miles over rough but passable dirt roads. They remain open all year, but should not be attempted during, or within a day of, a rainstorm.

assemble for public ceremonies. For most of the year, Chaco held a relatively small, high-caste population, and the upper floors of its pueblos were empty or used for storage; at festival times, they accommodated a large influx of temporary guests.

Evidence for this ceremonial role includes the extraordinary 450-mile network of **roads** that link Chaco with around 75 "**outlier**" communities. Averaging thirty feet in width, they were far wider than ordinary human foot-traffic could require; in fact they were more like causeways, built of hard-packed stone and running arrow-straight across cliffs, mesas, and canyons. Most are now only visible from the air. The longest stretched all the way to Aztec Ruins, 64 miles north (see p.100), but if that same line is extended *south*, it makes a virtually perfect alignment with the site known as either **Casas Grandes** or **Paquimé**, over 300 miles away in Mexico. Roadside beacons may have been lit to summon pilgrims to major festivals.

Navajo legends relate that Chaco was ruled by the despotic **Great Gambler**, who was born to a poor Chacoan woman, taught to gamble by his father, the Sun, and won control over the canyon and all it held. When he was eventually defeated, he was shot into the sky, where he once more accumulated great wealth and returned to the region in the shape of the Spaniards. Meanwhile, freed of their oppressor, the people of Chaco had dispersed.

Recently, ferocious archeological debate has focused on the signs of large-scale violence at Chaco. Human remains found in two thirds of the Great Houses appear to have been mutilated in a manner that suggests **cannibalism**. In the absence of evidence of warfare, they're seen as possible victims of ritual slaughter. The leading exponent of this theory, Christy Turner III, has even argued that a wandering group of Toltec refugees entered the region from the south around 900, and established a reign of terror at Chaco by introducing the bloodthirsty Mexican practice of **human sacrifice**.

Trying to guess why the Chacoans left the canyon when they did – from 1230 onwards – is probably futile, although it might only have taken a tiny reduction in rainfall to drive them out. Where they went, however, is no great mystery. Both Aztec, at its peak between 1110 and 1275, and Casas Grandes, an even richer commercial center occupied from 1250 to 1500, can be seen as successive "capital cities" of the same cultural tradition.

Ácoma Pueblo (see p.110) is just one of many modern pueblos that show a clear continuity with Chacoan culture. At least nine Hopi clans trace their origins back to what they remember as "the place beyond the horizon," while the Zuni say a medicine society known as the Sword Swallowers joined them from Chaco.

To approach from the **south**, leave I-40 at Thoreau, 28 miles northwest of Grants; follow Hwy-57 north for another 28 miles, beyond **Crownpoint**, then turn right onto Arrowhead Hwy-9 for 13 miles to **Seven Lakes**, at which point the dirt road to Chaco itself branches off to the left. Coming from the **north** or **east**, turn off US-550 (still shown on some maps as NM Hwy-44) at Nageezi, 36 miles south of **Bloomfield**.

The two routes meet inside the park on its eastern side at the **visitor center** (daily 8am–5pm; ☎505/786-7014, ⓦwww.nps.gov/chcu), where the **admission fee** of $8 per vehicle is payable. As well as picking up maps and brochures, plus schedules of summer-only ranger-led tours, you can watch videos such as *Sundagger*, which explains how rocks and petroglyphs atop nearby **Fajada Butte** were carefully sited to plot not only the annual solstices, but also the moon's 18.5-year cycle.

The basic first-come, first-served *Gallo* **campground** ($10), a short way east of the visitor center, is the only visitor facility the park has to offer; from April to October it's usually full by 3pm. Bring any firewood you require. Backcountry camping is forbidden.

Seeing the park

The gates of the canyon's eight-mile one-way **loop road**, which provides the only access to the ruins themselves, are immediately north of the visitor center, and open the same hours. The major stop is at the far end, where **Pueblo Bonito** ("beautiful town" in Spanish), can be explored on an easy half-mile trail. Work on this four-story D-shaped structure, almost perfectly aligned east–west, started in 850 and continued for around three hundred years. Speculation that hordes of slaves were forced to build it have been deflated by precise dating of its parts; even during its busiest era, a workforce of just thirty men, cutting and hauling trees for a full month each year, and quarrying and shaping stone for four months every two years, could have done the job.

The trail leads around the back of Pueblo Bonito, passing the spot where Threatening Rock, a colossal boulder whose collapse the ancient inhabitants staved off with prayer sticks and supporting walls, finally destroyed thirty rooms in 1941. Entering the ruin via its lowest levels, the path reaches its central plaza, which held at least three **Great Kivas** of the kind restored at Aztec (see p.100). From there, you can walk through the passageways and chambers of the pueblo proper, where the rows of neatly finished doorways, each framed by the next, are Chaco's most photographed feature.

A separate trail from the same parking lot heads to the smaller complex of **Chetro Ketl**, a quarter-mile east. Constructed over the course of a century, from 1010 onwards, this shows Chacoan masonry at its most sophisticated – or as some archeologists put it, at its most obviously influenced by MesoAmerican models. Its horizontal rows of large, squared-off stones are chinked with smaller, flatter stones and set into a bed of adobe mortar with a mosaic-like precision. Many original beams (*vigas*) remain in place, and a vivid fragment of an ancient mural is protected behind a glass panel.

Pueblo del Arroyo, the next stop along the loop road, is the only Great House to stand right beside Chaco Wash. Although it rarely holds much water, the stream channel is much deeper and broader than it was in Ancestral Puebloan days. Only half of the pueblo, raised on a small hillock and occupied between 1070 and 1105, has been excavated.

Casa Rinconada, perched on another mound as the road heads back down the canyon, is the canyon's largest **Great Kiva**, at 62 feet across. It now lies open to the sun, the subtleties of its astronomical alignments lost but its central features still clearly identifiable. Archeologists are unsure whether the two large vaults in the *kiva* floor served as foot drums, or to propagate seedlings.

Crownpoint

CROWNPOINT, almost forty miles southwest of Chaco Canyon and 24 miles north of the I-40 town of **Thoreau**, is the principal town along the eastern flank of the Navajo Nation. Its only conceivable appeal for tourists is as the site of the **Navajo Rug Auction**, held usually but not always on the third Friday of each month, at Crownpoint Elementary School (☎505/786-7386, ⊛ www.crownpointrugauction.com). Viewing is from 4pm until 6.30pm, with the auction at 7pm, and prices range from $100 up to perhaps $3000 (no credit cards).

Western New Mexico

Although the reality of today's **I-40** may not match the romance of its predecessor, **Route 66**, crossing **western New Mexico** still has its rewards. The interstate passes through memorable desert scenery, while successive detours to the south lead to crucial sites in Southwestern history. At **Zuni Pueblo**, Spanish conquistadors first encountered the region's indigenous inhabitants, and **El Morro National Monument** records centuries of further incursions. Above all, **Ácoma Pueblo**, the superbly sited "Sky City," makes it worth spending a night in the dreary interstate towns of **Gallup** or **Grants**.

Gallup

As the largest town in I-40's 300-mile run between Albuquerque and Flagstaff, the famous Route 66 stop of **GALLUP**, 25 miles from the Arizona state line, might be expected to offer a diverting break in a long day's drive. Don't get your hopes up; cheap motels make it a handy overnight pit stop, but there's nothing to hold your interest.

Gallup sprang into being when the railroad arrived in 1881, and its role as the major railhead for the Navajo Nation was augmented by the arrival of first Route 66, and later I-40. The interstate and the railroad tracks still run east–west through the heart of town, paralleled by a ten-mile stretch of the former Route 66 that's lined with endless budget motels and fast-food outlets.

In the week leading up to the second weekend in August, the Navajo and other local Native Americans come together in Gallup for the **Inter-Tribal Indian Ceremonial**, a six-day extravaganza centered on Red Rock State Park, four miles east of town. A two-day powwow is followed by four days of rodeo, craft shows, and dancing, culminating in a Saturday morning parade through town (information and tickets ☎505/863-3896, ⊛ gallup-ceremonial.org). Be sure to make motel reservations well in advance.

During the rest of the year, Gallup remains a major commercial center for the Navajo. An estimated eighty percent of all **silver jewelry** sold in the Southwest passes through the hands of traders like Shush Yaz, 1304 W Lincoln Ave (☎505/722-0130, ⊛ www.shushyaz.com), and Richardson's Trading Company, 222 W 66 Ave (☎505/722-4762, ⊛ www.richardsontrading.com). For more mundane shopping, head to the **Rio West Mall**, near exit 20 off I-40, which has the usual mall stores and a movie theater.

Practicalities

The Amtrak station at 201 E 66 Ave has one daily **train** to Flagstaff and one to Albuquerque. **Buses** along I-40 call in at the Greyhound station at 200 E 66 Ave (☎505/863-3761), which is also used by Navajo Transit System (☎505/729-4005) services to Window Rock, Arizona. Gallup's **visitor center** is in the adjoining Gallup Multi-Cultural Center, 201 E 66 Ave (summer daily 8am–5pm; winter Mon–Fri 8am–5pm; ☎505/863-3841 or 1-800/242-4282, ⓦwww.gallupnm.org and ⓦwww.indiancountrynm.org).

Absolutely *the* place to **stay** is *El Rancho Hotel and Motel*, 1000 E 66 Ave (♨ ☎505/863-9311 or 1-800/543-6351, ⓦwww.elranchohotel.com; ❹), built in 1937 by the brother of movie mogul D.W. Griffith. From the murals in its opulent Spanish Revival lobby to the gallery of signed photos of celebrity Hollywood guests – John Wayne, Humphrey Bogart, and Ronald Reagan among them – this sumptuous Route 66 roadhouse is bursting with atmosphere. As its original slogan, still proudly displayed above the door, put it, it combined "The Charm of Yesterday and the Convenience of Tomorrow." Its decorative **restaurant** serves burgers named after Wayne and Bogart, plus (separate) Lucille Ball and Errol Flynn sandwiches, and the usual range of barbecue, steaks, and shrimp priced at around $13. There's also a bar and a gift store. Some guest rooms are in the original ranchhouse, the rest in a less characterful two-story motel building alongside.

You can pay under $30 per night and still manage to avoid the dingiest of Gallup's other 2000 rooms by staying at the *Colonial*, 1007 W Coal Ave (☎505/863-6821; ❶). The best place to **camp** is Red Rock State Park, where a fully equipped site costs $10 (☎505/722-3839). *Earl's Restaurant*, 1400 E 66 Ave (☎505/863-4201), is an inexpensive diner on the east side of town, which serves plenty of chile-rich New Mexican specialties and is usually bustling with Navajo crafts sellers, while the *Oasis*, 100 E 66 Ave (☎505/722-9572), offers tasty, healthy Mediterranean specialties. If all you want is a snack or a cappuccino, head instead for the lively, arty *Coffee House*, in the heart of town at 203 W Coal Ave (☎505/726-0291).

▲ *El Rancho Hotel*, Gallup

Zuni Pueblo

Although few tourists make the effort to visit the remote and, superficially, unenthralling **ZUNI PUEBLO**, 35 miles south of Gallup and a short way west of Hwy-602, it occupies a pivotal role in Southwestern history. Here, in 1539, the black African **Esteban** became the first outsider to enter the Pueblo world, and was promptly killed and cut into strips by the Zuni. Fray Marcos de Niza, following close behind him, fled for his life back to Mexico, to report "this land … is the greatest and best of all that have been discovered." The Zuni call themselves *A:shiwi*, "the flesh," and their country *Shi:wona*, "the land that produces flesh." Fray Marcos, who garbled that name into Cíbola, announced that the six Zuni towns were the **Seven Cities of Cíbola**. Spanish conquistadors had long sought the legendary Seven Cities of Antilla, founded by bishops who sailed west to escape the Moorish invasion of Portugal in 714 AD and said to be rich in **gold**. In 1540, therefore, a Spanish expedition led by Francisco Vásquez de **Coronado** returned to Zuni. Turned back from the now-vanished town of Hawikku, the Spaniards defeated its inhabitants in the first battle ever fought between Europeans and Native Americans. For the full tale of the Coronado expedition, and more about Esteban's extraordinary life, see Contexts on p.499.

There was no gold at Zuni. The region was a major Pueblo trading center, where the peoples of the Rio Grande exchanged turquoise for birds, feathers, and shells brought up from the south. Life went on after Coronado departed, but, like the Hopi, the Zuni thereafter found themselves restricted to an ever smaller area by Navajo, Apache, Spanish, and Anglo newcomers. Today's **Zuni Indian reservation** encompasses around three percent of ancestral Zuni lands and, with agriculture rendered marginal by erosion and over-grazing, the Zuni now depend for most of their livelihood on the recently acquired skill of making **silver overlay jewelry**.

Visiting Zuni Pueblo

The dominant feature on the Zuni reservation, the red-and-white-striped mesa of **Dowa Yallane** or **Corn Mountain**, has long served as a refuge for the Zuni people in times of trouble. Immediately below, straddling Hwy-53 three miles west of Hwy-602, stands the main **village**. Now invariably known as **ZUNI**, it was founded as *Halona Idiwan'a*, or "Middle Place of the World," around 1700, when the Zuni came down from Corn Mountain after the Pueblo Revolt.

Simply driving along Hwy-53 through Zuni, it looks like just another rundown desert community. Almost none of the architecture is at all distinctive, though several buildings hold jewelry outlets, crafts shops, and simple diners. As even those structures used for ceremonial purposes are built to resemble new houses, you get little sense that the traditional life of the pueblo is continuing.

In recent years, however, the Zuni have made their culture more accessible to visitors. Head three blocks south from the highway at the town's only stoplight, along Pia Mesa Road, and just across the Zuni River, facing the *Halona Plaza* supermarket, you'll come to the **A:shiwi A:wan Museum and Heritage Center** (Mon–Fri 9am–6pm; donations welcome; ☏505/782-4403). A former trading post refitted as an excellent modern museum, it documents Zuni history for tribal members as well as for tourists, centering on a remarkable collection of artifacts that were excavated from the long-abandoned site of **Hawikku** during the 1920s, and only returned by the Smithsonian Institute in 2001. Enthusiastic staff are happy to talk you through the displays and also provide local information of all kinds.

Not far east, north of the river but still south of the main road, the adobe **Our Lady of Guadalupe Mission Church**, erected by the Spanish in 1629, has been restored to more or less its original appearance. In line with historical accounts, the interior once more holds "life-size" murals of Zuni *kachinas* (Mon–Fri 8am–4.30pm; for a guide, call Zuni Tourism, below; donation). An ancient five-story "apartment block," like the two at Taos Pueblo (see p.167), still stands nearby, but the bottom floors are now underground, while the upper levels are concealed beneath modern accretions; the only traditional pueblo structures you'll see are the beehive-shaped bread ovens scattered around the plaza.

On a typical day, few visitors make it to Zuni, and even fewer stay very long. Special events can draw crowds, however, most notably the **Zuni Tribal Fair** in late August and the all-night **Shalako** dance, held in late November or early December. Anthropologists believe that this winter-solstice celebration, in which the *kachina* cult appears to blend with Aztec elements, was introduced by Mexican Indians left behind by Coronado.

As for **Hawikku** itself, the mound that conceals its ruins is roughly twelve miles southeast of Zuni, just west of the dirt road leading to the agricultural community of **Ojo Caliente**. Only visit with permission from, and a guide supplied by, the Heritage Center. There's precious little to see, apart from multi-colored potsherds poking from the rubble, but once you know the history it's an extraordinarily evocative site. Standing at the edge of the Pueblo world, you get a real sense of what a shock it must have been when first Esteban, and later Coronado, appeared across the infinite grasslands.

Practicalities

For advance information on the Zuni, contact Zuni Tourism (℡505/782-7238, ⓦwww.zunitourism.com). You can also visit on a **guided tour** from Albuquerque, with the Indian Pueblo Cultural Center (see p.189; departs Wed, Sat & Sun 8am; $90; ℡505/843-7270, ⓦwww.indianpueblo.org).

While there are no **motels** on the reservation, it does hold a superb **B&B**. Spending a night at the *Inn at Halona*, tucked behind the *Halona Plaza* super-market at 23 B Pia Mesa Rd (⚒ ℡505/782-4547 or 1-800/752-3278, ⓦwww .halona.com; ④), is a memorable, indeed unmissable, experience for anyone with an interest in Zuni life. Eight charming and individually styled guest rooms, almost all en suite and sharing use of sitting rooms as well as a patio and an extensive library, are located in two separate buildings. The very hospitable owners, who are not themselves Zuni but whose roots here go back over a century, provide excellent breakfasts, and are a mine of information. The inn does not serve dinner, but simple restaurants along the highway include *Chu-Chu's Pizzeria*, 1242 B Hwy-53 (℡505/782-2100).

El Morro National Monument

Hidden away on Hwy-53 south of the Zuni mountains, 25 miles east of Zuni Pueblo and 42 miles west of Grants, **EL MORRO NATIONAL MONUMENT** feels as far off the beaten track as it's possible to be in the modern United States. It seems incredible, therefore, that this sheer sandstone cliff was a regular rest stop for international travelers before the Pilgrims landed at Plymouth Rock. The evidence is plain to see, however. It was first recorded by Spanish explorers in 1583 – *el morro* means "the headland" – and in 1605, **Don Juan de Onate**, the founder of New Mexico, carved the first of the many messages that earned it the American name of **Inscription Rock**.

Translations and explanations of El Morro's graffiti are displayed in the **visitor center** (daily: summer 8am–7pm; spring & fall 9am–6pm; winter 9am–5pm; admission $3 per person; ℡505/783-4226, ⓦwww.nps.gov/elmo). You can see the real thing on a half-mile **trail**, which stays open until an hour before the visitor center closes.

El Morro is technically a cuesta, a long sloping mesa terminating in an abrupt bluff. The trail's first stop explains why so many people passed this way: a cool, perennial pool of water, collected beneath a waterfall that tumbles through a cleft in the pale pink cliffs. In such a self-evidently sacred spot, it's no surprise to see ancient **petroglyphs** scraped into the desert varnish nearby.

An optional and much more demanding two-mile hike climbs the cliff beyond the last of the inscriptions to see the recently excavated **A'ts'ina Ruins**, up on top. Its builders, who abandoned it in 1350 AD, were among the ancestors of the modern Zuni.

At mile marker 46, a mile east of El Morro, the Inscription Rock Trading Post stocks Zuni crafts and holds a coffee bar (℡505/783-4706, Ⓦwww.inscriptionrocktrading.com).

El Malpais National Monument

If you had to pick one federal park in the Southwest *not* to visit, **EL MALPAIS NATIONAL MONUMENT** would be the obvious choice. Its creation in the 1980s was bitterly opposed by neighboring Ácoma Indians, who lost, in part, because they preferred not to reveal the whereabouts of sacred shrines. For tourists, however, the problem with El Malpais is more basic: it's **dull**.

El Malpais is Spanish for "the Badlands," and it preserves a tract of territory covered by **lava flows** from a volcanic eruption two or three thousand years ago – recent enough for the landscape to remain blackened and barren. Spelunkers delight in underground "lava tubes" up to seventeen miles long, but hiking any distance across the rough rock above is a pretty miserable business.

The map of El Malpais is a peculiar patchwork of desolate lava interspersed with pockets of grassland that the eruption missed. Confusingly, only the lava areas belong to the **national monument**, which is run by the National Park Service and served by a **visitor center** twenty miles east of El Morro on Hwy-53 (daily 8.30am–4.30pm; ℡505/783-4774, Ⓦwww.nps.gov/elma; admission free). The rest is administered as a **National Conservation Area** by the Bureau of Land Management, which has a **ranger station** on Hwy-17, nine miles south of I-40 exit 89 (daily 8am–4.30pm; ℡505/240-0300). Each of those roads skirts the periphery of the badlands; in an ordinary vehicle you can only get from one to the other via Grants.

On **Hwy-17**, the more interesting drive of the two, **Sandstone Bluffs Overlook** near the ranger station commands views westwards across the flatlands to the jagged peaks of the **Cerritos de Jaspe** and north to Mount Taylor. Not far beyond, **La Ventana Arch** is a chunky natural window three-quarters of the way up a cliff face east of the highway.

Grants

In general, **GRANTS**, sixty miles east of Gallup on I-40, looks better by night than it does by day. Daylight exposes an air of dereliction along its old Route 66 frontage that's concealed when the neon signs come on after dark. Even so, Grants has more character than Gallup and is a handy base for detours off the interstate.

Like Gallup, Grants started out as a railroad town. In the 1950s, just as a half-hearted **carrot** boom fizzled out, it struck rich in a rather less wholesome way. A Navajo shepherd, Paddy Martinez, picked up some yellow rocks on nearby Haystack Mountain, and Grants found itself sitting on half the US's reserves of **uranium**. Both the Anaconda mining company, which opened an enormous mine, and the Santa Fe Railroad, which owned the land, made a fortune; Martinez got a monthly pension and the title "official uranium scout."

Grants' uranium years have receded into history, but they're enjoyably recalled in the **New Mexico Museum of Mining** at 100 N Iron Ave (Mon–Sat 9am–4pm; $3). Visits consist of a faked descent into a mock-up mine, where you can poke around with no fear of radiation.

Practicalities

Grants' own **visitor center** adjoins the mining museum (Mon–Fri 9am–5pm; ℡505/287-4802 or 1-800/748-2142, Ⓦwww.grants.org). At the east end of town, just south of I-40 exit 85 at 1900 E Santa Fe Ave, the **Northwest New Mexico Visitor Center** offers information on the region's public lands (daily 8am–5pm; ℡505/876-2783).

Most of the town's more salubrious **motels** congregate east of downtown, across the railroad near exit 85 off the interstate. These include a good *Super 8*, 1604 E Santa Fe Ave (℡505/287-8811 or 1-800/800-8000; ❸), and a more upmarket *Holiday Inn Express*, 1496 E Santa Fe Ave (℡505/285-4676 or 1-800/465-4329; ❺).

The most popular place to **eat** is *La Ventana*, 110 Geis St in the Hillcrest Center (℡505/287-9393; closed Sun), which offers pretty much everything from steaks to fajitas, plus lighter sandwich lunches.

Ácoma Pueblo

The amazing **ÁCOMA PUEBLO**, south of I-40 fifteen miles east of Grants and fifty miles west of Albuquerque, encapsulates a thousand years of Native American history. Focused around the ancient village known as "**Sky City**," atop a magnificent mesa, it has adapted to repeated waves of invaders while retaining its own strong identity. Although the Acomans have long been happy to take the tourist dollar, so visitors seldom feel the awkwardness possible at other Pueblo communities, Ácoma is the real thing, and its sense of unbroken tradition can reduce even the least culturally sensitive traveler to awestruck silence.

A history of Ácoma Pueblo

Only certain Hopi villages can rival Sky City's claim to be the **oldest inhabited settlement** in the United States. This isolated mesa, 367ft high and 7000ft above sea level, was probably first occupied by Chacoan migrants at some point between 1100 and 1200, when the great pueblos of Chaco Canyon were still in use. The name Ácoma means "people of the white rock"; by the sixteenth century, it's thought to have held around six thousand inhabitants, living in five hundred or so three- to four-story houses.

The **Coronado** expedition of 1540 described the Acomans as "robbers, feared by the whole country round about." Noting the mesa's strong defenses – it could only be reached by climbing ladders through a narrow crevice – the Spaniards commented "no army could possibly be strong enough to capture the village."

In October 1598, Don Juan de **Oñate** visited Ácoma in peace, while exploring his recently proclaimed colony of New Mexico. A month later, however, his nephew Juan de **Zaldivar**, following with reinforcements, arrived at the foot of the mesa, demanded food, and was rejected. Depending on which version you believe, the Spaniards either tricked their way onto the mesa, or the Acomans invited them up and then ambushed them. In the ensuing fight, all the Spaniards were killed, save four who survived being hurled off.

When a punitive Spanish force of seventy men, equipped with cannons, stormed into the village in January 1599, over eight hundred Acomans died in a three-day house-to-house battle. Five hundred women and children and eighty men were taken prisoner. All were sentenced to twenty years of penal servitude, and each man had a foot publicly chopped off, in the plazas of the Rio Grande pueblos. Bitterness persists among the Pueblo peoples to this day; a statue of Oñate erected in Alcalde, New Mexico, in 1999 had its right foot removed within days.

Oñate was eventually called back to Mexico City and removed from office for his savagery. By 1629, Ácoma had a resident Spanish friar – Fray Juan Ramírez is said to have been accepted after he caught a child who fell off the mesa – and the Acomans were hard at work building a huge mission church. Ramírez's successors were driven out during the Pueblo Revolt, and a tyrannical eighteenth-century priest was thrown to his death, but in theory the pueblo was permanently converted to Catholicism.

The people of Ácoma clearly never felt inclined to follow the architectural example of the mission, whose mighty beams were carried 25 miles from Mount Taylor without once being permitted to touch the ground. Instead, they went on constructing the same multistory stone and adobe houses that can still be seen today.

Five hundred years since the Spanish arrived, the **Ácoma Indian Reservation** still has a population of six thousand. Most live in three communities that were originally sited for their proximity to fresh water but now stand conveniently close to I-40 – **ACOMITA**, **McCARTYS**, and **ANZAC**. Only thirteen families, forty people in all, live on the mesa itself, but others make daily trips to sell pottery or fry-bread, and many more return to their ancestral homes for feast days and other ceremonies. Eighty percent of Acomans call themselves Catholic, but the old religion endures; there are fourteen separate clans, and the Antelope Clan remains in charge of everything. Even today, the priest who serves the community is not himself an Indian, and is only permitted to visit the mesa once a week, on Wednesdays.

Arrival and information

Sky City is twelve miles south of the interstate, via any of three connecting roads. For the most dramatic approach, come in from the **west**, leaving I-40 at exit 102. When the mesa comes into view, glowing in the sunlight as you drop down a hillside roughly three miles distant, you'll understand why the first Spanish explorers spoke of cities of gold.

Before you take any photographs, however, you must first pay the relevant fees at the **Sky City Cultural Center**, at road's end below the mesa. You can only see Sky City itself on an hour-long **tour**; buses take groups up at regular intervals (daily: May–Oct 8am–6.30pm; Nov–April 8am–4.30pm; last tour leaves one hour before closing; $12, plus $10 for photo permit, no camcorders or video; ☏505/470-0181 or 1-800/747-0181, ⓦwww.skycity.com). The Cultural Center holds the excellent **Haak'u Museum** of Ácoma history and pottery (daily: May–Oct 8am–7pm; Nov–April 8am–4.30pm; $4), and also the good, inexpensive *Yaak'a Café*, where a bison or elk burger costs $9, and lamb stew $5. Note that Ácoma is **closed to all visitors** on June 24, June 29, July 10–13, July 25 during the first and/or second weekend in October, and the first Saturday of December.

The only **accommodation** available at Ácoma is up by the interstate, adjoining the tribal **casino**, in the large, comfortable, and stylish *Sky City Hotel* (☏505/552-6123 or 1-877/552-6123, ⓦwww.skycity.com; ❹). In the casino, the *Huwaka* **restaurant** offers cheap buffets as well as a full menu, and there's a coffee bar.

It's also possible to take a **guided tour** to Ácoma from Albuquerque, with the Indian Pueblo Cultural Center (see p.189; departs Tues & Thurs 9am; $80; ☏505/843-7270, ⓦwww.indianpueblo.org).

Sky City

While the original walls of **Sky City**'s oldest houses lie concealed beneath several centuries of replastering, the overall appearance of the village changed little in the last millennium. The high windowless wall of the main pueblo, at the northern edge of the mesa, protected its inhabitants against both the chill north wind and potential invaders. Three or four stories of terraced "apartments" face south to maximize the winter sun. Just one room still has its original tiny "windowpane" of translucent mica. Digging *kivas* down into the sandstone requires too much labor, so seven of the above-ground rooms are *kivas*, each shared by two clans and entered by a tall ladder pointing to the north. Ácoma's sparse rainfall collects in natural depressions in the rock; beside the largest of these cisterns is the mesa's only tree, a slender cottonwood.

Tour groups stroll more or less at will around the mesa-top, with plenty of opportunities to buy handmade pottery or ears of multicolored corn. Don't expect to enter any individual dwellings, however. The main stop is the still-active mission church of **San Esteban del Rey**, which measures 120ft long by 40ft wide, with seventy-foot-high walls that taper from 10ft thick at the base to 6ft at the top. The floor is made of hard-packed earth, while the whitewashed interior walls are decorated with a mixture of Christian images and Pueblo motifs. Ácoma's greatest treasure hangs above the altar – a painting of **St Joseph**, said to answer prayers for rain, which was borrowed by Laguna Pueblo in 1800 and only returned after the Acomans took Laguna all the way to the US Supreme Court. As no photography is permitted, you'll never have seen an image of the sublime view as you turn around from the altar, and won't be prepared for the glorious New Mexican light that streams in through the doorway to fill the cavernous space.

There's no soil on the mesa-top, so all the adobe bricks of the church were made with mud carried up from below, and its **cemetery** was filled with endless basket-loads of sand. Only honoured elders can now be buried here – not in coffins, but "replanted," facing east. At first, the churchyard wall looks crenellated, but in fact the bumps are "warriors," placed to guard the dead.

Legend has it that the forbidding **Enchanted Mesa**, visible to the east, once held its own Pueblo community. The only access to the top was via a spider's-web of ropes strung between the mesa itself and an adjoining rock pillar. When that pillar collapsed one day while the men were away from the village, two women and a child on top were left stranded, their cries for help fading as they starved.

If you prefer, you can walk rather than ride back down from Sky City, following the ancient footpath through clefts in the rock.

Laguna Pueblo

LAGUNA PUEBLO, just north of the interstate six miles east of Ácoma and 44 miles west of Albuquerque, is the **youngest** of the New Mexican pueblos. It was established in 1698 by refugees from several different pueblos, driven here by the disruption of the Pueblo Revolt and the threat of Navajo and Apache raids. It's also the **richest** pueblo, thanks partly to standing above the world's largest **uranium mine**, Anaconda's Jackpile mine, which closed in 1982, after operating for thirty years. However, **contamination** from mining has left a sorry legacy, with birth defects and cancer now major problems.

All of Laguna Pueblo, including its **San José Mission Church**, is visible from a rest stop on the west-bound side of I-40, halfway between the tribe's two **casinos** at exits 108 and 140, where traders sell crafts. There's no reason to explore any further.

Santa Fe and
northern New Mexico

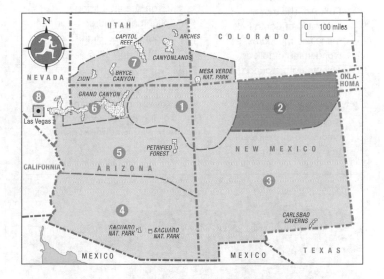

CHAPTER 2 # Highlights

✳ **La Fonda de Santa Fe** Splendidly atmospheric old hotel that once marked the end of the Santa Fe Trail. See p.121

✳ **The Palace of the Governors** The oldest public building in the country flew the flags of three other nations before the Americans moved in. See p.123

✳ **Museum of International Folk Art** The most enjoyable of Santa Fe's many fine museums; a wonderland of folk art objects from around the globe. See p.130

✳ **Coronado State Monument** When the fall colors are at their peak, the sunsets at this historic Pueblo settlement, beside the Rio Grande, are out of this world. See p.138

✳ **Bandelier National Monument** New Mexico's most appealing ancient site, where the ancestors of today's Pueblo peoples carved their homes into soft volcanic rock. See p.143

✳ **Santuario de Chimayó** Exquisite little adobe pilgrimage church beside the mountainous High Road from Santa Fe to Taos. See p.156

✳ **Taos Pueblo** The multistory adobe dwellings of Taos are a living legacy of New Mexico's extraordinary history. See p.167

▲ *Kiva*, Coronado State Monument

Santa Fe and northern New Mexico

B asking in the magical "**light**" that artists – and tourist boards – rave about, stretching beneath the flame-red peaks of the Sangre de Cristo mountains, **northern New Mexico** is the New Mexico of popular imagination, with its pastel colors, vivid desert landscape, and adobe architecture. Quite apart from its ravishing **beauty**, nowhere else in North America can boast such a sense of unbroken **history**. Native American pueblos and Hispanic colonial settlements have stood side by side along the Rio Grande for four hundred years, and the Yankees who arrived on the Santa Fe Trail still seem like relative newcomers.

State capital **Santa Fe**, the only city, more than lives up to its high-profile image as the epitome of Southwestern style, bursting with top-class museums, galleries and restaurants. Nonetheless, it remains less than a tenth the size of Albuquerque, and its central plaza is still recognizable as the frontier marketplace that welcomed trade caravans from Mexico and the Mississippi. **Taos**, 75 miles northeast and even smaller, is almost equally celebrated thanks to a remarkable twentieth-century influx of artists and writers such as **Georgia O'Keeffe** and **D.H. Lawrence**. It too has its share of museums and amenities and is a near neighbor to the Rio Grande's most striking pueblo, multistory **Taos Pueblo**.

Both Taos and Santa Fe are surrounded by spectacular scenery, and detours away from the river are rewarded with glimpses of countless fascinating communities. These range from the ancient **cliff dwellings** of **Bandelier National Monument** on the Pajarito Plateau west of the river, to Hispanic villages such as **Chimayó** on the **High Road** to the east, Wild-West towns like **Las Vegas**, and even the high-tech home of the H-Bomb, **Los Alamos**.

Santa Fe

SANTA FE has long ranked among the chic-est cities in the US, a favorite destination for upmarket travelers in particular. That appeal rests on a very solid basis; it's one of America's **oldest** and most **beautiful** cities, founded by Spanish adventurers and missionaries a decade before the Pilgrims reached Plymouth Rock. Spread across a high plateau at the foot of the stunning

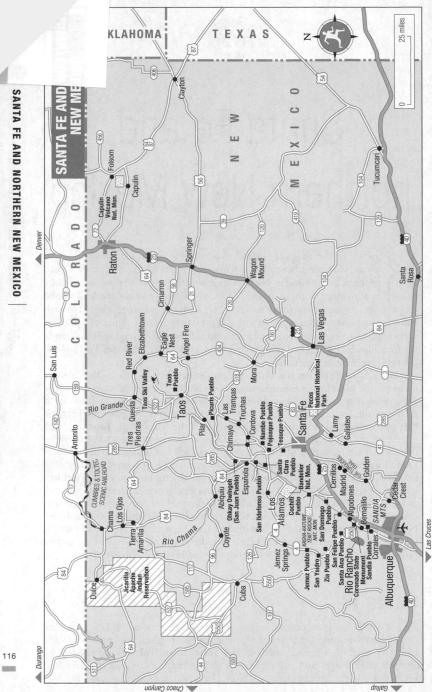

Sangre de Cristo mountains, New Mexico's capital still glories in the adobe houses and baroque churches of its original architects, now complemented by superb art museums and galleries. The busiest season is **summer**, when temperatures usually reach into the eighties Fahrenheit; in winter, the average daytime high is a mere 42°F, though with snow on the mountains the city looks more ravishing than ever.

With upwards of a million and a half tourists every year – not to mention twenty thousand daily commuters from Albuquerque – descending on a town of just seventy thousand inhabitants, Santa Fe has inevitably grown somewhat overblown. Long-term residents deplore the increased commercialization, and bemoan what's been lost, while first-time visitors, their initial impressions shaped by the depressing urban sprawl around the interstate, are inclined to wonder what all the fuss is about. Certainly, the rigorous insistence that every downtown building should look like a seventeenth-century Spanish colonial palace takes a bit of getting used to. This must be the only city in the world where it would be illegal to build a gas station that didn't resemble an Indian prayer chamber, and what on first glance appears to be a perfectly preserved ancient adobe turns out to be a multi-story parking lot.

There's still a lot to like about Santa Fe, however. Despite the summer crowds, the downtown area – clustered around its venerable **plaza** – still has the peaceful ambience of a small country town, while holding an extraordinary array of cultural and historic treasures. Above all else, it's rare indeed for it to be such fun simply to stroll around a Southwestern city.

A history of Santa Fe

The first homes of **La Villa de Santa Fe** ("Holy Faith") were erected above an abandoned Native American pueblo around 1604. In 1610, after previous Spanish settlements to the northwest had been deemed unsuitable, Santa Fe became the third capital of the infant colony of **New Mexico**. It was laid out as an imposing administrative city; as the **Palace of the Governors**, the *casas reales* or "royal houses" that commanded its parade-ground plaza went on to house Spanish, Pueblo, Mexican, and American rulers

---

Adobe

For many visitors, the defining feature of New Mexico is its **adobe architecture**, as seen in homes, churches, and even shopping malls and motels. While ancient pueblo villages were constructed using blocks of mud, cut from the riverbeds and mixed with grass, it was early Franciscan missionaries who introduced molded adobe **bricks**. The Spaniards had themselves learned the technique – in which a mixture of earth, sand, charcoal, and chopped grass or straw is left to bake in the sun in a wooden frame known as an *adobero* – from the Arabs. Built into walls, the bricks are set with a mortar of much the same composition, and then plastered over with mud and straw. The color of the soil used dictates that of the final building, and thus subtle variations can be seen all across the state. However, adobe is far from being a convenient material: it needs replastering every few years and turns to mud when water seeps up from the ground, so many buildings must be sporadically raised and bolstered by the insertion of rocks at their base.

These days, most of what looks like adobe is actually painted cement or concrete, but even that looks attractive in its own semi-kitsch way. Superb old adobes include the remote **Santuario de Chimayó** on the High Road between Santa Fe and Taos, the formidable church of **San Francisco de Asís** in Ranchos de Taos, and the multi-tiered dwellings of **Taos Pueblo**.

Santa Fe was the base from which horses, introduced to North America by the Spanish, spread across the continent and were acquired by Native American peoples. During its first two centuries the city presented an inviting target for mounted Apache, Ute, and Comanche raiders. Relations with the **Pueblo** peoples whom the Spaniards had come to convert were initially stable, but growing antagonism led to the **Pueblo Revolt** of 1680, when Santa Fe was besieged and conquered by an alliance of many different Indian groups. One thousand Spaniards fled south and lived in exile for twelve years at El Paso before returning under a new governor, **Don Diego de Vargas**. Their fight to regain control of the city is still celebrated in the annual **Fiestas de Santa Fe**.

Santa Fe was always a neglected outpost of the Spanish empire; at the time of Mexican independence in 1821, its garrison was armed merely with bows and

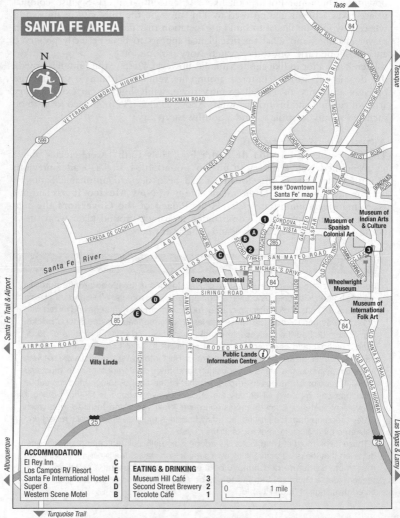

ACCOMMODATION
El Rey Inn	C
Los Campos RV Resort	E
Santa Fe International Hostel	A
Super 8	D
Western Scene Motel	B

EATING & DRINKING
Museum Hill Café	3
Second Street Brewery	2
Tecolote Café	1

0   1 mile

arrows. Attempts to improve the economy thereafter focused on the ever-expanding United States. Although American goods were soon pouring across the plains on the **Santa Fe Trail**, US citizens were forbidden to settle in the city. In 1843, the Mexican president ordered that the Santa Fe Trail be closed altogether, but a mere three years later New Mexico passed into American hands. A discreet payment of $50,000 to Governor Armijo ensured that there was no opposition to the entry of the US Army on **August 18, 1846**.

The Yankees set about transforming the squat, dusty Mexican town into something more conspicuously American, building in wood rather than adobe, but Santa Fe remained largely unchanged for the rest of the nineteenth century. Even when the old buildings started to disappear, the city was promptly seized by the conviction that it could only retain its identity by turning the clock back again – a campaign ironically inspired by the romantic notions of Anglo newcomers as to how Santa Fe *ought* to look. Since the 1930s, city mandates have ensured that almost every structure within sight of the plaza has been designed or redecorated to suit the **Pueblo Revival** mode. As a result, Santa Fe today – at least at its core – looks much more like its original Spanish self than it did a hundred years ago.

Arrival

Almost all visitors to Santa Fe arrive by **car**. Most drive an hour north on I-25 from **Albuquerque**, which in the absence of long-distance flights to Santa Fe's small municipal airport has the only major **airport** in New Mexico. The new Rail Runner **train** line, which opened in 2008, connects Albuquerque, both the airport and downtown, with Santa Fe, running partly along the I-25 median (journey time 1hr 30min; $7 one-way, $9 all-day pass; ☎1-866/795-7245, ⊛www.nmrailrunner.com). Its terminus, the Santa Fe Depot, is in the Railyard district, off Guadalupe Street half a mile southwest of downtown. Schedules are primarily designed for commuters, with no services on Sundays. Twin Hearts Express also runs **shuttle buses** from Albuquerque airport to Santa Fe ($25; ☎505/751-1201 or 1-800/654-9456, ⊛www.twinheartsexpress.com).

Amtrak trains do not serve Santa Fe itself, though daily arrivals at **Lamy**, seventeen miles southeast, are met by Lamy Shuttle vans ($18 one-way; ☎505/982-8829). **Buses** from all over the Southwest call at the Greyhound terminal at 858 St Michael's Drive (☎505/471-0008), a long way from the plaza. These include two daily buses to and from Albuquerque, which cost $19.50 one-way.

Information

Much the best place to pick up maps, brochures and information on Santa Fe and the whole state is the **New Mexico Department of Tourism**, in the Lamy Building at 491 Old Santa Fe Trail (daily: summer 8am–7pm; winter 8am–5pm; ☎505/827-4000 or 1-800/545-2040, ⊛www.newmexico.org). The **Public Lands Information Center**, 1474 Rodeo Rd (Mon–Fri 8am–5pm; ☎505/438-7840, ⊛www.publiclands.org), carries details on all public lands in New Mexico, including maps and brochures for state and national parks.

The main **post office** is also northwest of the plaza, at 120 S Federal Place (Mon–Fri 7.30am–5.30pm, Sat 9am–1pm; ☎505/988-6351).

Getting around

Most of what there is to see in Santa Fe lies within walking distance of the central plaza, but to get there from your hotel, or to see the farther-flung attractions, you may need to use the Santa Fe Trails **bus service**. All nine routes start from the **Downtown Transit Center**, a block northwest of the plaza on Sheridan Ave (Mon–Fri 6am–11pm, Sat 8am–8pm, Sun 10am–7.45pm; ☎505/955-2001, Ⓦsantafetrails.santafenm.gov), with a standard adult fare of $1, one-day passes for $2, and monthly passes for $20. The most useful for visitors are route #2, which runs up **Cerrillos Road** at half-hourly intervals, and route #M, which loops between the plaza and the **outlying museums**, again roughly every half-hour.

The only **taxi** company in town is Capital City Cabs (☎505/438-0000), while **bikes** can be rented at Mellow Velo, 638 Old Santa Fe Trail (☎505/995-8356, Ⓦmellowvelo.com).

Tours and excursions

Two-hour **walking tours** of town are conducted by the Friends of the Palace of the Governors, setting off from the Palace's blue gate on Lincoln Avenue (May–Oct Mon–Sat 10.15am; $10; ☎505/476-5109). Walk Through Time Tours, based at the *Inn at Loretto*, 211 Old Santa Fe Trail, run similar tours (daily 10am & 2pm; $10; ☎505/231-2770), and also Loretto Line **bus tours** (daily 10am, noon & 2pm; $15).

Excursion trains down to Lamy, drawn by diesel, not steam, leave from the old Santa Fe Depot at 410 S Guadalupe St (May–Oct Fri 11am & 6pm, Sat 11am & 5pm, Sun 2pm; March, April, Nov & Dec Fri & Sat 11am, Sun 2pm; Jan Sun 2pm; Feb Thurs 11am & Sun 2pm; $28–32; ☎505/989-8600 or 1-888/989-8600, Ⓦwww.sfsr.com). See the website for details of frequent extra services.

Accommodation

Even in winter, you won't find a room within walking distance of downtown Santa Fe for under $80, and in summer – when every bed in town is frequently taken – there's little under $125. **Cerrillos Road** (US-85), the main road in from I-25, holds most of Santa Fe's **motels** and its one **hostel**. Everything gets more expensive as you approach the center, though **B&Bs** make an attractive alternative to paying the sky-high prices demanded by the plush plaza-area hotels.

▲ *La Fonda de Santa Fe* hotel

Commercial **campgrounds** in the area include *Los Campos RV Resort*, 3574 Cerrillos Rd (mid-May to Sept; ☎505/473-1949 or 1-800/852-8160, ⓦwww .loscamposrv.com), which does not accept tenters, and the *KOA*, further east at I-25 exit 290 (March–Oct; ☎505/466-1419, ⓦwww.santafekoa.com). Camping nearby in the **Santa Fe National Forest** (☎505/438-7840, ⓦwww.fs.fed.us /r3/sfe) is cheaper and much more appealing. The *Black Canyon* campground (April–Nov; ⓦwww.recreation.gov; $10), which holds just under fifty tent sites and is unusual in offering advance reservations, is seven miles up Hwy-475, northeast of town. Two much smaller sites lie further on: *Big Tesuque* (year-round; free) is four miles beyond *Black Canyon*, and *Aspen Basin* (year-round; free) is another three miles beyond that, at the ski area (see p.131). Both have toilet facilities, but no showers.

B&Bs

Adobe Abode 202 Chapelle St ☎505/983-3133, ⓦwww.adobeabode.com. Small, playfully themed and very central B&B, with assorted folk-art-filled rooms both in a century-old house and in a separate newer building. **❼**

El Paradero 220 W Manhattan Ave ☎505/988-1177, ⓦwww.elparadero.com. Converted Spanish-era farmhouse near Guadalupe St. The rooms, especially those that open onto the central courtyard, are relatively plain and simple and furnished with folk art; twelve are en suite, while two share baths. **❺**

The Madeleine 106 Faithway St ☎505/986-1431 or 1-888/877-7622, ⓦwww.madeleineinn.com. Large Queen Anne inn with a peaceful garden setting behind the cathedral. The mixture of rooms (not all en suite) and cottages are all furnished with Pueblo and Mexican artworks. **❻**

Hotels

Eldorado Hotel & Spa 309 W San Francisco St ☎505/988-4455 or 1-800/955-4455, ⓦwww .eldoradohotel.com. Consummately stylish, taste-fully tiled upmarket hotel, a very short walk west of the plaza, offering spacious, well-appointed rooms – many with wood-burning *kiva* fireplaces – plus a rooftop swimming pool, spa with massage therapies, espresso bar, top-flight restaurant, and gym. **❾**

Hotel Santa Fe 1501 Paseo de Peralta at Cerrillos Rd ☎505/982-1200 or 1-800/825-9876, ⓦwww .hotelsantafe.com. Run by Picuris Pueblo, this attractive, elegant and very comfortable adobe hotel on the edge of downtown is within walking distance of the plaza, has its own good restaurant, *Amaya*, and stages free lectures by local experts. **❼**

Inn & Spa at Loretto 211 Old Santa Fe Trail ☎505/988-5531 or 1-800/727-5531, ⓦwww .innatloretto.com. This upmarket hotel rising between the plaza and the river is an extraordinary

spectacle, with its seven tiers, designed to resemble Taos Pueblo. Besides its opulent rooms and public spaces, a high-class restaurant, and the adjoining Loretto Chapel, it hosts a top-quality spa. **❾**

🏃 **La Fonda de Santa Fe** 100 E San Francisco St ☎505/982-5511 or 1-800/523-5002, ⓦwww.lafondasantafe.com. Gorgeous old inn on the southeast corner of the plaza, marking the end of the Santa Fe Trail; guests have ranged from Kit Carson to John F. Kennedy. Built in 1920 to replace the century-old original, it features hand-painted murals and stained glass throughout and plenty of nooks and crannies where you can sit and soak up the atmosphere. Each lavishly furnished room is different, with some lovely suites in the newer *La Terrazza* section, and there's a good restaurant plus the *Bell Tower* rooftop bar. **❾**

La Posada de Santa Fe Resort & Spa 330 E Palace Ave ☎505/986-0000 or 1-866/331-7625, ⓦwww.laposadadesantafe.com. Despite its size, this is downtown's most peaceful option, with individual adobe *casitas* (cottages) set in spacious gardens as well as ultra-modern spa rooms. **❾**

Old Santa Fe Inn 320 Galisteo St ☎505/995-0800 or 1-800/734-9910, ⓦwww.oldsantafeinn .com. Former Route 66 motor court, now an appealing mid-range inn; many of its tasteful, Mexican-themed rooms have their own gas fireplaces. Avoid the few rooms in the inadequately sound proofed two-story buildings. Breakfast included. **❼**

Hostel and motels

El Rey Inn 1862 Cerrillos Rd at St Michael's Drive ☎505/982-1931 or 1-800/521-1349, ⓦwww .elreyinnsantafe.com. This white-painted adobe, here since the 1930s, has the most character and best value of the Cerrillos Road motels, with surprisingly stylish and distinctive South-western rooms adorned with Art Deco tiles, some nice suites, complementary breakfasts, a pool,

and a large garden. Ask for a room away from the road. ❺

Garrett's Desert Inn 311 Old Santa Fe Trail ☎505/982-1851 or 1-800/888-2145, ⓦwww .garrettsdesertinn.com. Large, dull-looking two-story motel, with well equipped and reasonably appealing rooms, a pool and café. and great rates for such a central location. ❺

Santa Fe International Hostel 1412 Cerrillos Rd at Alta Vista ☎505/988-1153, ⓦwww .hostelsantafe.com. This old-fashioned hostel, housed in a ramshackle former motel a couple of miles southwest of the plaza, is one of those love-it-or-hate-it places. Some travelers find the staff unfriendly, the owner a control freak, and the rooms poorly furnished and dirty; others seem totally satisfied, say there's a good atmosphere, and don't mind the compulsory chores. Dorms beds cost $18, or you can get an en-suite room to yourself for $35 single, $45 double. In winter the whole place can be damp and cold. ❶–❷

🏃 **Santa Fe Motel & Inn** 510 Cerrillos Rd ☎505/982-1039 or 1-800/930-5002,

ⓦwww.santafemotel.com. To call this delightfully stylish yet inexpensive little adobe complex a "motel" barely does it justice; even its most conventional rooms are appealingly furnished, and some have their own kitchens, while there are also several gorgeous little casitas. The staff are very friendly, and the rates, which are great for such a quiet, central location, include a full cooked breakfast. ❺

Santa Fe Sage Inn 725 Cerrillos Rd at Don Diego ☎505/982-5952 or 1-866/433-0355, ⓦwww .santafesageinn.com. The most central chain motel, a mile or so from the plaza; large, clean, functional if not inspiring, with a pool and free breakfasts. ❹

Super 8 3358 Cerrillos Rd at Richards Ave ☎505/471-8811 or 1-800/800-8000, ⓦwww.super8.com. Thanks to its half-hearted adobe exterior, this hundred-room chain motel, four miles from downtown, looks strange, but it's a dependable bargain. ❹

Western Scene Motel 1608 Cerrillos Rd at Cochiti ☎505/983-7484. Rundown but inexpensive two-story adobe motel, a short way south of the hostel. ❹

The City

Even if it's not always easy to tell genuine historic buildings from modern counterfeits, there's a definite, romantic continuity between today's Santa Fe and the Spanish settlement of four hundred years ago. The most enjoyable way to start a visit is simply to wander the narrow streets of the old town. Before long you'll find plenty of specific diversions to capture your interest.

Once you've got your bearings in the **plaza**, the best places to get a sense of local history and culture are the **Palace of the Governors** and the **Museum of Fine Arts** downtown, and the museums of **Indian Arts and Culture** and **Folk Art** a couple of miles southeast. Two private museums, the **Museum of Spanish Colonial Art** and the **Georgia O'Keeffe Museum**, are also well

Santa Fe festivals

The first of the three major events in Santa Fe's annual calendar is **Spanish Market** (ⓦwww.spanishmarket.org), held during the last week in July, when examples of the traditional folk arts of Hispanic New Mexico are sold on the plaza, while contemporary works are on sale in the Palace of the Governors. A smaller-scale **Winter Spanish Market** takes place during the first weekend in December.

Indian Market (ⓦwww.swaia.org) fills the plaza on the weekend after the third Thursday in August, attracting over 100,000 buyers and craftspeople from all over the world for the premier showcase of Southwestern Native American arts and crafts. September's **Fiestas de Santa Fe** (ⓦwww.santafefiesta.org), which take place over the weekend after Labor Day, have been held annually since 1712 to celebrate the Spaniards' return after the Pueblo Revolt. The ceremonial burning of *Zozobra* ("Old Man Gloom") in Fort Marcy Park on the Thursday prior, which kicks off the parades and processions, is not a Catholic tradition; it was invented in the 1920s by atheist American intellectuals.

▲ Apache statue, Museum Hill

worth seeing. Alternatively, set about exploring Santa Fe's distinct neighborhoods, such as the old **Barrio Analco** just southeast of downtown, home to the **San Miguel Mission**; the **Canyon Road** arts district, just beyond; and funkier **Guadalupe Street** to the west, with its new **Railyard** development.

The plaza

Santa Fe's central **plaza** has been the heart of the city since 1610, though the original rectangular parade ground of the Spanish garrison was twice as large as the neat, leafy square of today. As well as witnessing many turning points in New Mexican history – from the public hanging of three Indian "witch-doctors" in 1675 (which helped to trigger the Pueblo Revolt five years later, when Pueblo Indians filled the plaza to lay siege to the Palace of the Governors), to the nineteenth-century celebrations of Mexican independence and annexation by the United States – it served as journey's end for countless weary travelers on the Santa Fe Trail. Just how contentious the city's history remains is illustrated by the **obelisk** at the center of the plaza, where unknown hands have chiseled the word "savage" out of an inscription that formerly honored "the heroes who have fallen in the various battles with savage Indians in the territories of New Mexico."

The plaza now serves as a pleasant public park, where visitors and office workers alike picnic on the grass as they watch the latest bemused arrivals spill out of their tour buses. Under the arcade of the Palace of the Governors, along its northern flank, **Native American traders** shelter from the summer sun or winter wind. They're strictly licensed, so the price, authenticity, and quality of their craftworks and jewelry compare favorably with the stores and galleries that line the other three sides of the square.

Palace of the Governors

The **Palace of the Governors** (Mon–Thurs, Sat, & Sun 10am–5pm, Fri 10am–8pm; closed Mon in winter; $8, free Fri 5–8pm; under-17s free; ☎505/476-5100, ⊛www.palaceofthegovernors.org), which fills the north side of the plaza, often fails to make an immediate impression on visitors. That this long single-story structure looks so much like every other building in central

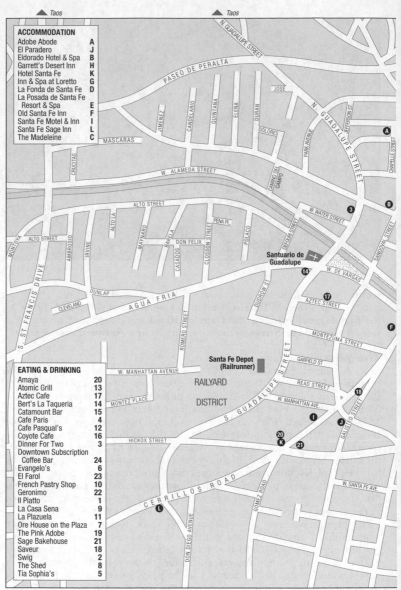

▲ Taos   ▲ Taos

ACCOMMODATION

Adobe Abode	A
El Paradero	J
Eldorado Hotel & Spa	B
Garrett's Desert Inn	H
Hotel Santa Fe	K
Inn & Spa at Loretto	G
La Fonda de Santa Fe	D
La Posada de Santa Fe Resort & Spa	E
Old Santa Fe Inn	F
Santa Fe Motel & Inn	I
Santa Fe Sage Inn	L
The Madeleine	C

EATING & DRINKING

Amaya	20
Atomic Grill	13
Aztec Cafe	17
Bert's La Taqueria	14
Catamount Bar	15
Cafe Paris	4
Cafe Pasqual's	12
Coyote Cafe	16
Dinner For Two	3
Downtown Subscription Coffee Bar	24
Evangelo's	6
El Farol	23
French Pastry Shop	10
Geronimo	22
Il Piatto	1
La Casa Sena	9
La Plazuela	11
Ore House on the Plaza	7
The Pink Adobe	19
Sage Bakehouse	21
Saveur	18
Swig	2
The Shed	8
Tia Sophia's	5

▼ Albuquerque, Turquoise Trail & other Cerrillos Road motels

Santa Fe is hardly surprising – it served as a blueprint for the remodeling of the city. It's also as much of a fake, in that until 1913, it was a typical, formal, territorial building with a square tower at each corner; its subsequent adobe "reconstruction" was based on pure conjecture.

Nonetheless, the palace is the oldest public building in the United States and now serves as a fascinating **historical museum**. Constructed in 1610 as the headquarters of the Spanish colonial administration, it was first occupied by

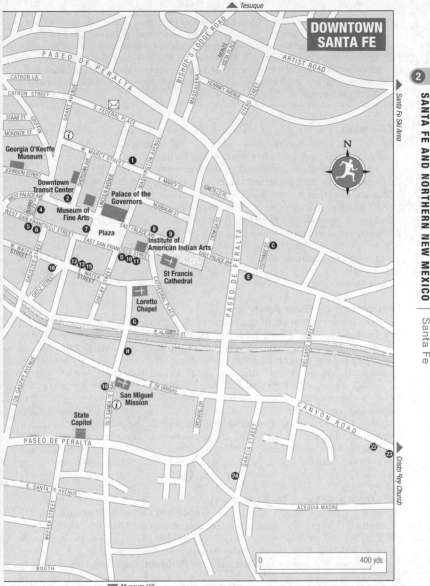

Governor **Pedro de Peralta**. To call it a "palace" may now seem an exaggeration, but it was originally much larger, an imposing adobe, with two towers and a sod roof, which formed part of a bigger defensive complex. After the **Pueblo Revolt** of 1680, the palace was taken over by Pueblo peoples, who sealed its doors and windows, divided its rooms, and dug still-visible storage pits into the floor, but it was soon back in Spanish hands, and later became home to first Mexican, and then American, governors of New Mexico. By the time Governor

②

A combination ticket, costing $18 and valid for four days, grants admission to five leading Santa Fe museums: the Palace of the Governors, the Museum of Fine Arts, the Museum of Indian Arts and Culture, the Museum of International Folk Art, and the Museum of Spanish Colonial Art. Alternatively, a $12 one-day ticket entitles you to visit *either* the Palace of the Governors and the Museum of Fine Arts, *or* the museums of Indian Arts and International Folk Art. No offers, however, include the Georgia O'Keeffe Museum.

Lew Wallace wrote part of *Ben Hur* here, during his term of office from 1878 to 1881, the palace had turned Victorian. Its balustrades, elaborate windows, and wallpaper were removed after it ceased to be the official Governor's residence in 1909, and was restored as part of the **Museum of New Mexico**.

Displays in its well-preserved interior are especially strong on Hispanic New Mexico, featuring a reproduction nineteenth-century chapel with a genuine 1830 altarpiece. Starting with the sixteenth-century Spanish *entrada* into the Southwest, the exhibits also serve to stress that the frontier experience of New Mexico lasted for three centuries, far longer than anywhere else in the United States. Be sure to visit the well-stocked bookstore (which you can also access without paying admission), and to wander into the peaceful open-air courtyard beyond, where the Palace Print Shop sells hand-printed cards and booklets (daily 9am–4.30pm).

Museum of Fine Arts

On the northwest corner of the plaza at 107 E Palace Ave, Santa Fe's **Museum of Fine Arts** (Mon–Thurs, Sat & Sun 10am–5pm, Fri 10am–8pm, closed Mon in winter; $8, free Fri 5–8pm, under-17s free; ⓦwww.mfasantafe.org) is housed in a particularly attractive adobe, with ornamental beams and a cool central courtyard. Erected in 1917, this was Santa Fe's first example of the "Pueblo Revival" school of architecture and remains unsurpassed to this day. It was also one of the few major art museums to be established by artists rather than educators or collectors, and it continues to concentrate on painting and sculpture by local artists. The main focus is on changing exhibits of contemporary work, though selections from the permanent collection, displayed upstairs, usually include an O'Keeffe or two, while the room devoted to painter and printmaker Gustave Baumann is especially fascinating. Once again, there's also a good shop selling Southwestern prints.

Georgia O'Keeffe Museum

The ten galleries of the showpiece **Georgia O'Keeffe Museum**, at 217 Johnson St, house the world's largest collection of O'Keeffe's work (Mon–Thurs, Sat & Sun 10am–5pm, Fri 10am–8pm; $8, free Fri 5–8pm; under-18s free; ☏505/946-1000, ⓦwww.okeeffemuseum.org). Highlights include many of the desert landscapes she painted near **Abiquiu**, forty miles northwest of Santa Fe (see p.154), where she lived from 1946 until her death in 1986. Most of the museum is given over to touring exhibitions devoted to differing aspects of O'Keeffe's work, so there's little guarantee as to which pieces may be displayed at any one time. The first two rooms however feature the permanent collection, with some New York cityscapes that make a surprising contrast among the more familiar sun-bleached skulls and iconic flowers. There's so much material that entire rooms concentrate on paintings of particular motifs, be it flowers or pink seashells, all characterized by O'Keefe's trademark close focus and voluptuousness.

St Francis Cathedral

Santa Fe only acquired its first Catholic bishop in 1851, after New Mexico joined the United States and ceased to belong to the Mexican diocese of Durango. As described in Willa Cather's novel *Death Comes for the Archbishop*, the arrival of **Jean Baptiste Lamy** – a Frenchman, previously resident in Kentucky – threw the overwhelmingly Hispanic church in New Mexico into turmoil.

Lamy's most lasting achievement, **St Francis Cathedral**, now makes an unlikely spectacle, looming two blocks east of the plaza at the top of San Francisco Street. Eschewing adobe, the first cathedral west of the Mississippi was built of solid stone, between 1869 and 1886, in the formal – and, frankly, dreary – Romanesque style of France. Its walls rose over and around those of its eighteenth-century predecessor, which was progressively removed as rubble. In the only part of that structure to survive, the side chapel of **Our Lady of the Rosary**, pride of place goes to a statue of the Virgin known as **La Conquistadora**. Brought from Mexico in 1625, she was credited by the Hispanic population of Santa Fe with facilitating both their escape from the Pueblo Revolt in 1680 and their subsequent reconquest of the province. The statue itself looks more like a Victorian doll than a venerated religious artifact – an effect enhanced by the practice of dressing it in different clothes at different times of the year. She is still paraded through the city each June, on the Sunday after Corpus Christi.

Institute of American Indian Arts Museum

The stimulating **Institute of American Indian Arts Museum**, 108 Cathedral Place (June–Oct Mon–Sat 10am–5pm, Sun noon–5pm; Nov–May Mon & Wed–Sat 10am–5pm, Sun noon–5pm; $5, under-16s free; ☏505/983-8900, Ⓦ www.iaia.edu/museum), is housed in a modern building – which naturally looks like adobe – facing the cathedral. Don't confuse it with the Museum of Indian Arts and Culture on the edge of town (see below); as they insist on telling you, "we're contemporary, not historical," and most of the artwork exhibited is less than a year old. Encompassing paintings, installations, collages, and mixed-media pieces, it's all a long way from the usual stereotyped notion of Native American art. The sculpture garden is especially recommended.

Loretto Chapel

A block from the plaza at the start of Old Santa Fe Trail, the **Loretto Chapel** (winter Mon–Sat 9am–5pm, Sun 10.30am–5pm; summer Mon–Sat 9am–6pm, Sun 10.30am–5pm; $2.50, ages 7–12 $2; Ⓦ www.lorettochapel.com) was built for the Sisters of Loretto under the auspices of Archbishop Lamy. Work was directed from 1873 onwards by **Projectus Mouly**, the 18-year-old son of the French architect responsible for St Francis Cathedral. In different accounts, he either drank himself to death, or was killed by Lamy's cousin. Either way, the completed chapel lacked any means of reaching the choir loft, twenty feet above the nave. Hence the legend of its **Miraculous Staircase**, an elegant wooden spiral – more of a spring, in a sense – which makes two complete 360 degree turns as it rises and was built without a single nail or any support at either the center or the sides. It's said to be the work of a mysterious carpenter who arrived in answer to the nuns' prayers and disappeared without demanding payment.

The story is more entertaining than the reality, however. The chapel is now deconsecrated and belongs to the upmarket *Inn at Loretto*, with direct access from the hotel, so it's always packed with irreverent tourists. What's more, the nuns found the staircase too frightening to climb, so they disfigured it by adding banisters. The whole thing is now propped up with a metal brace.

San Miguel Mission

Two blocks south of the Loretto Chapel, across the river, **San Miguel Mission** (Mon–Sat 9am–5pm, Sun 1.30–4pm; Mass on Sun at 5pm; $1, under-7s free) is said to be the oldest church in the United States to have remained in continuous use. The site is known to have been occupied in 1300 AD, while the church was built by Tlaxcalan Indians from central Mexico, who accompanied New Mexico's earliest Spanish settlers in 1610. Although its roof was destroyed during the 1680 Pueblo Revolt, parts of its graceful, sloping adobe walls survived. That said, before the church was "restored" to its current appearance in the nineteenth century, its external lines were much sharper than they are today; its rounded adobe look is not necessarily authentic.

Inside, a hole in the floor beneath the altar reveals the foundations of an ancient pueblo, as well as the original steps of the sanctuary, while the pale green *reredos*, or altarpiece, above was painted in 1798 to frame a statue of San Miguel brought by missionaries from Mexico. The mission also holds a buffalo hide and a deerskin, painted with depictions of Jesus on the cross, which date from around 1630. In addition, its gift shop contains what's said to be the oldest bell in the US, cast in Spain in 1356.

Kokopelli

Time was when you could hardly move in Santa Fe without someone trying to sell you a figurine of a colorful coyote howling at the moon. More recently, however, the coyotes have been superseded by a symbol more closely associated with Native American traditions – the hunchbacked flute player known as **Kokopelli**.

Although Kokopelli derives originally from ancient **rock art**, his image has been so extensively appropriated by non-Indian artists that he's now become an all-purpose icon for the Southwest. He's usually depicted in silhouette, as a solid block of a single color, whether printed, painted, cast in clay or cut from sheet metal. His flute is a simple extension of his face, each leg curves seamlessly from his trunk, and his head is crested with what might once have been feathers but are now often dreadlocks. You might see him cycling, skiing, or dressed in strange costumes, but his basic shape remains instantly recognizable.

But who was Kokopelli? There's no single answer. While he's often referred to as an "Anasazi flute-player" – "Anasazi" being the term formerly used for the Ancestral Puebloans – he dates back longer than that. You can see him in the pictographs in Canyonlands' Horseshoe Canyon (see p.440), created by so-called Archaic peoples more than 1600 years ago. Other ancient cultures familiar with Kokopelli included the Mogollon, the Sinagua, and the Hohokam.

Kokopelli has been viewed in many, inconsistent ways, but there's general agreement that he was not a hunchback, but a trader whose "hunch" is really a pack on his back, rather than a physical deformity. As they carried their goods north from Mexico, such traders, possibly carrying seeds for sale, announced their arrival in each new pueblo by blowing a **flute**. Some see him as a benevolent deity who introduced agriculture to the Southwest, bringing new crops to each village and explaining the rituals necessary to their cultivation. Others see him as much more of a trickster, a Pied Piper figure who used his flute to seduce impressionable women (hence the enormous phallus in many ancient images).

Today, however, Kokopelli is most associated with the Hopi, though even within that tribe different groups tell different stories. The Flute Clan currently based at Walpi on First Mesa, marked their successive homes (they trace their migrations back to Mesa Verde) by depicting their clan symbol, Flute Player, in rock art. They regard Flute Player as distinct from the mischievous Kokopelli, who is remembered by other Hopi clans as a kachina, and also exists in a female version – or perhaps it's his wife – Kokolmana.

The claims of a nearby adobe, immediately north of the church, to be the **oldest house in the United States** are generally dismissed, though it too probably stands on the ruins of the former pueblo. This whole district, the **Barrio de Analco**, is now an appealing residential neighborhood, abounding in two-hundred-year-old houses.

Guadalupe Street and the Railyard

A few blocks southwest of the plaza, the stretch of **Guadalupe Street** that runs south from the tiny Santa Fe River has become the focus of a characterful little district that caters more to local students and artists than passing tourists. It centers around the small **Santuario de Guadalupe** at Guadalupe and Agua Fria (May–Oct Mon–Sat 9am–4pm; Nov–April Mon–Fri 9am–4pm; donation), a shrine built between 1776 and 1795 to mark the end of the Camino Real, the trail from Mexico City that for centuries provided Santa Fe's only connection with the outside world. Remodeling in the 1880s added an incongruous New England-style spire and tall windows, and the church became a small museum of its own history to mark its (and the nation's) bicentennial in 1976. Since then it has hosted regular dance and music performances, with Mass celebrated only on the 12th of each month.

In the late nineteenth century, the surrounding neighborhood became the point of arrival into Santa Fe for trains on the Atchison, Topeka & Santa Fe, and Denver & Rio Grande railroads. Since it became Santa Fe's terminal for the Rail Runner system (see p.119), it has been redeveloped under the official name of **The Railyard**, with its former warehouses and small factories converted to house stores, galleries, and restaurants.

Canyon Road and Acequia Madre

Before Santa Fe ever existed, **Canyon Road**, which climbs a steady but shallow incline east from Paseo de Peralta, a few hundred yards east of San Miguel Mission, was an Indian trail that led to the pueblo at Pecos. Since the 1920s, however, it has been famous as the center of Santa Fe's **art colony**. It's now dominated by galleries and high-class stores – some of which are reviewed on p.135 – but even if you don't plan to buy anything it makes for an intriguing half-day stroll out from downtown.

At Canyon Road's far eastern end, the 1940 **Cristo Rey** church is the largest adobe building in the US. It's over three miles out, however, and most walkers prefer either to double back along Canyon Road at some earlier point, or return to town via **Acequia Madre**, one block south. The name of this ancient unpaved street literally means the "mother ditch;" following the course of the city's first irrigation canal, it's lined with beautiful adobe homes.

Museum of Indian Arts and Culture

The excellent **Museum of Indian Arts and Culture** (daily 10am–5pm; closed Mon in winter; $8, under-17s free; ☎505/827-6344, ⓦwww.miaclab.org) is on a raised plateau known as **Museum Hill**, two miles southeast of downtown, with extensive views of the hills and mountains that almost surround the city. It stands at the northern end of **Milner Plaza**, a landscaped area that also holds a good café (see p.133) and a giant bronze statue of an Apache Mountain Spirit Dancer.

The centerpiece of the museum, a permanent exhibition entitled **Here, Now, and Always**, provides comprehensive coverage of all the major Southwest tribes, including the 'O'odham, Navajo, Apache, Pai, Ute, and Pueblo peoples. It's intended as much for Native Americans themselves as for tourists – hence the taped messages that warn Navajo and Tewa visitors to skip certain sections in order to avoid contact with the world of their dead forebears. Myth and history are explained in copious detail, while contemporary realities are acknowledged in such forms as the inclusion of computer games, alongside music, architecture, and language, in the exhibit on the modern Apache way of life. Different parts of the exhibit focus on the topography of the Southwest, explaining how native peoples have thrived in such differing terrains as canyons, river basins, mesas, and deserts.

As well as hosting excellent temporary exhibitions, the museum also boasts a superb array of Native American pottery, from pristine thousand-year-old Ancestral Puebloan and Mimbres pieces up to the works of twentieth-century revivalists.

Museum of International Folk Art

The delightful **Museum of International Folk Art** (daily 10am–5pm; closed Mon in winter; $8, under-17s free; ☎505/827-6344, ⓦwww.moifa .org), across Milner Plaza, centers on the huge **Girard Collection** of paintings, textiles, and, especially, **clay figurines**, gathered from all over the world. These are arranged in colorful dioramas that include a Pueblo Feast Day, complete with dancing *kachinas* and camera-clicking tourists, and street scenes from countries such as Poland, Peru, Portugal, and Ethiopia featuring fabulously ornate churches and cathedrals. The sheer scale of the place has to be seen to be believed.

An equally eclectic array of folk art objects is on display in the Neutrogena Collection, where the specific artifacts displayed change each year. The traditional New Mexican crafts in the **Hispanic Heritage Wing** are also fascinating. Alongside the expected *santos* (religious depictions of saints, whether carved figures or painted panels of wood), you'll encounter eerie skeletal wooden figures of "Death Personified," associated with the Penitente brotherhoods (see p.157). Excellent temporary exhibitions focus on more recent works such as *paños* – handkerchiefs decorated with religious and secular images in magic marker or pencil by often-anonymous prison inmates.

Be sure to call in at the museum **gift store**, which stocks some of the best souvenirs in town.

Museum of Spanish Colonial Art

The **Museum of Spanish Colonial Art** stands immediately north of the Milner Plaza museums, (daily 10am–5pm; closed Mon in winter; $6, under-16s free; ☎505/982-2226, ⓦwww.spanishcolonial.org). Focusing on such traditional Hispanic religious artworks, long pervasive in the iconography of Santa Fe, as *retablos* (often-naïve painted images of religious scenes and figures) and *bultos* (carved wooden statues of saints), it makes a valiant attempt to place colonial art in a global context. Statuettes in its World of Art room are drawn from as far afield as Goa and Guatemala. Showcasing work by contemporary New Mexican schoolchildren, another gallery, El Futuro, proves local traditions are in no danger of dying out. The whole collection is appealingly laid out in a former private home, one room of which replicates the living room of an eighteenth-century Spanish captain in New Mexico (see below) and reveals so-called "Santa Fe style" to be more than a mere home decorating invention.

Sadly, however, given the abundance of Hispanic colonial art on display throughout Santa Fe, and in particular the superior exhibits in the neighboring folk art museum (see above), there may well be little here that isn't already familiar to you. In addition, being by definition largely vernacular, the pieces tend not to be of such exceptional quality as to merit a special trip.

Wheelwright Museum of the American Indian

The large, private **Wheelwright Museum of the American Indian** (Mon–Sat 10am–5pm, Sun 1–5pm; free; ☏505/982-4636, ⓦwww.wheelwright.org), is located down a short slope behind the folk art museum. Designed to resemble a Navajo *hogan* (see p.74), its original purpose was to record Navajo sand paintings and ceremonials. These days, however, its permanent collection is seldom on show, and it concentrates instead on changing exhibitions, usually of contemporary art that's similar to what you'll see in the galleries in town. The Case Trading Post downstairs sells jewelry, rugs, and *kachinas* of very high quality, at very high prices.

Rancho de las Golondrinas

Once a fortified *paraje* (stopping place) on the Camino Real, the **Rancho de las Golondrinas** (June–Sept Wed–Sun 10am–4pm; guided tours available by reservation, also in April, May & Oct; $5, ages 13–18 $4, under-13s $2; ☏505/471-2261, ⓦwww.golondrinas.org), fifteen miles south of Santa Fe, is now a living history museum. To reach it, turn right onto Hwy-599 from exit 276 on I-25; left onto Frontage Road; and follow Los Pinos Road to the right for three more miles.

The adobe farmstead at the center of the "Ranch of the Swallows" is thought to have welcomed the governor of New Mexico in 1698 and strongly resembles Pueblo architecture of the period. As La Cienaga Ranch, it belonged in the eighteenth century to Captain Manuel Delgado, whose living room is reproduced in the Spanish colonial art museum (see above). He was wealthy enough to own a wardrobe of thirteen velvet, cashmere, and silk suits.

Topped by a tall *torreon* (watchtower), the 200-acre farmstead incorporates a covered well and plenty of stables and livestock pens within its strongly defensive walls, while planted fields reach down to the river beyond. Other early Hispanic structures – many brought from elsewhere in New Mexico – include a watermill, a replica Penitente *morada* (chapel; see p.157), a smithy, and smaller farmhouses. The whole place is staffed by well-informed but unobtrusive "villagers" in period costume, with different sections maintained in the style of the seventeenth, eighteenth, and nineteenth centuries. It's an absolutely lovely spot, ranged across the meadows and woodland to either side of the river and bursting with wild flowers and sweet-smelling herbs.

The best time to visit Las Golondrinas is during one of the **theme** or **festival weekends** ($7), held on the first weekend of each month in summer, as well as several other weekends. Festival season starts with the Spring Festival in June and ends with October's Harvest Festival.

Santa Fe ski area

Santa Fe's **ski area**, located within the Santa Fe National Forest, is just sixteen miles northeast of the city, off the winding and very scenic Hwy-475. Boasting a 12,075ft summit and 1725ft of vertical skiing, its 69 runs are usually open from late November until early April (daily lift tickets $58 full-day, $42 half-day; information on ☏505/982-4429 or ⓦwww.skisantafe.com). Skiing is suitable for all levels, and there is a ski/snowboard school as well as multiday programs and workshops for both children and adults. Equipment can be rented on site, but there are **no resort facilities** apart from a café and a grill that provide soups, burgers, sandwiches, and the like.

Pecos National Historical Park

A short way north of I-25, 25 miles east of Santa Fe, a long, low ridge in the heart of the Sangre de Cristo mountains served for over a thousand years as one of the most significant cultural rendezvous in the Southwest. Excavations during the 1920s so precisely chronicled changes in pottery and architecture as to become the model for all other such digs, and **PECOS NATIONAL HISTORICAL PARK** is thus famed as the "birthplace of Southwestern archeology."

Ninth-century Basketmakers (see p.494) were the first to inhabit this spot, but between 1450 and 1550, as the pueblo of **Cicuyé**, it was home to over two thousand people, including five hundred warriors. Protected behind four-story walls, it was a major **trading center**, where Pueblo peoples exchanged turquoise, axes, and shells from as far west as the Pacific for bison meat, hides, and wood for bows brought by Plains nomads who camped outside the walls. As described on p.500, **Coronado** stayed here in 1541 and met a captive from the plains who lured his expedition east in search of the nonexistent gold of Quivira.

After Franciscan missionaries built a church alongside what they called **Pecos Pueblo** sixty years later, Spaniards too came to trade, but Apache and Comanche raids eventually forced Pecos into decline. Its last twenty survivors migrated 65 miles west to join Jemez Pueblo in 1838. Their descendants continue to elect a governor of Pecos Pueblo, and return for ceremonies.

The whole Pecos story is well told in the **visitor center** (daily: summer 8am–6pm; winter 8am–4.30pm; ☎505/757-6414, ⓦwww.nps.gov/peco; $3 per person), from where a mile-long trail loops onto the ridge itself. Much of the former pueblo area remains unexcavated, though some walls are exposed, and large buried structures are obvious everywhere. Beyond it, the trail leads around and through the high roofless walls of the **mission church**, stark in the bright sunlight and surrounded by the ruined *convento* buildings where its priests once lived. The *kiva* in the heart of the church was dug as a deliberate act of sacrilege during the Pueblo Revolt. Note that if you're pressed for time, you can park close to the church, and spare yourself the hike from the visitor center, by following the signs off the approach road to the "picnic area."

Two additional parcels of the park, not currently open to visitors, incorporate the site of the **Battle of Glorieta Pass**. Fought on March 28, 1862, it was the turning point of the **Civil War** in the Southwest, when four thousand Union soldiers repelled three thousand Confederate invaders who had already briefly occupied Santa Fe.

Eating

Santa Fe has been renowned as one of America's most exciting places to eat since the early 1980s, when a stupendous feat of marketing managed to make dishes such as banana-crusted sea bass seem quintessentially Southwestern. It's said to have more high-end restaurants per capita than anywhere else in the US, though that doesn't make it any easier to get a reservation at the latest hotspot in summer. In addition, the fact that so many diners are simply tourists, passing through, makes it hard for restaurants to develop much character. Nonetheless, there's some memorable dining to be had, and it doesn't have to be wallet-busting. The sheer inventiveness of the city's menus makes up for its shortage of ethnic alternatives (though you will find the odd adobe sushi bar here and there).

The **Santa Fe School of Cooking**, 116 W San Francisco St (☎505/983-4511 or 1-800/892-4688, ⓦwww.santafeschoolofcooking.com), offers lunchtime classes in preparing such Southwestern specialties as chile stuffed chicken or lamb adovada with chipotle sauce, culminating in the opportunity to eat the lot (2hr 30min; $40–80 depending on ingredients).

Cafés and coffeehouses

Aztec Cafe 317 Aztec St ☎ 505/820-0025.
Counterculture hangout in the Galisteo St district,
with wi-fi and a nice patio, and serving coffees,
pastries, smoothies, and light meals, with
occasional live music. Mon–Sat 7am–7pm, Sun
8am–7pm.

**Downtown Subscription Coffee Bar &
Newsstand** 376 Garcia St ☎ 505/983-3085.
Despite the name, this sprawling café, where
the large outdoor terrace is usually commandeered by local intellectuals, is a fair walk from
downtown, being just south of Canyon Rd. Daily
6.30am–7pm.

French Pastry Shop *La Fonda de Santa Fe*, 100 E
San Francisco St ☎ 505/983-6697. Though it feels
more like a diner than a coffeehouse, this hotel
café serves fabulous pastries and coffees, along
with breakfasts, sandwiches, and crêpes both
sweet and savoury. Daily 6.30am–5pm.

Sage Bakehouse 535 Cerrillos Rd ☎ 505/820-
7243. No-frills bakery on the southern fringe of
downtown, open early for delicious fresh-baked
bread and coffees on the small patio. Daily Mon–Fri
7am–5pm, Sat 7am–2pm.

Inexpensive

Atomic Grill 103 E Water St ☎ 505/820-2866.
Snack-oriented restaurant, with patio seating,
one block south of the plaza, that squeezes
burgers, sandwiches, and some reasonable $10
pizzas onto a menu that holds over fifty microbrews. Breakfasts such as *huevos rancheros*
are served all day, and it's a rare option for a
late-night meal. Mon–Thurs 10am–2am, Fri &
Sat 9am–3am, Sun 9am–1am.

Museum Hill Café 705 Camino Lejo ☎ 505/820-
1776. Spacious café, enjoying fabulous mountain
views from a terrace on the plaza between the folk
art and Indian arts museums southeast of town.
Inexpensive but good sandwiches, burgers, pasta
specials, and salads, and a large brunch on
Sundays. Daily except Mon 9am–3pm.

Saveur 204 Montezuma St ☎ 505/989-4200. High
quality café-cum-salad bar not far west of the
State Capitol, serving delicious cooked and raw
specialties by the pound, and offering major
discounts after 3pm. Mon–Sat 8am–3.45pm.

The Shed 113 E Palace Ave ☎ 505/982-9030.
Typical Mexican-flavored local restaurant in a
pleasant garden courtyard not far northeast of the
plaza, which serves a steady diet of chile enchiladas, blue-corn tortillas, and even low-fat
specialties. There's nothing over $9 on the lunch
menu, but dinner is a little more expensive.
Mon–Sat 11am–2.30pm & 5.30–9pm.

Tecolote Café 1203 Cerrillos Rd at Cordova
☎ 505/988-1362, ☻ www.tecolotecafe.com. This
inconspicuous joint, a couple of miles south of
downtown, is renowned for magnificent breakfasts
– burritos, *huevos rancheros*, creamy eggs
benedict, or shirred eggs (poached on a bed of
chicken livers). Daily except Mon 7am–2pm.

Tia Sophia's 210 W San Francisco St ☎ 505/983-
9880. Spicy, very inexpensive Mexican diner, a
block or two west of the plaza, that's hugely
popular with lunching locals. Daily breakfast
specials. Mon–Sat 7am–2pm.

Moderate

Bert's La Taqueria 416 Agua Fria ☎ 505/474-
0791. Very good, very stylish Mexican restaurant –
far from an ordinary cantina – that's housed in the
former convent of the Santuario de Guadalupe.
Unusual and delicious specialties include spiced
corn truffles with cheese, and even *chapulines*
(grilled grasshoppers), while they also serve more
conventional dishes like *queso fundido* or
chimichangas. Little costs over $10. Mon–Wed
5–9pm, Thurs–Sat 5pm–1am.

Café Paris Burro Alley ☎ 505/986-9162, ☻ www
.cafeparisnm.com. A great spot for a well-priced
lunch on a sunny day, this large, friendly French/
Mediterranean restaurant, on a pedestrian alley a
short walk west of the plaza, has lots of outdoor
seating, and serves zesty salads, pasta and
specials for under $15. Daily 8am–10pm.

Dinner For Two 106 N Guadalupe St ☎ 505/820-
2075. As the cutesy name suggests, this quiet,
intimate little place, not far south of the river, is
aimed primarily at couples rather than groups.
Serving contemporary Southwestern cuisine, with
dinner appetizers like crab cakes at around $10,
and entrees such as sea bass for $24–30, and a
wide range of set menus and specials, it also
features live classical duets most Fri and Sat
nights. Mon, Wed & Thurs 4–9pm, Fri–Sun
11.30am–9pm.

El Farol 808 Canyon Rd ☎ 505/982-9912,
☻ www.elfarolsf.com. Friendly *tapas* bar, a mile or
so down Canyon Rd, with a romantic patio at the
front and a livelier atmosphere indoors, where
there's live music that ranges from blues to
flamenco and a long bar. Authentic Spanish treats
like Cabrales cheese or octopus cost $7–10; the
idea is to share several with your party. Daily
11am–4pm & 5pm–2am.

Il Piatto 95 W Marcy St ☎ 505/984-1091.
Reasonably priced and very good Italian restaurant, festooned with cooking utensils and serving
pasta galore, such as a calamari spaghetti for
$17, plus specials like roast duckling for $25.

Mon–Fri 11.30am–2pm & 5.30–9pm, Sat & Sun 5.30–9pm.

La Plazuela *La Fonda de Santa Fe*, 100 E San Francisco St ☎505/982-5511. Delightful, beautifully furnished Mexican restaurant, which feels like an open-air courtyard even though it's covered by a glass ceiling. All the usual Mexican dishes are nicely prepared and sold for reasonable prices, with entrees at $12–16 at lunchtime, and some more expensive dinner items, such as *filet mignon*, costing up to $44. Mon–Fri 7–10.45am, 11.30am–2pm, & 5.30–10pm; Sat & Sun 7–10.45am, 11.45am–3pm, & 5.30–10pm.

Ore House on the Plaza 50 Lincoln Ave ☎505/983-8687. "Nueva Latina" restaurant whose menu ranges from $7 green chile stews up to elaborate $33 dinner entrees such as rack of lamb. The location is unbeatable: from the tiled tables on its *ristra*-garlanded balcony, on the southwest corner of the plaza, you can watch all the life of the city. Daily 11.30am–10pm.

The Pink Adobe 406 Old Santa Fe Trail ☎505/983-7712, ⓦwww.thepinkadobe.com. This 300-year-old adobe provides a deeply romantic setting for a hybrid New Mexican/Cajun menu that's not wildly inspiring. Open for lunch on weekdays only, with salads and sandwiches for around $9, and dinner nightly, when entrees such as grilled tuna or Southern fried chicken cost $25 and up. Mon–Fri 11.30am–2pm & 5.30–10pm, Sat & Sun 5.30–10pm.

Expensive

Amaya *Hotel Santa Fe*, 1501 Paseo de Peralta at Cerillos Rd ☎505/982-1200. Warm, inviting, restaurant in the lovely *Hotel Santa Fe*, serving a rich, hearty version of contemporary Southwestern cuisine. There's a lot of meat on the menu, with $30 entrees including tenderloin of elk or wild boar; the $29 Picuris mixed grill is a veritable menagerie. Daily 7–10.30am, 11.30am–2.30pm, & 5.30–10pm.

Cafe Pasqual's 121 Don Gaspar Ave ☎505/983-9340. Lovely, lively, and ever-innovative Old/New

Mexican restaurant that serves top-quality food in an attractive tiled dining room, a block from the plaza. Entrees range from vegetarian *enchiladas* ($19) to chile-rubbed *filet mignon* ($38) or chipotle prawn tostadas ($31). Appetizers include spicy Vietnamese squid and the delicious Pigs and Figs salad, made with bacon, figs, and mozzarella (both $14). They also serve large, tasty breakfasts. Mon–Thurs 7am–3pm & 5.30–10pm, Fri & Sat 7am–3pm & 5.30–10.30pm, Sun 8am–2pm & 5.30–10pm.

Coyote Café 132 W Water St ☎505/983-1615, ⓦwww.coyotecafe.com. Celebrity chef Mark Miller sold his showcase restaurant, just off the plaza, in 2007, but under new owners it remains as trendy as ever. The à la carte prices can be ferocious, with entrees like pan-seared white miso sea bass or elk tenderloin costing close to $40, and appetizers like scallop carpaccio for $15. Lunch, especially at the rooftop *Cantina* upstairs, is a better deal. It's possible to plot a vegetarian course through the menu, with a vegetable *torta* at $23, though you'll have to cope with the cowhide seats. Daily 11.30am–9pm.

Geronimo 724 Canyon Rd ☎505/982-1500, ⓦwww.geronimorestaurant.com. With its separate small dining rooms, this converted ancient adobe is Santa Fe's most intimate upmarket restaurant, with a streetfront patio and a cool inner courtyard. The menu is mostly contemporary fusion with the odd Mexican touch, with dinner entrees priced at $28–46. Daily, summer 5.30–9.30pm, winter 6–9.30pm.

La Casa Sena 125 E Palace Ave ☎505/988-9232. Lovely courtyard restaurant, a block from the plaza; zestful Southwestern lunches, with most entrees priced at $12–15, are the best deal; the $12 Sena Sampler plate is great value. Dinner entrees cost $17–28, and there's a $65 set menu ($95 with wine). At the adjoining, cheaper *La Cantina*, staff perform Broadway show tunes. Mon–Sat 11.30am–3pm & 5.30–10pm, Sun 11am–3pm & 5.30–10pm.

Nightlife and entertainment

Santa Fe has the somewhat limited range of **nightlife** you'd expect of a small city, though its **cultural scene** livens up during the summer tourist season. For full **listings** of what's going on, check the free weekly *Reporter* (ⓦwww .sfreporter.com) or the *Pasatiempo* section of Friday's *New Mexican*. The city runs its own ticket agency for local events (ⓦticketssantafe.org).

Year round, musical and theatrical performances – by touring artists as well as local groups – are hosted downtown at the **Lensic Performing Arts Center**, a strikingly converted former movie theater at 211 W San Francisco St (☎505/988-1234, ⓦwww.lensic.com). The much-anticipated **Santa Fe Opera** season runs from late June through August in a magnificent amphitheater seven miles north of town on US-84 (☏ 505/986-5900 or 1-800/280-4654, ⊛ www .santafeopera.org). July and August is also the time to catch the six-week **Santa Fe Chamber Music Festival** (☏ 505/983-2075 or 1-888/221-9836, ⊛ www .santafechambermusic.org).

Some of the most atmospheric places to **drink** in town are in the old hotels – the downstairs *La Fiesta* lounge and rooftop bar in *La Fonda* on the plaza are good bets – but otherwise conventional bars are surprisingly few and far between.

Bars and clubs

Catamount Bar 125 E Water St ☏ 505/988-7222. Downtown bar with plenty of microbrews on tap and live rock or blues most nights.

Evangelo's 200 W San Francisco St ☏ 505/982-9014. The only good bare-bones bar in easy walking range of the plaza, with a pool table and a jukebox, plus occasional live music.

Second Street Brewery 1814 Second St ☏ 505/982-3030. This lively brewpub is too far from the center to attract many tourists, which is half the reason it's so popular with young locals; there's also live music several nights a week.

Swig 135 W Palace Ave ☏ 505/955-0400. Very classy and expensive downtown DJs-and-martinis bar that also serves tasty Asian-style tapas. Tues–Sat 5pm–2am.

WilLee's Blues Club 401 S Guadalupe St ☏ 505/982-0117, ⊛ www.willees.com. Busy nightclub in the Guadalupe Street district that's open for live blues and jazz nightly except Sun.

Shopping

Secure in the knowledge that many visitors come specifically to **shop**, central Santa Fe is bursting with (generally high-priced) stores and galleries. The galleries alone turn over more than $200 million each year. The city remains largely the preserve of independents, however; few of the international names that move in seem to last long. Don't expect to make an early start; most stores and galleries don't open until 10am.

Almost everyone agrees that the best place to buy **Indian crafts**, such as silver and turquoise **jewelry**, is from the Native American sellers outside the Palace of the Governors, ideally during August's Indian Market (see p.153). If you're interested in **Hispanic folk art**, take a look at the gift store in the Museum of International Folk Art before you shop downtown.

The two main **malls**, neither of which is particularly large or interesting, are the **Villa Linda Mall**, southwest at 4250 Cerrillos Rd, and the **De Vargas Mall**, ten minutes' walk northwest of the plaza at N Guadalupe Street and Paseo de Peralta; there's also a Borders **bookstore** at 500 Montezuma near the Railyard.

Central Santa Fe

Andrea Fisher Fine Pottery 100 W San Francisco St ☏ 505-986-1234, ⊛ www.andreafisherpottery .com. Museum-like gallery, a block west of the plaza, which specializes in Native American pottery and boasts one of the nation's largest selections of Maria Martinez pieces.

Collected Works Bookstore 208B W San Francisco St ☏ 505/988-4226. Very central bookstore that's a great source for books on New Mexican history and culture.

Jackalope 2820 Cerrillos Rd ☏ 505/471-8539, ⊛ www.jackalope.com. A Southwestern legend for its pile-'em-high philosophy, this sprawling complex, centered on a disused church well out from downtown, completely takes the mystique out of purchasing folk art. However, the rock-bottom prices for its mostly Mexican and Peruvian arts, crafts, and downright junk make it the ideal spot to pick up inexpensive souvenirs.

Móntez Gallery 125 E Palace Ave ☏ 505/982-1828. Friendly little store near the plaza, specializing in good-quality antique Hispanic religious art, plus attractive and very inexpensive reproductions.

Posters of Santa Fe 111 E Palace Ave
℡505/982-6645 or 1-800/827-6745, ⓦwww
.postersofsantafe.com. The place to find the perfect
visual image of Santa Fe, whether it's a fine-art
print by Gustave Baumann or Georgia O'Keeffe, a
vintage cowboy or rodeo girl illustration, or a
simple card or notebook.

Canyon Road
Curiosa 718 Canyon Rd ℡505/988-2420. Quirky
little store with all sorts of well-priced gifts, jewelry
and oddities.
Hahn Ross Gallery 409 Canyon Rd ℡505/984-
8434, ⓦwww.hahnross.com. Enjoyable fine art
gallery, run by a children's book illustrator and
specializing in very bright paintings that blend the
fantastic with the naïve.
Kania-Ferrin Gallery 662 Canyon Rd ℡505/982-
8767. Native American antiques such as baskets
and rugs, antique Mexican *ex votos*, and even
carved canoe prows from New Guinea, all at prices
that run into thousands of dollars.

Nambe Showroom 924 Paseo de Peralta
℡505/527-4623. Factory outlet at the foot of
Canyon Rd with a large stock of Nambe ware –
shiny, futuristic table- and ovenware made from a
local alloy that looks like silver but has unique
heat-retaining properties.
Nathalie 503 Canyon Rd ℡505/982-1021,
ⓦwww.nathaliesantafe.com. Little of the Western
wear here would be at home on the range –
it's all a little too chic and decorative for life on
horseback – but it'll still look great when you wear
it back home.
Pachamama 223 Canyon Rd ℡505/983-4020.
Unusually cheap Hispanic crafts, mainly from
Mexico, including *retablos*, statues, and
lots of tin.
Silver Sun 656 Canyon Rd ℡505/983-8743,
ⓦwww.silversun-sf.com. Native American arts
and crafts, with a stand-out collection of
beautiful turquoise jewelry, and some very
affordable prices.

South to Albuquerque

Travelers embarking on the sixty-mile drive southwest from Santa Fe to
Albuquerque can choose between two routes. The **interstate**, I-25, is fast and
reasonably scenic, but for atmosphere and Old West charm it doesn't begin to
match the **Turquoise Trail**, which squeezes between the Sandia and Ortiz
mountains to the east.

The interstate route

While commuters may not give it a second thought, the hour-long journey
from Santa Fe to Albuquerque on **I-25** represents a major transition. When it
drops down the escarpment known as **La Bajada**, twenty miles from downtown
Santa Fe, the interstate leaves the Rocky Mountains and enters the desert. To
the north of La Bajada, the Rio Grande was traditionally known as the **Rio
Arriba**, or Upper River, and cuts through a deep rocky gorge; to the south, the
Rio Abajo or Lower River meanders across a broad floodplain.

La Bajada also marks the dividing line between the northern and southern
pueblos. Below it, the interstate runs through three separate Indian reservations. In 1996, when state legislators considered banning the casinos that have
finally brought the pueblos a degree of prosperity, pueblo authorities countered
by threatening to place **toll-gates** on the interstate at every boundary.

Cochiti Pueblo
COCHITI PUEBLO, ten miles west of the interstate on Hwy-16, at the foot
of La Bajada – a total of 24 miles from Santa Fe – is home to a thousand
Keresan-speaking Indians who trace their ancestry back to the cliff dwellers of
Bandelier. In the Keresan language, its name is *Kotyete*, meaning "stone *kiva*."
Visitors have free access to the pueblo in daylight hours; some residents sell
crafts outside their houses, but there are no formal stores. The mission church

of **San Buenaventura** still incorporates vestiges of its original adobe form, as built in 1628, but it has been greatly modified over the years, and the contemporary frescoes within are not all that enthralling.

A Cochiti potter, Helen Cordero, fashioned the first ceramic "**storyteller**" here in 1946. Each depicting a mother with up to thirty children, these rank among New Mexico's best-selling souvenirs and are made by over two hundred Indians, including around fifty Cochiti.

In the 1970s, the tribe was forced to lease part of its land to the federal government to create **Cochiti Lake**, by constructing what was then the world's largest earthen dam across the Rio Grande. Though the dam itself is something of an eyesore, the lake now attracts a million recreational users each year – almost exclusively New Mexico residents – and has a campground as well as a small **visitor center** (Mon–Fri 8.30am–3.30pm, Sat 10am–2pm, Sun noon–4pm; ☎505/465-0307).

Kasha-Katuwe Tent Rocks National Monument

In 2001, a previously little-known corner of Cochiti Pueblo became **KASHA-KATUWE TENT ROCKS NATIONAL MONUMENT** (daily: mid-March to Oct 7am–7pm, last admission 6pm; Nov to mid-March 8am–5pm, last admission 4pm; $5 per vehicle, national park passes accepted; ☎505/761-8700, ⓦwww.blm.gov/nm), jointly administered by the BLM and the pueblo. Kasha-Katuwe means "white cliffs" in Keresan and erosion has sculpted a canyon wall of pale, soft volcanic rock into cone-like shapes that range up to almost one hundred feet tall. Only a few are free-standing pinnacles; most are "hoodoos" that poke from the hillside. While nothing like as dramatic as, say, Utah's Bryce Canyon (see p.393), it makes an interesting half-day venture off the interstate.

To reach the monument, follow signs for Cochiti Pueblo. Just after a left turn signed to the actual pueblo, turn right at a painted water tower, onto Tribal Route 92, which becomes Forest Service Road 266. A 4.5-mile, unpaved spur road dead-ends at a parking lot, from which the easy two-mile

▲ Kasha-Katuwe Tent Rocks National Monument

Cave Loop Trail circles Peralta Canyon to pass the main formations. While it's not quite long or hard enough to count as a hike, wear decent shoes and carry water. If you want more exercise, follow the **Canyon Trail** at the furthest point of the loop, which climbs steeply through a narrow slot canyon for another mile to reach Vista Point, which grants an overview of the whole ensemble.

Santo Domingo Pueblo

Six miles south of Cochiti, **SANTO DOMINGO PUEBLO** is the largest Keresan pueblo, with a population approaching five thousand. For many centuries, its people have been renowned for their **jewelry-making**, and especially necklaces of delicate shell and turquoise *heishi* beads. By some accounts, Santo Domingans taught silversmithing to the Navajo in the nineteenth century, and they're now prominent among the Native American vendors in Santa Fe.

Santo Domingo doesn't have a visitor center or formal opening hours, but as well as an adobe church with a lovely painted facade, its central plaza holds several stores selling jewelry, pottery, and other crafts, and also a simple café, *Rosetta's Trading Post* (℡505/465-2504).

San Felipe Pueblo

SAN FELIPE PUEBLO, the next of the southern pueblos, stands another six miles downriver from Santo Domingo. Until 1250 AD, the San Felipeans were a single tribe with their fellow Keresan speakers now known as the Cochiti. Their subsequent migrations only ended in 1693, when they settled here for good after the Pueblo Revolt.

Daytime visits are always permitted here, but photography is not. On the pueblo's **feast day**, May 1, its plaza, worn down over the generations into a bowl-shaped depression, is thronged with dancers performing a day-long corn dance. The tribe runs a large **casino** and **travel center**, both of which house restaurants, at exit 252 off the interstate.

Algodones

Stretching languidly beside the river five miles southwest of San Felipe, the village of **ALGODONES** makes a tranquil base for visits to both Santa Fe and Albuquerque. *Hacienda Vargas*, 1431 El Camino Real (℡505/867-9115 or 1-800/261-0006, ⓦwww.haciendavargas.com; ④), is a relaxing rural **B&B**, set in a lovely adobe trading post. All seven rooms have en-suite facilities, in some cases including hot tubs.

Bernalillo and Coronado State Monument

BERNALILLO, an unexciting satellite community of Albuquerque five miles south of Algodones, is principally noteworthy as the site of **CORONADO STATE MONUMENT** (daily except Tues 8.30am–5pm; $3; ℡505/867-5351, ⓦwww.nmmonuments.org). In a spectacular setting a mile west of the interstate, on the west bank of the Rio Grande and with fabulous views of the Sandia Mountains to the east, the monument preserves what remains of the ancient pueblo of **Kuaua**. The Spaniards knew this region as **Tigüex**, and described it as a "broad valley planted with fields of maize and dotted with cottonwood groves;" Francisco de Coronado spent the winter of 1540 in the vicinity, though there's no evidence it was at this precise spot. Kuaua was then a thriving community of well over a thousand rooms; now it's a ruin, of which archeologists have exposed a few eroded adobe walls. The central feature is a restored *kiva*, decorated with vivid reproductions of its multicolored **murals**. The faded originals, preserved in the visitor center, include scenes of a rabbit hunt. Rabbits often represent the **moon** in Pueblo art, as Pueblo peoples see a "rabbit in the moon" rather than a "man in the moon." The monument is especially ravishing from late October onwards, when the fall colors along the riverbank are unbelievable.

While Bernalillo itself holds no **accommodation** options, the state's largest and most luxurious resort, the *Hyatt Regency Tamaya*, is just six miles up Highway 44 at Santa Ana Pueblo; for a full review, see p.149. Rates at the large but attractive riverfront **campground** near the monument entrance depend on the degree of comfort you require (☏505/867-3311; $14–22).

Bernalillo does boast one of New Mexico's finest **restaurants**. At the south end of town, east of the river – and, being close to exit 240 off I-25, an easy evening excursion from Albuquerque – the *Range Cafe*, 928 Camino del Pueblo (Sun–Thurs 7.30am–9pm, Fri & Sat 7.30am–9.30pm; ☏505/867-1700), is a brightly decorated hall that serves three meals daily. Huge Mexican-style appetizers like *chimichangas* cost $10 or less; strongly chile-flavored main dishes, like the fabulous *quesadillas* garnished with blue-corn chips, a little more. It's a very popular spot, so expect to wait. Another top-quality restaurant, the *Prairie Star*, stands only a mile or so northwest of the monument on Santa Ana Pueblo lands; see review on p.149.

Across the Rio Grande, just down from the monument entrance, the enormous Jackalope outlet (☏505/867-9813) is utterly unabashed about selling "Folk Art by the Truckload;" if you're looking for a large, cheap **souvenir**, and you haven't already sampled their Santa Fe store (see p.135), this is the place to come.

Rio Rancho

If you're unpleasantly surprised by the volume of traffic climbing US-550 past Coronado State Monument, that's probably because you've never heard of **RIO RANCHO**, reached via a turn-off a short way further up the hill. This ever-expanding community was founded in the early 1960s, after the AMREP Corporation purchased the Koontz cattle ranch for residential development. Though some of its earliest inhabitants, lured here from the East Coast by enticing advertising, were disappointed enough to sue AMREP (successfully) for fraud, Rio Rancho's population has mushroomed to over 75,000. With retirees joining Albuquerque commuters, and Intel opening the world's largest chip-manufacturing plant, Rio Rancho has overtaken Santa Fe to become New Mexico's third largest city. Although it holds half a dozen chain motels, however, there's no reason for tourists to visit.

Sandia Pueblo

SANDIA PUEBLO, between Bernalillo and Albuquerque, dates back to around 1300 AD and was visited by Coronado in 1540. *Sandía* is the Spanish for watermelon; differing stories have it either that the Spaniards mistook the squashes they saw here for watermelons, or they thought that at sunset the mountains to the east resembled segments of pink watermelon. The village's Tiwa name– **Nafiat**, meaning "dry or sandy place" – seems more appropriate to its dusty central plaza. After it was destroyed in 1692 by Spaniards returning after the Pueblo Revolt, many of its inhabitants took refuge with the Hopi, far to the west, and the settlement was not rebuilt for fifty years.

Today the main preoccupation of the three hundred Sandians is protecting their sacred sites in the nearby mountains from blundering hikers. Being so close to Albuquerque, they're also among the chief beneficiaries of the legalization of Indian gaming. The success of the 24-hour **Sandia Casino**, alongside the interstate, has enabled the tribe to open the striking **Sandia Resort**

(☎505/796-7500 or 1-800/526-9366, Ⓦwww.sandiacasino.com; ⑥), a luxury hotel and conference center with five restaurants and full spa facilities.

Other Sandia concerns include the *Bien Mur Trading Post* **crafts center**, on Tramway Road (Mon–Sat 9.30am–6pm, Sun 11am–6pm; ☎505/821-5400 or 1-800/365-5400, Ⓦwww.bienmur.com), which commands views of a **buffalo preserve** that holds the tribe's herd of buffalo.

The Turquoise Trail

The **Turquoise Trail** – less glamorously known as **Hwy-14** – is a modern name for what may be one of the oldest thoroughfares in North America, connecting **mines** along the eastern flanks of the Sandia Mountains with the settlements of the Rio Grande Valley. In the last two hundred years, these mines have yielded copper, coal, and even gold, but **turquoise** production dates back perhaps ten times as far. Long before the coming of the Spaniards, traders carried local stone all over the Southwest and down into Mexico, and wealthy pueblos lined the nearby streams.

Until the recent influx of artists, craftworkers, and small-scale entrepreneurs, communities along the trail had dwindled to become little more than **ghost towns**, but now funky **Madrid**, in particular, makes an appealing day-trip destination for visitors to Santa Fe. For general information on the trail, access Ⓦturquoisetrail.org.

Cerrillos

The northernmost Turquoise Trail town, **CERRILLOS**, is just over twenty miles south of Santa Fe, reached simply by continuing south on Cerrillos Road, which becomes Hwy-14, for fifteen miles beyond its intersection with I-25. The dusty rolling hillocks that surround it – the "little hills" of its name – hold one of the world's greatest concentrations of **turquoise**.

Archeologists estimate that ninety percent of the turquoise treasures seized by the Spaniards from the Aztec capital of Tenochtitlán were crafted using stone from this unprepossessing spot. Prehistoric miners scooped a hundred thousand tons of rock from **Mount Chalchihuitl**, two miles northeast, leaving a cavern 300 feet wide and 200 feet deep. Early Spanish settlers may have forced the Indians to work for them; a mine collapse around 1680, which killed up to eighty Indians, helped to precipitate the Pueblo Revolt. By the time the Spaniards returned, the Indians had deliberately hidden many of the shafts, and tales of fabulously wealthy "**lost mines**" still abound.

Today's Cerrillos, nestled amid the giant cottonwoods along the bank of the broad but usually dry Galisteo River, has changed little since its last boom in the 1890s. Mining not only turquoise but gold, silver, copper, and lead, it was briefly rich enough to support eight daily newspapers and numerous hotels and saloons. In 1988, its unpaved streets and falsefront wooden buildings made it an ideal location for the bratpack Western flick *Young Guns*.

There's still a bit of life in the old town; as recently as 1983, robbers made off with $500,000 worth of gold from the nearby Ortiz Mines. Tourists, however, have to content themselves with the **Casa Grande Trading Post**, **Turquoise Mining Museum**, **and Petting Zoo** (daily 9am–5pm; $2), an endearing shop-cum-museum that offers a random assortment of old bills and letters, porcupine quills, rattlesnake skins, and petrified wood, plus the chance to pet a llama or pull on a string to make a plaster Indian hammer on a rock.

The *Hacienda Dona Andrea*, 78 Vista del Oro (☎505/424-8995, Ⓦwww .hdasantafe.com; ⑥), is a luxury **B&B** where each of the nine en-suite guest rooms has its own fireplace.

Madrid

Between 1869 and 1959, the village of **MADRID**, three miles south of Cerrillos, made a good living from mining **coal**. In the early days, coal was hauled by wagon as far as St Louis; later it was consumed in vast quantities by the Santa Fe Railroad. Tunnels ran directly beneath the main street, while a mine shaft that burrows straight into the hillside can now be seen in the **Old Coal Mine Museum** at the south end of town (daily May–Oct only 9am–5.30pm; $5). The rest of the museum consists of several barns stuffed with ancient junk like obsolete X-ray machines and decrepit Model "T" Ford trucks, plus the **Engine House Theater**, which stages moustache-twirling **melodramas** on summer weekends, and assorted other performances in winter (℡505/435-3780, ⓦwww.themineshafttavern.com).

After the mine closed down, the whole town was auctioned off piecemeal, and the straggle of wooden cottages to either side of the narrow highway have progressively been taken over by New-Agey newcomers. Several hold genuinely interesting crafts and antiques stores; if you're close enough to home to carry **furniture**, there are some real bargains to be had.

One attractive old mining home, *Java Junction* (℡505/438-2772 or 1-877/308-8884, ⓦwww.java-junction.com; ❹), houses a **coffeeshop** downstairs, serving a limited array of bagels and pastries, and a **B&B** apartment upstairs, with kitchen and bathroom. *Mama Lisa's Ghost Town Kitchen* (℡505/471-5769) serves good salads and daily specials, while the lively *Mine Shaft Tavern*, attached to the museum (℡505/473-0743), claims to have the longest **bar** in New Mexico and stays open late every night, with live **music** on weekends. Burgers, fajitas, and the like are available until 8pm daily.

Golden

In 1825, **GOLDEN**, fifteen miles south of Madrid, was the site of the Wild West's first-ever gold rush. It has yet to revitalize to any great extent, and you might hardly notice that it's there as the highway races down its former main street. Look out, however, for the tumbledown **adobe church** on the hill at the north edge of town, which served the mining camp of **Tuerto** and has preserved its pioneer graveyard.

Sandia Crest and Cedar Crest

Ten miles south of Golden, the **Sandia Crest Scenic Byway** branches west from Hwy-14, to climb for eight tortuous miles up to the razorback ridge atop the Sandia Mountains. From the mile-high **observation deck** at road's end, you can survey the sprawling city of **Albuquerque**, with the Rio Grande flowing in from the north, and also look east across the endless plains, beyond the Ortiz Mountains. The adjacent *Sandia House* sells tasteless snacks and useless gifts. A fee of $3 is charged for day-use of the nearby trails, but most visitors stay for barely ten minutes before heading back down the hill; there's no through route to Albuquerque.

In winter, **skiers** exploring the eastern Sandia slopes base themselves down below, in **CEDAR CREST** at the foot of the Scenic Byway. *Elaine's*, 72 Snowline Estates (℡505/281-2467 or 1-800/821-3092, ⓦwww.elainesbnb .com; ❺), is a very comfortable B&B set in spacious grounds, while the *Sandia Mountain Hostel* (℡505/281-4117; ❶) offers dorm **accommodation** at $16 per bed, and *Kokopelli's Restaurant* (℡505/286-2691; closed Tues) serves all **meals**. The Turquoise Trail ends six miles south at the intersection with I-40, which sweeps the final dozen miles west to Albuquerque through **Tijeras** – "Scissors" – **Canyon**.

West of Santa Fe

The **Jemez Mountain Trail**, which loops through the mountains west of Santa Fe, can be enjoyed as a long day's excursion or a roundabout route down to Albuquerque. Potential stops range from modern **Los Alamos** – the top-secret "town that never was" – to the ancient dwellings of **Bandelier National Monument**; the scenery encompasses mountain meadows and desert canyons.

The **Pajarito Plateau**, the dominant feature of the landscape, was created just over a million years ago, when colossal **volcanic eruptions** buried four hundred square miles beneath a thousand feet of ash. This solidified into **tuff**, which has been eroded away ever since to form an intricate tangle of deep gorges and forested mesas. "Pajarito" means "little bird" in Spanish; it's a translation of the Tewa *tsirege*, the name of an abandoned local pueblo. Only one road climbs onto the plateau, **Hwy-502**, which branches west from US-84 near Pojoaque Pueblo, fifteen miles north of Santa Fe.

Visitors to both Los Alamos and Bandelier should take care to avoid the **rush-hour** traffic that heads up Hwy-502 until around 9am and comes back down again from 3pm onwards.

Los Alamos

The wealthy enclave of **LOS ALAMOS**, eighteen miles up Hwy-502, is not so much a town as the overgrown campus of the **Los Alamos National Laboratory**. Home during World War II to the **Manhattan Project**, which first developed the atomic bomb, it has remained the leading US center for the research and development of nuclear weapons.

Los Alamos is a confusing place to visit. Its layout – sprawling along several "fingers" at the edge of the Pajarito Plateau, separated by deep canyons – is bizarre in the extreme, and the fact that most of the complex is off limits to the public doesn't help. Most visitors call in at one of the two local **museums**, then head on to Bandelier.

The **Bradbury Science Museum**, at Central Avenue and 15th Street (Tues–Sat 9am–5pm, Sun–Mon 1–5pm; free), presents the authorized version of the laboratory's history. Opponents of nuclear proliferation are given space to state their case – forcefully argued rival displays debate the decision to drop atomic bombs on Japan – but overall the line is extremely gung-ho. The central exhibits are full-sized 1940s replicas of "Little Boy," which devastated Hiroshima, and "Fat Man," dropped on Nagasaki. The **visitors' book** is fascinating enough to have been published, while the excellent Otowi Station **bookstore** stands alongside.

Los Alamos Historical Museum, close to the visitor center at 1921 Juniper St (winter Mon–Sat 10am–4pm, Sun 1–4pm; summer Mon–Sat 9.30am–4.30pm, Sun 1–4pm; free), is housed in the former Los Alamos Ranch School. As well as displays on local history, it too covers the bomb in some detail. Exhibits range from a 360 degree aerial photo of Hiroshima to classic examples of atomic kitsch, such as a picture of the commander of the 1946 tests at Bikini cutting a mushroom-cloud shaped cake, some earrings made with "atomsite" fused glass from the Trinity site, and an A-bomb-shaped lamp.

Practicalities

Los Alamos' **visitor center** is at 109 Central Park Square (Mon–Fri 9am–5pm, Sat 9am–4pm; ☏505/662-8105 or 1-800/444-0707, ⓦvisit.losalamos.com).

As well as upmarket **motels** that cater largely to visiting scientists, like the *Best Western Hilltop House*, 400 Trinity Drive (☏505/662-2441 or 1-800/462-0936,

The Town That Never Was: Los Alamos and the Bomb

In 1942, the US and Britain decided to amalgamate the nine research efforts then racing to build the **atomic bomb**. Albert Einstein had suggested the idea to President Roosevelt three years earlier, and a team led by Enrico Fermi was achieving promising results beneath a disused football stadium in Chicago. The search was on for a suitable location in a sparsely populated area, away from the sea. **J. Robert Oppenheimer**, the scientific chief of the **Manhattan Project**, who had backpacked in New Mexico, recommended the exclusive Los Alamos Ranch School on the Pajarito Plateau, and the site was duly bought out. When its final class graduated in February 1943, the scientists moved in.

Working in the utmost secrecy – the words "Los Alamos" were forbidden, and newcomers were told merely to report to 109 Palace Avenue in Santa Fe – scientists took just over two years to make the bomb a reality. The first successful test took place at the **Trinity Site**, 200 miles south (see p.203), on July 16, 1945. Three weeks later, bombs were dropped on **Hiroshima**, on August 6, and **Nagasaki**, August 9; a complete Japanese surrender followed immediately.

For Oppenheimer, who described the development of the bomb with a quotation from the *Bhagavad Gita*, "I am become Death, the shatterer of Worlds," Los Alamos had served its purpose, and the laboratory could now close. Instead, as the Cold War set in, its energies were devoted toward the construction of the **H-Bomb**. Though security was more paramount than ever, ideologically motivated spies such as **Klaus Fuchs** and **David Greenglass** (whose sister and her husband, **Ethel** and **Julius Rosenberg**, were later executed) soon betrayed Los Alamos' secrets to the Russians. Paranoia grew to the point that employees were instructed to "Watch Your Liberal Friends," and Oppenheimer himself was barred by his successor Edward Teller from access to privileged information.

The gate house on the road up from Santa Fe that denied outsiders access to Los Alamos was finally removed in 1957. The laboratory business is still booming, spending well over half its two-billion-dollar annual budget on the research and development of nuclear weapons. While the lab has also drilled a 12,000-foot hole to "mine" heat from hot rocks deep in the earth and worked on the Human Genome Project, its public image remains firmly linked with nuclear experimentation.

Ⓦwww.bestwesternlosalamos.com; ❶), and *Holiday Inn Express*, 2455 Trinity Drive (☎505/661-1110; ❹), the town has a handful of **B&Bs**, such as *Adobe Pines B&B*, 3496 Orange St (☎505/661-8828 or 1-866/661-8828, Ⓦwww .losalamoslodging.com; ❹). The *Blue Window Bistro*, 813 Central Ave (☎505/662-6305; closed Sun), is the best-value place to **eat** in town, with sandwich lunches and tasty dinner entrees for under $15.

Bandelier National Monument

Long before the scientists descended on Los Alamos, the "finger canyons" of the Pajarito Plateau were home to Native Americans. At **BANDELIER NATIONAL MONUMENT**, ten miles south of Los Alamos – a fifty-mile drive from Santa Fe – **Ancestral Puebloans** enlarged natural cavities in the soft volcanic rock to create **cliff dwellings**, and also built free-standing pueblos beside the streams on the valley floors. Set amid delightful woodlands and framed against the rose-pink canyon walls, Bandelier's intriguing remains provide an ideal introduction to New Mexico's past. The **visitor center**, at the bottom of a narrow switchback road down from Hwy-4 (daily: June–Aug 8am–6pm; March–May, Sept & Oct 9am–5.30pm; Nov–Feb 9am–4.30pm; $12 per vehicle; ☎505/672-3861, Ⓦwww.nps.gov/band), gives an excellent

▲ Cave dwellings at Bandelier National Monument

overview of the monument, with displays of pottery and jewelry, models and reconstructions, and century-old photographs.

Although the Ancestral Puebloans are often said to have "disappeared" around 1300 AD, there's little mystery about where they went. Bandelier is a "missing link," occupied between roughly 1150, as the Four Corners region was being abandoned, and 1550, when many of today's pueblos were established. As successive itinerant groups streamed in, perhaps fleeing drought or invasion, they may have merged here to create the modern Pueblo culture. The peoples of **Cochiti** and **San Ildefonso** in particular trace their ancestry back via Bandelier to Mesa Verde, and it was a Cochiti guide who led amateur archeologist **Adolph Bandelier** to this site in 1880.

Frijoles Canyon

The monument's major sights are concentrated along a 1.5-mile loop trail through **Frijoles Canyon**, open daily from dawn to dusk. From the visitor center, the trail leads swiftly to the remains of **Tyuonyi** on the canyon floor. Only the ground floor and foundations survive of this circular, multistory, 400-room village, whose name means "place of agreement". It's seen as a center for trade and storage, common to the **Keresan**-speaking peoples, whose pueblos lay to the south, and the **Tewa** speakers to the north. Local obsidian was traded as far as the Dakotas and the Mississippi. Despite the apparently large number of dwellings, the canyon's maximum total population is estimated at between five and seven hundred. Tyuonyi may have still been in use when Coronado's soldiers reached the Southwest (see p.500), though they didn't come this far.

A side path from Tyuonyi leads up to dozens of **cave dwellings**, their rounded chambers scooped into the warmer, south-facing wall of the canyon. (As artificial creations, technically these are "cavates" rather than caves.) Ladders and walkways mean visitors can scramble up to, and even enter, some of them, to peer out across the valley.

The main trail continues to the **Long House**, an 800ft-long series of two- and three-story houses built against the cliffs. Though most of the upper stories have collapsed to expose the plastered walls, you can still see the mortised holes that held their pine roof beams or *vigas*. Above these, rows of petroglyphs and pictographs depict figures and abstract symbols.

Though the main trail doubles back to the visitor center, keen hikers can follow the stream for another half-mile, to the point where **Alcove House** nestles in a rocky overhang 150 feet above the canyon floor. Reaching it entails climbing three hair-raising ladders, as well as steep stairways hacked into the crumbling rock. At the top, *viga*-holes show that the cave once held several structures, but it's now bare except for a reconstructed *kiva*, set down in its sloping sandy floor, and entered by ladder.

Another trail drops south from the visitor center, coming out after a mile and a half at the **Lower Falls** – at their best in late spring – and then reaches the Rio Grande in another ten minutes. It's also possible to hike up into the backcountry above Frijoles Canyon; a very demanding trek of 6.5 miles each way leads to two very weathered but still remarkable **stone lions**, carved by ancient sculptors.

Tsankawi

The small, separate **Tsankawi** section of Bandelier lies a dozen miles northeast of the visitor center, just off Hwy-502 as it climbs from the Rio Grande valley up to Los Alamos. Visits consist of an hour-long loop hike onto an isolated mesa-top that holds the almost indiscernible ruins of an ancient pueblo. If the site itself is disappointing, however, the trail is not; following the same route once used by the Ancestral Puebloans, it's worn waist-deep into the soft tuff in places, and includes a number of prehistoric "stairways." Assuming you're happy to negotiate a couple of short ladders, you're also rewarded with lovely views down into the valley, as well as glimpses of the mysterious Los Alamos laboratories closer at hand.

Practicalities

Snacks and sodas are available at the monument visitor center, but there's no **accommodation** at Bandelier itself apart from the very pleasant *Juniper Campground*, just off Hwy-4 up on Frijoles Mesa (first-come, first-served; $12). Tsankawi, however, stands close to the tiny community of White Rock, which holds the gleaming white *Hampton Inn*, 124 Hwy-4 (☎505/672-3838 or 1-888/813-0912, ⓦwww.hamptoninnlosalamos.com; ⑤).

Valles Caldera National Preserve

Hwy-4 climbs west of Bandelier and Los Alamos, bursting unexpectedly out of the forests to skirt the long rim of **Valle Grande**. This 500-foot-deep, 176-square-mile caldera was created by a still-active volcano 1.2 million years ago. Its wide meadows form a lush counterpoint to the dry-as-dust terrain of most of New Mexico, and the basin was much prized by ancient peoples both as prime hunting territory and as a source of obsidian, a volcanic glass that can be chipped to form ultra-sharp blades.

The national government purchased the huge Baca Ranch here for $101 million in 2000, to create the 89,000-acre **VALLES CALDERA NATIONAL PRESERVE**. The basic aim is to run it as a self-sustaining wildlife reserve – it's home to a large elk herd in summer, as well as several rare bird species – funded through commercial activities. You don't need a permit to walk the short trails that lead from a couple of roadside pullouts on Hwy-4, but to take a longer hike, you have to reserve and pay a $10 fee at least 24 hours in advance (☎1-866/382-5537, ⓦwww.vallescaldera.gov). The altitude of 8750 feet makes all physical activity demanding, and lightning strikes are such a constant threat, thanks to the almost daily afternoon thunderstorms, that all hikers are advised to leave the area by 2pm. In practice, the preserve remains primarily a drive-through experience.

Spence Hot Springs

Perhaps the most obvious vestiges of the volcanic past around Valles Caldera are the many **hot springs** that bubble from beneath the ground. Among the most irresistible is **SPENCE HOT SPRINGS**, on a promontory above the Jemez River between mileposts 24 and 25 on Hwy-4, half an hour out of Los Alamos. Half a dozen waterfall-connected pools provide a range of temperatures to suit anybody, from the high 90°sF in the lower pools to a blissful 104°F at the top; local custom calls for bathing suits on weekend nights, otherwise it's clothing optional. To get there, cross the river over a fallen tree and then climb up the canyon, keeping to the left for about a ten-minute walk uphill.

Jemez Springs

Five miles downhill from Spence Hot Springs, Hwy-4 runs past the bizarre (and very smelly) **Soda Dam**, where calcified deposits all but block the Jemez River, to enter **JEMEZ SPRINGS**. This appealing hamlet, where the river is lined by glowing cottonwoods and flows between high canyon walls that flame gold and red, was once the site of the Towa-speaking pueblo of **Giusewa**, the "Place of the Boiling Waters." The most active of its hot mineral springs was enclosed in the 1870s by a **bath house**, where you can enjoy an hour-long soak for $15, or a massage for $37 (☎505/529-3303, ⓦwww.jemezspringsbathhouse.com).

The substantial shell of the mission church of **San Jose de los Jemez**, built by Franciscans in 1621 only to be destroyed almost immediately by Navajo raiders, is now preserved in **Jemez State Monument** (daily except Tues 8.30am–5pm; $3). Walls that once held bright frescoes are now just stumps, but the principal doorway has been reconstructed. Most of the ruins that surround it were convent outbuildings rather than pueblo dwellings, although you can still spot several subterranean *kivas*. Jemez Springs' religious tradition continues to this day, as it's home to large Christian monasteries as well as a Zen center.

Practicalities

Jemez Springs offers several small-scale **accommodation** options, including the lovely *Cañon del Rio–Riverside Inn*, 16445 Hwy-4 (T 505/829-4377, W www.canondelrio.com; ⑥), which has an outdoor hot tub. The *Laughing Lizard Cafe* (T 505/829-3108, W www.thelaughinglizard.com; ③) serves coffee and full meals on a nice terrace above both highway and river, and offers four inexpensive motel-style rooms, while the late-opening *Los Ojos Restaurant and Saloon* (T 505/829-3547) has food, pool tables, and cheap beer.

Jemez Pueblo

After Giusewa Pueblo was abandoned in 1630, its inhabitants built **JEMEZ PUEBLO**, fifteen miles downstream of Jemez Springs. There they participated in the Pueblo Revolt of 1680, sacking their church and killing its priest; when the Spaniards returned, they briefly retreated northwest, establishing cultural and family links with the Navajo that endure to this day. They also assimilated

▲ Saloon in Jemez Springs

the last twenty survivors of Pecos Pueblo in 1838 (see p.131). Jemez now has a population of around 3000 and is the only surviving Towa-speaking pueblo.

Home for the Jemez Indians is a gorgeous, lush canyon floor, surrounded by low cliffs of rich red rock. In honor of that scenery, they call themselves **Walatowa**, "people of the canyon," and that's also the name of their village. The pueblo itself is only open to visitors on feast days such as August 2, November 12, and December 12. An impressive **visitor center**, three miles north on Hwy-4 at **Red Rock** holds displays on their history, can arrange group tours, and sells a wide range of crafts (daily 8am–5pm; ⊤505/834-7235, ⓦwww .jemezpueblo.org). On weekends between April and mid-October, the **Jemez Pueblo Open Air Market**, also at Red Rock, sells food and artwork.

Heading west: Cuba

Hwy-4 meets US-550 at **San Ysidro**, six miles south of Jemez Pueblo. Turn left here, and in 23 miles you'll meet I-25 at Bernalillo, just north of Albuquerque. A right turn, on the other hand, carries you northwest toward Chaco Canyon (see p.102) or Mesa Verde (see p.86). The first stop on that route is the lonely farming community of **CUBA**, reached after a 43-mile drive through Indian lands.

Not much more than a curve in the highway, Cuba is nonetheless home to three rundown **motels**, of which the *Frontier* (⊤505/289-3474; ❷), at the north end of town across the Rio Puerco, is the most salubrious. Alongside it, the friendly *Frontier Cafe*, 6478 Hwy-44 (⊤505/289-3130), is smarter than it looks from the outside and makes an excellent stop for a Mexican lunch or dinner: a delicious *posole* stew, with chile and *sopaipillas*, costs barely $5. In the foothills five miles north, at 510 Los Pinos Road, the appealing *Circle A Ranch* **hostel** (May to mid-Oct; ⊤505/289-3350, ⓦwww.circlearanch.info; ❶–❸), is an adobe *hacienda* that offers dorm beds for $20 as well as private rooms with and without baths.

Zia Pueblo

Six miles south of San Ysidro, reached by a short spur road off US-550, little **ZIA PUEBLO** overlooks the Jemez River. Now 750 strong, the Zia Indians have occupied this spot since the sixteenth century. They're best known for the **sun symbol** that features on New Mexico's flag and license plates. Though they've failed to persuade the courts to grant them royalties for its use, they do at least earn some money as a movie location; both *All The Pretty Horses* and *Ghosts of Mars* were filmed here.

There's little reason for outsiders to visit Zia, but the tribe does maintain a small **visitor center** not far off the highway (Mon–Fri 8am–noon & 1–5pm; free; ⊤505/867-3304).

Santa Ana Pueblo

Zia's closest neighbors, at the equally small **SANTA ANA PUEBLO**, eight miles southeast along US-550, are also Keresan speakers, who moved in after the Pueblo Revolt. Only since the advent of Indian gaming in the 1990s have they made any effort to welcome visitors. Profits from the roadside **Santa Ana Star Casino** (ⓦsantaanastar.com), which holds four restaurants and a large bowling center, have enabled the tribe to branch out in several new directions. These include two top-quality golf courses, 22 soccer fields, and several crafts outlets.

The most conspicuous development of all, however, is New Mexico's most prestigious **luxury resort**, a joint venture between the pueblo and Hyatt.

As well as 350 opulent rooms and suites, the *Hyatt Regency Tamaya Resort & Spa*, at 1300 Tuyuna Trail (☎505/867-1234, ⓦtamaya.hyatt.com; ❸), features three swimming pools, a fitness center and spa, four restaurants, a championship golf course, and its own stables and hot-air balloon. It also holds the Tamaya Cultural Center (daily 9am–5pm), a free museum focusing on the people of Santa Ana.

Also on Pueblo land, the excellent *Prairie Star* restaurant, 288 Prairie Star Rd (Tues–Sun 5.30–9pm; ☎505/867-3327), resides in an adobe home northwest of the casino and offers contemporary Southwestern cuisine at around $30 per entree.

From the end of the Jemez Mountain Trail, when Hwy-44 meets I-25 at **Bernalillo** (see p.138), downtown Albuquerque is a sixteen-mile drive south, while Santa Fe is forty miles northeast, a drive described on p.136 onwards.

From Santa Fe to Taos: the northern pueblos

The quickest route between Santa Fe and Taos follows **US-84** as far as the Rio Grande, then continues northeast beside the river on **Hwy-68** – not that the switch from one road to the other, at **Española**, is discernible to the naked eye. US-84 passes through the heartland of the **northern pueblos**. The most interesting of these tiny Tewa-speaking villages for casual visitors are **Nambe**, near the impressive **Nambe Falls**, and **Pojoaque** beside the highway, where a museum and visitor center provide a quick taste of Pueblo culture. Serious collectors can head instead for **San Ildefonso** and its famous pottery.

Tesuque Pueblo

Nine miles north of Santa Fe, west of US-84, and overlooked by the remarkable **Camel Rock**, the traditional community of **TESUQUE PUEBLO** studiously turns its back on the city. Its name means "place of the cottonwood trees," and its people were the first to strike against the Spaniards during the Pueblo Revolt. There's no visitor center, but the tribe operates the **Camel Rock Casino** (☎505/984-8414, ⓦcamelrockcasino.com), which has a good buffet restaurant, and also holds an open-air colorful weekend **flea market**, selling everything from clothing to furniture to hot sauce (March to late Nov Fri–Sun).

Pojoaque Pueblo

POJOAQUE PUEBLO, twelve miles out of Santa Fe on US-84, was once one of the largest pueblos, but its original settlement was abandoned after a smallpox epidemic in 1895, and in terms of land it's now the smallest in the state. Though some ceremonial activities have resumed, most of the tribe's attention is devoted to running a busy roadside complex. Its **visitor center** covers the history and culture of all the Tewa peoples (Jan–March Mon–Sat 9am–5.30pm, Sun 10am–4pm; April–Dec Mon–Sat 9am–6pm, Sun 9am–4pm; ☎505/455-3460) and sells Native American artifacts. The similar, adjoining **Poeh Museum** (Mon–Fri 8am–5pm, Sat 4–9pm; ⓦwww.poehmuseum.com; $1) concentrates on craftworks from the northern pueblos, and stages **dance** performances at 11am and 1pm on summer Saturdays and Sundays. The complex includes the *O Eating House* restaurant.

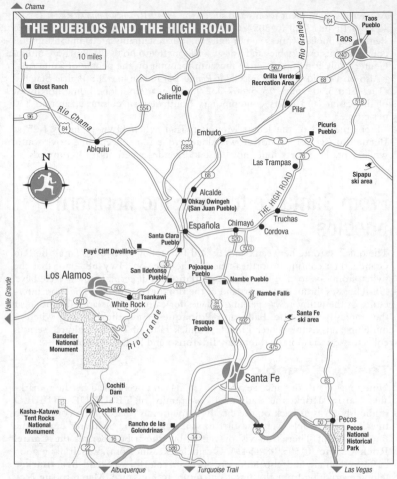

The Cities of Gold **casino**, alongside the museum (℡505/455-3313, Ⓦwww .citiesofgold.com), which contains another restaurant, has proved so lucrative that the tribe was able to buy the nearby Santa Fe Downs racetrack, adjoining the pueblo, in order to close it down. Across from the casino, the *Cities of Gold* **hotel** offers 124 comfortable but unexciting rooms (℡505/455-0515 or 1-877/455-0515; Ⓞ).

Nambe Pueblo

The most beautifully sited of the northern pueblos, **NAMBE PUEBLO**, is reached by turning right on Hwy-503 just beyond Pojoaque. Keep going up the hillside beyond the Sacred Heart church, and turn right after three verdant miles. The pueblo itself, 1.5 miles along, is not visible from the road; apart from a large *kiva*, not much remains in its old plaza area. After another 3.5 miles, you come to a ranger station, where an admission fee of $10 per vehicle is payable (daily: April & May 7am–8pm; June–Aug 6am–8pm; Sept & Oct 7am–7pm; still photography $5 extra; Ⓦnambefalls.com).

The steep five-minute hike up to the triple-decker **Nambe Falls** starts from the picnic area and campground just beyond. At the top of the climb, you can admire the waters as they tumble through a jagged cleft in the surrounding red rocks, but the view is somewhat marred by the colossal concrete dam that towers above. There's no way to reach the foot of the falls, let alone swim there. **Camping** back at the picnic area (April–Oct only) costs $20 per night.

San Ildefonso Pueblo

Five miles west of Pojoaque, before Hwy-502 crosses the Rio Grande and climbs up to Los Alamos, **SAN ILDEFONSO PUEBLO** is best known as the former home of potter **Maria Martinez**. From 1919 onwards, together with her husband Julian, she was responsible for revitalizing the Pueblo ceramic tradition; the finest collection of the pair's work is in Taos' Millicent Rogers Museum.

The people of San Ildefonso trace their ancestry back to Mesa Verde, by way of the Pajarito Plateau. In 1694, when the Spaniards returned after the Pueblo Revolt, refugees from San Ildefonso and its neighbors held out on a nearby mesa, **Black Rock**, until they were starved down.

San Ildefonso now consists of two plazas, one of which holds a replica of its original mission church. Individual artisans sell pottery from their own homes – look out for signs – or you can buy from the selection in the **Tewa Visitor Center** when you pay your pueblo admission fee (Feb–Oct daily 8am–5pm; Nov–Jan Mon–Fri 8am–5pm; $5 per vehicle, $10 photo permit, $20 video; ℡505/455-3549). The nearby **Tribal Museum** (Mon–Fri 8am–4pm; no additional charge) holds some of Martinez's original works.

Santa Clara Pueblo

Five miles north of San Ildefonso, or five miles west of Española, **SANTA CLARA PUEBLO** is known to its 1500 inhabitants as Kapo, "where the roses grow near the water." During the sixteenth century, they migrated here from Santa Clara Canyon, eleven miles west. Their previous home, consisting of two tiers of cliffside "apartments" plus a large mesa-top pueblo, at the edge of the Pajarito Plateau, remains remarkably well preserved. It closely resembles the better-known ruins at Bandelier National Monument (see p.143), which suggests that the Santa Clarans descended from the builders of Mesa Verde. Formerly open to visitors as **PUYÉ CLIFF DWELLINGS**, the site was closed in 2000 following severe forest fires. While it's worth contacting the pueblo on ℡505/753-7326 to see whether the cliff dwellings have reopened, that currently seems unlikely.

Assuming Puyé is still off limits, the only activity for visitors to the pueblo is to shop for pottery from outlets around the main plaza; the visitor center there can tell you which ones are open (Mon–Fri 8am–4.30pm). The pueblo also runs the successful Big Rock Casino in Española (ⓦwww.bigrockcasino.com).

Española

The only sizeable Hispanic settlement between Santa Fe and Taos is **ESPAÑOLA**, roughly halfway between the two and immediately south of the confluence of the Rio Chama and the Rio Grande. While most highway traffic continues northeast at this point toward Taos on Hwy-68, US-84 veers west across the river toward Chama (see p.173) and Colorado.

Other than watching the local youth cruising the streets in their customized "low-riders" or joining them in one of the dozens of neighborhood fast-food joints, Española has little to offer tourists. However, it can make an alternative

In 1540, the first Spaniards to explore what's now New Mexico encountered a settled population of around a hundred thousand people, living in a hundred or so villages and towns. These inhabitants did not see themselves as a single people, but the Spaniards collectively named them **Pueblo Indians**, from the Spanish for "village." Smallpox, war, and general disruption took their toll, but New Mexico is still home to around forty thousand Pueblo Indians, autonomous Pueblos.

Fifteen pueblos are concentrated along the Rio Grande north of Albuquerque. There's a long-standing division between the seven southern pueblos, south of Santa Fe, most of which speak Keresan, and the eight to the north, which mostly speak Tewa (pronounced *tay-wah*). Together with the four pueblos that lie further afield, they jointly promote themselves through Albuquerque's **Indian Pueblo Cultural Center** (see p.189; ☎505/843-7270, ⓦwww.indianpueblo.org).

Despite their fascinating history, most pueblos aren't the tourist attractions they're often touted to be. While the best-known, **Taos** and **Ácoma**, retain their ancient defensive architecture, the rest tend to be dusty adobe hamlets scattered around a windblown plaza. All the pueblos have to some extent incorporated **Catholicism**, as introduced by the Spanish, into their religious beliefs, and thus tend to center on an old adobe mission church. Rarely, however, does Christianity amount to more than a syncretic imposition upon more fundamental traditional beliefs, and you'll also see *kivas*, or prayer chambers, nearby.

If you can time your visit to coincide with a feast day, a trip to a pueblo is an extraordinary experience. The spectacle of hundreds of costumed, body-painted tribal members of all ages, drawn from other pueblos as well as the host village, performing elaborate dances in such timeless surroundings, seems like a genuine glimpse of the ancient life of the continent. You won't be allowed to photograph or even sketch the ceremonies, but stalls selling food, jewelry, ceramics, and other Pueblo crafts make it possible to take something away with you.

Otherwise, unless you are a knowledgeable shopper in search of Pueblo arts and crafts, visits can be disappointing. You'll certainly be made to feel unwelcome if you fail to behave respectfully – don't "explore" places that are off limits, such as shrines, *kivas*, or private homes.

Visitors to each pueblo are required to register at a visitor center; some charge an admission fee of $3 to $10, and those that permit such activities at all charge additional fees of about $5 for still photography, $10–15 for video cameras, and up to $100 for sketching. Many forbid the use of cell phones.

Southern pueblos

Cochiti; p.136	☎505/465-2244	ⓦpueblodecochiti.org
Jemez; p.147	☎505/834-7235	ⓦjemezpueblo.org
San Felipe; p.138	☎505/867-4706	ⓦsanfelipecasino.com
Sandia; p.139	☎505/867-3317	ⓦsandiapueblo.nsn.us
Santa Ana; p.148	☎505/867-3301	ⓦsantaana.org
Santo Domingo; p.138	☎505/465-2214	
Zia; p.148	☎505/867-3304	

Northern pueblos

Nambe; p.150	☎505/455-2036	ⓦnambefalls.com
Ohkay Owingeh; p.154	☎505/852-4400	
Picuris; p.159	☎505/587-2519	ⓦpicurispueblo.net
Pojoaque; p.149	☎505/455-3313	ⓦcitiesofgold.com
San Ildefonso; p.151	☎505/455-3549	
Santa Clara; p.151	☎505/753-7326	
Taos; p.167	☎505/758-1028	ⓦtaospueblo.com
Tesuque; p.149	☎505/983-2667	

Pueblos further afield

Ácoma; p.110	☏1-800/747-0181	ⓦskycity.com
Isleta; p.208	☏505/869-3111	ⓦisletapueblo.com
Laguna; p.112	☏505/552-6654	ⓦlagunapueblo.org
Zuni; p.107	☏505/782-7238	ⓦzunitourism.com

A pueblo calendar

Jan 1	Turtle Dance	Taos
Jan 1	Corn Dance	Santo Domingo
Jan 1	Cloud or Basket Dance	Ohkay Owingeh
Jan 6	Three Kings Day	Most pueblos
Jan 22–23	San Ildefonso Pueblo Feast Day	San Ildefonso
Jan 25	St Paul's Feast Day	Picuris, Ohkay Owingeh
Feb 2	Candelaria Day	Picuris, San Felipe
early Feb	Governor's Feast	Ácoma
early Feb	Deer Dance	Ohkay Owingeh
March 19	St Joseph's Feast Day	Laguna
Easter	Dances	Nambe, San Ildefonso, Santo Domingo, Zia
May 1	San Felipe Feast Day	San Felipe
May 3	Santa Cruz Feast Day	Taos
May 7	Santa Maria Feast Day	Ácoma
June 13	San Antonio Feast Day	Most pueblos
June 24	San Juan Feast Day	Ohkay Owingeh, Taos
June 29	San Pedro Feast Day	Santa Ana, Santo Domingo
July 4	Nambe Falls Celebration	Nambe
July (2nd week)	Taos Pueblo Pow-wow	Taos
July 14	San Buenaventura	Cochiti
July (3rd week)	Northern Pueblo Artist & Craftsman Show	Varying northern pueblos
July 25	Corn Dances	San Ildefonso, Taos
July 26	Santa Ana Feast Day	Laguna, Santa Ana, Taos
Aug 2	Santa Persingula Feast Day	Jemez
Aug 4	Santo Domingo Feast Day	Santo Domingo
Aug 10	Pueblo Revolt Anniversary	Most pueblos
Aug 10	San Lorenzo Feast Day	Ácoma, Picuris
Aug 12	Santa Clara Feast Day	Santa Clara
Aug 15	Assumption	Laguna, Zia
Aug (3rd week)	Indian Market	Santa Fe
Aug (3rd week)	Zuni Tribal Fair	Zuni
Aug 28	San Augustine Feast Day	Isleta
Sept 2	San Estéban Feast Day	Ácoma
Sept 4	Isleta Pueblo Feast Day	Isleta
Sept 8	Corn Dances	Laguna, San Ildefonso
Sept 19	Laguna Pueblo Feast Day	Laguna
Sept 25	Santa Isabela Feast Day	Laguna
Sept 29–30	Feast of San Gerónimo	Taos
Oct (1st week)	Harvest Festival	Zuni
Oct 3–4	San Francisco Feast Day	Nambe
Nov 12	San Diego Feast Day	Jemez, Tesuque
early Dec	Shalako Ceremony	Zuni
Dec 12	Guadalupe Feast Day	Pojoaque
Dec 24–25	Matachina Dance	Most pueblos
Dec 26	Turtle Dance	Ohkay Owingeh
Dec 28	Children's Dances	Picuris, Santa Clara

base to Santa Fe or Taos. Budget **motels** include a *Days Inn*, 807 S Riverside Drive (☎505/747-1242, ⓦwww.daysinn.com; winter ❷, summer ❸), while *Angelina's*, 1226 N Railroad Ave (☎505/753-8543), is a recommended New Mexican **restaurant**.

❷ Abiquiu and Ghost Ranch

Twenty miles up US-84 from Española, the landscape erupts into a riot of red-rock splendor. Cliffs and mesas of Chinle, Entrada, and Windgate sandstone soar above corrugated hillocks of gray, brown, and red clays, all strongly reminiscent of southern Utah and the Navajo badlands of northeast Arizona. Surprisingly few visitors pass this way, but it's hardly little-known. If it now appears definitively Southwestern, that's largely because the paintings of **Georgia O'Keeffe** have done so much to shape contemporary notions of the Southwest – and it was this very terrain that inspired those paintings. Of one peak near Abiquiu, the **Pedernal**, O'Keeffe said, "God told me if I painted that mountain enough, I could have it."

From 1946 until she died, at age 98, in 1986, O'Keeffe's life centered on the pretty adobe village of **ABIQUIU** (pronounced *a-beh-cue*), originally a settlement of *genízaros* (the Christianized descendants of Plains peoples captured by eighteenth-century Spaniards). She maintained homes both at **Ghost Ranch** fourteen miles north of Abiquiu, and in the village itself; the former is not open to the public, while the latter, perched on a hilltop south of the highway, can only be visited on guided tours. You must both reserve and pay in advance, and provide full names and addresses of all participants (July–Sept Tues–Fri; late March to June & Oct to late Nov Tues, Thurs & Fri; 9.30am, 11am, noon, 2pm & 3.30pm; $30; ☎505/685-4539, ⓦwww.okeeffemuseum.org).

Abiquiu village was a trading center on par with Taos in the late eighteenth and early nineteenth centuries, and was briefly New Mexico's third largest town. These days, it consists of little more than a small plaza, surrounded by tumbledown adobes and centered by the beautiful, restored church of **Santo Tomás**; photography is not permitted. There's **accommodation** at the *Abiquiu Inn*, 21120 Hwy-84 (☎505/685-4378 or 1-888/735-2902, ⓦabiquiuinn .com; ❻), which has nineteen comfortable guestrooms and a good restaurant, and arranges local tours.

Several religious groups have established retreats in the Abiquiu region, including the international Muslim community that erected the **Dar al-Islam mosque** on the mesa above the village; there's also a Presbyterian ministry at Ghost Ranch where there are also **museums** of local anthropology and paleontology (summer Tues–Sat 9am–5pm, Sun 1am–5pm; winter closed Sun and all Dec; ⓦwww.ghostranch.org; $3), and the Benedictine **Monastery of Christ in the Desert** (ⓦwww.christdesert.org), thirteen miles west of Ghost Ranch.

Ohkay Owingeh (San Juan Pueblo)

Set amid the cottonwoods on the east bank of the Rio Grande off Hwy-68, five miles north of Española, the largest Tewa pueblo, long known as **San Juan Pueblo**, has recently reverted to its Tewa name of **OHKAY OWINGEH**. This is the third village to have stood in this area since 1250, all of which have been called Ohkay, meaning "we are the brothers." The first two capitals of the colony of New Mexico were also built here in 1598. Before they relocated to Santa Fe in 1610, the Spanish took over Ohkay and called it San Juan, and then occupied nearby Yunge and renamed it **San Gabriel**. Later that century, San Juan was the birthplace of **Po'pay**, the medicine man who led the Pueblo Revolt.

The centerpiece of the plaza is the much-restored **mission church**, the first building in the Southwest to be made with adobe bricks as opposed to simple chunks of mud. It's flanked by two rectangular *kivas*, as well as a smaller Catholic chapel. Admission is free in daylight hours, but photography is by permission only.

Next to the **Ohkay Casino**, on Hwy-68 just outside Española, the *Ohkay Hotel Resort* (☎505/747-1668 or 1-877/747-1668, ⓦwww.ohkay.com; rooms ❹, suites ❻) offers one hundred conventional motel **rooms** and twenty more luxurious suites.

Alcalde

The previously low-profile community of **ALCALDE**, a couple of miles further up the Rio Grande from San Juan Pueblo, hit the local headlines in 1999. Shortly after the unveiling of a statue of New Mexico's first governor, Don Juan de Oñate, unknown assailants amputated its right foot – an obvious reference to the barbaric punishment Oñate meted out to the defeated menfolk of Ácoma Pueblo in 1599 (see p.111).

Embudo

Half a dozen miles on from Alcalde, the funky little village of **EMBUDO** has in recent years become something of an alternative artists' colony. Its handful of crafts and oddities stores include Gasoline Alley, whose forecourt display of 1950s gas pumps is a great little slice of Americana. Inside, you'll find what its owner calls the "shiny stuff," largely consisting of assorted neon and glass advertising signs from the Route 66 era. Open to no fixed hours, it's more of a museum than a shop, though some of the stock is for sale.

Just across the Rio Grande to the south, *Embudo Station* is a **brewpub** and **restaurant** housed in a former railroad station (March–Oct daily except Mon 11.30am–9pm;☎505/852-4707,ⓦwww.embudostation.com;❺).Commanding a lovely spot beside a bend in the river, its patio garden makes a great place to sit out on a summer's evening – be sure to try the sweet potato fries – and there are a couple of rental cabins if you fancy lingering longer.

Pilar and the Orilla Verde Recreation Area

PILAR, perched above the Rio Grande fifteen miles southwest of Taos, started out as a Jicarilla Apache farming village. On May 30, 1854, two or three hundred Jicarilla defeated sixty US dragoons nearby in the Battle of Cieneguilla. It took several more years of fighting before they signed a treaty that confined them to their current reservation to the west (see p.174). These days, Pilar is a base for summer **rafting** trips run by the operators listed on p.163, and also holds a simple roadside diner, the *Pilar Yacht Club*.

The main objective of the Bureau of Land Management **visitor center**, on the east side of Hwy-68 in Pilar (summer daily 8.30am–4.30pm; winter Fri–Sun 10am–3pm; ☎505/751-4899, ⓦwww.blm.gov/nm), is to inform travelers about the **Orilla Verde Recreation Area**. Reached by a minor road that drops from just across the highway, this stretches along both banks of the southern end of the **Upper Rio Grande Gorge**. Six miles along, a developed riverside **campground** charges $7 per vehicle.

Whatever your map may suggest, you can't continue toward Taos at this level, along the east bank of the river. However, it's possible to meet up with US-285 by following the dirt road that crosses the river beyond the campground. More to the point, the **Vista Verde Trail** shortly after the bridge is an enjoyable 1.25-mile hiking trail that leads across the sagebrush-topped west-bank mesa to an overlook above the Rio Grande Gorge. A longer trail, slightly further up the hillside, runs all the way to the Rio Grande Gorge Bridge (see p.172); at seven miles one way, it's better tackled on a bike or a horse than on foot.

The High Road

While the most direct route from Santa Fe to Taos heads straight up the Rio Grande Valley, the "**High Road**" over the forested Sangre de Cristo Mountains to the east makes a rewarding alternative if you have a couple of hours to spare. Winding through timeless **Hispanic villages**, it passes some splendid old **adobe churches** and offers good opportunities to sample traditional New Mexican food or buy local folk art. Shopping for crafts is a big deal year-round, reaching its peak in the **High Road Art Tour**, which takes place during the last two weekends of September (ⓦwww.highroadnewmexico.com).

Chimayó

The first and most famous of the High Road towns, **CHIMAYÓ** is 25 miles north of Santa Fe, eight miles northeast of **Pojoaque Pueblo** via Hwy-592 and Hwy-503, or eight miles east of **Española** on Hwy-76. Stretching luxuriantly through the fertile upland meadows that line the Santa Cruz River, and backed by scrubby red-tinged hills, it feels more of a piece with the Rio Grande Valley below than with the mountains to the east.

Chimayó was founded in 1740 as a sort of penal colony for Hispanic trouble-makers. In Tewa, the word *tsimayo* means "good flaking stone;" Indians from San Juan Pueblo quarried obsidian here, which they chipped to form sharp blades. They held a nearby dried-up hot spring sacred, claiming that the mud from around it, when eaten, had healing properties. Within the *barrio* (neighborhood) at Chimayó's southern end known as **El Potrero**, that spring is now the site of a spell-binding colonial chapel, the **Santuario de Chimayó** (daily: May–Sept 9am–5pm; Oct–April 9am–4pm).

The church was built between 1813 and 1816, after a visiting priest told the landowner, **Bernardo Abeyta**, about the shrine at Esquipulas in Guatemala, which had arisen at a similar spring venerated by Guatemalan Indians. As a result, Abeyta's church also centered on a crucifix known as **Nuestro Señor de Esquipulas**, supposedly found locally in 1810 (conceivably it had been buried during the Pueblo Revolt).

The church, the crucifix, and the still-exposed *posito*, or dust pit, swiftly became the focus of **pilgrimages** not only by Hispanic peasants but also by Pueblo Indians, for whom the sacred hole in the earth clearly echoed the ancient concept of the *sipapu* (see p.528). To this day, it remains the "**Lourdes of America**."

While devout New Mexican Catholics see Chimayó as much more than a picturesque tourist attraction, the Santuario is an undeniable delight to visit: a ravishing little round-shouldered, twin-towered, tin-roofed adobe beauty set in a walled churchyard beneath the rolling Sangre de Cristo foothills. At the heart of the altar within, the crucifix is framed by a gorgeous *reredos*, with a small equestrian statue of Santiago to the right. Two smaller **side chapels** are filled with mind-boggling votive offerings – paintings, photographs, statues, press cuttings, even discarded crutches. The hole containing the "Holy Dirt" is in the floor at the rear; pilgrims are allowed to take a scoop, as it's replenished regularly with earth from the hills. **Mass** is celebrated at noon on Sundays, and on all other days at 11am in summer, 7am in winter.

The smaller and more ramshackle **Santo Niño Chapel** (same hours), across the plaza, contains a diminutive statue of Santo Niño, the Lost Child – more of a doll, if truth be told – to whom expectant mothers bring offerings such as tiny pairs of shoes.

The Penitentes

During the nineteenth century, the remote hills above Chimayó were renowned as the heartland of the mysterious Hispanic Catholic sect known as the **Penitentes**. Anglo newcomers claimed to have glimpsed hooded figures filing along the ridges at dawn, **whipping** themselves as they went.

A large grain of truth lay beneath the lurid speculation. Self-mortification – the infliction of pain in order to share the suffering of Christ – was widespread in medieval Europe. The Spanish expedition that founded New Mexico performed public self-flagellation on Good Friday 1598, as it marched up through Mexico, and similar acts by early Franciscan missionaries attracted Pueblo Indian scorn. The Penitentes as such, however, emerged after Mexico achieved independence in 1821. Cut off from Spanish funding, the Franciscans vanished from New Mexico within twenty years, leaving the region almost devoid of priests. Hispanic Catholics formed **lay brotherhoods** to keep their faith alive.

The Penitentes – **Los Hermanos de Nuestro Padre Jesús Nazareno**, or the Brothers of Our Father Jesus of Nazareth – may well have modeled themselves on a Guatemalan example, introduced at the same time as the Guatemalan-influenced pilgrimages to Chimayó. From an initial emphasis on individual prayer and penance, they developed a complex system of rituals. While never administering the sacraments, they brought solace to Catholics forced to live – and die – without priests. The Penitente brotherhood in each village soon became a mutual-aid society, a cultural and political force as well as a spiritual one.

After the American takeover of New Mexico in 1846, the Penitentes were suddenly outsiders not only in their own country but even in their own church. The first Catholic bishop of Santa Fe, Jean-Baptiste **Lamy**, had little sympathy for the unorthodoxies of his Hispanic flock, and denied the sacraments to their most prominent spokesman, Father **Martínez** of Taos. Forced into **secrecy**, the Penitentes began to gather at night in remote spots. Lacking access to official church property, they met in plain adobe structures known as **moradas** – not necessarily distinguished with crosses or towers, but adorned with the handmade sacred images known as **santos**.

The focus of ritual activity was **Lent**, when all Catholics practice some form of self-denial, and the Penitentes attempted to experience the passion and death of Christ. For processions, they divided into *Los Hermanos de Luz* – the **Brothers of Light**, responsible for the candles and music – and *Los Hermanos de Sangre*, the **Brothers of Blood**, who scourged themselves with yucca whips or carried giant wooden crosses. Participants were hooded to ensure humility. Some re-enacted the **crucifixion**, albeit tied rather than nailed to the cross, while others dragged a **Death Cart** – a wooden wagon holding an effigy of Death, armed with a bow and arrow – laden with stones. The Death Cart also figured in the Penitentes' elaborate **funeral** processions. The wayside stone cairns, topped with crosses, seen throughout the High Country are not graves, as outsiders supposed, but *descansos* – places where the coffin-bearers would pause to rest.

A century of conflict ended in 1947, when the Penitentes were officially recognized by the Bishop of Santa Fe. Those that remain now regard themselves as members of the **Third Order of St Francis**, a lay branch of the Franciscan monastic order, and the most lasting Penitente legacy in New Mexico is the *santero* tradition of religious folk art.

Chimayó has specialized in **weaving** since 1805, when two weavers sent as teachers from Spain chose to live here in preference to Santa Fe. Outlets scattered through the village sell hand-woven goods; other galleries concentrate on wood carving and religious art. The High Road Marketplace, very close to the Santuario, is a community craft store stocking work by several local artists (closed Jan–March; ☎ 505/689-2689).

Practicalities

Two properties make Chimayó an appealing overnight destination. The *Rancho de Chimayó*, Hwy-503 (closed Mon Nov–April; ☎ 505/351-4444), has to be the best traditional New Mexican **restaurant** in the state, serving superb *flautas* and a mouthwatering *sopaipilla*, stuffed with meat and chiles, on a lovely sun-drenched outdoor patio. The *Rancho* offers seven appealing **rooms** in a separate building across the highway (☎ 505/351-2222 or 1-888/270-2320, ⓦ www.ranchodechimayo.com; ❹), but there's an even more tasteful **B&B** on the edge of town in the shape of *Casa Escondida* (☎ 505/351-4805 or 1-800/643-7201, ⓦ www.casaescondida.com; ❺). Its eight comfortable rooms feature *viga* ceilings, tiled floors, and *kiva* fireplaces, and all have their own private bathrooms.

Truchas

By the time you reach **TRUCHAS**, eight miles northeast of Chimayó on Hwy-76, you're well into the mountains; the views down and across the Rio Grande Valley are tremendous. Villagers from Las Trampas, further up, were granted permission to establish Truchas in 1754, on condition that it was enclosed within a walled square, to defend against Comanche attacks. The settlement took on its present form almost immediately, however, consisting of separate individual farms arrayed along a high ridge above the Río de las Truchas, or "river of trout." As one of New Mexico's least changed Hispanic communities, it was the movie location in 1987 for Robert Redford's *Milagro Beanfield War*.

Hwy-76 makes a right-angle bend to avoid Truchas, but a detour east onto the minor road up the valley takes you along a narrow street of adobe homes and barns – interspersed with the odd incongruous art gallery – and past the fields toward the 13,103-foot **Truchas Peak**.

Las Trampas

Truchas' parent community, the quiet hamlet of **LAS TRAMPAS**, is another eight miles along Hwy-76. It started life as an outpost used by fur-trappers pursuing beaver – hence its name, "the traps" – which by attracting Comanche raids doubled as an early-warning system for Santa Fe. Though no longer walled, its dusty central plaza, alongside the highway, still holds the evocative adobe church of **San Jose de Gracia** (daily 10am–4pm). Built in 1760, it features a choir loft that extends both inside and out, so that singers could accompany ceremonies on the square as well as in the church. Note the unattached *morada* – Penitente meeting place – beside the cemetery to the east. Las Trampas holds a couple of gift stores, plus a hideous auto scrapyard, but nowhere to eat or sleep.

Five miles on from Las Trampas, Hwy-76 meets Hwy-75 ten miles west of Hwy-68 and the Rio Grande. The quickest route to Taos, twenty miles north, is via Hwy-73 to the east, and then Hwy-518 to the north; more Hispanic villages line the way, but none is of interest to tourists.

Picuris Pueblo

Turn left at the junction where Hwy-76 meets Hwy-75, and half a mile toward the Rio Grande you'll come to tiny **PICURIS PUEBLO**. Tucked away in a side valley, this was the last pueblo to be "discovered" by the Spanish, and proudly insists that it has never signed a treaty with any government, the US included. Its population has never risen much above two hundred, and Picuris remains just a cluster of adobe houses spreading across the hillside around a whitewashed church. The best-known tribal enterprise is the excellent *Hotel Santa Fe* in Santa Fe, reviewed on p.121.

There's a model of the pueblo and a reconstructed *kiva* in the village **museum** (daily 9am–5pm; $3 suggested donation). The same building also holds a gift store and the *Hidden Valley Restaurant*, a snack bar with views over a small blue lake. A self-guided **pueblo tour**, which leads past a few active *kivas* – including an unusual 500-year-old tower *kiva* – costs $5, plus another $6 for a photo permit; with advance reservations, you can also take guided tours at similar rates (☎505/587-2519, ⓦpicurispueblo.net).

Sipapu

Turning right off Hwy-76 onto Hwy-75 brings you to Hwy-518, the final leg of the High Road to Taos. Pass Hwy-518 and in a couple of miles you'll enter the tiny **ski resort** of **SIPAPU**, tucked into the pretty mountain valley known as **Tres Ritos Canyon**. *Sipapu Lodge*, along the highway to either side of the Rio Pueblo (☎1-800/587-2240, ⓦsipapunm.com; ❶–❺), offers every conceivable grade of accommodation, from dorm beds through private camping cabins, motel rooms, and luxury duplexes. Lift tickets in season, which generally runs mid–December through March, cost $39. Taos is just 22 miles away.

Taos

Part Spanish colonial outpost, part hangout for bohemian artists and New Age dropouts, and home to one of the oldest Native American communities in the United States, tiny **TAOS** has become famous out of all proportion to its size. Not quite seven thousand people live in its three component parts: **Taos** itself, around the old plaza; sprawling **Ranchos de Taos** three miles south; and the Indian village of **Taos Pueblo** two miles north. There's one restaurant for every 45 inhabitants, and a massage therapist for every thirty.

Like Santa Fe, Taos – the name rhymes with "house" – stretches languidly across a glorious high-desert plateau. The approach from the south is especially spectacular, as you cross a final bluff on Hwy-68 to be confronted by the pine-forested Sangre de Cristo mountains soaring above the sun-bleached foothills. This far up, the **Rio Grande** is not yet meandering through a well-watered valley but lies deep in a craggy canyon west of town, occasionally glimpsed as a crack in the plateau.

Beyond the usual unsightly highway sprawl, Taos is a delight to visit. As well as museums, galleries, and stores to match Santa Fe, it still offers the unhurried pace and charm, and the sense of a meeting place between Pueblo, Hispanic, and American cultures, that attracted figures such as Georgia O'Keeffe and D.H. Lawrence.

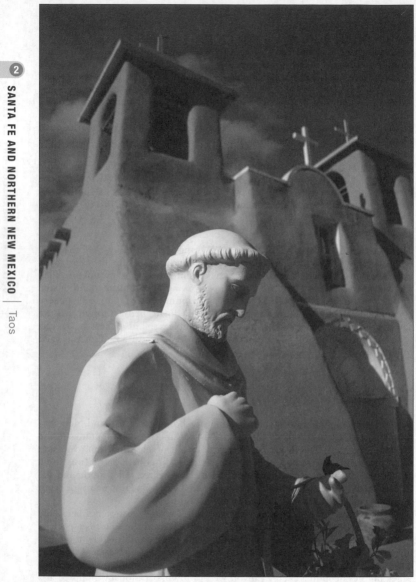

▲ St Francis statue, San Francisco de Asis, Ranchos de Taos

A history of Taos

As detailed on p.167, **Taos Pueblo** is around a thousand years old. Its first Franciscan mission was established in 1598. However, the modern town of Taos dates from the 1630s, when an uprising at the pueblo induced Spanish colonists to found the separate community of **Fernando de Taos** a few judicious miles south. Although its early history was dogged by Pueblo rebellions, the Spaniards and Pueblos eventually united to resist raids by "horse Indians" such as the Apache and Comanche. In the early nineteenth century, despite attempts by the Mexican authorities in Santa Fe to restrict contact with the outside world, Taos became the venue for annual **rendezvous**, at which "mountain men" and trappers from the Rockies traded with Indians from the pueblos and plains, and New Mexican merchants.

After the US takeover of New Mexico, Taos' Hispanic and Pueblo citizens once more found common cause. In **1847**, the territory's first American governor, Charles Bent, was killed in his Taos home, but the revolt failed to spread to Santa Fe, and the US Army launched an assault on the Pueblo that succeeded in suppressing further resistance.

Taos' reputation as an **arts colony** began at the end of the nineteenth century, with the arrival of the painter Joseph Henry Sharp. He was soon joined by two young New York artists, Bert Phillips and Ernest L. Blumenschein; legend has it that their wagon lost a wheel outside of Taos as they headed for Mexico in 1898, and they liked the place so much they never got around to leaving. The three men established the **Taos Society of Artists**, in 1915. Soon afterwards, society heiress and arts patron Mabel Dodge arrived and married an Indian from the Pueblo to become **Mabel Dodge Luhan**. In turn, she also wrote a fan letter to English novelist **D.H. Lawrence**, who visited in the early 1920s, and whose widow **Frieda** made her home in Taos after his death. New generations of artists and writers have "discovered" Taos ever since, the most famous being **Georgia O'Keeffe**, who stayed here in the 1920s before moving to Abiquiu (see p.154). Her renditions of the church at Ranchos de Taos in particular were a major influence on contemporary Southwestern art.

The influx of hippies who converged upon Taos in the late 1960s, was followed in subsequent decades by art-loving tourists, gallery-owning entrepreneurs, and wealthy divorcées. Even as the urban area has grown larger and more commercialized, however, the population has remained minimal.

Arrival and information

Hwy-68, the main route up to Taos from Santa Fe and Albuquerque, passes first through Ranchos de Taos, then becomes an uninspiring commercial strip as it approaches downtown and is renamed **Paseo del Pueblo Sur**. The well-equipped **visitor center**, two miles south of the plaza at the intersection of highways 68 and 585 (summer daily 9am–5pm, winter Mon–Sat 9am–5pm; ⊤505/758-3873 or 1-800/732-8267, Ⓦwww.taosvacationguide.com), holds countless brochures and maps, as well as useful and valuable **accommodation discount coupons**.

Greyhound and TNM&O **buses** from Albuquerque ($38) and Santa Fe ($28) arrive at **Taos Bus Center**, at 1386 Paseo del Pueblo Sur, opposite the visitor center on Hwy-68 (⊤505/758-1144).

Taos' **post office** is not far north of the plaza at 318 Paseo del Pueblo Norte (Mon–Fri 8am–4pm, Sat 9am–1pm; ⊤505/758-2081), while **internet access** is available at the Wired Coffee Shop, 705 Felicidad Lane (⊤505/751-9473, Ⓦwww.wiredcoffeeshop.com), near the visitor center.

Getting around

Walking is the best way to get around the compact center of Taos, though a public **bus** service covers the greater urban area. The hourly Chile Line bus runs along a twelve-mile stretch of Hwy-68, between Ranchos de Taos and Taos Pueblo, with a loop around the plaza in the middle (Mon–Sat 7am–9pm,

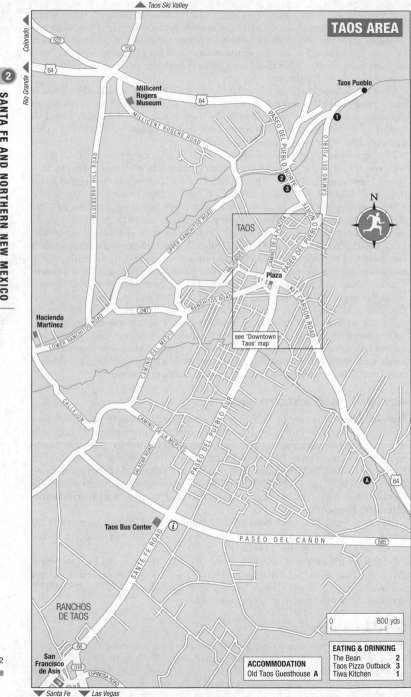

▲ Taos Ski Valley

Colorado ◄

Rio Grande ◄

TAOS AREA

522

150

64

Taos Pueblo ●

Millicent
Rogers
Museum

64

MILLICENT ROGERS ROAD

CAMINO DEL PUEBLO

PASEO DEL PUEBLO NORTE

❶

❷
❸

BLUEBERRY HILL ROAD

UPPER RANCHITOS ROAD

TAOS

CAMINO DE LA PLACITA

VALVERDE

PASEO DEL PUEBLO NORTE

N

Plaza

KIT CARSON ROAD

RANCHITOS ROAD

Hacienda
Martínez

240

LOWER RANCHITOS ROAD

see 'Downtown
Taos' map

CAMINO DEL MEDIO

CALLEJON

CAMINO DE LA MERCED

SALAZAR ROAD

PASEO DEL PUEBLO SUR

Ⓐ

64

Taos Bus Center ⓘ

PASEO DEL CAÑON

585

SANTE FE ROAD

Angel Fire & Carson National Forest ►

0   800 yds

RANCHOS
DE TAOS

68

San
Francisco
de Asis

518

ESPINOSA ROAD

▼ Santa Fe   ▼ Las Vegas

ACCOMMODATION
Old Taos Guesthouse A

EATING & DRINKING
The Bean	2
Taos Pizza Outback	3
Tiwa Kitchen	1

Sun 8am–5pm; 50¢ one-way; ☎505/751-4459); some services continue up to the Ski Valley in winter only. Another option is to rent a **bike** from Gearing Up, 129 Paseo del Pueblo Sur (☎505/751-0365, ⓦ www.gearingupbikes.com).

Tours and excursions

In summer, open-air **trolley tours** visit the main attractions (May–Oct daily 10.30am & 2pm from visitor center, 10.45am & 2.15pm at plaza; ☎505/751-0366, ⓦ www.taostrolleytours.com; $33, including entry fees). All the tours go to Taos Pueblo, except for those on Sundays and Monday afternoons, which visit the Millicent Rogers Museum and Martínez Hacienda instead.

Out of ski season, between mid-April and mid-July, many visitors go **white-water rafting**, through the Taos Box Canyon of the Rio Grande, which offers rapids up to Class V. Operators based at Pilar, south of town – see p.155 – include Far Flung Adventures (one-day trips Mon–Fri $105, Sat & Sun $125; ☎505/758-2628 or 1-800/359-2627, ⓦ www.farflung.com), and Cottam's Rio Grande River Trips (half-day $50, full-day $100; ☎505/758-2822 or 1-800/322-8267, ⓦ www.cottamsoutdoor.com).

Taos Indian Horse Ranch (☎505/758-3212 or 1-800/659-3210, ⓦ www .taosindianhorseranch.com) runs **horseback** excursions on Pueblo lands; short beginners' rides start at $50. Rafting, biking, kayaking, and, in winter, snowmobiling can also be arranged through Native Sons Adventures, 1033-A Paseo del Pueblo Sur (☎505/758-9342 or 1-800/753-7559, ⓦ www .nativesonsadventures.com).

The Pueblo Balloon Company (☎505/751-9877, ⓦ www.puebloballoon .com) offers hot-air balloon flights over the Rio Grande gorge, costing $225, or $100 for ages 6–12.

Accommodation

Taos has **accommodation** to meet all needs, at prices well below those of Santa Fe. However, midwinter rates are no lower than midsummer, and can even be considerably higher close to the ski area. **High season** runs from Christmas to mid-April and mid-June to mid-October; **low season** is the rest of the year.

There are no real **budget** options near the plaza, but the *Snowmansion* hostel, on the Paseo Del Pueblo Norte towards the Ski Valley to the north, offers bare-bones bunks or simple rooms. Otherwise, chain motels line Hwy-68 south of town, while three or four amusingly adobe-styled **motels** on Kit Carson Road just east of the plaza provide quieter alternatives; call in at the visitor center first to pick up discount coupons. For a few dollars more, you can avail yourself of atmospheric **B&B** inns – check out ⓦ www.taos-bandb-inns.com – or luxury **hotels**.

The best places to **camp** in the vicinity are the nine summer-only campgrounds in **Carson National Forest** (☎505/758-6200, ⓦ www.fs.fed.us/r3/carson), reached by following Kit Carson Road east until it becomes Hwy 64.

Taos

Abominable Snowmansion Hostel/HI-Taos Taos Ski Valley Rd, Arroyo Seco ☎505/776-8298, ⓦ www.abominablesnowmansion.com. Membership is not required at this pleasant, friendly HI-AYH hostel-cum-ski lodge. It's on a very tight curve in the road as you enter Arroyo Seco village on Hwy-150 up to the Ski Valley, five miles north of downtown. Office hours are daily 8–11am & 4–10pm, so don't arrive at midday. Dorm beds $15 in summer, $22 in winter, when rates include breakfast; teepees, and camping space out back; bargain private rooms and cabins come with and without en-suite facilities. ❶–❸

Best Western Kachina Lodge de Taos 413 Paseo del Pueblo Norte ☎505/758-2275 or 1-800/522-4462, ⓦ www.kachinalodge.com. Large, tasteful, family-oriented motel at the Taos Pueblo turn-off, with lots of Southwestern art, a reasonable restaurant, a pool, live music, and small-scale Pueblo dance performances every night in summer. ❹

El Pueblo Lodge 412 Paseo del Pueblo Norte ☏505/758-8700 or 1-800/433-9612, ⓦwww .elpueblolodge.com. Southwestern-themed motel, half a mile north of downtown near the Taos Pueblo; 1-, 2-, and 3-bedroom condos also available. Rooms ❹, condos ❽–❾

🏃 **Historic Taos Inn** 125 Paseo del Pueblo Norte ☏505/758-2233 or 1-888/519-8267, ⓦwww.taosinn.com. Gorgeous central Taos landmark, where several ancient adobes were welded together to create an atmospheric and very Southwestern hotel. Each of the 44 rooms plays some variation on the Pueblo theme; the *kiva* fireplaces are just for show, but a real fire burns downstairs, in the cozy, convivial lobby area that was once an open courtyard. Both the excellent *Doc Martin's* restaurant (see p.171) and the *Adobe Bar* are packed nightly. ❹–❼

Indian Hills Inn 233 Paseo del Pueblo Sur ☏505/758-4293 or 1-800/444-2346, ⓦwww .newmex.com/indianhillsinn. The only cheap-ish highway motel within walking distance of the plaza; if you're sensitive to noise, be sure to get a room well away from the street. ❹

La Doña Luz 114 Kit Carson Rd ☏505/758-4874 or 1-800/758-9187, ⓦwww.ladonaluz.com. Hispanic-flavored rooms of differing sizes and standards – all have en-suite facilities – in a peaceful adobe B&B a very short walk east of the plaza. ❸–❽

La Fonda de Taos 108 South Plaza ☏505/758-2211 or 1-800/833-2211, ⓦwww.lafondataos .com. Vintage 1930s hotel on the plaza that has been totally modernized to hold 24 luxurious suites, with Southwestern furnishings and tiled bathrooms. The lobby even holds a gallery of D.H. Lawrence paintings (see opposite). ❺

B&Bs

Casa de las Chimeneas 405 Cordoba Lane ☏505/758-4777 or 1-877/758-4777 ⓦwww .visit-taos.com. Luxurious eight-room B&B, set in adobe-walled gardens a couple of blocks southeast of the plaza, with a fitness room and spa. ❼

Laughing Horse Inn 729 Paseo del Pueblo Norte ☏505/758-8350 or 1-800/776-0161, ⓦwww .laughinghorseinn.com. 1887 *hacienda*, half a mile north of the plaza, that later became a print shop and is now a B&B inn. Ten bedrooms share three bathrooms, and there's also a penthouse suite, plus a Jacuzzi, psychic readings, and free mountain bikes. Rooms ❹, suite ❻

🏃 **Mabel Dodge Luhan House** 240 Morada Lane ☏505/751-9686 or 1-800/846-2235, ⓦwww.mabeldodgeluhan.com. Gorgeous 200-year-old adobe B&B complex, not far northeast of the plaza off Kit Carson Lane, where the lovely guestrooms are named in honor of former guests like Willa Cather and Ansel Adams. Two rooms, including the light-filled solarium, share a bathroom painted by D.H. Lawrence; the cheaper lodge annex has more modern fittings. The inn regularly plays host to creative workshops run by writer Natalie Goldberg among others. ❹–❽

Old Taos Guesthouse 1028 Witt Rd ☏505/758-5448 or 1-800/758-5448, ⓦwww.oldtaos.com. Vintage adobe *hacienda*, a couple of miles east of the plaza, now restored as a spacious B&B complex. Each of the nine rooms offers different facilities – all have private bath and handcarved furniture, some have *kiva* fireplaces – and there's an outdoor hot tub. Two-night minimum stay. ❺

Taos Ski Valley

Amizette Inn PO Box 756, Taos Ski Valley, NM 87525 ☏505/776-2451 or 1-800/446-8267, ⓦwww.amizetteinn.com. Small but comfortable ski lodge, just over a mile down the valley from the lifts, with an indoor hot tub and sweeping views from its verandas. Rates include breakfast. ❺

Edelweiss Lodge & Spa 106 Sutton Place, Taos Ski Valley, NM 87525 ☏505/737-6900 or 1-800/458-8754, ⓦwww.edelweisslodgeandspa .com. Intimate, luxurious hotel at the foot of the slopes with a winter-only bistro, plus sauna, Jacuzzi, and in-house masseuse. ❽

The Town

Downtown Taos still centers on the old Spanish **plaza**, which has been remodeled several times over the years, and migrated slightly eastwards in the process. The tiny square is now ringed by galleries and souvenir stores, and its tree-shaded benches make a pleasant spot from which to watch the world go by. The Stars and Stripes have flown day and night from the flagpole at its heart ever since it was erected by Kit Carson during the Civil War; the nearby bandstand was a gift from Mabel Dodge Luhan.

While there's little to see on the plaza itself, a short walk along the narrow, winding streets that stretch away in all directions is rewarded with glimpses of

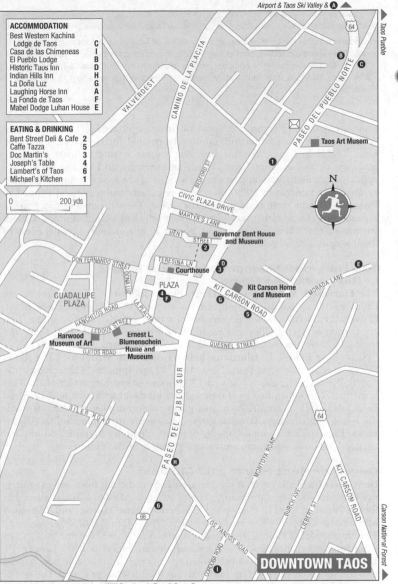

ACCOMMODATION

Best Western Kachina
  Lodge de Taos   C
Casa de las Chimeneas I
El Pueblo Lodge   B
Historic Taos Inn   D
Indian Hills Inn   H
La Doña Luz   G
Laughing Horse Inn   A
La Fonda de Taos   F
Mabel Dodge Luhan House E

EATING & DRINKING

Bent Street Deli & Cafe 2
Caffe Tazza   5
Doc Martin's   3
Joseph's Table   4
Lambert's of Taos   6
Michael's Kitchen   1

0   200 yds

N

Taos Art Musem

Governor Bent House
and Museum

Courthouse

Kit Carson Home
and Museum

PLAZA

GUADALUPE
PLAZA

Harwood
Museum of Art

Ernest L.
Blumenschein
Home and
Museum

DOWNTOWN TAOS

Taos as it used to be. The best central museum is the **Kit Carson Home**, while
the **Millicent Rogers Museum**, a few miles north, holds superb Native
American and Hispanic artworks.

La Fonda

Although **La Fonda** hotel, on the south side of the plaza, was built in 1937, well
after **D.H. Lawrence**'s death, a gallery in the lobby holds a unique collection of

②

Discount museum tickets

Under a scheme run by the Museum Association of Taos (⊛ www.taosmuseums.org), a **$25 combination ticket**, sold at each museum and valid for a year, buys admission to five Taos museums – the Millicent Rogers Museum, the Blumenschein Home, the Harwood Museum, the Taos Art Museum and Fechin Home, and the Hacienda Martínez.

paintings by the Nottinghamshire novelist (irregular hours; $3). Bought from his widow Frieda's second husband, most were painted in Italy rather than Taos. One, *The Holy Family*, was his first ever canvas; it shows. Apart from one landscape (a "collaboration" with Frieda and their friend Dorothy Brett), they depict sweaty, fleshy wrestlings such as *The Rape of the Sabine Women*. When first exhibited, in London in 1929, they were regarded as obscene and banned in Britain. They now seem tame, though the *Sunday Times'* original verdict remains accurate: "he can do rather less with a paintbrush than a child of seven without any natural flair." Lawrence's ashes are now held in a memorial chapel north of Taos, as described on p.175.

The Harwood Museum of Art and Ernest L. Blumenschein Home

The **Harwood Museum of Art**, two blocks southwest of the plaza at 238 Ledoux St (Tues–Sat 10am–5pm; Sun noon–5pm; $8, $25 combination ticket; ⊛ www.harwoodmuseum.org), combines works by twentieth-century Taos artists such as Bert Phillips and woodcarver Patrociño Barelo with *santos* and *retablos* by their nineteenth-century Hispanic counterparts.

Nearby, the **Ernest L. Blumenschein Home and Museum**, 222 Ledoux St (daily: May–Oct 9am–5pm; Nov–April 11am–4pm; $8, $25 combination ticket), preserves the much-restored 1790 house of the cofounder of the Taos Society of Artists. Paintings by Blumenschein, his daughter Helen, and Zuni and Hopi artists such as Fred Kabotie (see p.338) are on display, but the real star is the house itself. Though Taos has grown to obscure its original uninterrupted views, Blumenschein's studio, made gloriously light by its raised ceiling and enlarged windows, still commands a fine prospect of the mountains.

Governor Bent House and Museum

Bent Street, a block north of the plaza, takes its name not from any irregularities but from the first American governor of New Mexico, Charles Bent. His former home at no. 117 is now the **Governor Bent House and Museum** (daily: April–Oct 9.30am–5pm, Nov–March 10am–4pm; $2; ☎ 505/758-2376). The imposition of American rule was resented by Taos' Hispanic and Indian population alike, and Bent was killed here by an angry mob on January 19, 1847. Most of his family attempted to escape through a still-visible hole hacked into the adobe walls; they were captured, but their lives were spared. The rest of the small house is a ramshackle museum of frontier Taoseño life, holding Indian artifacts, antiquated rifles, and even an eight-legged lamb.

Kit Carson Home and Museum

Just east of the plaza, across the highway at the end of Taos' sole surviving stretch of wooden boardwalk, is the dusty but evocative adobe home of "mountain man," mason, and part-time US cavalry officer **Kit Carson** (daily 9am–6pm; $5; ⊛ www.kitcarsonhome.com). Born in Kentucky in 1809, Carson left home to join a wagon train to Missouri in 1826 – a one-cent reward was offered for the return of the teenage runaway – and spent the ensuing winter in Taos. He was to return repeatedly throughout his life, in between escapades like scouting for the 1840s Frémont expeditions and campaigning against the Navajo in the 1860s (see p.506).

Carson bought the house at the heart of today's museum in 1843, on his marriage to a local woman, Josefa Jaramillo. It was sold after their deaths in 1868 to support their seven orphaned children, and now holds a disappointingly small collection of press cuttings and photos relating to Carson himself, plus a mock-up of the family's living quarters, complete with *fogon de campaña*, a bell-shaped adobe fireplace.

Taos Art Museum and Fechin Home

Russian artist and woodcarver Nicolai Fechin (1881–1955) made his home in Taos between 1927 and 1933 – almost literally so, in that he sculpted and shaped virtually every inch of the interior. As the **Taos Art Museum and Fechin Home**, it's now open to the public at 227 Paseo del Pueblo Norte (daily except Mon 10am–5pm; $8, $25 combination ticket; Ⓦ taosartmuseum.org). Its ornate decorations are in themselves well worth a quick look, while its walls are adorned with choice pieces by Taos Society of Artists members, including a few lovely Gustave Baumann prints. The house makes a spectacular setting for chamber-music concerts on summer evenings.

Millicent Rogers Museum

Four miles north of the plaza, well past the Taos Pueblo turn-off and reached by a dirt road that angles into a tricky five-way intersection, the **Millicent Rogers Museum** (April–Oct daily 10am–5pm; Nov–March Tues–Sun 10am–5pm; $10, under-17s $2, $25 combination ticket; Ⓦ www.millicentrogers.org) is one of New Mexico's best galleries. Millicent Rogers – a former fashion model, granddaughter of a founder of Standard Oil and "close" to Cary Grant – lived here until her death in 1953.

Focusing on both Native American and Hispanic art, the museum traces how those cultures have been perceived. Its highlight is the family collection of San Ildefonso Pueblo potter **Maria Martinez**, whose black-on-black ceramics are the most famous (and valuable) Native American artworks of the twentieth century. Fascinating photos show her creating a pot step by step. Displays also outline the unbroken thousand-year tradition of Pueblo pottery, from the prehistoric Mimbres and Ancestral Puebloan peoples onwards. Other crafts include turquoise jewelry, and Navajo blankets.

The development of Spanish colonial religious art in the New World is shown through an array of rugs, looms, carved wooden furniture, *bultos*, and *retablos*, plus a "**Death Cart**" (see p.157), in which a skeleton, known as Doña Sebastiana, rides in a rickety wooden carriage and brandishes a bow and arrow.

Taos Pueblo

Tiwa-speaking peoples have lived at **TAOS PUEBLO**, just over two miles north of Taos plaza, for almost a thousand years. While they may have originally arrived from the east, across the plains, they have long been at the forefront of the **Pueblo Indian** cultural tradition. Together with Ácoma (see p.110) and the Hopi mesas (see p.80), the pueblo can claim to be the oldest continuously occupied settlement in the United States. It's also stunningly beautiful, centering

▲ Hispanic Death Cart, Millicent Rogers Museum, Taos

on two multistory adobe "apartment blocks" framed beneath the shining forested peak of Taos Mountain.

The northernmost New Mexican pueblo, Taos is among the few not to have been displaced by the coming of the Spaniards. Its survival has required a long hard struggle; the pueblo was abandoned for two years in the 1630s, to escape retaliation after the killing of a priest, and it later played a central role in the **Pueblo Revolt** of 1680 (see p.502). When the Spanish subsequently reconquered New Mexico, Taos Pueblo was almost completely destroyed. It revolted again under both Mexican and American rule. In 1837, Taos Indians cut off the head of the Mexican governor of New Mexico and used it as a football. Ten years later, they were heavily implicated in the rebellion against

Charles Bent (see p.166); when the retaliating US Army besieged and burned the pueblo's church, over 150 women, children, and elderly noncombatants were killed.

In the twentieth century, the pueblo was forced to campaign for the return of the sacred **Blue Lake**, high in the mountains. The source of the Río Pueblo de Taos that flows through the heart of the village, and the focus of an annual three-day pilgrimage, Blue Lake was unexpectedly incorporated into a federal forest reserve in 1906. When Richard Nixon finally handed it back in 1970, it marked the first time that land had ever been returned to Native Americans for religious reasons; access is now forbidden to outsiders.

Visiting the pueblo

Taos Pueblo is generally open from 8am until 5.30pm from Monday to Saturday, and between 8.30am and 5pm on Sunday, but it often closes for tribal events such as festivals or funerals, and remains closed between mid-February and early April; check with Taos Pueblo Tourism (☎505/758-1028, ⓦwww.taospueblo.com) before you visit.

The pueblo can be reached via two approach roads off Hwy-68. One continues north as the highway veers west at the *Best Western Kachina Lodge*, half a mile north of the plaza, while the other branches off at Jackie's Trading Post, another half-mile on. After entering the reservation, they meet and run together to the pueblo plaza, where you pay the **entrance fee** ($10 per person, plus $5 per still or video camera) and park your vehicle. That fee entitles you to join one of the regular **walking tours**, led by Pueblo residents. While taking a tour may help overcome any awkwardness you might feel, however, it won't take you beyond the limited public areas through which you're free to wander alone.

Visits focus on the two large **adobe complexes** – Hlaauma, the north house, and Hlaukwima, the south house – that stand to either side of the Río Pueblo de Taos, also known as Red Willow Creek. In their current form, they almost certainly date from the uncertain years that followed the Pueblo Revolt, at the start of the eighteenth century. This architectural design, consisting of individual dwellings stacked like dice and entered via rooftop ladders, was originally adopted for defense. While the homes have been adapted to include ground-level doorways and windows, their occupants still choose to live without toilets, running water, or electricity. Both complexes remained fully inhabited until the mid-1970s, but due to the lack of conveniences and the constant tourist intrusion, they now hold a mere ten families between them. The remainder of the reservation's population of three thousand live in newer homes nearby. Several rooms facing the plaza function as **craft shops**, but you can't penetrate any further, and you'll only glimpse the *kivas* (ceremonial chambers), distinguished by their long ladders, from a distance.

Visitors are encouraged to enter, but not photograph, the pretty little **Church of San Gerónimo** on the edge of the plaza. Murals inside feature traditional corn and sun motifs; mass, open to all, is celebrated every Sunday morning at 7am. Tours also lead to the ruins of the pueblo's previous church, all but destroyed by the US army in 1847. Its solitary belltower dominates a small dusty cemetery beside the adobe wall that surrounds the entire pueblo. Now just a few feet in height, the wall originally stood twelve feet tall. In the plaza itself, what look like makeshift awnings to shelter parked cars are in fact *ramadas*, wooden racks used for drying corn and chile peppers.

For most of the year, Pueblo life continues with scant regard for visitors, though (camera-less) outsiders are welcome at certain spectacular feast days and dances. Most of these take place in summer; the biggest are the **Corn Dances** (June 13 & 24, July 25 & 26), the **Taos Pueblo Pow Wow** (second weekend in July), and the **Feast of San Gerónimo** (Sept 29 & 30).

Taos Pueblo is one of the many pueblos that rushed to build its own **casino**, three-quarters of a mile northwest of the pueblo itself; it's a relatively small affair, with no accommodation and just a simple restaurant (℡505/737-0777, Ⓦwww .taosmountaincasino.com). As one unapologetic elder remarked, "poverty was never a part of Pueblo life until the Europeans came."

Ranchos de Taos

The distinct community of **RANCHOS DE TAOS**, which spreads to either side of Hwy-68 three miles southwest of central Taos, was founded when Indian farmlands were taken over by the Spanish to grow the crops that fed the townspeople of Taos. Each *rancho* or farm had its own main house, or *hacienda*, and even today Ranchos de Taos retains the feel of a rural village; you can still buy fresh hay for your animals from lots along the highway.

San Francisco de Asis

In Rancho's small unpaved plaza, the mission church of **San Francisco de Asis** turns its broad shoulders, or more accurately its massive adobe buttresses, to the passing traffic on Hwy-68. Built around 1776, it's one of colonial New Mexico's most splendid architectural achievements, with subtly rounded walls and corners disguising its underlying structural strength. Encountering genuine adobe, which crumbles away after heavy rain or snow, can come as a shock after so much fakery elsewhere in the state; the local congregation is obliged to replaster the whole thing yearly.

The ever-changing interplay of light and shade across the church's golden exterior has fascinated painters from Georgia O'Keeffe onwards. She observed in 1971 that "Everyone paints the Taos church. If you're in Taos for two days you have to paint the Taos church. I asked myself do I have to paint all that church? I'll just paint a little piece of it. That'll do just as well. And I did."

The church's **interior** is equally intriguing. Amid a clutter of devotional objects and artworks, a magnificently ornate green-and-red *reredos* (altarpiece) frames several individual paintings. It was painted by the nineteenth-century *santero* Molleno, who was also responsible for the altarpiece of the Santuario de Chimayó (see p.156). The **plaza** outside – remarkably peaceful considering that the highway is thirty yards away – holds a handful of restaurants and gift stores.

Hacienda Martínez

Two miles west of the highway, halfway between San Francisco de Asis and the downtown plaza on Ranchitos Road, the **Hacienda Martínez** is one of the few Spanish haciendas anywhere to be preserved in something like its original state (daily: April–Oct 9am–5pm; Nov–March 10am–4pm; $7, $25 combination ticket). It was built in 1804 by Don Antonio Martínez, an early mayor of Taos who was also the father of Padre Antonio Jose Martínez (see p.157). Within its thick, windowless, adobe walls – the place could be sealed like a fortress against then still-prevalent Indian raids – two dozen rooms are wrapped around two separate patios, holding animal pens and a well. Trade goods of the kind Don Antonio once carried south along the Rio Grande are displayed alongside tools, looms, and simple furnishings of the era, while the rooms farthest from the entrance contain a fine collection of Hispanic religious art.

Taos Ski Valley

Fifteen miles north of Taos, reached via an attractive road that winds up through a narrow gap in the mountains from the village of **Arroyo Seco**, rise the precipitous slopes of **TAOS SKI VALLEY**. Located on the north flank of **Wheeler Peak** – the highest point in New Mexico at 13,161 feet – the runs are usually open to skiers and snowboarders from late November until early April (daily lift tickets late Nov to mid-Dec and late March to early April $40, mid-Dec to late March $66; information ☏505/776-2291 or 1-866/968-7386, reservations ☏1-800/776-1111, ⓦwww.skitaos.org).

Experts rate Taos one of the most challenging ski resorts in the Rockies – just over half its 110 separate runs, served by twelve lifts, are rated for experts only – but the highly rated Ernie Blake Ski School (same telephone numbers) teaches novices aged 3 and upwards on the nursery slopes. If you've never skied, the **Yellowbird Beginner's Package** is an ideal way to try it out, with lessons, lift tickets, and ski rental costing $88 for one day or $148 for two days.

The road up into the Ski Valley dead-ends at a massive parking lot that serves several **lodges**, **hotels**, and **condo** blocks, some of which are listed on p.164. There are also a number of cafés, restaurants, and bars, including the casual *Rhoda's*, which serves snacks and full meals for lunch and dinner (☏505/776-2005) and the lively *Tim's Stray Dog Cantina* (☏505/776-2894). Most accommodation and dining options remain open year-round, but there's little point staying in summer.

Eating and drinking

Taos has a fine selection of **restaurants** in all price ranges and several **coffeehouses**. If your main priority is to **drink**, the *Adobe Bar* in the *Historic Taos Inn* (see p.164), with its roaring log fire and regular live music, is the coziest spot in town, while *Eske's*, a short way south at 106 Des Georges Lane (☏505/758-1517), is a **brewpub**, open nightly until 10.30pm, that also serves simple stews and snacks.

Coffeehouses

The Bean 900 Paseo del Pueblo Norte ☏505/758-7711, and 1033 Paseo del Pueblo Sur ☏505/758-5123. These serious coffee roasters sell espressos and pastries to a clientele composed largely of 40-somethings, including, at the northern outlet, Indians from the nearby pueblo. Mon–Fri 6.30am–6pm, Sat 7am–4pm, Sun 7am–2pm.

Caffe Tazza 122 Kit Carson Rd ☏505/758-8706. Welcoming central café with nice sunlit terraoo, serving coffees and light veggie meals to counter-cultural locals and assorted crazies. Live entertainment most evenings, with anarchic open-mike nights. Free local newspapers. Daily 6.30am–8pm.

Gypsy 360 482 Ski Valley Rd, Arroyo Seco ☏505/776-3166. Unlikely gourmet deli, in a tiny village on the road up to Taos Ski Valley, that offers espresso coffees, pricey but tasty pastries, and sandwiches. Tues, Wed & Sat 8am–4pm, Thurs & Fri 8am–8pm, Sun 9am–3pm.

Restaurants

Bent Street Deli & Cafe 120 Bent St ☏505/758-5787. Airy, partly outdoor place, just north of the plaza; good-value breakfasts, sandwich or pasta lunches, and tasty dinners like shrimp with garlic or organic roast chicken for $15–20. Mon–Sat 8am–9pm, Sun 11am–3pm.

Doc Martin's *Historic Taos Inn*, 125 Paseo del Pueblo Norte ☏505/758-1977. Delicious, inventive New Mexican food in romantic old adobe inn, on the main road just east of the plaza. Unusual breakfast options include the $8 Kit Carson (poached eggs on yam biscuits); dinner entrees, such as piñon-crusted salmon or roast chicken, cost $20–24. A four-course *prix-fixe* menu, with wine, costs $60. Daily 7.30–11am, 11.30am–2.30pm, & 5.30–9.30pm.

🏃 **Joseph's Table**, *La Fonda de Taos*, 108 South Plaza ☏505/751-4512, ⓦwww.hotellafonda.com. This delightful restaurant serves wonderful (if rich) food in a lovely setting, with very friendly service. Thanks to a creative use of fabric, the alcoves along one wall have been turned into "love shacks" that resemble tented pavilions, The fabulous parma ham risotto appetizer is $14, while full entrees like a crispy duck leg or pan-seared scallops cost around $30, but you can also order smaller portions from the separate *Joe's Bar* menu, like a buffalo burger for $14. Daily 5.30–10pm, lunch 11.30am–2.30pm May–Aug only.

Lambert's of Taos 309 Paseo del Pueblo Sur ☎505/758-1009. Cozy, low-key restaurant half a mile south of the plaza, with a classy but friendly atmosphere and art on the walls. The cuisine is New American rather than New Mexican, with grilled meat or fish entrees like pepper-crusted duck for $16–34, and opulent desserts. Mon–Sat 5.30–9pm.

Michael's Kitchen 304C Paseo del Pueblo Norte ☎505/758-4178. Inexpensive Mexican and Southwestern dishes in an old adobe kitchen a few blocks north of the plaza, plus fresh-baked pastries, cinnamon rolls, and coffee in the morning. Mon–Thurs 7am–2.30pm, Fri–Sun 7am–8pm.

Taos Pizza Outback 712 Paseo del Pueblo Norte ☎505/748-3112. Hard-to-find pizzeria tucked behind another building to the left of the highway a mile north of town. It has a welcoming youthful ambience and huge portions of great food – the $10 veggie *calzones* are amazing. Daily 11am–10pm.

Tiwa Kitchen Taos Pueblo ☎505/751-1020. Indian-run, largely organic restaurant on the road into Taos Pueblo, serving strong chile-flavored stews, traditional *horno*-baked bread, Indian fry bread, and lots of blue corn meal. Daily except Tues, summer 11am–7pm, winter 11am–5pm.

Shopping

If you're **shopping** for souvenirs, Taos may not have Santa Fe's range of stores, or anything like so many upmarket galleries, but it's just as much fun to walk around. As ever, the **museum stores** – especially at the Millicent Rogers Museum – are among the best in town.

Stores and galleries

Blue Rain Gallery 117 South Plaza ☎505/751-0066. The very best in Native American arts and crafts, alongside the plaza; unfortunately, the exquisite *kachinas* can run into thousands of dollars.

Coyote Moon 120C Bent St ☎505/758-4437. A riot of color, this is Taos' best selection of Mexican folk art, with plenty of Oaxacan carved animals and Day of the Dead souvenirs.

Dwellings Revisited 10 Bent St ☎505/758-3377. Quirky store where the owners have imported trinkets, oddities, furniture, and folk art from all over the world. Unusual Greek and Indian items sit alongside the more familiar Mexican stuff.

Horse Feathers 109B Kit Carson Rd ☎505/758-7457. A great source for all things Western, from Stetson hats and colorful cowboy boots at bargain prices, to off-the-wall antiques.

Moby Dickens 124A Bent St ☎505/758-3050. Central bookstore with a copious selection of local fiction and history, plus New Age material.

Taos Artisans Co-op 107A Bent St ☎505/758-1558. Individually styled jewelry, clothing, and sculpture by an assortment of Taoseño artists.

West of Taos

Assuming your plans already cover Santa Fe and points south, the obvious day-trip drive from Taos follows the **Enchanted Circle** to the northeast; see p.174. However, a longer and wilder route heads **west** on US-64, across the Rio Grande and over the dramatic **San Juan Mountains**. Branching west off Hwy-68 four miles out of downtown Taos, this reaches the awesome 650-foot-high **Rio Grande Gorge Bridge** seven miles on. Be sure to take the time to park at the end and walk out to the middle, otherwise you'll barely get a glimpse of the narrow chasm as you drive across.

After a magnificent seventy-mile mountain run, punctuated by scenic overlooks, US-64 finally drops into **Chama Valley**. From there, either head south into Georgia O'Keeffe country around **Abiquiu**, or north to **Chama** itself, the base for excursions on New Mexico's best-known **steam railroad**.

Tierra Amarilla

US-64 meets the north–south US-84 in **TIERRA AMARILLA** ("yellow earth"), at the foot of the sheer, furrowed **Brazos Cliffs**. This pastoral village, founded in 1832 when the valley was prone to constant Ute, Apache, and Navajo raids, provides a classic example of the consequences to New Mexico's Hispanic population of the American takeover of the territory. In 1860, the US Congress refused to recognize that shared grazing lands belonged to the community as a whole, and instead sold them off to a Yankee landowner from Santa Fe.

Bitter disputes have raged ever since, culminating in an incident commemorated by a defaced roadside marker in the heart of the village. In 1967, a group led by Chicano activist **Reies López Tijerina** seized a nearby campground in the Kit Carson National Forest. Declaring independence from the United States, they burned down Tierra Amarilla's Rio Arriba Courthouse, destroying land-grant records and injuring a policeman and a jailer. The government responded by sending in two hundred military vehicles, including tanks. After a controversial trial, Tijerina was acquitted of any involvement by an Albuquerque court. Although he has long since distanced himself from the campaign, passions still run high – hence the sign reading *TIERRA O MUERTE* ("Land or Death") on the outskirts of town.

While Tierra Amarilla remains the county seat, it has declined to the point where parts are all but derelict. In the nearby village of **LOS OJOS** – the scene of major civil disobedience in 1989 – one cooperative effort to revitalize the local economy has proved a resounding success. **Tierra Wools** maintains local **weaving** traditions by breeding Spanish Churro sheep in the valley, and selling hand-dyed rugs and clothing from the clearly signposted Los Ojos Trading Post (☎505/588-7231 or 1-888/709-0979, ⓦwww.handweavers.com), a mile west of US-84.

Chama

Tiny **CHAMA**, set in the meadows at the head of the Chama Valley, a dozen miles north of Tierra Amarilla and a total of 85 miles northwest of Taos, is a former mining camp that has reinvented itself as a base for summer hunters and winter skiers.

Chama's major appeal for out-of-state visitors is that the pretty yellow station just below the town center is the western terminus of the narrow-gauge **Cumbres & Toltec Scenic Railroad** (late May to mid-Oct; ☎505/756-2151 or 1-888/286-2737, ⓦwww.cumbrestoltec.com), the highest such railroad in the nation. This exhilarating, if not entirely comfortable, 64-mile steam-train ride crosses the High Brazos mountains into Colorado by way of **Cumbres Pass**, then runs through the deep **Toltec Gorge** and out onto the plains before ending in **Antonito**, Colorado. Its many movie credits include the opening sequence of 1989's *Indiana Jones and the Last Crusade*. The railroad is so frequently in financial jeopardy that you should check before you come whether it's still functioning. It's not possible to do the entire round-trip by train in one day; passengers either go by van to Antonito and return by train (depart Chama 8.30am; $83), or take the train through the most scenic segment as far as Osier, and pick up a return train there (depart Chama 10am; $74). Dress warmly; it gets pretty cold up in the mountains.

Practicalities

Chama's **visitor center** is half a mile south of town at the junction of US-64 and Hwy-17 (daily: summer 8am–6pm; winter 8am–5pm; ☎505/756-2306 or 1-800/477-0149, Ⓦwww.chamavalley.com). The comfortable *Vista del Rio* (Ⓣ505/756-2138 or 1-800/939-9943, Ⓦvistadelriolodge.com; ❺) is typical of the many **riverfront lodges** along US-64/84. In the heart of town, *Carlatte's* on Terrace Ave (Ⓣ505/756-2555) serves coffee and simple meals, and has an outdoor patio. The most convenient place to **camp** is the *Rio Chama RV Campground*, beside the river at the north end of town (Ⓣ505/756-2303).

The Cumbres Pass and Antonito, Colorado

North of Chama, **Hwy-17** follows much the same route as the railroad, first climbing far above the single track and then crisscrossing it repeatedly as it makes its way up to the 10,022-foot **Cumbres Pass**. In July 1848, legendary "mountain man" Bill Williams was injured here in a confrontation between the US Army and a combined force of Utes and Apaches.

Beyond the pass, highway and railroad part company, not to meet again until they reach **ANTONITO**, Colorado, fifty miles out of Chama – a dreary, depressing little town that's home to the **Cumbres & Toltec Scenic Railroad** terminus, the reasonable *Narrow Gauge Railroad Inn* (Ⓣ719/376-5441 or 1-800/323-9469, Ⓦwww.narrowgaugerailroadinn.info; ❸) and a few basic cafés.

Dulce and Jicarilla Apache Indian Reservation

US-64 and US-84 join forces for twelve miles **west of Chama**, then once across the Continental Divide – not at all dramatic at this point – US-64 continues alone for another fifteen miles to **DULCE**, the headquarters of the **Jicarilla Apache Indian Reservation**. Today's three-thousand-plus Jicarilla are descended from separate Apache groups who lived further east, some as Plains nomads in the Cimarron area, and some in adobe villages near the pueblos of the Rio Grande. Their name is often said to come from the little baskets (*jicarillas*) they now sell to tourists, but the Jicarilla say they started making baskets on being confined to this remote reservation in the nineteenth century, and that the name comes from a Mexican word connected with chocolate.

There's little for tourists to see or do on the Jicarilla reservation, whose economy is based on oil and gas revenues and raising sheep. Dulce itself is just a very sharp dog-leg in the highway, where US-64 turns south rather than climb onto sheer Archuleta Mesa; after a few miles the road turns west again to head through Vaqueros Canyon and Gobernador Canyon (see p.101). However, Dulce does hold the *Best Western Jicarilla Inn* (Ⓣ505/759-3663 or 1-800/742-1938; ❹), which has a good restaurant.

The Enchanted Circle

While the driving circuit through the Sangre de Cristo range northeast of Taos doesn't quite live up to its tourist-brochure billing as the **Enchanted Circle**, it does pass a handful of long-abandoned ghost towns amid the mountain scenery. Oklahomans and Texans flock to the closest **ski slopes** to home, but visitors from further afield are more likely to spin off east to the hard-bitten frontier town of **Cimarron**.

The Lawrence Ranch

Starting seventeen miles north of Taos on Hwy-522, a rutted, muddy road climbs for five miles east to the **Lawrence Ranch**. The English novelist **D.H. Lawrence** made three six-month visits to Taos in the early 1920s, having been enticed across the Atlantic by Mabel Dodge Luhan (see p.161). Staying at her mountain cabin, then known as Kiowa Ranch, he wrote "there are all kinds of beauty in the world, but for greatness of beauty I have never experienced anything like New Mexico." **Georgia O'Keeffe** was also a guest here, in 1929, when she painted the tree right in front of the main cabin as *The Lawrence Tree*. As seen from below, the painting makes the tree look more like a giant squid; it's usually on display in the Georgia O'Keeffe Museum in Santa Fe.

Lawrence died in France in 1930, but five years later his widow Frieda shipped his ashes back to New Mexico. They now rest in a small **shrine** that enjoys panoramic views of the upper Rio Grande valley, at the top of a zigzag cement footpath cleared through the forest; according to some stories, the ashes were actually poured into a wheelbarrow of cement, to ensure they could never be taken away. Frieda is said to have acquired the ranch from Mabel Dodge Luhan in exchange for the manuscript of *Sons and Lovers* – which Mabel in turn used to pay her psychiatrist – and lived in it until her death in 1956. It now belongs to the University of New Mexico, which holds weekend retreats in the main cabin; only the shrine is accessible to visitors, with no fixed hours or admission fee.

Red River

Half a dozen miles beyond the Lawrence Ranch, as Hwy-522 gathers itself for the final climb into Colorado, **Hwy-38** follows Red River east from **QUESTA**, an ugly little village ravaged by opencast mining. After twelve more attractive riverside miles, it reaches **RED RIVER**, a former gold-mining town whose rough-shod timber architecture is more authentic than it looks. Summer visitors hike in the surrounding forests, but Red River is at its busiest during the winter **ski** season, when there's cross-country skiing in the valley and a downhill resort in the mountains. The season typically lasts from late November until late March, with lift tickets costing $58 per day. For full details contact the information office (☎575/754-2223, ⑩redriverskiarea.com).

Appealing **accomodation** options include the *Alpine Lodge*, 417 W Main St (☎575/754-2952 or 1-800/252-2333, ⑩www.alpinelodgeredriver.com; ⑤).

Cimarron

Beyond Red River, Hwy-38 negotiates the 9820-foot **Bobcat Pass** – often closed in winter – then drops by way of the ruins of long-abandoned **Elizabethtown** down to **Eagle Nest**. Just a cluster of cabins and RV parks, Eagle Nest sprang up around a lake formed when the **Cimarron River** was dammed in 1920, and is popular with fishing enthusiasts. US-64 parallels the river to enter impressive **Cimarron Canyon** four miles east, beneath the towering 800-foot **Palisade Cliffs**. This route provided access to Taos for nineteenth-century travelers who split from the Santa Fe Trail's "mountain branch" at **CIMARRON** itself, 24 miles east of Eagle Nest.

Cimarron means "wild" or "untamed," and in its heyday the town was as wild as the West could be. It stood at the heart of the 1.7-million-acre **Maxwell Land Grant**, the largest private landholding in the US, accumulated by Lucien Bonaparte Maxwell after the American takeover of New Mexico. Maxwell's main business was cattle ranching, but with gold and silver mines booming and busting all over the mountains, Cimarron lured a vast profusion of gamblers, gunfighters, outlaws, and cowboys.

Cimarron's old downtown stands relatively intact half a mile south of the main highway. Its history is lovingly chronicled in the **Old Mill Museum** (June–Aug Mon–Wed, Fri & Sat 9am–5pm, Sun 1–5pm; May & Sept Sat 9am–5pm, Sun 1–5pm; $3). The most famous of other nearby relics is the **St James Hotel** opposite, at 17th and Collinson (℡505/376-2664 or 1-866/472-5019, ⓦwww .stjamescimarron.com; ❹). Built by President Lincoln's former White House chef in 1873, it has witnessed 26 murders; names in the guest register include Jesse James and Buffalo Bill. It now has its own grand, "tin-ceilinged" restaurant, and a less romantic motel annex.

Angel Fire

The Enchanted Circle loops back to Taos from Eagle Nest along US-64, passing, after ten miles, through the part-**golf**, part-**ski** resort of **ANGEL FIRE** in Moreno Valley, developed in the late 1960s. Despite recent upgrading, Angel Fire shows few signs of maturing beyond its current brash, unappealing sprawl, though the creature comforts of its centerpiece, the *Angel Fire Resort* itself, cannot be faulted (℡505/377-6401 or 1-800/633-7463, ⓦwww.angelfireresort.com; ❹). As at Red River, the ski slopes are usually active between late November and late March, but here they're considerably more suitable for novices, and there's also a snowboard park. Lift tickets cost $59 per day.

Northeast New Mexico

Successively traversed by Pueblo Indian traders, pioneers on the **Santa Fe Trail**, and passengers on the transcontinental railroad, the traditional route between New Mexico and the plains is now followed by the **I-25** interstate. The Wild West town of **Las Vegas** provides a good send-off into New Mexico's **northeast corner**, as the Sangre de Cristo mountains gradually recede below the western horizon and the Great Plains begin to unfurl in all their relentless monotony. There's no great reason to stray off the interstate until the Rockies start to loom above **Raton**, a hundred miles on, though with time to spare the detour to **Capulin Volcano** at that point is worth making.

Las Vegas

Seventy-three miles from Santa Fe, the sleepy backwater of **LAS VEGAS**, New Mexico, has more in common with its upstart Nevada namesake than may be immediately obvious. Once a wild, lawless frontier outpost, where almost anything went, it consists of two distinct sections. The **old Plaza** area, above the fertile meadows (*vegas*, in Spanish) that line the Gallinas River, was established in 1835, when Hispanic settlers drove away the Comanche and set about capturing trade on the burgeoning **Santa Fe Trail**. When the **railroad** arrived in 1879, focus shifted across the river to the grid of streets around the new station. Incomers included the legendary **"Doc" Holliday**, who briefly owned a saloon on Center Street before scurrying back to Dodge City to escape a murder charge. In a single month, Las Vegas witnessed 29 gunshot deaths.

At the end of the nineteenth century, Las Vegas was the principal city in New Mexico, and almost all its buildings still date from the Victorian era. The conspicuous lack of adobe makes it easy to forget you're in the Southwest, but it ranks among the state's most authentic Wild West towns, and while it offers no particular stand-out tourist attractions, it's a delight to stroll around.

Grand Avenue – the main business drag – and I-25 alike now closely parallel the railroad, leaving the **Plaza** high and dry a mile to the west. Its four-square layout resembles something from the Deep South, though a Victorian bandstand rather than a courthouse stands at its center. The only significant building on the perimeter is the *Plaza Hotel* (see below), but **Bridge Street**, which leads up from the highway, is lined with antiques stores and cafés.

Theodore Roosevelt recruited around forty percent of his volunteer **Rough Riders**, who invaded Cuba in 1898, in Las Vegas. Their exploits, plus the minutiae of local history, are recorded in the **City Museum**, 727 Grand Ave (Tues–Sat 10am–4pm; free).

Hwy-518 leads due north from Las Vegas into some of New Mexico's most appealing mountain scenery, and serves as an eighty-mile shortcut to **Taos**. The Hispanic farming village of **MORA**, thirty miles out, is the seat of Mora County, ranked by the *Wall Street Journal* as one of the three poorest counties in the US.

Practicalities

Two Amtrak **trains** pull into Las Vegas each afternoon, from Albuquerque and Chicago. Brochures at the **visitor center**, 513 Sixth St (Mon–Fri 9am–5pm; ☎505/425-8631 or 1-800/832-5947, ⓦwww.lasvegasnewmexico.com), detail **walking tours** of town.

The nicest place to **stay** is the restored, antiques-furnished *Plaza Hotel*, 230 Old Town Plaza (☎505/425-3591 or 1-800/328-1882, ⓦwww .plazahotel-nm.com; ❹), which offers substantial discounts for online bookings. Its *Landmark Grill* is Las Vegas' classiest **restaurant**, open daily for all meals. There are also plenty of **motels**, such as the *Super 8*, 2029 N Grand Ave (☎505/425-5288 or 1-800/800-8000, ⓦwww.super8.com; ❸). Local students huddle over lunchtime espressos in the Super Chief Coffee House, 514 Grand Ave (☎505/454-1360), while the *Rialto*, 141 Bridge St (☎505/454-0037; closed Sat), is more of a traditional diner.

Raton

Appealing little **RATON** is tucked into the foothills of the Rockies a hundred miles north of Las Vegas on I-25, a mere eight miles south of the Colorado border. Once a way-station on the Santa Fe Trail, it reached its present size after becoming the site of a railroad repair shop in 1880, and can have changed little since then.

Few passengers now bother to dismount from the sleek Amtrak Starliner that pulls into the Santa Fe Depot around noon daily, but an hour or two's stroll in **downtown Raton** can be fun. Photos and oddments in the **Raton Museum**, facing the station at 216 S First St (May–Sept Tues–Sat 9am–5pm; Oct–April Wed–Sat 10am–4pm; free), recall highlights from Raton's first century. Until 1938, the town was dominated by the seven-story *Hotel Swastika*, which then "found it necessary to change its name" to the *Yucca*, and is now a bank.

Taking an antique furnished room at the *Historic El Portal Hotel*, 101 N Third St (☎505/445-3631 or 1-888/362-7345, ⓦwww.elportalhotel.com; ❸), is the most atmospheric **lodging** option. Alternatively, **Trinidad**, twenty miles north in Colorado, makes an equally diverting stop.

Capulin Volcano National Monument

CAPULIN VOLCANO NATIONAL MONUMENT, thirty miles east of Raton on US-64/87 and then three miles north on Hwy-325, preserves the neatest and most symmetrical of a chain of cinder cones that last exploded around ten thousand years ago.

Most people drive straight past the **visitor center** (daily: summer 7.30am–6.30pm; winter 8am–4pm; $5 per vehicle; ☏505/278-2201, ⓦwww.nps.gov/cavo), on up the two-mile spiral of road that leads to the summit. Once there, a thousand feet above the plains, you can **hike** for a mile around the rim, enjoying views to the Sangre de Cristo mountains in the west and Oklahoma to the east, or make the slightly more demanding descent down to the vent where it all began.

Albuquerque and southern New Mexico

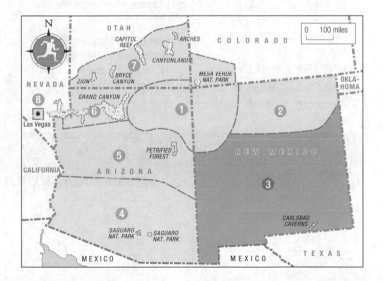

CHAPTER 3 # Highlights

✳ **Albuquerque International Balloon Festival** It's hard to imagine a more photogenic spectacle than hundreds of colorful hot-air balloons soaring above the Rio Grande on a crisp fall morning. See p.185

✳ **Indian Pueblo Cultural Center** Albuquerque's premier museum provides a great opportunity to learn about New Mexico's nineteen surviving pueblos. See p.189

✳ **Lincoln** This quintessential Wild West town has barely changed since Billy the Kid blasted free from the county courthouse. See p.196

✳ **White Sands National Monument** An utterly amazing landscape of pure white sand dunes, lined against the azure sky. See p.202

✳ **The Underground Lunch Room** A perfect slice of 1950s Americana, this space-age subterranean cafeteria makes a surreal climax to a tour of Carlsbad Caverns. See p.206

✳ **Silver City** Another wonderful Wild West relic, this mountain retreat from the heat of the desert is by far the most appealing town in southwest New Mexico. See p.214

✳ **Gila Cliff Dwellings** Remote ancient ruins, set in a lovely valley high in the mountains of southern New Mexico. See p.217

▲ Restroom at White Sands National Monument

Albuquerque and southern New Mexico

W hile New Mexico's tourist destinations lie largely to the north, its often-neglected central and southern portions hold many sites of interest. Prime among them is the state's largest city, **Albuquerque**, where the relics of its Route 66 heyday remain visible everywhere, and several stimulating museums celebrate a fascinating and varied history.

Much of the region remained dominated by the nomadic Apache until well into the nineteenth century. Even Albuquerque was founded long after Santa Fe, while towns such as **Silver City**, **Mesilla**, and **Lincoln** only really got going after New Mexico joined the United States in 1846. All three went on to play significant roles in the career of **Billy the Kid**, and all still look today much like the frontier outposts Billy must have known. Together with the pre-Columbian remains of the **Gila Cliff Dwellings** in the remote southwest corner, they're southern New Mexico's most appealing historic attractions, but it also holds a couple of **geological** wonders. The subterranean labyrinths of **Carlsbad Caverns National Park** lure a million tourists across the plains each year, while the dazzling dunes of **White Sands National Monument** make an extraordinary spectacle against the San Andres Mountains. Top-secret missile tests and bomb blasts give this desolate landscape an added sense of mystery, making its role in popular myth as the site of the notorious **Roswell Incident** a tiny bit more plausible.

Albuquerque

Sprawling at the heart of New Mexico, where the main east–west road and rail routes cross both the Rio Grande and the old road south to Mexico, **ALBUQUERQUE**, with half a million people, is the state's only major metropolis, even if it isn't the capital. Though many tourists race straight from

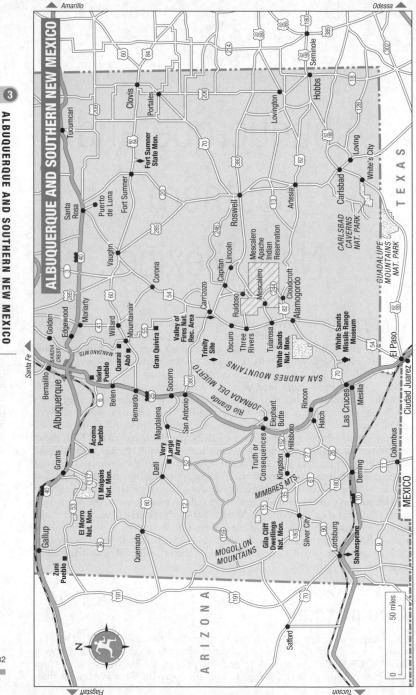

the airport up to Santa Fe without a thought for Albuquerque, the "**Duke City**" has a good deal going for it. Although, like Phoenix, it's grown a bit too fast for comfort, its original Hispanic core remains discernible, and its diverse, cosmopolitan population gives a rare cultural vibrancy. Even if its architecture is often uninspired, the setting is magnificent, sandwiched between the Rio Grande, lined by stately cottonwoods, and the dramatic, glowing **Sandia Mountains**. Specific highlights include the intact **Spanish plaza**, the neon-lit **Route 66** frontage of Central Avenue, the fascinating **Indian Pueblo Cultural Center**, and October's **hot-air balloon** extravaganza.

A history of Albuquerque

Three centuries ago, in 1706, Hispanic colonists named a new town beside a sweeping curve of the Rio Grande in honor of the Spanish **Duke of Albuquerque**. Albuquerque's earliest surviving adobe buildings, however, still the nucleus of **Old Town**, date from the 1790s, when it occupied a pivotal position on the **Camino Real** – the "Royal Road" from Mexico to Santa Fe, which later connected with the **Santa Fe Trail** from the Mississippi. Modern Albuquerque began to grow with the arrival of the railroad in 1880, when its epicenter shuffled a couple of miles east toward the new station. Around that time, Albuquerque managed to lose its first "r," possibly thanks to a misspelling by a railroad signpainter.

What really transformed Albuquerque was the decentralization of **defense** industries during World War II. Weapons research at **Sandia National Laboratories**, on the giant **Kirtland Air Force Base**, southeast of the city, brought a massive influx of money and jobs. In the 1950s, "Atomic City" was the best-educated city in the nation, in terms of PhDs per capita, and acquired enough federal offices to earn the nickname "Little Washington." It even achieved the dubious distinction of surviving an **H-bomb**: in 1957, a B-36 bomber accidentally dropped a 42,000-pound nuclear device near the air base. Its conventional explosives went off, creating a sizeable crater, but failed to trigger the intended one-megaton thermonuclear blast. Kirtland base these days is effectively a self-contained city, now more sealed off than ever from the rest of Albuquerque.

Arrival and information

Albuquerque's **International Sunport**, four miles southeast of downtown and New Mexico's principal airport, is served by all major US airlines. All the **rental car** chains (see p.32) have outlets here, while a **taxi** into the center with Yellow Cab (☎505/247-4888) costs around $12; Airport Shuttle (☎505/765-1234, ⓦwww.airportshuttleabq.com) runs door-to-door shuttles at similar rates. Many hotels and motels also have their own free shuttles.

Public transportation in Albuquerque has been transformed by the new **Rail Runner** light-rail system (fares from $1; ☎1-866/795-7245, ⓦwww.nmrailrunner.com). Commuter trains from its Downtown Albuquerque station, in the **Alvarado Transportation Center** at First and Central on the eastern edge of downtown, run south to Belen and north to Bernalillo, but the main appeal for tourists is that services also continue all the way north to Santa Fe, as detailed on p.119. The first Rail Runner stop south of downtown, the Bernalillo County/International Sunport station at 113 Rio Bravo SE, is a short ride from the airport on ABQ Ride bus #222; alternatively, bus #50 runs straight from the airport to the Downtown station.

Both Amtrak **trains** between Los Angeles and Chicago, and long-distance Greyhound **buses** (including 4 daily buses to Santa Fe; ☎505/243-4435; $28), also use the Alvarado Transportation Center.

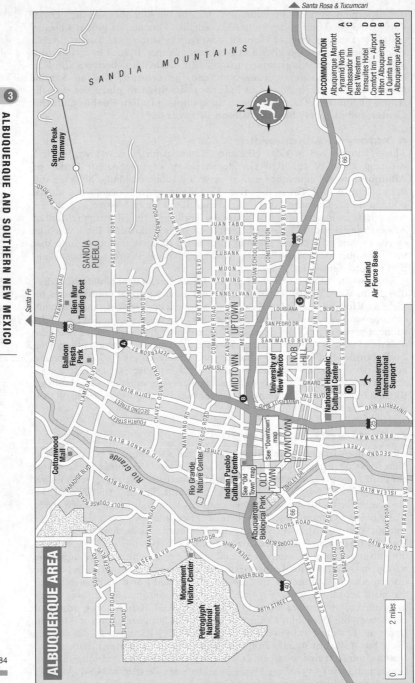

▲ Santa Rosa & Tucumcari

ALBUQUERQUE AREA

SANDIA MOUNTAINS

N

Santa Fe ▲

Sandia Peak Tramway

END ROAD

ACCOMMODATION
Albuquerque Marriott   A
Pyramid North   C
Ambassador Inn   D
Best Western   D
Imsuites Hotel   B
Comfort Inn – Airport   C
Hilton Albuquerque   B
La Quinta Inn   B
Albuquerque Airport   D

66

Kirtland
Air Force Base

TRAMWAY BLVD

JUAN TABO
MORRIS
EUBANK
MOON
WYOMING
PENNSYLVANIA

PASEO DEL NORTE
ACADEMY ROAD
SPAN ROAD

SANDIA
PUEBLO

Bien Mur
Trading Post

TRAMWAY ROAD

ROY

40

LOMAS BLVD

INDIAN SCHOOL ROAD

CONSTITUTION

CENTRAL AVENUE

LOUISIANA

SAN PEDRO DR.

SAN MATEO BLVD

ZUNI ROAD

GIBSON BLVD

C

MONTGOMERY BLVD
COMANCHE ROAD
CANDELARIA ROAD
MENAUL BLVD

SAN FRANCISCO
SAN ANTONIO DR

COMANCHE ROAD

CARLISLE

UPTOWN

MIDTOWN

25

Balloon
Fiesta Park

JEFFERSON ST

A

ALAMEDA BLVD

EDITH BLVD

CHAVEZ OSUNA ROAD

SECOND STREET

FOURTH STREET

MANTANO RD

GREGOS ROAD

TISHIZI

RIO GRANDE BLVD

NOB
HILL

University of
New Mexico

B

UNIVERSITY BLVD

GIRARD

YALE BLVD

KATHRYN

National Hispanic
Cultural Center

D

✈ Albuquerque
International Sunport

UNIVERSITY BLVD

Rio Grande
Nature Center

Indian Pueblo
Cultural Center

See "Old
Town" map

OLD
TOWN

See "Downtown"
map

DOWNTOWN

DINGLEY DR

BROADWAY

SECOND STREET

25

Cottonwood
Mall

PARADISE BLVD

N COORS BLVD

GOLF COURSE ROAD

Rio Grande

MANTANO ROAD

RIO GRANDE BLVD

Albuquerque
Biological Park

COORS ROAD

66

BRIDGE BLVD

RENAL ROAD

TOWER ROAD

SAGE ROAD

RIO BRAVO BLVD

BLAKE ROAD

ISLETA BLVD

SQUAW ROAD

UNSER BLVD

UNSER BLVD

UNSER BLVD

ATRISCO DR

LADERA DRIVE

40

S COORS BLVD

SCENIC ROAD

GILA ROAD

Monument
Visitor Center

Petroglyph
National
Monument

98TH STREET

CENTRAL AVENUE

0   2 miles

▼ Acoma & Gallup

The balloons of Albuquerque

First held in 1972 as a 50th anniversary stunt for a local radio station, when it featured just thirteen balloons, Albuquerque's annual **International Balloon Fiesta** has grown to become the most important event in world ballooning. By a freak of geography, the **"Albuquerque Box"** offers ideal conditions for balloonists. After takeoff, the prevailing winds consistently blow balloons toward the east, until they clear the top of the Sandia Mountains. Then stronger winds propel them back westwards, making it possible to land more or less where they were launched. As a result, Albuquerque regularly hosts major gas and hot-air ballooning championships, such as the unlikely sounding Coupe de Gordon Bennett.

A photographer's dream, the Balloon Fiesta lasts from the first Saturday until the second Sunday of October. It attracts roughly a thousand balloons and well over a million visitors, so book several months in advance if you need a room, or even a rental car, in early October. The fun focuses on **Balloon Fiesta Park**, half a mile west of I-25 and seven miles north of downtown. Admission costs $6 (under-12s free), with a further $10 for parking. The busiest times are the "mass ascensions" at 7am on the four weekend mornings, as well as the "Special Shapes" events, when balloons in shapes ranging from beer bottles to dumptrucks, and dragons to donuts, take to the air. Volunteers are always welcomed to help set the things up, and may be rewarded with a quick flight. For a full festival program, contact ☏1-888/422-7277, ⊛www .balloonfiesta.com.

Companies running hot-air balloon flights year round, from around $160 per person, include Rainbow Ryders (☏505/823-1111 or 1-800/725-2477, ⊛www .rainbowryders.com), and World Balloon (☏505/293-6800 or 1-800/351-9588, ⊛www.worldballoon.com).

The Alvarado Transportation Center is also the hub of the ABQ Ride **city bus** network (☏505/843-9200, ⊛www.cabq.gov/transit). Its free D-Ride route circles downtown, while commuter buses further afield cost $1 a ride.

Pick up **information** on Albuquerque from the Indian Pueblo Cultural Center (see p.189), or the **kiosks** in the Plaza Don Luis on Romero NW in Old Town (daily: April–Oct 9am–5pm; Nov–March 9.30am–4.30pm), and at the airport (daily 9.30am–8pm).

Accommodation

The twenty-mile length of **Central Avenue**, the old Route 66, is lined with the flashing neon signs of $40-per-night **motels**. Try to have a good look in daylight, to spot those that may turn scary at night. You'll have to pay a little extra to stay in the heart of **Old Town** – which holds few accommodation options – or downtown. Larger convention **hotels** are congregated along the interstates and near the airport – look out for discount coupons in New Mexico's welcome centers – while **B&Bs** are scattered across the city.

Albuquerque Marriott Pyramid North 5151 San Francisco Rd NE ☏505/821-3333 or 1-800/262-2043, ⊛www.marriott.com. Gigantic pyramid (stepped not smooth) near exit 232 off I-25 north of town, with a waterfall in the lobby, three restaurants, a fitness center, and over three hundred large rooms, geared especially toward business travelers. **❼**

Ambassador Inn 7407 Central Ave NE ☏505/265-1161. There's nothing fancy or exciting about the *Ambassador*, and it's well to the east of the liveliest part of Central Ave, but for a clean, presentable, ordinary motel room, the price is great. **❷**

Andaluz 125 Second St NW ☏505/242-9090 or 1-800/777-5732, ⊛www.hotelandaluz.com. As *La Posada de Albuquerque*, this historic, elegant hotel, built in Mexican style by Conrad Hilton in 1939, has long been downtown's most appealing upscale option. When this book went to press, it had yet to reopen following a major re-vamp, but the new owners promised it would retain its beautiful wood-paneled lobby, and top-class restaurant and bar. ⑥

Best Western Innsuites Hotel 2400 Yale Blvd SE ℡505/242-7022 or 1-800/780-7234, ⓦwww .bestwestern.com. Pleasant courtyard motel, quieter than you might expect from its location so close to the airport, and offering a free airport shuttle. ⑤

Casas de Sueños 310 Rio Grande Blvd SW ℡505/247-4560 or 1-800/665-7002, ⓦwww .casasdesuenos.com. Beautifully furnished, exotic, and friendly B&B, very close to Old Town, with themed adobe *casitas* (cottages) and smaller rooms. ⑤

Comfort Inn – Airport 2300 Yale Blvd SE ℡505/243-2244 or 1-800/221-2222, ⓦwww .comfortinn.com. Good-value motel, served by free shuttles from the airport across the road, and offering complimentary breakfasts. ④

Hilton Albuquerque 1901 University Blvd NE ℡505/884-2500 or 1-800/445-7667, ⓦwww .hilton.com. Midtown high-rise near the intersection of I-40 and I-25. Good rooms, three restaurants, and several busy bars. ⑥

La Quinta Inn Albuquerque Airport 2116 Yale Blvd SE ℡505/243-5500 or 1-800/531-5900, ⓦwww.lq.com. Large, upscale motel, served by frequent shuttles from the nearby airport, and offering safe, good-value accommodation. ④

Monterey Nonsmokers Motel 2402 Central Ave SW ℡505/243-3554 or 1-877/666-8379, ⓦwww.nonsmokersmotel.com. Clean, fifteen-room motel, two blocks west of Old Town, with pool, laundry, and a strict nonsmoking policy. ②

Old Town Bed and Breakfast 707 17th St NW ℡505/764-9144 or 1-888/900-9144, ⓦwww .inn-new-mexico.com. Friendly, very small-scale B&B in mock-adobe home a couple of blocks from the heart of Old Town. Both guestrooms have private bathrooms, though one is a more extensive suite. ④–⑤

Route 66 Hostel 1012 Central Ave SW ℡505/247-1813, ⓦwww.rt66hostel.com. Albuquerque's only hostel, a friendly place between Old Town and downtown, offers dorm beds for $17, kitchen facilities, and very plain but bargain-priced private doubles. Office hours daily 7.30–10.30am & 4–11pm. ①

The City

Albuquerque consists of several distinct districts, interspersed between anonymous residential areas and threaded through by the twenty-mile artery of **Central Avenue**, the most authentic surviving remnant of the classic Route 66, alive with flashing neon. **Old Town** remains the most interesting area for visitors, with **downtown** two miles to the east and the **university district** and the fashionable **Nob Hill** area beyond that. Further east, the **Sandia Mountains** finally call a halt to the Sunbelt sprawl. The city has instead pushed west of the Rio Grande, where only **Petroglyph National Monument** holds any interest for tourists.

Old Town

Albuquerque's tree-filled **Old Town Plaza** may lack the cachet of its counter-part in Santa Fe, but makes an appealing focus for the old Spanish settlement. Adobe buildings on all four sides have been restored as souvenir stores and tourist restaurants, with crafts sellers congregating under the porticos on the eastern side. The whole ensemble is still presided over by the twin-towered facade of **San Felipe de Neri church** to the north.

To get a sense of the city's past, spend an hour or two at the **Albuquerque Museum of Art and History**, a couple of blocks northeast of the plaza at 2000 Mountain Rd (daily except Mon 9am–5pm; $4, free Sun 9am–1pm; ⓦwww.cabq .gov/museum). As well as an impressive array of the armor and weaponry carried by the Spanish conquistadors – though the paucity of local finds means that the exhibits are drawn from sixteenth-century Europe rather than New Mexico – it holds delicate religious artifacts, plus paintings and photos showing Albuquerque through the centuries. There's a lot on the history of weaving along the Rio Grande; Coronado brought five thousand sheep on his expedition here in 1542, so the region has the longest tradition of sheep-rearing of anywhere in the US.

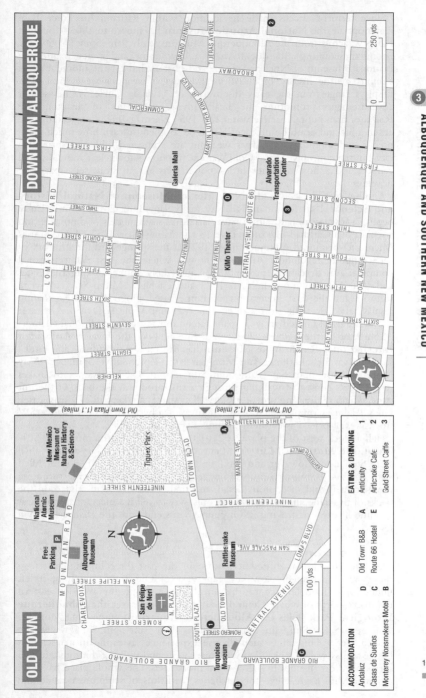

DOWNTOWN ALBUQUERQUE

GRAND AVENUE
TIJERAS AVENUE
BROADWAY
COMMERCIAL
MARTIN LUTHER KING JR BLVD

Galeria Mall

FIRST STREET
SECOND STREET
THIRD STREET
FOURTH STREET
FIFTH STREET
SIXTH STREET
SEVENTH STREET
EIGHTH STREET
KELEHER

LOMAS BOULEVARD

ROMA AVENUE
MARQUETTE AVENUE
TIJERAS AVENUE
COPPER AVENUE

KiMo Theater

CENTRAL AVENUE (ROUTE 66)

Alvarado
Transportation
Center

GOLD AVENUE
SILVER AVENUE
LEAD AVENUE
COAL AVENUE

FIRST STREET
SECOND STREET
THIRD STREET
FOURTH STREET
FIFTH STREET
SIXTH STREET

D
E
3

0   250 yds

N

Old Town Plaza (1.1 miles) ▲   Old Town Plaza (1.2 miles) ▲

OLD TOWN

New Mexico Museum of Natural History & Science

National Atomic Museum

Free Parking P

Albuquerque Museum

Tiguex Park

MOUNTAIN ROAD
CHARLEVOIX
SAN FELIPE STREET
NINETEENTH STREET
OLD TOWN ROAD
SEVENTEENTH STREET
MARBLE AVE.
EIGHTEENTH ST.

ROMERO STREET
N. PLAZA
San Felipe de Neri
SOUTH PLAZA
OLD TOWN
ROMERO STREET

Turquoise Museum

RIO GRANDE BOULEVARD

Rattlesnake Museum

SAN PASCALE AVE.
LOMA S BLVD

CENTRAL AVENUE

N

0   100 yds

i

1
A
C
G
B

ACCOMMODATION

Andaluz
Casas de Sueños   C
Monterey Nonsmokers Motel B

Old Town B&B   D
Route 66 Hostel   C

EATING & DRINKING

Anticuity   1
Articnoke Café   2
Gold Street Caffe   3

A
E

Since terrorist attacks made its location within Kirtland Air Force Base inappropriate, the **National Atomic Museum** has moved to 1905 Mountain Rd NW, across from the Albuquerque Museum (daily 9am–5pm; $6; @www .atomicmuseum.org). It's due to have a new home and a new name, the National Museum of Nuclear Science and History, but for the moment all its exhibits on the history of radiation and nuclear weapons are behind glass. Displays range from the early discoveries of Madame Curie, via newspaper advertisements promoting the health-giving properties of drinking the Radithor brand of radioactive water, to a 1953 *Life* magazine cover reading "we are in a life and death bomb race." You'll be soothed to learn how much more precise and sophisticated today's weapons are compared with the "primitive city-busting concepts" of the Cold War era, just how safe nuclear waste disposal can be, and a host of other little-known facts. A gift store sells space-age novelties.

Another two blocks east, the **New Mexico Museum of Natural History and Science**, 1801 Mountain Rd NW (daily 9am–5pm; closed Mon in Jan & Sept; $7; @www.nmnaturalhistory.org), has full-scale models of dinosaurs, and a replica of a Carlsbad-like snow cave. Its fascinating "Start Up" exhibition uses Microsoft's origins in Albuquerque in 1977 as the springboard for a history of the computer revolution. Albuquerque was where the first Altair personal computer was developed, prompting an incredibly young-looking Bill Gates and Paul Allen to move here in 1977 and establish "Micro-Soft" to write software for the first generation of home-based programmers. Fascinating displays also cover the stories of the internet and Apple. A Dynamax theater shows the usual limited array of giant-screen movies for an additional charge.

Southeast of the plaza at 202 San Felipe St NW, the bizarre **American International Rattlesnake Museum** has live rattlers on display and rattlesnake curios for sale (June–Aug Mon–Sat 10am–6pm, Sun 1–5pm; Sept–May Mon–Fri noon–6pm, Sat 10am–6pm, Sun 1–5pm; $3.50; @www.rattlesnakes .com). Visits consist of walking through a small room at the back of the gift store, where spiders and scorpions as well as snakes are kept in tiny glass cases. Gus's Trading Company, across the highway nearby at 2026 Central Ave SW, stocks a well-priced assortment of Indian crafts and jewelry.

Half a block west of the plaza, at 2107 Central Ave NW, the intriguing little **Turquoise Museum** (Mon–Sat 10am–4pm; $4) looks like just another mall store. Step inside, however, and you'll find you've entered a fortified vault, filled with rare and beautiful turquoise nuggets. The story of worldwide turquoise production is told in copious detail, and there's lots of useful advice on the tricks of the trade; unfortunately, the only way to tell if a piece of turquoise is genuine involves destroying it. Of course, visits end with the chance to buy a few trinkets.

The riverfront

The Rio Grande has shifted its course in the past three hundred years, so there's an unexpectedly low-key gap **west** of Old Town, much of it left undeveloped in deference to the unruly river. Along the wooded eastern riverbank, north of where Central Avenue crosses the river, the **Albuquerque Biological Park** holds the **Albuquerque Aquarium** (June–Aug Mon–Fri 9am–5pm, Sat & Sun 9am–6pm; Sept–May daily 9am–5pm; $7; @www.cabq .gov/biopark). This offers such diverse experiences as eating in a restaurant beside a glass-walled tank filled with live sharks, and walking through a tunnel surrounded on all sides by fierce-eyed moray eels. The whole place has been designed with a great eye for aesthetics, with lots of sculpture outside and beautifully lit tanks filled with ethereal, wispy jellyfish within. Across the central plaza, the **Rio Grande Botanic Garden** (same hours, same ticket) consists of two large conservatories – one holding rare plants from the Sonoran and Chihuahua deserts, the other more temperate Mediterranean species plus a series of formal walled gardens. Disappointingly, the river itself is not visible from either section.

Two miles north of Old Town, by way of Rio Grande Boulevard, the **Rio Grande Nature Center** (daily 8am–5pm; $3 per vehicle; ⓦ www.rgnc.org) has informative displays describing local wildlife. Two short but pleasant nature trails follow the riverside, feeling far removed from the city.

Indian Pueblo Cultural Center

The **Indian Pueblo Cultural Center**, at 2401 12th St NW, across I-40 a few blocks north of Old Town (ⓣ 505/843-7270, ⓦ www.indianpueblo.org), is a highly informative **museum** (daily 9am–4.30pm; $8) and **crafts market** (daily 9am–5.30pm; free), collectively run by the nineteen New Mexican pueblos. Its horseshoe-shaped design deliberately echoes the architecture of the Ancestral Puebloan city of Pueblo Bonito, in Chaco Canyon.

This is New Mexico's one major museum about Native Americans to be curated by Native Americans, and the displays downstairs have a clear and distinct point of view. The shared heritage at the root of Pueblo culture is explained in detail, as is the impact of the Spanish conquistadors. Describing the Pueblo Revolt of 1680 as the "first civil war," it states that by allowing the defeated Spaniards to leave unharmed, the Pueblo peoples "showed them more mercy than they showed us." There's also as good an explanation as you're ever likely to get of a topic Pueblo Indians rarely discuss with outsiders; how indigenous Pueblo religion has managed to coexist with imported Catholicism. Videos illustrate modern Pueblo life, while a separate display case is devoted to each individual Pueblo.

An outstanding selection of pottery and jewelry is sold in the stores upstairs, which you can visit without paying the museum admission fee. A separate **art gallery** hosts changing exhibitions of Native American art. The good-quality *Pueblo Harvest* café on site is reviewed on p.191. On weekends throughout the year, **Pueblo dances** take place in the central courtyard.

The National Hispanic Cultural Center

A mile south of Old Town, still on the east side of the river, the Barelas neighborhood traditionally marked the point where the Camino Real trail from Mexico entered Albuquerque. Whether you choose to visit the impressive **National Hispanic Cultural Center**, at 1701 Fourth St, is likely to depend on what's on in its spacious **art gallery** (daily except Mon 10am–5pm; $3; ⓦ www.nhccnm .org). Stimulating temporary exhibitions complement permanent displays that focus on "Hispanidad," with lots of New Mexican religious iconography. A good **café**, *La Fonda del Basque*, serves breakfast and lunch daily.

Downtown

Downtown Albuquerque may be where New Mexico's largest city conducts its daily business, but it holds little that's likely to detain tourists for long; unless you're staying in a hotel nearby, you may bypass it altogether.

The University District

A couple of miles east of downtown, the campus of the **University of New Mexico** stretches along the northern side of Central Avenue. The 25,000-strong student body keeps the southern side of the highway lively around the clock with funky hangouts of all kinds, from bookstores and laundromats to cafés and diners.

Of the six museums on campus, non-academic visitors are most likely to enjoy the **Maxwell Museum of Anthropology** (Tues–Fri 9am–4pm, Sat 10am–4pm; free; ⓦwww.unm.edu/~maxwell), which documents the peoples of the Southwest, past and present. There's some fine Mimbres pottery (see p.216), as well as material from Chaco Canyon, while the Ancestors segment traces human evolution from the three-million-year-old Lucy, just 3ft 7in tall, unearthed in Ethiopia.

The Sandia Mountains

The forested **Sandia Mountains** tower 10,500ft over Albuquerque to the east; views from the summit are especially beautiful at and after sunset, when the city lights sparkle below. In summer it's a good 25°F cooler up here than in the valley, while in winter you can go downhill or cross-country **skiing** (mid-Dec to mid-March; lift tickets $48; ☎505/242-9052, ⓦwww.sandiapeak.com).

The most exciting way to reach the top is by riding the world's longest tramway, the 2.7-mile **Sandia Peak Tramway**, which departs from the end of Tramway Road a dozen miles northeast of town. During the uppermost 1.5 miles of its exhilarating 15-minute climb, not a single support tower interrupts the progress of the cable car (summer daily 9am–9pm; winter Mon & Wed–Sun 9am–8pm, Tues 5–8pm; $17.50).

If you'd rather **drive** to the top of the mountains, you have to circle around the back on I-40, then approach from the east, by way of the Turquoise Trail – a route described on p.141.

Petroglyph National Monument

Beneath a chain of burned-out cinder cones thrown up by a 150,000-year-old volcanic eruption, a low seventeen-mile escarpment west of the Rio Grande, protected as the **PETROGLYPH NATIONAL MONUMENT**, holds some unusually accessible ancient Native American **rock art**. Apart from the spectacular views of the valley and mountains, there's no need to go to its **Las Imágenes visitor center** (daily 8am–5pm; ☎505/899-0205, ⓦwww.nps .gov/petr), reached by crossing the river on I-40 then driving four miles north on Unser Boulevard. Instead, continue to the petroglyphs themselves, another mile north in **Boca Negra Canyon** (same hours; Mon–Fri $1 per vehicle, Sat & Sun $2).

Three short trails off the canyon's one-way loop road lead up to the escarpment, which on close inspection turns out to consist of tumbled black lava boulders; only the half-hour **Mesa Trail** demands any energetic climbing. Most of the crudely scratched images you'll pass, ranging from simple spirals to masked figures and eagles with Bart Simpson hairdos, date from 1300 to 1680 AD. During the eighteenth century, shepherds from the nearby Hispanic settlement of Atrisco added a number of Christian crosses and symbols.

Petroglyph National Monument has for many years been the focus of intense controversy, because city boosters see it as a major obstacle to any future westward expansion of Albuquerque. Despite opposition from the nineteen New Mexican pueblos as well as local activists, the Paseo del Norte road was indeed extended onto monument land in 2007.

Eating

The chefs of Santa Fe may be trying to redefine Southwestern cuisine, but Albuquerque still knows what it likes – mountainous **Mexican** meals. This is the place to come to grips with what real New Mexican food is all about, with family diners all over the city competing to create the spiciest *chile rellenos*, enchiladas, and *sopaipillas*. If you don't mind driving a few miles out of town, fine dining options within easy reach of Albuquerque include the *Range Cafe* in Bernalillo (see p.138) and *Prairie Star* at nearby Santa Ana Pueblo (see p.148).

Coffeehouses

Gold Street Caffe 218 Gold Ave SW ℡505/765-1633. Oddly formal downtown espresso café, where you have to Wait To Be Seated – but it's worth it, for great coffee, wonderful pastries, and full breakfasts. Mon–Fri 7am–2pm, Sat & Sun 8am–2pm.

Satellite Coffee 3513 Central Ave NE ℡505/256-0345. University District coffee bar, marked by the sign of the flying saucer, which also serves daily specials like split pea soup. Branches all over the city. Daily 6am–8pm.

Budget restaurants and diners

Duran Central Pharmacy 1815 Central Ave NW ℡505/247-4141. Mexican dining counter attached to a working drugstore, not far from Old Town, with delicious, inexpensive tortillas, enchiladas, and plenty of chile, both green and red. Mon–Fri 9am–6.30pm, Sat 9am–2pm.

Flying Star 3416 Central Ave SE ℡505/255-6633. Lively, crowded University District café serving eclectic international cuisine to a largely student clientele. The vast menu ranges through breakfast specialties, salads, and blue-plate specials such as Vietnamese noodles or pasta pomodoro for $10.

Other branches throughout the city. Sun–Thurs 6am–11pm, Fri & Sat 6am–midnight.

Frontier 2400 Central Ave SE ℡505/266-0550. Legendary diner across from the university, where an unceasing parade of characters chow down on burgers, burritos, and great vegetarian enchiladas. Formerly open 24hr, it now closes between 5am & 8am.

Pueblo Harvest Cafe Indian Pueblo Cultural Center, 2401 12th St NW ℡505/843-7270. While still serving Pueblo specialties like Indian fry-bread at lunchtime, this unusual Native American restaurant now stays open for fine dining in the evening, with braised bison ribs among its good $20–30 entrees. Mon–Thurs 8am–9pm, Fri & Sat 8am–10pm, Sun 8am–4pm.

Sadie's 6230 Fourth St NW ℡505/345-5339, Ⓦwww.sadiessalsa.com. Huge, great value Mexican restaurant – the stuffed *sopaipillas* are irresistible, as indeed are the margaritas. It's too bright and loud, with giant TV screens, to be romantic, but it's a good place to bring kids. Mon–Sat 10am–10pm, Sun 10am–9pm.

66 Diner 1405 Central Ave NE ℡505/247-1421, Ⓦwww.66diner.com. Classic Fifties diner near the university, with white-capped waiting staff, a soda fountain, and a lively late-night clientele.

▲ The KiMo Theater, Albuquerque

Mon–Fri 11am–11pm, Sat 8am–11pm, Sun 8am–10pm.

Fine dining

Antiquity 112 Romero St NW ☏505/247-3545. Old Town cottage turned romantic restaurant, serving French cuisine, some of it given a New Mexican twist by a leavening of chile. Entrees typically cost $18–27. Dinner only, nightly from 5pm.
Artichoke Café 424 Central Ave SE ☏505/243-0200, ⓦwww.artichokecafe.com. Simple but classy restaurant in the heart of downtown, serving a good, varied menu of California-influenced modern American cuisine; typical entrees cost $18–30. Mon 11am–2.30pm & 5.30–9pm, Tues–Fri 11am–2.30pm & 5.30–10pm, Sat 5.30–10pm, Sun 5.30–9pm.

High Finance 40 Tramway Rd NE ☏505/243-9742. Pricey seafood and steak restaurant in unparalleled location, at the top of the Sandia Peak Tramway – see p.190 – with eagle's-eye views of the sunset over Albuquerque. Daily: summer 11am–9pm; winter 11am–8pm.
Scalo 3500 Central Ave SE ☏505/255-8781. Large but romantic and stylish Northern Italian restaurant near the university. Appetizers like steamed mussels or beef carpaccio cost $10, entrees such as roasted salmon are more like $25, and there are plenty of pasta and vegetarian options. Thurs 11am–2pm & 5–10pm, Fri & Sat 11am–2pm & 5–11pm, Sun 11am–2pm & 5–9pm.

Drinking and nightlife

Many of downtown Albuquerque's **bars** and **nightclubs** have long doubled as small theaters or music venues. Sadly a disastrous fire in 2008 saw *Puccini's Golden West Saloon* destroyed and other clubs severely damaged, but the spectacularly restored KiMo Theater should not be missed. The free weekly *Alibi* magazine (ⓦwww.alibi.com) carries full listings of what's coming up or going down.

The Anodyne 409 Central Ave NW ☏505/244-1820. Downtown's most popular bar offers pool tables, pinball, a good jukebox, and an eclectic mix of customers, from beer guzzlers to martini sippers.
Brewster's Pub 312 Central Ave SW ☏505/247-2533. Raucous downtown bar, where on any night except Monday – reserved for football – you've a good chance of hearing live jazz, Latin, or blues.
Burt's Tiki Lounge 313 Gold Ave SW ☏505/247-2878, ⓦwww.burtstikilounge.com. Tuesday is the big tiki-bar cocktail night here, though the Polynesian decor makes a good backdrop for live bands for the rest of the week. Mon–Sat 8pm–2am.
Caravan East 7605 Central Ave NE ☏505/265-7877, ⓦwww.caravaneast.com. Enormous honkytonk, where tenderfeet can do the two-step with throngs of urban cowboys. Live bands play Thurs–Sat. Tues–Sat 4.30pm–2am.
El Rey Theater 620 Central Ave SW ☏505/242-2353, ⓦwww.elreytheater.com. Live music from salsa to country, and all points in between.

Exhale 6132 Fourth St NW ☏505/342-0049, ⓦwww.exhaleabq.com.Albuquerque's top lesbian bar is also very welcoming to gay men, and boasts one of the city's largest dancefloors. Closed Mon & Tues.
KiMo Theater 423 Central Ave NW ☏505/768-3522, ⓦwww.cabq.gov/kimo. Gorgeous, city-owned "Pueblo Deco" theater, dating from the late 1920s, which puts on an eclectic program of opera, dance, and theater performances, kids' movies, and also regular live bands.
The Launchpad 618 Central Ave SW ☏505/764-8887, ⓦwww.launchpadrocks.com. Dance and live music space that showcases touring indie and world music bands; there's also a cluster of pool tables.
Midnight Rodeo 4901 McLeod Rd NE ☏505/888-0100. Huge country-music club – the largest in the Southwest – with a great old-fashioned race-track dancefloor, though all the music comes from DJs rather than live bands. Wed–Sat 8pm–2am. Cover $8, Fri & Sat only.

East of Albuquerque

The first twenty miles of I-40's eastward run from Albuquerque are scenic, as the interstate threads between the Sandia Mountains. Once through the hills, however, if you don't turn north onto the **Turquoise Trail** toward Santa Fe – see p.140 – you're in for a long hard slog out into the plains. The only place before Texas that might pique your curiosity is **Fort Sumner**, which played a heart-rending role in Navajo history and also holds the grave of **Billy the Kid**.

Santa Rosa

A hundred unutterably boring miles east of the Sandia Mountains, weary drivers reach their first potential overnight stop. South and west of the interstate, a four-mile stretch of the former Route 66 runs through **SANTA ROSA**. At **Parker Avenue** in the small downtown, and **Will Rogers Drive** further east, it's dotted with diners and motels, but there's little to see, apart perhaps from the restored classic cars at the **Route 66 Auto Museum**, 2866 Route 66 (daily: April–Oct Mon–Sat 7.30am–6pm, Sun 10am–5pm; Sept–April Mon–Sat 8am–5pm, Sun 10am–5pm; $5; ⓦ www.route66automuseum.com).

Scuba-divers desperate for a dip cross the plains to plunge into Santa Rosa's **Blue Hole**, a crystal-clear natural pool that's sixty feet across and eighty feet deep, though to anyone who's seen the ocean it may come as an anti-climax. You'll find it by turning left off Fifth Street, south of the main drag, onto Blue Hole Road.

Practicalities

Santa Rosa's **visitor center** is at 244 S Fourth St (Mon–Fri 8am–5pm; ⓣ 505/472-3763, ⓦ www.santarosanm.org). Its dozen or so **motels** include a reasonable *Super 8*, 1201 Historic Rte 66 (ⓣ 505/472-5388, ⓦ www.super8 .com; ❸), and the more upscale *Best Western Adobe Inn*, 1501 Historic Rte 66 (ⓣ 505/472-3446 or 1-800/780-7234; ❹). The *Lake City Diner*, downtown at 101 Fourth St (ⓣ 505/472-5253; closed Sun), is a spotless, good-value, dinner-only "Nuevo Mexicano" **restaurant**, housed in a converted bank and straight out of a Norman Rockwell painting.

Tucumcari

Sixty miles east of Santa Rosa, **TUCUMCARI** is the definitive Route 66 pit-stop. If you expect its abundant truck stops, diners, and motels to yield a kitsch fascination, you'll be sorely disappointed, but their glittering neon signs make a welcome sight as dusk descends on the plains. No one in their right mind stays two nights in Tucumcari; an hour spent admiring the barbed-wire collection of the **Tucumcari Historical Museum**, 416 S Adams St (Mon–Sat 8am–5pm; $2.50), should convince you it's time to hit the road again.

Practicalities

Route 66, also known as Tucumcari Boulevard, cuts a broad five-mile swath through town, passing 34 motels along the way, as well as the **visitor center** at 404 W (Mon–Fri 9am–5pm; ⓣ 505/461-1694, ⓦ www.tucumcarinm.com). Among the more salubrious places with **rooms** for around $50 or less is the classic Route 66 *Blue Swallow* motel, 815 E Route 66 (ⓣ 505/461-9849, ⓦ www.blueswallowmotel.com; ❸). Slightly more upscale options include the *Best Western Discovery Inn*, 200 E Estrella Ave (ⓣ 505/461-4884 or 1-800/780-7234; ❹). **Dining** choices are plentiful yet limited; *Del's Family Restaurant*, 1202 E Route 66 (ⓣ 505/461-1740; closed Sun), is as good a diner as you're going to find.

Fort Sumner

A 45-mile detour south of I-40 near Santa Rosa brings you to modern **FORT SUMNER**, a small town named after a nineteenth-century Army outpost that stood seven miles southeast, on what's now **Fort Sumner State Monument** (daily 8.30am–5pm; $5; ⓦwww.nmmonuments.org). The fort was infamous as the headquarters of the **Bosque Redondo Indian reservation**, where nine thousand Navajo and Mescalero Apache captives were incarcerated during the 1860s after being rounded up by General James Carleton and Kit Carson and forced here on the Long Walk (see p.517). The idea was for the reservation to be self-sufficient and for the Indians to become accustomed to an agricultural lifestyle. In fact, the Pecos River proved too salty to drink, let alone use for irrigation. In the words of Navajo headman Barboncito:

Whatever we do here causes death. Some work at the *acequias*, take sick, and die; others die with the hoe in their hands; they go to the river to their waists and suddenly disappear; others have been struck and torn to pieces by lightning.
A rattlesnake bite here kills us; in our country a rattlesnake before he bites gives warning which enables us to keep out of its way and if bitten, we readily find a cure – here we can find no cure.

The Mescalero escaped in November 1865, only to be chased by Carson and suffer further slaughter. The Navajo remained until General William T Sherman arrived to replace Carleton on May 28, 1868; the treaty that allowed them to return home was signed on June 1. Over three thousand prisoners had died.

Only a low ridge of adobe bricks on the eastern riverbank remains of the fort the Navajo built for their captors, but the dead are honored by a large visitor center-cum-museum. The **Bosque Redondo Memorial** details the whole sorry story, including photos of soldiers guarding large groups of Native American captives.

After the reservation closed, rancher Lucien Maxwell bought the fort and surrounding land. **Billy the Kid** was hiding in his son Peter's bedroom here in 1881 when **Pat Garrett** tracked him down and shot him dead. His **grave** is located in the backyard of the **Old Fort Sumner Museum**, a few hundred yards east of the fort (daily 9am–5pm; $3.50). Billy was buried alongside two fellow outlaws, Tom O'Folliard and Charlie Bowdre; all remain imprisoned to this day, as their joint tombstone, poignantly inscribed "*PALS*," is protected from would-be thieves behind steel bars. Originally erected by film director King Vidor, the tombstone was stolen so often that participants in an annual festival, held on the second weekend of June, now compete to "steal" an eighty-pound replica, and then throw it as far as possible.

The museum itself holds jumbled items that may or may not have belonged to Billy, plus displays relating to local history, as does the rival **Billy the Kid Museum**, back in town at 1601 E Sumner Ave (mid-May to mid-Sept daily 8.30am–5pm; mid-Sept to mid-May Mon–Fri 8.30am–5pm, Sun 11am–5pm; $4). The latter museum, however, is vast, with endless warehouses full of old cars, wagons, typewriters, and other rusty hardware. For the full saga of Billy the Kid, see p.196.

Practicalities

While there's no earthly reason to choose to spend a night in Fort Sumner, were you to be trapped by a desert thunderstorm, you could shelter in one of its unexciting **motels**, such as the *Coronado*, 309 W Sumner Ave (☏505/355-2466; ❶), or the *Super 8*, 1599 E Sumner Ave (☏505/355-7888, ⓦwww .super8.com; ❷). Later on, you'd probably end up eating a cheap Mexican **meal** at *Sadie's*, 1112 E Sumner Ave (☏505/355-1461).

Southeast of Albuquerque

Although the Rio Grande Valley, south of Albuquerque – and covered on p.208 onwards – has always held a larger human population, the terrain **southeast** of the city offers greater scenic and historic appeal. Here you'll find the ancient pueblos of **Salinas National Monument**, the eerie gypsum wastelands of **White Sands**, and the mountain resorts of **Ruidoso** and **Cloudcroft**. Most compelling of all, however, is the rough-hewn frontier town of **Lincoln**. Scene of the bloodiest exploits in the career of **Billy the Kid**, it has remained all but untouched since his death.

Salinas National Monument

Early Spanish colonists ranked the precious salt deposits of **Salinas Valley**, east of the Manzano Mountains seventy miles southeast of Albuquerque, among New Mexico's greatest treasures. Franciscan missionaries targeted the Pueblo peoples of the valley, erecting massive churches atop their existing settlements, but due to epidemics and Apache raids, the entire region had been abandoned before the Pueblo Revolt of 1680. Three separate ruined pueblos now form **SALINAS NATIONAL MONUMENT**. Each has its own "contact station" (daily: summer 9am–6pm; winter 9am–5pm; free), and they share a **visitor center** (daily 8am–5pm; free; ☎505/847-2585, ⓦwww.nps.gov/sapu) in little **MOUNTAINAIR**, 36 miles east of I-25 on US-60.

Only at the largest Salinas pueblo, **Gran Quivira**, on a low hill 26 miles south from Mountainair along Hwy-55, has the pueblo itself been more than minimally excavated. That process has revealed an impressive 300-room structure complete with hidden *kivas*, built in secret to avoid the wrath of the Spanish priests. The adjoining Mission of San Buenaventura church probably remained incomplete when the pueblo was abandoned. Juan de Oñate, who visited Gran Quivira in 1598, reported that its inhabitants painted stripes on their noses.

The main feature of **Quarai**, a mile west of Hwy-55 eight miles north of Mountainair, is the fortress-like stone church of La Purísima Concepción, whose golden walls tower above the rubble-strewn mounds that conceal the pueblo village. At **Abó**, just north of US-60 nine miles west of Mountainair, the church of San Gregorio dominates an even more tantalizing expanse of ruins.

Carrizozo and the Valley of Fires

Fifty miles southeast of Gran Quivira, where US-54 meets US-380, the parched desert outpost of **CARRIZOZO** replaced better-known Lincoln as the seat of Lincoln County in 1909. There's nothing much to it, apart from the *Outpost Bar & Grill*, a rather gloomy saloon at 415 Central Ave (☎505/648-9994) that's renowned for its green chile burgers, and *Carrizozo Joe's*, 133 Central Ave (☎505/648-5637), a friendly espresso café.

The **Valley of Fires Recreation Area**, four miles northwest (daily dawn–dusk; $3, or $5 per vehicle; ☎505/648-2241), preserves a jet-black river of lava that poured for over forty miles down the Tularosa Valley 5000 years ago. Though it ranges from four to six miles wide and up to 150 feet deep, the one trail across the lava is less than a mile long. It's so rough underfoot, and so exposed to the sun, that you're unlikely to want to hike any further, but there's a good **campground** alongside ($12). At its southern end, the lava flow abuts the utterly contrasting White Sands National Monument; see p.202.

Capitan

A twenty-mile drive up into the mountains east of Carrizozo brings you to the crossroads known as **CAPITAN**, notable only as the birthplace of a little bear named **Smokey**. Rescued from a forest fire in 1950, the five-month-old Smokey was taken to the National Zoo in Washington DC, where he survived another 26 years and became a national fire prevention symbol. His words of wisdom, seen on anti-fire billboards across the country – "Only YOU Can Prevent Forest Fires" – live on. Smokey's grave is the centerpiece of **Smokey Bear Historical State Park**, which also features exhibits on his life and a short nature trail (daily 9am–5pm; $2; ⓦ www.smokeybearpark .com). Capitan is plagued, incidentally, by a running feud between people who say "Smokey Bear" (good) and willful misfits who insist on "Smokey *the* Bear" (bad).

The *Smokey Bear Restaurant and Motel*, 316 Smokey Bear Blvd (ⓣ 505/354-2253 or 1-800/766-5392, ⓦ www.smokeybearmotel.com; ③) offers simple but appealing cabin-style **rooms** and dining near the park.

Billy the Kid and the Lincoln County War

The Hispanic farming community of Las Placitas del Río Bonito, founded during the 1850s, was renamed **Lincoln** in 1869. It became the seat of **Lincoln County**, which at 27,000 square miles was the largest county in the United States, occupying a quarter of New Mexico. Rival Anglo ranchers and their political allies were then competing for economic control throughout the Wild West. The **Western Civil War of Incorporation** pitted large cattle-raising conglomerates, federal lawmen, and Republican capitalists against small-scale Democrat ranchers and cowboys. Such tensions were everywhere exacerbated by individual antagonisms; Tombstone's **Gunfight at the OK Corral** is a classic example (see p.261).

Lincoln in the 1870s was dominated by a "ring" of men that centered on the mercantile, or store, of **Lawrence G. Murphy**, an Irish former theology student, Freemason, and alcoholic whose business affairs were run by **James J. Dolan**. Their racketeering included rustling cattle from rancher **John Chisum** to supply beef at knock-down prices to the US Army at nearby Fort Stanton. The arrival of a wealthy 23-year-old Englishman, **John Tunstall** (born in Dalston, east London, in 1853), who opened a rival mercantile in Lincoln with lawyer **Alexander McSween**, triggered the **Lincoln County War**.

On February 18, 1878, Tunstall was murdered on the road to Ruidoso by a posse of Dolan's men. Among Tunstall's hired hands who witnessed the slaying was the gunslinger **Billy the Kid**, born Henry McCarty in Brooklyn in 1859, Billy had been brought west by his mother, who married William Antrim in Santa Fe in 1873. Within a year she had died in Silver City, and young Billy Antrim was cast adrift. A life of petty teenage crime culminated with the shooting in 1877 of a bullying Irish blacksmith in Fort Grant, Arizona. As **Billy Bonney**, the fledgling outlaw fled to Lincoln.

After Tunstall's death, his men formed the **Regulators** and were deputized by the local justice of the peace to seek out his killers. Ten of them, including Billy, killed the two chief culprits in March, then gunned down **Sheriff William Brady**, a Dolan man, on Lincoln's main street on April 1. That July, forty of Dolan's supporters laid siege to the Regulators in the adobe home of Alexander McSween; after five days, they summoned soldiers from Fort Stanton, who trained a Gatling gun on the house and set it ablaze. McSween and three Regulators were killed trying to escape, but Billy and ten others sprinted to safety.

Lincoln

Though not strictly speaking a ghost town, tiny **LINCOLN**, twelve miles east of Capitan on Hwy-380, is a perfectly preserved Wild West settlement. During the late nineteenth century, around 750 people made their home in this cattle-ranching center and Army outpost of **Fort Stanton**, including the legendary outlaw Billy the Kid. Bypassed by the railroads, however, it soon dwindled, and time seems to have stood still ever since. No new buildings have joined the venerable false-front structures that line Main Street, and the entire town is now **Lincoln State Monument**. Visitors can stroll its length at any time, while the cheapest way to visit its various historical sites is via a joint admission ticket, sold at each (each site $3.50, joint admission to all sites $5; not all sites remain open throughout the winter; ☎505/653-4372, ⑩www.nmmonuments.org & ⑩www.hubbardmuseum.org).

The **Historic Lincoln Visitors Center** (daily 8.30am–5pm), at the east end of town, offers the fullest displays on local history, and its short opening video makes a good introduction to Lincoln's complicated story. After exhibits

Billy spent two years on the run, mostly rustling cattle near Fort Sumner, where he also dealt cards in the saloon of Texan buffalo hunter **Pat Garrett**. In 1880, New Mexico's governor **Lew Wallace** offered an amnesty to all participants in the Lincoln County War who would testify against Dolan. Billy accepted the deal and surrendered, only to escape when he realized that Wallace – then busy writing *Ben Hur* – was not going to keep his word. Later that year, Garrett was elected as sheriff of Lincoln County, on a pledge to recapture Billy (who naturally lobbied for his opponent). Garrett knew exactly where to look. Just before Christmas, after ambushing and killing two of Billy's friends at Fort Sumner, he duly captured Billy himself at nearby Stinking Springs. Reporting his arrest, the *Las Vegas Gazette* made the first-ever reference to "Billy the Kid."

Billy was taken by train to Santa Fe and on to **Mesilla**, where he was convicted of Sheriff Brady's murder. As he awaited the hangman's noose in Lincoln's courthouse – the former Murphy store, its owner James Dolan having by now taken over the Tunstall mercantile down the street – Billy pulled off his most daring **escape**. Taking advantage of a trip to the outhouse, on April 28, 1881, he shot Deputy J.W. Bell with his own gun. Meanwhile, Marshal Bob Olinger, a long-time Dolan ally, was having lunch with prisoners in the *Wortley Hotel*. Hearing the shots, he raced across the street, to be felled by a blast from an upper window. Billy then struggled unsuccessfully for an hour to break his shackles, repeatedly falling off the horse he was attempting to commandeer, watched all the while by a crowd who dared not intervene.

With a $500 reward on his head, Billy fled back to Fort Sumner. Late on the night of July 14, Garrett crept into the bedroom of rancher Pete Maxwell, whose family owned Fort Sumner, to ask if he had seen his friend Billy. Moments earlier, Billy had climbed through the window to find out if Maxwell knew Garrett's whereabouts. Garrett recognized the voice that called *"quien es?"* (who's there?), and shot Billy dead.

The next year, Garrett wrote a bestseller, *The Authentic Life of Billy The Kid, the Noted Desperado of the Southwest*. He was not re-elected as sheriff, however, and embarked on a life of wandering that saw him ranching in Texas, a guest of Theodore Roosevelt at the White House, and a customs collector in El Paso, before he was eventually murdered for no apparent reason near Las Cruces in 1908. Strangely enough, the man who shot him, William Brazel, was the uncle of the main "witness" of the Roswell UFO crash in 1947 (see p.204).

▲ Billy the Kid still haunts Lincoln's County Courthouse

covering Hispanics, cowboys, "Buffalo Soldiers" – the black cavalrymen stationed at Fort Stanton – and Apaches, the museum moves on to the Lincoln County War. Its account of Billy's life is extremely thorough, extending to the coroner's handwritten report on the men shot during his April 1881 escape; however, none of the artifacts definitely belonged to Billy himself.

Alongside the museum stands Lincoln's oldest building, the **Torréon**. While resembling the masonry of Ancestral Puebloans, this circular tower was erected by Hispanic settlers during the 1850s, as a refuge against Apache raids. It's too small to admit visitors; a glance from the street makes it easy to imagine quite how cramped it must have been and speaks volumes about the miserable, unglamorous reality of frontier life.

A few yards further west, the **Tunstall Store** is an extraordinary time capsule (March–Nov daily 9am–5pm). The "mercantile" over which the Lincoln County War was fought must have failed to sell a single item in the ensuing century. It remains stocked with dusty date-expired groceries, plus Victorian paraphernalia like weighing scales and cash registers, cases of photos and artifacts, and even Lincoln County's first-ever light bulb, installed in 1914 and allegedly still capable of burning. The wounded Billy the Kid hid beneath the floorboards after shooting Sheriff William Brady on the street outside, on April 1, 1878.

After Dolan took over Tunstall's operation, L.G. Murphy's original store, across the road and a hundred yards west, became the **Lincoln County Courthouse** and served as Billy's prison when he was brought back from Mesilla to be hanged (daily 8.30am–5pm). Billy felt he was being railroaded; his increasingly bitter letters to Governor Lew Wallace are displayed upstairs in the courtroom where his cell formerly stood. A bullethole at the foot of the stairs shows where he shot Deputy Bell during his famous escape. You can stand at the window through which he then shot Marshal Olinger. Stones in the garden mark where the two men died. That the courthouse is now so old and musty only adds to the atmosphere of it all.

Practicalities

Lincoln doesn't have its own visitor center; call the monument offices for general information. On the first weekend of August, its streets echo with gunfire once again during the three-day **Old Lincoln Days** festival which features living history demonstrations, fiddle competitions, and the like.

Near the courthouse, the *Wortley Hotel* – once owned by Pat Garrett – offers seven plain but appealing hotel rooms, furnished with functional Victorian antiques (April to mid-Oct only; ☎505/653-4300, ⓦwww.wortleyhotel .com; ❹). Its dining room serves simple stews and sandwiches at lunchtime only, including the pot roast and mashed potatoes that constituted Marshal Bob Olinger's final meal. The *Lincoln Grille*, a tiny shack close to the Torreón, serves simple lunchtime burgers and burritos (☎505/653-4805).

Ruidoso

For visitors from the flatlands of west Texas and Oklahoma – not to mention valley towns like Alamogordo – the hilltop community of **RUIDOSO**, nestling almost 7000 feet up in the forested Sacramento Mountains thirty miles southwest of Lincoln, offers an enticing retreat from the heat of summer. As a result, motels and mountain lodges line several miles of the Ruidoso ("Noisy") River. Tourists from further afield, however, may well feel it lacks interest, though it makes a reasonable overnight stop en route to Carlsbad.

Ruidoso's major claim to fame is the **All-American Futurity**, which was, until the 1980s, the world's richest **horse race** of any kind – and with prize money totaling around $2 million, it remains the highest-paying event for quarter horses. (Quarter horses, the world's most popular breed, are so-called because they excel at quarter-mile races.) The race takes place each Labor Day at the **Ruidoso Downs** racetrack, just east of town, as the climax of a 77-day season that runs from late May to early Sept (ⓦwww.ruidownsracing.com). Also at the track, the **Billy the Kid Casino** offers year-round slot-machine gambling.

Outside the **Hubbard Museum of the American West**, alongside the racetrack (daily 10am–5pm; $6; ☎505/378-4142, ⓦwww.hubbardmuseum .org), stands a sculpture ensemble of eight lifesize galloping horses, *Free Spirits* *of Noisy Water*. Inside, you'll find displays on all aspects of Western history, with a particular emphasis on horses. In winter, attention turns to the 12,000ft slopes of **Ski Apache** (T505/464-3600, Wwww.skiapache.com), a downhill ski area northwest of town where lift tickets cost around $54 per day. Though operated by the Mescalero Apache, it's not on tribal land.

Practicalities

Ruidoso's **visitor center** is at 720 Sudderth Ave (Mon–Sat 9am–5pm, Sun 1–4pm; Wwww.ruidoso.net), while **motels** include the inexpensive *Apache*, 344 Sudderth Ave (T505/257-2986 or 1-800/426-0616, Wwww.ruidoso.net/apache; ③). The glitzy *Inn of the Mountain Gods*, three miles southwest on Carrizo Canyon Road (T505/257-5141 or 1-888/324-0348, Wwww.innofthemountaingods.com; ⑤) is, like the ski resort, owned by the Mescalero Apache, and holds a lucrative casino as well as fine dining and luxury accommodation. Other eating possibilities range from the classy French cuisine of *Le Bistro*, 2800 Sudderth Drive (closed Sun; T505/257-0132), to the sandwiches and coffee at the *Ruidoso Roastery*, 113 Rio St (lunch only, closed Sun; T505/257-3576).

Mescalero Apache Indian reservation

Immediately south of Ruidoso, US-70 runs for around fifteen miles through the highlands of the **Mescalero Apache Indian reservation**. The Mescalero trace their history as a distinct Apache group back to the early eighteenth century, when they were driven from the plains by the Comanche and turned to a lifestyle split between farming and raiding Pueblo and Hispanic settlements. In 1862 Kit Carson rounded up 500 Apaches to be confined with the Navajo at Bosque Redondo (see p.194). The Apache were eventually granted this small reservation in 1873, which was too high to grow or gather many traditional foods. The Mescalero were later joined by other Apache refugees, such as those remnants of Geronimo's Chiricahua who chose to return to the Southwest in 1913 from their enforced exile in Oklahoma.

Thanks to their successful investments in Ski Apache and the *Inn of the Mountain Gods*, the Mescalero's tribal economy has greatly strengthened in recent years. Tourists don't see much from the highway, and most roads leading off it are barred to outsiders. It's well worth driving through the open-range country between Ruidoso and Cloudcroft, however, where wildflowers dot the quasi-Alpine meadows and Apache cowboys gallop in pursuit of their errant cattle.

Cloudcroft

Much smaller and cozier than Ruidoso, the picturesque mountain village of **CLOUDCROFT** – forty miles further south, and almost two thousand feet higher – has been a vacation resort from the word go. It was built in 1898, after a railroad spur was pushed up into the Sacramento Mountains to carry timber down to El Paso, and immediately attracted day-trippers escaping the sweltering valley below. The railroad is long gone, but drivers still twist their way up US-82 from Alamogordo, leaving behind the bare sandstone hills, scattered with creosote bushes, as they penetrate the forested uplands.

Cloudcroft itself is a pretty little Western community in which to while away an afternoon. The souvenir stores and cafés that line the boardwalk of **Burro Avenue**, one block north of the highway, get a bit more kitschy each year, so **hiking** makes an increasingly enjoyable alternative to shopping. Cloudcroft stands at the heart of the southern segment of the Lincoln National Forest, which features maintained and waymarked trails of varying lengths. Starting near the west end of town, the **Cloud Climbing Rail Trail** follows the old railroad route for a mile down to a vast ruined trestle that drivers on US-82 may have already noticed. Spectacular views extend right across the valley; it's usually possible to glimpse the White Sands (see p.202), as a thin white line at the foot of the San Andres Mountains on the far side.

Practicalities

Cloudcroft's **visitor center** is housed in a log cabin beside US-82 on the eastern approaches to town (Mon–Sat 10am–5pm; ☎505/682-2733 or 1-866/874-4447, ⓦwww.cloudcroft.net).

Most overnight visitors rent individual **cabins**; all cabins have heating and en-suite facilities, many also offer kitchenettes or extra bedrooms. *Buckhorn Cabins* (☎505/682-2421, ⓦwww.zianet.com/buckhorn; ③) is on the highway in the town center – and has a sideline in selling large carved wooden bears – while *Spruce Cabins* is tucked up in the hills further east (☎505/682-2381, ⓦwww.sprucecabins.com; ④). Six miles west of town, perched in the woods down towards Alamogordo, the blue-painted double-decker *Cloudcroft Mountain Park Hostel* (☎505/682-0555, ⓦwww.cloudcrofthostel.com; ①–②; cash only) is a smart motel-style **hostel** that offers dorm beds for $17 and private rooms for $30. The closest Lincoln National Forest **campground** to town, about a mile northeast of the center along Hwy-244, is *The Pines* (☎505/682-2551; mid-May to mid-Sept; $9).

South of the highway, a mile up Hwy-130, *The Lodge at Cloudcroft* (☎505/682-2566 or 1-800/395-6343, ⓦwww.thelodgeresort.com; ⑥) is a prestigious **historic hotel**. As well as well-priced B&B rooms, it features some absurdly plush suites and private cottages, and also *Rebecca's*, an attractive continental restaurant with panoramic views. It even has its own golf course, at an elevation of 9000ft.

Cloudcroft has relatively few **restaurants**. On Burro Avenue, the *Front Porch Pizza and Grill* (☎505/682-7492) serves espresso coffee as well as pizza, while the *Western Bar & Cafe* (☎505/682-2445), is a friendly all-purpose diner.

Alamogordo

Sprawled at the foot of the Sacramento Mountains seventy miles northeast of Las Cruces, **ALAMOGORDO** is, like Los Alamos, a child of the Bomb. Once a quiet ranching center, it has grown since World War II to a town of well over thirty thousand inhabitants, most of whom owe their living to the military bases and research facilities tucked away in the surrounding deserts. It's conservative enough to have held public burnings of the Harry Potter books in 2002.

Alamogordo's original central streets remain surprisingly unchanged, but they're a neglected backwater compared to the frenzy of commercial activity along the five-mile strip of US-54, here known as **White Sands Boulevard**. Given pride of place at the **Tularosa Basin Historical Society Museum**, 1301 N White Sands Blvd (Mon–Sat 10am–4pm; free), an old electric toaster from *Howards Café* bears witness to quite how little ever happens around these parts.

Any five-story building in Alamogordo would probably be a tourist attraction; that the gleaming glass cube on the hillside east of town holds the **New Mexico Museum of Space History** is gilding the lily (daily 9am–5pm; museum $6, movie theatre/planetarium $6; ⓦwww.spacefame.org). Displays inside trace the history of rocketry from eleventh-century China onwards, covering New-Mexico-based pioneers Robert Goddard and Wernher von

Braun – one snap of von Braun's cheery crew sitting astride a V-2 rocket is straight out of *Dr Strangelove* – up to the craft that will offer the first commercial space flights. A diorama depicts the unfortunate Ham, the first chimp in space, who was trained at Alamogordo in 1961 by receiving electric shocks or banana-flavored pellets according to which lever he moved. The adjoining **Clyde W. Tombaugh Imax Theater** shows giant-screen movies and doubles as a **planetarium**; there's also a "garden" of abandoned rockets outside.

Practicalities

Alamogordo's **visitor center** is alongside the Tularosa Basin museum at 1301 N White Sands Blvd (Mon–Fri 8am–5pm; ☏505/437-6120, ⓦwww.alamogordo .com). **Motels** along US-54 range from the *White Sands*, 1101 S White Sands Blvd (☏505/437-2922; ❷), to the friendly, high-standard *Best Western Desert Aire*, at 1021 S White Sands Blvd (☏505/437-2110, ⓦwww.bestwestern.com; ❹), which has an outdoor pool.

As for **food**, it's more fun to head downtown than to eat at the diners along the main highway. *Memories*, 1223 N New York Ave (☏505/437-0077; closed Sun), is a "Continental" restaurant set in a very floral old house, where all entrees, such as steaks, salmon, or swordfish, cost under $20 including soup or salad.

White Sands National Monument

The glistening, towering dunes of **White Sands** fill 275 square miles of the broad Tularosa Basin, between the Sacramento and San Andres mountains. Though their whiteness is beyond dispute, they're not sand but fine **gypsum**, deposited on an ancient sea bed 250 million years ago. Anywhere else, the gypsum would have dissolved and been carried off by rivers; here, however, it's trapped in a riverless ring of mountains. The southern portion of this surreal landscape has been set aside as **WHITE SANDS NATIONAL MONUMENT**, entered north of US-70 fourteen miles west of Alamogordo. Be warned that roughly twice each week, US-70 **closes** for up to two hours while missile tests are under way.

Beside the highway, the **visitor center** (daily: summer 8am–7pm; winter 8am–6pm; ☏505/479-6124, ⓦwww.nps.gov/whsa) illustrates the unique life-forms that populate this pallid environment. From there, it takes five more miles along the paved portion of **Dunes Drive** (daily: summer 7am–9pm; winter 7am–sunset; $3 per person) before you reach the heart of the dunes. In this initial stretch, as you get your first glimpses of white sand beneath the scrubby vegetation, you may wonder what the fuss is about. Unless you have either an abundance of time or walking difficulties, skip the unenthralling nature trail along the **Interdune Boardwalk**.

A little further along, the plants thin out, and you come to a bizarre world of dazzling white knife-edge ridges and graceful slopes. The drive now loops around a six-mile one-way labyrinth, where the roadway is at times hundreds of yards wide, and then narrows again to a slender channel, as the west winds that constantly replenish the dunes pile sand in your path in luxuriant drifts. Plentiful pull-outs, some equipped with fabulous 1950s-style curving picnic shelters, enable you to leave your vehicle and plough through pristine sand to the top of the ridges, which offer long-range mountain views. Slipping and sliding back down again is even better.

There's no developed **campground** at White Sands, but backcountry camping is allowed, by permit only. Once or twice a year, rangers lead vehicle convoys up to Lake Lucero, the actual source of the sands.

White Sands Missile Range Museum

A couple of miles north of the national monument boundary, on the top-security White Sands Missile Range – the largest military installation in the US – the **White Sands Space Harbor** holds one of the three seven-mile runways where the **Space Shuttle** is able to land. A back-up facility to the regular landing sites in California and Florida, it's usually used for training; but it has welcomed one actual landing, the Space Shuttle *Columbia*, in 1982.

For the full story of what goes on here, head for the **White Sands Missile Range Museum**, thirty miles west of the monument en route to Las Cruces, and four miles south of US-70 (Mon–Fri 8am–4pm, Sat & Sun 10am–3pm; free; ☎505/678-8824, ⓦ www.wsmr-history.org). The open-air **Missile Park** alongside displays all the missiles ever tested at White Sands. These date back to "Vengeance Weapon 2," the **V-2** rocket, almost four thousand of which were fired across the English Channel by the Nazis during World War II. After the war, the weapon's designer, Dr Wernher von Braun, directed the firing of sixty more V-2s at White Sands – one went astray and crashed across the border near Ciudad Juarez, Mexico. He moved on to Huntsville, Alabama, in 1950.

The southeast corner

East of the mountains, at the edge of the Great Plains, **southeast New Mexico** has little in common with the rest of the Southwest. It's not quite as dull as it looks, however; all its treasures are tucked away underground, from its oil and mineral wealth to the fairytale labyrinth of **Carlsbad Caverns National Park**. Traditionally, Carlsbad was the only reason tourists ever strayed this way, but these days a steady influx of pilgrims come to contemplate the extra-terrestrial wonders of **Roswell**.

Trinity Site

Twice each year, sightseers make a peculiar pilgrimage to the **Trinity Site**, out on the **White Sands Missile Range** in the desert thirty miles west of Carrizozo (see p.195), where the first **atomic bomb** was detonated at 5.30am on July 16, 1945. Brought by road from Los Alamos in the back of a '42 Plymouth, the bomb, code-named **Fat Man**, was not dropped but placed atop a steel tower. As well as destroying a nearby "doom town" built to study its effects, the blast was strong enough to shatter windows in Silver City, 120 miles west, and to fuse the sands below "Ground Zero" into a thick slab of radioactive green glass known as **trinitite**. The eight-feet-deep crater it created was subsequently filled in to minimize radiation.

The Missile Range has witnessed thousands more weapons tests since then, and remains off limits to nonmilitary personnel except for the first Saturdays of April and October. Visitors on those days can either join a "caravan" that sets off from **Alamogordo** at 8am, or enter the range unaccompanied via the **Stallion Gate** (8am–2pm), on US-380 fifty miles west of Carrizozo. You're forbidden to stop or take photos other than at the site itself, or to make political speeches, and urged not to pick up any trinitite you may spot. Not only is it part of a National Historic Landmark, it's radioactive.

For more information on tours, and on the range itself, access ⓦ www.wsmr.army .mil – where the authorities helpfully explain "In the end, if it's a missile, we fire it" – or drop in at the White Sands Missile Range Museum (see above).

Roswell

Fifty-seven miles east of Lincoln, and seventy-five miles north of the national park at Carlsbad, the small ranching town of **ROSWELL** is renowned as the spot near which an **alien spacecraft** supposedly crashlanded on the night of July 4, 1947. The commander of the local air force base authorized a press statement announcing that the wreckage of a flying saucer had been retrieved and taken away for examination. Despite a follow-up denial within a day, claiming that it was in fact a weather balloon – and more recent statements such as President Clinton's categorical assertion that "No, an alien spacecraft did not crash in Roswell, New Mexico, in 1947" – the story of the so-called "**Roswell Incident**" has kept running. As 100,000 *X-Files* fanatics descended upon Roswell in 1997 for a six-day festival to mark the "Incident's" fiftieth anniversary, the US Air Force revealed that the errant balloon had been monitoring the atmosphere for evidence of Soviet nuclear tests. Witnesses were also said to have confused the balloon crash with parachute experiments in 1953, which involved dropping dummies from high-altitude planes. UFO theorists, however, remain unconvinced. Incidentally, considerable vagueness surrounds exactly where the crash took place. Since a local entrepreneur bought up one purported site, the original witnesses have started to "remember" that it all happened somewhere else entirely. With TV series such as *Roswell* and *Taken* perpetuating the myth, Roswell's curious tourist boom shows no signs of abating.

Despite its best intentions, and the wishful thinking of the truly weird clientele who drift in from the plains, the central **International UFO Museum**, 114 N Main St (daily 9am–5pm; $5; ☎505/625-9495, ⓦwww.roswellufomuseum.com), inadvertently exposes the whole tawdry business as transparent nonsense. Set up by the military press officer responsible for the 1947 announcement, it reveals such gems as that John F. Kennedy was shot because he was about to reveal the secret, and that Neil Armstrong, astonished at encountering flying saucers on the moon, blurted out "Boy, were they beige!" (You'd have to assume that "big" was the word he was fumbling for.) Murals depict "what might have happened," while the showpiece exhibit is a model of a so-called "**alien autopsy**." Note the "fiction" and "non-fiction" sections in the museum bookstore.

By way of contrast, the long-standing **Roswell Museum**, 100 W 11th St (Mon–Sat 9am–5pm, Sun 1–5pm; free), boasts an excellent, multifaceted collection with nary an alien corpse to be seen. Its most sensational section celebrates pioneer rocket scientist **Robert Goddard** (1882–1945), one of whose early experiments prompted the newspaper headline "*Moon Rocket" Man's Test Alarms Whole Countryside*. His entire laboratory has been reconstructed, and an entertaining video shows him wheeling a rudimentary rocket in a wagon to the launch pad, then racing to escape the blast in a model T Ford. There's also a huge, top-quality **art gallery**, displaying Southwestern landscapes by Henriette Wyeth and Peter Hurd as well as a solitary Georgia O'Keeffe, *Ram's Skull With Brown Leaves*.

Practicalities

Roswell's **visitor center**, at 912 N Main St (Mon–Fri 8am–5pm; ☎505/624-6860, ⓦwww.roswellnm.org), is active in promoting the town's annual **UFO Festival**, held on the weekend of July 4 (ⓦwww.uforoswell.com). The finest **motel** in town, the *Best Western Sally Port Inn*, 2000 N Main St (☎505/622-6430 or 1-800/548-5221, ⓦwww.bestwestern.com; ❸), also has a good restaurant. The *Cattle Baron*, 1113 N Main St (☎505/622-2465), is a large, good-value **steakhouse**, while *Farley's*, just up the hill at 1315 N Main St (☎505/627-1100), is a livelier sci-fi-themed pub and diner.

Carlsbad

Considering that a million tourists per year pass through **CARLSBAD** en route to Carlsbad Caverns National Park – covered below – the town itself is astonishing in its blandness. A century of ranching and potash-mining has given it a sizeable if characterless downtown area, but the one significant attraction is the **Living Desert State Park**, a couple of miles northwest (daily: summer 8am–8pm; winter 9am–5pm; last admission 1hr 30min before closing; $5). This botanical garden of desert plants doubles as a zoo that houses elk, rattlesnakes, a prairie dog village, and even "Maggie the Painting Bear."

Carlsbad also possesses the dubious distinction of being home to the **Waste Isolation Pilot Plant** (Ⓦ www.wipp.energy.gov). Hollowed from a thick layer of salt two thousand feet below ground level, this subterranean facility is the world's first repository for radioactive waste created during the production of nuclear weapons.

Practicalities

Carlsbad's **visitor center** is at 302 S Canal St (Mon–Fri 8am–5pm; Ⓣ 505/887-6516, Ⓦ www.carlsbadchamber.com). Cheap **motels**, like the clean, comfortable *Super 8*, 3817 National Parks Hwy (Ⓣ 505/887-8888 or 1-800/800-8000, Ⓦ www.super8.com; ❸), line US-62/180 to the southwest. More central alternatives include the large *Best Western Stevens Inn*, 1829 S Canal St (Ⓣ 505/887-2851 or 1-800/730-2851, Ⓦ www.stevensinn.com; ❹), where rates include a full breakfast at the *Flume Room* **restaurant**, which is as good a place to eat as you're likely to find. In the heart of town, the *Blue House Bakery*, 609 N Canyon St (closed Sun; Ⓣ 505/628-0555), serves coffee and pastries from 7.30am.

Carlsbad Caverns National Park

CARLSBAD CAVERNS NATIONAL PARK consists of a tract of the Guadalupe Mountains that's so riddled with underground caves and tunnels as to be virtually hollow. Tamed in classic park-service style with concrete trails and electric lighting, this subterranean wonderland is now a walk-in gallery, where tourists come in droves to marvel at its intricate limestone tracery. Before you decide whether to join them, however, be sure to grasp that the park is a *long* way from anywhere else – three hundred miles southeast of Albuquerque and 150 miles northeast of El Paso, Texas.

The Guadalupe Mountains are the remnants of the **Capitan Reef**, a 400-mile-long horseshoe-shaped reef that formed beneath a primeval ocean. Made up of algae and sponges rather than coral, it was thrust above the plains a mere three million years ago. Surface moisture has trickled through the resultant cracks ever since, gnawing at the rock within.

Almost all park visitors confine their attention to the main cave, **Carlsbad Cavern** itself, where the summer crowds can be intense. Strangely, though, that's part of the fun – coming to Carlsbad feels like a real throwback to the 1950s boom in mass tourism. If you're not convinced, wait until you see the gloriously kitsch **Underground Lunchroom**.

Arrival and information

To reach the park headquarters, drive twenty miles southwest of the town of Carlsbad on US-62/180, then turn west at **White's City** to climb another seven miles. This narrow, twisting road ends atop the mountains, with sweeping views east across the plains. Part of a complex that includes a restaurant, a gift store, a crèche, and even a kennel, the **visitor center** is the place to pay

▲ Carlsbad Caverns National Park, New Mexico

entrance fees and pick up details of the day's program of tours (daily: June to late Aug 8am–7pm; late Aug to May 8am–5pm; ☎505/785-2232, ⓦwww.nps .gov/cave).

The standard park fee of $6 for three days covers access to **Carlsbad Cavern** by elevator or on foot; the passes described on p.41 are sold and accepted. For additional fees ranging $7–20 you can also join guided tours to otherwise inaccessible parts of the main cavern, or of **Slaughter Canyon Cave**, as detailed opposite. Some tours require participants to carry flashlights or even to wear kneepads. All tours can be reserved in advance, online or on ☎1-877/444-6777. Note that there's no **camping** at the national park; the nearest campgrounds and motels are at White's City and Carlsbad.

Carlsbad Cavern

The centerpiece of Carlsbad Cavern, the **Big Room**, lies 750 vertical feet below the visitor center – as it's inside the mountain, it's also 400ft horizontally from the open air in some places. Measuring up to 1800ft long and 250ft high, it's festooned with stalactites, stalagmites, and countless unnameable shapes of swirling liquid rock. All are a uniform stone gray; the rare touches of color are provided by slight red or brown mineral-rich tinges, improved here and there with gentle pastel lighting. Most visitors take an hour or so to complete the reasonably level trail around its perimeter. Whatever the weather up top – summer highs exceed 100°F – the temperature down here is always a cool 56°F, so dress warmly.

Direct **elevators** drop to the Big Room from the visitor center (summer first down 8.30am, last up 6.30pm; winter first down 8.30am, last up 4.55pm). They arrive alongside the **Underground Lunchroom**, a vast formation-free side cave paved over in the 1950s to create a diner-cum-souvenir-store that sells indigestible lunches in polystyrene containers, plus Eisenhower-era souvenirs such as giant pencils and Viewmaster reels. To modern eyes, this strange installation seems absurd, but moves to close it down have been stymied by its place in popular affections.

To get a better sense of the depth of the cavern, eschew the elevator and **walk** down via the **Natural Entrance Route** (last entry summer 3.30pm, winter 2pm). This steep paved footpath switchbacks into the guano-encrusted maw of the cave, a short way from the visitor center. It takes fifteen minutes to reach the first formations and another fifteen to reach the Big Room itself. $3 buys you a recorded audio tour. All visitors are obliged to ride the elevator back out.

The walk-down trail once meandered through beautiful side caves such as the **King's Palace**, filled with translucent "draperies" of limestone. However, formations were broken at the rate of two thousand per year, so these have been closed to casual visitors. They're now open on guided tours only, which start from the Big Room (daily 10am, 11am, 2pm, & 3pm in summer, diminishing to 10am & 2pm in winter; $8). Additional tours can take you along the **Left Hand Tunnel** route down from the visitor center ($7), or on a much more demanding descent into either **Spider Cave** or the **Hall of the White Giant** (both $20).

The rest of the park

The park's other readily accessible cave is 25 miles southwest of the visitor center. Much less frequented, and much less developed, **Slaughter Canyon Cave** can only be explored on two-hour guided tours (late May to mid-Aug daily 10am & 1pm; mid-Aug to late May Sat & Sun 10am; check schedules on Ⓦ www.nps.gov/cave; $15). To get there, drive five miles south of White's City on US-62/180, then eleven miles west on Hwy-418, and finally hike the steep half-mile up to the cave entrance.

Slaughter Canyon Cave still appears as "New Cave" on some maps, but it's been renamed to avoid confusion since the discovery of **Lechuguilla Cave**. Revealed after cavers cleared a thirty-foot plug of bat dung and rubble in 1986, the astonishing Lechuguilla cave system is not only deeper than Carlsbad Cavern but, at 1600ft, has turned out to be the deepest in the US. Over a hundred miles of tunnels have been mapped so far, but they're so dangerous that Lechuguilla is off limits to all but the experts. It's expected to remain a "wilderness cave" – even its location is kept secret – so the rest of us will have to content ourselves with the marvelous pictures of its delicate crystalline formations in the visitor center.

White's City

Twenty miles southwest of Carlsbad at the turn-off for Carlsbad Caverns, **WHITE'S CITY** is not a town but a privately owned tourist complex that provides the closest accommodation and camping to the national park. A notorious eyesore, it was built in 1926 by entrepreneur Charlie White, who cannily anticipated the imminent advent of automobile tourism and bought up the land at this crucial road junction without ever having seen it. The park service has deplored its very existence ever since and has attempted to avoid the same situation arising at parks elsewhere.

Current components of White's City (all ☎505/785-2291 or 1-800/228-3767, Ⓦwww.whitescity.com) include the mock-adobe *Best Western Cavern Inn*, on both sides of the highway (❸), which has its own water park for guests; the *White's City RV Park*, which has tent camping space; and the *Velvet Garter Restaurant*.

White's City also boasts the ultratacky **Million Dollar Museum** (daily 7am–8pm; $3), an assortment of decrepit dolls' houses, two-headed snakes, old shoes, arrowheads, the twelfth largest moose ever shot in Wyoming, and even a human corpse, in the nauseating form of a "7000-year-old cliff dwelling baby."

The Rio Grande valley

The 260-mile route between Albuquerque and the Mexican border at El Paso, Texas, follows one of America's oldest and most romantic trails. For 250 years, the **Camino Real** or "Royal Road" beside the Rio Grande gave the Hispanic colonists of New Mexico their one tenuous link with the outside world. However, travelers on the Camino Real were so prone to Apache attack if they followed the curve of the Rio Grande between **Socorro** and **Las Cruces** that they preferred to take a hundred-mile shortcut behind the mountains that lie east of the river. This route too had its perils – not least a complete lack of water – and became known as the **Jornada del Muerto**, or Dead Man's Route, after Juan de Oñate's chaplain Fray Cristóbal de Salazar died here in the early 1600s. To this day there's no north–south road through the desert. The Camino Real is now paralleled by I-25, a monotonous four-hour drive relieved only by distant views of the mountains. You don't even see much of the river itself, except where it's been dammed to form incongruous turquoise lakes around the town of **Truth or Consequences**. Of the old way-stations en route, only **Socorro** in the north and **Mesilla** in the south are particularly worth visiting.

Isleta Pueblo

The only New Mexican pueblo south of Albuquerque, **ISLETA PUEBLO** (☎505/869-3111, Ⓦisletapueblo.com), lies just off the interstate a dozen miles from downtown, to which it's also connected by the RailRunner light rail system (see p.183; Ⓦwww.nmrailrunner.com). The sole survivor of the many pueblos encountered by Spanish explorers along the lower Rio Grande, it served in the seventeenth century as a refuge where Tiwa peoples gathered to resist the threat of Apache raids. During the Pueblo Revolt, some Isletans accompanied the Spanish retreat southwards to found the pueblo of **Tigua**, outside El Paso, while others fled west to join the Hopi. Isleta itself was repopulated in 1718 and remains home to almost four thousand people.

Although the tribal lands mark a verdant interruption amid the dormitory communities that line the interstate's first fifty miles, the reservation is plagued by river-borne pollution from the industries of Albuquerque. Economically, it's dependent on its huge neighbor; a high proportion of Isletans work in the city, and the tribe also runs a 24-hour **casino** (T 505/724-3800 or 1-877/747-5382, W isleta-casino.com; **6**), which holds a luxury hotel plus a gourmet restaurant and an all-you-can-eat buffet. Every day during daylight hours, visitors have free access to the principal pueblo village – also known as **SHIAW-IBA** – where the main attraction is the white-walled **mission church** of San Agustín de Isleta. In addition, Isleta stages major festivals on August 28 and September 4.

Socorro

Historic **SOCORRO**, eighty miles south of Albuquerque, received its unusual name – "help," in Spanish – from Don Juan de Oñate in 1598, after local Pueblo peoples fed his expeditionary party from their reserves of corn. The first Hispanic settlement was destroyed during the Pueblo Revolt of 1680, where-after the site was abandoned for over a century. The picturesque **plaza** at its core, a block west of the main road, California Street, and the spruced-up adobe church of **San Miguel**, a couple of blocks north (daily 6am–6pm; free), were rebuilt during the 1820s. Sixty years later, triggered by the arrival of the railroads and the discovery of extensive **silver** deposits nearby, Socorro briefly became New Mexico's largest town. When the silver ran out, so too did most of the population, leaving behind some fine Victorian architecture.

Practicalities

For a self-guided walking tour of Socorro, call in at the **visitor center**, a block west of the plaza at 217 Fisher Ave (Tues–Fri 9am–5pm, Sat 10am–2pm; T 575/835-8927, W www.socorronm.gov). **Motels** include the *Super 8*, 1121 Frontage Rd NW (T 575/835-4626 or 1-800/800-8000, W www.super8.com; winter **2**, summer **3**), and the newer, smarter *Holiday Inn Express*, 1040 N California St (T 575/836-4600 or 1-800/465-4329, W www.ichotelsgroup .com; **5**). As for **food**, the *Socorro Springs Brewing Company*, 1012 California St (T 575/838-0650), serves calzones and pizzas from its wood-fired oven, along with sandwiches, to go with its home-brewed beers.

The Very Large Array (VLA)

Astronomy enthusiasts, or simply fans of the unusual, should head fifty miles west of Socorro, on the lonely US-60, to where the aptly named **Very Large Array**, or VLA, spreads across the Plains of San Agustin. One of the world's most powerful observatories, it comprises 27 separate moveable radio dishes, each 25 metres across, which can be arranged in permutations that vary from a dense cluster to a twenty-mile line. The array's visitor center (daily 8am–sunset; T 505/835-7243, W www .aoc.nrao.edu), clearly signed on Hwy-52 just south of US-60, holds assorted displays, but is usually not staffed. Instead, visitors can simply followed a well-marked walking route that takes them closer, but not right up to, however many dishes are currently nearby. Guided tours only take place on the first Saturdays of April and October, to coincide with the Trinity Site tours detailed on p.203.

While the VLA makes a striking, photogenic spectacle, reaching it requires a long detour from the interstate. Neither **Magdalena**, twenty miles east of the array, nor **Datil**, fifteen miles west, hold much for visitors apart from a basic diner or two, so the trek is probably only worth it if you're en route to or from Arizona. Springerville is around a hundred miles west on US-60, while Hwy-12 heads southwest from Datil, and makes a possible route southwards towards either Silver City in New Mexico or, ultimately, Tucson.

Bosque del Apache Wildlife Refuge

As they continued southwards from Socorro along the Camino Real, beside the Rio Grande, Hispanic colonists avoided the encampments at Bosque del Apache (forest of the Apaches) by crossing the river twenty miles south of Socorro and heading towards the Jornada del Muerto trail. This point off Hwy-1 is now the **Bosque del Apache Wildlife Refuge**, the Southwest's most spectacular **bird-watching** site (open daily from 1hr before sunrise to 1hr after sunset; visitor center Mon–Fri 7.30am–4pm, Sat & Sun 8am–4.30pm; $3 per vehicle; ☎575/835-1828, ⓦwww.fws.gov or www.friendsofthebosque.org). As many as twenty thousand sandhill cranes and almost fifty thousand snow geese migrate here in early December for the winter; and even in summer its riverine marshes and forests are bursting with birds and mammals.

El Camino Real International Heritage Center

The whole story of the Camino Real, which is very much the history of New Mexico as a Spanish colony, is recounted in lavish and fascinating detail at the impressive **El Camino Real International Heritage Center**, thirty miles south of Socorro, overlooking the Rio Grande from near exit 115 off I-25 (daily except Tues 8.30am–5pm; $5; ☎575/854-3600, ⓦwww.caminorealheritage .org). The trail was the lifeblood of New Mexico, linking Santa Fe with Mexico City, 1500 miles south, and the exhibits stress ongoing cultural connections. Smaller-scale trails have been laid out nearby as short nature hikes.

Truth or Consequences

Until 1950, the minor spa town seventy miles south of Socorro was appropriately known as **Hot Springs**. Then the radio show *Truth or Consequences* promised that any community prepared to change its name would receive the meager reward of hosting its tenth anniversary edition. Hot Springs prostituted itself for fifteen minutes of fame, and **TRUTH OR CONSEQUENCES** was saddled with the world's worst name – though locals habitually abbreviate it these days to "**T or C**."

Several **thermal springs** – where Apache warriors such as Geronimo once soaked away the worries of the warpath – are now run as private bathhouses, with prices starting at around $3 for a twenty-minute session. Native American memorabilia, including Mimbres pottery (see p.216), form a prominent part of the historical collection at the **Geronimo Springs Museum**, 211 Main St (Mon–Sat 9am–5pm, Sun 11am–4pm; $5; ⓦwww.geronimospringsmuseum .com). You can also learn fascinating snippets about **Ralph Edwards**, the late presenter of the long-defunct *Truth or Consequences* show, who managed to return each year for the first fifty times the **Truth or Consequences Fiesta** was celebrated, on the first weekend in May. He died aged 92 in 2005.

Practicalities

T or C's small downtown consists of a couple of blocks sandwiched between two busy one-way streets, Broadway and Main Street. The **visitor center** is alongside the museum (Mon–Fri 9am–noon & 1–5pm, Sat 11am–4pm; ☎575/894-1968). Most of the better **motels** – like the *Hot Springs Inn*,

The Final Frontier

Appropriately enough, given its long-standing association with cutting-edge technology, frontier adventurism, and strange alien spacecraft, New Mexico will become home to the world's first **commercial space flights**. The state government and Virgin Galactic are building **Spaceport America** in the empty desert of the Jornada del Muerto, roughly 45 miles northeast of Las Cruces and 25 miles southeast of Truth or Consequences.

If the first flights meet the optimistic schedule of taking place in 2010, they may launch from California's Mojave desert rather than New Mexico. The craft used, SpaceShipTwo, is an updated version of the prototype which in 2004 became the first space vehicle to fly to an altitude of over 100km twice within two weeks, thereby claiming the $10 million Ansari X-Prize. Carried aloft by the WhiteKnightTwo launch plane, the ship is released and then fires its own rocket engines to reach suborbital space. Amazingly, it uses a combination of nitrous oxide – laughing gas – and solid rubber as fuel. Virgin Galactic is ultimately hoping to operate a fleet of five spacecraft from New Mexico, each capable of carrying eight astronauts, and to offer its space voyagers a "five-star destination experience" on the ground as well. The actual flight will last around three hours, culminating in perhaps three minutes of weightlessness; it won't go into Earth orbit. Reservations for US$200,000 tickets are already being accepted; contact ⓦwww .virgingalactic.com for details. Prospective passenger **Paris Hilton** has observed:

"I'm very scared to do it. What if I don't come back? ... With the whole light-years thing, what if I come back 10,000 years later, and everyone I know is dead? I'll be like, 'Great. Now I have to start all over.'"

2270 N Date St (☎575/894-6665, ⓦ www.thehotspringsinn.com; ❸), where there's a pool – are well to the north, near interstate exit 79. The *Sierra Grande Lodge & Spa*, 501 McAdoo St (☎575/894-6976, ⓦwww.sierragrandelodge .com; ❺), is a gorgeously restored 1920s lodge with luxury rooms and suites and mineral baths, while the lovely *Riverbend Hot Springs*, beside the Rio Grande in the heart of town at 100 Austin St (☎575/894-7625, ⓦwww.nmhotsprings .com; ❶–❹), offers comfortable suites as well as "semi-private" rooms that share baths, and boasts spring-fed hot tubs. The dining room at the *Sierra Grande* has to be the best **restaurant** in town, serving contemporary American cuisine at around $20 per entree; *La Piñata*, 1990 S Broadway (☎575/894-9047), is a good Mexican alternative.

Hillsboro

Hwy-152 branches west from I-25 fifteen miles south of T or C, crossing the Mimbres Mountain en route to **Silver City** (see p.214). **HILLSBORO**, less than twenty miles off the interstate in the fertile foothills, is a former gold-mining settlement that has since turned its hand to apple-growing instead, as celebrated in an annual **Apple Festival** held on Labor Day weekend. Now no more than a village, with a small crop of arts-and-crafts galleries, Hillsboro also boasts the *Barbershop Café*, 200 Main St (☎575/895-5283), a friendly local **restaurant**.

Hatch

Forty miles south of T or C, along I-25 en route to Las Cruces, tiny **HATCH** is noteworthy only as the home of New Mexico's leading **chile farms**. All year, roadside stalls sell fresh peppers and the dried garlands known as *ristras*, while Labor Day weekend sees a **Chile Festival** (☎575/267-5050,

@www.hatchchilefest.com) with fiercely competitive chile cook-offs. *B&E Burritos*, 303 N Franklin St (@575/267-5191), is renowned for fiery Mexican cuisine.

Fort Selden State Monument

Another twenty miles down I-40, by which time you're just fifteen miles north of downtown Las Cruces, Fort Selden State Monument stands on the east bank of the Rio Grande just south of **RADIUM SPRINGS**. It preserves the ruined adobe walls of a US Army fort built to protect Las Cruces in 1865 (daily except Tues 8.30am–5pm; $3; @575/526-8911). Its small museum focuses largely on the black troops stationed here just after the Civil War, who became known as Buffalo Soldiers, and are also commemorated by a bronze statue outside. The fort was decommissioned in 1891, so it basically consists of rounded stumps surrounding its former parade ground, but it still comes alive on summer weekends during regular re-enactments.

Las Cruces

Named after "the Crosses" that marked the graves of early travelers killed by the Apache, **LAS CRUCES** is now a major crossroads, where the east–west I-10 meets the north–south I-25. Once a riverside farming community, it has grown beyond recognition, though the boom in industrial and military employment has been at the expense of any scenic beauty Las Cruces may once have possessed. It has very little to offer visitors. As New Mexico's second largest city, it boasts a wide array of shops and services, but they're all housed now in the malls that line I-25 to the east, leaving downtown a rather desolate sprawl. Any time you can spare for sightseeing is better spent in neighboring Mesilla.

Practicalities

Las Cruces' downtown **visitor center** is at 211 N Water St (Mon–Fri 8am–5pm, Sat 9am–1pm; @575/541-2444, @www.lascrucescvb.org). The cream of the **motels** has to be the *Best Western Mission Inn*, 1765 S Main St (✈ @575/524-8591 or 1-800/390-1440; ❸); it may not look all that special from the outside, but the large rooms are surprisingly attractive, featuring lovely Mexican tilework and murals. Rates include a full cooked breakfast. *Lundeen's Inn of the Arts*, 618 S Alameda Blvd (@575/526-3326 or 1-888/526-3326, @innofthearts.com; ❹), is a **B&B inn** where each room is named for regional artists, such as Maria Martínez or Georgia O'Keeffe, and furnished appropriately.

As for **dining**, the most promising area is along University Avenue, which marks the northern limits of the New Mexico State University campus at the south end of town. *Mix-Pacific Rim*, 1001 E University Ave (@575/532-2042), specializes in Japanese and Asian cuisine, with a sushi bar, and entrees like Thai green curry priced at anything up to $20. The adjoining *Mix Express* (same phone) serves cheaper takeout. The whole neighborhood is buzzing with student-oriented **coffeehouses**. Elsewhere, the slogan of *Nellie's Café*, 1226 W Hadley Ave (@575/524-9982) – "*Chiles with Attitude*" – tells you what to expect: sublimely spicy Mexican food.

Mesilla

The little-changed Hispanic village of **MESILLA** stands just south of I-10 two miles south of Las Cruces, an easy drive down Avenida de Mesilla from downtown. When New Mexico passed into American hands in 1846, the

Mesilla Valley still belonged to Mexico; Mesilla itself was founded in 1850 by New Mexicans who preferred to remain Mexican. Under the **Gadsden Purchase**, however, signed here in 1853, it passed to the US and soon became one of the Southwest's largest towns, with over eight thousand inhabitants. During the Civil War, Mesilla even served briefly as the Confederate capital of the territory of Arizona, but it went into swift decline when the railroad bypassed it in favor of Las Cruces in 1881.

Mesilla's Old West **plaza** has a real frontier feel, though most of the old adobes that surround it – including the former courthouse where **Billy the Kid** was tried and sentenced to death in 1881 – now house art galleries and souvenir shops. Gift stores stock interesting Southwest souvenirs and jewelry leavened with some much cheaper Mexican crafts, while the Mesilla Book Center has an excellent selection of local literature. Two blocks east at 1875 Boutz Rd, the small **Gadsden Museum** (Mon–Sat 9–11am & 1–5pm, Sun 1–5pm; $2) recounts the town's history and details the events that lead to the Gadsden Purchase.

Practicalities

Mesilla has its own small **visitor center**, at 2231 Avda de Mesilla (daily 9am–5pm; ☎575/524-3262, ⓦwww.oldmesilla.org). The *Mesón de Mesilla*, five minutes' walk east of the plaza at 1803 Avda de Mesilla (☎575/525-9212, ⓦwww.mesondemesilla.com; ❹–❼), is a **B&B** with fifteen rooms of varying degrees of luxury, gorgeous mountain views, and an outdoor pool. **Restaurants** on the plaza include the *Double Eagle* (☎575/523-6700), which has indoor and outdoor seating and serves steaks or salmon as well as burgers, salads, and Mexican dishes for lunch and dinner daily. *La Posta* is a Mexican *cantina* in the former offices of the Butterfield Stage Coach (☎575/524-3524).

Southwest New Mexico

Most of New Mexico's sparsely populated **southwest corner** – also known as the "**Bootheel**" – consists of open rangeland. Interstate towns like **Deming** and **Lordsburg** are entirely forgettable, though a detour north into the mountains takes you to the mining historic town of **Silver City** and the ancient **Gila Cliff Dwellings**.

Deming

A bonanza of billboards sixty miles due west of Las Cruces announces your arrival at **DEMING**, a typical desert outpost scattered with motels and diners. Half-hearted attempts at agriculture have left their traces on the landscape, but the main sign of activity comes from the ever-present swirling dust devils (as the noncommittal highway signs would have it, "Dust Storms May Exist"). If you're ready for a break, however, the **Deming Luna Mimbres Museum**, 301 S Silver Ave (Mon–Sat 9am–4pm, Sun 1.30–4pm; $2), has some surprisingly good displays, including cabinets of Mimbres pottery (see p.216) and a great show of minerals and gemstones.

Assuming you have a pickax handy, you're allowed to take away whatever agates, onyx, or geodes you can prise from the arid slopes of **Rockhound State Park**, ten miles southeast (daily 7.30am–dusk; $5). Any easy pickings have long since been carted away, leaving this as perhaps the most frighteningly boring park in the whole Southwest.

Practicalities

Deming is served by Amtrak **trains** and more frequent Greyhound **buses**, which call at the Chevron station at 1216 W Pine St (☎575/546-3881). The **visitor center**, 800 E Pine St, is at the east end of downtown (Mon–Fri 9am–5pm, Sat 9–11am; ☎575/546-2674 or 1-800/848-4955, ⓦwww.demingchamber.com). In Deming's biggest event of the year, late August's **Great American Duck Race** (ⓦwww.demingduckrace.com), live ducks waddle down a dry track and paddle down a wet one. If your duck wins – they're assigned by a lucky draw – you can win big money.

Budget **motels** along the main drag, parallel to the interstate, include the central *Anselment's Butterfield Stage*, marked by a flashing neon sign at 309 W Pine St (☎575/544-0011; ❶); the large *Holiday Inn* at the eastern interstate exit at 4600 E Pine St (☎575/546-2661, ⓦwww.ichotelsgroup.com; ❸) is the best of the bunch and has a decent **restaurant**, too. A block south of the main drag at 122 E Spruce St, *Joe Perk Coffee Shop* (☎575/544-0141; closed Mon) sells smoothies and pastries.

Pancho Villa State Park

Sleepy Columbus, thirty miles south of Deming, just north of the Mexican border, is where Mexican revolutionary Pancho Villa led five hundred guerrillas in an attack on the US cavalry on March 9, 1916. "Raid Day" commemorates the anniversary each year in **PANCHO VILLA STATE PARK** (daily 8am–5pm; ☎575/531-2711; $5; camping $10). A small museum chronicles the last invasion of the US, and the adjoining sixty-acre desert botanical garden makes a nice place to **camp** (except in summer, when it's baking hot).

If you fancy a *cerveza* or two, the frontier with neighboring **LAS PALOMAS**, three miles south in Mexico, remains open day or night. Border formalities are minimal, though foreign travelers must be sure to carry their passports.

Silver City

Six thousand feet up in the Mogollon Mountains, **SILVER CITY** stands roughly fifty miles from either Deming or Lordsburg on I-10. As you drive up from the interstate, however, it's easy not to notice that you're climbing – the region has been so extensively **mined** that many of the hills that once lay south of Silver City have now been completely carved away.

Ancient peoples knew this region as a source of top-quality **turquoise**, but the Hispanic settlement of La Cienaga de San Vicente was only founded in 1804, after friendly Apaches showed the Spanish soldier Jose Manuel Carrasco where to find **copper**. The Santa Rita copper mine was repeatedly attacked by the Apache, however, and was abandoned altogether in 1838. Only when **silver** was discovered after the Civil War was the town reestablished, with a new name and a rip-roaring reputation. **Billy the Kid** spent most of his childhood here; he's said to have committed his first robbery – of a Chinese laundry – in Silver City, and also his first murder.

Things having calmed down when the silver ran out, Silver City today is a rundown, but nonetheless appealing, Victorian relic, scattered with ornate old buildings. The two thousand students of Western New Mexico University, whose campus is on the western edge of downtown, keep things reasonably lively for most of the year, and they're replaced in summer by a large influx of tourists. Copper mining, meanwhile, continues unabated; neighboring Santa Rita, a fully fledged community in its own right that was the birthplace of

Apollo 17 astronaut Harrison Schmitt, disappeared into the bowels of an open-pit copper mine in 1966.

Arrival and information

Silver City's **visitor center** is on Hwy-90 as it enters downtown, at 201 N Hudson St (April–Oct Mon–Fri 9am–5pm, Sat 10am–2pm, Sun noon–1pm; Nov–March Mon–Fri 9am–5pm; ☎575/538-3785 or 1-800/548-9378, ⓦwww.silvercity.org). The annual **Blues Festival** attracts big names at the end of each May (ⓦwww.mimbresarts.org).

Accommodation

Room rates are surprisingly inexpensive in Silver City, but with most of the **motels** strung along US-180 east of town there's a dearth of options within walking distance of downtown.

Bear Mountain Lodge Bear Mountain Rd ☎575/538-2538 or 1-877/620-2327, ⓦwww .bearmountainlodge.com. A 1920s ranch house four miles northwest of downtown, owned and operated by the Nature Conservancy of New Mexico. The eleven B&B guest rooms include four luxurious suites. On-site naturalists run regular guided tours. ❺
Holiday Inn Express 1103 Superior St ☎575/538-2525, ⓦwww.hiexpress.com /silvercitynm. The best of the chain motels, with a heated spa and free continental breakfasts. Three miles east of downtown, it's hard to find, hidden behind a *Wendy's*. ❺
Palace Hotel 106 W Broadway ☎575/388-1811, ⓦwww.zianet.com/palacehotel. Small, nicely restored nineteenth-century hotel, located downtown. Some rooms have showers instead of baths, and they all have historic rather than contemporary fittings, but the ambience – and the rates – are great. ❷

The Town

A massive flood ripped the heart out of downtown Silver City in 1895, washing away its original Main Street. No buildings survive from the days of **Billy the Kid**; Wild West devotees have to settle instead for inspecting the places where they *used* to be. The former site of Main Street is now occupied by **Big Ditch Park**; stand on its eastern edge, at 11th and Hudson, and you're on the spot where Billy grew up, in a simple one-room cabin. His mother is buried in the town cemetery, on Memory Lane a couple of miles east. After her death, Billy found work as a busboy in the *Star Hotel*, which survives in much-altered form at Broadway and Hudson, but soon turned to crime. The jail where he was imprisoned, and from which he made the first of his many escapes, stood at 304 N Hudson St.

Two good museums explore local history in considerable depth. The **Silver City Museum**, 312 W Broadway (Tues–Fri 9am–4.30pm, Sat & Sun 10am–4pm; $3), concentrates on the boom-and-bust mining years, with photos of the frontier era and personal accounts of the vanished community of Santa Rita. It also holds Indian pottery, rugs, and basketry. The emphasis at the **Western New Mexico University Museum**, 12th and Alabama (Mon–Fri 9am–4.30pm, Sat & Sun 10am–4pm; free), is on an absolutely beautiful collection of **Mimbres pottery**, tracing its development over a thousand-year period.

Eating and drinking

What few interesting **restaurants** and **diners** Silver City has are concentrated downtown, along with a few hair-raising **bars**, so don't expect to find anything more exciting along the highways further out.

Buckhorn Saloon and Opera House 62 Main St, Pinos Altos ℗575/538-9911. Enjoyable Wild West-themed steakhouse in the ghost town of Pinos Altos, seven miles north of Silver City (see below). Open Mon–Sat for dinner only, with live music every night except Tues.

Diane's Restaurant and Bakery 510 N Bullard St ℗575/538-8722. Friendly downtown restaurant where the menu ranges from steak and meatloaf via Italian seafood stews to Thai green curries; lots of wine by the glass, and they have their own

bakery across the street. Closed Sun pm, & all Mon.

Javelina Coffee House 210 N Bullard St ℗575/388-1350. Wi-fi-equipped community rendezvous in the heart of downtown, open daily from 6am.

Shevek and Mi 602 N Bullard St ℗575/534-9168. A full menu of Mediterranean and, especially, Italian dishes, including seafood, with patio seating in summer. Closed Wed; breakfast & lunch on Sat & Sun only.

Into the mountains

North of Silver City, the volcanic **Mogollon** and **Mimbres mountains** are among the remotest wilderness areas in the US, mostly belonging to the **Gila National Forest**. Until the late nineteenth century, this was an Apache stronghold; **Geronimo** was born at the headwaters of the Gila River and returned throughout his free adult life. Before that, they were home to the **Mogollon**

The Mogollon and the Mimbres

Archeologists identify the three major cultures of the prehistoric Southwest as the **Ancestral Puebloans** of the Colorado Plateau, the **Hohokam** of the Salt River Valley around modern Phoenix, and the **Mogollon**, based in the **Mogollon mountains** of what's now southwest New Mexico. Thanks to their proximity to Mexico, Mogollon peoples were among the first to acquire both **agriculture** – in the shape of corn and squash, around 1200 BC – and **pottery** – around 200 AD.

At its peak, between 100 AD and 1300 AD, the Mogollon culture extended well into modern Arizona and Mexican Chihuahua. Its heartland, however, remained the **Gila** and **Mimbres** rivers, north and east of modern Silver City. The Mogollon sub-group known as the **Classic Mimbres** culture is considered to represent the ancient Southwest's finest artistic flowering. Above all, the Mimbres people – their name comes from the Spanish for "willows" – were superb **potters**. While the intricate stylized borders of their plates and bowls are typical of many pueblo peoples, their vivid naturalistic images of birds, insects, and animals are quite extraordinary. Usually executed in black on white, they also hint at a complex mythology; some show bees or rabbits juxtaposed with strange humanoid creatures, others are what may be prototype *kachina* figures (see p.78), and there are even scenes of decapitation suggesting human sacrifice.

The Mimbres culture reached its apogee around 1100 AD, with around five thousand people farming beside the Mimbres River. As well as a dozen or so walled villages, each of which held up to two hundred rooms, they occupied several smaller, more isolated settlements. While depictions of Pacific fish suggest they traveled extensively, there's little evidence of trade. No Mimbres ceramics have been discovered elsewhere, and it's believed that the finest bowls were created for specific individuals at birth, used in ceremonies throughout their lifetime, and finally **buried** with them. The bowl would be inverted over the head of the corpse, always with a "**kill hole**" punched through it, which according to modern Pueblo Indians released its "spirit" to accompany that of the deceased. As a result, undamaged Mimbres bowls are extremely rare, and Mimbres pottery in general is so valuable that the few known Mimbres sites have been extensively looted, rendering the detective work of archeology almost impossible. As far as anyone can tell, the Mimbres stopped producing pottery around 1150 AD, and left the valley soon afterwards, possibly because overuse had depleted its soil.

Pueblo peoples
ancient and modern

The chance to experience Native American cultures up close is one of the Southwest's greatest attractions. Besides holding around fifty diverse Native American reservations, most of them far removed from clichéd ideas of poverty, the Southwest is filled with relics of long-vanished times, in the shape of the extraordinary, often spellbindingly beautiful, architecture and artefacts left by its earliest inhabitants. Visiting only the most important and accessible ancient sites would take months, while many more remain hidden in remote corners of the desert, seen only by intrepid adventurers.

Betatakin pueblo, Navajo National Monument ▲

Ancestral Puebloan pottery ▼

Early settlers

The first humans to reach the Southwest were hunters, up to fourteen thousand years ago, who swiftly harried the continent's original "mega-fauna" of mammoths, giant sloth and the like to extinction. The nomadic hunter-gatherers who followed were supplanted in turn when agriculture arrived from Mexico around two thousand years ago, triggering the emergence of more sedentary cultures. Prime among these were the **Ancestral Puebloans** – a people archeologists used to call the **Anasazi**, until they realized that Navajo word meant "ancient enemies" – who spread across the Four Corners region, the high country where Arizona, New Mexico, Utah, and Colorado now meet. To the south, the **Hohokam** were desert farmers, who irrigated the huge valley that now holds modern Phoenix, but were ultimately forced by drought to abandon the area. Further east, the **Mogollon** inhabited the high country in what's now eastern Arizona and western New Mexico.

While no Southwestern civilization ever matched the Aztecs or Maya, cultural influences continued to filter up from Mexico. The art of making **pottery** arrived less than two thousand years ago. A Mogollon sub-group, the **Mimbres**, remain celebrated for their sublime ceramics to this day. Along endless dusty trails, from Mexico's Pacific coast to the Rio Grande, the Aztec traders known as *pochteca* plodded north in search of turquoise, and it's even suggested that Toltec refugees, fleeing the destruction of their empire, may have brought the *kachina* religion still practiced by many Pueblo peoples.

Ancient sites

By around 1100, the highly sophisticated Ancestral Puebloans were building multi-storied **pueblos** (now named using the Spanish word for "village"), in which hundreds of families lived in contiguous "apartments" The largest pueblos, such as in New Mexico's **Chaco Canyon**, functioned as ceremonial centers, which had small permanent populations but attracted many visitors for special occasions. Sites like Chaco, **Hovenweep**, and **Wupatki** also held significant alignments, reflecting the Ancestral Puebloans' astronomical expertise. At much the same time, construction began on the astonishing cliff dwellings for which the Ancestral Puebloans are best remembered. Important ancient sites include:

Navajo National Monument, Arizona. Hike or ride to spectacular lost cities, set in vast rocky alcoves. See p.61.

Canyon de Chelly. Dramatic cliff dwellings in a red-rock canyon. See p.69.

Hovenweep, Utah. Enigmatic towers poised above a Four-Corners canyon. See p.82.

Mesa Verde, Colorado. Magnificent cliff "palaces," perched like eagle's nests in soaring canyon walls. See p.86.

Chaco Canyon, New Mexico. The largest free-standing pueblos, far out in the desert. See p.102.

Bandelier National Monument, New Mexico. Precarious ladders climb to cavelike dwellings hollowed into the rock. See p.143.

Wupatki, Arizona. Several small pueblos, built following a volcanic eruption. See p.292.

Montezuma Castle, Arizona. Ravishing pink "castle," created by the Sinagua people. See p.303.

▲ Canyon de Chelly

▼ Cliff Palace, Mesa Verde National Park

▼ Wupatki Pueblo, Wupatki National Monument

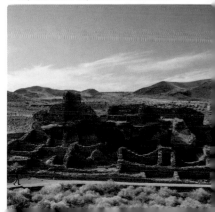

Taos Pueblo ▲

Pictographs, the Great Gallery ▼

Dancer from Ácoma pueblo, Gallup Inter Tribal Ceremonial ▼

Modern pueblos

No great mystery surrounds the so-called "disappearance" of the Ancestral Puebloans from the Four Corners in the thirteenth century. They simply migrated away, both east to the Rio Grande in northern New Mexico, where they still inhabit nineteen pueblos, and south to the villages of Ácoma, Zuni, and Hopi. The surviving pueblos retain much of their traditional way of life, blending ancient beliefs with Catholicism. Some, like the amazing "Sky City" of **Ácoma**, and the twin multistoried pueblos of **Taos**, have barely changed in the last millennium, and are now year-round tourist attractions. Others are less immediately spectacular, but burst vibrantly into life during their annual feast days, celebrated with dazzling dances and public ceremonies.

Rock art

Rock art long predates the invention of writing. The deserts of the Southwest abound in both **petroglyphs**, images scratched or chipped onto stone surfaces, and painted **pictographs**. At Utah's exceptional **Great Gallery**, Archaic shamen daubed enigmatic, ghost-like figures onto remote canyon walls. Other locations include the "Newspaper Rocks" in Utah and Arizona, carvings in Monument Valley, and painted panels in Capitol Reef. The best-known motif in Ancestral Puebloan rock art is the "hunchback" flute-player Kokopelli; see p.128.

The rock art tradition continued into recent times; the sandstone walls of the Canyon de Chelly are marked with Navajo depictions of nineteenth-century Spanish raids, and the Spaniards added their own carvings to the remarkable **Inscription Rock** at El Morro.

peoples, and the main reason to make the fifty-mile dead-end trip into the mountains on **Hwy-15** is to see the dramatic Mogollon ruins of the **Gila Cliff Dwellings National Monument**.

Hwy-15 is, however, a beautiful drive in its own right, albeit a slow one. It's never especially steep, let alone dangerous, but the twists and turns seem endless. Potential stops along the way include **Pinos Altos** – a fun little semi-ghost town in the woods a few miles out of Silver City that's home to the *Buckhorn Saloon* (see above) – and the **Vista Viewpoint** above the Gila River near the far end.

Gila Cliff Dwellings National Monument

Occupied for just a brief moment in history, between 1270 AD and 1300 AD, the Mogollon pueblo now preserved as the **GILA CLIFF DWELLINGS NATIONAL MONUMENT** is southern New Mexico's most spectacular archeological site. While not on the scale of the Ancestral Puebloan "cities" of the Four Corners region – see Chapter 1 – it's much less visited, and you may well have the place to yourself. To modern eyes, ancient Southwestern peoples often seem to have chosen to live in inhospitable places, but here there's no such problem. The dwellings are tucked into sheltered south-facing recesses along the wall of a shallow canyon, a couple of hundred feet above a perennial creek and thus in earshot of running water and the constant rustle of small game. "Gila," incidentally, is pronounced "heela," and comes from an Apache word meaning mountain.

Even when there's no traffic, driving the full fifty miles from Silver City can take two hours. You won't have time to see the monument if you set off from Silver City later than 4pm in summer, or 2pm in winter. If you're coming from the east, Hwy-35, which branches off Hwy-152 fifty miles west of I-25, is not so slow or mountainous, but it's still a hell of a long drive. Either way, the final eight miles follow the broad valley of the Gila River. The **visitor center**, poised near the confluence of its Middle and West forks, is the place to pay the entrance fee of $3 per person or $10 per family (daily: summer 8am–5pm; winter 8am–4.30pm; ☎575/536-9461, ⊛www.nps.gov/gicl).

The **trail** to the dwellings (daily: summer 8am–6pm; winter 9am–4pm) starts a mile further on, crossing the Gila on a long footbridge. Only half a mile along the creek do you get your first glimpse of the pueblo. What from below looks like three separate caves turns out after you climb the hillside to be a single, deep, long alcove with three entrances. Each entrance was sealed with stones and mortar, but behind them lay around forty interconnected rooms, sharing a communal – and presumably very dark – plaza at the rear. As the trail leads into and through the complex, keep an eye out for the pictographs that mark certain dwellings, as well as a granary that still holds a desiccated cache of tiny corn.

Practicalities

The Forest Service maintains two small, free **campgrounds** beside the Gila River, five miles south of the monument, equipped with running water in summer only. Three miles further south, the *Gila Hot Springs Vacation Center* (☎575/536-9551, ⊛www.gilahotspringsranch.com; ❸), holds another pretty campground with tent camping for $4, plus RV hookups and a couple of comfortable, large rental units at bargain rates. The owners offer hunting and horseback trips to the mountains.

Seventeen miles southeast of the intersection of Hwy-35 and Hwy-15, a total of 34 miles south of the monument, or eleven miles up Hwy-35 from

Hwy-152, the *Pueblo on the Mimbres Bed & Breakfast* (☎575/536-9391, ⓦwww
.puebloonthemimbres.com; ⑤) offers three separate Western-themed B&B
units, with full kitchen and shared indoor and outdoor seating areas.

Lordsburg

Sixty miles down the interstate from Deming, 44 miles southwest of Silver City,
and just twenty miles short of Arizona, **LORDSBURG** is southwest New
Mexico's last gasp. John Wayne went to a lot of trouble to get here in *Stagecoach*,
but the desultory strip of gas stations and motels today make you wonder why
he bothered. Far more redolent of the Old West is **SHAKESPEARE**, two
miles south, a privately owned **ghost town** that's only open for infrequent
guided tours (March–Dec only, on the second Sat & Sun of each month, plus
occasional other weekends, 10am & 2pm; $4; ☎575/542-9034, ⓦwww
.shakespeareghostown.com). If you go at any other time, there's no access to the
site and nothing to see.

Practicalities

The **New Mexico Welcome Center**, south of the interstate at the west end of
town (daily 8am–5pm; ☎575/542-8149), is the best place to pick up information on Lordsburg and the region. If you need a **bed**, the few blocks south of
I-10 on Main Street hold much better options than the dismal mom-and-pop
motels on Motel Drive, with a reasonable *Super 8*, 110 E Maple St (☎575/542-
8882 or 1-800/800-8000, ⓦwww.super8.com; ③), and a big *Holiday Inn Express*,
1408 S Main St (☎575/542-3666, ⓦwww.hiexpress.com; ④), with large rooms.
Kranberry's, opposite at 1405 S Main St (☎575/542-9400), is the best of a
humdrum crop of **diners**, and serves a tasty $8 green chile stew.

4

Phoenix and southern Arizona

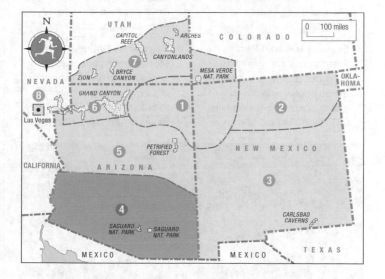

CHAPTER 4 # Highlights

✳ **The Heard Museum** Arizona's finest collection of Native American artifacts, including hundreds of superb Hopi *kachinas*. See p.229

✳ **Desert Botanical Garden** A tremendous assortment of fascinating desert plants thrives in the heat of the Valley of the Sun. See p.231

✳ **Hotel Congress** Downtown Tucson's hippest hangout; not just a hotel and a hostel, but also a great café and nightclub. See p.244

✳ **Saguaro National Park** There's nowhere quite like it; hordes of towering multi-armed saguaro cactuses march across the desert hills of Tucson. See p.248

✳ **San Xavier del Bac** The spectacular "White Dove of the Desert" has to be the Southwest's most beautiful mission church. See p.252

✳ **Tombstone** From the OK Corral to *Big Nose Kate's*, Tombstone is an irresistible throwback to the wildest days of the West. See p.260

✳ **Bisbee** Atmospheric old mining town that has reinvented itself as a cozy, arty, mountain hideaway for overheated Arizonans. See p.263

✳ **Chiricahua National Monument** Apaches such as Geronimo and Cochise once hid among the weird rock formations of this remote mountain fastness. See p.265

▲ Rock formations at Chiricahua National Monument

Phoenix and southern Arizona

D espite every conceivable geographic and climatic disadvantage, ninety percent of Arizonans live in **Southern Arizona**, mainly concentrated in two of the most unlikely cities on earth – **Phoenix** and **Tucson**. Not only does Southern Arizona for the most part lack the compelling scenery of the state's northern half, it also lacks the **water** to support either Phoenix or Tucson. However, although the very existence of either city defies normal logic, they have accrued sufficient political leverage to persuade the federal government to spend ever more money on vast canal projects to meet their needs.

Phoenix in particular can be seen as the bloated spider at the center of the web, sucking the juices from the rest of the state. By far the largest city in Arizona, it has minimal appeal for tourists. **Tucson** at least has a spark of life, thanks to its long and fascinating history; it started out as a Mexican frontier outpost, and is still surrounded by such missionary relics as the churches of **San Xavier del Bac** and **Tumacácori**. It's also at ease with its desert surroundings, accessible in **Saguaro National Park** and the **Arizona-Sonora Desert Museum**. Beyond Tucson, **southeast Arizona** is the one area of southern Arizona where the landscapes rival those of the Colorado Plateau, and as well as intriguing flora and fauna its "sky islands" hold evocative Wild West sites like **Tombstone**, now an entertaining if slightly tacky theme park of a town, and the mining settlement of **Bisbee**.

Phoenix's fragile grip on reality is highlighted by the fact that it was built on the ruins of a long-lost desert civilization. Until 1350 AD, the valleys of southern Arizona were home to the **Hohokam** people and crisscrossed by sophisticated irrigation canals. The Hohokam eventually depleted the land too much for their way of life to endure. Their name means "people who have vanished" in the language of the **'O'odham** (once known as the Pima and the Papago) who later took their place. The 'O'odham now occupy vast reservations in southwest Arizona, while their old enemies, the **Apache**, dominate the mountains to the east.

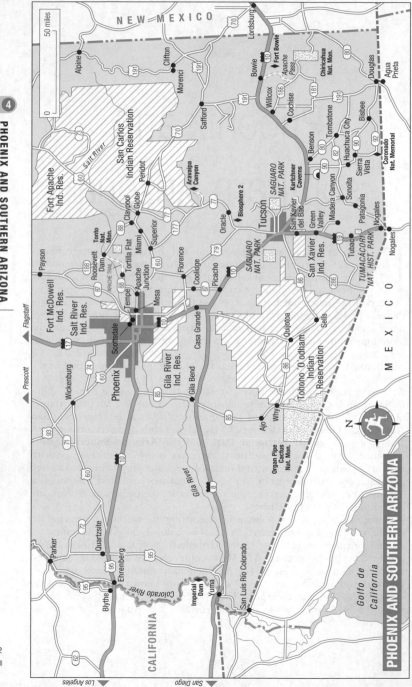

PHOENIX AND SOUTHERN ARIZONA

Phoenix

When it began life in the 1860s, **PHOENIX** must have seemed like a good idea. The sweltering little farming town stood in the heart of the **Salt River Valley**, which measures forty miles east to west and twenty miles north to south, with a ready-made irrigation system left by ancient Indians and plenty of room to expand. Within a century, however, Phoenix had turned into what writer Edward Abbey called "the blob that is eating Arizona," acquiring as it did so the money and political clout to grow way beyond its natural limitations. Today, Arizona's capital has filled the entire valley and is the fifth largest city in the US. Over 1.5 million people live within the city boundaries, and around four million people inhabit the twenty separate incorporated cities, such as **Scottsdale**, **Tempe**, and **Mesa**, which together make up the metropolitan area. Note that although the entire Phoenix area is known colloquially as the **Valley of the Sun**, the term has no official meaning.

Perhaps the single most defining characteristic of Phoenix, even more than its sheer size, is that it's **hot**; between June and August daytime highs average over 100°F, making it one of the world's hottest cities outside the Middle East. While that may put off visitors in summer, when local room rates are at their lowest, tourists flock here from colder climes in winter, to enjoy temperatures that rarely drop below 65°F. They pay vast sums to warm their bones in the luxury resorts and spas, concentrated especially in Scottsdale, that are the modern equivalent of the 1930s dude ranches. Unlike golf, tennis, and shopping at one of the city's plentiful upscale malls, **sightseeing** rarely ranks high on the agenda. In fact, apart from the **Heard Museum**'s excellent Native American displays, the cactuses at the **Desert Botanical Garden**, and Frank Lloyd Wright's architecture studio at **Taliesin West**, Phoenix is short of must-see attractions. If you're on a touring vacation, there's no reason to spend more than a night or two, and you could easily choose to bypass it altogether.

A history of Phoenix

Phoenix epitomizes the Western maxim that "water flows uphill to money," with a history that revolves around its maneuverings to obtain ever more water, from ever further afield. The first Anglo-American settler in the Salt River Valley was John Smith in **1865**, who supplied hay to Camp McDowell, thirty miles northeast. However, the obvious traces of over three hundred miles of **canals** dug by the ancient **Hohokam** people (see p.497) made it clear that the valley had once supported a large population. By clearing one such canal in 1867, Confederate deserter Jack Swilling established **Phoenix**. It was named by British adventurer "Lord" Darrel Duppa, who saw it as rising like the mythical bird from the ashes of the Hohokam civilization.

Phoenix was laid out in 1870 on a 98-block grid measuring one mile long by half a mile wide. Avenues and streets (now numbered) were named for Indian tribes, and cross streets for presidents. By 1889 it was **capital** of Arizona, and home to over ten thousand people. Catastrophic floods and droughts during the 1890s convinced the city-dwellers that their future depended on ensuring a safe, dependable source of water. The building of the **Roosevelt Dam** in the mountains to the east, in 1911 (see p.236), was the first step in a process that culminated with the completion of the **Central Arizona Project**, a 336-mile canal from the Colorado River to Phoenix, in the 1990s.

By the 1920s Phoenix was promoting itself as the "winter playground of the Southwest," a healthy refuge from the smog-laden cities of the East. Its citizens were exhorted to landscape their properties with gardens, under the slogan

"**Let's Do Away With the Desert**," and lavish resort hotels began to open. Exponential growth truly began during World War II, when the city acquired three major air bases, and **industrialization** continued apace during the 1950s. The development of **air-conditioning** finally made the desert heat bearable, and the population swelled from 107,000 to 439,000 between 1950 and 1960 alone. As it swallowed a host of neighboring communities, the city's endless sprawl swiftly covered the "golden fields of ripened grain" described in one

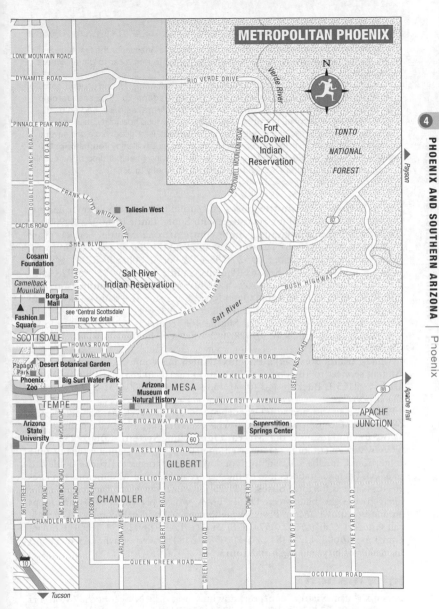

1940s guidebook. By the time it topped one million, around 1990, it had grown by over four hundred square miles in forty years.

Arrival and getting around

Sky Harbor International Airport (☎602/273-3300, ⓦwww.phxskyharbor .com), three miles east of downtown, holds outlets of all the major **rental car**

Excursions from Phoenix

If a family visit or business trip to Phoenix brings you to Arizona for the first time and you'd like to see a little more of the state, you'll have to rent a car to get anywhere interesting.

Great **day-trips** include driving a hundred miles north on I-17 and visiting some combination of **Montezuma Castle** (see p.303), **Sedona** (p.295), and **Jerome** (p.301), or following the **Apache Trail** northeast from Mesa, as described on p.235. With a **weekend** to spare, the **Grand Canyon** is an obvious possibility, though it is a 450-mile round-trip excursion. Alternatively, **Flagstaff** is a good base for several lesser known attractions (see p.285), while Wild West fans will enjoy **Tombstone**, 180 miles southeast (p.260). Best of all, if you're up to driving three hundred miles each way, is northeast Arizona's stupendous **Canyon de Chelly** (p.68).

chains. Door-to-door **shuttle buses** cost around $10 for downtown destinations and more like $20 for Scottsdale, with SuperShuttle (☎602/244-9000 or 1-800/258-3826, ⓦwww.supershuttle.com). Arizona Shuttle Services runs frequent shuttles south to **Tucson** (daily 6.30am–11.30pm; one-way $30 with 7-day advance reservation; ☎520/795-6772 or 1-800/888-2749, ⓦwww .arizonashuttle.com); the Sedona–Phoenix Shuttle (one-way $50; ☎928/282-2066 or 1-800/448-7988 in AZ, ⓦwww.sedona-phoenix-shuttle.com) runs eight daily services to **Sedona**; Open Road Tours runs five daily services up to **Flagstaff** (one-way $42, round-trip $76; ☎602/997-6474 or 1-800/766-7117, ⓦwww.openroadtours.com); and Shuttle "U" connects with **Prescott** (one-way $34, round-trip $56; ☎928/442-1000 or 1-800/304-6114, ⓦwww .shuttleu.com).

Amtrak **trains** don't serve Phoenix, though bus connections coincide with Amtrak services to Tucson (see p.243) and Flagstaff (p.285). Greyhound **buses** arrive at 2115 E Buckeye Rd (☎602/389-4200 or 1-800/231-2222), close to the airport.

Phoenix is so vast, and so utterly dependent on car travel, that it's much easier to drive than to use **public transport** – even driving, it can take hours to get across town. However, the **Metro Light Rail System** (☎602/253-5000, ⓦwww.valleymetro.org) commenced operations in 2008, along a twenty-mile route, from Camelback Road north of downtown Phoenix to Apache Boulevard in Mesa. There's a station close to the airport at 44th and Washington, and fares are the same as for local **buses**, at $1.25 for a one-way ride. Tourists are more likely to use the blue/green DASH buses, which ply two extravagant loops around downtown (Mon–Fri 6.30am–8pm; free). Local **cab** companies include call Checker Cab (☎602/257-1818) or Ace Taxi (☎602/254-1999). Contact Gray Line (☎602/437-3484 or 1-800/777-3484, ⓦwww.graylinearizona.com) for details of **city** and **regional tours**.

Information

Phoenix's main **visitor center** is downtown at 125 N Second St (Mon–Fri 8am–5pm; ☎602/254-6500 or 1-877/225-5749, ⓦwww.visitphoenix.com); there's also an office at 2502 E Camelback Rd, near the northeast corner of the Biltmore Fashion Park (Mon–Fri 10am–9pm, Sat 10am–6pm, Sun noon–6pm; ☎602/955-1963). **Scottsdale** has its own visitor center at 4343 N Scottsdale Rd (Mon–Fri 8am–5pm; ☎480/421-1004 or 1-800/782-1117, ⓦwww .scottsdalecvb.com); **Tempe** has one at 51 W Third St (Mon–Fri 8am–5pm; ☎480/894-8158 or 1-800/283-6734, ⓦwww.tempecvb.com); as does **Mesa**, at

120 N Center St (Mon–Fri 8am–5pm; ☎480/827-4700 or 1-800/283-6732, Ⓦwww.visitmesa.com).

Accommodation

Metropolitan Phoenix is so huge that it's worth making sure that your **accommodation** is near the places you want to visit. Downtown Phoenix is one of the more affordable areas of the city, with cheap motels lining the somewhat rundown Van Buren Street a few blocks north of the center. Room rates are considerably more expensive in **winter**, when snowbirds from all over the US fill the upscale **resorts** of Scottsdale in particular. If you're driving in from elsewhere in the Southwest, pick up discount lodging coupons at state welcome centers, and courtesy phones at the baggage claim area in Sky Harbor airport offer bargain rates too.

Central Phoenix

Arizona Biltmore Resort & Spa 2400 E Missouri Ave ☎602/955-6600 or 1-800/950-0086, Ⓦwww.arizonabiltmore.com. Extraordinarily lavish 500-room resort, built under the influence of Frank Lloyd Wright in the 1930s and still retaining its Art Deco trimmings and extravagant gardens despite subsequent renovations. It is showing its age, however, and many guests resent the extra charges for almost everything. Two golf courses, three restaurants, plus tennis and spa. ⑨

DOWNTOWN PHOENIX

ACCOMMODATION
Best Western Central Phoenix — A
Budget Lodge Motel — C
Hotel San Carlos — D
Metcalf House Hostel — B

EATING & DRINKING
Alice Cooper'stown — 5
Arcadia Farms — 2
Cibo — 3
Drip Coffee Lounge — 1
Pizzeria Bianco — 4

0   800 yds

Best Western Central Phoenix Inn & Suites
1100 N Central Ave ☎602/252-2100 or
1-800/780-7234, ⓦwww.bestwestern.com. Rates
remain constant year-round at this good-value
business-oriented hotel, close to downtown a
quarter-mile north of the Heard Museum, with pool
and free breakfasts. ⑤

Budget Lodge Motel 402 W Van Buren St
☎602/254-7247 or 1-800/780-5733, ⓦwww
.budgetinn.com. Reasonably attractive rooms at
very attractive rates, in an unexciting motel setting
within walking distance of the downtown core,
though you won't want to walk here after dark. ③

Holiday Inn Express Phoenix Airport 3401 E
University Drive ☎602/453-9900, ⓦwww
.hiexpress.com. This very presentable, good-value
motel, between Phoenix and Tempe, may not be
somewhere to spend very long, but it's a handy
overnight stop before or after a flight from nearby
Sky Harbor, with a pool and complimentary
breakfast. ⑦

Hotel San Carlos 202 N Central Ave ☎602/253-
4121 or 1-866/253-4121, ⓦwww.hotelsancarlos
.com. To appreciate this historic, very central 1920s
hotel, you have to be the kind of traveler who
positively prefers an old-fashioned, frazzled and
often noisy downtown hotel to a crisp, new, deathly
quiet motel. That said, rooms are very tastefully
furnished, and there's a nice café, and a rooftop
swimming pool. ⑦

Metcalf House Hostel, 1026 N Ninth St above
Roosevelt St ☎602/254-9803, ⓦwww.home
.earthlink.net/~phxhostel/. Dorm beds at $18 for
HI/AYH members, $25 non members, in a slightly
rundown location in a residential district, 15min
walk north of the Arizona Center. No phone reservations, but space is usually available in the
ten-bed men's dorm and four-bed "ladies" dorm.
No curfew, plus use of kitchen and laundry. Check
in 5–10pm, or, usually but not always, 7–10am.
Closed July & Aug. ①

Super 8 Phoenix 965 E Van Buren St ☎602/252-
6823 or 1-800/800-8000, ⓦsuper8.com. Dependable chain motel, in a rundown neighborhood very
close to downtown, with a pool; there are seven
other *Super8s* in the Phoenix area. ③

Scottsdale

**Days Inn Scottsdale Resort at Fashion Square
Mall** 4710 N Scottsdale Rd ☎480/947-5411 or
1-800/329-7466, ⓦwww.scottsdaledaysinn.com.
Though not all that prepossessing, this two-story
motel, immediately north of Fashion Square Mall –
just stroll across the street – has perfectly acceptable rooms, plus an outdoor pool with bar and
beach volleyball court, and can be a real bargain. ⑤

**Four Seasons Resort Scottsdale at Troon
North** 10600 East Crescent Moon Drive
☎480/515-5700, ⓦwww.fourseasons.com
/scottsdale. Magnificent desert resort, with very
luxurious rooms and suites arrayed in separate
casitas around spacious swimming pools in the
cactus-studded mountains to the north of Scottsdale,
plus a good spa and fine restaurants. ⑨

Hermosa Inn 5532 N Palo Cristi Rd ☎602/955-
8614 or 1-800/241-1210, ⓦwww.hermosainn
.com. Former guest ranch, poised between Phoenix
and Scottsdale in Paradise Valley, that's been
converted into a tranquil 35-room boutique hotel,
with a genuine Southwestern ambience to its large,
luxurious rooms and a good restaurant. ⑨

The Inn at Pima 7330 N Pima Rd ☎480/948-
3800 or 1-800/344-0262, ⓦwww.zmchotels.com.
Smart low-rise motel, with comfortable conventional rooms and pricier suites, a few miles
northwest of central Scottsdale but offering free
local shuttles. ⑦

Motel 6 On Camelback 6848 E Camelback Rd
☎480/946-2280 or 1-800/466-8356, ⓦwww
.motel6.com. Cut-price lodgings are few and far
between in Scottsdale, so this totally unremarkable
budget motel, just off I-17 close to downtown
Scottsdale, is well worth considering. ③

The Phoenician 6000 E Camelback Rd
☎480/941-8200 or 1-800/888-8234, ⓦwww
.thephoenician.com. Gorgeous 250-acre resort,
spread out at the base of Camelback Mountain at
the northern end of Scottsdale and offering every
conceivable luxury, with golf course, waterfalls, and
lush gardens as well as lavish rooms and
restaurants. ⑨

Tempe

Fiesta Resort Conference Center 2100 S Priest
Drive ☎480/967-1441 or 1-800/528-6481,
ⓦwww.fiestainnresort.com. Recently upgraded for
conference use, this upscale resort still has an
appealing Southwestern ambience, and remains
less expensive than its Scottsdale counterparts,
offering large rooms plus two restaurants, pool,
tennis, and spa. ⑦

Hyatt Place Tempe 1413 W Rio Salado Parkway
☎480/804-9544, ⓦphoenixairport.place.hyatt
.com. Handy for both the airport and downtown
Tempe – and connected to both by free shuttles –
this crisp, new hotel offers upscale facilities at
surprisingly affordable prices. ⑦

Sleep Inn Airport 2621 S 47th Place ☎480/967-
7100 or 1-800/631-3054, ⓦwww.sleepinn.com.
Above-average chain motel, three miles south of
the airport but served by 24hr free shuttles;
breakfast is free. ⑥

Tempe Mission Palms Hotel 60 E Fifth St
ⓣ480/894-1400 or 1-800/547-8705, ⓦwww
.missionpalms.com. Very comfortable Southwestern-themed, largely business-oriented hotel in

Tempe's revitalized Mill Ave district, with a rooftop
swimming pool. Good value in summer, but pricier
in winter. ⑨

Central Phoenix

Although **Downtown Phoenix** – defined as the few blocks east and west of
Central Avenue and north and south of **Washington Street** – remains too hot
and too spread out to walk around in any comfort, determined efforts have
been made to regenerate and revitalize the area. A ninety-block district, focusing
on two massive side-by-side sports stadiums, the **US Airways Center** and
Chase Field (home respectively to the Phoenix Suns and Arizona Diamondbacks; see p.234) has even been rebranded with a new name – **Copper Square**.
Adjoining the two is the one significant downtown **mall**, the **Arizona
Center**, on Van Buren Street between Third and Fifth.

What little remains of Phoenix's nineteenth-century architecture now constitutes **Heritage Square**, a couple of blocks southeast of the Arizona Center at
115 N Sixth St. Rather than original adobe ranch houses, however, it preserves
a quaint assortment of Victorian homes converted into tea rooms and toy
museums. You can get a better impression of the early days at the **Phoenix
Museum of History**, across the street at 105 N Fifth St (Tues–Sat 10am–5pm;
$6; ⓣ602/253-2734, ⓦwww.pmoh.org), which displays a "calendar stick" used
by Pima Indians and features the city's first jail – a rock with a chain attached –
as well as early town plans and a steam-powered bicycle.

Immediately south, at 600 E Washington St, the **Arizona Science Center**
(daily 10am–5pm; adults $9, ages 3–17 $7; ⓣ602/716-2000, ⓦwww.azscience
.org) ranks as Arizona's second-favorite tourist attraction, welcoming barely
fewer visitors each year than the Grand Canyon. Aimed primarily at children,
it's a hands-on museum of learning games and interactive gimmicks that centers
on a giant-screen movie theater.

Two more significant attractions lie a mile or so north of downtown (and
north of I-10, though you won't see the interstate as it burrows beneath Central
Avenue). The permanent collection at the vast and hugely rewarding **Phoenix
Art Museum**, 1625 N Central Ave (Tues 10am–9pm, Wed–Sun 10am–5pm;
adults $10, ages 6–17 $4; free Tues 3–9pm, and also open free first Fri of month
6–10pm; ⓣ602/257-1222, ⓦwww.phxart.org), is sensibly rooted in an
extensive array of Western art, starting with David Hockney's rendition of the
Grand Canyon and including an enjoyable room devoted to Arizona artist
Philip Curtis. Anish Kapoor's black sculpture *Upside Down Inside Out* is another
highlight, and temporary exhibitions range through all eras and styles. A top-
quality gift store stocks Mexican crafts items and jazzy modern ceramics.

Three blocks north, the **Heard Museum**, 2301 N Central Ave (daily
9.30am–5pm; $10; children 6–12 $3; ⓣ602/252-8848, ⓦwww.heard.org), has
been greatly enlarged in the last few years, while still showcasing its lovely old
original buildings. It provides a good introduction to the culture of the **Native
Americans** of the Southwest, and their arts and crafts in particular.
A sumptuous pottery collection includes stunning Mimbres bowls (see p.216),
clay dolls made by the Quechan and Mohave peoples as souvenirs for
nineteenth-century railroad passengers, and modern Hopi ceramics. You'll also
find a complete Navajo *hogan* (see p.74), some fine old Havasupai baskets,
Apache beadwork, and painted buffalo-skin shields from New Mexican pueblos.
Best of all are the Hopi **kachina dolls** – see p.78 – four hundred of which were

▲ Hopi *Kachina* dolls, Heard Museum, Phoenix

donated by arch-conservative Arizona senator Barry Goldwater. Additional galleries upstairs tell the heartbreaking story of how the federal government shattered traditional family life by shipping Native American children to boarding schools. Once again, the museum also holds a superb store, and a good *Arcadia Farms* café (see p.232).

Scottsdale

Now home to almost 250,000 people and stretching more than twenty miles from north to south, the town of **SCOTTSDALE**, founded ten miles northeast of Phoenix in the 1880s, is a remarkable success story in its own right. Despite being almost wholly subsumed into the metropolitan maw, it has carved itself an eccentric double niche as both the city's chic-est destination, home to opulent resorts and designer-led malls, and its most determinedly "Western" quarter.

Southeast of **Camelback Mountain** and the **Scottsdale Fashion Square** mall, downtown Scottsdale centers on a few pleasant blocks of sidewalk cafés and souvenir stores. West of Scottsdale Road counts as the **Main Street Arts and Antiques District**; to the east, **Old Town** plays the Wild West theme for all it's worth. At 7374 E Second St, the **Scottsdale Museum of Contemporary Art** (Tues, Wed, Fri, & Sat 10am–5pm, Thurs 10am–8pm, Sun noon–5pm; closed Tues June–Aug; $7, free Thurs & Fri in summer, Thurs in winter; ☏480/994-2787, ⊛www.smoca.org) is a showcase for stimulating modern art, hosting changing temporary exhibitions rather than a permanent collection.

Whatever its general appearance may suggest, Phoenix has managed to attract some visionary designers. Notable among them was **Frank Lloyd Wright**, who came to the city to work on the *Biltmore Hotel* and returned to spend the winter for most of the 25 years before his death in 1959. His studio, **Taliesin West** – located at 114th Street and Frank Lloyd Wright Boulevard, at Scottsdale's far northeastern edge – is now an architecture school and a working design studio, with multimedia exhibits of the man's life and work (Oct–May daily 10am–4pm; June & Sept daily 9am–4pm; July & Aug Mon & Thurs–Sun 9am–4pm; ☏480/860-2700, ⊛www.franklloydwright.org). It can only be seen on guided visits, the main options being the hour-long "Panorama Tour" (daily 10am, 12.15pm & 2.15pm; $27); the ninety-minute "Insight Tour" (daily 9am–4pm, every hour May–Oct, every half-hour Nov–April; $32), which grants access to Wright's private living area; and the three-hour "Behind The Scenes Tour" (Mon, Thurs & Sat 9.15am; $60). Seventy years after Wright first came here, Taliesin West is still a splendidly isolated spot, where his trademark "organic architecture" makes perfect sense. Wright and his students camped out and assessed the terrain long before building any permanent structures, and the complex blends seamlessly into the desert. The expertise and enthusiasm of the guides makes the experience well worth the price.

ACCOMMODATION
Days Inn Scottsdale	A
Motel 6 On Camelback	B
The Phoenician	C

EATING & DRINKING
Bandera	3
Cowboy Ciao	1
Malee's on Main	2

CENTRAL SCOTTSDALE

Designed by **Paolo Soleri**, an Italian-born former student of Wright, and constructed out of rammed earth and concrete, the buildings at the **Cosanti Foundation**, four miles southwest at 6433 Doubletree Ranch Rd, have a similar organic feel (Mon–Sat 9am–5pm, Sun 11am–5pm; $1 donation; ☎480/948-6145, ⓦ www.arcosanti.org). Crafts workshops cast bells and bronzes, and a small museum shows drawings and models of Soleri's life work: the planned community of **Arcosanti**, described on p.304.

In **Papago Park** at the south end of Scottsdale **Papago Park**, the fascinating **Desert Botanical Garden**, 1201 North Galvin Parkway (daily: May–Sept 7am–8pm; Oct–April 8am–8pm; adults $10, ages 3–12 $4; ☎480/941-1225, ⓦ www.dbg.org), is filled with an amazing array of cactuses and desert flora from around the world. Prime specimens include spineless "totem pole" cactuses from the Galápagos Islands and "living stone" plants from South Africa that at a glance you'd never suspect were alive. Separate enclaves are devoted to **butterflies** – seen at their best in August and September – and to **hummingbirds**, of which Arizona boasts fifteen indigenous species.

Nearby, the relatively minor **Phoenix Zoo** (June–Sept Mon–Fri 7am–2pm, Sat & Sun 7am–4pm; Oct & mid-Jan to May daily 9am–5pm; Nov daily 9am–4pm; Dec to mid-Jan daily 9am–4pm & 6–10pm; adults $16, ages 3–12 $7; ☎602/273-1341, ⓦ www.phoenixzoo.org) offers four monkey islands, some giant Galápagos tortoises, and a half-hour ride on a Safari Train.

Tempe

Contemporary Phoenix's major success story has been the transformation of the community of **TEMPE** into the liveliest and most dynamic portion of the Valley of the Sun. It lies south of Scottsdale, across I-60, and six miles east of downtown Phoenix. The fifty thousand students of **Arizona State University**, keep the cafés, clubs, stores, and restaurants of the red-brick **Mill Avenue** constantly buzzing. Several minor museums and galleries are dotted across the college campus, immediately east, while a couple of blocks north the Salt River has been dammed and its surroundings landscaped to create an appealing park, the **Tempe Town Lake**.

Mesa

Built on the site of the Mormon settlement of Fort Utah, which lasted for three years from 1877, **MESA**, east of Tempe, is now Arizona's third-largest city. Covering more than a hundred square miles, it has a population of over 450,000. Hidden among its endless broad boulevards are twenty golf courses, several large malls, some of Phoenix's most affordable residential districts, and dozens of cheap motels. With the Superstition Mountains rising to the east, it's not a bad base for passing visitors.

As well as displays on dinosaurs and the Hohokam, the enjoyable **Arizona Museum of Natural History**, 53 N MacDonald St (Tues–Sat 10am–5pm, Sun 1–5pm; $6; ☎ 480/644-2230, ⊛ www.arizonamuseumofnaturalhistory.org), features a reconstruction of a block of Mesa's Main Street as it looked a century ago.

Eating

Unless you're prepared to pay resort prices, it's hard to find a good **restaurant** in Phoenix with very much atmosphere. Apart from a block or two in central Scottsdale, and Tempe's lively Mill Avenue, no areas of the metropolis are small enough to walk around while you look for a place to eat, but if you're happy to drive, neighborhood diners – especially Mexican – can still be found, and the major thoroughfares are the usual fast-food heaven.

Central Phoenix

Alice Cooper'stown 101 E Jackson St ☎ 602/253-7337, ⊛ www.alicecooperstown.com. Barbecue restaurant-cum-sports bar, owned by the rock star and local resident, and located alongside downtown's US Airways Center. While far from fine dining, the food's better than you might expect, with entrees priced at up to $15, and the atmosphere is fun, with waiters in full Alice make-up. Sun–Thurs 11am–10pm, Fri & Sat 11am–11pm.

Arcadia Farms Heard Museum, 2301 N Central Ave ☎ 602/251-0204, ⊛ www.arcadiafarmscafe.com. This small, bright museum café – an offshoot of the Scottsdale original (7014 E First Ave; ☎ 480/941-5665), which has another branch nearby at the Phoenix Museum of Art – serves healthy Southwestern breakfasts and lunches, with salads, sandwiches and entrees, including daily specials like crab cakes and quesadillas, priced at around $12. Daily 9.30am–3.30pm.

Barrio Café 2814 N 16th St ☎ 602/636-0240, ⊛ www.barriocafe.com. Reservations are not taken at this wildly popular little local Mexican place, but it's worth the wait – you can always sample the huge array of tequilas – to enjoy authentic southern Mexican food, including succulent *cochinita pibil* (pork), and guacamole freshly made at your table. Tues–Thurs 11am–10pm, Fri 11am–10.30pm, Sat 5–10.30pm, Sun 11am–9pm.

Cibo Restaurant 603 N Fifth Ave ☎ 602/441-2697, ⊛ www.cibophoenix.com. This appealing restored downtown house, with a nice patio, serves gorgeous *saltimbocca* sandwiches and salads for lunch, then $12 pizzas plus a wide range of antipasti for dinner. Mon 11am–2pm & 5–9pm, Tues–Thurs 11am–2pm & 5–10pm, Fri 11am–2pm & 5–11pm, Sat 5–11pm.

Coup des Tartes 4626 N 16th St ☎ 602/212-1082, ⊛ www.nicetartes.com. Unassuming 1930s farmhouse that conceals a romantic little dinner-only restaurant, serving classic French appetizers like brie with caramelized apples ($12), a broader range of entrees from Moroccan lamb shank ($23) to lobster risotto ($36), and succulent French tarts ($9). Bring your own wine, with a corkage charge of $9 per bottle. Tues–Sat 5.30–10pm.

Drip Coffee Lounge 2325 N Seventh St ☎ 602/795-9905, ⊛ www.dripcoffeelounge.com. Stylish, hip coffee bar which also serves simple snacks near the Heard Museum downtown. Daily except Mon 7.30am–3pm.

Durant's 2611 N Central Ave ☎ 602/264-5967, ⊛ www.durantsaz.com. This old-style downtown restaurant is a venerable institution for Arizona's elite, specializing in rich all-American food such as oysters Rockefeller ($16.50) and steaks, at $31 and up; if you can down the 48-oz Porterhouse, your name gets added to a plaque on the wall. Locals also drop in for late-night drinks at the atmospheric central bar. Mon–Thurs 11am–midnight, Fri 11am–1am, Sat 5pm–1am, Sun 4.30pm–midnight.

Pizzeria Bianco Heritage Square, 623 E Adams St ☏602/258-8300, ⓦwww.pizzeriabianco.com. High-quality pizzas in a very convenient downtown location, with ultra-fresh ingredients including home-made mozzarella; no wonder it's so popular. No reservations. Tues–Sat 5–10pm.

Sierra Bonita Grill 6933 N Seventh St ☏602/264-0700, ⓦwww.sierrabonitagrill.com. Hearty Southwestern food, intended to evoke the ranches of yesteryear, with south-of-the-border staples like tamales and quesadillas alongside cowboy stew and buttermilk chicken, and several lighter options. Most appetizers cost under $10, most entrees under $20. Mon–Thurs & Sun 11am–10pm, Fri & Sat 11am–11pm.

Vincent's Market Bistro 3930 E Camelback Rd ☏602/224-3727, ⓦwww.vincentsoncamelback .com. This very inexpensive but high-quality French-style bistro/deli, with a tiny outdoor seating area, is attached to a thriving farmers' market, and squeezed around the back of *Vincent's* much more upscale fine-dining restaurant (also recommended). Lunchtime salads and omelets cost around $8, $10 nightly dinner specials include seafood kebab or paella. Mon–Fri 7am–8pm, Sat & Sun 7am–2pm; closed Mon June–Sept.

Scottsdale

Bandera 3821 N Scottsdale Rd ☏480/994-3524. Chicken cooked in the wood-burning oven ($16) is the specialty in this busy, inexpensive rotisserie on the southeast edge of downtown, though other meats and fish are almost as good. Sun–Thurs 4.30–10pm, Fri & Sat 4.30–11pm.

Binkley's 6920 E Cave Creek Rd ☏480/437-1072, ⓦwww.binkleysrestaurant.com. This expensive but utterly sublime restaurant regularly wins accolades as the finest in Phoenix, combining the best of classic French and contemporary American cuisine. The one snag is that it's a twenty-mile drive north of downtown Scottsdale. Typical entrees like poached sablefish cost around $40, while tasting menus start at $65. Tues–Sat 5.15–9.30pm.

Cowboy Ciao 7133 E Stetson Drive at Sixth ☏480/946-3111, ⓦcowboyciao.com. Appropriately enough, considering a decor that blends an Old West roadhouse with an Italian feel, this hip downtown option serves "modern American food with global influences." At lunchtime, a burger or seared tuna sandwich costs $13; the $12 "Stetson" chopped salad is also available in the evening, when a stuffed pork rib chop is $26 and the grilled

lamb loin $30. Mon–Thurs & Sun 11.30am–2.30pm & 5–10pm, Fri & Sat 11.30am–2.30pm & 5–11pm.

El Chorro Lodge 5550 E Lincoln Drive ☏480/948-5170, ⓦelchorrolodge.com. Spacious, classy Paradise Valley lodge that's been catering to Phoenix sophisticates since 1937; dine al fresco in summer, or by the cozy fireside in winter. The signature Eggs Benedict cost $17, while entrees range from $14 burgers and $19.50 chicken livers up to prime rib at $30–37. Sunday brunch is a local tradition. Mon–Fri 11am–2pm & 5–9.30pm, Sat 5.30–10pm, Sun 9am–2pm (Oct–May only) & 5.30–10pm.

Malee's on Main 7131 E Main St ☏480/947-6042, ⓦwww.maleesthaibistro.com. Somewhat inconspicuous but very popular and dependably good Thai place downtown, serving all the usual items – pad thai noodles, chicken green curry – at reasonable prices. There's another branch at Desert Ridge Marketplace. Mon–Wed 11.30am–2.30pm & 5–9pm, Thurs & Fri 11.30am–10pm, Sat noon–10pm, Sun 5–9pm.

Talavera *Four Seasons Resort Scottsdale at Troon North*,10600 East Crescent Moon Drive ☏480/515-5700. It's worth the long drive up into the hills of northern Scottsdale to reach this very classy, sophisticated resort restaurant, where the terrace enjoys unparalleled views over the valley. You'll pay premium prices for classic dishes like seared *foie gras* or mighty steaks prepared to your specifications, but they're uniformly superb. Daily 6–10pm.

Yasu Sushi Bistro 4316 E Cactus Rd, Ste. B–4 ☏602/787-9181. Besides delicious, inexpensive sushi and sashimi, this tiny but smart Japanese place near the Paradise Valley mall specializes in unusual charcoal-grilled *sumibiyaki* items like scallops or chicken meatballs. Mon–Thurs 11.30am–2.30pm & 5–9.30pm, Fri 11.30am–2.30pm & 5–10.30pm, Sat 5–10.30pm.

Tempe

House of Tricks 114 E Seventh St ☏480/968-1114, ⓦwww.houseoftricks.com. Tiny modern-American place in the University district, named for chefs Robin and Robert Trick, with lots of vegetarian options. Dinner entrees range from $21 for pasta with pesto up to $34 for pistachio-crusted rack of lamb. Daily except Sun 11am–10pm.

Monti's La Casa Vieja 3 W First St ☏480/967-7594, ⓦwww.montis.com. Tempe's oldest adobe house, built beside the Salt River ferry landing in 1873, is now an atmospheric Western-themed diner, serving a conventional steak-and-chicken menu at surprisingly low prices. Mon–Thurs & Sun 11am–10pm, Sat & Sun 11am–11pm.

Ra 411 S Mill Ave ☏480/303-9800, ⓦwww .rasushi.com. Lively, trendy Japanese restaurant in the heart of downtown Tempe – as well as four other Valley locations – where you can get two soft-shell crabs for around $10, and a full bowl of noodles for under $15, while sushi hand rolls cost around $10 and sushi platters are under $20. Daily 11am–11pm.

Mesa

The Landmark Restaurant 809 W Main St ☎ 480/962-4652, ⊛ www.landmarkrestaurant.com. Classic mid-American diner housed in a former Mormon church, serving hearty baked and roasted meats for $16–25, including a trip to the excellent salad bar. Mon–Thurs 11am–8pm, Fri & Sat 11am–9pm, Sun 11am–7pm.

The Seafood Market 1910 S Gilbert Rd ☎ 480/890-0435. A feast of fresh fish, flown in from all over the world and prepared simply at reasonable prices. Also at 1356 W Southern Ave (☎ 480/890-0435). Daily 11.30am–9pm.

Nightlife, entertainment, and sports

Phoenix's **nightlife** has less of a Western identity than you might expect, with Tempe and Scottsdale respectively cultivating an alt-rock, college crowd, and a glitzier clubbing scene. For a rundown of what's happening musically, pick up the free weekly *New Times* (⊛ www.phoenixnewtimes.com), or check out the bars and clubs listed below.

Both the **Phoenix Symphony Hall**, 225 E Adams St (☎ 602/495-1999, ⊛ www.phoenixsymphony.org), and the **Scottsdale Center for the Performing Arts**, 7380 E Second St (☎ 480/994-2787, ⊛ www.scottsdalearts.org), adjacent to the Museum of Contemporary Art, put on classical music, theater, and ballet. The **Arizona Diamondbacks** play major league baseball beneath the retractable roof of air-conditioned Chase Field at 401 E Jefferson St (☎ 602/514-8400, ⊛ www.azdiamondbacks.com), while the **Phoenix Suns** play NBA basketball at the US Airways Center, 201 E Jefferson St (☎ 602/379-7900, ⊛ www.suns.com), and football's **Arizona Cardinals** are based at Glendale's new, state-of-the-art University of Phoenix Stadium (☎ 602/379-0102, ⊛ www.azcardinals.com).

Bars and clubs

Bar Smith 130 E Washington St, Phoenix ☎ 602/229-1265, ⊛ www.barsmithphoenix.com. The best thing about this stylish downtown bar and lounge is its fabulous outdoor dance floor. Mon–Thurs 11am–2pm, Fri 11am–2am, Sat 10pm–2am.

Bikini Lounge 1502 Grand Ave, Phoenix ☎ 602/252-0472. A real gem of a dive bar, this veteran tiki bar attracts a fascinating, eclectic mix of local characters.

Chez Nous 915 Grand Ave ☎ 602 266 7372, ⊛ www.cheznouscentral.com. Dark, deeply atmospheric old-style cocktail lounge, with a steady soul and Motown soundtrack and live R&B bands. Mon–Thurs 3pm–1am, Fri 3pm–2.30am, Sat 6pm–2.30am, Sun 6pm–1am.

e4 4282 N Drinkwater Blvd, Scottsdale ☎ 480/734-9181, ⊛ www.e4-az.com. The city's hottest dance club is a massive, eye-popping affair, designed around the elements of air, earth, fire, and water, and holding a Vegas-style "ultra-lounge" downstairs as well as the *Liquid* dance club with cascading waterfalls. Tues & Wed 9pm–2am, Fri & Sat 9pm–2am. Cover $5 Wed & Thurs, $10 Fri & Sat.

Marquee Theatre 730 N Mill Ave, Tempe ☎ 480/829-0607, ⊛ www.luckymanonline.com. The best venue to see big-name touring acts, with an open floor rather than seating, and good beer.

Last Exit Bar & Grill 1425 W Southern Ave, Tempe ☎ 480/557-6656, ⊛ www.lastexitlive.com. Rock-oriented live music venue in an unpromising mall, where acts range from country-rock to local punks. Mon–Fri 3pm–2am, Sat & Sun 5pm–2am.

Shopping

With the city's great outdoors being too hot and sprawling to take for more than a few minutes at a time, you'll probably find yourself looking for a nice cool **mall** at some point.

The biggest of the lot is the **Metrocenter** (⊛ www.metrocentermall.com), just east of I-17 at 9617 Metro Parkway, nine miles north of downtown. The central mall building contains the usual outlets and large department stores, while countless more stores and restaurants line the oval ring road around it. When you tire of shopping, try the Desert Storm rollercoaster in **Castles'n'Coasters** alongside (June–Aug Fri 5–11pm, Sat noon–11pm, Sun 5–9pm; Sept–May Sun–Thurs 10am 10pm, Fri & Sat 10am–midnight; $25 or pay per ride; ☎602/997-7575, ⊛www.castlesncoasters.com).

The **Biltmore Fashion Park** (⊛www.shopbiltmore.com), north of Camelback Road at 24th Street, halfway between downtown Phoenix and Scottsdale, concentrates on designer names and has a giant *Borders* bookstore, while the **Scottsdale Fashion Square** (⊛www.fashionsquare.com), further east at 7000 E Camelback Rd, is (slightly) more affordable. Also in Scottsdale, a couple of miles north, the smaller **Borgata** mall is notable for its extraordinary mock-Italian architecture, while the **Main Street Arts and Antiques District** is full of pricey galleries, largely specializing in Southwestern and cowboy art. Tempe's **Arizona Mills** mall offers the valley's best discount shopping. Finally, the downtown **Arizona Center** (see p.229) may be short on interesting shops, but at least it has a 24-screen movie theater and busy restaurants.

East of Phoenix

Almost two hundred miles of mountainous terrain stands between Phoenix and New Mexico to the east, much of it belonging to two huge Apache reservations. Although sweltering Phoenicians spend summer weekends in hill towns like Payson and Pinetop to the northeast (both covered in Chapter 5), there's little to detain ordinary tourists on the long drive east.

US-60 and US-70 are the quickest routes to New Mexico, but if you want a quick escape from the desert heat, head instead up the **Apache Trail** into the **Superstition Mountains**, the site in legend of the **Lost Dutchman Mine**. Two German prospectors, Jacob Waltz and Jacob Weiser, supposedly discovered rich deposits of gold around 1870 and turned up repeatedly in the town of Florence bearing priceless nuggets. Before his death in Phoenix in 1890, Waltz is said to have murdered not only Weiser but another seven men who tried to shadow him back to the motherlode. Ever since, expeditions have attempted to follow his deathbed directions to the mine – guarded, according to different accounts, by pygmies or a never-discovered group of Apaches – and thirty gold-seekers are rumored to have lost their lives.

The Apache Trail

The closest accessible wilderness to central Phoenix lies along **Hwy-88**, which climbs northeast into the Superstition Mountains from Apache Junction, almost twenty miles east of Mesa and a good thirty miles from downtown Phoenix. This fifty-mile highway was constructed in 1904 as a direct route to the Roosevelt Dam, then being built at the confluence of Tonto Creek and Salt River. After the dam's completion in 1911, it was renamed **The Apache Trail** in a bid to drum up tourists, and became a popular scenic drive. It's still a long, slow haul, tortuous enough to take around two hours end to end.

Just four miles up from Apache Junction, at 4650 N Mammoth Mine Rd as the cactus-studded foothills start to rise, ramshackle **Goldfield Ghost Town** provides an appealing photo opportunity, complete with discarded mine machinery and a street of tumbledown timber-frame stores (daily 10am–5pm; ⊛www.goldfieldghosttown.com). Much of what you see is either fake or brought from somewhere else, but it's all quite atmospheric. **Activities** including descents into mine shafts, and train rides cost from around $6 per person, and various on-site businesses offer pricier jeep tours, horse rides or even helicopter flights in the vicinity. Alternatively, you can pick up a snack or a meal at the *Coffee Cantina and Bakery* (☎480/983-8777) or the *Mammoth Steak House* (daily 10am–8pm; ☎480/983-6402).

Many day-trippers go no further up the Apache Trail than **Canyon Lake**, fifteen miles along. Created by a more recent dam, it's a bit too narrow to satisfy pleasure-boaters, who find themselves having to turn around every time they get up a bit of speed. However, if you're happy to take it easy, a cruise on *Dolly's Steamboat* (☎480/827-9144, ⓦwww.dollysteamboat.com) is an enjoyable way to pass a couple of hours. Cruises run five days weekly at noon, costing $20; twilight dinner cruises cost $57.

TORTILLA FLAT, at the east end of the lake, is not so much a town as a hundred-yard stretch of boardwalk with an Old West flavor. Its saloon, diner, and souvenir store are all operated by the same management (☎480/984-1776, ⓦwww.tortillaflataz.com). Named for the nearby flat-topped boulders, Tortilla Flat has no connection with the Steinbeck novella.

Beyond Tortilla Flat, as the mountains finally start to get serious, Hwy-88 responds by turning to gravel. After a few hair-raising hairpin bends, with stomach-lurching views across the saguaro-studded canyons, it returns to undulating gently along beside the river. An optional detour drops down to **Apache Lake**, another busy boating and picnicking spot. Keep going to reach **Roosevelt Dam** itself, which was recently raised and strengthened to cope with Phoenix's bottomless thirst for water.

Tonto National Monument

Three miles east of Roosevelt Dam, the **cliff dwellings** of **TONTO NATIONAL MONUMENT** (daily 8am–5pm; $3 per person) stand high above Hwy-88, overlooking Theodore Roosevelt Lake. From the **visitor center** (same hours; ☎928/467-2241, ⓦwww.nps.gov/tont), a very steep trail, which shuts an hour before closing time, climbs half a mile upwards. Not a walk

▲ Town Jail, Tortilla Flat

to schedule for the middle of a summer's day, it leads to the remarkably complete **Lower Ruin**, set in a deep alcove near the top of the rocky ridge, with great saguaro cactuses standing sentinel.

This large pueblo, dating from the mid-fourteenth century, was built by the **Salado** Indians, now regarded as less sophisticated than the Ancestral Puebloans to the north. Their masonry is much cruder, using lumps of rock that had fallen from the cliff face and were then thickly plastered with mud that still bears thousands of ancient fingerprints. Visitors can walk through several rooms of the ruin, some of which retain their original beams and saguaro-rib ceilings. "Shelves" and storage niches are tucked into the cave walls, as well as notches that once supported additional rooms.

Between November and April only, rangers lead guided hikes to the **Upper Ruin**, reached by a separate trail up the next ridge along.

Globe

Hwy-88 rejoins US-60, the direct route east from Phoenix, thirty miles southeast of Tonto National Monument, just outside **GLOBE**. This mining town sprang into being in the 1880s, when a twelve-mile strip of land on which a globe of pure silver had just been discovered was grabbed from the Apache reservation; since the silver and gold ran out, it has made its living from copper.

Downtown Globe's few central blocks still hold several Victorian-era brick structures, though the claim that these include "the West's oldest Woolworth's" betrays quite how little there is of interest. On the northern outskirts, the small **Gila County Historical Museum**, 1330 N Broad St (Mon–Fri 10am–4pm, Sat 11am–3pm; free), explores local history in punitive detail.

That Native Americans lived here before the Apache is shown by the ruins of **Besh-Ba-Gowah**, a mile southeast of town, home first to the Hohokam and later to the Salado. Their modern Apache name means "metal-its-house." Visitors can enter reconstructed living quarters and a *kiva* (daily 9am–5pm; $3).

If you prefer your Wild West utterly unvarnished and unromantic, head a mile or two west of Globe to the twin communities of **CLAYPOOL** and **MIAMI**. All but engulfed by monstrous mountains of copper-mine tailings, these flyblown towns are packed with gun stores, all-day saloons, and pick-up trucks, and are certainly not a vacation destination to be chosen in preference to Miami, Florida.

Practicalities

Globe's **visitor center** stands in front of the museum on Hwy-88, at 1360 N Broad St (Oct–April Mon–Fri 8am–5pm, Sat & Sun 10am–4pm; May–Sept Mon–Fri 8am–5pm; ☎928/425-4495 or 1-800/804-5623, ⓦwww .globemiamichamber.com). The most salubrious of its dozen or so **motels** is the *Days Inn*, 1630 E Ash St (☎928/425 5500; ❼). Downtown **cafés** include the Mexican bakery *La Luz del Dia*, 304 N Broad St (☎928/425-8400), where the burritos are made with fresh tortillas, while *Java Junction*, at Broad and Center (closed Sun; ☎928/402-8926), serves coffee and sandwiches. On the third weekend in October, Native Americans from all over the Southwest pour in for the three-day **Apache Days** fair.

Superior

Fifteen miles southwest of Miami on US-60 – or, if you're driving up from Phoenix, forty miles east of the foot of the Apache Trail – another former silver-mining town, **SUPERIOR**, holds the **Boyce Thompson Arboretum** (daily:

May–Aug 6am–3pm; Sept–April 8am–5pm; last entry 1hr before closing; $7.50, ages 5–12 $3; ☎520/689-2723, ⓦag.arizona.edu/bta). This landscaped public garden spreads through two parallel canyons, and contains desert plants from around the world. Cactuses are of course abundant, but there are also spectacular oddities like the towering boojum tree from Baja California. A brisk walk along the main hiking trail takes around an hour, though you could spend much longer exploring additional side trails like the themed "Plants of the Bible" walk. The fall colors are usually at their best during the last two weeks of November and the first week of December.

A mile or so east of the arboretum, **Buckboard City** is a mock-up Western steak-and-barbecue restaurant that also runs the adjoining "**World's Smallest Museum**," basically a shed filled with all sorts of weird stuff (Wed–Sun 8am–1.30pm; donations; ⓦwww.worldssmallestmuseum.com).

San Carlos Indian Reservation

The two-million-acre **SAN CARLOS INDIAN RESERVATION**, which extends a hundred miles east and north of Globe, was created in 1872 to protect the **Apache** from such outrages as the Camp Grant massacre of 1871 (see p.520). In the words of one tribal member, the reservation was "the worst place in all the great territory stolen from the Apache. If anybody ever lived there permanently, no Apache knew of it. The heat was terrible. The insects were terrible. The water was terrible."

Around eight thousand Apache now live on the reservation, which offers few activities for tourists apart from sailing or fishing on **San Carlos Lake**, twenty miles east of Globe, or **camping** beside it at *Soda Canyon Point* (☎928/475-2756; $5). After the original reservation town of **San Carlos** was drowned when the lake arose behind the new Coolidge Dam in 1930, the community previously known as **Rice**, ten miles north, was simply renamed San Carlos. Today, it's just an administrative center; to learn more about the Apache, visit the **San Carlos Apache Cultural Center** in **Peridot**, on US-70 nearby (ⓦwww.sancarlosapache.com; Mon–Fri 9am–5pm; $3).

Aravaipa Canyon

The beauty of **ARAVAIPA CANYON**, which lies just below the southern boundary of of the San Carlos Reservation, belies its sad history as the site of one of the most notorious tragedies in the whole sorry tale of Anglo–Apache relations. In 1871, when it was home to a semipermanent Apache encampment under the nominal protection of the US Army, 144 women and children were slaughtered in the **Camp Grant massacre**. Their killers were an unholy party of Tucson vigilantes who called themselves the Committee of Public Safety; for more on the so-called "Tucson Ring" that lay behind it, see p.243.

Reached along a well-maintained eleven-mile dirt road that heads east from Hwy-77 fifty miles south of Globe, Aravaipa Canyon is now a **wilderness area**. The terrain ranges from sun-drenched hillsides covered with saguaros to the deep-red gorge carved by Aravaipa Creek – a rare perennial desert stream – and lined by giant cottonwoods. Visitors keen to experience the desert in its wild state need to come prepared; the canyon has no trails, no established campgrounds, and no signs, and is home to rattlesnakes and scorpions. Only fifty people can enter the thirty-square-mile wilderness at any one time; obtain a **permit** ($5 per day, with a maximum two-night stay) from the BLM, 711 Fourteenth Ave, Safford AZ 85546 (☎928/348-4400, ⓦwww.blm.gov/az/aravaipa).

From Phoenix to Tucson

The hundred-mile sprint from Phoenix to Tucson along the **I-10** interstate is one of Arizona's less inspiring drives. The chief distraction en route is the molar-shaped promontory of **Picacho Peak**, at the base of which the roadside Rooster Cogburn Ostrich Farm is as good a place to stretch your legs, and possibly buy a feather duster, as any (daily except Wed 9am–5.30pm; ⓦwww .roostercogburn.com). If you don't mind taking a slightly more circuitous route, however, it's possible to break the journey at a couple of equally unlikely and enigmatic structures – ancient **Casa Grande** and ultra-modern **Biosphere 2**.

Casa Grande Ruins National Monument

On the outskirts of **Coolidge**, fifteen miles east of interstate exit 185, or twenty miles north of exit 210, **CASA GRANDE RUINS NATIONAL MONUMENT** preserves the most substantial surviving example of **Hohokam** architecture (daily 8am–5pm; $5 per person; ☎520/723-3172, ⓦwww.nps .gov/cagi). It shares its name – Spanish for "Great House" – but little else, with the I-10 pit stop of Casa Grande, thirty miles southwest, and the much larger ancient site of Casas Grandes, far south in northern Mexico.

The Casa Grande itself is a four-story building, made of the concrete-like natural stone known as caliche, that was completed early in the fourteenth century. Spanish priest Father Eusebio Kino, who passed this way in 1694 – by which time the site had been abandoned for three centuries – said the main structure was "as large as a castle", and surrounded by thirteen smaller houses and many ruins. It was clear to him that "in ancient times there had been a city here." The house stood in a walled compound in the flood-plain of the **Gila River**, where villagers used a network of canals to grow crops, harvested fruit from saguaro cactuses, and traded for shells and macaws with peoples from the south. It's now protected beneath a spider-like canopy; visitors can enter the compound but not the structure itself. Its exact purpose is unknown, though as its windows and wall niches are aligned with key moments in the cycles of both the sun and moon, archeologists think it was an astronomical observatory that doubled as a fortress.

Biosphere 2

Hwy-79 heads southeast from the small farming community of **FLORENCE**, ten miles east of Casa Grande monument, to meet **Hwy-77** roughly thirty miles north of Tucson. Turning east toward Oracle at this point gives tourists the chance to catch up with the latest developments in the extraordinary science-fiction saga of **BIOSPHERE 2**, at mile-marker 96.5 on Hwy-77 (daily 9am–4pm; $20, ages 6–12 $13; ☎520/838-6200, ⓦwww.b2science.org).

When it was completed, in 1991, this vast complex of Plexiglas pyramids was extensively publicized as a major laboratory for environmental science. Containing five separate "**biomes**," or self-contained ecosystems – rainforest, marsh, savannah, desert, and a 25-foot-deep ocean – it was designed as a miniature working model of Biosphere 1, planet Earth itself, and stocked like a real-life Noah's ark with almost four thousand species of plants and animals. Investigative journalists soon revealed, however, that it was staffed largely by ex-actors from an experimental theater group, assembled by a certain "Johnny Dolphin" in the hope of colonizing Mars and thus escaping nuclear holocaust on Earth. A hundred million dollars' worth of support from Texas oil tycoon Ed Bass got this farfetched scheme off the ground, and top academics were recruited to add a veneer of respectability.

Eight "Biospherians" were sealed into Biosphere 2 in 1991, their "mission" being to survive in isolation for two full years. This they more or less did, growing 88 percent of their own food, and losing 13.65 percent of their body weight. Much of what transpired was replete with irony; hungry Biospherians found themselves planting bananas and papayas in what they had resolved would be the inviolate wilderness of the rainforest and destroying parts of the desert to boost oxygen, while the ocean proved impossible to keep clean. As for their fellow inhabitants, the bush babies caught the hummingbirds, and the only birds to survive were unwanted sparrows that snuck in during construction. After "crazy ants" killed all the pollinating insects, all the plants had to be pollinated by hand.

By the time the next crew moved in, conditions had degenerated into farce. Two of the original crew, who had been acrimoniously fired, broke the Biosphere's seals from the outside, thus aborting the second mission after just six months; they later sued and won compensation for their dismissal.

Though Biosphere 2 briefly ranked among Arizona's most popular tourist destinations, now that no one is locked inside, the crowds have dwindled. Run by the University of Arizona, it's primarily a historical attraction. Even so, the standard two-and-a-half-hour guided tours are still worth taking. Most of that time is spent peering into the greenhouses hoping to spot any sign of life larger than an ant, and marveling at the fact that, whatever you may have assumed, Biosphere 2 is not solar powered but depends on an external natural-gas power plant. Tunnels take you down beneath the "Coral Biome;" the guides insist it isn't an aquarium, but it doesn't half look like one. Visitors are also allowed into the Biospherians' futuristic living quarters, tacked like a space capsule onto the back of the main block, where they appear to have suffered no privations whatsoever.

The all-day *Cañada del Oro* café serves good **meals** on an appealing terrace.

Tucson

For over two hundred years, under five separate flags **TUCSON** has been southern Arizona's leading city. Spreading across a mountain-ringed basin at the northern limits of the **Sonoran Desert**, its 900,000-plus inhabitants pride themselves on being cosmopolitan, cultured, and liberal than those of its upstart rival Phoenix. Like Phoenix, the "Old Pueblo" has grown way past the point where the flow of the region's rivers, such as the Santa Cruz, is sufficient to quench its thirst. All are now dry sandy washes for most of the year, though flash floods still rage through the cross-town culverts after summer thunderstorms. However, Tucson embraces rather than denies the desert, eschewing lawns and fountains in favor of directing visitors toward the landscapes of **Sabino Canyon** and the **Arizona–Sonora Desert Museum** and the cactus-strewn hillsides of **Saguaro National Park**.

By Southwestern standards, Tucson (pronounced *too-sonn*) is a diverse, attractive, and lively city, home to the 37,000 energetic students of the **University of Arizona** as well as a large influx of retirees, and strongly influenced by its long association with Mexico, a mere sixty miles south. Although it suffers from the same Sunbelt sprawl as Albuquerque and Phoenix, it still has a compact and recognizably historic center, some good parks and museums, affordable accommodation and enjoyable restaurants, and even a pretty good nightlife.

A history of Tucson

The valley of the Santa Cruz had already been inhabited for many centuries by the time Spanish priest Eusebio Kino visited the **Pima Indian** settlement of *Stjukshon*, or "dark spring," in 1700. Recent archeological excavations west of downtown have even suggested that this may be the oldest inhabited site in North America. In 1776, under the direction of **Hugo O'Conor**, one of the Catholic "Wild Geese" who had fled English-controlled Ireland to fight for Spain, the Spanish relocated their main Arizonan fortress here from Tubac (see p.254). That forty-mile move northwards brought them closer to **Apache** territory, and the energies of the Hispanic and Pima citizens of **San Agustín de Tucson** were largely devoted to resisting Apache raids and sieges. The severed heads of Apache warriors were displayed as trophies on the city walls.

When Tucson was sold to the US in the **Gadsden Purchase** of 1854 (see p.505), the incoming Anglos were generally welcomed. Most of the valley's Mexican farmers remained in Arizona, and were even joined by more of their former compatriots. Soon, however, travelers were describing Tucson as "a place of resort for traders, speculators, gamblers, horse-thieves and vagrant politicians … a paradise of devils."

Although the **Confederates** who occupied southern Arizona in 1862 were swiftly driven away by Union forces from California, suspicions of lingering Confederate sympathies led to Tucson being passed over as capital of the new Territory. Conflict with the Apache continued, and a vigilante force of Mexicans, Anglos, and 'O'odham Indians from Tucson was responsible for the notorious **Camp Grant massacre** of 144 Apaches in Aravaipa Canyon in 1871 (see p.238). US Army commanders came to believe that a shadowy

▲ Harris hawk, Arizona-Sonora Desert Museum, Tucson

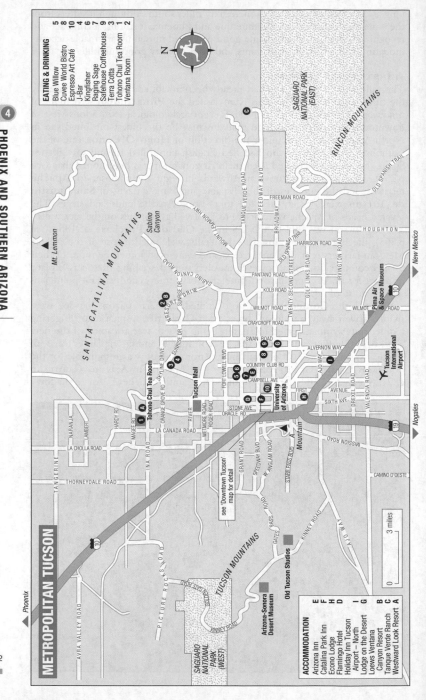

METROPOLITAN TUCSON

▲ Phoenix

EATING & DRINKING

Blue Willow	5
Cuvee World Bistro	8
Espresso Art Café	10
J-Bar	4
Kingfisher	6
Raging Sage	7
Safehouse Coffeehouse	9
Terra Cotta	3
Tohono Chul Tea Room	1
Ventana Room	2

ACCOMMODATION

Arizona Inn	E
Catalina Park Inn	F
Econo Lodge	H
Flamingo Hotel	D
Holiday Inn Tucson Airport – North	I
Lodge on the Desert	G
Loews Ventana Canyon Resort	B
Tanque Verde Ranch	C
Westward Look Resort	A

SANTA CATALINA MOUNTAINS

Mt. Lemmon

Sabino Canyon

RINCON MOUNTAINS

SAGUARO NATIONAL PARK (EAST)

SAGUARO NATIONAL PARK (WEST)

TUCSON MOUNTAINS

Arizona-Sonora Desert Museum

Old Tucson Studios

Tucson Mall

University of Arizona

Pima Air & Space Museum

Tucson International Airport

New Mexico

▲ Nogales

see 'Downtown Tucson' map for detail

0   3 miles

N

"**Tucson Ring**" of businessmen was consistently provoking the Apache in order to profit from the resultant military spending.

The end of the Apache Wars in the 1880s coincided with the coming of the transcontinental **railroad** and the reorientation of the commerce of Tucson along east–west routes. Its role as an entrepôt for trade with Mexico rapidly declined, and the Mexican merchants who had been its wealthiest citizens were driven out of business. Ever since, Mexican laborers have streamed back and forth across the border as the economy expands and contracts, but Tucson has become ever more American. Outstripped by Phoenix during the 1920s, and home to under forty thousand people (in an area of just nine square miles) as recently as 1940, by conventional standards the city has nonetheless grown at a phenomenal rate.

Arrival, information, and city tours

Tucson International Airport, eight miles south of downtown (☏520/573-8100), receives flights from all over the Southwest, but in terms of long-distance services it very much plays second fiddle to Phoenix. It's connected to central Tucson by the slow Sun Tran **bus** #6 or #11 ($1) and the $25 shuttle vans of Arizona Stagecoach (☏520/889-1000, ⓦwww.azstagecoach.com). For **taxi** service, call Allstate Cab (☏520/798-1111).

The Amtrak station, downtown at 400 E Toole Ave, is served by three **trains** weekly in each direction between Los Angeles and points east; connecting Amtrak buses run north to Phoenix. Greyhound **buses** also stop very centrally, at 471 W Congress St (☏520/792-3475). Arizona Shuttle Services runs a shuttle-van service between Tucson and **Phoenix**'s Sky Harbor airport (one way $30; ☏520/795-6771 or 1-800/888-2749, ⓦwww.arizonashuttle.com).

Most of downtown can be explored on foot, but on weekends you can ride the **Old Pueblo Trolley** (Fri 6–10pm, Sat noon–midnight, Sun noon–6pm; $1 per trip or $2.50 all day; ☏520/792-1802, ⓦwww.oldpueblotrolley.org) from Eighth Street and Fourth Avenue out to the university, a mile east of the center.

Tucson's downtown **visitor center**, in the lurid little La Placita development at 100 S Church Ave (Mon–Fri 9am–5pm, Sat & Sun 9am–4pm; ☏520/624-1817 or 1-800/638-8350, ⓦwww.visittucson.org), has free maps and information, and is the starting point for two-hour **walking tours** at 10am daily. Grayline (☏520/622-8811 or 1-800/276-1528, ⓦwww.graylinearizona.com) offers $59 **city tours** by bus, as well as trips further afield in southeast Arizona.

North of the university, Tucson Map & Flag Center, 3239 N First Ave (☏520/887-4234, ⓦwww.mapsmithus.com), stocks Arizona's best selection of maps and local guides. The main **post office** is at 141 S Sixth Ave.

Accommodation

Tucson offers a broader range of **accommodation** than Phoenix, with plenty of reasonably priced **hotels** and **motels** downtown as well as some atmospheric **B&Bs** both in the historic center and out in the surrounding desert. It also has its fair share of **resorts** and **dude ranches**. Once again, rates drop when the mercury rises.

Hostels and B&Bs

Catalina Park Inn 309 East First St ☏520/792-4541 or 1-800/792-4885, ⓦwww.catalinaparkinn .com. A beautiful yet not overly fussy six-room historic B&B across from a quiet park. Within walking distance of the university and happening

Fourth Ave. Closed mid-June to late Sept. ⑥
El Presidio Inn 297 N Main Ave ☏520/623-6151 or 1-800/349-6151, ⓦwww.bbonline.com/az /elpresidio. Four tastefully furnished Spanish colonial suites in historic downtown adobe B&B, with spacious wraparound veranda. ⑤

Hotel Congress 311 E Congress St ☏520/622-8848 or 1-800/722-8848, ⊛www.hotelcongress.com. Central, bohemian hotel, an easy walk from Amtrak and Greyhound, with vintage Art Deco furnishings. In the 1930s, bank-robber Dillinger was arrested here after pleading for his strangely heavy luggage to be rescued from a blaze on the third floor; now it offers forty plain en-suite guest rooms, with vintage radios rather than TVs. With the *Cup Café* (see p.250) and Club Congress (see p.251) downstairs, this is one of the hottest spots in town, with loud music and dancing at night. ❹

Roadrunner Hostel 346 E Twelfth St ☏520/628-4709, ⊛www.roadrunnerhostelinn.com. Small and very central independent hostel in a downtown home, offering space in six-bed dorms for $24 per night or $144 per week, and private rooms for $48, plus wi-fi. ❶–❷

Hotels and motels

Econo Lodge 3020 S Sixth Ave ☏520/623-5881 or 1-800/553-2666, ⊛www.econolodge.com. With its pleasant rooms and well-maintained pool, this inexpensive motel, west of the airport, represents the best value you're likely to find close to downtown. ❷

Flamingo Hotel 1300 N Stone Ave ☏520/770-1910, ⊛www.flamingohoteltucson.com. Despite recent renovations, this Western-themed motel remains at heart a plain budget option, but it does have a pool and spa, and stands barely a mile north of downtown Tucson. ❸

Holiday Inn Tucson Airport – North 4550 S Palo Verde Blvd ☏1-520/746 1161 or 0871/423-4896, ⊛www.ichotelsgroup.com. Six-story, Southwestern-styled hotel with reasonable rooms, a nice pool, and a waterfall in the lobby, located roughly halfway between the airport – served by free shuttles – and downtown. ❺

Ranches and resorts

Arizona Inn 2200 E Elm St ☏520/325-1541 or 1-800/933-1093, ⊛www.arizonainn.com. Elegant

desert oasis that's been a winter favorite for numerous presidents, Rockefellers, and the Duke and Duchess of Windsor, but with just 95 rooms remains surprisingly unstuffy and not all that expensive in low season. Rates include gourmet breakfast. ❾

Lodge on the Desert 306 N Alvernon Way ☏520/325-3366 or 1-800/978-3598, ⊛www.lodgeonthedesert.com. 1930s adobe resort a couple of miles east of downtown, tastefully restored to resemble a Mexican hacienda, with large, comfortable rooms, and a good restaurant. ❽

Loews Ventana Canyon Resort 7000 N Resort Drive ☏520/299-2020 or 1-800/234-5117, ⊛www.loewshotels.com. Grand red-brick resort, reaching majestically across a hundred acres at the foot of the Santa Catalina mountains northeast of the city, with its own on-site waterfall. Four restaurants, two golf courses, plus tennis and spa, and the desert on your doorstep. ❼

Tanque Verde Ranch 14301 E Speedway Blvd ☏520/296-6275 or 1-800/234-3833, ⊛www.tanqueverderanch.com. Arizona's most authentic dude ranch, an irresistibly romantic 400-acre spread adjoining Saguaro National Park twenty miles east of downtown. The accommodations in individual *casitas* are luxurious and the stable is home to more than a hundred horses. Rates include all meals and a full program of rides, from early-morning cowboy cookouts to all-day pack trips; there's also tennis, swimming, and hiking. Three-day minimum. ❾

Westward Look Resort 245 E Ina Rd ☏520/297-1151 or 1-800/722-2500, ⊛www.westwardlook.com. Plush resort, in attractive landscaped grounds north of the city, that retains its atmospheric 1912 core while modernized to hold almost 250 extra-large rooms and suites in very private low-slung *casitas*. The emphasis on physical fitness, and tennis in particular, doesn't preclude having a top-quality restaurant. ❼

Downtown Tucson

Downtown Tucson, which centers on the area where the east–west Congress Street and Broadway Boulevard cross the north–south Stone Avenue, is largely characterized by undistinguished modern architecture, though the 1928 **Pima County Courthouse** on Church Avenue is an eclectic mix of Southwestern and Moorish influences. The adobe fortress of San Agustín de Tucson occupied what's now the four-block **El Presidio Historic District**, a couple of blocks northwest. None of its original structures is still standing, but several of their successors, dating from the nineteenth century when Tucson passed into American hands, have been restored as cafés, art galleries, and B&Bs.

Access to much of El Presidio is controlled by the **Tucson Museum of Art**, alongside at 140 N Main Ave (Tues–Sat 10am–4pm, Sun noon–4pm; $8, under-13s free; free first Sun of month; Ⓦwww.tucsonmuseumofart .org). The main building is used for changing exhibitions of modern painting and sculpture, and the gift shop stocks interesting contemporary crafts. An adjoining adobe, the **Palice Pavilion**, displays magnificent pre-Columbian artifacts, including ceramics with extraordinarily life-like faces

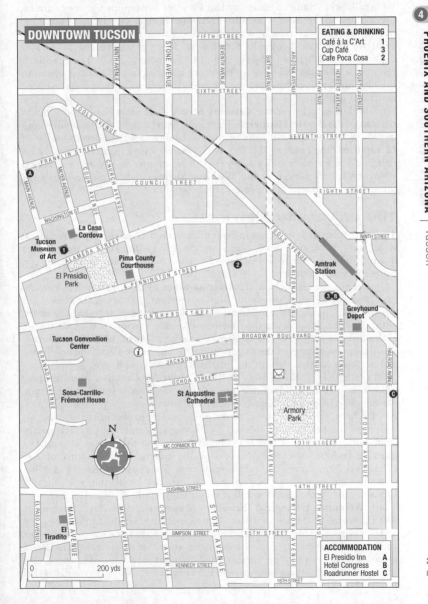

DOWNTOWN TUCSON

EATING & DRINKING

Café à la C'Art	1
Cup Café	3
Cafe Poca Cosa	2

La Casa Cordova

Tucson Museum of Art

El Presidio Park

Pima County Courthouse

Amtrak Station

Greyhound Depot

Tucson Convention Center

Sosa-Carrillo-Frémont House

St Augustine Cathedral

Armory Park

N

El Tiradito

0   200 yds

ACCOMMODATION

El Presidio Inn	A
Hotel Congress	B
Roadrunner Hostel	C

produced by the Mochica culture of northern Peru, textiles from the later Peruvian Chancay culture, and gold from Colombia and Costa Rica. Mexican artifacts range from masks and effigies created by the ancient Olmec and Mixtec peoples, to eighteenth-century religious pieces and nineteenth-century oil-on-tin family portraits. The oldest house in the complex, **La Casa Cordova** at 175 N Meyer Ave (same hours), contains displays on the city's Mexican heritage.

Three blocks south, engulfed by the Tucson Convention Center complex, the solitary adobe **Sosa-Carrillo-Frémont House** (Wed–Sat 10am–4pm; free) is the sole survivor of a neighborhood torn down during the 1960s. Built for merchant Leopoldo Carrillo in 1858, it was rented by former explorer turned Arizona governor John C. Frémont in 1878. Though much restored, it offers a vivid sense of the more civilized side of frontier life, from the high-quality furniture and the saguaro-rib ceilings to the fig-tree-shaded courtyard gardens.

Still within walking distance, **Cushing Street**, three more blocks south, marks the start of the **Barrio Historico**. The city's 1880s business district holds plenty of century-old adobes, but its most notable landmark is the sidewalk shrine of **El Tiradito**, "the castaway." Said to mark where a young man was killed by his father-in-law for committing adultery with his mother-in-law, and was buried where he fell, it's famous as the **Wishing Shrine**. Light a candle that burns through the night, and your prayers will be answered.

The university district

The other main area of interest in central Tucson is the **University of Arizona**, which spreads between Sixth Street and Speedway Boulevard a mile east of downtown. Park Avenue, on its western flank, is lined with funky cafés and stores that cater to students.

On campus, the highlight is the **Arizona State Museum** at 1013 E University-sity Blvd (Mon–Sat 10am–5pm, Sun noon–5pm; $3; ⓦwww.statemuseum.arizona.edu). Its Pottery Project traces the history of Southwestern ceramics, with a stunning case devoted to fabulous "burden carrier" pots made by the Hohokam between 850 and 1000 AD. The large **Paths of Life** exhibition illuminates the cultures of the major Native American peoples of the Southwest and northern Mexico, though the emphasis is heavily on Arizona.

Just north, at 1030 North Olive Rd, the **Center for Creative Photography** holds one of the world's finest photography archives (Mon–Fri 9am–5pm, Sat–Sun noon–5pm; $2 suggested donation; ⓦwww.creativephotography.org). Ansel Adams left his negatives, prints, and journals to the university, and his collection has been complemented by photographs from all eras. Temporary exhibitions only show a tiny selection, however, and the archive is primarily intended for serious scholars. Next door, the eclectic **UA Museum of Art** (Thurs–Fri 9am–5pm, Sun noon–4pm; free; ⓦartmuseum.arizona.edu) has some morbid Spanish *retablos* as well as canvases by Rembrandt, Picasso, O'Keeffe, and Warhol, and some fine cubist sculpture by Jacques Lipchitz.

The **Arizona Historical Society Museum**, across Park Avenue at 949 E Second St (Mon–Sat 10am–4pm; $5; ⓦwww.arizonahistoricalsociety.org), surveys the history of southern Arizona with a replica mine tunnel, and a good "Oxcart to Auto" exhibit on travel in the frontier era. If it's specifically the history of Tucson itself that interests you, it's worth also calling in at the museum's downtown offshoot, at 140 N Stone Ave (Tues–Fri 10am–4pm; $3).

Northern Tucson and the Santa Catalina Mountains

Metropolitan Tucson's northern boundary is formed by the natural barrier of the **Santa Catalina Mountains**, whose bare, dusty slopes are eventually crowned with pine forests. At the edge of the mountains, eight miles north of downtown, **Tohono Chul Park**, a block west of Oracle Road at Ina Road, is a former private estate that has been converted into a desert garden (daily 8am–sunset, last admission 5pm; $7; ⓦ www.tohonochulpark.org). The name means "desert corner" in the Tohono 'O'odham language, and it's now filled with yucca, prickly pear, and other cactuses, and a-flutter with hummingbirds. The park's *Tohono Chul Tea Room* is reviewed on p.251.

For an enjoyable taste of the mountains, head to **Sabino Canyon**, at the far end of Sabino Canyon Road in the Coronado National Forest, ten miles northeast of downtown (daily dawn–dusk; free, but parking $5; ☏ 520/749-2861, ⓦ www.sabinocanyon.com). The canyon was cut into the lower reaches of Mount Lemmon by Sabino Creek, which manages to flow for up to eleven months of the year, and is lined by green vegetation. Assorted trails lace into the hills from a four-mile riverbank road – barred to private vehicles, but served by jump-on, jump-off **tram rides** ($8.50) – that's popular with early-morning joggers.

Eastern Tucson: Pima Air & Space Museum

While the main attraction in eastern Tucson is the eastern segment of Saguaro National Park – see p.249 – it's also worth admiring the vintage and modern aircraft displayed at the **Pima Air & Space Museum**, 6000 E Valencia Rd (daily 9am–5pm; Nov–May adults $13.50, ages 7–12 $9; June–Oct adults $12, ages 7–12 $8; ☏ 520/574-0462, ⓦ www.pimaair.org). From I-10, take the Valencia Road exit and drive two miles east. Some exhibits, like the Wright Brothers' 1903 Flyer and the Apollo capsule, are replicas, but the great majority are the real deal, including plenty of World War II bombers, prototype helicopters, and the superfast X-15 fighter. The whole place is so huge you may well prefer to pay $6 extra to tour it by tram.

Western Tucson: Old Tucson and the Arizona-Sonora Desert Museum

Twelve miles west of the university on Speedway Boulevard, en route to Saguaro, **Old Tucson Studios**, 201 S Kinney Rd (daily 10am–4pm; $17, under-12s $11; ⓦ www.oldtucson.com), is an entertaining Wild West theme park. Its focus is a movie-set mock-up of the "Old Pueblo," constructed for the 1939 western *Arizona*, which has been used for TV shows and movies up to *Tombstone* and *Geronimo*. Visitors can ride a stagecoach or a coal-fired steam train, and watch gunfights on Main Street or a bawdy show in the saloon. Since Old Tucson had to be almost entirely rebuilt after a fire in 1995, it's now even more spurious than ever. Kids love it all the same.

Part zoo, part garden, the much more satisfying **Arizona-Sonora Desert Museum** stands two miles further west in Tucson Mountain Park (daily: June–Aug Sun–Fri 7.30am–5pm, Sat 7.30am–10pm; March–May & Sept 7.30am–5pm; Oct–Feb 8.30am–5pm; $9.50, ages 6–12 $2 June–Aug; $13, ages 6–12 $4 Sept–May; ⓦ www.desertmuseum.org). Displays in the museum proper explain regional geology and history, while dioramas are filled with tarantulas, rattlesnakes, and other creepy crawlers. In enclosures along the loop path beyond – a hot walk in summer – bighorn sheep, mountain lions, jaguars, and other seldom-seen desert denizens prowl in credible simulations of their natural habitats, and impish prairie dogs go about their impenetrable business. Hawks and bald eagles fly about a large aviary, thankfully separated from the greenhouse full of hummingbirds. Spectacular displays by free-flying Harris hawks are scheduled most winter afternoons. The outdoor terrace of the museum's restaurant makes a great stop-off for a light lunch; it also has a good coffee bar.

Saguaro National Park

Flanking Tucson to either side, the two sections of **SAGUARO NATIONAL PARK** offer visitors a rare and enthralling opportunity to stroll through desert "forests" of monumental, multilimbed **saguaro** (pronounced *sa-wah-row*) **cactuses**. Both tend to be seen on short forays from the city; there's no lodging, or even permanent campground, in either segment, and in summer, it's far too hot to do more than pose for photographs, dwarfed beneath some especially eccentric specimen.

As saguaros prefer sloping foothills, which offer a little run-off after rain, to level desert, both sections include rugged mountain tracts. Most of the **Rincon Mountain District** in the east, which became a national monument in 1933, is much higher, and the one road only penetrates its low-lying fringes. It was joined in 1961 by the **Tucson Mountain District** in the west, which incorporates the world's densest stand of saguaro.

Admission to either or both sections of the park, valid for a week and payable at the visitor centers (Ⓦ www.nps.gov/sagu), costs $10 per vehicle. **Backcountry camping** is by permit only; contact park rangers for details.

The western park: Tucson Mountain District

The **Tucson Mountain District** of Saguaro National Park is fifteen miles west of downtown Tucson, on the far side, logically enough, of the Tucson Mountains. The Red Hills **visitor center** (daily 8am–5pm; ☎ 520/733-5158), stands two miles along Kinney Road from the Desert Museum. 1.5 miles further on, turn right off the highway to start the six-mile **Bajada Loop Drive**, which although not fully paved is always passable to ordinary vehicles, and leads through a wonderland of weird saguaro, offering plentiful short hiking trails and photo opportunities. Although you can join the road at either of its two intersections, which are less than half a mile apart, its central mile or so is one-way, so the only way to complete a full loop is by starting at the south.

The easiest walk, the **Desert Discovery Nature Trail**, sets off just before the one-way section. It follows a small gully before climbing onto a low brow for sweeping westward views, with abundant saguaro all around; in principle it's half a mile long, though you can choose how far you want to walk before you turn back. If you've only time for one hike in the park, however, head further along the road and walk at **Signal Hill** instead, ideally timing your arrival to enjoy its magnificent sunset panoramas. You're not the first to pass this way; boulders at the top are marked with Hohokam petroglyphs. True gluttons for punishment can follow the longer **Hugh Norris Trail** up a ridge to the 4687ft summit of Wasson Peak.

Branching onto Golden Gate Road from the northeastern limit of the loop drive brings you in around five miles to Picture Rocks Road, which joins **Ina Road** a few more miles along and thus makes an alternative route back to northern Tucson.

▲ Mighty Saguaros at Saguaro National Park

The eastern park: Rincon Mountain District

To reach the eastern section of Saguaro National Park, the **Rincon Mountain District**, drive seventeen miles east of downtown Tucson along first Broadway Boulevard and then Old Spanish Trail. The **visitor center** is at the end of the road (daily 8am–5pm; ☎520/733-5153).

Although short trails such as the quarter-mile **Desert Ecology Trail** lead off the eight-mile **Cactus Forest Drive** (daily: April–Oct 7am–7pm; Nov–March 7am–5pm), this area of the park is less immediately rewarding for casual visitors than its western counterpart. Instead, most of those who make their way here

The saguaro cactus; a desert saga

As the mighty, multi-armed **saguaro cactus** is unique to the Sonoran Desert, and Tucson stands near the desert's northeastern extremity, the Tucson region is one of very few places in the Wild West where real-life saguaro grow. Whatever you may have seen in the movies, you can drive a long way in Arizona without seeing a saguaro; the thrill when you finally encounter a thousand at once is deeply satisfying.

Each saguaro can grow up to fifty feet tall and weigh up to eight tons, but it reaches that size at the slowest of rates. A teenage cactus is a foot high, a 50-year-old more like seven feet. At 75, it sprouts the first of what may amount to forty "arms," and it only reaches its full height at around 150, with perhaps another fifty years to go before it dies. Its roots radiate as much as a hundred feet in all directions, barely three inches below the surface, and can draw enough water from one rainstorm to last the plant for two years.

Each year from the age of 30 onwards, between late April and June, a saguaro grows up to a hundred white flowers, each of which blossoms for a single night and dies by the next afternoon. In its lifetime, each saguaro produces as many as forty million seeds, though few, if any, are likely to germinate and thrive. It's also home to an intricate community of birds, insects, mammals, and reptiles. Woodpeckers and owls burrow holes into the trunk for their nests, which the cactus heals over with hardened "scar tissue" to create permanent hollows. The **Tohono 'O'odham** Indians traditionally cut away these depressions for use as bowls; they also mashed the saguaro's succulent crimson fruit to make jam, syrup, and even wine, and used its long, wood-like ribs to construct dwellings and fences.

Thanks to the thriving black market in selling stolen saguaros to property owners, officials announced in 2008 that many cactuses in Saguaro National Park were to be micro-chipped against theft.

come specifically to hike far from the road, up into the mountains. The saguaro cactuses thin out almost as soon as you start climbing the **Tanque Verde Ridge Trail**, which leads in due course to a hundred-mile network of remote footpaths through thickly forested canyons. All six of the district's wilderness campgrounds are only accessible on foot or by horse, and can only be used if you pay $6 per night for a permit. Water is seasonally available – check with rangers – but should be treated before you drink it.

Eating

Though downtown Tucson shuts down pretty early each evening – it's hard to find anywhere to eat after 9pm – the city has a fine selection of **restaurants**. Mexican joints and cowboy-style Wild West steakhouses abound in the central districts, while fancier restaurants congregate further north in the Foothills, and especially in the resort hotels.

Coffeehouses

Cup Café *Hotel Congress*, 311 E Congress St ☎520/798-1618. Jazzy downtown café, straight out of the 1930s but updated to include an espresso bar, that makes a good breakfast rendezvous. Sun–Thurs 7am–10pm, Fri & Sat 7am–midnight.

Espresso Art Café 942 E University Blvd ☎520/624-4126. Grungy, alternative coffee bar, in the heart of the University District, with a sideline in selling artworks and regular live music. Mon–Fri 7am–11pm, Sat & Sun 8am–11pm.

Raging Sage 2458 N Campbell Ave ☎520/320-5203. Lively, pricey, family-run coffeehouse; the smell alone is irresistible. Daily 7am–5pm.

Safehouse Coffeehouse 4024 E Speedway Blvd ☎520/318-3090. Relaxed local coffeehouse, where excellent coffee and a good range of snacks attract an eclectic late-night crowd. Sun–Thurs 7am–2am, Fri & Sat 7am–3am.

Cafés and diners

Blue Willow 2616 N Campbell Ave ☎520/327-7577, 🌐www.bluewillowtucson.com. Tasty, fruity breakfasts and light lunches and dinners, served on a pleasant garden patio. Mon–Fri 7am–9pm, Sat & Sun 8am–9pm.

Café à la C'Art Tucson Museum of Art, 150 N Main Ave ☎520/628-8533. With such a good café in the art museum courtyard, serving sandwiches, salads and daily specials, there's no need to look further afield. Mon–Fri 11am–3pm.

Café Poca Cosa 110 E Pennington St ☎520/622-6400, 🌐cafepocacosatucson .com. Popular and stylish downtown café that serves tasty but inexpensive Mexican – or to be more precise, Sonoran – cuisine with a great deal of contemporary Southwestern flair. Typical highlights on the short blackboard menu include shredded beef, or cod with clams. Lunch entrees are around $10; at dinner they're more like $20. Tues–Thurs 11am–9pm, Fri & Sat 11am–10pm.

Tohono Chul Tea Room Tohono Chul Park, 7366 N Paseo del Norte ☎520/797-1222. Attractive adobe café in small desert park (see p.247) on the northern fringes of town that's ideal for breakfast, a $10 lunch special, or a scones-and-jam afternoon tea. Daily 8am–5pm.

Restaurants

Cuvee World Bistro 3352 E Speedway Blvd ☎520/881-7577, 🌐www.cuveebistro.com. The eclectic menu at this playfully opulent yet casual bistro samples pretty much any tasty world cuisine. Typical entrees, from crispy sea bass to mahogany

roasted duck, are priced at $18–25, and there's live music at weekends. Mon–Sat 11am–10pm.

J-Bar Westin La Paloma Resort, 3770 E Sunrise Drive ☎520/615-6100, 🌐www.janos.com. Terrific southwest-Mex cuisine by Tucson's nationally acclaimed chef Janos Wilder at half the price of his upscale restaurant, Janos, next door – thus his Yucatan plantain-crusted chicken with green curry costs just $15.50. That and the view make it work the trip north to the Foothills. Mon–Sat 5–9.30pm.

Kingfisher 2564 E Grant Rd ☎520/323-7739, 🌐kingfishertucson.com. Upmarket restaurant that serves seafood – from Maine lobsters and Maryland soft-shell crabs to Oregon oysters – with an eclectic mix of American cooking styles from Cajun to New Pacific. Entrees cost from $19, and strict meat-eaters can opt instead for barbecue chicken or ribs. The reduced late-night menu can be a life-saver. Mon–Fri 11am–11pm, Sat & Sun 5–11pm.

Terra Cotta 3500 Sunrise Drive ☎520/577-8100, 🌐www.dineterracotta.com. Inventive Southwestern cuisine, a long way north of downtown in the Foothills. The menu ranges from gourmet pizzas cooked in a wood-burning oven to meats grilled with chiles, with typical entrees priced around $20. Daily 4–10pm.

Ventana Room Loews Ventana Canyon Resort, 7000 N Resort Drive ☎520/615-5494, 🌐www .ventanaroom.com. Showcase resort dining room, commanding a panoramic view from the northern Foothills. Continental-style grilled meats and fish from $35 per entree, or go for the prix fixe menus from $89. Tues–Thurs 6–9pm, Fri & Sat 6–10pm.

Entertainment and nightlife

Downtown, Tucson **nightlife** focuses on Congress Street with its gaggle of arty cafés and nightclubs; most venues double as bars or restaurants. A handful of student places can be found near the university, while country saloons are scattered on the outskirts of town. Check listings in the free *Tucson Weekly* (🌐www.tucsonweekly .com). The Tucson Convention Center Music Hall, 260 S Church Ave (☎520/791-4101), features orchestral concerts, opera, and ballet, while the city's prime **theater** venue is the Temple of Music and Art, 330 S Scott Ave (☎520/622-2823). The Tucson Jazz Society (🌐www.tucsonjazz.org) promotes jazz gigs all over town.

Cactus Moon 5470 E Broadway ☎520/748-0049, 🌐www.cactusmoon.net. As befits the Western decor, country music is normally the order of the day at this large dancehall-cum-bar, though Wed can be anything from metal to hip-hop, and attracts a college crowd. Tues–Sat 5pm–2am.

Club Congress Hotel Congress, 311 E Congress St ☎520/622-8848. Hectic, trendy, late-opening bar with live music, including some surprisingly big names, a couple of nights each week.

Gentle Ben's Brewing Co 865 E University Blvd ☎520/624-4177, 🌐www.gentlebens.com. Microbrewery, regularly packed with students, and serving simple food.

IBT's 616 N Fourth Ave ☎520/882-3053, 🌐www .ibts.net. Tucson's premier gay downtown dance club features contemporary DJs most nights and also puts on drag acts and revue. Daily noon–2am.

Kon Tiki Lounge 4625 E Broadway ☎520/323-7193. Tiki bar with fun South Seas theme and

killer cocktails. Mon–Sat 11am–1am, Sun
4pm–1am.
Rialto Theatre 318 E Congress St ☎520/740-1000,
Ⓦ www.rialtotheatre.com. 1920s vaudeville theater
that's reopened as Tucson's hottest venue for
touring bands. Daily except Mon.

South to Mexico: the Mission Trail

The tract of southern Arizona between Tucson and the Mexican border was the
first part of the state settled by the Spanish, and remained Arizona's most
populous region until well into the nineteenth century. The Spanish called this
area **Pimería Alta**, and its scattered **mission churches** and abandoned forts
still testify to their efforts to Christianize its **Pima** inhabitants from 1692
onwards. Epidemics and Apache raids meant that of the early towns, only
Tucson grew to any size, but as recently as 1870, the Pima were still Arizona's
largest ethnic group.

Twelve thousand Pima – now known as the **Akimel 'O'odham** – survive on
the **San Xavier Reservation** a few miles south of Tucson. The magnificent
church of San Xavier – the "White Dove of the Desert" – is the prime attraction for modern travelers who drive the 65 miles down to Mexico on the **I-19**
interstate, but the artistic community at **Tubac**, and the atmospheric border
town of **Nogales**, help to make for an entertaining international day-trip.

San Xavier del Bac

Even today, the white-plastered walls and towers of **San Xavier del Bac**, the
best-preserved mission church in the US, seem like a dazzling desert mirage.

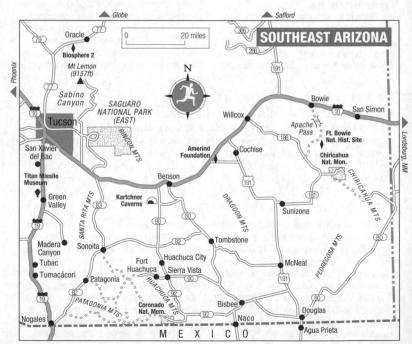

▲ San Xavier del Bac

How much more dramatic they must have been two centuries ago, when to Christian missionaries and Apache warriors alike they symbolized the Spanish quest to subdue and convert the native peoples of the Southwest.

Located a mere nine miles south of downtown Tucson, just west of I-19, the church stands on the eastern fringes of the arid San Xavier Reservation. The Jesuit **Father Eusebio Kino** founded it in 1700, beside the Santa Cruz River and next to the Pima village of W:ak ("where the water emerges"), which soon became Bac. Kino's church was destroyed by Apaches in 1767; what survives is its replacement, built for the Franciscans between 1783 and 1797. No one knows the name of the architect responsible for its Spanish Baroque, even Moorish lines – it consists almost entirely of domes and arches, making only minimal use of timber – let alone the 'O'odham craftsmen who embellished its every feature.

Although the church attracts a constant stream of tourists (daily 7am–5pm; donation), the ideal time to come is on Sunday morning, when masses at 8am, 11am, and 12.30pm pack in the parishioners from the reservation. As you approach the main entrance across the dusty plaza, with saguaro cactuses to the right and ocotillo to the left, take a moment to appreciate its ornate facade. On the top level, a cat squats on the spiral flourish to the right, eyeing a mouse in the corresponding position on the left. The tower on the right was never completed, possibly to avoid the need to pay a levy to the authorities back in Mexico.

Inside the church, the left alcove holds a recumbent, articulated statue of **St Francis Xavier**, covered with metal *milagros* (images of healed body parts). Devout Catholics can lean in and lift his head. Two naive gilt-headed lions guard the approach to the main altar, representing the royal lions of León and Castille in Spain. The altar itself holds a telling example of the intermingling of Catholicism with traditional beliefs; a gilded monstrance that incorporates a wickerwork surround bearing the 'O'odham "man in the maze" design.

Still within the mission walls, to the right of the church, a small **museum** (daily 8.30am–4.30pm; donation) displays a gigantic illuminated sheepskin psalter and photos of other remote churches on the Tohono 'O'odham reservation.

The little hillock immediately east is now topped by a replica of the shrine of Saint Bernadette at Lourdes, France. Juan Mateo Manje, who accompanied Father Kino to W:ak, described finding a white stone on top of this hill in November 1699:

We guessed it might be some idol that the heathen Indians worshipped, so with great effort we pulled out the stone, thereby exposing a large hole. At the time, we did not know what it could be. While we were coming down the hill, a great and furious hurricane developed. We could scarcely walk because of the terrific windstorm. None of the Indians had gone with us to the top of the hill; but when the furious wind arose they started to yell, saying in sort of rebellion, "*Vbiriqui cupioca*," which meant that the House of the Wind (god) had been opened.

The major **feast days** at San Xavier Mission are those of St Francis of Assisi, on October 4, and St Francis Xavier, December 3.

The Titan Missile Museum

Sixteen miles south of San Xavier, the main attraction at the **Titan Missile Museum** (daily: May–Oct 8.45am–5pm; Nov–April 8.45am–5.30pm; $9.50; ⓦtitanmissilemuseum.org) is an underground silo that, until 1982, held two Titan II nuclear missiles. Each was primed and ready to fire at a choice of three specific targets, as much as five thousand miles away; what those targets were remains classified even today, but they never changed during the 22 years that the site was operational. A total of 54 such missiles were deployed at 27 separate locations, in Arizona, California, and Arkansas, but only this site survived the end of the Cold War. One of its missiles is actually still down there – no longer primed, of course – and can be examined close up on hour-long subterranean **guided tours**.

The whole installation was designed to remain functional in a nuclear war. Its vast sliding door could open through eight feet of post-holocaust debris; the crew could live beneath the surface for up to thirty days; and the whole place could even operate on two 28-volt batteries in case of electrical outage. Tours culminate in the control room, still scattered with top-secret manuals, where two keys had to be turned simultaneously to fire the missile.

As you might imagine, inspecting colossal rocket launchers and other military hardware is very much a "guy thing." Casual visitors who take the tours may well run out of steam before the excitable gun nuts in the crowd find time to draw breath. Check out the website for details of the twice-monthly, five-hour, "Top-to-Bottom" tours ($70).

Tubac

These days, the village of **TUBAC**, fifty miles south of San Xavier, is a thriving **arts colony**. Originally, however, this was the first permanent Spanish settlement in Arizona, founded in 1752 as a **presidio** or fortress to guard against repetitions of the previous year's Pima Revolt against the Jesuits. In 1775, its commander, Juan Bautista de Anza, launched the expedition that established **San Francisco**, but Tubac soon declined, after its garrison was shifted to the new city of Tucson in 1776. For the next century, it was alternately abandoned and resettled as Apache raids permitted.

Tubac's successful new incarnation has enabled it to grow almost beyond recognition, with all new real-estate developments echoing Taos and Santa Fe in their use of the faux-adobe architectural style. The broad streets in its central core are now paved and lined with studios, galleries, folk-art stores, and boutiques, while each year yet another identical little plaza seems to sprout from the surrounding fields. Most of what's on sale lies firmly within the established genres of contemporary Southwestern arts and crafts – lurid O'Keeffe-esque sunsets and blanket-swathed native Americans, turquoise ironwork, and the like – but there are also plenty of inexpensive imports, especially ceramics, from south of the nearby Mexican border. For more formal exhibitions by local artists, visit the **Tubac Center of the Arts**, 9 Plaza Rd (Sept to mid-May Mon–Sat 10am–4.30pm, Sun 1–4.30pm; closed mid-May to Aug; free; ⓦtubacarts.org).

The foundations of the original adobe fortress now lie beneath an earthen mound, but can be admired from a cool underground viewing gallery in the **Tubac Presidio State Historic Park** (daily 8am–5pm; winter $3, summer $2). The large museum alongside contains pieces from all periods of Tubac's long history, including beautiful naive *retablos*, the press that was used to print Arizona's first newspaper, *The Weekly Arizonan*, in 1859, and a crucifix depicting the black "Christo Negro" – a Native American Christ. On alternate Sundays between October and March, from 1pm until 4pm, costumed locals re-enact the daily life of the eighteenth-century presidio.

Practicalities

Pick up local information at the state park or the **visitor center**, in the small mall on Plaza Road, the main road into town (Mon–Fri 10am–5pm, Sat & Sun 10am–2pm; ⓣ520/398-2704, ⓦtubacaz.com). Each year, in early February, the town hosts the weeklong **Festival of the Arts**. The nicest of the **B&Bs** in the old center is the timber *Tubac Country Inn*, at 13 Burruel St, where five very spacious en suite rooms share a common veranda and use of an attractive garden (ⓣ520/398-3178, ⓦtubaccountryinn.com; closed Aug; ❹).

The *Tubac Deli & Coffee Company*, 4 Plaza Rd (daily 6.30am–7pm; ⓣ520/398-3330), is a friendly, busy coffeehouse and snack place across from the visitor center. For a fuller meal, head for *Shelby's Bistro*, nearby at 19 Plaza Rd (Mon, Tues & Sun 11am–4pm, Wed–Sat 11am–4pm & 5–9pm; ⓣ520/398-8075), where the long, consistently good menu ranges from delicious black bean soup via pizzas up to substantial meat and seafood entrees – but watch for bugs on the cooled outdoor patio.

Tumacácori National Historical Park

A **Spanish mission** founded by Father Kino in 1691, before its more celebrated neighbor at San Xavier (see above), is now the focus of the **TUMACÁCORI NATIONAL HISTORICAL PARK**, three miles south of Tubac (daily 9am–5pm; $3 per person; ⓦwww.nps.gov/tuma). Like San Xavier, the church here was built at the end of the eighteenth century, but having failed to withstand Apache raids, Tumacácori was abandoned in 1848, five years before the region passed into US control.

It's now an evocative ruin, topped by a whitewashed dome but home only to the birds that fly down from the Patagonia Mountains. Behind its weather-beaten red-tinged facade, the plaster has crumbled from the interior walls to reveal bare adobe bricks. A few traces of a mural can be discerned in the raised sanctuary, but little remains of the priests' living quarters alongside.

A fascinating **museum** holds a replica of a banner carried by missionaries; one side depicts the Madonna and Child, the other shows an Indian burning in hell. Opposite the gate, the *Tumacácori Restaurant* serves Mexican and Greek specialties as well as deli sandwiches.

Nogales, Arizona, and Nogales, Mexico

Twenty miles south of Tumacácori, an hour from Tucson, sits the largest of the Arizonan–Mexican border towns, **NOGALES** – in effect two towns, one in the US and one across the border in Mexico. Known jointly as *Ambos Nogales* (both Nogales), they were founded in 1880, and still see vast quantities of freight traffic daily. Over four million vehicles pass through the checkpoints each year, while an astonishing 7.7 million people enter from Mexico on foot. Tourists, too, head south from Arizona in considerable numbers, though with cheap Mexican crafts now so widely available in the US, the day-trippers these days tend to be looking for cut-price medicines rather than rugs or hammocks.

There's nothing in particular to see on either side of the border, though the contrast between the sedate, ordered streets of the American town and the jumbled whitewashed houses clinging to the slopes in Mexico hits you as soon as you come in sight. Nogales, Arizona – the birthplace of iconoclastic jazz great **Charles Mingus** – is a dreary little community, while Nogales, Mexico, is basically a lively, large-scale street market.

Crossing the border is straightforward, as only travelers heading more than 21km south of the border require Mexican visas. US citizens must, however, carry their passports, while foreign visitors should check their visa status entitles them to re-enter the US; if you're on or eligible for the Visa Waiver Scheme (see p.47), you're fine. There's no need to **change money**; US dollars are freely accepted by stores and businesses in Mexico. If you plan to set off further south, pick up a **tourist visa** just beyond the border crossing. Then take a taxi (around $10) a couple of miles to the **long-distance bus station**, from which regular buses head to **Hermosillo**, **Guaymas** on the Pacific (a good overnight stop), and **Los Mochis**, the start of the Copper Canyon Railroad.

Although there's no scheduled **rail** connection with Guaymas, in recent years the *Sierra Madre Express* has run eight-day excursions from Nogales in deluxe private trains, including an ascent of the Copper Canyon Railroad. Due to the recession, a question mark currently hangs over its future plans (☎1–800/666-0346, ⓦwww.sierramadreexpress.com; from $4000 per person).

Practicalities

Nogales' **visitor center** is at 123 W Kino Park at the north end of town (Mon–Fri 9am–5pm; ☎520/287-3685, ⓦwww.thenogaleschamber.com). Four daily direct **buses** to Tucson (1hr) are operated by Citizens/Grayline Bus, 35 N Terrace Ave ($10.50; ☎520/287-5628).

None of the Arizona-side **motels** stands within a mile of the border; the closest is the *Best Western Siesta Motel*, 673 N Grand Ave (☎520/287-4671 or 1-888/215-4783; ❹), while the cluster near the interstate three miles out includes the smart hundred-room *Holiday Inn Express*, 850 W Shell Rd (☎520/281-0123 or 1-800/465-4329; ❹).

Most visitors prefer to **eat** in Mexico, where abundant cafés and diners line the busy central streets. Classier dining is offered by the unusual *La Roca*, hollowed into the rocky hillside just east of the railroad, a couple of blocks from the border at Calle Elias 91, where a full seafood meal still costs under $20. The best restaurant on the Arizona side is the Italian *Bella Mia*, 204 W Mariposa Rd (☎520/761-3535).

Sonoita Valley and Patagonia

A longer but even more attractive route back from Nogales to Tucson avoids the interstate by following highways 82 and 83 northeast from Nogales through the lush **Sonoita Valley**, in the craggy mountains of the Coronado National Forest.

The appealing little Wild West mining and cattle-ranching town of **PATAGONIA**, twenty miles up from Nogales, attracts weekend crowds of **birdwatchers**. At the far southwestern end of a mile-long dirt road that leads off Fourth Street, the **Patagonia-Sonoita Creek Sanctuary** is a dense riverbank stand of oaks and cottonwoods that's home to an amazing range of songbirds and raptors, including finches and flycatchers, kingbirds and kestrels, and woodpeckers and cardinals (April–Sept Wed–Sun 6.30am–4pm; Oct–March Wed–Sun 7.30am–4pm; $5; ☎520/394-2000). With all this colorful collection to choose from, the sighting most prized by twitchers is a drab little specimen called the northern beardless tyrannulet.

Twelve miles north of Patagonia, **SONOITA** itself is a wide-open desert crossroads, lined with a few false-front stores, at the point where Hwy-83 veers northwest to rejoin I-10 two miles east of Saguaro National Park, while Hwy-82 cuts east toward Tombstone, 35 miles away (see p.260).

Practicalities

Welcoming little **B&B**s in Patagonia include the three-room *Duquesne House*, a century-old adobe boarding house at 357 Duquesne Ave (☎520/394-2732, ⓦwww.patagoniaaz.com; ❹). The *Stage Stop Inn*, 303 W McKeown Ave (☎520/394-2211 or 1-800/923-2211 in AZ, ⓦwww.thestagestopinn.com; ❹), is a convenient **hotel**, built in the 1970s as a Western-movie set, which has its own funky restaurant, the Home Plate (Thurs–Sun only). *Gathering Grounds*, nearby at 319 W McKeown Ave (Sun–Wed 7am–5pm, Thurs–Sat 7am–9pm; ☎520/394-2097), is handy for a lunchtime snack or an evening meal of steak, fish or *clayudas*, a kind of Mexican pizza.

Sonoita holds further accommodation options, like the eighteen-room, cowboy-themed *Sonoita Inn* at the crossroads, which has its own steakhouse (☎520/455-5935 or 1-800/696-1006, ⓦwww.sonoitainn.com; ❺). Just west of town at 3280 Hwy-82, *Café Sonoita* (Tues & Wed 11am–2pm, Thurs–Sat 11am–2pm & 5–8pm; ☎520/455-5278) has a high reputation for its creative cuisine, with succulent barbecued ribs or pan-seared trout for around $12, and some fancier specialties.

The southeast corner

Although the **I-10** interstate remains consistently dull as it crosses **southeast Arizona**, the rugged territory to the south holds some spectacular scenery and memorable historic sites. While the much-mythologized Wild West outpost of **Tombstone** does its best to entertain the hordes of cowboy fanatics who troop this way, the mining town of **Bisbee** is in many ways a more evocative relic of frontier times. Meanwhile the opening of **Kartchner Caverns** has transformed previously quiet interstate towns such as nearby **Benson**.

Further east, the **Chiricahua Mountains** witnessed the final saga of Native American resistance to federal encroachment, in the 1880s guerrilla campaign of Geronimo's **Apaches**. The Chiricahua is merely one of around a dozen separate ranges that soar from the deserts, known as "**sky islands**" because each harbors its own unique ecosystem of plants, birds, and animals.

Benson

Forty miles southeast of Tucson on I-10, sleepy little **BENSON** serves primarily as an overnight base for visitors to Kartchner Caverns. There's nothing much to do in the town itself, though the Singing Wind, a couple of miles north, up Ocotillo Avenue (daily 9am–5pm; ☎520/586-2425), is a farmhouse **bookshop** that's bursting with volumes about Southwestern history and culture.

Practicalities

Benson's **visitor center** is at 249 E Fourth St (Mon–Sat 9am–5pm; ☎520/586-2842, ⓦwww.bensonchamberaz.com). The classiest of its near-identical chain **motels** is the *Holiday Inn Express*, 630 South Village Loop (☎520/586-8800 or 1-888/263-2283, ⓦwww.hiexpress.com; ⑤). Four miles southeast of town, the *Astronomer's Inn* is a one-of-a-kind **B&B** (☎520/586-8551, ⓦwww .astronomersinn.com; ⑤). Located on a hilltop next to the private Vega-Bray **astronomical observatory**, it offers guests (for an additional fee the chance to have exclusive use of the observatory equipment.

Back in town, the chief exception to a pitiful run of fast-food **diners** is the *Chute Out Steak House*, 161 S Huachuca St (☎520/586-7297).

Kartchner Caverns

When **Kartchner Caverns** – signposted west off Hwy-90 seven miles south of Benson – was designated Arizona's newest state park in 1999, it was expected to become one of the state's premier tourist attractions. Unlike counterparts such as Carlsbad Caverns in New Mexico, these caves are very unusual in being "live;" they're still being hollowed out of the Whetstone Mountains by each new dose of rainfall, and the formations within are still growing. While the caves may be an exciting novelty for local residents, however, they're not really worth traveling across the country – let alone the world – to see, and with a visit for a family of four costing at least $60, they're also wildly overpriced.

Kartchner Caverns were discovered in 1974 when local cavers Gary Tenen and Randy Tufts, investigating a strange-smelling hole in the mountainside, squeezed into what turned out to be a vast open space. Eventually the two explorers mapped out the subterranean complex at over two miles long, with around 13,000 feet of passageways. They told no one until 1987, whereupon it took a further twelve years, and $28 million, for the Arizona state authorities to prepare the caverns for display.

Admission to the park costs $5 per vehicle, but you can only see the caves themselves on one of the two distinct **guided tours** detailed below. Overall numbers are limited, and during busy periods all tours may be booked months ahead, though two hundred unreserved "walk-ins" are allowed each day. Try to reserve as far in advance as possible, by phone or online (Mon–Fri 8am–5pm; ☎520/586-2283, ⓦwww.azstateparks.com). You have to pay the full fee by credit card when you book; the fees are not refundable, though you can change the precise time of your tour. If you're hoping to turn up without a reservation, call on your chosen day to assess your chances; if you fail to get in, you can at least content yourself with the displays in the large **Discovery Center** instead (daily 7.30am–6pm).

The shorter of the two tours, the **Rotunda/Throne Room** tour, follows a narrow, switchbacking cement trail of a third of a mile through the caverns' two upper "rooms" (adults $19, $10 ages 7–13). It lasts for something over an hour, including a tram ride to the cave entrance and 45 minutes spent underground. Formations en route include precarious stalactites (the ones that dangle from the ceiling) and towering stalagmites (which rise from the floor) – to add to the confusion, there's also a 21ft hollow soda straw, a combination of both that stretches from floor to ceiling. However, the most spectacular feature is the striated **coloring** of the cavern walls, created by eons of unseen flooding and illuminated by the dramatic sound-and-light show with which the tour culminates.

The longer **Big Room** tour delves deeper into the cave system, and requires visitors to pass through no fewer than six separate airlock doors (mid-Oct to mid-April only; adults $23, $13 ages 7–13). It takes ninety or more minutes, and goes into a little more technical detail, while showcasing unusual wet formations such as a bizarre "fried egg."

The Amerind Foundation Museum

If you choose to continue east from Benson on I-10, the one point of interest on the barren run to New Mexico comes 25 miles later (65 miles from Tucson), in the shape of the **Amerind Foundation Museum** (daily except Mon 10am–4pm; $5; ☎520/586-3666, ⓦwww.amerind.org). This privately run anthropological museum is in the remote Texas Canyon, a mile southeast of exit 318. Not that you'll see anything as vulgar as a roadside billboard to announce its presence: it's a rather highbrow affair, with the declared ambition to "increase the world's knowledge of ancient man by excavation and collection." Displays cover native cultures from North, Central, and Southern America, but specialize in the Southwest, featuring fine Apache, Navajo, and Hopi crafts, plus older pieces from the Mimbres and Hohokam peoples. While not quite on a par with the museums in Flagstaff, Phoenix, or Santa Fe, it's worth an hour or two of your time if you're passing this way.

Sierra Vista and Ramsey Canyon Preserve

The characterless modern town of **SIERRA VISTA**, 30 miles south of Benson on Hwy-90, has grown in tandem with the Army base at **Fort Huachuca**. One of the few nineteenth-century military outposts to remain active, the fort still employs over thirteen thousand people. As the headquarters of the United States Army Intelligence Center, it's widely reported to have played a major role in developing the interrogation techniques made infamous at Abu Ghraib – not that you'll find much on the subject in the **US Army Intelligence Museum** (Mon–Fri 9am–4pm, Sat & Sun 1–4pm; $2 donation).

A much more enjoyable hour or two can be spent at the **Ramsey Canyon Preserve**, squeezed into a slender gorge in the Huachuca Mountains, off Hwy-92 seven miles south (March–Oct daily 8am–5pm; Nov–Feb Thurs–Mon 9am–4pm; $5; ☎520/378-2785, ⓦwww.nature.org). Owned by the Nature Conservancy, this well-watered spot is dedicated to safeguarding local wildlife in general, but the main reason everyone comes here is for its mind-boggling summer array of colorful **hummingbirds**, which reach their peak population in August. Guided walking tours explore the preserve in summer only (March–Oct Tues, Thurs & Sat 9am). Be warned that there's not much room for cars; the 23 parking spaces are first-come, first-served, so there's a risk you'll be turned away.

Practicalities

Plenty of **motels** in town cater to visiting service families and nature-lovers. The *Windemere Hotel*, 2047 S Hwy-92 (☎520/459-5900 or 1-800/825-4656, ⓦwindemerehotel.com; ❹), is the newest and largest. Just outside the preserve, seven miles south, the *Ramsey Canyon Inn*, 29 Ramsey Canyon Rd (☎520/378-3010, ⓦ ramseycanyoninn.com; ⓪), is a plush six-room **B&B** where a battery of sugar–water feeders attracts countless hummingbirds in summer.

Coronado National Memorial

Tucked into the southernmost notch of the Huachuca Mountains, five miles off Hwy-92, twenty miles from Sierra Vista, **CORONADO NATIONAL MEMORIAL** commemorates the approximate spot where in May 1540 the expedition of **Francisco Vásquez de Coronado** first entered what is now the United States (see p.500). Displays in the **visitor center** (daily: summer 8am–5pm; winter 8am–4pm; free; ☎520/366-5515, ⓦ www.nps.gov/coro) explain the history, but the memorial basically exists to offer a selection of scenic **hiking trails**. The best short hike climbs south from **Montezuma Pass**, the highest point along the washboard dirt road west of the visitor center. The 0.4-mile **Coronado Peak Trail** culminates in huge views in all directions, and especially to the pyramidal Mexican mountains across the border.

Tombstone

Perhaps the most famous town in the Wild West, **TOMBSTONE** lies 22 miles south of I-10 on US-80, 67 miles southeast of Tucson. Well over a century has passed since its mining days came to an end, but "The Town Too Tough to Die" clings to an afterlife as a tourist theme park. With its dusty streets, wooden sidewalks, and swinging saloon doors, it's surprisingly unchanged, though these days the emphasis is on entertaining kids with tacky dioramas and daily shoot-outs. While much more commercialized than Lincoln, its counterpart in New Mexico (see p.196), to be honest it's also more fun.

Prospecting in the Dragoon Mountains in 1877, **Edward Schieffelin** was told by soldiers stationed nearby that all he'd find would be his own tombstone. Hence the name of the town that rose from the desert when he made Arizona's

▲ Stagecoach, Tombstone

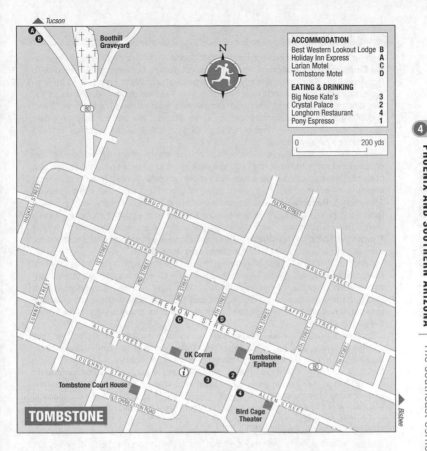

largest **silver** strike, in March 1878. Schieffelin sold his stake for $500,000, but the mine yielded $30 million in seven years, and by 1880 Tombstone was home to over ten thousand people. Drifters arrived from the played-out gold fields of Canada and Australia, and gamblers came in from Dodge City, only for the mine to hit water 500 feet down in 1886, and be flooded beyond repair.

Most of the buildings that fill modern Tombstone's simple grid date from the early 1880s. Decaying wagons are parked on the street corners, and signs along the boardwalks mark the sites of famous shoot-outs. It's all quite surreal, as groups of disconsolate, ornery **gunslingers** still pace the streets, snarling at each other, and generally creating enough trouble that the town council has repeatedly attempted to outlaw public gunfighting. Assuming you visit when no ban is in place, whenever a posse of cowboys manage to round up enough tourists, usually at around $4 per head, they gun each other down on some appropriate vacant lot. During **Helldorado Days**, held on the third weekend of each October, you can hardly move for corpses.

Although the real gunfight at the OK Corral in fact took place on Fremont Street, the **OK Corral** itself, on Allen Street between Third and Fourth, remains a big attraction (daily 8.30am–5pm; gunfights Tues–Thurs 2pm & 4pm, Fri–Mon 2pm & 5pm; $5.50, or $9 with gunfight; Ⓦ www.ok-corral.com). The first thing you see on entering is the hearse used to take the victims away. In

The gunfight at the OK Corral

Despite the fame of the **gunfight at the OK Corral** – which ended the feud between the **Earps** and the **Clantons** – how the clannish dispute began remains obscure. To Hollywood, the Earps have always been the heroes, with Wyatt Earp played by firm-jawed stars like Henry Fonda and Kevin Costner. They were, after all, officers of the law, although it was **Virgil** who was Tombstone's marshal, and his brothers **Wyatt** and **Morgan** merely temporary deputies. Ike Clanton, his brother Billy, and their "gang" were freebooting cattle rustlers, who raided Mexican ranches to feed Tombstone's hungry miners.

Such family-based clans were typical of the West, where individuals seldom prospered alone but trustworthy partners were few and far between. Just as typically, both factions had allied themselves with more powerful forces. Though the Earps dreamed of establishing their own cattle empire, they were the hired guns of Tombstone's **Republican** elite. For the owners and managers of the local mines, a federally imposed end to Arizona's frontier anarchy was essential for future investment. Their mouthpiece, Republican mayor John Clum, was also editor of the *Tombstone Epitaph*. The Clantons, like most cowboys and small-scale ranchers, were aligned with the county sheriff, **Democrat** John Behan.

In the spring of 1881, masked gunmen held up a stagecoach near Tombstone and killed two passengers. Some say the robbers were Clanton associates; others, that a familiar cough betrayed one as **John "Doc" Holliday**, a consumptive dentist from Georgia who was close to the Earps, and that the victims were Clanton's men. The hold-up may even have been a joint operation by both groups, who fell out when the plan went awry.

By October, each faction had sworn to shoot the other on sight. The final showdown came at 2pm on **October 26, 1881**. Virgil, Wyatt, and Morgan Earp, together with Doc Holliday, confronted the Clanton brothers, Tom and Frank McLaury, and Billy Claiborne, not in the OK Corral itself, but on Fremont Street nearby. Two of the Clanton group were unarmed, whereas all the Earps had pistols, and Holliday was carrying a shotgun. The Earps fired first. When the shooting stopped, Billy Clanton and the McLaury brothers were dead; Virgil and Morgan Earp and Doc Holliday were wounded, and Ike Clanton had fled.

Under the headline "Three Men Hurled Into Eternity in the Duration of a Moment," the next day's *Tombstone Epitaph* reported that "the feeling among our best citizens is that the Marshal was entirely justifiable." However, Wyatt and Holliday were charged with murder and were held in jail before being acquitted toward the end of November.

In March 1882, Morgan Earp was killed as he played billiards in Tombstone's *Campbell & Hatch* saloon. Three days later, Wyatt Earp shot the chief suspect, Clanton associate Frank Stilwell, in Tucson. He also killed two more of the Clanton gang that summer before leaving Tombstone with his surviving brothers, and moving to Los Angeles. Lionized by early moviemakers, he died in 1929. Tombstone's Episcopalian minister at the time of the shoot-out – Endicott Peabody – went on to be Franklin Roosevelt's White House chaplain.

the second of two baking-hot adobe–walled courtyards beyond, crude dummies show the supposed locations of the Earps and the Clantons. In the original studio of photographer C.S. Fly alongside, you can pose for your own souvenir photo or tintype (Thurs–Mon 10am–5pm; $25).

At Allen Street and Sixth Avenue, the **Bird Cage Theater** (daily 8am–6pm; $10) was Tombstone's leading venue for entertainment of all kinds. Seven "bird cages," much like theater boxes but curtained off and used by prostitutes, hang from either side of the main hall. Those on the left were frequented by the Earps and their cronies, while the ones on the right were the preserve of Sheriff Behan and the Clantons. The theater now holds a motley collection of curiosities, including a revolting foot-long "merman" from China and another ornate hearse, while downstairs you can see the old gaming tables and bordello rooms.

The **Tombstone Courthouse State Historic Park** (ⓦwww.pr.state.az .us/parks/TOCO/) at Third and Toughnut (daily 8am–5pm; $3) holds displays on the Apache and early outlaws, and documents several rough episodes of frontier justice.

Boothill Graveyard, half a mile north on US-80, closed in May 1884, having been filled by 276 burials. In keeping with the souvenir store that now guards the entrance, several of the graves bear dubious jokey epitaphs, and country music is piped from concealed speakers, the losers at the OK Corral still rest in relative peace (daily 7.30am–6pm; free).

Practicalities

Tombstone's **visitor center** is at Allen and Fourth (daily 9am–5pm; ☏520/457-9317 or 1-888/457-3929, ⓦwww.tombstone.org). Very central, standard **motels** include the *Tombstone Motel*, 502 E Fremont St (☏520/457-3478 or 1-888/455-3478, ⓦwww.tombstonemotel.com; ❸), and the *Larian*, 410 E Fremont St (☏520/457-2272; ❹). A mile north on US-80 you'll find two classier mountain-view alternatives, the *Best Western Lookout Lodge* (☏520/457-2223 or 1-877/652-6772, ⓦwww.bestwesterntombstone.com; ❹), and the *Holiday Inn Express* (☏520/457-9507, ⓦwww.ichotelsgroup.com; ❹).

Among old-style **saloons** serving steaks and beer in as raucous an atmosphere as they can manage are the very fancy *Big Nose Kate's* at 417 E Allen St (☏520/457-3107), where the waitresses wear period costume, and country musicians entertain most afternoons; and the *Longhorn Restaurant*, diagonally opposite at 501 Allen St (☏520/457-3405). *Pony Espresso*, 424 Allen St (☏520/457-3648), serves espresso coffees, pastries, and deli sandwiches.

Bisbee

Crammed into a narrow gorge 25 miles south of Tombstone, **BISBEE** is among Arizona's most atmospheric Victorian towns, rivaled only by Jerome (see p.301). Its fortunes were similarly built on a century of mining mundane, dependable **copper** from the surrounding mountains, rather than a few ephemeral years of gold and silver. Its solid brick buildings testify to the days when Bisbee was the largest city between New Orleans and San Francisco, its population of twenty thousand outstripping both Phoenix and Tucson.

George Warren, who first discovered copper in Mule Pass Gulch, the site of modern Bisbee, in 1877, swiftly lost his claim in a fit of drunken bravado, betting he could outrun a man on horseback. The Copper Queen and Phelps Dodge companies soon moved in, then amalgamated rather than fight over which owned a vast ore body found between their two mines.

Phelps Dodge finally closed down in 1975, having extracted over six billion dollars' worth of metals. As the miners moved away, however, artists and retirees moved in, preserving Bisbee's original architecture while turning it into a thriving, friendly little community that caters to tourists without being overwhelmed by them.

Walking Bisbee's narrow central streets, lined with galleries and antiques stores, is a pleasure in itself, though you may grow weary of climbing the high staircases built by the WPA during the 1930s. If you'd like to know more about local history, call in at the **Bisbee Mining and Historical Museum**, 5 Copper Queen Plaza (daily 10am–4pm; $7.50). You can also join

▲ *Shady Dell RV Park*, Bisbee

hour-long **underground tours** of the actual mines, with Queen Mine Tours, 111 Arizona St (daily 9am, 10.30am, noon, 2pm, & 3.30pm; adults $12, ages 4–15 $5; ☎520/432-2071, ⓦwww.queenminetour.com).

Practicalities

Bisbee's **visitor center**, at 2 Copper Queen Plaza (Mon–Fri 9am–5pm, Sat & Sun 10am–4pm; ☎520/432-3554 or 1-866/224-7233, ⓦwww.discoverbisbee .com), has details of **B&B**s like the quirky *School House Inn*, in a converted school a mile west at 818 Tombstone Canyon (☎520/432-2996 or 1-800/537-4333, ⓦwww.schoolhouseinnbb.com; ❹). A grander alternative is the venerable *Copper Queen Hotel*, in the heart of town at 11 Howell Ave (☎520/432-2216, ⓦwww.copperqueen.com; ❻), which has a plush bar and a good restaurant with terrace seating; the only drawback is the antiquated plumbing. And there's some truly unique accommodation on the southern outskirts of town, in the nine beautifully restored, irresistibly kitsch 1950s trailers at the *Shady Dell RV Park*, 1 Douglas Rd (🏕☎520/432-3567, ⓦwww.theshadydell.com; ❸–❻). This is not a place to bring your own RV, but a great opportunity to sample how a Southwest road trip used to be. *Dot's Diner* alongside (☎520/432-1112) serves authentic Fifties fare.

Once-notorious **Brewery Gulch**, which runs north from Main Street, still holds a handful of spit-and-sawdust saloons and diners, while the less atmospheric **Copper Queen Plaza** mall to the south has its own brewpub and espresso café. Nearby, *Café Cornucopia*, 14 Main St (Mon & Thurs–Sun 10am–5pm; ☎520/432-4820), serves good, simple salads, sandwiches and smoothies, or you can get a much fancier four-course meal for around $20 at the trendy modern *Café Roka*, 35 Main St (☎520/432-5153; summer Fri–Sat 5–9pm; spring & fall Wed–Sat 5–9pm; winter Thurs–Sat 5–9pm).

Douglas

As you'll see from the endless tailings that spill from the canyons to the south, room to build in or near Bisbee was extremely limited. In 1900, therefore, the new town of **DOUGLAS** was constructed 25 miles east, nestled against the Mexican border, to hold a smelter that processed copper from Bisbee's mines. Although Douglas has diversified into ranching and industry, the relocation of Phelps Dodge following a bitter 1980s strike has left the local economy too depressed for it to make an appealing stop for tourists.

Illegal trade with the much larger city of **AGUA PRIETA** across the border – home to almost 100,000 people – is a major source of income. One notorious drug smuggler hired surveyors and laborers to dig a deep tunnel between his houses in either town, then had them executed to preserve his secret.

Douglas has long been renowned as the number-one port of entry for **illegal immigrants** from Mexico. In a single month, the 275 agents of the Border Patrol stationed in Douglas arrested 61,000 such entrants – a rate of almost one hundred per hour, but nonetheless a small proportion of those who attempted the crossing. A major US crackdown, initiated in 1994 and given added impetus since September 2001, has involved the construction of a permanent border wall in the vicinity, and forced ever-more would-be migrants to attempt to cross the fearsome Sonora Desert on foot. Around 250 per year die of dehydration, while Douglas is racked by controversy, and unauthorized vigilante patrols vie with church and humanitarian groups to find distressed wanderers.

As for legal border traffic, cars and pedestrians alike cross into Mexico at the foot of Pan American Avenue, a mile or so southwest of downtown Douglas; US citizens should carry passports. With its whitewashed adobe homes and churches, Agua Prieta is a considerably more attractive place to stroll around than Douglas, and offers plenty of opportunities to eat spicy Sonoran food and buy cheap souvenirs.

Practicalities

Douglas has a **visitor center** at 345 Sixteenth St (Mon–Fri 8am–5pm, Sat 8am–1pm; ℡520/364-4927, ⓦwww.douglasaz.gov). The only building of any distinction is the 160-room *Gadsden Hotel*, 1046 G Ave (℡520/364-4481, ⓦhotelgadsden.com; ❸), which opened in 1907 and still boasts an extraordinarily opulent lobby with a white marble staircase leading to a 42ft Tiffany glass window. The guest **accommodation** is not nearly so classy, but both its *Saddle and Spur Lounge* and *El Conquistador* **restaurant**, which serves reasonable meals for around $10, have a real frontier-town air. A few more downmarket motels are scattered along Hwy-80 to the east.

Chiricahua National Monument

Stretching northeast of Douglas toward New Mexico, the **Chiricahua Mountains** were the homeland and stronghold of the **Chiricahua Apache**. Led by legendary warriors like **Cochise** and **Geronimo**, the Chiricahua – the name means "land of wild turkeys" – were the last Native Americans to hold out against the US Army. The 25-year **Apache Wars** began at Apache Pass in 1861, when Cochise met Lt. George Bascom under a flag of truce, and was falsely accused of kidnapping a 12-year-old boy. He escaped into the mountains, but his brother and two nephews were hanged, precipitating a vicious cycle of raids and killings that only ended with Geronimo's fourth and final surrender in 1886.

Had the small Chiricahua band not fought so long and hard, they might still be living on the **Chiricahua reservation**, established during a period of relative peace in 1872. Occupying the entire southeastern corner of Arizona, it was disbanded in 1876, when the Chiricahua were forcibly decamped to join their distant cousins on the San Carlos Reservation to the north. No sign of the

Apache presence remains, but the core of the former reservation now constitutes **CHIRICAHUA NATIONAL MONUMENT**, entered off Hwy-186 27 miles southeast of Willcox. The monument was designated to protect the bizarre **rock formations** created in the 27 million years since volcanic eruptions covered the landscape with a 2000ft coating of dark rhyolite rock. That layer has now cracked and fragmented into strange towers and columns of stacked and balanced stones, a bewildering maze that always defeated Army attempts to pursue the Apache into the mountains.

Although Chiricahua National Monument is not as spectacular as the desert canyons of Utah, this remote fastness preserves a tract of barely touched wilderness that conjures up haunting images of the Wild West, and it's also a sanctuary for rare animals and birds. These include a colony of thick-billed **parrots**, once common here and reintroduced in 1986.

Just one paved road – the eight-mile **Bonita Canyon Drive** – penetrates, but does not cross, the mountains, and stays open 24 hours. From the monument entrance it runs for two miles to the **visitor center** (daily 8am–4.30pm; $5 per person; ⊕520/824-3560, ⓦwww.nps.gov/chir), then follows Bonita Canyon east before climbing south to reach **Massai Point**, 6870ft up. This high vantage point looks out over the main concentration of rocky pinnacles, in **Echo Canyon** and **Heart of Rocks**; trails drop from the parking lot to circle the promontory below.

Only if you have a few hours to spare, however, does Massai Point make a good spot from which to start **hiking**; it is possible to walk down into the labyrinth from here, but then you're faced with either a long climb to get back out again, or a one-way walk of at least four miles to reach the visitor center. For a shorter and less demanding stroll, set off instead along **Echo Canyon Trail**, which starts half a mile or so back down the road. This level footpath leads in ten minutes to some dramatic formations, and you can turn back whenever you've had your fill. The highest peak in the monument at 7310ft, **Sugarloaf Mountain**, can be climbed on a separate mile-long trail, but it's a much less rewarding hike.

No food, gas, or lodging is available in the monument, and overnight backpacking is forbidden, but you can **camp** year-round at the small *Bonita Canyon Campground* (first-come, first-served; $12). Alternatively, the *Sunglow Ranch* is a 400-acre **guest ranch** just south of the monument at 14066 S Sunglow Rd, Pearce (⊕520/824-3344 or 1-866/786-4569, ⓦsunglowranch .com; ❼), which holds three luxurious guest *casitas* of varying sizes; the plushest has two bedrooms and bathrooms and a cozy fireplace area. Rates include dinner at the on-site *Sunglow Café*.

Fort Bowie

The ruins of **FORT BOWIE** (daily 8am–5pm; free), the original focus of the Chiricahua Reservation and now a national historic site, lie just beyond the northern boundary of Chiricahua National Monument. They're reached by a demanding but exhilarating 1.5 mile trail that starts on the north side of **Apache Pass**, a total of 22 miles from the monument visitor center or, if you're coming from the north, thirteen miles from the somewhat desolate I-10 pitstop of **Bowie**.

Apache Pass today is an insignificant back route. The central nine miles of the **Apache Pass Road** across it are not even paved, though when it hasn't been raining they're usually passable to ordinary vehicles. This low saddle between the Dos Cabezas and Chiricahua mountains is currently overgrown with mesquite bushes, but when the Apache were here it ran through clear, open grassland. Its perennial natural **springs** made it a crucial way station for the **Butterfield Overland Mail**, which started regular runs through Apache Pass in 1857, as part of a 25-day, 2800-mile service between St Louis and San Francisco. The US Army soon established a permanent military presence at the pass.

Allow at least two and a half hours for the round-trip hike. The first significant relic comes after half a mile, with the stone walls of the **Apache Pass Stage Station**, built in 1858. Shortly after crossing the old stage route, now a mere furrow in the soil, you reach the **cemetery** where Little Robe, Geronimo's two-year-old son, lies alongside several US soldiers. Not far beyond, the trail reaches the glorious lush creek that flows from **Apache Spring** – the source of all the trouble, but now the preserve of a myriad of playful coatis and bobcats.

There are no views to speak of as you climb; instead, the **fort** itself sits in a deep, broad bowl, ringed by mountains and dominated by a granite knob known as **Helen's Dome**. Only the rounded, sun-baked stumps of its adobe walls now survive, though a flag still flutters above the parade ground, and a visitor center nearby provides much-needed shade and water. An optional, slightly longer route back continues up the adjacent hillside before circling down to the trailhead. En route, you step over the geological fault that created the springs, and the surrounding vegetation instantly transforms from yucca and flowering cactuses (on limestone) to beargrass (on granite).

Willcox

Only one significant community interrupts I-10 in its ninety-mile run east from Benson to the New Mexican border: **WILLCOX**, 36 miles out from Benson. In its small but atmospheric downtown area, the **Chiricahua Regional Museum**, 127 E Maley St (Mon–Sat 10am–4pm; $2 donation), is a storefront that holds informative displays on both Cochise and Geronimo.

Practicalities

Willcox's Chamber of Commerce runs a **visitor center** at 1500 N Circle I Rd, close to exit 340 off the interstate (Mon–Sat 9am–5pm; ☏520/384-2272 or 1-800/200-2272, ⓦwillcoxchamber.com). Chain **motels** nearby include a *Super 8*, 1500 W Fort Grant Rd (☏520/384-0888 or 1-800/800-8000, ⓦsuper8.com, ⊙). Back in town, *Rodney's* is a friendly hole-in-the-wall **barbecue** place at 118 N Railroad Ave (☏520/384-6317; closed Mon), while *Bucko's*, 114 S Railroad Ave (☏520/384-2575; closed Mon), is a friendly espresso café housed in a charming old store just along the street, opposite the railroad depot.

Southwest Arizona

Two interstates, **I-8** and **I-10**, run west across central and southern Arizona toward California, 35 miles apart near Phoenix and more than twice that by the time they reach the state line. There's virtually nothing of interest in these vast desert plains, apart perhaps from the strange prototype military airplanes glimpsed above the Barry M. Goldwater Air Force Range, which stretches south from I-8 to Mexico. A long detour south will take you to the wild terrain of **Organ Pipe Cactus National Monument**, but the only town you might conceivably want to visit is **Yuma**, a venerable river crossing on the far southwest border with California, whose mundane present fails to live up to its wild past.

Tohono 'O'odham Indian Reservation

The high country to the east of Tucson, known as **Papaguería** to the Spanish, is now dominated by the **TOHONO 'O'ODHAM INDIAN RESERVA-TION** (formerly known as the Papago Indian Reservation). The **Tohono 'O'odham**, whose name means "desert people," are one of three related groups who together call themselves the **'O'odham** – "The People." Unlike the Akimel **'O'odham** (or Pima), the "river people" who lived in permanent villages, the Tohono **'O'odham** were traditionally "two-villagers," who divided their time between a summer "field" village in the valleys and a winter "well" village near a spring in the foothills. Apart from the mission at San Xavier del Bac, described on p.252, the **'O'odham** are best known these days for the music they call *waila*, derived from Mexican accordion and polka music, which may be more familiar as "**chicken scratch**."

Around ten thousand Tohono 'O'odham now live on the reservation, which was established in 1916. They share it with the less numerous **Hia C–ed 'O'odham**, formerly known as the Sand Papago – desert nomads who in 1976 accepted $26 million as compensation for the loss of the lands now enclosed by Organ Pipe Cactus National Monument and the Barry Goldwater Air Force Base.

For tourists, the only reward in driving the hundred-mile width of the reservation, which starts 25 miles out of Tucson on **Hwy-86**, is its sheer sense of desolation. The only signs of human occupation, since most Tohono **'O'odham** live far from the road, are a handful of roadside buildings at **Sells**, the administrative headquarters 56 miles southwest of Tucson, and **Quijotoa**, another 23 miles northwest.

Organ Pipe Cactus National Monument

Hwy-86 ends at **Hwy-85**, fifty miles south of Gila Bend, at a Y-shaped intersection that has over the years acquired the formal name of **WHY**. A twenty-mile detour south from here through the straight, flat **Sonoyta Valley**, between the jagged ridge of the dry Ajo Mountains to the east and the lower Puerto Blanco Mountains to the west, climbs in due course to reach **ORGAN PIPE CACTUS NATIONAL MONUMENT**, right on the Mexican border.

Located at the heart of the Sonoran Desert, the five-hundred-square-mile monument is a treasure-trove of rare desert plants and animals, but focuses especially on the **organ pipe**, found almost nowhere else in the United States. Where the saguaro stands alone, the organ pipe grows in clusters of tubular "pipes," thrusting up from a shared central root system.

The $8 per vehicle monument **entrance fee** is payable only if you leave the main road. From the **visitor center**, just west of the highway (daily 8am–5pm; ☎520/387-6849, ⓦwww.nps.gov/orpi), two separate **scenic drives** loop off into the mountains. Both are unpaved and steep, but generally passable for ordinary vehicles; the 21-mile **Ajo Mountain Drive** takes around two hours to complete, the 53-mile **Puerto Blanco Drive** at least half a day. This remote area is so prone to illegal border crossings that it receives virtually constant attention from security forces; roads are often closed altogether for significant periods, and even when they're not the activities of the border patrols may make you feel too uncomfortable to linger.

In summer, **hiking** anything more than the hundred-yard nature trail at the visitor center would be far too grueling to consider, but between October and April, you might feel more inclined to walk several short trails that lead further afield. The cooler months are also the only time when the **campground** (first-come, first-served; $12), a mile south of the visitor center, is likely to fill up.

Ajo

Ten miles north of Why, almost halfway to Gila Bend and the interstate, **AJO** is a former copper-mining town that's nicer than the hideous open-pit mine to the south might suggest. Hispanic settlers were digging for copper by 1750; they named the town in honor of the garlic (*ajo*) that grows wild in the hills nearby.

Since Phelps Dodge closed the mine in 1984, after a bitter strike, Ajo has defied the sceptics and clung to life by attracting a steady trickle of tourists and retirees. There's a welcoming bustle about its tidy, grassy plaza, surrounded by palm trees and holding two whitewashed Spanish-colonial churches, even if the streets behind hold little of interest.

Practicalities

Two clean, simple **motels** stand either side of the highway a couple of miles north of Ajo. The *Marine Resort* is tucked behind a screen of cactuses at 1966 N Hwy-85 (℡520/387-7626, ⓦwww.marinemotel.com; ❸), while *La Siesta* is a little further along at 2561 N Hwy-85 (℡520/387-6569; ❸). Back in town, the *Guest House Inn*, 3 Guesthouse Rd (℡520/387-6133, ⓦwww.guesthouseinn .biz; ❹), is a comfortable **B&B** with four en-suite rooms. The *Copper Kettle* on the plaza, at 23 Plaza St (℡520/387-7000), is the best **restaurant**, serving mainly Mexican dishes.

Gila Bend

At the intersection of Hwy-85 and I-8, **GILA BEND** is a minor farming community whose rather scanty history is celebrated in the tiny **museum** that adjoins its rudimentary **visitor center** at 644 W Pima St (daily 8am–4pm; ℡520/683-2002, ⓦwww.gilabendaz.org).

While not a destination in itself, Gila Bend has the widest array of **motels** in almost two hundred miles of interstate. The *Best Western Space Age Lodge*, 401 E Pima St (℡520/683-2273 or 1-866/683 7722, ⓦwww.bestwesternspaceagelodge .com; ❹), is a dramatic Fifties relic, where the Sputnik motif extends to a giant neon flying saucer sign.

Yuma

The sheer size of **YUMA**, a hundred miles west of Gila Bend, surprises most visitors; its numbered streets start a full fifty miles out from the center, and while its population remains under 100,000, it's Arizona's third largest conurbation. According to the *Guinness Book of Records*, it's also the sunniest place on earth, with less than three inches of rain per year and 339 sunny days. Average July highs are 107°F (42°C), while the record maximum is 124°F (51°C).

Commanding the confluence of the Gila and Colorado rivers, this site was recognized as being significant as early as 1540, when **Hernando de Alarcón**, in charge of the naval wing of Coronado's expedition (see p.500), sailed past its high bluffs. It later became the major river crossing for California-bound travelers, though Spanish attempts to establish a permanent mission settlement were destroyed by the **Yuma Revolt** of 1781, when **Quechan** Indians (known to the Spaniards as the Yuma) massacred over 150 settlers during Mass.

At the height of California's **Gold Rush**, sixty thousand passengers in a single year paid $2 each to be ferried across the Colorado at **Yuma Crossing**. This lucrative trade was at first controlled by the Quechan, but freebooting entrepreneurs wrested it out of their hands, with the US Army at Fort Yuma on hand to stifle Indian resistance. (A phenomenally bloodthirsty account of the struggle appears in Cormac McCarthy's novel *Blood Meridian*; see p.526.) Known initially as Colorado City, and later Arizona City, Yuma took on its current name in 1873, by which time it was experiencing a gold rush of its own.

Now that intricate hydraulic engineering has tamed the Colorado – one California-bound canal actually siphons beneath the river – it would take a major dam-burst to cause a repeat of the river's formerly devastating floods. In theory, Arizona could use its share of the Colorado's water to irrigate the land around Yuma and create a rival to California's nearby **Imperial Valley**, one of the world's richest farming areas; instead, although Yuma's economy is indeed largely founded on agriculture, the vast bulk of the water is channeled across the desert to Phoenix and Tucson at astronomical expense.

Yuma is not a vacation destination in the usual sense, but its warm, dry winters, when temperatures seldom drop below the mid-70°s F, have made it a goal for hordes of "**snowbirds**" who keep an astonishing 72 local RV and trailer parks busy. During summer, on the other hand, Yuma is too much of an inferno for anyone to linger very long.

Arrival and information

Yuma's **visitor center**, downtown at 139 S Fourth Ave (May–Oct Mon–Fri 9am–6pm, Sat 9am–2pm; Nov–April Mon–Fri 9am–6pm, Sat 9am–4pm, Sun noon–4pm; ℡928/783-0071 or 1-800/293-0071, ⓦvisityuma.com), doubles as an Arizona welcome center. Amtrak **trains** from LA to Tucson stop nearby at 281 Gila St, at hideously unsocial hours, while Greyhound **buses** run from 170 E 17th Place (℡928/783-4403) to Phoenix, Tucson, and San Diego.

Yuma River Tours (℡928/783-4400, ⓦwww.yumarivertours.com) runs various **Colorado cruises** from Fisher's Landing, 32 miles upstream from Yuma, including trips on jet boats (five-hour $75, seven-hour $95, both starting at 10am daily) and a replica sternwheeler (three-hour, $48; 11am daily).

Accommodation

As well as a plethora of RV parks, the "business loop" that parallels the interstate for six miles through the heart of Yuma holds dozens of **hotels** and **motels**, with plusher chains along its east–west segment on **32nd Street**, and old-fashioned budget options on the north–south **Fourth Avenue** closer to the river.

Best Western Coronado Motor Hotel 233 Fourth Ave ℡928/783-4453 or 1-877/234-5567, ⓦbwcoronado.com. Veteran, nicely updated, central motel, within easy walking distance of downtown, and built in appealing Mission Revival style, with a little museum of pioneer life. ❹
Hotel Lee 390 S Main St ℡928/726-6336. Antique-furnished, old-fashioned and not fully modernized downtown hotel – there's no elevator, for example – where not all the rooms have en-suite baths. ❷
Yuma Cabaña 2151 S Fourth Ave ℡928/783-8311 or 1-800/874-0811, ⓦwww.yumacabana .com. Traditional roadside motel, with a lovely old neon sign, a couple of miles up from the river. Clean, quiet, and very good value. ❸

The Town

Yuma is not an attractive town; it's much too large to explore on foot, while its historic downtown is small and insignificant, and only the new Gateway Park, of more interest to locals than visitors, offers appealing access to the riverside. Instead, the best place to get a feel for the town's tempestuous past is the **Yuma Territorial Prison State Historic Park**, set high above the Colorado a few blocks east of downtown (daily 8am–5pm; $4). Built in 1876, the "Hell Hole of Arizona" was the state's principal prison for 33 years. Its restored wooden guard tower gives great views of the green-lined river meandering in from the north; this spot originally marked the precise confluence of the two rivers, but that has now shifted five miles further upstream. The "Ocean to Ocean" bridge here was built in 1915, not only superseding the ferry but also completing the southern-most transcontinental railroad route.

Inside the prison compound's adobe walls, fascinating displays tell the stories of its three thousand prisoners. These ranged from teenage burglars to Harvard lawyers and included nine Mormon polygamists, several Mexican revolution-aries, and a handful of women, such as the colorful Pearl Hart, who served five years for committing Arizona's last stagecoach robbery in 1899. You can also enter several cells.

Yuma's former **Quartermaster Depot**, on Fourth Avenue near the river bridge, is now a state park (daily 9am–5pm; $4). All supplies originally reached Yuma via a fifty-mile river journey from the ocean via Port Isabel on the Gulf of California; the depot still holds two warehouses where Colorado paddle steamers used to moor. Various ancient wagons, carriages, and even trains have been stabled indoors or set out to pasture on the lawns, but unless transportation history is your thing, it's not desperately exciting.

Yuma's most unusual attraction has to be the **Saihati Camel Farm**, roughly four miles south of town on Ave 1E (Oct–May Mon–Sat 9am–5pm; $3; ☎928/627-7511). Until you get within smelling distance, it's fiendishly difficult to find: Avenue 1E only starts, as a dirt road, south of the airport. Assuming you do manage to get here, you'll be able to inspect a large herd of slobbery, drooling dromedaries, bred here for circuses and zoos – there's no camel riding here – plus a cross section of other wildlife such as ostriches, water buffalo, and Watusi cattle.

Finally, many visitors like to take a day-trip south into **Mexico**, whether to little **Algodones**, across from California a mere ten miles east, or to the much larger city of **San Luis**, 23 miles south. Both offer the usual array of souvenir stores and restaurants, together with cut-price drugstores.

Eating

Yuma is no place to expect memorable **eating**, though cruising up and down Main Street will take you past every fast-food option imaginable.

The Coffee Bean 2450 S Fourth Ave ☎928/317-0284. Friendly little coffee-and-pastries joint on the main drag.

Garden Cafe 248 S Madison Ave ☎928/783-1491. Tasteful café with indoor and outdoor seating, behind a small free museum of pioneer life, that's open for breakfast and lunch only and serves salads, sandwiches, and espresso coffees. Closed Mon & June–Sept.

Lutes Casino 221 Main St ☎928/782-2192. This downtown landmark may look like a dull old barn from the outside, but inside it's bursting with quirky oddities and paraphernalia, and does a brisk trade in surprisingly tasty hamburgers. There's no gambling, but plenty of pool and domino players. Mon–Thurs 10am–8pm, Fri & Sat 10am–9pm, Sun 10am–6pm.

River City Grill 600 W Third St ☎928/782-7988. Bright "international" restaurant, serving an eclectic and relatively expensive menu that concentrates on Asian-influenced seafood options like Thai crab cakes or seared *ahi*. Outdoor dining available. Mon–Fri 11am–2pm & 5–10pm, Sat & Sun 5–10pm.

North from Yuma: Quartzsite

North of Yuma, three **wildlife refuges** – the Kofa, Cibola, and Imperial – line the Colorado River. Established to protect mule deer and bighorn sheep as well as migratory Canadian geese, the parks aren't really designed for visitors, and are virtually inaccessible without a four-wheel-drive vehicle. Granted that you'd rather not get caught up in the tank battles staged by the army in its **Yuma Proving Grounds**, there's nowhere to stop on the main north–south highway, **US-95**, until you reach **QUARTZSITE**, eighty miles out of Yuma.

With the Colorado now twenty miles west, Quartzsite is even bleaker and drier than Yuma, While it has a nominal population of two thousand, it, too, experiences a major winter influx of snowbirds. Literally hundreds of thousands of RV-owners descend on this desert outpost between early January and mid-February each year, ostensibly to bargain for precious, semi-precious, and merely pretty stones, but also to ride out the coldest months with like-minded fellow retirees.

In Quartzsite's dusty, central **cemetery**, a pyramidal monument topped by a brass camel commemorates an odd episode in Southwestern history. Inscribed "The last camp of **Hi Jolly**, born somewhere in Syria about 1828, died Quartzsite December 16 1902," it marks the grave of Haiji Ali, who arrived at Indianola, Texas, in 1856, in charge of 33 **camels** that had been requisitioned by the then Secretary of War, Jefferson Davis. Although they adapted well to the desert, army mule handlers and cowboys lacked the patience or inclination to care for them properly, and experiments to test their suitability as beasts of burden petered out during the Civil War. "Hi Jolly" became just another prospector; the abandoned camels bred in the wild into the twentieth century. To this day, it remains against the law to shoot a camel in Arizona.

Despite its endless expanse of RV parks, Quartzsite has just four tiny and flyblown **motels**, with fewer than ten rooms each.

Parker

Quartzsite's winter crowds spill over to **PARKER**, beside the river 35 miles north. The main activity here is boating on the placid waters downstream of the **Parker Dam**, a Depression-era project designed to divert Colorado water to the thirsty cities of southern California. Since 1985 the dam has also provided water for the **Central Arizona Project**, whose 336 miles of aqueducts stretch as far as Phoenix and Tucson. Almost twenty miles out of Parker, it's the deepest dam in the world, dug 235 feet into the riverbed. Jet-skiers glide up to its base for a closer look, and it can also be seen on free self-guided **tours** (daily 7.30am–4pm).

Parker started life in 1905 as the principal settlement on the **Colorado River Indian Reservation**. Not far from the dam, clearly signposted from Hwy-95, visitors can examine prehistoric rock art, or **intaglios**, made by "carving" the darker top layer of rock away from the desert floor, to reveal lighter layers of sand beneath (daily 8am–sundown; $3). The figures are so huge (up to 160ft) that it's hard to tell what you're looking at, but gaze long enough and you can discern a four-legged animal, and a human and spiral design.

Overlooking the Colorado just under two miles northwest of town, the *Bluewater Resort & Casino*, 11300 Resort Drive (☎928/669-7000 or 1-888/243-3360, Ⓦwww.bluewaterfun.com; Sun–Thurs ❷, Fri & Sat ❻), is a huge casino resort, owned by the Colorado River Indians, that has its own indoor water park.

⑤

Flagstaff and central Arizona

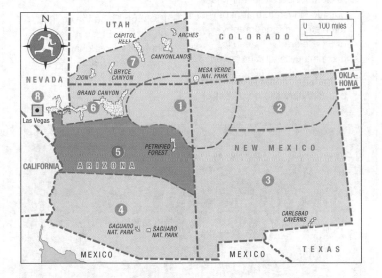

CHAPTER 5

Highlights

✳ **La Posada** Glorious old restored hotel, straight from the heyday of Route 66, that's a great reason to spend a night in Winslow. See p.283

✳ **Downtown Flagstaff** Flanking both sides of Route 66 and the Santa Fe Railroad, Flagstaff's bustling downtown streets abound with the flavor of the West. See p.287

✳ **The Museum of Northern Arizona** Superb museum, just outside Flagstaff, that explains the history and geography of the Colorado Plateau in fascinating detail. See p.288

✳ **Wupatki National Monument** Extraordinary site northeast of Flagstaff, where the ancient Sinagua people raised multi-story pueblos out of the desert floor. See p.292

✳ **Verde Canyon Railroad** Take a delightful half-day train ride into the wilderness of little-known Verde Canyon. See p.301

✳ **Jerome** Former mining town, now turned artists' colony, perched high on a hillside with magnificent views. See p.301

✳ **Prescott** Once the capital of Arizona, Prescott remains one of its most charming little towns. See p.305

▲ *The Museum Club*, Flagstaff

Flagstaff and central Arizona

With the state's northernmost hundred miles, from the rugged Navajo and Hopi reservations across to the Grand Canyon, impassable to east–west traffic, the **I-40 corridor** is the focus of a huge tract of north and central Arizona. Before the interstate was pushed through, the legendary **Route 66** followed much the same path; before either road, there was the Santa Fe Railroad; and before the railroad arrived, not much more than a century ago, there were no significant Anglo settlements in the region at all.

Even today, only charming, characterful **Flagstaff** of the I-40 towns, set in the world's largest stand of sweet-smelling ponderosa **pine forest**, amounts to much more than an overnight pit stop. It also makes a great base for visits not only to the Grand Canyon (detailed in Chapter 6) but to the dramatic ancient sites of **Wupatki** and **Walnut Canyon**, and the superbly positioned New Age mecca of **Sedona**.

The highlight of the long drive between Flagstaff and New Mexico is **Petrified Forest National Park**, where giant fossilized remains lie strewn like matchsticks across the eerie desert badlands. To the west, the road to California is less inspiring; it makes sense to detour south by way of the historic hilltop mining town of **Jerome** and pristine Victorian **Prescott** or, further west, to take a timewarp spin along Route 66 to the ghost town of **Oatman**.

East of Flagstaff

During its 150-mile run west from the New Mexican border to Flagstaff, **I-40** passes few towns of any size, let alone interest. The **landscape**, however, while barren in the extreme, is consistently beautiful, with double rainbows reaching across the desert plain and fiery dawns blazing along the horizon. The most accessible section of this **Painted Desert** lies within **Petrified Forest National Park**, which makes an intriguing half-day detour.

For many, this relentless desolation is exactly what they came to see; few join the locals in escaping south to the cool uplands of the **White Mountains**.

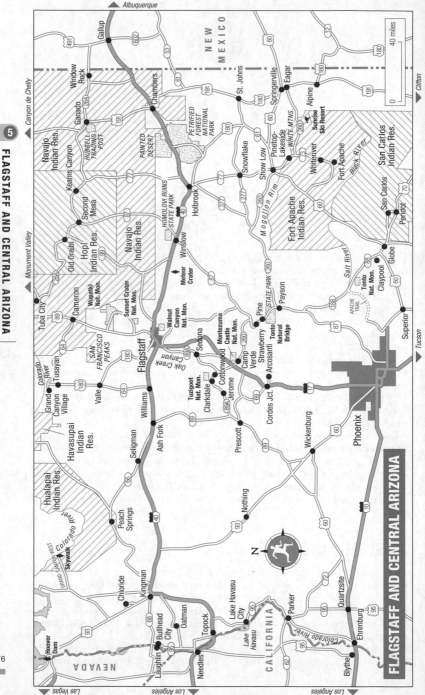

FLAGSTAFF AND CENTRAL ARIZONA

5

Petrified Forest National Park

Straddling the interstate 25 miles east of Holbrook, **PETRIFIED FOREST NATIONAL PARK** serves a dual purpose. While its chief role is to protect a prehistoric "forest" of fossilized trees, south of I-40, it also stretches north to include picturesque stretches of the Painted Desert, an ill-defined area of multicolored badlands that covers much of northeast Arizona. Its blue-tinged clays and crumbling sands support little vegetation or life, and continue to erode at a fearsome rate. Each year, more and more lithified logs are exposed to view, lying in haphazard profusion on the barren slopes. Petrified wood is not in fact all that rare, but its sheer abundance here is extraordinary; the wood-bearing layer, also rich in dinosaur bones and other fossils, extends three hundred feet beneath the ground.

The gigantic trees of Petrified Forest, drawn from long-extinct species such as *Auracarioxylon*, *Woodworthia*, and *Schilderia*, date back 225 million years. This is not, however, the site of an actual forest. Its mighty trunks are horizontal, not vertical; they didn't grow here, they accumulated as a vast log jam in an ancient river. Settling onto the riverbed, they were buried by layers of silt and ash, thereby slowing decay. Bit by bit, silica seeped in and replaced the original wood cells, then crystallized into quartz.

Cross sections of petrified wood, cut with diamond saws and then polished, look stunning; prize specimens are displayed in the park's two visitor centers, while lesser examples, gathered outside the park, are sold in commercial outlets nearby. As seen on the ground from trails along the park's **27-mile Scenic Drive**, however, the trees themselves are not always all that exciting. Segmented, crumbling, and very dark, they can just seem like a bunch of logs lying in the sand, even if they are stone logs. The best viewing comes in late afternoon, when the setting sun brings out rich red and orange hues.

Petrified Forest became a national park in 1962 when large-scale **pilfering** threatened to deplete its stocks altogether. A similar park in the Dakotas had to close in the 1930s after visitors carried off all its fossil treasures, and even today twelve tons of rock disappears from the Petrified Forest each year. In theory, rangers can search your vehicle as you leave and impose heavy fines on anyone caught with a pocketful of petrified wood-chips. They rarely bother, however, preferring the subtler approach of displaying letters in the visitor centers from repentant rock thieves who have been punished by the loss of hair, health, pets, or progeny.

Arrival and information

Although the main road through the park crosses I-40, there's no access to or from the interstate at that point. Instead, the park has two separate entrances, at the north and south ends of its scenic drive. Which you use will depend on how much time you can spare, and which way you're heading. If you're coming from New Mexico, turn north off the interstate at exit 311, 22 miles west of Chambers, and within a mile you'll come to the **Painted Desert Visitor Center** (daily: summer 7am–7pm; winter 8am–5pm; ☎928/524-6228, ⓦwww.nps.gov/pefo). If you're heading east and only have time for a quick look, you can use that same entrance, but if you want to see the entire park it makes more sense to leave I-40 at Holbrook (see opposite) and take US-180 for twenty miles southeast to the southern entrance, near the **Rainbow Forest Museum** (daily 8am–5pm).

Displays at both visitor centers explain the geology of the park and forest. The **admission fee** of $10 per vehicle, or $5 for motorcyclists, cyclists, and pedestrians, is levied at roadside kiosks nearby, where you can also buy National Parks passes (see p.41).

▲ Painted Desert, Petrified Forest National Park

Simple snacks are available at the Rainbow Forest Museum, but the Painted Desert Visitor Center holds most of the park's few facilities, including a *Fred Harvey* **restaurant** that serves overpriced café meals all day, a large gift store, and a gas station. There are no **lodges** or **campgrounds** in the park; the only way to spend a night is to camp in the backcountry, with a free permit from the visitor center.

Exploring the park

Petrified Forest effectively divides into three sections, with an area rich in ancient Indian remains separating the desert in the north from the forest in the south. To see its full range, you have to complete the entire 27-mile scenic drive, but there's no need to stop at every overlook along the way.

Assuming you enter the park in the north, beyond the Painted Desert Visitor Center, you'll soon find yourself skirting the edge of a giant mesa, which drops away northwards to reveal long-range views across the **Painted Desert** itself. At different times of day, the undulating expanse of clay-topped mounds takes on different colors, with an emphasis on blueish shades of gray and reddish shades of brown. It's best admired through the panoramic windows of the **Painted Desert Inn** (daily 9am–5pm), a mile or two along, a long-defunct adobe hotel that has been restored as a museum. Mexican-style murals inside, painted by Hopi artist Fred Kabotie in 1948, depict Hopi pilgrimages and dances, while a stone slab bears a thirteenth-century petroglyph depiction of a fierce-clawed mountain lion. From the promontory behind the inn, **Kachina Point**, backcountry **trails** drop down into the Painted Desert Wilderness. Only by walking these can you truly appreciate the scale of the place, but even the shortest hike involves a hot climb back up again.

After six miles of similar overlooks, the road crosses first the interstate, and then, in quick succession, the Santa Fe Railroad and the broad but usually dry Puerco River. At the **Puerco Indian Ruin**, just beyond, a short trail leads around a small, partially excavated pueblo, abandoned in 1300 AD by its Ancestral Puebloan inhabitants. Patches of black desert varnish on nearby rocks show well-preserved petroglyphs, including one you'd swear depicted a stork bringing a baby.

A little further along, a bunch of bigger petroglyph-covered boulders – known collectively, like many such sites, as **Newspaper Rock** – lie at the foot of a rocky incline. Closer access is forbidden, but free binoculars allow you to peer at the indistinct scribbles. In time, some resolve themselves into male and female figures.

By the time you've passed the bizarre pyramidal hillocks of the **Teepees**, you've finally reached the **Petrified Forest**. At roadside halts from here on, rough concrete walkways have been laid over the terrain – and often over the tree trunks too – so visitors can ramble through the larger concentrations of logs. At **Blue Mesa**, certain tree-trunks are raised on muddy "pedestals" above the surrounding desert; at **Agate Bridge**, one even spans a little gully.

The park's busiest trail, the **Long Logs Walk** near the southern entrance, is so popular that its parking lot is closed in the mornings, and hikers have to walk a few hundred extra yards up from the Rainbow Forest Museum. Here at the edge of the desert, a little grass manages to survive, making the half-mile main

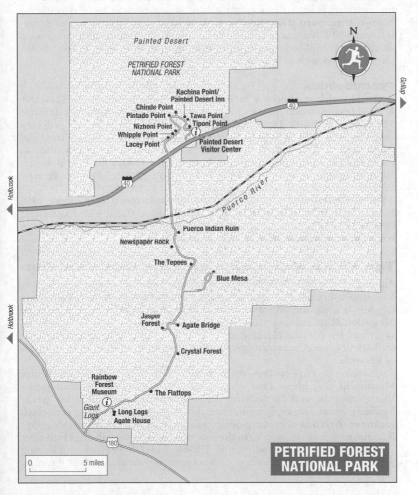

PETRIFIED FOREST
NATIONAL PARK

trail especially surreal. The large, shattered logs – which when alive resembled ponderosa pines – are simply strewn across the grasslands, with not another stone or rock in sight. A side trail leads in another half mile to a knoll holding the remains of a seven-hundred-year-old Indian pueblo constructed entirely from petrified wood. **Agate House** might sound amazing, but, thanks perhaps to its clumsy restoration, it's oddly banal.

When the Long Logs Walk looks busy, the **Crystal Forest** trail, five miles north, makes a good alternative.

Holbrook

From 1886 to 1900, **HOLBROOK**, halfway between Gallup and Flagstaff, was the rowdy headquarters of the "Hashknife" cattle outfit, the third largest in the country. Not much seems to have happened since, but traffic on Route 66 and I-40 has kept Holbrook ticking.

Unless you're ready to stop for the night, there's no great reason to stray off the interstate, though a romantic patch of Route 66 frontage survives along **Navajo Boulevard**. The **Old West Museum**, housed in the former courthouse at 100 E Arizona St (Mon–Fri 8am–5pm, Sat & Sun 8am–5pm; free), is an appealing small-town melange of Ancestral Puebloan pots, fading photographs, and dioramas of Wild West shootouts.

Practicalities

Holbrook's **visitor center** is in the museum (same hours; ☎928/524-6558, ⓦwww.azjournal.com). By far the most unusual place to **stay** is the *Wigwam Motel*, 811 W Hopi Drive (⚞ ☎928/524-3048, ⓦgalerie-kokopelli.com /wigwam; ❷), a Route 66 relic in which each room is a miniature teepee of white concrete; it's all enjoyably retro, though it would be nicer if they made an exception and bought new mattresses. There's also a *Holiday Inn Express*, up the hill north of the interstate at 1308 E Navajo Blvd (☎928/524-1466, ⓦwww .hiexpress.com; ❹), with other chain motels.

The best **restaurant** in Holbrook is the self-explanatory *Mesa Italiana*, 2318 Navajo Blvd (☎928/524-6696). The *Butterfield Stage Co*, 609 W Hopi Drive (☎928/524-3447), open for lunch and dinner in summer, and dinner only in winter, serves espresso coffees as well as steaks.

The White Mountains and the Mogollon Rim

Although the spellbinding northern Arizonan desert appears to stretch away forever to either side of I-40, the southern limit of the Colorado Plateau is in fact just beneath the horizon to the south – the 2000ft escarpment of the **Mogollon Rim**, curving two hundred miles from west to east and extending well into New Mexico. Heading south from I-40 feels like you're heading into the back of beyond, but you're soon within a hundred miles of the megalopolis of **Phoenix**.

For sweltering city-dwellers, the highland forests – especially in the **White Mountains**, near **Show Low** – make ideal destinations for weekend breaks. Visitors from beyond the Southwest rarely stray this way, and unless you're looking to hunt, fish, or, in winter, ski, the only point in doing so is to reach **southern Arizona** without passing through Phoenix. While no Mogollon Rim town amounts to more than the sum of its dreary parts, all do at least offer abundant motels. Both roads south, **US-60** and **US-191**, are exhilarating drives, passing through untamed mountainous terrain that evokes the early days of the Wild West.

Springerville and Eagar

The easternmost White Mountain towns, **SPRINGERVILLE** and neighboring **EAGAR**, stand near the edge of the plains in **Round Valley**, a few miles west of New Mexico. They're only significant as base camps for trips into the mountains, which you'll encounter a couple of miles south on US-191, or ten miles west on Hwy-260, across the innocuous Little Colorado River.

Springerville's **visitor center**, 418 E Main St (Tues–Sat 8am–4pm; ☎928/333-2123, ⓦwww.springerville-eagarchamber.com), can provide details of nearby attractions. It also holds a tiny museum devoted to **Casa Malpais**, a partially underground pueblo built by the Mogollon people, and serves as the base for up to three daily guided tours of the site itself, a couple of miles north ($7). The best value among half a dozen **motels** is the friendly *Reed's Lodge*, 514 E Main St (☎928/333-4323 or 1-800/814-6451, ⓦwww .k5reeds.com; ❸). As for **restaurants**, the nearby *Safire*, 411 E Main St (☎928/333-4512), serves meats and beers to match any hunter's appetite.

Coronado Trail Scenic Road

South of Springerville, the tortuous high-mountain US-191, designated the **Coronado Trail Scenic Road**, doesn't so much follow the route taken by Francisco de Coronado in 1540 – see p.500 – as vaguely parallel it. Driving all the way to **Clifton**, 120 miles south can take up to four hours, but so long as you fill up on gas first you're sure to enjoy it.

At the only village to interrupt the pine woods – **Alpine**, 25 miles south of Springerville – US-180 branches off west into New Mexico. Just a tiny T-junction in a meadow, Alpine is said to be the chilliest spot in Arizona. It holds a handful of motels, including *Sportsman's Lodge* near the intersection (☎928/339-4576 or 1-877/560-7626; ❸), and *Tal-Wi-Wi Lodge*, three miles north (☎928/339-4319 or 1-800/476-2695, ⓦtalwiwilodge.com; ❹).

Beyond Alpine, snow frequently closes US-191 between mid-December and mid-March. When it's open, roadside trailheads, used mainly by hunters, make it possible to hike into the **Apache-Sitgreaves National Forest**, which also holds several rudimentary campgrounds (call ☎928/339-5000 for details). The most scenic spot is the **Blue Vista** pull-out, in the twistiest stretch of road twenty miles south of Alpine, which commands sweeping views of the misty mountains. It lies just south of the **Hannagan Meadow** clearing, where the big red-timber *Hannagan Meadow Lodge* (☎928/339-4370, ⓦwww .hannaganmeadow.com; ❸) rents out rooms and cabins in summer and has a reasonable restaurant.

Show Low

SHOW LOW, fifty miles south of Holbrook on Hwy-77 and 43 miles west of Springerville on US-60, is the largest town on the Mogollon Rim. It stands on the site of a 100,000-acre ranch, whose cofounders played cards in 1876 to decide who should get to keep it. With the game all square, one invited the other to "show low and take the ranch;" his rival drew the deuce of clubs and duly took possession. He went on to sell the ranch to the Mormon church, which built a small settlement before selling it on again.

Show Low is basically a strip of motels and diners ranged along US-60, or **Deuce of Clubs Avenue**. Inexpensive places to stay include the central *KC Motel*, 60 W Deuce of Clubs Ave (☎928/537-4433 or 1-800/531-7152, ⓦwww.kcmotelinshowlow.com; ❸). **Restaurant** options include *Fiesta Mexicana*, 350 E Deuce of Clubs Ave (☎928/532-3424), while *High In The Pines*, 1191 E Hall (☎928/537-1453), serves deli lunches and good coffee.

Fort Apache Indian Reservation

One reason why the mountains of eastern Arizona are not better known is that a large proportion of the central massif still belongs to the **Apache**. The Apache are not a single "tribe", however, so there are two separate but contiguous reservations here. The **FORT APACHE INDIAN RESERVATION**, which starts just a mile or two out of Pinetop and Show Low, stretches south to the Salt and Black rivers; beyond it the **San Carlos Indian Reservation** extends for another hundred miles past Globe.

The Fort Apache Reservation is headquartered in the town of **WHITE-RIVER**, cupped in a mile-high valley twenty miles south of Pinetop and home to the *White Mountain Apache Motel & Restaurant* (☎928/338-4927; ❸). What few visitors make it this far, however, are drawn a few miles further southwest, to **FORT APACHE** itself, at the confluence of the north and east forks of the White River. This US Army outpost was founded in 1870 to support the campaigns of General Crook, who though allied with the White Mountain Apache wanted to keep an eye on them. Several buildings survive, and hold displays on the period (summer Mon–Sat 8am–5pm; winter Mon–Fri 8am–5pm; $5). The **tourist office** nearby (same hours; ☎928/338-1230 or 1-877/338-9629, ⊛www.wmat.us) can direct you toward crafts stores and other sites.

Two more contemporary attractions form the backbone of the reservation's tourist trade. The **Hon-Dah Resort Casino** (☎928/369-0299 or 1-800/929-8744, ⊛hon-dah.com; ❺), at the junction of highways 260 and 73 three miles southeast of Pinetop, is a 24-hour gaming facility with its own attached hotel, restaurant, and pool. Arizona's most popular **ski resort**, the **Sunrise Park Resort** (☎928/735-7669 or 1-800/772-7669, ⊛www.sunriseskipark.com; Sun–Thurs ❸, Fri & Sat ❺), is thirty miles east via Hwy-273, a short spur south of Hwy-260. The 65 runs are generally open between November and March. Lift tickets cost $49.

Hwy-60, the only north–south road across the reservation, is also the most direct route between northeast Arizona and Tucson. All of its 87-mile run from Show Low to **Globe** (see p.237) is awe-inspiring, but the most dramatic moment comes fifty miles along, where it takes five miles of switchbacks to get to the bottom of gaping **Salt River Canyon**.

Payson

Until 1959, **PAYSON**, ninety miles west of Show Low on Hwy-260, was a sleepy cowboy town that had started out in a gold-rush frenzy and then relaxed into a yearly round of ranching punctuated by the odd rodeo. Then the paving of Hwy-87 placed Payson within two hours' drive of Phoenix, eighty miles southwest. It's now a mountain retreat whose population doubles or triples at weekends, as urban refugees flock to their second homes or at least rent cabins in the forest.

On first glance, Payson, if not exactly appealing, is at least mildly impressive but somehow as you drive down its long, broad streets, passing representatives of every national fast-food and lodging chain, you never seem to find a compelling reason to stop.

Payson's **visitor center** is at 100 W Main St (Mon–Fri 9am–5pm, Sat & Sun 10am–2pm; ☎928/474-4515 or 1-800/672-9766, ⊛www.rimcountrychamber.com). Its best-value **motel** is the *Best Western Payson Inn*, 801 N Beeline Hwy (☎928/474-3241, ⊛www.bestwesternarizona.com; ❹). No local **restaurant** is all that exceptional. Weekenders from Phoenix tend to dine Italian-style at *Cucina Paradiso*, 512 N Beeline Hwy (☎928/464-6500).

Tonto Natural Bridge

The world's widest and longest (but not quite highest) **travertine bridge**, formed from minerals deposited by constantly flowing springs, is preserved in **TONTO NATURAL BRIDGE STATE PARK**, fifteen miles north of Payson on Hwy-87 (daily: May–Aug 8am–7pm; April, Sept, & Oct 8am–6pm; Nov–March 9am–5pm; $4; ☏928/476-4202, ⓦwww.azparks.gov). In 1877, a Scottish gold prospector, David Gowan, supposedly hid in a cave inside the bridge as he fled the Apaches who used the surrounding meadows as a summer camp. He stayed and built a cabin nearby. When a description of the natural wonder appeared in an English newspaper in 1896, David Goodfellow spotted the name of his long-lost uncle and wrote to Gowan, who offered him the site. Goodfellow's ten-room lodge no longer accepts guests but still serves as the park's giftshop and visitor center (same hours).

The bridge itself, reached by a network of short trails, doesn't really live up to the build-up. Spanning a gully that's roughly 150ft wide, it's more of a tunnel, or a dank cave with openings at both ends. With effort, you can scramble down to a boardwalk at the base, but you can't go through it.

Winslow

Back on I-40, thirty miles west of Holbrook and 56 miles east of Flagstaff, **WINSLOW** is another Route 66 town kept alive by transcontinental truckers. It's also the closest the interstate comes to the Hopi mesas (see p.77), which jut from the desert across sixty miles of butte-studded wilderness to the north.

Winslow was founded as a railroad stop in 1882, not far from the recently established Mormon community of **Brigham City**, now lying derelict a mile northeast. If you only know of it thanks to the line about "standin' on the corner in Winslow, Arizona," in the Eagles' *Take It Easy*, you'll be glad there's an official **Standin' on the Corner Park** at Kinsley Avenue and Second, where you can have your photo taken with a bronze statue of a guitar-toting hitch-hiker. Local history is recalled in the diverting **Old Trails Museum**, nearby at 212 Kinsley Ave (Tues–Sat 10am–4pm; free).

Three miles northeast, **Homolovi Ruins State Park** (daily 8am–5pm; $5 per vehicle; ☏928/289-4106) holds four pueblo villages and hundreds of lesser sites that were occupied by the Hisatsinom people – the ancestors of today's **Hopi** – until perhaps the fourteenth century. Most remain unexcavated, though archeologists are usually hard at work between June and July, when visitors are welcome to join them.

Practicalities

Winslow's Amtrak station still welcomes one daily **train** west to Flagstaff and one east to Albuquerque. Greyhound **buses** along I-40 stop at the McDonald's at 1616 N Park Drive. The local **visitor center** is currently at 101 E Second Rd (Mon–Fri 8am–5pm; ☏928/289-2434, ⓦwinslowarizona.org), though it's scheduled to re-locate in the near future.

Winslow's grandest **accommodation** option, *La Posada*, 303 E Second St (🛏☏928/289-4366, ⓦlaposada.org; ⑤), is so totally magnificent that it's worth going a very long way out of your way to spend a night here. It was originally designed during the late 1920s by Mary Jane Colter of Grand Canyon fame (see p.323), though she invented an entire fictional history of its former life as a Spanish hacienda. The last and greatest of the railroad hotels built for the Fred Harvey company, it closed in 1959 when the railroads had been superseded by private cars. In 1999, however, it was restored as a true labor of love by a small group of enthusiasts who proclaim "we are not hoteliers – for us this is about

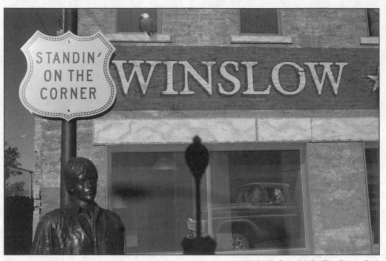

▲ Winslow's Standin' On The Corner Park

art." Dazzlingly colourful modernist canvases by one of them, Tina Mion, bedeck the public spaces, but the whole place is so enormous that there's also plenty of the earthy Southwestern style you might expect. The surrounding gardens are a delight too, while doors from the lobby lead straight to the old railroad platform. Best of all are the guest rooms, where the fixtures and fittings, and especially the tiling, feel like a real throwback to the heyday of transcontinental travel. All are named for illustrious former visitors ranging from Clark Gable to Roddy McDowell, and have en-suite baths or even whirlpool tubs, but they're without phones. The *Posada's* **restaurant**, the *Turquoise Room* (☎928/289-2888), serves all meals daily, and it too is irresistible in terms both of its decor and contemporary Southwestern cuisine. Dinner entrees can cost well over $20, but it's in a different league from anywhere else along a hundred-mile stretch of highway.

Most of the other, older **motels** in town are now pretty decrepit, so unless you're determined to pay rock-bottom rates you'd do better to head a little further west to the *Super 8*, 1916 W Third St (☎928/289-4606 or 1-800/800-8000, ⓦwww.super8.com; ❸). The pick of the all-day **diners** is the *Falcon Restaurant*, 1113 E Third St (☎928/289-2628), while the best **campground** is at Homolovi Ruins (see above; $10), where water is available in summer only.

Meteor Crater

Around 22,000 years ago, a meteorite slammed into northern Arizona, blasting a huge hole, nearly a mile across and over five hundred feet deep, into the scrubby plateau. The site of that impact, **METEOR CRATER** (daily: late May to early Sept 7am–7pm; early Sept to late May 8am–5pm; $15, under-18s $7; ☎1-800/289-5898, ⓦwww.meteorcrater.com) now lies six miles south of the interstate, eighteen miles west of Winslow and 38 miles east of Flagstaff.

Though the staff dress up in mock Park Service uniforms, Meteor Crater is privately owned and frankly offers poor value for money. A modern gallery beside the parking lot holds the unimaginative **Astronauts Hall of Fame**, which commemorates the fact that the first men on the moon were trained on the cavity's otherworldly surface (some skeptics claim that they faked their entire mission here). Walkways climb from there to the lip of the abyss, where you'll probably find that there's a limit to how long you can spend staring at a featureless hole in the ground. Hour-long guided walking tours set off hourly from 9.15am to 2.15pm, but you can't hike into the actual crater.

Flagstaff

Northern Arizona's liveliest and most attractive town, **FLAGSTAFF**, occupies a superbly dramatic location beneath the San Francisco Peaks, halfway between New Mexico and California. Straddling the I-40 and I-17 interstates, and a major waystation for tourists en route to the Grand Canyon eighty miles northwest, it's also a worthwhile destination in its own right.

Downtown, where barely a building rises more than three stories, oozes Wild West charm. Its main thoroughfare, Santa Fe Avenue, used to be **Route 66**, and before that the pioneer trail west. A stroll around its central few blocks is gloriously evocative of the past, though these days the diners and saloons are interspersed with outfitter stores and coffee bars, and local cowboys and Indians share the sidewalks with liberal-minded students from Northern Arizona University. Just to add to the atmosphere, the tracks of the Santa Fe Railroad still divide downtown in two, so life in Flagstaff remains punctuated both day and night by the mournful wail of passing trains.

Flagstaff's first settlers arrived in 1876, lured from Boston by reports of mineral wealth and fertile land. They soon moved on, disappointed, toward Prescott, having stayed long enough to celebrate the centenary of US independence by flying the Stars and Stripes from a towering pine tree. As this flagpole became a familiar landmark on the route west, the town became known as Flagstaff. Right from the start, it was a cosmopolitan place, with a strong black and Hispanic population working in the (originally Mormon-owned) lumber mills and the cattle industry, and Navajo and Hopi heading in from the nearby reservations to trade.

Modern Flagstaff, with a population of a little over fifty thousand, makes an ideal base for travelers. As well as the abundant hotels, hostels, restaurants, diners, bars and shops within easy walking distance of downtown, outlets of the national food and lodging chains line the interstates slightly further afield. There are also a couple of good museums nearby, together with wonderful scenery and ancient sites in the close vicinity. Just one word of warning: at almost seven thousand feet above sea level, the nights may well be colder than you're expecting. It can even snow in July.

Arrival, information, and getting around

Though the Santa Fe Railroad is still busy with freight, Amtrak's daily **Southwest Chief** between Chicago and Los Angeles is now the only passenger **train** that stops at Flagstaff's venerable wooden stationhouse, in the heart of town. In summer, the eastbound service leaves at 5.11am for Albuquerque and the westbound at 8.57pm for Los Angeles; winter times are one hour later. In addition, Horizon Airlines (Ⓦwww.horizonair.com) flies daily to Pulliam Airport, off I-17 five miles south of downtown Flagstaff, from Los Angeles.

Open Road Tours & Transportation (☎928/226-8060 or 1-800/766-7117, Ⓦwww.openroadtours.com), based at the Amtrak station, runs twice-daily **bus service** via Williams to the Grand Canyon. The first bus leaves Flagstaff at 8am, the second at 3.45pm; the one-way fare is $27 for adults, and $19 for children 11 and under. Open Road also offers tours to Sedona and Monument Valley and around Flagstaff itself, as well as five daily **buses** between Flagstaff and **Phoenix** ($42), and three daily to Sedona ($25). As detailed below, two local hostels, the *DuBeau* and the *Grand Canyon*, can arrange inexpensive excursions to the Grand Canyon and Sedona. Greyhound, a few blocks south of downtown at 399 S Malpais Lane (T 928/774-4573), runs five daily buses to Phoenix and also heads east toward Albuquerque and west to Las Vegas, LA, San Diego, and San Francisco.

Flagstaff's helpful **visitor center** occupies half of the Amtrak stationhouse at 1 E Route 66 (Mon–Sat 8am–5pm, Sun 9am–4pm; T 928/774-9541 or 1-800/379-0065, W www.flagstaffarizona.org). Even when it's not staffed, the building remains open for rail passengers, so visitors can still pick up brochures and **discount coupons** for local motels. You'll also find a courtesy phone in the Amtrak lobby for making hotel and hostel reservations (daily 8am–5pm).

The least expensive **car rental** agency is Budget, 175 W Aspen Ave (T 928/213-0156); Avis, Hertz, Enterprise, and National also have outlets. Absolute Bikes, 202 E Route 66 (open daily; T 928/779-5969, W www .absolutebikes.net), rents out **mountain bikes**. Perhaps the best of several local **outfitters** offering equipment for outdoor activities and backpacking expeditions is Aspen Sports, 15 N San Francisco St (T 928/779-1935).

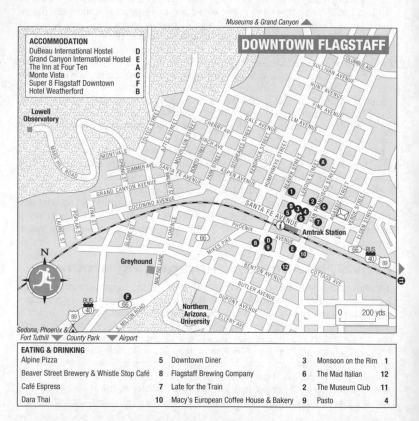

Accommodation

As Flagstaff is considerably more than just another interstate pit stop, its dozens of **motels** and **B&Bs** charge higher rates than its I-40 neighbors. They're still not bad value, however, while **budget** travelers can choose between two hostels. Most chain motels are clustered well to the east, but staying close to downtown is much more fun. It's worth knowing that if you do manage to find a room where the lonesome whistle of freight trains doesn't wake you up in the night, it's unlikely to be anywhere near Flagstaff.

If you arrive without a reservation, use the free **courtesy phones** in the visitor center (see above) to compare options. Above all, plan ahead on summer weekends, when the town is likely to be booked solid.

The nicest local **campground** lies three miles south on US-89A, at *Fort Tuthill County Park* (May–Sept; ℡928/774-3464), though Flagstaff also holds the year-round Flagstaff KOA at 5803 N AZ-89A (℡928/526-9926 or 1-800/562-3524, ⊛www.koa.com). Best of all, contact the Coconino National Forest for details of its "Room With A View" **cabin rentals** in the nearby woods (℡928/527-3600, ⊛www.fs.fed.us/r3/coconino).

DuBeau International Hostel 19 W Phoenix Ave ℡928/774-6731 or 1-800/398-7112, ⊛www .dubeauhostel.com. Welcoming independent hostel just south of the tracks, whose spotless, appealingly converted en-suite motel rooms serve as four-person dorms – $20 per bed in summer, $18 in winter – or private doubles at $45 Sun–Thurs or $48 Fri & Sat. Internet access is available, and breakfast is free, but the common areas can get noisy at times. Free pick-up from Greyhound. For tours, see the *DuBeau's* sister property, the *Grand Canyon International Hostel*, below. Open weekends only from Nov–Feb. ❷

Grand Canyon International Hostel 19 S San Francisco St ℡928/779-9421 or 1 888/442 2696, ⊛www.grandcanyonhostel.com. Independent hostel, under the same friendly management as the similar nearby *DuBeau*, that offers dorm beds at $20 in summer or $18 in winter and six private rooms priced at $38–45. Free pick-up from Greyhound, car rental discounts, and tours to the Grand Canyon (March–Oct Mon, Wed, Fri & Sat; Nov–Feb Tues, Thurs & Sat; $75) and Sedona (Sun, plus Thurs March–Oct only; $55). ❷

The Inn at Four Ten 410 N Leroux St ℡928/774-0088 or 1-800/774-2008, ⊛www.inn410.com. Bright ranch home operating as a luxurious antique-furnished B&B; all ten rooms are en suite, most with fireplaces and three with whirlpool tubs. On summer evenings, the porch and patio make welcoming, convivial retreats. ❼

Monte Vista 100 N San Francisco St ℡928/779-6971 or 1-800/545-3068, ⊛www.hotelmontevista .com. Attractive landmark 1920s hotel in the heart of downtown. The assorted restored rooms, with and without attached bathrooms, are named for celebrity guests, from Bob Hope to Michael Stipe; Paul McCartney stayed here in August 2008. Many of the guests are young international travelers, drawn by the local nightlife, including the hotel's own bar (see p.290). Weekend rates rise by as much as $20. ❸–❺

Super 8 Flagstaff Downtown 602 W Route 66 ℡928/774-4581 or 1-800/800-8000, ⊛www .super8.com. Attractive chain motel centered on an enclosed swimming pool, adjacent to a Barnes & Noble bookstore less than a mile southwest of downtown, just past the US-89 turnoff toward Sedona. ❹

Super 8 I-40 Flagstaff Mall 3725 N Kasper Ave ℡928/526-0818 or 1-888/324-9131, ⊛www .super8.com. Decent budget motel four miles east of downtown, right where Route 66 joins US-89. ❹

Hotel Weatherford 23 N Leroux St ℡928/779-1919, ⊛www.weatherfordhotel.com. Attractive old downtown hotel, with elegant wooden fittings, which bit by bit is restoring its fading rooms to offer tasteful accommodation; three large but basic ones share a bathroom and lack telephones or TVs, the rest are en suite. The upstairs lounge offers Wild West ambience, but can make for a noisy night. ❸–❻

The Town

Flagstaff's little-changed **downtown** stretches for a few red-brick blocks north of the railroad. Filled with cafés, bars, and stores selling Route 66 souvenirs and Native American crafts, as well as outfitters specializing in tents, clothing, and other contraptions for outdoor adventures, it's a fun place to wander around, even if it holds no significant tourist attractions. Few specific buildings are historic; by the time you've browsed a few bookstores, downed a few coffees, and peeped into the old *Weatherford* and *Monte Vista* hotels, you may well be ready to move on. Your most lasting impression is likely to be of the magnificent volcanic **San Francisco Peaks**, rising smoothly from the plains on the northern horizon, and topped by a jagged ridge.

Museum of Northern Arizona

The exceptional **Museum of Northern Arizona**, three miles northwest of downtown on US-180 (daily 9am–5pm; $7, under-18s $4; ☎928/774-5213, Ⓦwww.musnaz.org), makes an essential first stop for any visitor to the Colorado Plateau. Although it covers local geology, geography, flora, and fauna – and can help you come to grips with the various theories as to the origins of the Grand Canyon – its main emphasis is on documenting **Native American** life. It provides an excellent run-through of the Ancestral Puebloan past and contemporary Navajo, Havasupai, Zuni, and Hopi cultures, with rooms devoted to pots, rugs, *kachina* dolls, and silver and turquoise jewelry. There are also temporary shows of local (not always Native American) arts and crafts, a well-stocked bookstore, and a **nature trail** that runs through the small piñon-fringed canyon outside.

Ever since it was established, in 1928, the museum has encouraged the development of traditional and new skills among Native American craftworkers. The exquisite inlaid silver jewelry now made by the Hopi, for example, is the result of a museum-backed program to find work for Hopi servicemen returning from World War II. During its annual Native American Marketplaces, every item is for sale; the **Hopi** show takes place on the weekend closest to July 4, the **Zuni** one in late May, and the **Navajo** one at the start of August.

For details of **Museum of Northern Arizona Ventures**, an extensive program of tours and expeditions, which include multi-day Grand Canyon trips, check on Ⓦwww.mnaventures.org.

The Pioneer Museum

Alongside US-180, a little closer to town than the Museum of Northern Arizona, an impressive steam train guards the **Pioneer Museum** (Mon–Sat 9am–5pm; $3; Ⓦwww.arizonahistoricalsociety.org). Run by the Arizona Historical Society, and housed in what was once the county hospital, the museum holds a random but reasonably entertaining assortment of objects and images from old Flagstaff.

Lowell Observatory

Flagstaff's **Lowell Observatory**, located in the pine forest atop Mars Hill, a mile west of downtown, is famous as the place where the existence of the dwarf planet Pluto was first confirmed. Many of the necessary calculations were performed by Dr Percival Lowell, who founded the observatory in 1894 and also deluded himself that he'd discovered canals on Mars. Lowell died in 1916 – he's buried in a small domed mausoleum of blue glass on the hilltop – and Pluto was eventually spotted in 1930 by Clyde Tombaugh.

From the **visitor center** (daily: March–Oct 9am–5pm; Nov–Feb noon–5pm; $6, under-18s $3; ☎928/774-3358, Ⓦwww.lowell.edu), where only very technically minded visitors are likely to get much joy from playing with computers or watching explanatory videos, the **Pluto Walk** footpath climbs up to the tiny original observatory. Signs tick off the relative positions of the planets; if it kept going on the same scale, it would have to extend over six hundred miles, beyond Boise, Idaho, to show the position of the nearest star, Alpha Centauri.

Astronomy remains a passion in Flagstaff, and the town has won awards for minimizing night-time light pollution. The observatory reopens most evenings for after-dark **stargazing sessions** (June–Aug Mon–Sat 5.30–10pm; Sept–May Mon, Wed, Fri & Sat 5.30–9.30pm; no additional charge).

Eating

While surprisingly short of high-end **restaurants**, central Flagstaff holds a lively assortment of both old-style Western **diners** and eclectic **budget** options. Thanks to all those students, the area around San Francisco Street, both north and south of the tracks, is filled with vegetarian cafés and espresso bars.

Alpine Pizza 7 N Leroux St ☎928/779-4109. Raucous downtown student hangout, with decent pizzas and lots of different beers. Mon–Sat 11.30am–2pm & 5–11pm, Sun 5–11pm.

Café Espress 16 N San Francisco St ☎928/774-0541. Great vegetarian breakfasts, then salads, sandwiches, and veggie specials for the rest of the day, plus espresso. Mon, Tues & Sun 7am–3pm, Wed–Sat 7am–9pm.

Charly's Pub & Grill *Hotel Weatherford*, 23 N Leroux St ☎928/779-1919. Café-restaurant in a classy Western setting, serving good, inexpensive meals accompanied by live music (cocktail piano at lunch, bands at night). Daily 8am–10pm.

Dara Thai 14 S San Francisco St ☎928/774-0047. Large Thai place just south of the tracks, where the service is great and a plate of delicious pad Thai noodles costs just $8 at lunch, $10 at dinner. Mon–Sat 11am–10pm, Sun noon–9pm.

Downtown Diner 7 E Aspen Ave ☎928/774-3492. Classic Route 66 diner a block north of the main drag, featuring leatherette booths and hefty burgers and sandwiches. Mon–Sat 5.30am–9pm, Sun 7am–6pm.

Late for the Train 107 N San Francisco St ☎928/779-5975. Little coffee bar that serves

excellent house-roasted coffee and pastries to a slightly older, literary crowd. Daily 6am–9pm.

Macy's European Coffee House & Bakery 14 S Beaver St ☎928/774-2243. Not merely superb coffee, but heavenly pastries to go with it, in a chaotic but friendly, student-oriented atmosphere. Substantial vegetarian dishes include black bean pizza and even couscous for breakfast. You'll also find free wireless internet and an adjacent coin laundry. Daily 6am–10pm.

Monsoon on the Rim 6 E Aspen Ave ☎928/226-8844. This pan-Asian, sushi-centered restaurant, with huge plate-glass windows, has more to do with the new West than the Old West. While pretty good rather than wonderful, the food is surprisingly cheap, with most of the Thai and Chinese options priced around $8 at lunchtime, $10 in the evening, and the people-watching is fun. Daily 11.30am–9pm.

Pasto 19 E Aspen Ave ☎928/779-1937. Downtown Italian joint, with pasta specials and chicken, shrimp, and vegetarian entrees for $17–22. A tasting menu for two costs $60. Mon–Thurs & Sun 11.30am–2.30pm & 5–9pm, Fri & Sat 11.30am–2.30pm & 5–9.30pm.

Nightlife

Milling with international travelers in summer and students the rest of the year, Flagstaff is the liveliest **nightspot** between Las Vegas and Santa Fe. Wander a block or two to either side of San Francisco Street downtown, and you can't go wrong. Besides the *Monte Vista Lounge*, hotel bars that feature live music include both the *Exchange Pub* and the upstairs *Zane Grey Ballroom* at the *Weatherford*.

Beaver Street Brewery & Whistle Stop Café 11 S Beaver St ☎928/779-0079. Popular micro-brewery that also serves inventive and inexpensive food, with an outdoor summer barbecue in the beer garden. Daily 11.30am–midnight.

Flagstaff Brewing Company 16 E I-40

☎928/773-1442. Bustling downtown pub, with outdoor seating, big windows, and live music Thurs–Sun.

The Mad Italian 101 S San Francisco St ☎928/779-1820. Highly sociable downtown bar with several pool tables.

Monte Vista Lounge *Monte Vista*, 100 N San Francisco St ℡ 928/779-6971. Hip little bar and dance club in the basement of a venerable old hotel, with frequent live music or DJs.
The Museum Club 3404 E Route 66 ℡ 928/526-9434, ⓦ www.museumclub.com. A real oddity, this log-cabin taxidermy museum, popularly known as "The Zoo," somehow transmogrified into a classic Route 66 roadhouse, saloon, and country music venue that's a second home to hordes of dancing cowboys. Daily 11am–2am.

Around Flagstaff

The area around Flagstaff is extraordinarily rich in natural and archeological wonders, with three national monuments – Sunset Crater, Wupatki, and Walnut Canyon – within 25 miles, and the San Francisco Peaks overshadowing them all. All are generally seen as day-trips from Flagstaff; the monuments offer almost no practical facilities, with only Sunset Crater having so much as a campground.

The San Francisco Peaks

The **San Francisco Volcanic Field**, north of Flagstaff, consists of four hundred distinct volcanic cones, which have appeared over the past two million years. During that time, the region has also been covered by glacial ice three times, shaving three thousand feet off the top of the volcanoes.

The serrated **SAN FRANCISCO PEAKS** are the remnants of a single mountain; their highest point today, at 12,643 feet, is the summit of **Mount Humphreys**. They were named by Spanish missionaries in honor of St Francis of Assisi, though the Hopi already knew them as *Nuvatukya'ovi*, the home of the *kachina* spirits, and to the Navajo this was *Dook'o'oosliid*, one of the four sacred mountains. Seen from afar, topped by a semi-permanent layer of clouds, it's obvious why the Hopi and Navajo regarded them as the source of life-giving rain. Ironically, it's because the mountains were sacred sites for both tribes that they now belong to neither; as federal law stipulates that Native American reservations can only include lands of which a tribe can prove it has "exclusive use," the very fact that both held them holy precluded either from claiming them, and left them open to Yankee exploitation.

The Hopi in particular still make annual pilgrimages on foot from their mesas, 65 miles east, to shrines hidden in the mountains.

Arizona Snowbowl

Considering that the San Francisco Mountain, which has not erupted for 220,000 years, is dormant rather than extinct, the time may come when the gods decide that Flagstaff's own **ski resort**, the **Arizona Snowbowl**, is a desecration no longer to be tolerated. For the moment, it survives, nestling between Mount Humphreys and Mount Agassiz at the end of a seven-mile spur road north of US-180, and featuring ski runs such as "Boo-Boo" and "Bambi." There's not enough water to make artificial snow – an early name for the peaks was the **Sierra Sinagua**, or "waterless range" – so the season typically runs from mid-December through early April. That may change if the Forest Service is permitted to make snow here using treated wastewater from Flagstaff's municipal sewage system; Hopi and Navajo tribal leaders consider the plan a violation of sacred lands, and the resultant lawsuits had reached the US Supreme Court as this book went to press.

The *Ski Lift Lodge* provides both food and cabin lodgings (℡ 928/774-0729; ❺), while lift tickets cost $49 for a full day (9am–4pm) or $41 for the afternoon. For more information, call ℡ 928/779-1951 or visit ⓦ www.arizonasnowbowl.com.

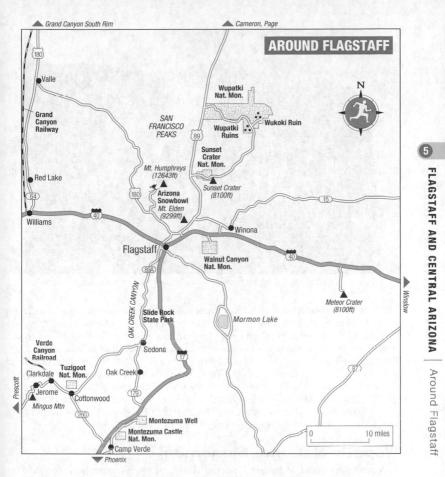

Valle

Grand
Canyon
Railway

SAN
FRANCISCO
PEAKS

Wupatki
Nat. Mon.

Wupatki
Ruins

Wukoki Ruin

Sunset
Crater
Nat. Mon.

Red Lake

Mt. Humphreys
(12643ft)

Arizona
Snowbowl
Mt. Elden
(9299ft)

Sunset Crater
(8100ft)

Williams

Winona

Flagstaff

Walnut Canyon
Nat. Mon.

Meteor Crater
(8100ft)

Slide Rock
State Park

Mormon Lake

Verde
Canyon
Railroad

Sedona

Clarkdale

Tuzigoot
Nat. Mon.

Oak Creek

Jerome

Mingus Mtn

Cottonwood

Montezuma Well

Montezuma Castle
Nat. Mon.

Camp Verde

▼ Phoenix

◄ Prescott

OAK CREEK CANYON

Winslow ▶

N

5

FLAGSTAFF AND CENTRAL ARIZONA | Around Flagstaff

In summer, the longest of the Snowbowl's four chairlifts, which climbs to within a few hundred feet of the 12,350ft summit of Mount Agassiz, remains open as the **Scenic Skyride** (mid-May to mid-Sept daily 10am–4pm; mid-Sept to mid-Oct Fri–Sun 10am–4pm; $12 adults, $8 under-13s). To protect the fragile vegetation, onward hiking is prohibited, but you'll find plenty of other day-use **trails** in these mountains, most of them also open to mountain-bikers. One switchbacks to the summit of Mount Humphreys for seventy-mile views to the Grand Canyon and beyond.

Sunset Crater National Monument

The focus of **SUNSET CRATER VOLCANO NATIONAL MONUMENT**, three miles down a side road that heads east off US-89 twelve miles north of Flagstaff, is the youngest of the San Francisco volcanoes. Its most recent eruption, in 1065 AD, had a profound impact on the local population. Thick deposits of ash opened previously infertile land to cultivation, accelerating – if not triggering – a land rush that threw different Native American cultures into contact for the first time.

▲ Wukoki Pueblo, Wupatki National Monument

John Wesley Powell named Sunset Crater for its multicolored cone, which swells from a black base through reds and oranges to a yellow-tinged crest. Unfortunately, however, its shifting cinders are too unstable to allow hikers to climb up to the rim. Instead, the one-mile **Lava Flow Trail** at its base offers a close-up look at the jagged black lava that streamed out across the desert, and the steeper one-mile **Lenox Crater Trail** ascends a lesser cone nearby.

The monument's visitor center is near the start of the road (daily 8am–5pm; ☎928/526-0502, ⓦwww.nps.gov/sucr) opposite the forest service's Bonito campground (early May to mid-Oct; $16; ☎928/527-0866). The monument admission fee of $5 per person also covers entry to Wupatki.

Wupatki National Monument

A dozen miles north of Sunset Crater, a cluster of several exceptionally well-preserved ancient ruins, dramatically poised between the volcanoes and the desert, jointly constitute **WUPATKI NATIONAL MONUMENT**. They appear to testify to a period in which different tribal groups lived side by side in harmony. At some time after the Sunset Crater eruption the Sinagua people already present here, who surely witnessed the explosion, were joined by many others, including the Ancestral Puebloans and the Hohokam. When the rich new soil had been exhausted, around 150 years later, all moved on once more.

Although the first of the five separate pueblo complexes you see as you approach from Sunset Crater is Wukoki (see below), it's best to start your visit at the monument's excellent **visitor center**, slightly further along the highway (daily: summer 8am–7pm; winter 8am–5pm; $5 per person, including Sunset Crater; ☎928/679-2365, ⓦwww.nps.gov/wupa). This explains the history of the Sinagua and their neighbors, placing them firmly with the context of the traditional migration story of their modern descendants, the Hopi.

A paved loop trail leads down from the visitor center to the main three-story, hundred-room pueblo block of **Wupatki** ("long cut house") itself, molded to a sandstone hillock and thereby concealing a number of natural caves. The site's most intriguing features, however, lie a little further along. First comes what seems to be an amphitheater, a walled circular plaza of unknown purpose. Beyond it is an oval **ball court**, the northernmost such court ever found. Similar arenas throughout central America were used for a game – part ritual, part sport – in which players tried to propel a rubber ball through a stone hoop high on a wall, using their knees and elbows alone, much like modern basketball (except that the losers were sacrificed at the end). Alongside the ball court, cracks in the ground have created a natural **blowhole**, through which air is either sucked or blown depending on pressure and temperature. The audible "breathing" of the earth made this a sacred shrine for Wupatki's ancient inhabitants.

Wukoki, at the end of its own 2.5-mile spur road, takes its name from a modern Hopi word meaning "big house." Reminiscent of the castle-like structures at Hovenweep in southern Utah, it's located within sight of a procession of rounded cinder cones, but was probably positioned for its commanding prospect of the Painted Desert to the north and east. Windows in its central tower – again molded to the contours of a red-rock outcrop, and built with bricks of the same material – look out in all directions. Archeologists believe some are precisely aligned to monitor the sunrise at significant moments. With the Little Colorado River a full five miles distant, the pueblo's inhabitants must have been desperately short of water.

The loop road past Sunset Crater and Wupatki rejoins US-89 twenty miles south of Cameron (see p.353). Outcrops along its final few miles hold more pueblos, such as one known for obvious reasons as **The Citadel**, perched on and fully occupying a hilltop. While its interior, which appears to contain a large circular *kiva*, remains unexcavated, much of its outer wall is still standing, incorporating striped bands of black lava boulders. It too is dotted with tiny "windows" that may have served defensive or astronomical purposes.

Walnut Canyon National Monument

Another Sinagua site, as spectacular in its own way as Wupatki, can be seen at **WALNUT CANYON NATIONAL MONUMENT**, just south of I-40 ten miles east of Flagstaff. It can also be reached by driving eight miles out from downtown Flagstaff on Route 66. Between 1125 and 1250 AD, this shallow canyon was home to a thriving Sinagua community, who lived in small family groups rather than in communal pueblos. Literally hundreds of their **cliff dwellings** still nestle beneath overhangs in the canyon sides of the. They simply walled off alcoves where softer strata of rock had eroded away, and put up partitions to make separate rooms. No single dwelling is on the same scale as at Wupatki, and only a handful are accessible to visitors, but cumulatively they make an impressive spectacle.

A large scenic window in the **visitor center** (daily: June–Aug 8am–6pm; March–May & Sept–Nov 8am–5pm; Dec–Feb 9am–5pm; $5; ☏928/526-3367, ⓦwww.nps.gov/waca) gives an excellent overall view. **Walnut Creek** itself, long since diverted to provide Flagstaff's drinking water, now runs dry, but you can see how fertile this valley must have been when the Sinagua first arrived. Trees cling to the porous rock to shade the ancient dwellings, and the vegetation thickens down to a valley floor dense with black walnut and oak.

Only visitors who arrive an hour or more before closing time are allowed to set off down the mile-long **Island Loop Trail**; as the dwellings are at their most photogenic in late afternoon, that calls for careful timing. Having dropped steeply down from the visitor center, the trail crosses a narrow causeway to an isthmus of rock high above a gooseneck of the creek. Once there, you can go inside a few Sinagua homes; note the T-shaped doorways, which could only be entered headfirst, and the ceilings blackened by the smoke of generations of fires. Petroglyphs have been found in the other ruins visible on all sides, but none remain on the trail.

Between June and August each year, rangers lead two to three-hour **guided hikes** to lesser-known and otherwise inaccessible sites within the monument (Tues, Sat & Sun at 10am; call to confirm).

No accommodation, and only minimal snack food, is available at the canyon.

South of Flagstaff

US-89A threads its way south from Flagstaff down **Oak Creek Canyon** to emerge after 28 miles at **Sedona**, on the threshold of the extraordinary **Red Rock Country**. Up from the valley rise giant mesas and buttes of stark red sandstone, where Zane Grey set several Wild West adventures. The boom-and-bust mining town of **Jerome** looks down from a mountainside to the south. Hwy 260 links both US-89A and I-17 and the haunting Sinagua ruins of **Tuzigoot** and **Montezuma Castle**.

Oak Creek Canyon

Local claims that **OAK CREEK CANYON**, the largest of several slender chasms that cut into the 2000ft escarpment of the **Mogollon Rim**, is a serious rival to the Grand Canyon are somewhat exaggerated. However, you *can* drive right through it, and with its sheer walls striped in vivid bands of color, its sparkling streams and densely wooded glens, and its facilities for camping, eating, and general playing around, this would be an unmissable attraction anywhere else in the world.

Lookout Point, its northern end, appears suddenly a dozen forested miles south of Flagstaff on US-89A. Native American craft stalls surround the parking lot, and several overlooks within easy walking distance command prospects of the narrow gorge below. The road then switchbacks sharply down to run alongside **Oak Creek** itself. The lowest level in the rocks to either side, often obscured by maples, cedars, oaks, and pine, is the bright-red Supai sandstone. Above that, layers of white sandstone, buff limestone, and finally black basalt testify to a geological history which has fluctuated from harsh desert to sea bottom. Temperatures are cool enough to make fishing, picnicking, and hiking expeditions welcome escapes.

Seven miles before Hwy-89A reaches Sedona, **Slide Rock State Park** is a natural water chute, where you can swim and slide across smooth boulders set in the riverbed (daily: March to mid-May 8am–6pm; mid-May to mid-Oct 8am–7pm; mid-Oct to Feb 8am–5pm; $8 per vehicle in winter, $10 in summer; Ⓦazstateparks.com). The absence of still water in Oak Creek means that it's almost insect-free.

Practicalities

The canyon's narrow floor has been heavily developed, though leisure facilities are hidden where possible by careful landscaping. The loveliest place to **stay** of all has to be a cabin at *Garland's Oak Creek Lodge*, across a small ford half a mile north of Slide Rock (late March to mid-Nov; closed Sun; ☎928/282-3343, Ⓦgarlandslodge.com; ❽). Rates include breakfast and dinner in the top-quality dining room. Forest Service **campgrounds** at river and road level include *Pine Flat* (reservations ☎1-877/444-6777, Ⓦwww.recreation.gov; early March to mid-Nov; $20), and the first-come, first-served *Bootlegger* (April–Oct; $18).

Sedona

There's no disputing that the New Age resort of **SEDONA** enjoys a magnificent setting, amid definitive Southwestern canyon scenery. Sadly, however, the town itself adds nothing to the beauty of its surroundings. In fact, it's a real mess, with several miles of ugly sprawl interrupted by the occasional mock-historical mall monstrosity. Some visitors, particularly Europeans, experience a strong negative reaction, feeling there are plenty of beautiful landscapes elsewhere in the Southwest that haven't been sullied by this sort of over-development. Other travelers, by contrast, absolutely love it, for its combination of luxurious accommodations and fancy restaurants, and almost limitless opportunities for active outdoor vacationing. In particular, artists, healers, and wealthy retirees have flocked here in the last few decades. Whether you love it or hate it may depend on whether you share their wide-eyed awe for angels, crystals, and all matters mystical – and whether you're prepared to pay over-the-odds prices for the privilege of joining them. Whatever your attitude, Sedona is still an intriguing place to visit, where even the most hard-nosed commercial operation can seem a front for the real business of holding earnest conversations about the state of each other's psyches. **John McCain** certainly likes it; he spends almost every weekend on his ranch nearby.

Established in 1902 by Theodore Schnebly and named after his wife, Sedona remained a small farming settlement for most of the twentieth century, unmarked on most maps. German surrealist painter **Max Ernst** moved here in the 1940s – the bizarre backdrops of his later canvases seem less surreal once you've seen where they were painted – and Hollywood moviemakers filmed in the area from the 1950s onwards. Elvis Presley came here to shoot his 27th movie, *Stay Away Joe*, in 1967.

Arrival and information

Sedona is 28 miles south of Flagstaff on Hwy-89A and 120 miles north of Phoenix. It centers on the intersection known as the "**Y**," above Oak Creek, where Hwy-89A branches southwest toward Cottonwood and Prescott, and Hwy 179 continues by way of the village of Oak Creek to meet I-17, fourteen miles south. This road system is utterly unable to cope with the level of visitation; expect bumper-to-bumper traffic on weekends.

Just north of the "Y," in the area known as **uptown** – the one part of Sedona where the stores and businesses are close enough together to make walking a possibility – the **visitor center** is at Hwy-89A and Forest Road (Mon–Sat 8.30am–5pm, Sun 9am–3pm; ⓣ928/282-7722 or 1-800/288-7336, Ⓦvisitsedona.com).

New Age Sedona

Sedona's big break as a destination for **New Age** travelers came in 1981, when Page Bryant, author and psychic, "channeled" the information that Sedona is in fact "the heart *chakra* of the planet." Since pinpointing her first **vortex** – a point at which, it is claimed, psychic and electromagnetic energies can be channeled for personal and planetary harmony – the town has achieved its own personal growth and blossomed as a focus for New Age practitioners of all kinds. Huge crowds came to Sedona in 1987 for the "Harmonic Convergence," paying up to $75 for a seat on Bell Rock at the time when it was supposed to launch itself to the galaxy of Andromeda. (Dissatisfied customers are said to have included one gentleman who brought his mouth organ, under the impression that it was a harmonica convergence.)

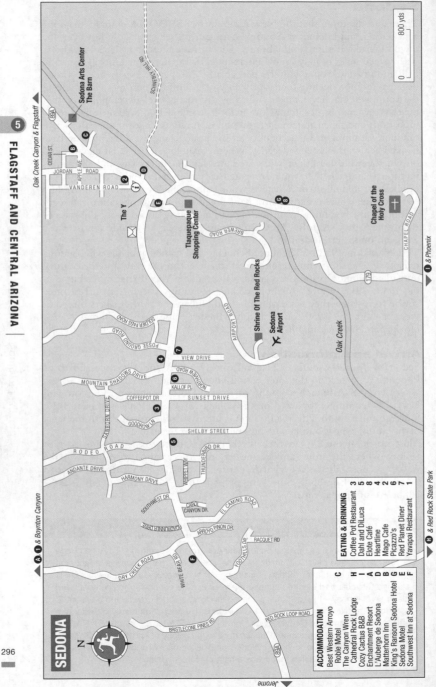

SEDONA

N

296

Oak Creek Canyon & Flagstaff ▲

Jerome ▲

▲ *& Boynton Canyon*

Sedona Arts Center
The Barn

CEDAR ST.
JORDAN ROAD
APPLE AVE.
VANDEREN ROAD
The Y

Tlaquepaque Shopping Center

Shrine Of The Red Rocks

Sedona Airport

BREWER ROAD
AIRPORT ROAD

Chapel of the Holy Cross

CHAPEL ROAD

179

SCHNEBLY HILL RD.

▼ *& Phoenix*

Oak Creek

SOLDIER PASS ROAD
POSSE GROUND ROAD
MOUNTAIN SHADOWS DRIVE
VIEW DRIVE
NORTHVIEW ROAD
KALLOF PL.
COFFEEPOT DR.
SUNSET DRIVE
SANBORN DRIVE
GOODROW LN.
SHELBY STREET
THUNDERBIRD DR.
WEBBER WAY
RODEO ROAD
ANDANTE DRIVE
HARMONY DRIVE
SOUTHWEST DR.
CAROL CANYON DR.
EL CAMINO ROAD
ROADRUNNER DRIVE
ARROYO PINON DR.
FOOTHILLS DR.
RACQUET RD.
WHITE BEAR RD.
DRY CREEK ROAD
BRISTLECONE PINES RD.
RED ROCK LOOP ROAD
89A

▼ *& Red Rock State Park*

ACCOMMODATION

Best Western Arroyo Roble Motel	C
The Canyon Wren	H
Cathedral Rock Lodge	I
Cozy Cactus B&B	A
Enchantment Resort	D
L'Auberge de Sedona	B
Matterhorn Inn	G
King's Ransom Sedona Hotel	E
Sedona Motel	F
Southwest Inn at Sedona	

EATING & DRINKING

Coffee Pot Restaurant	3
Dahl and DiLuca	5
Elote Café	8
Heartline	4
Mago Cafe	2
Picazzo's	6
Red Planet Diner	7
Yavapai Restaurant	1

0   800 yds

The Sedona–Phoenix Shuttle (☎928/282-2066 or 1-800/448-7988 in AZ, ⓦwww.sedona-phoenix-shuttle.com), an eight-daily **bus** service between Sedona and Phoenix Airport, costs $50 one-way.

The Sedona Trolley runs two different 55-minute **tours** from the visitor center (daily 9am–5pm; hourly tours, $12; ☎928/282-4211, ⓦwww.sedonatrolley .com). Companies that rent out **bikes** include Bike & Bean, 6020 Hwy-179 (☎928/284-0210, ⓦbike-bean.com), which has its own espresso bar. Sedona Jeep and Car Rentals (☎928/282-8700, ⓦwww.sedonajeeprentals.com) can provide **4WD** vehicles.

Accommodation

Sedona is an expensive place to **stay**, and away from the "Y" it's too spread out to walk around. There's no hostel, so budget travelers can get better deals at Cottonwood and Jerome (see p.300 & p.301); for those who don't mind spending well over $100, however, Sedona has some extremely fancy options, including around twenty upscale **B&Bs** and several full-service **resorts**.

Best Western Arroyo Roble Motel 400 N US-89A ☎928/282-4001 or 1-800/773-3662, ⓦwww .bestwesternsedona.com. This comfortable multi-tiered motel, stacked up above Oak Creek not far north of uptown Sedona, has a separate deluxe wing, Arroyo Roble North. ❼

The Canyon Wren 6425 N US-89A ☎928/282-6900 or 1-800/437-9736, ⓦcanyonwrencabins .com. Individual two-person cabins, each with a whirlpool tub, six miles north of Sedona in Oak Creek Canyon. ❻

Cathedral Rock Lodge 61 W Los Amigos Lane ☎928/282-7608 or 1-800/352-9149, ⓦcathedralrocklodge.com. Small, friendly B&B-cum-New-Age retreat in spacious grounds on the Red Rock Loop Road, with two double rooms, a suite, and a separate cabin – and a resident *reiki* practitioner. ❻–❾

Cozy Cactus B&B 80 Canyon Circle Drive ☎928/284-0082 or 1-800/788-2082, ⓦcozycactus.com. Ranch house B&B at the edge of the woods near the foot of Castle Rock, offering five themed, en-suite double rooms. ❼–❾

Enchantment Resort 525 Boynton Canyon Rd ☎928/282-2900 or 1-800/826-4180, ⓦenchantmentresort.com. Extremely luxurious resort, equipped with four pools and seven tennis courts, that has taken over ravishing Boynton Canyon eight miles west of town. Accommodation is in fully equipped one- and two-bedroom adobe *casitas*. ❾

King's Ransom Sedona Hotel 771 Hwy-179 ☎928/282-7151 or 1-800/846-6164, ⓦkingsransomsedona.com. Predictable upper-range motel, a mile or so south of town, with rather small rooms – most with balconies – but a nice garden and a reasonable restaurant. ❺

L'Auberge de Sedona 301 L'Auberge Lane ☎928/282-1661 or 1-800/905-5745, ⓦwww .lauberge.com. Plush two-part resort in the heart of the town, with fancy if somewhat incongruous French-themed motel rooms at road level looking out onto the red rocks, and a cable-car connection to the individual guest cottages ranged along the tranquil banks of Oak Creek below. ❽

Matterhorn Inn 230 Apple Ave ☎928/282-7176 or 1-800/372-8207, ⓦmatterhorninn.com. Central motel, on the right as you come into town on Hwy-89A from the north, with two tiers of rooms that face across to the red rocks. ❺

Sedona Motel 218 Hwy-179 ☎928/282-7187 or 1-877/828-7187, ⓦwww.thesedonamotel.com. Small motel, amazingly inexpensive by local standards, in an ideal and attractive location close to the "Y" uptown. ❸

Southwest Inn at Sedona 3250 W US-89A ☎928/282-3344 or 1-800/483-7422, ⓦwww .swinn.com. The classiest of Sedona's many highwayside motels, with very welcoming staff and comfortable sound-proofed rooms; to get a view, though, you have to pay a bit extra. ❻

Exploring Sedona

Sedona itself holds little to detain sightseers, though strolling the two or so blocks that count as **uptown**, just north of the "Y," is pleasant enough. Above the roaring traffic, you can usually still hear the synchronized chirruping of crickets in **Oak Creek** below, while your eyes are repeatedly drawn to the superb red rocks that tower above the banal buildings along Hwy-89A. A little way south of the "Y," on Hwy-179, **Tlaquepaque Shopping Center** is a very upscale mall, modeled on a Mexican village near Guadalajara, that offers Sedona's most distinctive (and expensive) shopping.

The prevailing pay-no-taxes ethos of Sedona's ardent libertarians has ensured that few of the side roads off the main highways are paved. That dovetails neatly, of course, with the booming business in off-road tours, as listed opposite. Nonetheless, much of the best scenery is visible from the highway, and in any case many jeep roads are perfectly passable in ordinary vehicles. So long as you're happy to remain in ignorance as to which rocks are really electro-magnetic tuning forks vibrating in harmony with Alpha Centauri, there's no great need to take a commercial tour.

The major problem is **parking**. The National Forest Service requires anyone parking in the forests around Sedona – which means anyone using the majority of roadside pullouts in the vicinity, for anything more than "incidental stopping", reckoned at fifteen minutes or more – to buy a **Red Rock Pass**, which costs $5 for a day, $15 for a week, or $20 for a year. The passes are sold in local visitor centers, stores, motels, and B&Bs, and also by vending machines in parking lots; you can find full details on ⓦ www.redrockcountry.org. Annual national park passes (see p.41) are also accepted, but must be displayed in the parked car. Just to complicate matters further, four popular scenic spots – Banjo Bill, Grasshopper Point, Red Rock Crossing (site of Crescent Moon Ranch), and Call O' The Canyon (trailhead for the West Fork Trail) – are on private land, and charge their own fees of up to $7; a $40 Red Rock Grand Pass covers those areas as well, but the national park passes do not.

The closest **vortex** to town is on **Airport Mesa**. Turn left up Airport Road from Hwy-89A as you head west, a mile past the "Y," and the vortex is at the junction of the second and third peaks, just after the cattle grid. Further up, beyond the precarious airport, the **Shrine of the Red Rocks** looks out across the entire valley.

Three and four miles further along Hwy-89A, two successive turnings to the left mark the Upper and Lower sections of the seven-mile **Red Rock Loop Road**, all of which is paved barring a bumpy but not too difficult mile in the middle. Its prime attraction is reached via a spur road a couple of miles down Lower Red Rock Loop Road. **Red Rock State Park** (daily: summer 8am–6pm; winter 8am–5pm; $7 per vehicle or $2 per person; ⓦazstateparks.com) may be the obvious name for a park in the Sedona area, but it's not in fact the best place to see red rocks. Instead it preserves a sweeping curve of **Oak Creek**, where the riparian environment survives reasonably intact. Its flora and fauna are explained in the prominent **visitor center** (same hours), which holds stuffed hawks and owls and some live fish. Two miles from the highway on Upper Red Rock Loop Road, a picturesque ford in Oak Creek known as **Red Rock Crossing**, which has featured in many movies, is alongside the Crescent Moon Picnic Area (daily 8am–8pm; $8). **Cathedral Rock**, on the far side of the stream, used to be called Courthouse Rock, and is another vortex.

Dry Creek Road, which heads north off Hwy-89 a mile closer to town, runs north past **Capitol Butte** to reach **Boynton Canyon**. While the lavish *Enchantment Resort* has impaired the magic of Boynton Canyon itself – which has its own vortex – several neighboring canyons are still perfect for short desert hikes. The resort office can provide trail maps marking Sinagua ruins in **Red Canyon**, or point the way to **Doe Mesa** or **Loy Butte Canyon**, both of which offer great views of the whole Sedona valley.

To enjoy the area's most spectacular scenic drive, turn left off Hwy-179 as soon as it crosses Oak Creek south of the "Y," onto the unpaved **Schnebly Hill Road**. In summer, the road remains open all the way to I-17, twelve rough

Within you or without you: experiencing Red Rock Country

Dozens of competing Sedona-based operators offer close encounters with Red Rock Country. The most popular option is a **jeep tour**, but you can also take scenic **flights** – in balloons, airplanes, or helicopters – ride on **horseback**, or trek with a llama. There's also a choice between a traditional tour, on which you'll see formations such as "Snoopy" and "Garfield," and a New Age **vision quest**, in which the same rock may be a "sacred energy area" or a "beacon vortex." Some guides even eschew vehicles altogether, in favor of taking you on a **spiritual journey** instead.

Arizona Helicopter Adventures ☏928/282-0904 or 1-800/282-5141, ⓦarizonaheli copteradventures.com. Chopper flights, from the 12min Red Rock RoundUp ($67) to the 30min Sedona Deluxe ($157).

Earth Wisdom Jeep Tours ☏928/282-4714 or 1-800/482-4714, ⓦearthwisdomtours .com. Choose either sightseeing or insighting – "more than ordinary tours, these are journeys ... in the way of our Native American friends ... learn of the ancestral secrets of the Medicine Wheel" – from $49.

Legends of Sedona Ranch ☏928/282-6826 or 1-800/848-7728. "Where horses are free ... but rides ain't"; 1hr $79, 2hr $99.

Mystic Tours with Rahelio ☏928/282-6735, ⓦrahelio.com. Since he "received guidance from the Star people," Rahelio has been offering "vortex empowerments" at $55 for 2hr, $75 for 3hr.

Northern Light Balloon Expeditions ☏928/282-2274 or 1-800/230-6222, ⓦnorthern lightballoon.com. Relatively unspiritual balloon trips from $195, with champagne picnics.

Pink Jeep Tours (☏928/282-5000 or 1-800/873-3662, ⓦpinkjeep.com). You can't miss this lot in uptown Sedona. Quite exceptionally garish "4-wheelin' vehicles" crunch around in off-road tours, from $45.

Red Rock Biplane Tours ☏928/204-5939 or 1-888/866-7433, ⓦwww.sedonaairtours .com. Fly over Sedona in an open-cockpit biplane, from $129 for 30min.

Sedona Red Rock Jeep Tours ☏928/282-6826 or 1-800/848-7728, ⓦredrockjeep .com. Jeep trips from 1hr ($45) up to the 3hr Ultimate ($105). Not only do you get to bomb around the desert, you can "focus on the need to offer love and healing to our earth, as well as each other," and participate in a traditional "smudging" ceremony. Also horseback and hiking tours.

Sedona Vortex Tours ☏928/282-2733 or 1-800/943-3266, ⓦsedonaretreats.com. Tour the vortex sites; "use the earth energies for personal transformation." 3hr tour $89.

Trail Horse Adventures ☏928/634-5276 or 1-866/958-7245, ⓦwww.trailhorse adventures.com. Horseback trips, largely geared around eating (in traditional cowboy style), in Cottonwood's Dead Horse Ranch State Park, from $65 up to $125.

miles east. Alternatively, continue south for three miles and then take Chapel Road to the left, which soon brings you to the **Chapel of the Holy Cross**. This tall and very narrow concrete chapel, whose facade is shaped like a massive cross, is squeezed into a cleft in the red cliffs (daily 9am–5pm). Another two miles down the highway, **Bell Rock**, on the east as you enter the village of Oak Creek, is Sedona's fourth major vortex.

Eating

Sedona is bursting with expensive Southwestern-style **restaurants**, not all of which are particularly good, and still has a smattering of old-fashioned diners. There's a shortage of places where you can just sit and watch the world go by over a coffee and a sandwich; most of its cafés are twee little places intended mainly to entice tourists into pastel-trimmed gift stores.

Coffee Pot Restaurant 2050 W Hwy-89A
☎928/282-6626. Sedona's largest, oldest diner –
named for a nearby rock formation – serves a
hundred kinds of omelets, and all the burgers,
Mexican dishes, and fried specials you could hope
for. Daily 6am–2.15pm.
Dahl and DiLuca 2321 W Hwy-89A ☎928/282-
5219. Northern Italian dinners served in a romantic
mock-up of a Tuscan villa; entrees cost up to $28,
but you can dine well for much less. Daily 5–10pm.
Elote Café *King's Ransom Sedona Hotel*, 771
Hwy-179 ☎928/203-0105. High-quality Mexican
restaurant a mile south of town, including delicious
salsa verde shrimp and smoked chicken
enchiladas. Tues–Sat 5–9.30pm.
Heartline 1610 W Hwy-89A ☎928/282-0785.
Tasteful white-table-linen restaurant, with an
attractive garden courtyard, that serves determinedly healthy – though not exclusively vegetarian
– Southwestern cuisine. Daily 4.30–10pm.

Mago Cafe 207A N Hwy-89A ☎928/204-1600.
Very central coffeehouse, near the visitor center,
with a pleasant terrace, and serving organic coffee
and oriental teas, plus sandwiches, salads and
Korean tofu specialties. Summer daily 8am–8pm;
winter daily 8am–6pm.
Picazzo's 1855 W Hwy-89A ☎928/282-4140.
Part of an arty Arizona chain, this fancy pizza place
enjoys pretty red-rock views. Sun–Thurs 11am–
10pm, Fri & Sat 11am–11pm.
Red Planet Diner 1595 W Hwy-89A ☎928/282-
6070. Enjoyably sci-fi-themed burger and chile
parlor. Daily 10am–11pm.
Yavapai Restaurant *Enchantment Resort*, 525
Boynton Canyon Rd ☎928/204-6000. Showcase
resort restaurant, serving top-class Southwestern
cuisine at around $40 per entree; plenty of beans
and chile to go with the freshest meats and fish.
Mon–Sat 6.30am–2.15pm & 5.30–9.15pm, Sun
brunch only, 10.30am–2.15pm.

Cottonwood

Describing **COTTONWOOD**, eighteen miles southwest of Sedona, the 1930s
WPA guide to Arizona wrote, "Familiar figures in the town are the cowboys
from the range and the prospector or 'desert rat' who wanders in from his camp
in the mountains to break the monotony of his lonely life." Today's Cottonwood is not nearly so romantic, though thanks to an influx of retirees it's much
larger. It's not really even the same place, as the former downtown is stranded a
couple of miles north of Hwy-89A, now lined by modern strip development.

Cottonwood does, however, make an inexpensive base for Sedona and Jerome,
and its old main street still possesses a certain charm. The *Best Western Cottonwood
Inn*, 993 S Main St, is a dependable chain **motel** (☎928/634-5575 or 1-877/377-
6415, ⓦbestwesterncottonwoodinn.com; ❹), while latterday desert rats break the
monotony with a coffee or snack at the friendly *Old Town Cafe* nearby, housed in
a small gallery at 1025A N Main St (closed Mon; ☎928/634-5980).

Tuzigoot National Monument

During the fourteenth century, there were fifty major pueblo sites in the Verde
Valley, occupied by the ancient people now known as the **Sinagua**. One of the
largest, perched on a hillock across the Verde River from **Clarkdale**, three miles
northwest of Cottonwood, now constitutes **TUZIGOOT NATIONAL
MONUMENT** (daily: summer 8am–6pm; winter 8am–5pm; $5; ☎928/634-
5564, ⓦwww.nps.gov/tuzi).

The ground floor alone had 86 rooms; with fifteen more rooms on the upper
level, it may have been home to some 225 people. Some archeologists think it
was a final enclave, where the Sinagua gathered against encroaching drought
before abandoning the area early in the fifteenth century. Artifacts at the visitor
center include turquoise mosaics and shell jewelry. Unfortunately, Tuzigoot is
among the least satisfying of such sites. When it was restored in a 1930s make-
work program, a little too much work was done, and a broad cement trail was
laid over, across, and through the pueblo. Furthermore, while the river, lined
with cottonwoods, still flows past the pueblo, the "fields" below are just a sickly
orange mass of tailings from the nearby copper mines.

Verde Canyon Railroad

Clarkdale, although an unremarkable little place itself, is the starting point for Arizona's most scenic vintage **train ride**. The **Verde Canyon Railroad** operates 25-mile round-trip excursions year-round, along the otherwise inaccessible Verde Canyon as far as Perkinsville, with plenty of dramatic red-rock scenery and archeological ruins en route. Call ahead for precise schedules, and note that the actual trains are powered by diesel engines, not steam ($55, ages 2–12 $35; ☎928/639-0010 or 1-800/320-0718, ⓦwww.verdecanyonrr.com).

Jerome

The tiny mining town turned arts colony of **JEROME**, high above the Verde Valley on Hwy-89A, is conspicuous from quite a distance; not only is an

▲ Verde Canyon Railroad

enormous letter "J" etched deep into the hillside above it, but a large chunk of that hillside is missing altogether, having been blown apart for **opencast copper mining**. This land abounds in mineral wealth – thick veins of copper are interspersed with gold and silver, and an endless supply of limestone is still extracted for cement – but serious exploitation only started in 1876. The **United Verde** mine was partly financed by New Yorker Eugene Jerome (a cousin of Winston Churchill's mother, Jennie Jerome), who insisted the new town bear his name. The United Verde has been called "the richest mine ever owned by an individual"; it made William Clark $100 million, and by 1953 had produced enough copper to give a thirteen-pound lump to every person on earth. Until the tortuous highway was built, the only way up to Jerome was the rail line that corkscrewed down from the mine to the world's largest copper smelter, at Clarkdale.

Jerome was a hard-drinking, hard-living town. The young **Pancho Villa** started out in life by supplying its drinking water, using a relay of two hundred burros, and the International Workers of the World (the "**Wobblies**") were briefly a strong presence; several hundred miners and "outside agitators" were literally railroaded out of town in 1917 and dumped unceremoniously in the remote deserts of southwest Arizona.

Harsh economic realities have always determined local fortunes. Plenty of copper remains in the earth; although the Depression hit hard, the mine was only closed in the 1950s, when imported copper made it uneconomic to continue, and as prices rise, it may reopen. To keep the mineral rights from reverting to the state, the present owners are obliged to keep on researching and prospecting; in fact, they do more than they have to, and reportedly find enough gold to cover their expenses.

As recently as the 1970s, Jerome was a **ghost town**, where it was possible to turn up and move into an empty house. Many who did so are still here, making a living from arts and crafts, and the town itself has made a dramatic recovery. The fact that it's now solely geared towards the needs of visitors makes it something of a tourist trap, but it's nonetheless fascinating to explore.

Arrival and information

Though on paper, Hwy-89A is a direct through route between **Sedona**, thirty miles northeast of Jerome, and **Prescott**, thirty miles southwest, the formidable **Mingus Mountain** makes reaching Jerome a slow business. Coming from Cottonwood, it's a painstaking switchback climb; if you approach from Prescott, you descend into Jerome, with gorgeous views of the valley spread out below.

Hwy-89A branches in two in the heart of town, where a one-way system takes westbound traffic along **Hull Avenue** and eastbound along **Main Street**. The **visitor center** is at 310 N Hull Ave (Mon–Fri 10am–4pm, Sat & Sun 11am–3pm; ☎928/634-2900, ⊕jeromechamber.com).

Accommodation

There's no room to build **motels** on Jerome's uncertain slopes, so accommodation is restricted to a couple of turn-of-the-century hotels and a few former homes converted into **B&Bs**.

Connor Hotel 164 Main St ☎928/634-5006 or 1-800/523-3554, ⊕connorhotel.com. Small central hotel, offering twelve attractive antique-furnished rooms, each with a tasteful tiled private bathroom, above the *Spirit Room* bar, which gets busy on weekends. ❹

Ghost City Inn 541 N Main St ☎928/634-4678 or 1-888/634-4678, ⊕www.ghostcityinn.com.

Century-old house, at the entrance to town as you come up from Cottonwood, with huge views from its wooden veranda. Some of the six guest rooms are resolutely Western, others more flowery, but all have en-suite bathrooms. ⑤
Jerome Grand Hotel 200 Hill St ☏ 928/634-8200 or 1-888/817-6788, ⓦ jeromegrandhotel.com. Restored hotel, housed in a former hospital that spills down five stories from the highest point in town; the views are fabulous, but the accommodation merely evokes bygone days, rather than being particularly luxurious. There's also a good on-site restaurant; see below. ⑤
Surgeon's House B&B 101 Hill St ☏ 928/639-1452 or 1-800/639-1452, ⓦ www.surgeonshouse .com. Smart, upmarket B&B, set in lovely gardens at the top of town; three of the four plush en-suite rooms enjoy dramatic views. ⑤

The Town

Thanks to the steep angle of the hillside, Jerome's streets are stacked one atop the other, and its stone houses tend to have two stories at the front and four or five at the back. Under the concussion of two hundred miles of tunnels being blasted into the mountainside, the whole town used to slip downhill at the rate of five inches per year; the **Sliding Jail** on Hull Avenue came to rest 225 feet from where it was built (it's still there, but it's not open to the public).

Built for mine owner "Rawhide Jimmy" Douglas in 1917, the **Douglas Mansion**, on Mine Museum Road below town, is now open as **Jerome State Historic Park** (daily 8am–5pm; $3). Given the sweeping views, it can be hard to concentrate on the displays detailing the history of the mines and the lifestyles of the bosses. Up in town, the **Mine Museum**, beneath the pressed-tin ceiling of the former *Fashion Saloon* at 200 N Main St (daily 9am–4.30pm; $2), displays an amateurish but enjoyable collection of oddities.

Many of Jerome's **shops** only stock souvenirs, but there are some interesting **crafts** showrooms around, such as the Knapp Gallery at 408 Lower Main St, and Made in Jerome Pottery, 103 Lower Main St higher up opposite the post office. The Jerome Artists Cooperative Gallery at 502 Lower Main St is a mixed bag of all the town has to offer, with some real bargains.

Eating and drinking

Day-trippers tend to fill Jerome's tearooms and snack bars at lunchtime – especially on weekends – but come the evening you can still get a faint sense of its riproaring past.

The Asylum *Jerome Grand Hotel*, 200 Hill St ☏ 928/639-3197, ⓦ theasylum.biz. "Fun" restaurant that makes the most of its dramatic, quirky setting in a former hospital, but nonetheless serves excellent Southwestern cuisine. All that plus a fabulous wine list and astonishing views – what more could you ask for? Dinner entrees range $17–26; lunch salads and sandwiches cost more like $10. Daily 11am–3pm & 5–9pm.
English Kitchen 119 Jerome Ave ☏ 928/634-2132. Supposedly Arizona's oldest restaurant, built in 1899, and successively an opium den and a meeting hall for the Wobblies. Now it's open for breakfast and lunch Tues–Sun, with salads, sandwiches, and great home-made pies, and a terrace offering commanding views.
Flatiron Cafe 416 N Main St ☏ 928/634-2733. Small, friendly joint at the southern apex of the one-way system. Espresso coffees, scrambled-egg breakfasts, and fancy salad-and-sandwich lunches for around $8. Mon, Tues & Fri–Sun 8.30am–3pm, Wed & Thurs 8.30am–11.30am.
Grapes 111 N Main St ☏ 928/634-8477. Inexpensive pizzas and deli items, plus espresso coffee and and extensive wine list.
Paul & Jerry's Saloon 206 N Main St ☏ 928/634-2603. Old-style saloon dating from 1889, with glorious ornate pool tables and a fine old bar with period trimmings. Open daily.

Montezuma Castle National Monument

Toward the east end of the Verde Valley, two dramatic ancient sites jointly constitute **MONTEZUMA CASTLE NATIONAL MONUMENT**. Roughly five miles apart, each now stands just east of I-17, forty miles south of Flagstaff and twenty miles southeast of Sedona.

The northernmost of the two, **Montezuma Well**, is a natural lake 368 feet across by 55 feet deep. Set like a volcanic crater into a small hill, it formed when the roof of an underground cave collapsed 11,000 years ago. It's still fed by a spring that produces a phenomenal 1.9 million gallons of warm water per day, naturally heated to a constant 75°F.

Not surprisingly, the well was sacred to Native Americans; the **Yavapai** people (see p.344) say they emerged into the world here. The **Hohokam**, who arrived around 600 AD, were the first to divert its water for irrigation, while the **Sinagua** followed in 1125 AD. Traces of their ruined pueblos can be discerned on the hilltop, reached by a five-minute walk from the parking lot, and a more complete **cliff dwelling** is set into the inner crater wall. It's now inaccessible, though you get a good view from the staircase that leads down to the lakeside, where a couple more dwellings stand at ground level. No fee is charged to visitors.

Five miles south, in an idyllic setting above Beaver Creek, **Montezuma Castle** itself is a superbly preserved Sinagua **cliff dwelling** from the same era. Filling a hillside alcove with a wall of pink adobe, and originally reached by three separate ladders from the valley floor, its five stories taper up to fit the contours of the rock. Apparently, the sycamore beams are still in place, and the fingerprints of the masons are still visible on the bricks, but visitors are not permitted to climb up.

The ruins of a much larger, though now much less photogenic, dwelling "next door" were exposed to view by a fire in about 1400 AD. Once again you can't go inside, but holes in the limestone show that it had 45 rooms, as well as little "cupboards" recessed into the walls. It may have housed a hundred people, as opposed to thirty or so in the castle.

Displays on the Sinagua in the castle **visitor center**, where you pay your entry fee (daily: summer 8am–6pm; winter 8am–5pm; $5; ℡928/567-3322, Ⓦwww.nps.gov/moca), are stylish and modern, if not all that detailed. The collection includes a macaw skeleton, which suggests trade with the Mexican civilizations thousands of miles south. There's no connection with the Aztec ruler Montezuma, though the well is said to appear on a deerskin map that belonged to Cortes himself.

Arcosanti

Two miles east of the interstate at **Cordes Junction**, 27 miles south of Montezuma Castle, the space-age project known as **ARCOSANTI** has been gradually rising from the rim of a beautiful high desert canyon since 1970. Designed to be (someday) a self-sufficient community of five thousand people, Arcosanti is the clearest embodiment of **Arcology**, a blend of architecture and ecology created and still overseen by Italian architect **Paolo Soleri**, a former student of Frank Lloyd Wright. His bell foundry at Cosanti, near Phoenix, is described on p.231.

Though far from any sizeable settlement, Arcosanti is intended as a model of future urban environments. Part construction site, part theme park, with buildings shaped to maximize the benefit of the sun's energy, it can be seen on hour-long guided tours (daily 9am–5pm; tours hourly 10am–4pm except noon; $8 donation; ℡520/632-6217, Ⓦwww.arcosanti.org). If you like what you see, you can also sign up for one of the five-week, $1350 workshops and help with the construction. A spacious **café** serves healthy and tasty meals, and you can stay in the on-site **motel** for as little as $35 for a basic double room. It's often booked up by groups, so be sure to reserve in advance. In summer, Arcosanti also hosts a popular series of outdoor **concerts**.

Prescott

The neat little Victorian town of **PRESCOTT** makes an unlikely sight in the Arizona wilderness, a hundred miles north of Phoenix by way of I-17 and Hwy-69 (which branches off the interstate at Cordes Junction). In 1863, when President Lincoln acceded to pressure from mining interests and granted Arizona territorial status, he chose to establish a new capital well away from Tucson, the obvious choice, which he saw as a hotbed of Confederate sympathizers. His first pick, **Fort Whipple**, was replaced in 1864 when gold was discovered near Prescott, which became the site of both fort and capital. It was named in honor of William H. Prescott, author of the classic *History of the Conquest of Mexico*, who never visited the town.

Although Tucson duly supplanted it as capital within three years, Prescott survived, with cattle ranchers joining the gold miners to make it a rowdy, liquor-loving town. Those days are long gone, however, and while Prescott refused to die, neither has it grown.

Still centering on its venerable courthouse square, it's a charming little town with a real Wild West flavor. While few out-of-state visitors find their way here, as it's not on any obvious itinerary, it makes a rewarding overnight stop, with a thriving infrastructure of hotels and restaurants.

Arrival and information

Coconino/Yavapai Shuttle **buses** connect Prescott with **Flagstaff** (3 daily Mon–Fri, 1 on Sat; $25 one-way, $40 round-trip; ☎928/775-8929 or 1-888/440-8929, ⓦcoconinoyavapaishuttle.com), while Shuttle "U" runs here from Phoenix's Sky Harbor Airport ($34 one-way, $56 round-trip; ☎928/442-1000 or 1-800/304-6114, ⓦwww.shuttleu.com). The **visitor center** stands at 117 W Goodwin St on Courthouse Plaza (Mon–Fri 9am–5pm, Sat & Sun 10am–2pm; ☎928/445-2000 or 1-800/266-7534, ⓦwww.prescott.org).

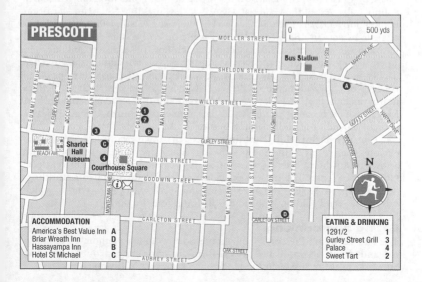

Accommodation

For a small town, Prescott has an ideal range of **accommodation** options. Besides assorted historic **hotels** around the main square, several small-scale **B&Bs** lurk in Victorian homes in the surrounding streets. The usual chain motels can be found on the fringes, but it would be a shame to stay too far from the center.

America's Best Value Inn 1105 E Sheldon St ☏ 928/776-1282 or 1-888/315-2378, ⊛ www .americasbestvalueinn.com. Chain motel on the eastern edge of town, as you approach from the interstate. ❸

Briar Wreath Inn 232 S Arizona St ☏ 928/778-6048, ⊛ www.briarwreath.com. Quaint century-old house run as a four-room B&B, where each nicely furnished room offers a surprising amount of space and light. ❻

Hassayampa Inn 122 E Gurley St ☏ 928/778-9434 or 1-800/322-1927, ⊛ hassayampainn.com.

Grand 1920s hotel just off the square, offering very comfortable, individually styled guest rooms and plenty of Art Deco flourishes amid its overall South-western theme. The *Peacock Room* serves upscale, expensive Continental cuisine. ❻

Hotel St Michael 205 W Gurley St ☏ 928/776-1999 or 1-800/678-3757, ⊛ www.stmichaelhotel .com. Atmospheric old downtown hotel – some say it's haunted – with a wide range of inexpensive rooms, all en suite, plus its own coffee bar and mall of antique and specialty stores. Rates include breakfast, and are cheaper on weekdays. ❸

The Town

Downtown Prescott focuses on the kind of **Courthouse Square** you'd expect to find in the Deep South, not the Wild West. Apart from the Courthouse itself, its central feature is the **Rough Rider Memorial Monument**, a bronze equestrian statue that commemorates William Owen "Buckey" O'Neill. While mayor of Prescott, this frontier character recruited many of Theodore Roosevelt's Rough Riders in 1898 and was killed in Cuba at the Battle of San Juan Hill. A colorful timeline set into the concrete footpath nearby traces local history from a visit by the Spanish explorer Espejo in 1581 up to the opening of the "Automated Flight Service Station" in 1985. Especially on summer weekends, the square plays host to community events and arts fairs.

The best place to get a feel for Prescott's past is the **Sharlot Hall Museum**, a short walk west of the center at 415 W Gurley St (Mon–Sat 10am–4pm, Sun noon–4pm; $5; ⊛ sharlot.org). Sharlot Hall herself arrived in Prescott with her pioneer parents in 1882, aged 12, and went on to become Arizona's official historian. She also started this collection, which now fills a dozen buildings and an entire city block. In its modern headquarters, you can admire the attractive flapper-esque gown of copper she wore when taking Arizona's three electoral college votes to Washington DC to elect Calvin Coolidge in 1925. Structures nearby include the 1864 Governor's Mansion and the contemporaneous Fort Misery, which became Arizona's first law office and courthouse as well as a church, general store, and boarding house.

The main **Sharlot Hall Building** covers the town's early history and also explores the travails of the Yavapai, tracing their story from baskets, bows, and arrows up to their current ownership of two casinos and the luxurious local Conference Center. The most popular section, the **Transportation Building**, holds a gorgeous Wells Fargo stagecoach, painted red with yellow wheels, which was in use – and held up by bandits – in Tombstone in 1881.

Eating and drinking

The streets around Prescott's Courthouse Square hold a plethora of places to **eat** and **drink** at reasonable prices. **Bars** are concentrated on Montezuma Street on its western side, in the block once known as **Whiskey Row**.

1291/2 1291/2 N Cortez St ☏ 928/443-9292. Styling itself "An American Jazz Grille", this sophisticated restaurant serves classic upper-crust American cuisine such as steaks for around $25 or balsamic calves' liver for $19. Live jazz nightly except Mon. Mon–Fri 11am–2pm & 5–10pm, Sat & Sun 5–10pm.
Gurley Street Grill 230 W Gurley St ☏ 928/445-3388. Large, extremely popular restaurant, downhill from the center, where several dining rooms cater to almost every taste, style, and budget, from foreign tourists to students on dates to farmers celebrating anniversaries. The menu includes chicken, ribs, and steaks, as well as pizzas, pasta specials, and stir-fries, all prepared to above-average standards. Daily 11am–late.
Palace 120 S Montezuma St ☏ 928/442-9208. Majestic old saloon, complete with double swinging doors, was originally the centerpiece of Whiskey Row. Still a genuine Western bar, it now also serves lunchtime salads and burgers as well as full meaty dinners. Sun–Thurs 11am–3pm & 4.30–9.30pm, Fri & Sat 11am–3pm & 4.30–10.30pm.
Sweet Tart 125 N Cortez St ☏ 928/443-8587. Attractive French bakery a block north of the square, serving sandwiches, salads, and, above all, delicious raspberry, blueberry, and lemon tarts – to name but a few. Tues–Sat 7am–4pm, Sun 8am–3pm.

Wickenburg

WICKENBURG, sixty miles southwest of Prescott and as far northwest of downtown Phoenix, is another former mining and ranching town now kept humming by tourism. It's only a little higher, and a little cooler, than Phoenix, so the main visitor season is in winter, between November and April.

Wickenburg stands beside the **Hassayampa River**, whose Apache name, meaning "river that runs upside down," refers to the fact that it often flows underground. This spot marks the "pumpkin patch" where Prussian prospector Henry Wickenburg built a mill in 1864 to process the gold he'd discovered in the Vulture Mountains, fifteen miles south. His **Vulture Mine** was seldom profitable, and finally closed down in 1942. By then, however, Wickenburg had established a successful sideline running **dude ranches**, where well-heeled Easterners could dabble with the Wild West lifestyle for a few carefree days.

In general, Wickenburg is spruce and prosperous, with little sense of a desert outpost, though the wooden sidewalks and false-front stores along **Frontier Street** in the heart of town must look much as they did in Wickenburg's heyday. You can still see the mesquite tree that served as the original town "jail"; miscreants were simply chained to its trunk. Local history is recalled at the **Desert Caballeros Western Museum**, 21 N Frontier St (Mon–Sat 10am–5pm, Sun noon–4pm; closed Mon May–Aug; $7.50; ⓦwesternmuseum.org), which features a 1900s street scene as well as paintings by Remington and Russell, lots of sculptures of noble native American warriors, several little dioramas, masses of spurs and bits and hats and chaps, and all the barbed-wire you could eat.

The **Vulture Mine** itself can also be visited (May–July Sat & Sun 8am–4pm; Sept–April daily 8am–4pm; closed Aug; $8). Its long-abandoned workings rear from the streets of the well-preserved ghost town of **Vulture City**. Stick to the walking trail as you wander round; the various buildings, which include a blacksmith's shop and the mine's head office, are not as sturdy as they appear.

Practicalities

Wickenburg's **visitor center** is housed in the former railroad station at 216 N Frontier St (summer Mon–Fri 9am–5pm; winter Mon–Fri 9am–5pm, Sat 9am–2pm, Sun 10am–3pm; ☏928/684-5479 or 1-800/942-5242, ⓦwww .outwickenburgway.com).

Only one working cattle ranch now accepts paying guests, the *Flying E Ranch*, 2801 W Wickenburg Way (Nov–April only; ☏928/684-2690 or 1-888/684-2650, ⓦflyingeranch.com; ◉), where rates include all meals but not riding. *Rancho de los Caballeros*, at 1551 S Vulture Mine Rd, is a purpose-built luxury resort, complete with its own golf course and stables (mid-Oct to mid-May; ℡928/684-5484 or 1-800/684-5030, ⓦwww.sunc.com; ⑨). Of conventional **motels**, the *Best Western Rancho Grande*, 293 E Wickenburg Way (℡928/684-5445 or 1-800/854-7235, ⓦbwranchogrande.com; ④), is the most attractive, part genuine adobe and part Spanish colonial mock-up. For a slap-up ranch-style **meal**, head out to *Charley's Steakhouse*, 1187 W Wickenburg Way (℡928/684-2413; closed Mon & June to mid-Oct; dinner only).

Joshua Forest Parkway

Northwest of Wickenburg, US-93 runs for 108 dramatic miles across some of Arizona's wildest and most scenic mountains, to meet I-40 twenty miles east of Kingman (see p.311). If you're heading up from Phoenix, this slow two-lane highway bears witness to just how much of the state remains wilderness. Apart from the hamlet of **NOTHING** – which might sound enticing on the map, but really is nothing, other than the home base of a towing company that rescues unfortunate stranded motorists – there's almost no sign of human life. Instead, the vegetation is the main source of interest, with saguaro and ocotillo **cactuses** scattered across the impressive rocky outcrops. These eastern fringes of the Mojave Desert are among the few places in Arizona where you'll encounter an abundance of **joshua trees** – hence the road's official designation as the **Joshua Forest Parkway**.

West of Flagstaff

Though the two hundred miles of I-40 that run **west from Flagstaff** to California are kept busy by traffic heading to, from, and between the Grand Canyon and Las Vegas, few towns along the way are especially interesting. However, most became reliant on tourism during the heyday of **Route 66**, and driving through any of them can bring on a frisson of that era's romance.

If you have the time to indulge your 1950s fantasies, then take the 120-mile side trip on the longest surviving section of what John Steinbeck called the "**Mother Road**," which starts at **Seligman**, loops back down to **Kingman**, and then crosses wild and mountainous country to the ghost town of **Oatman**. Otherwise, it makes little difference where or even whether you choose to take a break from the interstate.

Williams

Although Flagstaff is generally regarded as the obvious base for visitors to the Grand Canyon's South Rim, the closest interstate town to the national park is **WILLIAMS**, 32 miles west. While it can't boast half the charm or pizzazz of its neighbor, it's a nice enough little place, filled with Route 66-era motels and diners and retaining a certain individuality despite the stream of tourists. Its setting helps, cupped in a high grassy valley amid pine-covered hills; the largest peak, the 9264-foot **Bill Williams Mountain** to the south, was named for pioneer trapper and "mountain man" Bill Williams (1787–1849), and gave its name in turn to the town, founded thirty years after his death.

Like Flagstaff, Williams originally based both its architecture and its economy on the ponderosas of the surrounding forests. Since 1901, however, when the Santa Fe Railroad first connected it with the canyon rim, sixty miles due north, Williams has lived off tourism. Though the railroad went out of business in 1968, it reopened in 1989 as the **Grand Canyon Railway**, promoted as a fun ride rather than a serious means of transportation. Most people who spend the night in Williams are here to take the morning train up to the canyon.

Arrival and information

Amtrak's *Southwest Chief* **train** calls in at **Williams Junction**, three miles east of town, twice daily, heading east at 5.20am and west at 10.33pm. The *Grand Canyon Railway Hotel* (see below) runs free connecting shuttle buses into town.

Schedules and prices for the **Grand Canyon Railway** (℡928/773-1976 or 1-800/843-8724, ⓦwww.thetrain.com), which sets off daily, usually at 9.30am, from the **Williams Depot** in the center of town, appear on p.325.

Williams' **visitor center**, near the railroad depot at 200 W Railroad Ave (daily: summer 8am–6.30pm; winter 8am–5pm; ℡928/635-4061 or 1-800/863-0546, ⓦwilliamschamber.com), hands out brochures, and doubles as an entertaining **museum** of neighborhood history.

Marvelous Marv's Tours run daily **guided van tours** of the South Rim from Williams, with the $85 adult rate including park admission (℡928/707-0291, ⓦmarvelousmarv.com).

Accommodation

Although the *Grand Canyon Railway Hotel* is Williams' leading **accommodation** option, plenty of alternatives exist. The downtown streets are lined with vintage motels as well as the odd B&B, while national chains congregate near the interstate exits at either end of town.

Best Western Inn of Williams 2600 W Route 66 ℡928/635-4400 or 1-800/635-4445. Spacious, well-equipped motel resort, with a pool and hot tub, perched near I-40 exit 161 at the west end of town. **❼**

Grand Canyon Railway Hotel 1 Fray Marcos Blvd ℡928/635-4010 or 1-800/843-8724, ⓦwww .thetrain.com/hotel. The Grand Canyon Railway's flagship hotel opened in 1908 as the *Fray Marcos*; rebuilt and renamed, it lacks character, though the large open lobby is pleasant enough, and there's also an indoor pool, spa, and saloon. All rooms provide two queen beds. **❼**

Red Garter Bed & Bakery 137 W Railroad Ave ℡928/635-1484 or 1-800/328-1484, ⓦredgarter .com. Plush four-room B&B in a former downtown bordello, serving fresh-baked breakfasts from its own downstairs bakery. Closed mid-Dec to mid-Feb. **❺**

Rodeway Inn 201 E Route 66 ℡928/635-4041 or 1-877/424-6423, ⓦwww.rodewayinn.com. Though from outside this very central chain motel looks much like any other, the actual rooms have been well renovated and are very comfortable and good value. **❺**

The Town

Williams holds a definite romantic appeal as the very last town on the old **Route 66** to have been bypassed by the I-40 interstate. Until October 13, 1984, when Bobby Troup of (*Get Your Kicks On*) *Route 66* fame fronted a closing ceremony, the only stoplight on the interstate between Chicago and Los Angeles stood outside the Williams visitor center.

Much of the former Route 66 frontage remains barely changed, with quirky antiques stores selling vintage memorabilia alongside Native American crafts and jewelry. However, while it's fun to explore the central blocks along the two main one-way streets – Route 66, running west to east, is paralleled by the east–west **Railroad Avenue** – an hour's evening or morning stroll is enough; Williams is not really a place to spend the day.

For rail enthusiasts, the Williams Depot holds the slowly expanding **Grand Canyon Railway Museum** (daily 7.30am–5.30pm; free). As well as great hand-tinted old photos, it's bursting with vintage tools and implements, with cases of ancient arm-rests and window catches.

Highlights of Williams' annual calendar are **Rendezvous Days**, on Memorial Day weekend in late May, when locals dress up as pioneer "buckskinners," and the Labor Day **rodeo**.

Eating

Williams's **restaurant** selection is frankly disappointing. A few places conjure up the feel of its Route 66 heyday, but nowhere serves interesting food.

▲ Pies at Williams' Pine Country Restaurant

Grand Depot Café Williams Depot ☎928/635-8970. Adequate but dull family restaurant aimed at speedily satisfying hungry tour groups. All-you-can-eat buffets are available at every meal, and you can also order predictable à la carte options. Daily 6.30am–9pm.

Pancho McGillicuddy's 141 W Railroad Ave ☎928/635-4150. Popular but very average Mexican cantina, housed in an attractive tin-ceilinged building downtown, with its own authentic-looking saloon. South-of-the-border standards like flautas, tostadas, tamales, or carnitas, cost around $10, while mixed platters go for $16; also serves steaks and grills. Daily 11am–10pm.

Pine Country Restaurant 107 N Grand Canyon Blvd ☎928/635-9718. Traditional central diner with friendly waitstaff, where the food is actually pretty good, and the home-made pies are irresistible. Daily 5.30am–9pm.

Ash Fork

The ranching community of **ASH FORK**, stretched along a brief curving fragment of Route 66 north of the interstate another twenty miles west of Williams, is smaller, less picturesque and far less involved in catering to travelers. By this point I-40 has pulled clear of the forests, so downtown Ash Fork is constructed from yellowish local sandstone rather than timber.

The major **motel** chains haven't bothered to set up shop, but Ash Fork holds a few homespun alternatives, including the large, pink *Ash Fork Inn*, at the west end of town near I-40 exit 144 (☎928/637-2514; ❷). There's also a *KOA* **campground** at 783 Old Route 66 (☎928/637-2521), and a couple of basic diners in the thick of what few things Ash Fork has to its name.

Seligman

Starting a few miles west of Ash Fork, the old Route 66 parallels its modern replacement at a discreet distance for the twenty or so miles to **SELIGMAN**. This dusty desert halt now feels more than a little stranded, a mile or two north of the interstate, but if you're in the mood to be seduced by its kitsch diners and drive-ins, it makes a mildly diverting stop in a long day's drive. Every business strives to outdo the others with eye-catching displays – mannequins of Elvis and Marilyn waving from oddball parked vehicles and the like – and the passing traffic is worth watching, too, with all kinds of vintage roadsters making pilgrimages along the "Mother Road."

You might even choose to follow Route 66's original course as it curves northwards, through a dozen fading villages and part of the **Hualapai reservation** (see p.351), and back south to Kingman. That's a total drive of 88 miles, as opposed to the dreary 65-mile run west on I-40. It also provides access to **Havasu Canyon**, in the depths of the Grand Canyon, which as described on p.343 is one of the Southwest's least-known marvels.

Seligman offers I-40's only **accommodation** between Ash Fork and Kingman, though motels like the *Historic Route 66*, 500 W Route 66 (☎928/422-3204; ❸), are all much of an indifferent muchness. The wackiest local **diner** has to be *Delgadillo's Snow Cap* at 301 E Route 66 (☎928/422-3291; closed Dec–Feb), where every malt or burger comes with a side order of outrageous puns and put-ons.

Kingman

With a population of over thirty thousand, **KINGMAN**, 65 miles on from Seligman and thirty miles short of California, ranks second to Flagstaff among Arizona's I-40 towns. As all traffic between Phoenix or the Grand Canyon and **Las Vegas** – a mere hundred miles northwest on US-93 – is obliged to pass this way, Kingman's thirty-plus motels stay busy year-round. The best that can be said for it, however, is that it's not particularly ugly – apart from the long sprawl beside the railroad tracks north of the interstate – and it's not lifeless. Apart from that, it's a humdrum pit stop with a slight tinge of Route-66 quaintness.

Kingman's main street, curving alongside the railroad tracks, is named in honor of native son **Andy Devine**, the actor who drove the eponymous *Stagecoach* in John Ford's 1939 movie. As a local brochure puts it, "there must be somebody who hasn't heard of Andy Devine, but that person sure doesn't live in Kingman." His career, the culture and basketwork of the Hualapai, and other unlikely components of Mohave County's heritage, are explored in the **Mohave Museum of History & Arts**, 400 W Beale St (Mon–Fri 9am–5pm, Sat 1–5pm; $4). 1939 was clearly a big year for Kingman: Carole Lombard and Clark Gable were married here on March 29.

Arrival and information

Kingman's large **Powerhouse visitor center**, at the western edge of downtown at 120 W Andy Devine Ave (daily: March–Oct 9am–6pm; Nov–Feb 8am–5pm; ☎928/753-6106, ⊛kingmantourism.org), also sells lots of Route 66 memorabilia. The central Amtrak station still welcomes **trains** between Flagstaff and LA, but only at unearthly hours of the night, while Greyhound **buses**, between Phoenix and Las Vegas as well as east–west, use a terminal near the interstate at 3264 E Andy Devine Ave (☎928/757-8400).

Accommodation

Granted that you're unlikely to spend more than one night in Kingman – or linger in the morning, either – its ordinary but inexpensive **motels** should easily meet your needs. There's also beautiful **camping** in the hills five miles southeast of town, in the county-run **Hualapai Mountain Park** (☎928/681-5700, ⊛www.mcparks.com), which also holds the *Hualapai Mountain Lodge Resort* (☎928/757-3545; closed Mon; ❹).

Best Western A Wayfarer's Inn 2815 E Andy Devine Ave ☎928/753-6271 or 1-800/548-5695, ⊛www.bestwesternarizona.com. Upscale hundred-room chain property, a couple of miles northeast of town near I-40 exit 53, charging very reasonable rates for its smart if anonymous rooms, and offering a pool and indoor spa. ❹

Brunswick 315 E Andy Devine Ave ☎928/718-1800, ⊛hotel-brunswick.com. This century-old "historical boutique hotel" is downtown Kingman's characterful lodging, but it's best suited to budget travelers who will appreciate its rock-bottom, single-bedded cowboy or cowgirl options, with shared bathroom; the more lavish suites are overpriced considering the railroad noise. Rates include breakfast. ❷–❼

Quality Inn Kingman 1400 E Andy Devine Ave ☎928/753-4747 or 1-800/228-5151, ⊛qualityinn .com. Standard motel a half-mile from downtown, with small but adequate rooms, that offers a bit of character via a strong Route 66 theme, including a retro breakfast room. ❹

Super 8 3401 E Andy Devine Ave ☎928/757-4808 or 1-800/800-8000, ⊛super8.com. Reliable, inexpensive chain motel well east of town, just north of I-40 exit 53. ❸

Eating

Most Kingman **restaurants** play on the Route 66 angle. It's all too spread out to wander around comparing menus, but hop in your car and you'll find something.

Dambar & Steakhouse 1960 E Andy Devine Ave ☎928/753-3523. Classic Western steakhouse atop the hill, all sawdust and bare timber, serving grilled and barbecued ribs and chicken, as well as massive steaks. Entrees around $20 at dinner, more like $10 at lunch. Daily 11am–10pm.

Hubb's Café *Brunswick*, 315 E Andy Devine Ave ☎928/718-1800. The *Brunswick's* attractively restored dining room prepares eclectic international cuisine, from rich Continental sauces to spicy Asian curries, as well as American standards. Typical dinner entrees cost around $20. Mon–Fri 11am–2pm & 5–9pm, Sat 5–9pm.

Mr D'z Route 66 Diner 105 E Andy Devine Ave ☎928/718 0066. Loving re-creation of a classic Route 66 roadhouse, across from the visitor center and bursting with memorabilia, neon, and lurid molded trimmings. Good burgers and shakes, malts and floats, and fries with everything. Daily 7am–9pm.

Chloride

Fifteen miles northwest of Kingman, as US-93 tears through the flat, prosaically named **Detrital Valley** toward Las Vegas, a paved road climbs away into the mountains to the right. Its goal, the former silver mining center of **CHLORIDE** four miles up, was established in 1864 and boasts Arizona's oldest still-functional post office. As well as silver, vast quantities of gold, copper, lead, and turquoise were also extracted from the roadless **Cerbat Mountains** beyond, but Chloride these days lives by its wits, exploiting its ramshackle Wild West appearance to attract tourists.

Some of Chloride's erstwhile neighbors – such as **Cerbat** and **Mineral Park** – have become genuine **ghost towns**. In Chloride itself, the epicenter of the visitor industry is *Shep's* (☎928/565-4251 or 1-877/565-4251, ⓦwww .shepsminersinn.com; ❷), an antiques store that doubles as a **B&B**.

Bullhead City and Laughlin

While both the old Route 66 and the interstate head southwest from Kingman, Hwy-68 barrels due west for thirty miles to **BULLHEAD CITY** on the Colorado River. Built as a work camp for the construction of nearby Davis Dam, Bullhead City somehow survived the dam's completion in 1953 and is prospering these days due to its proximity to the casinos of **LAUGHLIN**, Nevada, just across the river.

In terms of temperature, **Bullhead** is the hottest town in the US, exceeding 120°F day after day each summer. In most other respects, however, it's not the least bit hot. Thirty thousand people now live along a ten-mile riverfront stretch of Hwy-93; why on earth you'd join them, even for a night, is hard to imagine.

Not that **Laughlin** is much better, despite the endless hype of its tourist authorities. If you've never been to Las Vegas, you may well be impressed by the dozen or so huge, glittering **casinos** that jostle for position beside the Colorado. They lack the panache of their Vegas counterparts, however, as well as the will to cater to anyone other than hardened gamblers. The only real reason to come here is that **accommodation** rates are so cheap, though it is also fun to take a **paddle-wheeler cruise** on the Colorado, costing about $10 for a little over an hour, from either the *Riverside Resort* or the *Edgewater Hotel*.

Practicalities

Laughlin's **visitor center**, across from the *Riverside* at 1555 S Casino Drive (daily 8am–4.30pm; ☎702/298-3321 or 1-800/452-8445, ⓦwww.visitlaughlin.com), offers free phone connections to all Laughlin hotels, and carries information on Las Vegas as well.

At least eight casinos in Laughlin offer well over a thousand **rooms** each, with weekday rates that can drop below $30 per room. The oldest, which traces its ancestry all the way back to an eight-room motel that opened in 1966 but has consistently kept pace with the rest, is *Don Laughlin's Riverside Resort Hotel*, 1650 S Casino Drive (☎702/298-2535 or 1-800/227-3849, ⓦwww.riversideresort.com; Mon–Thurs & Sun ❷, Fri & Sat ❸). Neighbors include the counterfeit Mississippi steamboat that is the *Colorado Belle*,

2100 S Casino Drive (℡702/298-4000 or 1-877/460-0777, ⓦcoloradobelle
.com; Mon–Thurs & Sun ❶, Fri & Sat ❸), and the top-of-the-range *Golden
Nugget*, 2300 S Casino Drive (℡702/298-7222 or 1-800/950-7700,
ⓦgnlaughlin.com; Mon–Thurs & Sun ❷, Fri & Sat ❸). Each casino holds
several **restaurants** ranging from buffet joints whose all-you-can-eat specials
start at under $5, to steakhouses and dimly lit Italian schmoozeries. It's really
not worth eating anywhere other than where you're staying, however – it
takes a long time to walk from one casino to the next, and you'll only find
the same bland choices you had before you set off.

Oatman

If you're in no great hurry to get to California from Kingman, following Route
66 over the **Black Mountains** is much more enjoyable than skirting south
then west on I-40. While **Needles**, California, is only fifty miles away on the
"Mother Road," however – as opposed to 64 on the interstate – it's a long, slow
drive, with lots of tricky mountain bends.

The eastern approaches to the mountains, at the edge of the Sacramento
Valley, are guarded by a splendid solitary rock pinnacle that was a beacon to
early travelers. Following a laborious climb up to a gap between the peaks,
the road twists down the far side and eventually enters **OATMAN**. This
former gold-mining community, which was established in 1906 and went
bust in 1942, is one of Arizona's most appealing **ghost towns**; a second
career as a movie backdrop and tourist stop-off has ensured that it's never
truly been abandoned. The streets are still roamed by semi-wild burros
descended from animals left by the miners; stores sell carrots, the only food
you're allowed to offer them.

Gift and craft stores now occupy most of the false-front structures along
Oatman's raised wooden boardwalk, with snacks available at *Olive Oatman's
Restaurant and Saloon* and the *Route 66 Deli and Espresso Shop*. The *1902 Oatman
Hotel* (℡928/768-4408; ❷) – a restored adobe that was in fact rebuilt after a fire
in 1920 – still rents out basic **rooms**, including the one where Clark Gable and
Carole Lombard spent their wedding night in 1939.

Lake Havasu City

Forty miles southwest of Kingman on I-40, ten miles from the California
border, a twenty-mile detour south on Hwy-95 brings you to the most incongruous sight of the Southwestern deserts. At **LAKE HAVASU CITY**, the old
gray stones of **London Bridge** reach out across the stagnant waters of the
dammed Colorado River. However, it's not often you see anything quite as
boring in Arizona as London Bridge; unless you've never seen a bridge before,
it's one to miss.

Lake Havasu City has an undeniable attraction for the parched urbanites of
cities such as Phoenix, who flock to fish on the lake or charge up and down in
motorboats and on jet skis, but it holds minimal appeal for travelers from further
afield. What's more, between March and June, it's almost permanently filled with
students on **Spring Break**, drinking and partying around the clock.

Only when you cross the bridge onto the island, and look back, do you appreciate how large Lake Havasu City has grown, sprawling up the gentle slope away
from the river. Most of those broad hillside streets are lined with condo blocks
and minor malls; the only place tourists bother to visit is the **English Village**,
a mock-Tudor shopping mall, which also holds a handful of riverview restaurants, at the base of the bridge. Out on the island, if you head south from the

London Bridge is falling down

Californian chainsaw manufacturer **Robert P. McCulloch** moved his factory to the remote Arizona desert in 1964, to try out his new sideline in outboard motors on Lake Havasu. Three years later, he heard Johnny Carson mention that London Bridge was up for sale; in the words of the nursery rhyme, it really was falling down, unable to cope with all those newfangled automobiles. McCulloch bought it for $2,460,000, and painstakingly shipped ten thousand numbered blocks of granite across the Atlantic. Lacking anything for the bridge to span, he dug a channel that turned a riverbank promontory into the island of **Pittsburg Point**. Despite the jibes that McCulloch thought he was buying London's picturesque Tower Bridge – the turreted one that opens in the middle – his investment in London Bridge, merely the latest in a long line of London Bridges and dating only from 1831, paid off handsomely. The bridge now ranks second among Arizona's tourist attractions, after the Grand Canyon, and Lake Havasu City has become a major vacation resort and retirement center, with a population of over fifty thousand. For its part, London Bridge is listed in the **Guinness Book of Records** as the largest antique ever sold.

bridge you'll soon come to **London Bridge Beach**. The "beach" is more grit than sand, and few people swim from it. With its bizarre fringe of date palms, however, and its panorama of weird desert buttes and the Chemehuevi Mountains, it does at least linger in the memory.

Practicalities

The **visitor center** at 420 English Village can tell you anything you want to know about Lake Havasu (Mon–Sat 8.30am–4pm; ℡928/453-3444 or 1-800/242-8278, ⓦgolakehavasu.com). Several operators offer short **river cruises** from the quayside of the English Village, and **jet ski** rentals are also widely available.

Lake Havasu City has a good 25 or so **motels**, though few are immediately obvious from Hwy-95. They range from the surprisingly hip *Agave Inn*, 1420 W McCulloch Blvd (℡928/854-2833 or 1-888/898-4328; ❹), to the extravagant riverfront *London Bridge Resort*, 1477 Queen's Bay Rd (℡928/855-0888 or 1-866/331-9231, ⓦlondonbridgeresort.com; ❻), where the lobby is all but filled by a gilt replica stagecoach. Note that rates are usually higher on weekends than on weekdays.

For a night out, the districts at either end of London Bridge are your best bet. The *City of London Arms* (℡928/855-8782) is a lively pub in the English Village on the mainland, while the *Mudshark Brewing Co*, not far south at 210 Swanson Ave (℡928/453-2981) is a slightly more upscale brewpub with better beer. *Shugrue's* (℡928/453-1400), across the bridge in the Island Fashion Mall, serves good fresh fish – even sushi – as well as salads and pasta.

6

The Grand Canyon

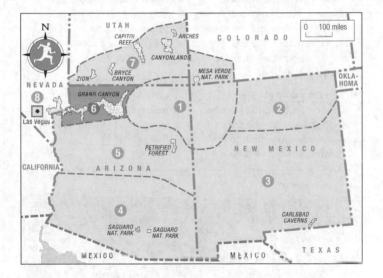

CHAPTER 6 # Highlights

✳ **El Tovar Hotel** The jewel of Grand Canyon Village, this historic hotel provides the South Rim's best food and lodging. See p.331

✳ **Shoshone Point** Little-known viewpoint, accessible only on foot, that feels a world away from all the other South Rim overlooks. See p.337

✳ **Desert View Watchtower** Circular mock-Puebloan tower, blending into the rocks at the east end of the South Rim, that provides stunning canyon views. See p.338

✳ **The Bright Angel Trail** Deservedly the most popular hiking trail within the park; a superb introduction to life below the rim. See p.340

✳ **The South Kaibab Trail** This hair-raising descent to the canyon floor offers the finest day-hikes in the park. See p.342

✳ **Havasu Falls** Astonishing, lush turquoise waterfalls buried deep within the canyon on the Havasupai reservation. See p.348

✳ **Cape Royal** The perfect vantage point from which to appreciate the overall shape of the canyon. See p.358

✳ **Toroweap Point** The remotest canyon overlook within the national park offers unique views into the Inner Gorge. See p.361

▲ Shoshone Point, South Rim

The Grand Canyon

lthough almost five million people come to see the **GRAND CANYON OF THE COLORADO** every year, it remains beyond the grasp of the human imagination. No photograph, or statistics, can prepare you for such vastness. At more than one mile deep, it's an inconceivable abyss; varying from four to eighteen miles wide; an endless expanse of bewildering shapes and colors, glaring desert brightness and impenetrable shadow, stark promontories and soaring, never-to-be-climbed sandstone pinnacles. While no one is disappointed with their first stunning sight of the chasm, visitors often struggle to understand what can appear as a remote and impassive spectacle. They race frantically from viewpoint to viewpoint, constantly imagining that the next one will be the "best," the place from which the whole thing will finally make sense. The secret to transcending that initial frantic excitement is to slow down, to appreciate whatever small portion of the canyon may be displayed in front of you at any one moment, and to allow enough time for the bigger picture to develop. And visiting the Grand Canyon need not be a passive experience. In addition to touring the **overlooks** along each rim, the views from all of which shift and change unceasingly from dawn to dusk, you can **hike** down into the depths; ride down on a **mule**; hover above the canyon in a **helicopter**; raft through the **whitewater rapids** of the river itself; spend a night at **Phantom Ranch** on the canyon floor; or swim beneath the waterfalls of the idyllic **Havasupai reservation**.

Mapping and defining precisely what constitutes the "Grand Canyon" has always been controversial; **Grand Canyon National Park** covers a relatively small proportion of the greater Grand Canyon area. Only in the past forty years has it included the full 277-mile length of the Colorado River from Lees Ferry in the east to Grand Wash Cliffs near Lake Mead in the west, and even now it's restricted for most of that way to the narrow strip of the inner gorge. Ranchers whose animals graze in the federal forests to either side, mining companies eager to exploit the mineral wealth hidden in the rocks, engineers seeking to divert the river to irrigate the deserts, and the Native Americans who live in the canyon, have combined to minimize the size of the park.

Admission to Grand Canyon National Park, valid for seven days on either rim, costs $25 for one private, noncommercial vehicle and all its passengers, or $12 per pedestrian or cyclist. All the park-service **passes** detailed on p.41 are sold and valid.

For an even more detailed account of the entire Grand Canyon region, see the **Rough Guide to the Grand Canyon**, also by Greg Ward.

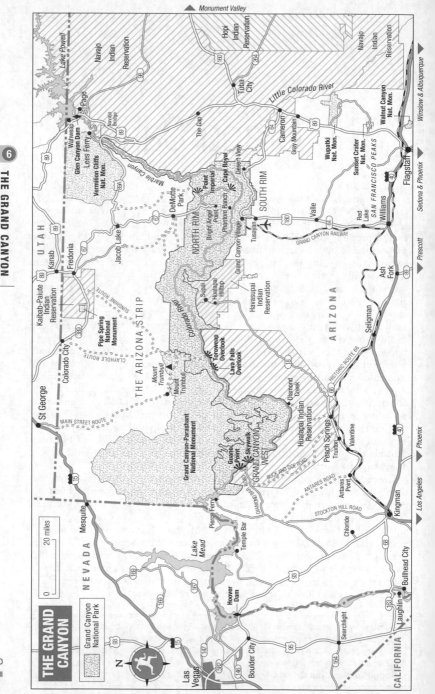

THE GRAND CANYON

Grand Canyon National Park

Grand Canyon National Park

N

0   20 miles

Monument Valley

Lake Powell

Page

Wahweap

Glen Canyon Dam
Lees Ferry
Vermilion Cliffs Nat. Mon.

Navajo Bridge

Marble Canyon

Kanab

Fredonia

Kalbab-Paiute Indian Reservation

Pipe Spring National Monument

Colorado City

St George

Mesquite

NEVADA

Las Vegas

Boulder City

Hoover Dam

Lake Mead

Temple Bar

Pierce Ferry

Grand Canyon-Parashant National Monument

Mount Trumbull

Mount Trumbull

THE ARIZONA "STRIP"

SUNSHINE ROUTE

MAIN STREET ROUTE

CLAYHOLE ROUTE

Jacob Lake

DeMotte Park

NORTH RIM

Colorado River

Toroweap Overlook

Lava Falls Overlook

Point Imperial

Bright Angel Point

Phantom Ranch

Cape Royal

Desert View

SOUTH RIM

Supai

Hualapai Hilltop

Havasupai Indian Reservation

Grand Canyon Village

Tusayan

GRAND CANYON WEST

Guano Point

Skywalk

DIAMOND BAR ROAD

BUCK AND DOE ROAD

Diamond Creek

Hualapai Indian Reservation

Peach Springs

Truxton

Valentine

Antares Point

ANTARES ROAD

STOCKTON HILL ROAD

Chloride

Searchlight

Bullhead City

Laughlin

Kingman

CALIFORNIA

Los Angeles

Phoenix

Prescott

Sedona & Phoenix

Winslow & Albuquerque

Flagstaff

Williams

Ash Fork

Seligman

ARIZONA

HISTORIC ROUTE 66

Valle

Red Lake

SAN FRANCISCO PEAKS

Walnut Canyon Nat. Mon.

Sunset Crater Nat. Mon.

Wupatki Nat. Mon.

Gray Mountain

Cameron

The Gap

Little Colorado River

Tuba City

UTAH

Lake Powell

Navajo Indian Reservation

Hopi Indian Reservation

Navajo Indian Reservation

GRAND CANYON RAILWAY

The vast majority of visitors arrive at the **South Rim** – it's much easier to get to, holds far more facilities (mainly at **Grand Canyon Village**, inside the park), and remains open year round. Another lodge and campground are located at the **North Rim**, which by virtue of its isolation can be a lot more atmospheric, but at one thousand feet higher this entire area is usually closed by snow from November until mid-May. Few people visit both rims on a single trip; to get from one to the other demands either a three-day hike down one side of the canyon and up the other, or a 215-mile drive. On both rims, the main activity consists of gazing over the gorge from lookouts spaced along the canyon-edge roads. In the 1920s the average visitor stayed for two or three weeks, whereas these days it's more like two or three hours – of which forty minutes are spent actually looking at the canyon.

If you're visiting the Grand Canyon as part of a longer Southwest itinerary, you may be wondering whether you "should" visit both rims, or which rim is "better." It really depends on how much time you have and what time of year it is. Though wilderness enthusiasts tend to find the summer crowds at the South Rim unbearable, even there it's possible to escape the throng, and there's great scope for day-hiking. The North Rim is convenient to Zion and Bryce parks and northeast Arizona and has nicer accommodation options. It's probably best to choose whichever rim fits in with your planned route, and not to feel you ought to see the other one as well

A history of the Grand Canyon

It may look forbidding, but the Grand Canyon is teeming with life – sheep and rabbits, eagles and vultures, mountain lions, and, of course, spiders, scorpions, and snakes all thrive here. The earliest signs of any **human** presence are twig figurines of animals, found hidden in caves in the canyon walls. Dated to around 2000 BC, they were probably created to ensure successful hunting. Remains of later dwellings built by the **Ancestral Puebloans** are scattered throughout the canyon – the most accessible to modern visitors is **Tusayan Ruin** (see p.338). A separate tribal group, the **Havasupai** (see p.344), arrived around 1300 AD.

In 1540 – less than twenty years after Cortés conquered the Aztecs of Mexico – the first **Spaniards** reached the Southwest. At the Hopi mesas, a detachment of Coronado's company were told of a great river not far west, inhabited by people with very large bodies (presumably the Havasupai, who tend to be significantly bigger than the Hopi). A small party, led by **García López de Cárdenas**, was despatched to investigate. Their Hopi guides led them to a spot somewhere near Grandview Point, but chose not to reveal the trails down to the river. The Spaniards spent three days on the South Rim, only appreciating the scale of the canyon after an abortive attempt to reach the river. They identified the Colorado as being the Tíson or "Firebrand" River, up which a simultaneous naval expedition was attempting to sail (it managed 225 miles, reaching what's now the site of the Hoover Dam).

When jurisdiction over the Grand Canyon passed from Mexico to the United States in 1850, it had never been surveyed and did not even have a fixed **name**. To the Havasupai, it was *Wikatata* ("Rough Rim"); Spanish maps showed it as *Río Muy Grande* ("Very Big River"); and trappers and prospectors knew it as the Big Cañon. The name Grand Canyon, first used on a map in 1868, was popularized by the one-armed Civil War veteran **John Wesley Powell**, whose expeditions along the fearsome and uncharted Colorado, in 1869 and 1871–72 – see p.433 – captured public imagination.

As the Grand Canyon was being recognized as the most extraordinary natural wonder in the US, American settlers arrived nearby in ever greater numbers.

Although the Grand Canyon could be called the world's clearest geological textbook, scientists continue to argue over how to read the story written in the stone. Layer upon layer of different rocks, readily distinguished by color, and each with its own fossil record, recede down into the canyon and back through time, until the riverbed lays bare some of the oldest exposed rocks on earth. Almost all the successive strata of sandstone and limestone were deposited during periods when the entire region was submerged beneath shallow primeval seas. The bottom layer, the two-billion-year-old **Vishnu Schist**, is so ancient that it contains no fossils; it dates back to the Precambrian era, when life had barely begun.

That same tale of sedimentation, of course, holds true for much of the planet. Two major factors transformed what, until five million years ago, was an unremarkable landscape into the Grand Canyon. First of all, the chronic shortage of rain in this desert area stopped vegetation growing to bind the brittle surface together. Secondly, there was the fast-flowing **Colorado River**, cascading down from the Rocky Mountains with a gradient over 25 times steeper than the Mississippi. In full flood, charged with mighty boulders, it can blast deep crevices into the earth.

However, a crucial mystery remains. The Colorado Plateau is not flat at this point; it's an enormous hill, known to the Paiute Indians as the **Kaibab**, or mountain with no peak, which slopes southwards from a ridge that runs roughly a dozen miles north of the North Rim. Thus the Colorado has eaten away a chunk of the hillside, around a third of the way up the southern slope – which explains why the North Rim is a thousand feet higher than the South. Why, or how, the Colorado River cuts straight through that hill, rather than flowing around it, has long perplexed geologists. The hypothesis currently in favor, "**stream piracy**," suggests that until five million years ago, the river did indeed skirt the Kaibab – along some unknown course – but was then "captured" by another river and began to flow through it instead. That may have occurred when a powerful stream, at the head of its own canyon, cut so far back that it breached the barrier that separated it from the Colorado. The Colorado would then rush through, abandoning its own course and usurping this alternative channel.

Crudely speaking, while the Colorado is responsible for the **depth** of the canyon – and continues to scour its way deeper – it did little to create its **width**, which owes more to flash-flooding along its tributary streams and extreme cycles of heat and cold. Vast slabs of stone are chiseled away when water that trickles into cracks in exposed rock later freezes and expands, thereby sculpting the fantastic pyramids and mesas that tower above the central gorge. Some layers of rock are much harder than others; thus the solid Tapeats Sandstone of the **Tonto Platform**, a mile-wide shelf above the river that runs through most of the national park, was left behind when the weaker Bright Angel Shale above it eroded away. Because the general slope of the Kaibab runs from north to south, rain that falls north of the canyon flows down toward the gorge, while rainfall to the south flows away. As a result, the **North Rim** is deeply cut by tributaries and pushed back further from the Colorado, while the lower **South Rim** is much more regular.

The most striking features were named for their supposed resemblance to the great temples of India and China – **Brahma Temple**, **Shiva Temple**, **Vishnu Temple**, and so on – by Clarence Dutton, a student of comparative religion who wrote the first Geological Survey report on the canyon in 1881. The tradition was followed by later cartographers such as François Matthes, who named **Krishna Shrine** and **Walhalla Plateau**.

Tensions have arisen ever since between this new permanent population, determined to survive in such an unforgiving environment, and visitors hoping to find unspoiled wilderness. Broadly speaking, **logging** and **grazing** interests retain control of the plateau forests, while in the canyon itself most attempts at

mining were defeated by the difficulty of the terrain, and **tourism** soon proved a far more lucrative proposition.

When the **railroad** first crossed northern Arizona in 1882, visitors were taken by stagecoach from the nearest station to the Grand Canyon, at **Peach Springs**, to stay at the *Diamond Creek Hotel* by the river. With the growth of the timber towns to the east, that site soon declined; by the 1890s, **Flagstaff** was the main terminus, connected with the canyon by three weekly stages. The railroad reached the canyon itself, via a branch line from **Williams**, in 1901. That triggered the growth of **Grand Canyon Village**, built by a subsidiary of the Santa Fe Railroad. The Fred Harvey Company's grand *El Tovar Hotel* – still the showpiece canyon-edge lodging – opened in January 1905, and its early marketing strategies influence the experience of Canyon visitors to this day. Following an internal memo to "get some Indians to the Canyon at once," the Hopi House souvenir store was built, modeled on the Pueblo village of Old Oraibi (see p.80) and staffed with Hopi craftspeople. Similarly, Navajo weavers were exhorted to produce rugs to suit tourist tastes, using previously unfavored "earth" colors such as brown. Pseudo-Pueblo architecture became the dominant theme, with a single architect, **Mary Jane Colter**, designing such structures as Hermit's Rest (1914), the Desert Watchtower (1932; see p.338), and *Bright Angel Lodge* (1935).

Late nineteenth-century proposals to create a **Grand Canyon National Park** aroused vigorous local opposition. In due course, however, naturalist **John Muir** – who declared the Grand Canyon to be "unearthly … as if you had found it after death, on some other star" – found a powerful ally in President **Theodore Roosevelt**. Only entitled to protect sites of historical, rather than geological, interest, Roosevelt used the pretext of preserving Ancestral Puebloan ruins to proclaim Grand Canyon National Monument in 1908. Arizonan politicians finally came round to the idea after Arizona achieved statehood in 1912. Even then, by the time the boundaries of the Grand Canyon National Park were fixed in 1919, they had trimmed away large tracts of grazing land. The new park covered around 1000 square miles and included just 56 miles of the actual canyon.

Meanwhile, tourism to the South Rim had not stood still. Thanks to his bogus mining claims, **Ralph Cameron** was charging a toll of $1 to riders on the Bright Angel Trail. In 1905, he built his own hotel alongside the railroad terminal, thereby forcing the Fred Harvey Company to relocate the station out of sight of the upstart rival. Cameron continued to be a thorn in the side of the new national park. Elected to the US Senate in 1920, he spent a few years hacking at its budget before his mining claims were eventually invalidated. His presence had by then spurred the development of the **Kaibab Trail**, stretching from rim to rim of the canyon by way of the Kaibab suspension footbridge (see p.342). Plans to pave that route never materialized, but a small enlargement of the park in 1927 permitted the construction of a road east to Desert View, which with the completion in 1928 of the Navajo Bridge across Marble Canyon reduced the previous 600-mile drive between the rims to a more feasible 215 miles.

The first **automobile** arrived at the Canyon in 1902, despite running out of gas twenty miles short. By 1926, more visitors were coming by car than by train, and Flagstaff was once again the major point of access. Advance reservations for both mule rides and lodging have been necessary since 1938; annual visitor numbers first exceeded a million in 1956, and ran at over five million through most of the 1990s. Anticipating that visitation would continue to increase, the park service drew up plans for a huge new tourism complex close to the South Rim, to be known as "**Canyon Forest Village**," and also a **light rail** network. However, for reasons no one can explain, numbers then dropped back down below five million, and the political will to make major changes has disappeared.

The South Rim

When someone casually mentions visiting the "Grand Canyon," it's almost certainly the **South Rim** to which they're referring. To be more precise, it's the thirty-mile stretch of the South Rim that's served by a paved road; and most specifically of all, it's **Grand Canyon Village**, the small canyon-edge community, sandwiched between the pine forest and the rim, that holds the park's **lodges**, **restaurants**, and **visitor center**.

The reason nine out of every ten canyon visitors come here is not, however, because this is a uniquely wonderful spot from which to see the canyon. In terms of views, it's as good a place to start as any – every visit begins with an eager rush to catch that first breathtaking glimpse of the abyss – but really Grand Canyon Village just happens to be where the canyon's tourist facilities have been concentrated ever since the arrival of the railroad a century ago.

As the millennium approached – and despite the emergence of **Tusayan**, just outside the park, as a rival accommodation center – it looked as though the village could no longer take the strain. An ambitious scheme was therefore drawn up under which visitors would explore the South Rim using a **light rail** network rather than their own vehicles. As described above, however, visitor numbers dropped instead, and the plan will probably never be implemented. As a result, the park remains in a strange state of limbo. All that's happened is that a large open-air **Canyon View Information Plaza** has been constructed, well away from the village center, and not beside the rim either. It looks great, but as you're supposed to drive into the village and then catch a bus back to the plaza, it's done nothing to relieve traffic congestion, and it doesn't even meet the basic requirement of making an easy first stop.

On a more positive note, the canyon is as majestic as ever, to be admired from countless differing vantage points, not only within the village but also along the eight-mile **Hermit Road** to the west and the 23-mile **Desert View Drive** to the east. The facilities in the village are of a pretty high standard, and generally well priced; the village itself is also more attractive than you might imagine, and once the day-trippers have gone rarely feels as crowded as the horror stories might suggest.

Getting to the South Rim

The South Rim is separated from I-40 by the sixty-mile expanse of the **Coconino Plateau**, covered by the largest **ponderosa pine forest** in the world. Crossing this undramatic landscape, you get no sense of the impending abyss until you reach the very edge of the canyon.

The vast majority of visitors reach the park entrance at Tusayan by **driving** north from I-40. AZ-64 from **Williams** (52 miles south; see p.308), also known as the Bushmaster Memorial Highway, joins US-180 from **Flagstaff** (75 miles southeast; see p.285), at **Valle**, thirty miles south of the canyon itself. The route from Flagstaff, by way of the San Francisco Peaks (see p.290), is more scenic, and is followed by most commercial **buses**. It's also possible to drive to Grand Canyon Village from the east, by turning onto AZ-64 from US-89 at **Cameron** (see p.353). Flagstaff is served by Amtrak trains, while a separate **rail** service connects Williams with the canyon itself.

There are direct **flights** to Tusayan from Las Vegas and other points in the Southwest.

By train

Amtrak **trains** come no closer to the South Rim than the stations at **Flagstaff** and **Williams**. In summer, westbound services, originating in Chicago, arrive at Flagstaff at 8.51pm and Williams Junction at 9.33pm daily, while eastbound trains, which start in LA, call at Williams Junction at 4.20am and Flagstaff at 5.06am daily. Times in winter are one hour later. Bus connections are detailed below.

Trains on the restored **Grand Canyon Railway** (☎928/773-1976 or 1-800/843-8724, ⊛thetrain.com) run for 64 miles from a separate station in the heart of **Williams** to the picturesque station at Grand Canyon Village. The railway is a tourist attraction in its own right, with passengers riding in historic cars of varying levels of comfort and entertained throughout the day by Wild West shoot-outs, hold-ups, pistol-packing marshals, singing conductors, and the like. The scenery en route – part desert scrubland, part pine forest – is far from spectacular, and you never actually see the canyon from the train, but it's a fun way to visit the park without having to drive. Services operate daily all year, with varying schedules but typically leaving Williams at 9.30am and arriving back at 5.45pm. Only in summer is the train pulled by **steam engines**. Round-trip fares range from $65 in Coach Class (under-13s $35) up to $170 (under-13s not permitted) in the Luxury Parlor Car. No Amtrak passes are accepted, and, unless you have a national park pass, an additional fee of $8 is charged for park admission.

By bus

Open Road Tours and Transportation (☎928/226-8060 or 1-877/226-8060, ⊛openroadtours.com) runs two **bus services** each day from the Amtrak station in **Flagstaff**, via the Grand Canyon Railroad Depot in **Williams**, to the IMAX movie theater in **Tusayan**, and the **Maswik Transportation Center** in Grand Canyon Village. The first service leaves Flagstaff at 8am daily, calling at Williams at 8.30am and reaching Maswik at 9.45am; the second leaves Flagstaff at 3.45pm and Williams at 4.30pm, reaching Maswik at 5.45pm. Return services leave Maswik at 10.15am and 6.15pm, arriving at Williams at 11.30am and 7.30pm respectively, and Flagstaff at noon and 8pm. Tickets cost $27 each way from Flagstaff for adults, or $22 from Williams, and $19 or $17 respectively for accompanied under-12s.

Companies that operate **one-day tours** to the Canyon from Flagstaff and Williams are listed on p.286 and p.309 respectively.

By air

The small **airport** at Tusayan – six miles from the South Rim, just outside the park boundary, and used primarily by "flight-seeing" tour companies (see p.327) – also welcomes scheduled services, especially from **Las Vegas**. Unlike the tours, these flights do not pass directly above the park, but they still give good views. Standard fares are around $150 one way and $250 round trip, but special offers can cost as little as $60 and $100, respectively. The major Vegas operator is Scenic Airlines (☎702/638-3300 or 1-800/634-6801, ⊛www.scenic.com).

Park bus tours

To reserve a guided South Rim **bus tour**, contact the "transportation desk" in any lodge, or call ☎928/638-2631. The **Desert View Tour**, a 52-mile, 4 hour round-trip along the East Rim, stops at Yavapai Observation Station and Lipan Point, as well as at Desert View at the far end, and costs $40. The 2 hour **Hermit's Rest Tour**, west of the village along the same route as the free Hermit's Rest shuttle bus (see p.328), costs $23. Shorter **Sunrise** and **Sunset** tours head east and west of the village respectively, with an adult fare of $18. Adults can take any two tours, not necessarily on the same day, for $50, while accompanied under-17s travel free.

Horse riding

Apache Stables (☎928/638-2891, @www.apachestables.com), based at *Moqui Lodge* in Tusayan (which is itself permanently closed), charges $450.50 for a one-hour trail ride through the Kaibab Forest, and $85.50 for two hours, and in the evening offers campfire rides on horseback for $55.50, or by wagon for $25.50.

Mule rides

Places on the **mule rides** down the Bright Angel Trail are limited; reserve as far in advance as possible, on ☎928/638-2631. One-day round-trips as far as Plateau Point cost $154, including lunch, while overnight trips to Phantom Ranch, including accommodation and all meals, cost $420 for one person, $743 for two. Two-night rides, available mid-November to March only, cost $593 for one, $991 for two. If you arrive without a reservation, join the waiting list at the Transportation Desk at *Bright Angel Lodge* and turn up there at 6am on the morning you want to ride; there are normally a few last-minute cancellations.

Grand Canyon Field Institute

The **Grand Canyon Field Institute** offers well-priced, expert-led guided tours and hikes in and around the canyon. Different tours, some restricted to women only, specialize in geology, history, natural history, photography, wilderness techniques, and other topics. Most involve camping and backpacking, others include lodge accommodation or even llama trekking; all are graded according to the difficulty of any hiking involved. Typical prices range from $485 for a three-night hike down to Indian Garden to $660 for a four-night rim-to-rim backpack. For full details, access @grandcanyon.org/fieldinstitute or call ☎928/638-2485 or 1-866/471-4435.

Flight-seeing tours

For safety reasons and to diminish **noise**, strict **regulations** surround flights above the national park. Airplanes and helicopters have to fly at different altitudes; no one

Arrival and information

While the obvious first port of call when you arrive at the South Rim is **Canyon View Information Plaza** (daily: May to mid-Oct 7.30am–6pm; mid-Oct to April 8am–5pm; ☎928/638-7888, @www.nps.gov/grca), it can be impossible in mid-summer to park anywhere near it. In fact, there's no need to stop at the visitor center so long as you have the park's **free newspaper**, *The Guide*, handed out at the two **entrance stations** on AZ-64 (one's just north of Tusayan, the other a mile east of **Desert View**).

As well as listing opening hours and shuttle-bus schedules, *The Guide* carries a full program of **park activities** such as ranger talks and guided hikes. On a typical day in high season, around fifteen talks or hikes take place, at venues

can fly below the level of the rim; and 75 percent of the park, including the airspace above the South Rim lookouts and the central rim-to-rim "Corridor," is off-limits.

Helicopter companies based at Tusayan include **Papillon** (℡702/736-7243 or 1-888/635-7272, ⊕www.papillon.com) and **Maverick** (℡928/638-2622, ⊕www .maverickhelicopter.com). They typically fly three standard routes: a half-hour western tour, straight across the canyon and back a few miles west of the village, for around $125 per adult ($90 per child); a forty-minute eastern tour, flying along the rim as far as the confluence of the Colorado and Little Colorado rivers, for roughly $145 ($100); and a fifty-minute loop trip that combines the two by flying across the forest of the North Rim, for perhaps $170 ($120). In addition, Papillon also runs amazing $555 day-trips to the Havasupai reservation, described on p.346.

The main **airplane** or "fixed-wing" tour operators at Tusayan are **Air Grand Canyon** (℡928/638-2686 or 1-800/247-4726, ⊕www.airgrandcanyon.com) and **Grand Canyon Airlines** (℡928/638-2359 or 1-866/235-9422, ⊕www.grandcanyonairlines.com). Such tours can cover much greater distances than helicopter companies, but are obliged to fly at least one thousand feet above rim level, and thus tend not to offer quite such good views. Fixed-wing tour prices are lower, ranging from $85 per adult ($55 per child) for a half-hour up to about $200 ($105) for ninety minutes.

Whitewater rafting

Places on commercial whitewater rafting trips tend to be reserved as much as a year in advance. Such trips vary in length from three days to three weeks, with the main choice being whether to cut the 300-mile voyage from Lees Ferry to Diamond Creek in half by leaving or joining the expedition at Phantom Ranch. An estimated 161 sets of rapids interrupt the full route. You can also choose between a quieter, slower oar-powered trip or a motorized expedition; both tend to cost around $225 per person, per day. A list of authorized operators, most of whom offer trips of both kinds and of varying lengths, appears below; you can also find the current list online at ⊕www .nps.gov/grca/planyourvisit/river-concessioners.htm.

It's also possible to arrange your own expedition, but the demand for that is so great that the park service runs a hugely intricate lottery to determine who gets to go, detailed on the park website.

No **one-day** rafting trips are available within Grand Canyon National Park. There are two alternatives, however, one at either end of the canyon. Colorado River Discovery, based in Page, Arizona, offers one-day trips that start below **Glen Canyon Dam** and finish at **Lees Ferry** ($70; ℡928/645-9175 or 1-888/522-6644, ⊕www.raftthecanyon .com), while further west, the tribal-run Hualapai River Runners arranges pricey one-day trips on the Hualapai Reservation, starting at Diamond Creek ($328; ℡928/769-2219 or 1-888/255-9550, ⊕www.destinationgrandcanyon.com).

ranging from shuttle bus stops and overlooks to the visitor center or the canyon rim in the village. All are free, and well worth attending.

In addition to the plaza, further **information desks** can be found at Kolb Studio, Yavapai Observation Station (see p.328), Tusayan Museum (see p.338), and Desert View (see p.338). For details of the **Backcountry Office**, which issues permits for backpacking and camping in the canyon, see p.339.

Most of these places, as well as several lodges and souvenir stores, sell a wide range of **books** about the canyon, including the comprehensive *Rough Guide: Grand Canyon*, as well as guides to the various hiking trails. None of the free **maps** on offer is adequate for backcountry hiking, so invest in the detailed hiking maps produced by Earthwalk Press (*Bright Angel Trail*; $9.95) or National Geographic–Trails Illustrated (*Grand Canyon National Park*; $9.95). For even greater resolution, get hold of the appropriate **US Geological Survey** quadrant map, each of which covers a square measuring seven miles by seven (☎1-888/275-8747, ⓦwww.usgs.gov).

Getting around the South Rim

Grand Canyon Village is always accessible to private vehicles and so, too, is the road **east** from the village to Desert View. Both the road **west** from the village to Hermit's Rest, however, and the short access road to **Yaki Point**, east of Mather Point, are only open during the months of December, January, and February. You're almost certain, therefore, to use one of the park's three free **shuttle bus** routes.

The first of these, the **Village Route**, loops between Grand Canyon Village and the information plaza, also stopping at *Maswik* and *Yavapai* lodges and the campground, from an hour before sunrise until 11pm in summer, 10pm otherwise. The second, the **Kaibab Trail Route**, connects the information plaza with Yaki Point, from an hour before sunrise until an hour after sunset. A quicker early-morning **Hikers Shuttle** service runs direct to Yaki Point from *Bright Angel Lodge* and the Backcountry Information Center; see *The Guide* for current hours. Finally, from March until November, buses follow the eight-mile **Hermit's Rest Route** road west of the village to eight different canyon overlooks, again from before sunrise until after sunset. You can get on and off as often as you choose. Park **bus tours** for a fee are detailed on p.326, while a 24-hour **taxi** service can be reached on ☎928/638-2822.

Grand Canyon Village and around

For almost a century after the *El Tovar Hotel* opened in 1905, at the heart of what became **GRAND CANYON VILLAGE**, most South Rim visitors got their first glimpse of the canyon from the rim-edge footpath alongside the hotel. These days, your initiation may well come at **Mather Point** instead, near the information plaza two miles east. That's no cause for regret; the sweeping canyonscape visible from there is far more comprehensive than any from the village.

Mather Point faces northeast, toward Bright Angel Canyon on the far side, which is the route followed by the North Kaibab Trail down from the North Rim (see p.355). Two other rim-to-river trails can be spotted closer at hand. To the east, the South Kaibab Trail zigzags down from Yaki Point, while the further west of the two visible stretches of the Colorado River marks the point where it's reached by the Bright Angel Trail. From there, the trail heads east to Phantom Ranch, which is also visible, nestling close to the other tiny patch of river.

Turn left and walk west for ten minutes from Mather Point to reach **Yavapai Point**, where as well as similar long-range views that now take in two different segments of the river, you'll find the **Yavapai Observation Station** (daily; hours vary from 8am–8pm in summer down to 8am–5pm in winter; free), in which displays explain how the canyon may have been formed. A further ten minutes' walk west brings you within sight of the village.

Grand Canyon Village is located at the inner end of a large, curving "alcove" that cuts into the rim, with a long, rising promontory to either side. As a result, from the paved, railed terrace that follows the rim for the length of the village you can only see straight across the canyon. Down below, the Bright Angel Trail

▲ Mather Point, South Rim

threads through the oasis of Indian Gardens before disappearing into a deep crevice, while another long trail leads across the flat, pale-green Tonto Platform to Plateau Point. Although the mighty walls of the Inner Gorge – the granite chasm that holds the Colorado – are visible on the far side, you can't see their full 1300ft depth, and the river remains out of sight at the bottom. *Grand Canyon Lodge*, on the North Rim, is visible however, though you're only likely to spot it after dark, when the lights come on.

The original core of Grand Canyon Village, consisting of self-consciously rugged log-and-boulder buildings such as the *El Tovar* hotel and the Kolb photographic studio, has since been joined by less attractive but stylistically similar structures; the whole place is carefully laid out to avoid seeming too crowded. Tucked away in the woods across the road, well back from the canyon, lie several more lodges, stores, restaurants, and the campground, together with the well-hidden residential area used by park employees.

Seven miles from Grand Canyon Village, a mile south of the park entrance, **TUSAYAN** is an unattractive strip-mall that holds nothing of interest beyond an IMAX cinema which continuously runs a mildly entertaining 35-minute movie on the canyon (daily: March–Oct 8.30am–8.30pm; Nov–Feb 10.30am–6.30pm; $12, $9 under-11s).

Accommodation

Roughly two thousand **guest rooms** are available close to the South Rim: half of them in and around **Grand Canyon Village**, and a further thousand in Tusayan. Given the choice, the best place to stay has to be on the very lip of the canyon, but very few rooms indeed enjoy canyon views, and they tend to be booked as much as two years in advance. In fact, for most of the summer it's very unusual for any same-day bookings to be available in the park. While the more basic in-park lodges, away from the rim, still make more convenient bases than Tusayan, the hotels in Tusayan do tend to be more modern and better equipped. On the other hand, some of the rates available inside the park represent extraordinarily good value.

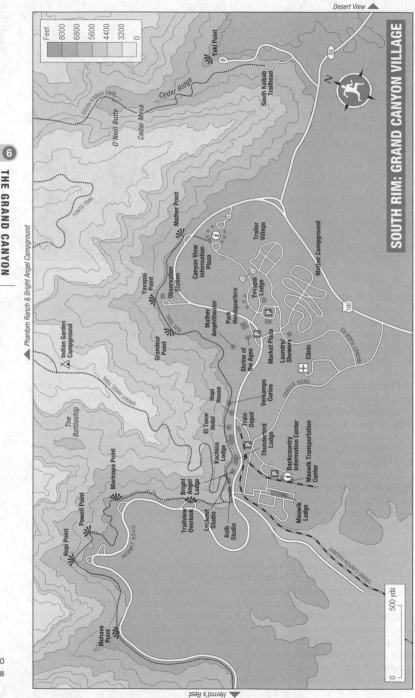

SOUTH RIM: GRAND CANYON VILLAGE

Feet
8000 6800 5600 4400 3200 0

Desert View

N

Yaki Point

Cedar Ridge

SOUTH KAIBAB TRAIL

O'Neill Butte

Cedar Mesa

South Kaibab Trailhead

TONTO TRAIL

Mather Point

Phantom Ranch & Bright Angel Campground

Indian Garden Campground

Canyon View Information Plaza

Trailer Village

Yavapai Point

Observation Station

RIM TRAIL

Mather Amphitheater

Yavapai Lodge

Park Headquarters

Market Plaza

Mather Campground

180

Tusayan

BRIGHT ANGEL TRAIL

Grandeur Point

Shrine of the Ages

Laundry/ Showers

Clinic

CENTER ROAD

The Battleship

Hopi House

Verkamps Curios

El Tovar Hotel

Train Depot

Thunderbird Lodge

Backcountry Information Center

Maswik Transportation Center

Maricopa Point

Kachina Lodge

Bright Angel Lodge

Trailview Overlook

Lookout Studio

Kolb Studio

Maswik Lodge

HERMIT ROAD

Powell Point

Hopi Point

GRAND CANYON RAILWAY

Mohave Point

500 yds

0

Hermit's Rest

Williams

All South-Rim accommodation options within Grand Canyon National Park are run by **Xanterra**. For all **reservations** for lodges or RV camping at Grand Canyon Village, and for Phantom Ranch, contact Xanterra (same-day ☎928/638-2631, advance 303/297-2757 or 1-888/297-2757, Ⓦwww.grandcanyonlodges.com).

If you are stuck, other possibilities include **Cameron** (see p.353), **Flagstaff** (p.285), and **Williams** (p.308).

In Grand Canyon Village

Bright Angel Lodge Individual "rustic" but comfortable log cabins, clustered around an imposing 1935 lodge that also holds some more basic rooms, many sharing bathrooms. Best of all is the Bucky O'Neill Suite, which has two front doors opening right onto the rim. Lodge rooms and historic cabins ❹, Rim Cabins ❻, Bucky O'Neill Suite ❾

El Tovar Hotel Log-built canyon-edge hotel, named for an early Spanish explorer, that has since 1905 exuded both rough-hewn charm and elegant sophistication. Only three suites enjoy extensive canyon views; the rest of the 78 tasteful rooms come in two sizes, but almost all hold only one bed. ❼, suites ❾

Kachina Lodge Anonymous but perfectly adequate motel-style rooms in a low two-story block, near the rim and run in conjunction with *El Tovar*. A few upstairs rooms offer canyon views. ❼

Maswik Lodge Larger complex, a few minutes' walk from the rim at the southwest end of the village. Two distinct blocks of motel-style rooms – *Maswik North* is considerably nicer than the small, cramped *Maswik South* – plus basic summer-only cabins, some of which sleep up to four guests. South ❹, North ❼

Thunderbird Lodge Long, low, box-like lodge that shares the lobby of, and is run with, *Bright Angel Lodge*. Well-equipped if characterless rooms, separated by twenty yards of grass from the canyon edge; a few have views. ❼

Yavapai Lodge 350 reasonable rooms in two quiet motel-type buildings, well back from the rim in the woods. By far the most likely to have availability at short notice, *Yavapai* closes either partially or completely according to demand in low season. ❺

In Tusayan

Best Western Grand Canyon Squire Inn 100 Hwy-64 ☎928/638-2681 or 1-800/622-6966, Ⓦgrandcanyonsquire.com. Tusayan's most lavish option, with outdoor pool, indoor spa, and bowling alley. Spacious and comfortable, if not all that characterful. ❻

The Grand Hotel Hwy-64 ☎928/638-3333 or 1-888/634-7263, Ⓦthe-grand-hotel-grand-canyon.pacificahost.com. Smart modern hotel; the rooms themselves are no better than elsewhere, but the indoor pool is nice, and it's home to a decent restaurant. ❼

Red Feather Lodge 106 Hwy-64 ☎928/638-2414 or 1-888/561-2425, Ⓦredfeatherlodge.com. Long-established motel with adjoining large new hotel

Camping on and around the South Rim

Tent and RV camping (without hookups) is available at the park service's year-round **Mather Campground**, south of the main road through Grand Canyon Village. Sites for up to two vehicles and six people cost $18 per night between March and mid-November, when it's possible, and strongly recommended, to make a reservation (☎1-877/444-6777, Ⓦwww.reservations.nps.gov). No reservations are accepted between mid-November and February, when sites are first-come, first-served, and the fee drops to $15 per night. The adjacent **Trailer Village** consists exclusively of RV sites with hookups, costing $30 per site per night for two people, plus $2 extra for each additional adult; reserve on ☎303/297-2757 or Ⓦwww.grandcanyonlodges.com. In summer, additional first-come, first-served, camping sites, without hookups, are on offer 25 miles east of Grand Canyon Village at the **Desert View Campground** (mid-May to mid-Oct; no reservations; $12).

Outside the park, the Kaibab National Forest runs the minimally equipped, first-come, first-served, **Ten-X Campground** (mid-April to Sept; no hookups or showers; $10 per night), two miles south.

block, sharing a pool; the newer rooms are pretty good. ⑥
Seven Mile Lodge 56 Powell Ave ☎ 928/638-2291. Tusayan's last little roadside motel; very plain and unadorned and the least expensive option

around. No reservations are accepted; rooms are simply given out from 9am daily. Despite the slight premium charged for housing three or four guests in the same room, it's still great value for groups of (close) friends. ④

Eating and drinking

Grand Canyon Village offers a reasonably wide choice of places to **eat**, and prices in the budget cafeterias are not bad. Summer crowds can lead to endless queueing, however, and it's worth bringing at least some food with you. A few stores – notably the Canyon Village Marketplace, which has a pretty good **deli counter** (summer daily 7am–6pm, otherwise daily 8am–5pm) – sell basic supplies. Tusayan holds several fast-food options in addition to the places listed below.

Both the *Bright Angel* and the *El Tovar* have atmospheric, traditional **bars** open until 11pm nightly, while *Maswik Lodge* has a "sports lounge" with big-screen TV.

Arizona Steakhouse *Bright Angel Lodge*. Informal, good-quality restaurant, a few yards from the rim but with no views to speak of, specializing in conventional meat and seafood entrees at $14–25. No reservations accepted, so you may have to wait two hours or more. Daily 11.30am–3pm (summer only) & 4.30–10pm. Closed early Jan to mid-Feb.
Bright Angel Restaurant *Bright Angel Lodge*. Straightforward, windowless diner that serves pretty much anything you might want, from snacks and salads for under $10 to steaks at around $15. No reservations, daily 6.30am–10pm.
Canyon Coffee House *Bright Angel Lodge*. Early-morning organic coffees and scones, served in the *Bright Angel's* bar. Daily 5.30–11am.
Canyon Star *Grand Hotel*, Tusayan ☎ 928/638-3333. Large, attractive hotel restaurant, where dinner is a choice between "hardy ranch fare," like $30 steaks or $18 ribs, or lighter salads and fish dishes. Lunchtime salads, sandwiches, and Mexican staples mostly cost under $10.

"Native American Experience" dances at 6.30pm and 8pm nightly. Daily 7–10am, 11am–2pm, & 5–9pm.
El Tovar *El Tovar Hotel* ☎ 928/638-2631 ext 6432. Grand, classy, and expensive dining room, looking out over the canyon; reservations, accepted for dinner only, tend to be grabbed days in advance. The food itself is very rich, especially at dinner, when entrees, such as roast duck or veal scallopini, cost $21–35. Appetizers, like deviled crab cakes or Navajo blue-corn tamales, are a bit more imaginative. Daily 6.30am–10pm.
Maswik Cafeteria *Maswik Lodge*. Self-service fast food, with separate Mexican and Italian sections as well as burgers and standard plate lunches. Breakfast can come in under $5, but lunch and dinner entrees are closer to $10. Daily 6am–10pm.
Yavapai Cafeteria *Yavapai Lodge*. Large cafeteria that's slightly preferable to the *Maswik's* for its salad bar and fried chicken – and with slightly lower prices for burgers and daily specials. Summer daily 6am–9pm, spring and fall daily 7am–8pm, shorter hours and probable closures in low season.

Other in-park facilities

Bank In Market Plaza, with a 24hr ATM machine. Mon–Thurs 9am–5pm, Fri 9am–6pm.
Camping equipment Can be bought or rented at the Canyon Village Marketplace. Daily: summer 7am–8.30pm, spring & fall 8am–8pm, winter 8am–7pm.
Travelers with disabilities The *Accessibility Guide*, available at all visitor centers and lodges, provides full accessibility details; for further information, call ☎ 928/638-2631 or look online at ⓦ www.nps.gov/grca. At either park entrance

station, you can request a permit to park at the Canyon View Information Plaza. Once there, you can obtain a further permit enabling you to drive on Hermit Road. Most shuttle buses cannot accommodate wheelchairs; request an accessible bus by calling ☎ 928/638-0591 two days in advance.
Gas The closest gas stations to the South Rim are in Tusayan and at Desert View.
Internet access Wi-fi access at all lodges; free public computers in Park Headquarters.

Laundromat Near *Mather Campground*. Daily: summer 6am–11pm; spring and fall 7am–9pm; winter 8am–6pm.
Medical help Call ☎911 for emergencies; ☎928/638-2551 for the village clinic (daily 8am–6pm; emergencies only at other times); ☎928/638-2460 for the pharmacy; and ☎928/638-2395 for dentist.

Post office In the Market Plaza. Mon–Fri 9am–4.30pm, Sat 11am–1pm; lobby, with stamp machines, daily 5am–10pm.
Showers Coin-operated showers, available to all visitors, are located in the laundromat building (hours as above).

Hermit Road

The eight-mile, dead-end scenic drive officially known as **Hermit Road** – and also unofficially as the **West Rim Drive** – starts a hundred yards west of *Bright Angel Lodge*, just as Grand Canyon Village peters out. Offering a succession of very different but consistently impressive canyon panoramas, it's the most obvious, and most enjoyable, half-day sightseeing trip from the village. As the only vehicles allowed access in summer are the free Hermit's Rest Route **shuttle buses**, detailed on p.326, the Xanterra bus tours, and those displaying disabled permits, it also makes a welcome escape from the crowds and traffic elsewhere along the rim.

While for most of its length the road runs within a few yards of the canyon, it's paralleled, as ever, by the **Rim Trail**, even closer to the edge. No one walks

Sunset and sunrise

"What's the best place to watch the sunset?" is probably the single question Grand Canyon park rangers most tire of being asked. There is no best place, neither for sunset, nor for sunrise. How could there be? Each rim of the canyon is almost three hundred miles long. Every yard of the way, the views are different, while the weather, cloud cover and visibility change every day.

That said, the Grand Canyon *does* look especially dramatic at the start and end of each day. When the sun is high in the sky, the colors tend to be bleached out, and heat and dust diminish visibility. By contrast, when the sun is low, the rich reds and oranges of the sandstone formations emerge, etched against sharp black shadows, and the whole spectacle can be simply stunning.

It's definitely worth ensuring that you're at a major canyon viewpoint as sunset approaches, and, to a lesser extent, at dawn. On the South Rim, that means getting away from the village itself, which does not command long-range canyon views to either east or west. Ideally, it's best to have both, at somewhere like Hopi, Mohave or Pima points to the west, or Yavapai, Yaki or Desert View to the east. The most popular spots tend to be Hopi Point for the sunset and Yavapai for sunrise; the down side of that, however, is that often a thousand or more people cram into those single small areas at the relevant moment. It's always better to play things by ear, and simply hope to find a quiet area where you can wander at will, rather than jostle for position. Ghostione Point is strongly recommended; because it's a twenty-minute walk from the nearest road, it rarely sees more than a handful of visitors.

Finally, bear in mind that it's not the sunset that's the spectacle, it's the canyon; if you aim to arrive five minutes before the precise time the sun goes down, you'll see very little. To illuminate anything within the canyon itself, the sun has to be significantly above the horizon, so the finest viewing comes in the final hour or so before sunset, and it comes from looking east, away from the sun and towards those buttes and temples that continue to catch direct sunlight, not west into the shadows. Similarly, it doesn't matter if you miss the moment of dawn; it's the ensuing hour, in which the rising sun picks out the pinnacles one by one, that will live in your memory.

The return of the condor

Of all the awesome spectacles along the South Rim, few can match the sight of a fully grown **California condor** soaring on the canyon updrafts. These magnificent birds, with a wingspan of more than nine feet and a lifespan of up to sixty years, were reintroduced to Arizona in 1996. They can frequently be seen hovering above Grand Canyon Village, or perching just below the rim.

The birds were native to the canyon, and indeed to most of North America, for thousands of years, but their population was dwindling long before the first Europeans arrived. The last condor in the Grand Canyon area was recorded as nesting near Lees Ferry in the 1890s, while a solitary bird was seen circling Williams in 1924. During the 1980s, the last remaining 22 individuals of the species were trapped in California. A captive breeding program reintroduced the birds first in California, and subsequently in northern Arizona. At the Arizona release site, located on the Vermilion Cliffs fifty miles northeast of the South Rim – see p.355 – scientists keep contact between condors and humans to a minimum, so the birds don't learn to associate humans with food. Condors are very inquisitive creatures, however, and to the delight of tourists almost all the Arizona birds spend much of their time near the village. Project workers and park rangers discourage them from approaching too close, and leave animal carcasses out for them in remote places. These natural scavengers also manage to find carrion by themselves.

Progress has been slow but certain. Around sixty free-flying, but tagged and monitored, condors now live in the Grand Canyon. For the latest news, call in at park visitor centers, or contact the Peregrine Fund (☎928/355-2270, ⓦwww.peregrinefund.org).

the entire eight miles, but since you can get on and off the bus at any of eight designated stops, the ideal way to explore is to combine shuttle bus rides with stretches of **walking**. Traveling the full length of Hermit Road without getting off the bus takes about ninety minutes. To allow for a couple of short hikes, and a stop at Hermit's Rest, give yourself perhaps three hours. Alternatively, you need never get on a bus at all; the four-mile round-trip hike from the village to Hopi Point, for example, takes under two hours. And finally, **cycling** is permitted year-round.

The first two viewpoints along the way, known as **Trailview I** and **II**, show prospective Bright Angel Trail hikers (see p.340) exactly what they're in for, with its red-dirt switchbacks clearly etched against the canyon walls below. After just over a mile, as you round the corner to pass out of sight of Grand Canyon Village, the railed, rocky overlook at **Maricopa Point** commands an almost 360° view, though only the tiniest sliver of the churning Colorado is visible. This is a prime spot for identifying the majestic buttes on the far side of the river, such as the Brahma and Zoroaster "temples," each with its capping layer of hard red sandstone.

Beyond Maricopa, road and trail alike have long detoured inland around relics of the **Orphan Mine**, which started out mining copper in 1893 but became America's largest uranium producer in the 1950s. Production stopped in 1969, and the mine was acquired by the park in 1988. As this book went to press, the ruins were finally being cleared away. At the far end, **Powell Point** marks the spot where the park was officially dedicated on April 30, 1920, and holds a memorial to the crews of John Wesley Powell's two Colorado expeditions (see p.433).

Beneath the curved terrace at **Hopi Point**, two miles out from the village and the busiest of the western viewpoints, several distinct stretches of the Colorado are exposed to view. The most dramatic lies immediately below Plateau Point (see p.341), the last few yards of the trail to which are also visible. It's hard to believe that the river is 350ft wide down there, lying at the foot of gnarled and impossibly ancient walls of black schist, streaked through with vertical pink faults. To the west, the river threads its tortuous way toward the ocean between interleaved spurs of red rock, and a maze of lesser canyons twists among the mighty buttes.

Road and trail curve gracefully west of Hopi Point for three-quarters of a mile to **Mohave Point**, a large railed promontory from which the long-range vista remains substantially unchanged. **Pima Point** is four miles further on, beyond a sheer-walled recess known as **The Abyss**. The river is by now less than two miles from the South Rim – look almost straight down to admire the three-quarter-mile Granite Rapid – but from the far bank it's another twelve labyrinthine miles to the North Rim.

Hermit Road ends slightly over a mile beyond Pima Point, at the **Hermit's Rest** way station, appealingly laid out in 1914 to evoke the dwelling of some imaginary canyon prospector, which sells gifts and simple snacks (daily: summer 8am–7.30pm; otherwise 9am–sunset). **Hermit Trail**, abandoned by the Santa Fe Railroad in 1931 but still popular with inner-canyon hikers (see p.343), starts a short way further along.

Desert View Drive

Desert View Drive, which runs for 23 miles east from Mather Point to Desert View itself, just inside the park's eastern boundary, is the one part of the South Rim that's open year-round for self-guided driving tours. Allow two hours at the very least to get to the end and back.

The first lookout along the way, **Yaki Point**, is accessible in your own vehicle only between December and February, though it's served year-round by free shuttle buses. Two miles east of Yavapai Point, it commands much the same

▲ California condor, seen from the South Kaibab Trail

trans-canyon views as its neighbor. The most prominent of several inner-canyon trails on show is the **South Kaibab Trail** (see p.342), which starts its quickfire descent to Phantom Ranch from its own separate parking lot nearby. From the main overlook, you can spot it far below, switchbacking down an exposed scree slope of red rock between two buttes. Scramble out onto the rocks beyond the viewpoint for clearer views down to the trail's principal staging post, O'Neill Butte.

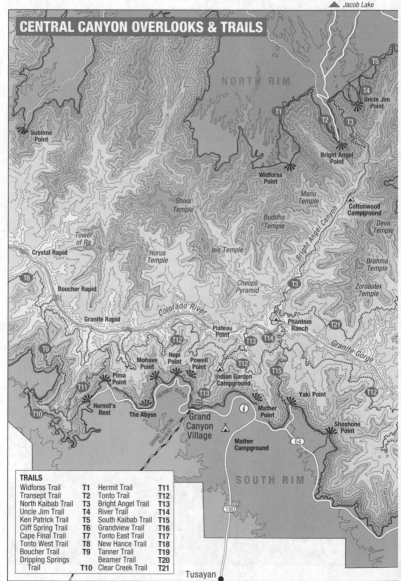

▲ Jacob Lake

CENTRAL CANYON OVERLOOKS & TRAILS

NORTH RIM

SOUTH RIM

Colorado River

Granite Gorge

Bright Angel Canyon

Williams & Flagstaff

TRAILS

Widforss Trail	**T1**	Hermit Trail	**T11**
Transept Trail	**T2**	Tonto Trail	**T12**
North Kaibab Trail	**T3**	Bright Angel Trail	**T13**
Uncle Jim Trail	**T4**	River Trail	**T14**
Ken Patrick Trail	**T5**	South Kaibab Trail	**T15**
Cliff Spring Trail	**T6**	Grandview Trail	**T16**
Cape Final Trail	**T7**	Tonto East Trail	**T17**
Tonto West Trail	**T8**	New Hance Trail	**T18**
Boucher Trail	**T9**	Tanner Trail	**T19**
Dripping Springs		Beamer Trail	**T20**
Trail	**T10**	Clear Creek Trail	**T21**

Shoshone Point, a couple of miles east of Yaki Point, is the least-known and least-visited of the South Rim viewpoints, for the simple reason that it's only accessible on **foot**, along an easy one-mile trail from Desert View Drive. It's an absolute gem of a place, offering beautiful views along with an unparalleled sense of peace and privacy. The trail to Shoshone Point begins from an unpaved parking lot 1.4 miles east of the turn-off to Yaki Point; look for a silver gate barring a dirt road, and a brown park notice reading "Site Use by Permit Only."

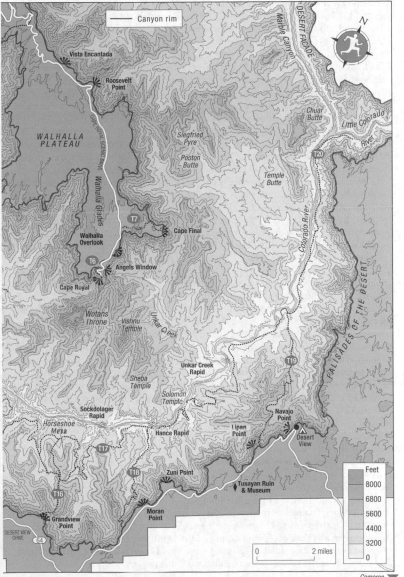

The sign is there because the park service does not publicize Shoshone Point to casual visitors, as it's used for weddings in summer, but there's no system for issuing permits to hikers. Instead, you're simply asked to respect the privacy of any group that may be out there, and not to hike out at all if there are a lot of cars at the parking lot. The point itself is truly spectacular. A solitary pale hoodoo marks the tip of its slender neck, while the sublime views range along the full panoply of the North Rim.

Eight miles east of Yaki Point, a total of twelve miles out from the village, **Grandview Point** was where Europeans first saw the Grand Canyon, in 1540 (see p.343). It's suggested that their Hopi guides deliberately led them to a spot from which no trails were visible, to make the canyon appear even more impassable. Grandview was also the place where Grand Canyon tourism first took off, after prospector Peter Berry constructed the Grandview Trail down to his Last Chance copper mine in 1892, and visitors began to gravitate to the site. In terms of views, it's inarguably superior to Grand Canyon Village. The Colorado makes a broad and langorous entrance off to the east before disappearing westwards into the stunning sandstone labyrinth, while down below the twin prongs of **Horseshoe Mesa** reach out toward the North Rim.

Tusayan Ruin, ten miles further east, in the forest south of the highway (and not to be confused with modern Tusayan), is what remains of a genuine **Ancestral Puebloan pueblo**. One of two thousand known such sites in the Grand Canyon area, it's not comparable in scale to relics elsewhere in the Southwest, but its very existence enabled President Theodore Roosevelt to accord National Monument status to the entire Grand Canyon. Only low stone walls survive of the original complex of buildings, occupied for perhaps 25 years by a group of up to thirty people, around 1185 AD. A small museum (daily 9am–5pm; free) holds displays on the contemporary Navajo and Hopi, as well as 4000-year-old twig figurines and Ancestral Puebloan pottery found nearby.

Desert View, 25 miles east of Grand Canyon Village, is the last viewpoint along Desert View Drive. As Hwy-64, however, the road continues another 34 miles to meet US-89 at Cameron (see p.353), so Desert View also provides visitors approaching from the east with their *first* opportunity to see what all the fuss is about. To the north, four miles distant, the Colorado River can be seen approaching its sudden westward turn. Just north of its last visible curve lies the confluence of the Colorado and Little Colorado rivers. The stark cliffs known as the **Palisades of the Desert** delineate the South Rim, while above them the pallid plains of the **Marble Plateau** stretch to the horizon, beneath an overwhelming sky. Sixty-five million years ago, this entire landscape was buried beneath an additional four or five thousand feet of sandstone. Thanks to erosion, all that remains are a few tiny vestiges, such as reddish **Cedar Mountain**, a mile or two back from the rim. Over to the west, the Colorado disappears deep into the Inner Gorge, engulfed on all sides by buttes and mesas, temples, shrines, and tabernacles.

Rather than the canyon itself, however, what immediately draws the eye is the remarkable **Desert View Watchtower** perched at its very lip, built in Ancestral Puebloan style by Mary Jane Colter in 1932. Stairs from the gift store at its base (daily 8am–7.30pm) climb through three circular chambers, decorated with authentic murals by the Hopi artist Fred Kabotie, as well as reproduction petroglyphs. Nearby stand an **information center** and bookstore (daily: summer 9am–7pm; spring and fall 9am–6pm; winter 9am–5pm); a **general store** (daily 9am–5pm); a **gas station** (daily: summer 9am–6pm; winter 9am–5pm); and a gift store-cum-**snack bar** (daily 7.30am–6pm). The **Desert View Campground** (see p.331) is at the end of a short spur road from the gas station.

South Rim hikes: into the canyon

Hiking any of the trails that descend into the Grand Canyon offers more than just another view of the same thing. Instead you pass through a sequence of utterly different landscapes, each with its own climate, wildlife, and topography. However, while the canyon can offer a wonderful wilderness experience, it's a hostile and very unforgiving environment, grueling even for expert hikers.

Park rangers have one simple message for all would-be hikers: **Don't try to hike to the river and back in one day**. It might not look far on the map, but it's harder than running a marathon. Several hikers each year die in the attempt, and several hundred more receive emergency medical treatment. If you do want to reach the Colorado, it's best to reserve campgrounds for two nights, so you have a day to recover before the trek out.

The South Rim is 7000 feet above sea level, an altitude that most people find fatiguing in itself. Furthermore, all hikes start with a long, steep descent – which can come as a shock to the knees – and unless you camp overnight you'll have to climb all the way back up again when you're hotter and wearier. As a rule of thumb, keep track of how much time you spend hiking down and allow twice that much to get back up again. Average summer temperatures inside the canyon exceed 100°F; to hike for eight hours in that sort of heat, you have to drink an incredible thirty pints of water. Always carry at least a quart per person – and much more if there are no water sources along your chosen trail. You must have food as well, as drinking large quantities without also eating can cause water intoxication. Ideally, the best seasons to hike are spring and fall.

Eight major trails lead into the canyon from the South Rim, but most either start from inaccessible places or are in poor condition. Traffic is heaviest on the **Bright Angel** and **South Kaibab** trails, the two **"Corridor Trails"** that link up in the gorge to lead to Phantom Ranch. They can be combined with the North Kaibab Trail to form a continuous route between the South and North rims. If you do want to hike from rim to rim, bear in mind that Transcanyon Shuttle runs from one to the other, so you can get back where you started (see p.356). The Corridor trails also offer the best **day-hikes** in the canyon; down

---

Backcountry camping

Backcountry camping below the canyon rim is by permit only, with permits costing $10, plus $5 per person per night. Applications are accepted in person, by mail (PO Box 129, Grand Canyon, AZ 86023), or by fax (Ⓕ 928/638-2125), but not by email or phone. Full details can be found online at Ⓦ www.nps.gov/grca, or in the park's free Backcountry Trip Planner newspaper.

All applications have to specify an exact itinerary, detailing where you'll spend each night – either named campgrounds or the wider-ranging "Use Areas" coded on official park maps, also available online. Between March and mid-November, there's a limit on the most popular trails of two nights per party per campsite.

Mailed or faxed applications are accepted for dates until the end of the fourth complete month after they're submitted; thus if you're planning a trip in the peak month of July, you'd better mail your application on March 1. To apply in person, turn up at either the **Backcountry Information Center**, in the Maswik Transportation Center near Maswik Lodge in Grand Canyon Village (daily 8am–noon & 1–5pm; Ⓣ 928/638-7875; or at the **North Rim Backcountry Office**, a quarter-mile north of the North Rim Campground (daily 8am–noon & 1–5pm; Ⓣ 928/638-7868). Even in peak season, your chances of a last-minute cancellation are pretty good. Your name is added to a waiting list, and each morning at 8am that day's cancellations are reassigned – though you have to be there on the spot to get one.

▲ Sunset at the South Rim

the Bright Angel Trail as far **Indian Garden**, or at most out to **Plateau Point**, and down the South Kaibab Trail to **Cedar Ridge**.

The Bright Angel Trail

By far the busiest inner-canyon hiking route – with mules as well as hikers – the **Bright Angel Trail** starts in Grand Canyon Village, alongside the wooden shack that once served as the Kolb photographic studio. An old Havasupai route, it was improved by miners a century ago, and then operated as a toll trail when the mines failed to prosper.

Although the side canyon immediately below the village makes access to the Tonto Platform relatively straightforward, it's still a long, hard climb. Most

day-hikers content themselves with walking to either of the two resthouses in the first three miles, but with an early start you should be able to manage the round trip of nine miles to Indian Garden, or even twelve miles to Plateau Point. In summer, you can obtain water along the trail and only need to carry one quart of water per person; in winter, when there is none, you should carry two. Only try to reach the river – 7.8 miles from the trailhead, with Phantom Ranch almost two miles beyond that – if you've reserved a campsite for the night.

The trail begins with a long, exposed set of switchbacks down the dry, rocky hillside, which changes from pale pink to sheer red. Two short tunnels punctuate its first mile. After another mile, you start to see more wildlife – deer, rodents, and the ubiquitous ravens – while various rock surfaces hold pictographs, all but obscured by graffiti. Both the basic 1930s **resthouses**, after 1.6 and 3.1 miles, have water in summer (May–Sept) and emergency phones, but only the 1.6-mile one has restrooms.

Beyond the second resthouse, a set of switchbacks known as **Jacob's Ladder** carry you down the sheer Redwall cliff, a major obstacle throughout almost the entire canyon. Then, finally, the trail starts to level out, and the vegetation gets greener, with yellow- and red-blossomed cacti scattered to either side. Soon you hear the astonishing sound of trickling water in Garden Creek, lined by dazzling green trees.

The spring at **Indian Garden**, 4.6 miles from the rim, is why this trail exists. Native peoples really did have a garden here, planted in prehistoric times and used by the Havasupai from around 1300 AD until the nineteenth century. Now this unexpected little oasis holds a ranger station, restrooms, separate camping and day-use areas, and a staging post for mules.

Plateau Point

From Indian Garden, the Bright Angel Trail continues to the river (see below), while the **Tonto Trail** runs both east and west along the flat, arid Tonto Platform. A spur trail off the Tonto Trail – reached by heading left at Indian Garden, crossing Garden Creek, and then turning right at an obvious intersection three-quarters of a mile along – threads its way out to **Plateau Point**, a superb overlook above the Inner Gorge from which it is not possible to descend any further. Constructed to give day-tripping mule riders a view of the river, this trail also makes an ideal route for hikers, who should allow at least eight hours for the full day-hike from the rim and back. Barren even by inner-canyon standards, the desert landscape is spectacular, with agave and yucca plants shooting up from the sandy soil, and the mighty red buttes and mesas of the canyon now framed against the blue sky.

Shortly after you get your first awesome glimpse of the black tumbling walls of the gorge, the trail comes to an end. Precariously perched on the rocky outcrops, you can see a long stretch of the dark-green Colorado, though both the bridges and Phantom Ranch lie out of sight around the next promontory to the east.

Devil's Corkscrew and the Colorado River

The continuation of the Bright Angel Trail beyond Indian Garden first drops through the fertile margins of Garden Creek, then switchbacks down the **Devil's Corkscrew**, hacked into the rock during the 1930s to create a shortcut to the river. Once beside the Colorado, dwarfed beneath thousand-foot walls of dark-gray granite, it undulates through sand dunes scattered with yucca and prickly pear.

Hikers can cross the river around a mile along, using the 1960s **Silver Bridge**; mules, which balk at the prospect of seeing the river between its slats, have to continue a little further. The 400ft **suspension bridge** they prefer was set in place in 1928, hanging from twin cables that were carried down the Kaibab Trail on the shoulders of 42 Havasupai. Not far away on the other side – though you'll have to cross Bright Angel Creek twice to reach it – is **Bright Angel Campground**, with **Phantom Ranch** a short distance up beyond.

The temperature at river level tends to be around 20°F higher than on the South Rim, and there's significantly less rainfall. The **ecology** down here has changed since Glen Canyon Dam was completed in the mid-1960s (see p.422). Previously, up to a million tons of earth and rock hurtled past Phantom Ranch each day. Now it's more like 40,000; trees that would previously have been swept away are establishing themselves, and fish that were perfectly adapted to such conditions are now becoming extinct.

Phantom Ranch

Bright Angel Creek flows down Bright Angel Canyon from the North Rim to meet the Colorado below Grand Canyon Village. John Wesley Powell named it in 1869, contrasting this "clear beautiful creek" with the muddy Dirty Devil River, upstream in Utah, and identified a small **Ancestral Puebloan ruin** that's still visible today.

This confluence now marks the only place where inner-canyon hikers and mule riders can not only cross the Colorado River but also camp and even sleep in a real bed at the bottom of the canyon. **Phantom Ranch**, beside Bright Angel Creek, consists of assorted cabins, corrals, and outbuildings clustered amid huge cottonwoods and fruit orchards around a central lodge.

First call on the fully equipped individual **cabins** (❹) goes to riders on the **mule trips** detailed on p.326, but they're also let to hikers when available, which is more likely in winter. Otherwise, hikers can get beds for $36 per night in one of the four ten-bunk, single-sex **dormitories** – two for men and two for women – with bedding, showers, towels, and soap provided. **Reservations** are essential; as for the South Rim lodges, they're handled by Xanterra (☎303/297-2757 or 1-888/297-2757, Ⓦwww.grandcanyonlodges.com). **Cancellations** are handed out first-come, first-served, at the *Bright Angel Lodge* early each morning. All supplies reach *Phantom Ranch* the same way you do, so family-style **meals** in its **restaurant** are expensive, a minimum of $18.50 for breakfast and up to $38 for dinner.

All **camping** at the beautiful *Bright Angel Campground*, a little closer to the Colorado, is by **permit** only, as detailed on p.339. Do not hike down without a reservation.

South Kaibab Trail

The **South Kaibab Trail**, the most direct route from the South Rim to Phantom Ranch, is never as busy as the Bright Angel Trail. And no wonder – taking just six miles to drop to the river, it's an even steeper haul, and the trailhead lies three miles east of the information plaza. If you plan to combine the Bright Angel and South Kaibab trails in hiking to and from Phantom Ranch, make the Kaibab the one you go *down*. Even if you can only spare the time for a short day-hike, however, you'll be rewarded by superb views.

The trail starts by descending slightly west of **Yaki Point**, but once past the end of the promontory it runs along the top of **Cedar Ridge**. This high crest surveys a thirty-mile stretch of the canyon in both directions and also faces straight up Bright Angel Canyon toward the North Rim. In the absence of any water en route, most hikers turn back after 1.5 miles. If you keep going, down a precipitous and very exposed slope, you meet the **Tonto Trail** 4.4 miles down. A long, if level, trek east enables backpackers to connect with the Grandview Trail (see below) but the obvious way to go is west. At a spot known as the **Tipoff**, a few hundred yards along, you're poised to plunge down into the Inner Gorge. The river, and the 1928 suspension bridge that leads to Phantom Ranch, are little more than a mile away. Alternatively, continue on the Tonto Trail for four miles to **Indian Garden** (see p.341), and climb back up to the village from there.

Grandview Trail

The **Grandview Trail**, down from Grandview Point (see p.338), was built during the 1890s to aid copper mining on **Horseshoe Mesa**, which remains littered with abandoned mine workings. Although it's possible, by connecting with other trails, to use the Grandview to reach the Tonto Platform and thus eventually the Colorado, it's not itself a rim-to-river route. Instead, the hike down to the mesa and back is a popular **day-hike**. That doesn't mean it's easy, however; now officially "unmaintained," it's a very demanding trail. Several of its switchbacks were constructed by inserting metal rods deep into the canyon wall, then covering them with juniper logs, stones, and dirt. At times it can be a little hair-raising, but it has stayed surprisingly sturdy for over a century. Reckon on six hours for the whole round trip.

Hermit Trail

Named in honor of Louis Boucher, a nineteenth-century prospector, the **Hermit Trail** is another unmaintained trail. Built in 1912 by Fred Harvey for mule riders from the *El Tovar* and abandoned in 1931, much of its engineering remains in good shape. It's now used mainly by solitary types, setting off on long backcountry camping expeditions away from the crowds.

From the Hermit's Rest parking lot at the end of Hermit Road (see p.335), the trail drops into a side canyon, then switchbacks into Hermit Gorge and slowly descends a high rock wall far above Hermit Creek. A detour less than two miles along allows for the popular day-hike to **Dripping Spring**, not recommended for anyone with a fear of heights. Alternatively, if you press on, rockfalls tend to make for slow progress, but the resthouse at **Santa Maria Spring**, 2.3 miles down from the trailhead, is a lovely day-hike destination. Beyond that, views of the Inner Gorge eventually open up. The *Hermit Camp* is not far west of the junction with the Tonto Trail, 7.7 miles along. Turning right (north) shortly before the campground brings you to the Colorado itself, just under nine miles from the trailhead, at **Hermit Rapid**, where the wave-like surge of the river can reach over twenty feet high.

The Havasupai reservation

Havasu Canyon, one of the most spellbindingly beautiful places in the entire Southwest, nestles deep in the Grand Canyon a mere 35 miles west of the park headquarters. The only approach is from the southwest, however, so it's a road trip of almost two hundred miles; once you leave the interstate, the last ninety miles lie across the endless Coconino Plateau.

Those visitors who brave the eight-mile desert hike down into the canyon are rewarded by a stunning oasis of turquoise waterfalls and lush vegetation,

The Havasupai

The **Havasupai** – the "people of the blue-green water" – trace their occupation of Havasu Canyon back at least as far as 1300 AD. The word **"Pai"** means people and refers to a Yuman-speaking group that reached the Southwest via California well over a thousand years ago. They soon quarreled, splitting to form the **Hualapai** ("People of the Tall Pines") of northwest Arizona, and the **Yavapai** ("Almost-People," who no longer quite deserved to be regarded as people) who settled along the Colorado further south. The Hualapai established close links with Pueblo groups such as the Hopi and Zuñi, from whom they eventually acquired the art of raising sheep and horses, as well as the seeds and skills to grow such crops as peaches. Until the Havasupai were allocated their own reservation toward the end of the nineteenth century, they regarded themselves not as a separate "tribe" but as just another band of Hualapai.

Although the Havasupai took their name from the turquoise river that watered their fields, they only lived on the canyon floor in summer, in houses of hide-covered branches. In winter, the canyon made a cold, miserable home, lacking big game and wood for fuel and receiving as little as five hours of sunlight per day. Instead, the Havasupai moved up onto the plateau to hunt deer, elk, and antelope. Their territory extended beyond the San Francisco Peaks (near modern Flagstaff) and took in the region now occupied by Grand Canyon Village.

In the summer of 1776, as the Declaration of Independence was being signed in Philadelphia, the Havasupai welcomed their first white visitor. **Father Francisco Tomás Garcés**, a missionary from San Xavier del Bac near Tucson, was greeted by five days of feasting. Describing the Grand Canyon as a "calaboose of cliffs and canyons," he dubbed it the Puerto de Bucareli in honor of the Viceroy who had despatched him; more enduringly, he was the first to name the Río Colorado. Meanwhile, as Garcés explored the canyon, the rest of his expedition blazed a trail to California, where they founded San Francisco.

The Havasupai then remained undisturbed for eighty years, until Anglo prospectors and surveyors began to enter the region. Conflict arose in 1866, when Congress granted the Atlantic and Pacific Railroad company ownership of swathes of land adjoining its tracks across northern Arizona. Native resistance escalated into **war**, and the defeated Hualapai spent several years confined to a reservation near Ehrenberg on the Colorado. Because the Havasupai did not participate in the fighting, they were allowed to remain in their traditional territory. In negotiations over

a Shangri-La that has been home for centuries beyond record to the same small group of Native Americans. They're here thanks to a geological fluke; although the canyon receives only nine inches of rain each year, all the water that falls for three thousand square miles around funnels down into this one narrow gorge, to create the year-round torrent of Havasu Stream.

Havasu Canyon forms the heart of the **Havasupai reservation**, said by a 1930s anthropologist to be "the only spot in the United States where native culture has remained in anything like its pristine condition." Since then, tourism has become the mainstay of the tribal economy, but visitor numbers are kept deliberately low, at about 35,000 per year. Suggestions of building a road – or even a tramway – down into the canyon have always been rejected, to minimize the impact on the traditional way of life. Instead, the five hundred or so Havasupai earn their keep by ferrying nonhikers up and down the trail on horses and pack mules, and by operating a thriving **campground** beside the stream as well as a comfortable lodge in the village of **Supai**. Although visitors should not expect sweeping views of the Grand Canyon itself – or to have

the extent of a permanent Havasupai reservation, the US government was as usual only prepared to acknowledge Native American "ownership" of land that held permanent settlements and cultivated fields. Areas used for hunting, gathering, or even grazing, especially if use was shared by more than one band, was never included in reservations. Fearful of being deported themselves, the Havasupai settled in 1882 for a tiny 518-acre plot at the bottom of Havasu Canyon. Restricted to a fraction of their former range, they were obliged to farm as intensively as possible.

During the ensuing century of hardship, the Havasupai repeatedly petitioned to have their reservation enlarged. Suffering great spiritual uncertainty, both the Havasupai and Hualapai took part in the 1890s **Ghost Dance** movement, joining in trance-like rituals designed to ensure that white men would vanish from the land and the old ways would return. The Havasupai also briefly adopted the rain-making *kachina* dances of the Hopi (see p.78), until a catastrophic **flood** on January 1, 1910, destroyed their village, which then stood half a mile from its current site.

At first, the creation of **Grand Canyon National Park** placed yet more restrictions on Havasupai use of traditional lands. The Havasupai survived largely through disobeying whatever unenforceable regulations outsiders sought to impose, continuing to spend their winters up on the plateau. Many Havasupai in due course found jobs in Grand Canyon Village, while tourism to Havasu Canyon itself became an important element in the tribal economy.

After endless legal battles – and a lobbying campaign to persuade environmentalist groups that Native Americans could look after wilderness lands every bit as well as the Park Service – the Havasupai finally won their struggle in 1975. Almost 200,000 acres were added to the reservation, the largest tract of land ever returned to Native Americans. It came only just in time; almost immediately, the Grand Canyon region experienced a boom in **uranium** mining, with over 3500 claims filed in the Arizona Strip during the ensuing decade.

In 1988, Energy Fuels Nuclear was granted rights to develop a uranium mine to be known as **Canyon Mine**, at a site outside the reservation, close to **Red Butte** in the Kaibab National Forest, which is sacred to the Havasupai as *Mat Taav Tijundva*. The mine was built but never went into operation, due to a drop in prices caused by the worldwide glut of uranium. Havasupai fears that it could contaminate Havasu Stream, Havasu Canyon, and ultimately the Colorado itself, helped to trigger a joint resolution of Congress in 2008 that banned uranium mining from the Grand Canyon area.

much interaction with the tribal members – for spectacular desert scenery and sheer romance, the Havasupai reservation is beyond compare.

Getting to the reservation

The only way to reach the Havasupai reservation by road is from I-40, turning off at **Seligman** (see p.311), if you're coming from Flagstaff or Grand Canyon Village, or at **Kingman** (see p.311) from Las Vegas or California. Stock up with food, water, and gas when you leave the interstate, then follow Hwy-66 – the only surviving segment of **Route 66** not superseded by newer roads – to the poorly marked intersection with **Arrowhead Hwy-18**, six miles east of **Peach Springs** (see p.352).

Hwy-18 runs for its entire 56-mile length with barely a building in sight, across bare sagebrush desert interrupted by patches of thick ponderosa forest. It's paved throughout, and there's no possibility of losing your way. Eventually, the road winds down through burgeoning canyonlands to end at the large

Havasupai tours and excursions

An expensive but undeniably wonderful way to see Havasu Canyon if you're short on time is to take a one-day **helicopter** trip from Tusayan, just outside Grand Canyon Village on the South Rim, with Papillon Grand Canyon Helicopters (adults $555, under-12s $535; ☎702/736-7243 or 1-888/635-7272, ⊛www.papillon.com). While your flight from Tusayan won't take you over the main body of the Grand Canyon, the descent into Havasupai via assorted side canyons is an exhilarating adventure. Once you're on the ground, you can either ride to Havasu Falls and back, or hike; either way, there's time to linger by the various falls. Meals are not included. When lodge accommodation is available, it's also possible to stay overnight and fly back the next day.

In addition, various organizations offer **guided expeditions** to the reservation. Especially recommended is the Grand Canyon Field Institute (see p.326), which typically runs three four-day hiking and camping tours each summer, one of which is reserved for women only, for a fee of around $655 (☎928/638-2485 or 1-866/471-4435, ⊛grandcanyon.org/fieldinstitute).

Some commercial operators promise a more luxurious experience. Arizona Outback Adventures (☎480/945-2881 or 1-866/455-1601, ⊛www.aoa-adventures.com) offers two-, three-, and four-day trips with accommodation at their own "Base Camp." Various options including hiking and/or helicopter transport cost from $1297 up to $1696. Discovery Treks (☎520/404-1151 or 1-888/256-8731, ⊛discoverytreks.com) arranges three-day trips with a choice of hiking, horseback riding and helicopter rides, and camping or staying in the lodge. Prices range from $900 upwards.

plateau known as **Hualapai Hilltop**. Although this is no more than a small cluster of dilapidated shacks, there are usually far more vehicles parked here than you might anticipate for such a remote spot.

Hualapai Hilltop commands a long view of the white-walled **Hualapai Canyon**, cutting into the tablelands as it stretches away north. From the end of the parking lot, the Hualapai Trail to Supai zigzags steeply down the hillside to the right and can then be seen threading its way across the valley floor below. Do not attempt to go down unless you have already reserved accommodation.

Hikers are free to set off whenever they choose. If you prefer to **ride** down on either horse or mule, make a reservation when you book your accommodation. The mule train leaves the hilltop at some point between 10am and noon; if you arrive any later than noon, you won't be able to ride down, and you'll lose both your reservation and your deposit. To ride as far as the **village** costs $70 per person one-way and $120 round-trip, and should be arranged with the management of the lodge (☎928/448-2111); riding to the **campground** costs $75 one-way, $150 round-trip, and is arranged by the **Havasupai Tourist Enterprise** (☎928/448-2121 or 2141, ⊛havasupaitribe.com). Riders' baggage weighing over ten pounds has to be carried separately – one animal can carry up to four packs, again for $70 one-way, $120 round-trip – and many hikers also arrange to have their bags carried.

A **helicopter shuttle** service also operates between Hualapai Hilltop and Supai village. Schedules are posted on ⊛havasupaitribe.com. In recent years, it's been active between 10am and 1pm on Thurs, Fri, Sun, and Mon between mid-March and mid-October, and on Fri & Sun only between November and mid-March. Passengers are carried on a first-come, first-served basis, without any advance reservations, for a one-way fare of around $85. Call AirWest Helicopters on ☎623/516-2790 to check whether the service is currently operational.

The trail to Supai

Beyond its initial switchbacks, the **Hualapai Trail** is not especially difficult. It is, however, a long eight-mile walk, with no shade for the first three miles and no reliable water source until very near the end. Allow around three hours to reach Supai village (and four or more to come back up again), and be sure to carry enough food and water for a day in the desert.

The route is very obvious and kept busy throughout the day with small supply trains of mules and horses. Once on the valley floor, it follows the bed of a dry wash between red-rock walls that slowly but inexorably climb to form a deep, narrow canyon. The sand underfoot is so thick that it shifts at every step, but the potential for flash floods is clear from the much-scoured rocks to either side. Mighty boulders occasionally all but block the path, while solitary cottonwoods reach up toward the thin strip of sky overhead.

After almost seven miles, the trail reaches the intersection where Havasu Canyon comes in from the right; until 1910, this was the site of Supai village (see below). Do not continue straight ahead into Cataract Canyon at this point – it took three weeks to find a dehydrated camper who did so in 1975. Bear left instead, at a dense cluster of small trees. The sound of rushing water soon signals the emergence of Havasu Stream from hidden crevices in the rock; before long it's flowing through the parched landscape in all its blue-green splendor.

Not far beyond, you cross a low rise to be confronted by the meadow that holds the modern village, and the two red-rock pillars that watch over Supai from the high canyon wall on the far side. Known as the **Wigleeva**, these twin sentinels are regarded as the guardian spirits of the Havasupai.

Supai

Though located in a superb natural setting – a wide flat clearing surrounded on all sides by forbidding walls of red sandstone – the village of **SUPAI** is not in itself attractive. The Havasupai were only obliged to build a year-round settlement down in the canyon after losing their lands on the plateau above (see p.344), and this site was their second choice after the first proved prone to flooding. It too has suffered repeated damage ever since, most recently in the catastrophic flood of 2008. It therefore consists of just a scattering of basic timber-frame houses and prefabricated cabins. Even the name itself is a flimsy fabrication; "Supai" is a meaningless abbreviation of "Havasupai," invented by the US Post Office.

Once the Hualapai Trail, running alongside a line of irrigation ditches, has shepherded you into the village, the first building you come to holds the tribal **registration office**. Campers and lodge guests alike pay the $35 reservation **entrance fee** here. A back room holds a small **museum** (daily 7am–7pm; $1), with a reasonably interesting assortment of early twentieth-century photos and cuttings. Although the Havasupai are famous for crafts such as basketmaking, the museum can no longer afford ancient artifacts; instead, the finest old Havasupai baskets in Arizona are in Phoenix's Heard Museum (see p.229).

Fifty yards further on, beyond the only post office in the US still to receive its mail by pack mule, lies Supai's dusty, wind-blown **plaza**. Benches outside the village's one **grocery store** form its main social center, where the older Havasupai gather each evening. The younger set, together with a vast population of dogs, are more likely to be found on the terrace of the **café**, opposite. Once past that, the trail skirts the edge of the village school, then branches left down toward the campground. Visitors are forbidden to wander off the main trail into the farm lands around the village.

Practicalities

All visitors, whether planning to camp or stay in the lodge, must make advance reservations by calling either **Havasupai Tourist Enterprises** (☏928/448-2121 or 2141, ⓦhavasupaitribe.com) or the lodge. Space is at a premium in summer, and is often fully reserved several months in advance. All prices on the Havasupai Reservation are subject to an additional ten percent **tribal sales tax**.

Havasupai Lodge (☏928/448-2111 or 448-2201, ⓦhavasupaitribe.com; ❻) stands slightly apart from things on the edge of the village, close to the canyon wall behind the school. It's a simple two-story structure, much like a typical national park lodge, where the reasonable motel-style rooms are without phones or TVs. All sleep four people.

The *Lodge* has a pleasant little garden, but the only place to get a **meal** in Supai is at the *Tribal Café* (daily: hours vary from 6am–7pm in summer down to 8am–5pm in winter; ☏928/448-2981). Here the food is far from exciting, with fried breakfasts, and a lunch or dinner of beef stew, Indian fry-bread, or burritos; pretty much everything seems to cost $8, or more if you want grated cheese on top. The grocery store has a limited selection of processed items, all carried in by mule and priced accordingly. Both café and store accept credit cards.

Spending a night at the **campground** – see below – costs $17 per person.

Below Supai

All the **waterfalls** for which the Havasupai reservation is famous lie further down the canyon beyond Supai. The riverbed immediately below the village is forever being reshaped by flash floods and fresh erosion, and the first set of falls you come to, **Navajo Falls**, tend to look different one day to the next. You'll probably hear it thundering from the left about a mile and a half into your descent from the village. Clearings in the undergrowth at regular intervals should enable you to see their foaming white tumbling, but these days it's seldom possible to approach them any closer. The falls were named for Chief Navajo, who led the Havasupai at the time the reservation was established, and died in 1900.

Havasu Falls

Beyond Navajo Falls, the trail soon reaches the stupendous double cascade of **Havasu Falls**. First seen from an overlook more or less level with the top, this is an absolutely breathtaking sight. The stream foams white as it hurtles over a 150ft cliff, to crash into shallow terraces filled with perfectly clear turquoise water. The rock formations all around are formed from water-deposited limestone known as **travertine** – the same stuff that creates the stalactites of Carlsbad Caverns and clogs the inside of domestic kettles. It's the light travertine coating on the riverbed that gives the water its astonishing blue-green

---

Stop Press – 2008 Flash Flood

At the time this book went to press, all trails on the reservation were closed for reconstruction following a flash flood in August 2008, which necessitated the emergency evacuation of 406 tribal members and visitors. To check that they have reopened, access ⓦhavasupaitribe.com. The detailed trail descriptions given here may no longer be accurate; in particular, it may not currently be possible to descend alongside Mooney Falls and continue towards the river.

▲ Havasu Falls, Havasupai Indian Reservation

glow. Be sure not to walk barefoot on it, however; travertine is horrendously sharp stuff.

In the days when it was known to the park service as **Bridal Veil Falls**, Havasu Falls used to be a long broad expanse of water, which explains the solidified sheets and curtains of travertine that run right across its wide brim.

Then a flash flood punched out a notch right in the center, through which the falls now gush to either side of a small outcrop that's knitted together by a frail cottonwood sapling. Side trails off the main path lead down to an idyllic shaded "beach" beside the largest, deepest pool, where the ceaseless roar makes conversation difficult, but swimming is all but irresistible. On the far side of the natural travertine dams that divide the various terraces – partially reconstructed after a flood in 1993, using artificial groynes now buried beneath new deposits – picnic tables stand in a cottonwood grove at a side canyon's mouth.

It's possible to take a short **horseback tour** from Supai village down to Havasu Falls, at a cost of $60; for reservations, contact Havasupai Tourist Enterprise (see p.348).

The campground

A short distance beyond Havasu Falls, two miles down from Supai village, you finally reach the Havasu **campground**, set in an especially narrow and high-walled segment of the canyon. Once a tribal burial ground, this site was only added to the reservation in 1975, having originally been considered to be too rich in mineral deposits to be left to the Indians.

The campground stretches for almost a mile, with tents pitched in clearings in the woods to either side of the stream. Facilities are primitive in the extreme, with no showers or campfires, but it's a wonderful spot, with treatable drinking water provided by fresh springs in the canyon wall. Although villagers are barred from the area in summer by tribal edict, groups of horses stand tethered at the entrance, waiting to carry campers back up the hill.

Mooney Falls and the Colorado River

Havasu campground is brought to an abrupt end by the 200ft **Mooney Falls**. This natural barrier was long regarded as virtually impassable; its modern name comes from an unfortunate prospector who fell to his death here in 1880, after a rope snagged as he was being lowered to the bottom. Colorful stories that he dangled for three days before the rope broke are untrue, but it did take many months before his companions managed to retrieve his body, which lay by then beneath a coating of limestone.

The trail to the bottom remains difficult today. Assuming it has been repaired following the 2008 flood (see p.348), you can scramble down the travertine ledges to reach two successive tunnels, made by Mooney's cohorts, which drop through the cliff face. Next you'll come to a sheer section that was blasted away in the flood of 1993 and now consists of a vertical series of footholds, aided by an iron chain fixed into the rock. The prospect of having to climb back up is terrifying enough to make many hikers to turn back at this point; if you press on, there are also two steep ladders to contend with. Assuming you do make it to the bottom, the pools and swimming holes at the foot of the falls are once again gorgeous.

A long dayhike from the campground continues on for three miles to **Beaver Falls**, a quick-fire set of rapids that's as far as the Havasupai recommend any visitors should try to go. Negotiating an onwards route involves climbing up to and along a high ledge, after which it takes four more miles to reach the Colorado itself. Quite possibly, you'd be greeted by river-runners who preferred to get here the easy way, shooting 157 miles of whitewater from Lees Ferry (see p.354).

The Hualapai reservation: "Grand Canyon West"

Immediately west of the Havasupai reservation, and also inhabited by descendants of the Pai people, the **Hualapai Indian reservation** spreads across almost a million acres, bounded to the north by a 108-mile stretch of the Colorado River.

A cluster of overlooks above that river frontage is promoted as **Grand Canyon West**, or the "**West Rim**" of the Grand Canyon. While it's been tremendously hyped in the last few years, thanks to the construction of the glass-floored **Skywalk** over the canyon, it's very far from being a must-see attraction – and it's also extraordinarily **expensive** and time-consuming to visit. If you're an outdoors type, eager to immerse yourself in the magnificent desert wildernesses of the Southwest, this probably isn't for you. If you're happy to pay premium prices for a once-in-a-lifetime thrill, on the other hand, it may be.

It can't be emphasized enough that Grand Canyon West bears no relation to the canyon at its best. This far west, the canyon is starting to peter out; it lacks the colossal depth and width of its central section, and holds none of the towering mesas, buttes, and temples so conspicuous from the South or North Rim viewpoints. The so-called West Rim is really just a canny piece of marketing aimed at Las Vegas's 37 million annual tourists. This is the closest spot to Las Vegas where it's possible to see the Grand Canyon, and most of its visitors are day-trippers who don't realize this isn't the canyon proper. That said, the West Rim is undeniably an impressive spectacle, and offers several unique experiences, including helicopter flights down to the Colorado, and short river trips, as well as the Skywalk.

Getting to Grand Canyon West

Several companies fly day-trip **air** tours **from Las Vegas** to the rudimentary airstrip alongside the West Rim headquarters. *Papillon Grand Canyon Helicopters* (☎702/736-7243 or 1-888/635-7272, ⓦwww.papillon.com), *Maverick Helicopter Tours* (☎702/261-0007 or 1-888/261-4414, ⓦwww.maverickheli copter.com), and *Sundance Helicopters* (☎702/736-0606 or 1-800/653-1881, ⓦwww.helicoptour.com) provide **helicopter** tours at $250–500, while **fixed-wing** operators, using small airplanes, include *Scenic Airlines* (☎702/638-3200 or 1-800/634-6801, ⓦwww.scenic.com), whose cheapest Skywalk package costs $194.

The best **driving** routes approach Grand Canyon West not via Peach Springs, but along paved roads from the west and the south. The busiest of the pair, **Pierce Ferry Road**, heads east from **US-93** thirty miles north of Kingman and forty miles south of the Hoover Dam. If you'd rather not drive from here, you can **park and ride**, taking a Hualapai bus to Grand Canyon West ($10 round-trip; reserve on ☎1-877/716-9378). Assuming you do continue in your own vehicle, follow Pierce Ferry Road for 28 miles, then turn right (east) onto **Diamond Bar Road**. From there, a rocky 14-mile climb – unpaved but graded, and normally suitable for all vehicles other than RVs – leads through foothills scattered with Joshua trees and up the Grand Wash Cliffs, leads to the Hualapai reservation, where you reach Grand Canyon West five miles later. Alternatively, you can take the forty-mile **Stockton Hill Road** due north from central Kingman and join Pierce Ferry Road 42 miles up, still 26 miles short of Grand Canyon West.

The sheer cost of visiting Grand Canyon West

Any independent traveler planning to visit Grand Canyon West needs to be aware that it's much, much more expensive than any other outdoors destination covered in this book.

If you drive to Grand Canyon West, you have to park your vehicle at the airport, and pay $20. All visitors also have to pay an $8 "impact fee", and buy the $30 **Hualapai Legacy** package, which includes a bus tour to Eagle Point and Guano Point, but *not* the Skywalk or any food.

The **Skywalk** costs an additional $30; a half-hour **horseback** ride costs $34 (1hr $74, 3hr $150); a half-hour **Hummer** off-road trip costs $59 (1hr $89); and a **helicopter** flight down to the river, for a pontoon **boat** ride, costs $159. A tribal tax adds ten percent to all charges.

Thus two adults who drive to the West Rim, and walk on the Skywalk, will pay a minimum of $170 for the day, excluding any drinks, meals or gas. With no reductions for children, families can expect to pay double that.

Seeing Grand Canyon West

The only entrance to Grand Canyon West is at the **airport**, a few hundred yards short of the rim. To reach the Skywalk and other viewpoints, further down the road, you have to join a **bus tour** from here. If you've flown in, some package will already be included in the overall price you've paid; otherwise, the prices are outlined in the box below.

The **Skywalk** itself is a short distance from the terminal, at **Eagle Point**. Unveiled in 2007 by astronaut Buzz Aldrin, it's a horseshoe-shaped glass-bottomed walkway that juts out a short way from the rim, four thousand feet above the canyon floor. However, whatever impression the publicity may give, it's not on the main canyon rim, and not directly above the Colorado, but on one rim of a narrow, unnamed side canyon, the cliff face on the other side of which bears an uncanny resemblance to a massive eagle with its wings outstretched. Supposedly to protect its glass floor, **cameras are forbidden** on the walkway, so if you to pay an official photographer if you want to capture the big moment.

At the dead end of the road, two miles from the terminal, the unfortunately named **Guano Point** surveys long stretches of the Colorado in both directions. Though the Grand Canyon looks as if it could go on forever, in fact it comes to an end not far beyond the next bend in the river to the west, where it bisects the Grand Wash Cliffs.

The Colorado River

No hiking trail connects Grand Canyon West with the Colorado River below, but many visitors take the four-minute **helicopter** ride down from the terminal. The flight in itself is a major adventure, and it's also a real thrill to find yourself walking down by the river in the depths of the inner gorge.

A short footpath leads down from the landing site to the river's edge, where wooden jetties act as the base for the pontoons and jet boats that sweep visitors out for a quick swirl on the river. The adjoining beach is the terminus for the Hualapai's one-day rafting trips, detailed on p.327; participants fly out from here.

Peach Springs

The only town on the Hualapai reservation, **PEACH SPRINGS**, is fifty miles southeast of Grand Canyon West as the crow flies, but not connected to it by road. Instead you have to reach it along Route 66 from I-40, by heading either 50 miles northeast of Kingman, or 35 miles northwest of **Seligman**. Home to just under a thousand of the total Hualapai population of around 1500, Peach Springs is no more than a straggle of buildings along the highway, of which the most prominent is the shiny, modern *Hualapai Lodge*, which has sixty good-sized motel bedrooms and a reasonable restaurant (☎928/769-2230 or 1-888/255-9550, ⓦwww.destinationgrandcanyon.com; April–Oct ❺, Nov–March ❹). The **Hualapai Office of Tourism** in the lodge (Mon–Fri 9am–5pm; ☎928/769-2219, same website) serves as the headquarters for one-day **rafting trips** on the Colorado (departs daily mid-March to mid-Oct at 8am; $328).

The road between the rims

Although the South and North rims stand just eleven miles apart, the shortest driving route between them takes 215 miles, and at least four hours. Very few towns lie along the way, but the scenery is seldom less than spectacular. Starting from Grand Canyon Village, you follow first Desert View Drive and then AZ-64 east, which runs close to the gorge of the **Little Colorado** (look out for Navajo trinket stalls) until it meets US-89 at **Cameron**. Head north to cross **Marble Canyon** on Navajo Bridge, then continue west on US-89A to **Jacob Lake**, where you take AZ-67 44 miles south to the North Rim. As most of this route is on the Navajo reservation, which observes daylight savings time, for six months of each year, clocks at any establishment en route are set one hour later than at the Grand Canyon.

Cameron

Tiny **CAMERON**, which amounts to little more than a handful of buildings, lies a mile or so north of the intersection of AZ-64 and US-89, on the south side of the suspension bridge spanning the Little Colorado River.

The **Cameron Trading Post** here, established in 1911, stocks a huge array of Southwest arts and crafts, from mass-produced trinkets and jeans to genuine Hopi *kachinas* and museum-quality Navajo rugs. While busy with tourists in summer, it remains at heart a trading center for the Navajo Nation, still conducting some of its business by barter. In addition, beautifully landscaped gardens surround a large **motel** complex (☎602/679-2231 or 1-800/338-7385, ⓦcamerontradingpost.com; ❹) where all the rooms are smart, and those on the upper floors have large balconies that look out across the Little Colorado. There's also **RV** parking for $15. A pleasant **dining room** with tin ceiling and large fireplace serves all meals, though the food itself is nothing special (daily: summer 6am–10pm; otherwise 7am–9.30pm).

There's further accommodation at **GRAY MOUNTAIN**, ten miles south of Cameron, in the motel-like *Anasazi Inn* (☎928/679-2214 or 1-800/678-2214, ⓦanasaziinn.com; ❸), with a restaurant and outdoor pool.

Marble Canyon and Navajo Bridge

Fifteen miles north of Cameron, US-160 branches northeast toward Monument Valley and Colorado via **Tuba City** (see p.61). Continuing north, after another forty miles of emptiness US-89 climbs up the mesa to the right, heading for Page and Glen Canyon Dam (see p.426). US-89A, however, presses on at the foot of the **Echo Cliffs**, to reach **Navajo Bridge** after a further fifteen miles.

There are in fact two Navajo Bridges. The 1929 original is now reserved for pedestrians only; a wider facsimile opened 150ft downstream in 1995. The Colorado at this point cuts through the chasm of **Marble Canyon** – it's such a narrow interruption in the vast flat plains that you can't tell it's there until you're right on top of it.

On the west bank, the **Navajo Bridge Interpretive Center** (mid-April to Oct daily 8am–5pm; early April & Nov Sat & Sun 10am–4pm; closed Dec–March; ☏928/608-6404, ⓦwww.nps.gov/glca) holds hair-raising photos of Navajo steelworkers at work on the 1995 bridge, plus displays on the Glen Canyon region. A little further on, *Marble Canyon Lodge* (☏928/355-2225 or 1-800/726-1789, ⓦwww.leesferryflyfishing.com; ❸) has more than fifty conventional motel-style rooms; it can also arrange river and fishing trips. The atmospheric *Lodge* itself has an adequate but unexciting **restaurant**, open for all meals daily, with a 6am start to feed the river-runners.

Lees Ferry

Before the construction of Navajo Bridge, ferries struggled across the river at **LEES FERRY**, six miles north. Mormon elder Jacob Hamblin was guided to this remote spot – the only place within hundreds of miles to offer easy land access to both banks of the Colorado – by Naraguts, a Paiute, in 1858.

Thirteen years later, **John Doyle Lee** was sent here to set up a ferry service to help Mormon missionaries en route south into Arizona. Lee was on the run after the **Mountain Meadows Massacre** in Utah in 1857, when a wagon train of would-be settlers was slaughtered by an armed white band clumsily disguised as Indians, Lee among them. He was finally arrested in 1874 and executed in 1877, but his (seventeenth) wife Emma remained here, at the place they knew as **Lonely Dell**. Determined not to honor Lee, Congress passed a special act to remove the apostrophe from what used to be "Lee's Ferry."

The ferry service was always perilous, with the boats in constant danger of being swept downstream, and was finally abandoned after a fatal accident in 1928. A crucial piece of equipment needed to finish the bridge on the left bank was stranded on the right bank; the only way to get it across was to take it eight hundred miles by road, via Las Vegas.

Lees Ferry marks the confluence of the Paria River with the Colorado; **Paria River Beach**, at the foot of the gently sloping road from Marble Canyon, is the official start of the Grand Canyon. To the south, the broad Colorado picks up speed as it squeezes into Marble Canyon. A few hundred yards north, across the Paria, the large parking lot is where **whitewater rafting** expeditions set off into the Grand Canyon – the first point where boats can get out again is at Diamond Creek, twelve days away by muscle power. A fairly basic **campground** ($10; ☏928/355-2334) is located nearby.

From the far end of the lot, a trail leads within a couple of hundred yards to sturdy **Lees Ferry Fort**, erected in 1874 as defense against Navajo attacks that never materialized. However, John Lee lived not here, but in the much more congenial surroundings of the **Lonely Dell Ranch**, nestled in a fertile curve of the Paria River around half a mile up from the confluence. His original **log cabin** stands not far beyond a replanted approximation of his **orchards**, rich with apple, pear, plum, and peach trees. For serious backpackers, this marks the end of an epic four- to six-day hike that traces the full length of the **Paria Canyon**, starting at the White House trailhead off AZ-89 between Kanab and Page (see p.391).

The Vermilion Cliffs

West of Marble Canyon, US-89A curves beneath the southernmost section of the **Vermilion Cliffs**. These soaring sandstone walls glow a magnificent red at sunrise and sunset, but the road itself is featureless. Only a couple of small **motels** offer any incentive to get out of your car. Both *Lees Ferry Lodge* (☎928/355-2231 or 1-800/451-2231, ⓦwww.vermilioncliffs.com; ❸) – three miles west of Marble Canyon, and smaller and slightly lower-priced than the *Marble Canyon Lodge* (see opposite) – and *Cliff Dweller's Lodge* (☎928/355-2261 or 1-800/962-9755, ⓦwww.cliffdwellerslodge.com; ❹), half a dozen miles beyond, have their own stores and restaurants.

Once past the southernmost promontory of the cliffs, the highway runs straight as an arrow across the broad sagebrush desert. Just under forty miles from the river, it hits the Kaibab Mountains and climbs through thick forest for the final eleven miles to Jacob Lake.

Jacob Lake and DeMotte Park

Deep in the pine forest 44 miles north of the North Rim, the crossroads community of **JACOB LAKE** looks more like a Canadian logging camp than anything you'd expect to find in Arizona. In winter, when AZ-67 down to the Grand Canyon is closed by snow, Jacob Lake goes into hibernation; in summer, however, it makes a good living from the constant stream of tourists.

The *Jacob Lake Inn*, a sprawling but welcoming complex of timber-frame buildings at the road junction, stays open year round (☎928/643-7232, ⓦwww.jacoblake.com). As well as its simple **motel** rooms (❺) and log cabins (❹), it incorporates some pricier family units capable of sleeping up to six (❻), plus a gas station, a general store, an old-fashioned diner counter, and a restaurant where chicken, trout, or steak entrees cost well under $20. Alongside it, the Forest Service's **Kaibab Plateau Visitor Center** has information on the area (daily 8am–5pm; ☎928/643-7298, ⓦwww.fs.fed.us/r3/kai) and is responsible for the lovely *Jacob Lake Campground*, on US-89A just west of the intersection, which caters to **tent campers** only (mid-May to Oct; ☎928/643-7395; $12).

Jacob Lake is named for Jacob Hamblin, a Mormon missionary to the Paiutes and Navajo. The Mormons made little use of the forests to the south, however, apart from grazing their cattle in the large meadow-like clearings along the road to the canyon. One of these, **DEMOTTE PARK**, 27 miles from Jacob Lake, is now home to *Kaibab Lodge* (mid-May to Oct only; ☎928/638-2389 in summer, ☎928/526-0924 in winter, or 1-800/525-0924, ⓦwww.kaibablodge.com), which offers two kinds of cabin – characterful older ones with bare wooden floors (❹), and a few slightly more expensive ones with motel-style trimmings (❺) – plus a simple restaurant open for breakfast and dinner daily. The park entrance is another five miles down the road, with visitor facilities nine miles beyond that.

The North Rim

Higher, bleaker, and much more remote than the South Rim, the **North Rim** of the Grand Canyon is accessible to travelers for barely half the year. Once **AZ-67**, the only road in, has been blocked by the first major snowfall of the winter, the area remains closed until the following spring. Although that first snow used to arrive toward the end of October, in several recent years the area has received a mere fraction of its official average annual snowfall of 140 inches, and the road has been known to close as late as December 9. The one accommodation option on the North Rim, *Grand Canyon Lodge*, continues to operate on a more rigid schedule, opening during the second week of May and closing on October 15. After it closes, the park itself remains open until the snow comes, but no food, gas, or lodging other than camping is available, and visitors must be prepared to leave at a moment's notice.

Even in peak season, the North Rim offers a sense of splendid isolation, and it receives less than a tenth as many visitors as the South Rim. You won't have the place to yourself, but you can still feel as though you're venturing into unexplored wilderness. The canyon itself is significantly different this side of the Colorado. Erosion is much more active: twice as much rain falls, and it freezes more often. As the Kaibab Plateau slopes south, the water flows toward the rim, which has cut twice as far back from the river, so the North Rim is far more indented with massive side canyons. The basic experience of visiting, however, is the same, with a cluster of venerable park-service buildings at **Bright Angel Point**, where the main highway reaches the canyon, and another rim-edge road where drivers can take their pick from additional lookouts.

North Rim practicalities

Visitor activity on the North Rim focuses on the glorified log cabin known as **Grand Canyon Lodge**, perched above the canyon at **Bright Angel Point**. As you approach the lodge complex, the park **visitor center** is the first building on the left (daily May to mid-Oct 8am–6pm; ☎928/638-7864, ⓦwww.nps.gov /grca). **Guest rooms** are not in the main lodge building but in individual cabins and larger motel-style blocks. Each of the well-appointed Western Cabins (❻) has a full-size bathroom and a porch and can sleep up to four people; a mere four offer canyon views, the only North Rim accommodation options to do so, and tend to be booked up to two years in advance. The more spartan Frontier Cabins (❺) can accommodate three guests each and have smaller bathrooms, while the similar Pioneer Cabins (❺) have two separate bedrooms. In addition, a couple of two-story blocks located furthest from the lodge hold twenty motel rooms apiece (❺), each with a queen bed and private bathroom. Only the Frontier cabins and the motel rooms have telephones. **Reservations** for all are essential (☎480/337-1320 or 1-877/386-4383, ⓦgrandcanyonlodgenorth .com). Cancellations are frequently available at short notice, so keep calling if you can't get a room or the precise kind of room you want.

Inside the main building, the magnificent **Dining Room** with rough hewn wood and stone walls is open daily for all meals (☎928/638-2611, or 928/645-6865 out of season; dinner reservations essential, well in advance); the prices aren't bad, and the food is better than in the **snack bar**, entered separately from the driveway. The *Lodge* also holds a **saloon** and **espresso bar**, but its best feature is the **viewing lounge** downstairs, with an array of comfortable armchairs facing vast picture windows.

A little over a mile north, the very pleasant **North Rim Campground** holds 87 car-camping sites ($18), spaced out through the forest. Although all are often reserved in advance (same-day ☎928/638-2611, advance ☎1-877/444-6777 or, from outside the US, ☎515/885-3639, ⓦwww.reservations.nps.gov), additional room is always available for backpackers, bicyclists, and others traveling without their own vehicles, who pay $5 per person.

No organized sightseeing tours are available at the North Rim, and there's no equivalent to the viewpoint shuttle buses that operate along the South Rim. The only long-distance public transportation is provided by the Transcanyon Shuttle

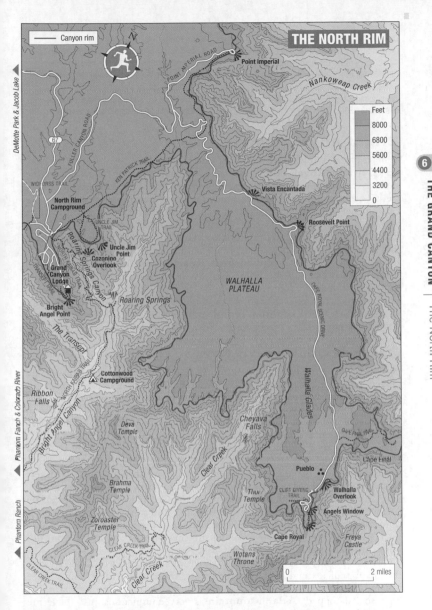

(☎602/638-2820, ⓦwww.trans-canyonshuttle.com), whose van service to the **South Rim** leaves from outside *Grand Canyon Lodge* at 7am daily. Having reached the South Rim at 11.30am, it departs again at 1.30pm, and arrives back at the North Rim at 6pm. A one-way trip costs $80, and the round trip $150.

Ask at the information desk for details of **mule rides** (1hr $40, half-day $75, full-day canyon expeditions $165; ☎435/679-8665, ⓦwww.canyonrides.com).

Other North Rim facilities

Camping equipment Can be bought at the General Store, opposite *North Rim Campground*.
Camping permits The North Rim Backcountry Office is just over a mile up the highway from *Grand Canyon Lodge*, not far north of the campground. Daily 8am–noon & 1–5pm; ☎928/638-7868.

Gas Near *North Rim Campground* (daily 7am–7pm).
Laundromat and showers Near *North Rim Campground*. Showers $1.50. Daily 7am–9pm.
Medical help There is no health clinic on the North Rim. Call ☎911 for emergencies.
Post Office In *Grand Canyon Lodge* (Mon–Fri 8–11am & 11.30am–4pm, Sat 8am–1pm).

Bright Angel Point

A short paved trail leads from the left side of *Grand Canyon Lodge* to the very tip of **Bright Angel Point**. In places, the trail fills the full width of the slender spit of land, with sheer drops to either side. After four hundred level yards, you reach the sanctuary of a railed viewing area, looking out across the canyon. Because the North Rim is a thousand feet higher than the South, views stretch way south to the plateaus of Arizona and the San Francisco Peaks, but it's hard to spot a sign of life at Grand Canyon Village, eleven miles distant. The Colorado is too deeply buried in the canyon to be seen; if you hear rushing water, it's coming from **Roaring Springs**, much closer to hand, which supply all the water used by the park on both rims. To either side, trees somehow cling to the near-vertical red ridges, while high buttes in the canyon proper reach almost to the level of the rims; most prominent of all is neat-capped **Brahma Temple** straight ahead, framed between two lesser specimens.

Cape Royal Scenic Drive

Apart from Bright Angel Point, all the North Rim's **canyon overlooks** are ranged along the eastern edge of the **Walhalla Plateau**, a considerable drive east from *Grand Canyon Lodge*. This long, high headland is reached by turning east onto **Fuller Canyon Road**, three miles north of the *Lodge*. At a junction five miles along, **Point Imperial Road** branches off to the left, while **Cape Royal Road** winds into the cool dense woods to the right.

Even if your time is limited, it's well worth making your way right to **Cape Royal**, fifteen miles from the junction at the end of Cape Royal Road. From the unremarkable parking lot, an even, paved footpath leads first to **Angels Window**, a natural archway just below the top of a rocky spur. As you approach, you can look through it all the way down to the Colorado River. An extremely narrow railed pathway that detours off the main trail a little further along leads onto the top of the "window," for views across to the flatlands of the Navajo reservation. Two broad, green-trimmed stretches of river are visible from this point, including the foaming Unkar Creek Rapid.

Views from **Cape Royal** itself, a couple of hundred yards further along the main trail, extend much further west, though the intervening ridge immediately west obscures Bright Angel Point. The canyon is much narrower here, so flat-topped **Cedar Mountain** is very conspicuous, just above the South Rim.

Other possible halts along Cape Royal Road include **Walhalla Overlook**, a mile or so from the end, where a very short forest trail ends at the foundation walls of a small **Ancestral Puebloan dwelling place**. **Roosevelt Point**, halfway between Walhalla and Fuller Canyon Road, looks across Marble Canyon toward the Echo Cliffs.

Point Imperial

Turn left at the intersection of Fuller Canyon and Cape Royal roads (see opposite) for a gradual three-mile climb to **Point Imperial**. Although at 8803ft this is the highest spot along either rim of the entire canyon, the actual overlook lies just below the parking lot. A long red sandy ridge pokes out beneath your feet, with a stark butte at the end, while to the right is the thickly wooded ridge that ends at Cape Royal. Looking down, the landscape is as dry as dust, a labyrinth of spurs and buttes in which it's virtually impossible to guess which is the main gorge of the Colorado. The plateau of the Navajo reservation on the far side is almost three thousand feet lower, so it spreads for miles, pierced by further chasms and gorges. To the southeast, the Little Colorado emerges from its own canyon to join the main onward rush of the Colorado.

North Rim hikes

Hikers on the Grand Canyon's North Rim should take the same precautions – and be as aware of their capabilities – as their counterparts on the South Rim (see p.324). There tends to be less scope for getting into difficulties here, however, as almost all the North Rim trails suitable for day-hiking stay on top of the plateau. On the only route that descends into the canyon itself, the **North Kaibab Trail**, hiking to the river and back in a single day is completely out of the question – it's a 28-mile round-trip with a 6000ft change in elevation.

The North Kaibab Trail

Some version of the **North Kaibab Trail**, following Bright Angel Creek down to the Colorado, has been in use for over a thousand years. Its current route, which starts by descending through Roaring Springs Canyon from a roadside trailhead two miles north of *Grand Canyon Lodge*, was established in the late 1920s. Parking at the trailhead is limited, but a limited, early-morning **hiker shuttle** service leaves *Grand Canyon Lodge* at 5.20am and 7.20am daily, costing $8 for the first person in each group, plus $5 per additional passenger.

Planning a day-hike on the North Kaibab, it's easy to be overambitious; the mileages may not sound that great, but the gradient is steep from the word go. Many people go no further than the **Coconino Overlook**, just 1.4 miles down

▲ Hikers on the North Kaibab Trail

through the fir forests, a high rocky vantage point from which you can see the junction of Roaring Springs and Bright Angel canyons. The gorgeous waterfalls at **Roaring Springs** come after another 3.6 miles, during which the trail burrows through the **Supai Tunnel**, crosses the suspended **Redwall Bridge**, and makes some spectacular cliffside traverses. Water from the springs is pumped up to the *Lodge* and also piped over to the South Rim, but there's enough left over to tend the "gardens" downstream that were originally planted by the Ancestral Puebloans.

The well-shaded **Cottonwood Campground**, 2.5 miles beyond the springs, is a major way-station for transcanyon hikers. The highlight of the final seven-mile segment to **Phantom Ranch** (see p.342) is lacy **Ribbon Falls**, reached via a short spur trail a mile past the campground.

Rim-edge trails

The ten-mile **Ken Patrick Trail**, the best canyon-edge trail near Bright Angel Point, alternates dramatic views with dense forest as it leads from the North Kaibab Trailhead all the way to Point Imperial. The four-mile **Uncle Jim Trail** branches off it to reach a viewpoint that overlooks the North Kaibab Trail, while the **Widforss Trail** heads the other way, west from the inland end of Bright Angel Point to the tip of the next headland along.

The Arizona Strip

By any logic, you'd expect the **Arizona Strip** – the anomalous area sandwiched between the North Rim of the Grand Canyon and the Utah state line – to belong to Utah rather than Arizona. In 1864, Mormon leader Brigham Young called on Congress to grant the Mormons all territory that lay within two degrees of latitude of either side of the Colorado; the boundary was drawn instead along the 37th parallel, and that remains the Utah–Arizona border. Repeated attempts to incorporate the Strip into Utah failed, largely because this remote region became a stronghold of renegade Mormons who didn't accept their church's abandonment of multiple marriage (see p.509). Effective isolation from the state authorities of both Utah and Arizona suited these die-hard polygamists just fine.

Virtually no roads cross the Strip, and those that do hold just a few tiny, secretive, and often semi-derelict hamlets. Although you have to pass this way in order to complete a full tour around the Grand Canyon, the majority of visitors tend to be racing between the Grand Canyon and the national parks of southern Utah. Few are aware that they're missing perhaps the most spectacular section of Grand Canyon National Park: the **Tuweep** district, home to two stunning overlooks at **Toroweap Point** that provide a rare opportunity to see the canyon's innermost core.

Fredonia

As Hwy 67 north of Jacob Lake drops off the edge of the Kaibab Plateau, it offers tremendous views across southern Utah. Tier upon tier of cliffs rise one behind the other into the distance, making it abundantly clear why geologists call the entire region the **Grand Staircase**. First comes the red sandstone of the Vermilion Cliffs, the formation pierced by Zion Canyon (see p.373); next are the White Cliffs, which form the Kolob Canyons district of Zion National Park; and beyond them, forty miles away, stand the softer Pink Cliffs, sculpted into the hoodoos of Bryce Canyon (see p.393).

The largest town on the Arizona Strip, **FREDONIA**, stands thirty miles northwest of Jacob Lake. With the bigger and much more interesting community of **Kanab** a mere seven miles north, across the Utah border (see p.389), it's hard to see why anyone would choose to spend the night here, but Fredonia does hold a few small motels. A helpful **welcome center**, near the state line at the north end of town (℡928/643-7241; Mon–Sat 9am–5pm), can advise on the Strip's backcountry routes, and sells the necessary maps.

Pipe Spring National Monument

Thirteen miles west of Fredonia, just off AZ-389, **Pipe Spring National Monument** (daily: June–Aug 7am–5pm; Sept–May 8am–5pm; $5; ℡928/643-7105, ⓦwww.nps.gov/pisp) marks the site of one of the very few water sources on the Arizona Strip. Ownership of this precious spring has been much contested; Mormon rancher Dr James Whitmore, who appropriated it from the Paiutes in 1863, was killed three years later by Paiute and Navajo raiders. The Mormons subsequently enclosed the spring in a fort, known as **Winsor Castle**. They retained control until it was declared a national monument in the 1920s, as much because it stood halfway between the Grand Canyon and Zion national parks as for any intrinsic interest.

Pipe Spring is now surrounded by, but distinct from the **Kaibab Paiute Indian reservation**. The buildings remain in good condition and serve as a rather unenthralling museum of early ranching life, of most appeal to students of Mormon history.

Colorado City

AZ-389 continues northwest from Pipe Spring, making it the most direct route from the North Rim to the I-15 interstate between Las Vegas and Salt Lake City. A mile or so before it reaches Utah, a spur road to the right runs up to the staunchly traditional Mormon community of **COLORADO CITY**. Set beneath the towering bluffs of the Vermilion Cliffs, this is a surreal-looking place, laid out with a small grid of extremely broad streets that see very few cars but plenty of gingham pinafores.

As the virtual fiefdom of a small group of polygamists, Colorado City has been the subject of furious controversy. Until his death in 2002, the octogenarian self-styled "Prophet" Rulon Jeffs was its effective ruler. Not only did he assign the town's young women, often in their early teens, as brides to his middle-aged and already multiply-married cronies, but he also presided over a system in which the local young men were run out of town as they came of age so they could not rival their elders. Rulon's son Warren, who succeeded him as Prophet and "inherited" around sixty of his wives, is currently serving a ten years-to-life sentence in Utah State Prison for similar offences, and set up the notorious polygamist compound in Eldorado, Texas, that was raided by the FBI in 2008. If you visit, everyone will assume you're a journalist hoping to write a sensational article, and you'll find no encouragement to linger.

Toroweap

The Arizona Strip holds one tremendous prize for visitors prepared to venture off the paved highways: **Toroweap Point**, the only place where you can drive to the very lip of the canyon's Inner Gorge and peer down sheer 3000ft cliffs to the Colorado River. As the crow flies, it's slightly under sixty miles west of Bright Angel Point, but by road it's almost 150 miles, and even a fleeting visit requires at least six hours of laborious driving on gravel roads.

▲ The Inner Gorge, as seen from Toroweap Overlook

There are two main routes: the eastern **Sunshine Route**, which starts by following **BLM road 109** south from AZ–389 seven miles west of **Fredonia** and then runs for 61 miles southwest, and remains open all year, and the more scenic but longer western **Main Street Route**, which takes a total of ninety miles from **St George**, Utah, but is closed by snow in winter. Both roads are generally passable in ordinary vehicles; if 4WD is necessary at all, it will be for the last few miles only. Be sure to inquire locally about driving conditions before you set off; carry plenty of food, water, and gas, and pack a spare tire and emergency repair kit.

Both routes eventually converge to enter the **Tuweep Area** of Grand Canyon National Park. Five very rough miles on, a free, **primitive campground** holds ten first-come, first-served sites. The road comes to a halt a mile after that at a wide, rocky hilltop known as the **Toroweap Overlook**, which at 4600ft is the lowest viewpoint within the national park. The view here may lack the usual buttes and pyramids or labyrinthine spurs and mesas, but tiptoe to the southern edge of the parking lot, and the ground suddenly drops 3000ft from your feet. Though you can see the river approaching from the east and flowing away to the west, it's so directly below that you may have to lie full length and peep over the edge to see it right here.

A five-minute hike west leads to the stupendous west-facing **Lava Falls Overlook**. The view of the river here, turning from green to blue as it recedes toward the horizon, and interspersed with mighty white rapids, is so spell-binding that you may not at first notice the most awesome feature of the landscape. Straight ahead, a colossal black **lava cascade** spills over the North Rim and pours down to within a few feet of the Colorado. On at least eight separate occasions, volcanic eruptions here have filled the Grand Canyon to a depth of as much as 2330ft, and thus blocked the Colorado. The largest flow, around 1.2 million years ago, created the long-vanished Prospect Dam, which backed the river up to form a lake that stretched all the way east to Lees Ferry. It took an estimated 23 years to fill to the brim; then the Colorado burst over the top and, eventually, wore the dam entirely away.

Southern Utah

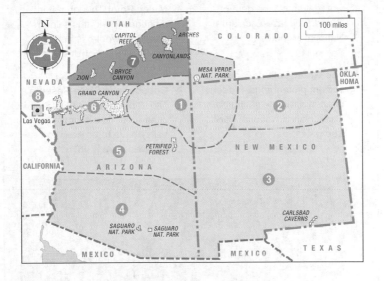

CHAPTER 7

Highlights

✳ **Zion Canyon** Whether you admire it from the roadside, or hike up its soaring walls, Zion is pure magic. See p.373

✳ **Bryce Canyon** Towering incandescent sandstone hoodoos make this one of the most extraordinary-looking places on earth. See p.393

✳ **Calf Creek Falls** An easy trail leads to a magnificent waterfall that's the gem of Grand Staircase-Escalante National Monument. See p.411

✳ **The Great Gallery** Eerie ancient pictographs, hidden deep in a remote section of Canyonlands National Park. See p.441

✳ **Delicate Arch** The hike up to this free-standing natural arch is the crowning glory of a visit to Arches National Park. See p.450

✳ **Rafting in Canyonlands** Penetrate the mysterious wilderness at the heart of Utah on float trips down the Green or Colorado rivers. See p.458

✳ **Muley Point** Though not in a national park, this seldom visited viewpoint is perhaps the finest in all of Utah. See p.467

✳ **Goosenecks State Reserve** The convolutions of the San Juan River near Monument Valley have to be seen to be believed. See p.467

▲ The Scenic Drive, Capitol Reef National Park

Southern Utah

S outhern Utah is a peculiar combination of the mind-boggling and the mundane. Its scenery is stupendous, a stunning geological freakshow where the earth is ripped bare to expose cliffs and canyons of every imaginable color; unseen rivers gouge mighty furrows into endless desert plateaus; and strange sandstone towers thrust from the sagebrush. The tiny Mormon towns scattered across this epic landscape, on the other hand, are almost without exception boring in the extreme. Each has its cluster of characterless motels and dull-as-ditchwater diners; they're not unfriendly places, but finding ways to while away your evenings can truly tax the imagination.

Most visitors therefore spend as much time as possible **outdoors**. Southern Utah has the greatest concentration of **national parks** in the US; in fact there have been serious proposals for the entire area to become one vast national park. The five parks that currently exist are not necessarily the most beautiful or spectacular spots in the state – their boundaries are the result of devious behind-the-scenes wrangling, and exclude lands prized by the ranching and mining conglomerates. Taken together, however, they make an ideal focus for a first tour of Utah, each with its own well-maintained infrastructure of hiking trails and scenic overlooks

In southwest Utah, **Zion National Park** centers on an awe-inspiring and richly fertile canyon, backed by barren highlands of sun-scorched white sandstone, while **Bryce Canyon** is a roaring inferno of flame-like orange pinnacles. Over to the east, **Arches** holds an eroded desertscape of graceful red-rock fins and spurs, all on a more manageable scale than the astonishing hundred-mile vistas of neighboring **Canyonlands**. Both lie within easy reach of **Moab**, a disheveled former mining town that has become Utah's hippest destination. The fifth park, **Capitol Reef**, stretches down the massive rainbow-tinted Waterpocket Fold in the middle of the region, pierced by slender, ravishing canyons.

Lesser-known but equally dramatic wildernesses include **Dead Horse Point** and **Muley Point**, on the eastern side of the state, and vast **Grand Staircase–Escalante National Monument** to the west. The most spellbinding wonder of them all, **Glen Canyon**, has been drowned since the 1960s beneath **Lake Powell**, an elongated reservoir whose turquoise waters, lapping desultorily against the red desert rocks, are a playground for houseboaters and jet-skiers.

The time in Utah is one hour later than Nevada all year round, and one hour later than Arizona from April to October; from November to March, it's the same as Arizona.

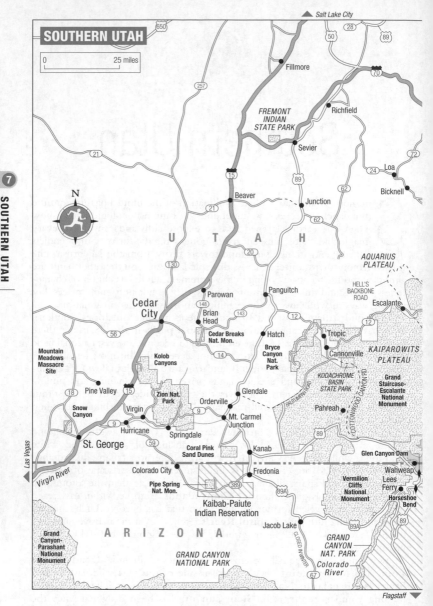

The defining topographical feature of southwest Utah is the **Grand Staircase**. Named by pioneer river-runner John Wesley Powell, it consists of a series of plateaus, stacked tier upon tier, that climb from the North Rim of the Grand Canyon. The **Chocolate Cliffs**, near the border with Arizona, are followed by the dazzling **Vermilion Cliffs**, then the **White Cliffs** – a 2000ft wall of Navajo

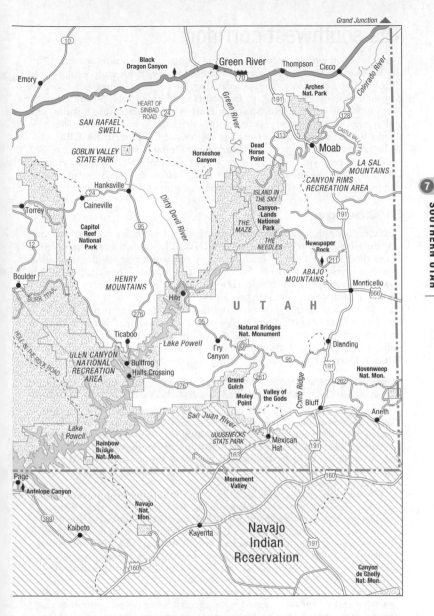

Sandstone, best seen at Zion Canyon – the **Grey Cliffs**, and finally the **Pink Cliffs** of Bryce Canyon. Although it took a billion years of sedimentation for these rocks to form, the staircase itself has only been created in the last twelve million years, by the general upthrust of the **Colorado Plateau**, which stretches away to the east.

The southwest corridor

Though now the most accessible and densely populated area of southern Utah, the far southwestern corner was a forbidding prospect for early explorers. In October 1776, close to modern Cedar City, fathers Domínguez and Escalante despaired of finding their way to California and headed back toward Santa Fe. Not until 1830 did the **Old Spanish Trail** establish a permanent route west, and it was another twenty years before Brigham Young ordered Mormon settlers to establish a string of towns at the foot of the **Hurricane Cliffs**.

The largest of those towns, **St George** and **Cedar City** (covered on p.386), stand fifty miles apart on I-15, the busy interstate that links Las Vegas with Salt Lake City. Both depend on tourism for their livelihood – catering especially to visitors to Zion National Park – despite lacking any great appeal themselves.

St George

Spreading beneath a long sandstone escarpment, nine miles north of Arizona, the venerable Mormon town of **ST GEORGE** has grown from a population of ten thousand in 1970 to around seventy thousand today. While this influx, largely of retirees, has made St George cosmopolitan by Utah standards, however, anywhere else it would seem like a conservative country backwater, albeit with a surprising number of motels.

St George was named not for England's dragon-slaying patron but for a Latter-Day saint, Apostle George A. Smith, who was sent here in 1861 to establish a colony, with 309 families. The original plan being to make Utah self-sufficient in **cotton**, this appropriately southern region became known as "**Utah's Dixie**." However, cotton from the Deep South flooded the market after the Civil War, and St George quietly prospered through growing other crops. It also became a winter refuge for aging Mormon elders such as Brigham Young, whose much-restored adobe **Winter Home** still stands at 200 North 100 West, complete with contemporary furnishings and artifacts (daily 9am–7pm; free).

Pride of place among St George's broad thoroughfares and sturdy well-spaced homes belongs to the gleaming white **Mormon Temple**, 440 South 300 East, the only LDS temple completed during Young's lifetime. Half fortress, half cathedral, it was a defiant statement that the settlers were here to stay. Young presided over its dedication shortly before his death in 1877, and it remains a powerful symbol to all Mormons. As with all Mormon temples, non-Mormons can't go inside; there is a visitor center (daily 9am–9pm; free), however, where the staff may well be so eager to convert you that the problem might be getting out rather than getting in.

Practicalities

As well as a **Utah Visitor Center**, alongside I-15 just inside the state line south of St George (daily: summer 8am–9pm; winter 8am–5pm; ℡435/673-4542, @utah.com), St George has its own **visitor center** at 1835 Convention Center Blvd, near I-15 exit 8 (Mon–Sat 9am–5pm; ℡435/634-5747 or 1-800/869-6635, @utahstgeorge.com).

Greyhound **buses** between Las Vegas and Salt Lake City stop outside *McDonald's* at 1235 S Bluff St (℡435/673-2933), while the St George Shuttle connects with Las Vegas nine times daily (℡435/628-8320 or 1-800/933-8320, @www.stgshuttle.com; $20).

Red Rock Shuttle (℡435/635-9104, @redrockshuttle.com) offers one-day **bus tours** and shuttle trips to Zion ($80), Bryce ($99), and the Grand Canyon ($99), while Southern Utah Scenic Tours (℡435/867-8690 or 1-888/404-8687, @www.utahscenictours.com) runs multi-day trips through southern Utah.

Virtually all St George's commercial life takes place along the main drag, St George Boulevard. With forty-plus **motels**, finding a room is usually easy, though summer weekends get busy. Reliable options include the central *Best Western Coral Hills*, 125 E St George Blvd (℡435/673-4844 or 1-800/542-7733, @coralhills.com; ❸) which has two pools, and the cheaper, veteran *Dixie Palm* at no. 185 E (℡435/673-3531; ❷). The *Seven Wives Inn* is an upscale, period-furnished **B&B** at 217 North 100 West (℡435/628-3737 or 1-800/600-3737, @sevenwivesinn.com; ❺).

Dining out in St George tends to be a question of which highway steakhouse or fast-food outlet catches your eye; there's plenty of choice, but not much excitement. The *Pizza Factory* is among a handful of lively restaurants in the central Ancestor Square development, 1 W St George Blvd (℡435/628-1234; closed Sun).

Snow Canyon State Park

One of Utah's most attractive state parks lies within ten minutes' drive of downtown St George. Don't expect to see snow in **SNOW CANYON STATE PARK**; it's a classic red-rock canyon, where the most distinctive feature is the layer of jet-black lava that flakes off the tops of its sun-baked sandstone pinnacles, left by a volcanic eruption 10,000 years ago.

The park's six-mile **scenic drive**, which remains open day and night, drops left from Hwy-18 seven miles north of St George. Winding down past overlooks and rounded monoliths, it reaches the **park headquarters** after a couple of miles, where you pay the $5-per-vehicle entrance fee. Reservations for the pleasant, shaded 36-space *Shivwits* **campground** alongside are recommended in spring and fall, but things get quieter during the hottest months (℡435/628-2255 or 1-800/322-3770; $16).

An excellent hour-long (1.5-mile) round-trip hike, the **Hidden Pinyon Trail**, starts a hundred yards further on. After cutting between the craggy outcrops into a peaceful meadow, it zigzags up and over a ridge to enter a heavily eroded landscape reminiscent of Canyonlands' Needles District (see p.443).

If it's too hot to hike, pull off another two miles on instead, where a cluster of lurid **red sand dunes** threatens to drift across the road. Kids especially will enjoy sliding down the slopes, which doubled for central Asia in Howard Hughes' movie *The Conqueror*, which starred John Wayne as Genghis Khan. It was filmed in 1954, when the Nevada Test Site, just ninety miles west, was at its busiest; Wayne, Hughes, and three-quarters of the cast probably died from cancers caused by fall-out from the nuclear explosions.

The road to Zion

The main road to Zion National Park, **Hwy-9**, a lovely thirty-mile drive, heads east from the I-15 interstate seven miles northeast of St George. None of the pioneer villages along the way is especially exciting, but the scenery is great, with the cottonwood-fringed Virgin River to the south and gigantic sandstone cliffs to the north. Be warned that you have to pay the admission fee to Zion if you want to continue east beyond the park on Hwy-9.

Hurricane

The westernmost town along Hwy-9 is **HURRICANE**, ten miles off the interstate at the junction with Hwy-59. While not actually on the Virgin River, it's connected to it by a seven-mile canal, conceived in 1863 but not completed until 1906. Only then was the town site settled, and it's still much the same agricultural community a hundred years on.

With the recent spurt in tourism, Hurricane's early timber-frame homes have been joined by **motels**, including the *Comfort Inn Zion*, on the hilltop west of town at 43 N Sky Mountain Blvd (℡435/635-3500 or 1-800/635-3577, ⓦwww.comfortinnzion.com; ❸).

Southeast from Hurricane, Hwy-59 takes twenty miles to reach the Arizona border, marked by the polygamist community of **Colorado City** (see p.361). The **North Rim** of the Grand Canyon is a hundred miles beyond (see p.355).

Virgin, Rockville, and Grafton

You'll probably barely notice **VIRGIN**, seven miles east of Hurricane – close to the foot of the **Kolob Terrace Road** north into the Zion backcountry, described on p.384 onwards – and notorious for having introduced a law making gun ownership compulsory. The same goes for **ROCKVILLE**, ten miles beyond Virgin. In fact, it's hard to keep your eyes on the road at all as you come closer to the wonders of Zion. Rockville is nevertheless a pretty little town, with several small-scale **B&Bs** along its tree-lined central avenue, such as the *Hummingbird Inn*, 37 W Main St (℡435/772-3632 or 1-800/964-2473, ⓦwww.infowest.com/hummingbird; ❹), where all four rooms have private baths.

South across the river from Rockville, turn right off Bridge Road onto an unpaved track, to reach the photogenic little ghost town of **GRAFTON**. Mormon farmers abandoned the struggle against floods and Indians around 1900, but Rockville residents have kept an eye on it ever since. It's also been touched up by Hollywood crews shooting movies like *Butch Cassidy and the*

Sundance Kid; this is where Paul Newman rode a bicycle to the tune of "Raindrops Keep Falling On My Head."

Just beyond Rockville, Hwy-9 veers north at the confluence of the North and East forks of the Virgin River, and heads for the maw of Zion Canyon.

Springdale

SPRINGDALE, the last town before Zion, spreads along a leafy three-mile stretch of the Virgin River just south of the park entrance. Rounding the final corner into town gives you your first stupendous view of Zion Canyon itself. Settled at the same time as the canyon, in the early 1860s, Springdale is now devoted almost exclusively to pampering tourists.

With its clashing and totally discordant architecture, Springdale is a classic national-park gateway community, but it's still somehow very appealing. Here and there green fields nestle right up to the highway – some even hold grazing cattle – while the occasional imposing private home punctuates the motels, inns, and restaurants. The whole ensemble is dwarfed into insignificance by the magnificent canyon walls that loom on either side of the river. By the time you've driven up and down the only road, Zion Park Boulevard, a couple of times, you'll have seen everything Springdale has to offer, but this lively, friendly community makes by far the nicest base in southwest Utah, and spending three or four nights here is no hardship whatsoever.

Arrival and information

Springdale has its own **visitor center**, at 118 Zion Park Blvd (Mon–Fri 9am–5pm; ☎435/772-3757 or 1-888/518-7070, ⓦzionpark.com), but for information on Zion you'd do better to go straight to the park (see p.375). The Zion Canyon Theatre, 145 Zion Park Blvd, shows a pointless but strangely popular giant-screen movie about the park (daily: April–Oct 11am–8pm; Nov–March Tues–Sat 1–6pm; $10; ☎435/772-2400, ⓦzioncanyontheatre.com).

Zion Cycles, at 868 Zion Park Blvd (☎435/772-0400, ⓦzioncycles.com), offers **bike rental**, while the Zion Adventure Company, at the same address (☎435/772-0990, ⓦzionadventures.com), rents out gear and runs a shuttle-van service for prospective Narrows hikers (see p.382), and also offers **guided bike tours** and **canyoneering**, though park regulations mean that such tours can only be outside park boundaries.

Accommodation

As Zion Park Boulevard runs straight between the burgeoning canyon walls toward the park, all the **motels** and **B&Bs** along the way offer the same attractive views. A couple of new properties appear each year, so except in high summer you should have no difficulty finding a room to suit your budget. Compared to the rest of southern Utah, standards are exceptionally high.

For details of staying at the in-park *Zion Lodge*, and of camping in Zion, see p.377. In Springdale, the shaded Zion Canyon Campground, half a mile outside the park at 479 Zion Park Blvd (☎435/772-3237, ⓦwww.zioncamp.com), offers year-round tent camping ($30) and RV hookups ($35), and has its own laundry and pizzeria.

Best Western Zion Park Inn 1215 Zion Park Blvd ☎435/772-3200 or 1-800/934-7275, ⓦzionparkinn .com. Modern convention-style hotel at Springdale's southern end, offering spacious rooms with panoramic windows and a heated swimming pool. ⑤

Cliffrose Lodge & Gardens 281 Zion Park Blvd ☎435/772-3234 or 1-800/243-8824, ⓦcliffroselodge.com. The closest motel to the park makes a pretty place to stay, with separate units spreading down the hillside to the cottonwoods that line the Virgin River. It also has its own pool and wild gardens. ⑥

🏃 **Desert Pearl Inn** 707 Zion Park Blvd
☎435/772-8888 or 1-888/828-0898,
ⓦwww.desertpearl.com. Extremely stylish riverside hotel, offering 61 very arty rooms, with high ceilings, wooden floors, huge windows and balconies, and facing a lovely turquoise pool plus hot tubs. ⑥

🏃 **El Rio Lodge** 995 Zion Park Blvd
☎435/772-3205 or 1-888/772-3205,

ⓦelriolodge.com. Small, very friendly, spotless, and cozy mom'n'pop motel, in walking distance of several restaurants. The rooms aren't fancy, but they're great value. ③

Harvest House 29 Canyon View Drive
☎435/772-3880 or 1-800/719-7501,
ⓦharvesthouse.net. Classy, non-smoking B&B in modern home, tucked beneath the sandstone cliffs. Four en-suite rooms, an outdoor hot tub, and gourmet breakfasts. ⑤

Eating

Springdale lacks national chains, offering instead a refreshing choice of individually styled **restaurants**.

Bit & Spur Restaurant & Saloon 1212 Zion Park Blvd ☎435/772-3498. Hectic dinner-only Mexican restaurant and bar, across from *Zion Park Inn* at the south end of town, where the food has a creative edge – try the zuni stew, made with pork, corn, and delicious vegetables, or the pumpkin and yam tamales – and the margaritas are top-notch. From the outdoor patio, you can watch the moon rise over the mountains. Daily 5–10pm.

Mean Bean Coffee House 932 Zion Park Blvd ☎435/772-0654. Small, friendly espresso bar in the heart of town that's a morning rendezvous for energetic locals; the raised outdoor seating area makes a wonderful place to greet the day. Daily 6.30am–5pm.

🏃 **Spotted Dog Cafe** *Flanigan's Inn*, 428 Zion Park Blvd ☎435/772-3244. High-quality

traditional restaurant, at the park end of town, that's much larger than it looks – the open-air patio is just the tip of the iceberg. Dinner entrees such as braised lamb shank or rabbit have a zesty, continental feel, and cost $16–26, while the home-made breakfast granola is fabulous. Daily 7–11.30am & 5–10pm.

Tsunami Juice and Java 180 Zion Park Blvd ☎435/772-3818. Small, but convenient and well-priced café immediately outside the park entrance, with smoothies, espressos, and bulging $8 wraps served hot or cold. Daily 8am–8pm.

Whiptail Grill 445 Zion Park Blvd ☎435/772-0283. Small central diner in a former gas station, with a few outdoor tables, which serves surprisingly good meals that range from pizza to tacos, with organic and wheat-free options. Daily 11am–7pm.

Zion National Park

With its soaring cliffs, riverine forests, and cascading waterfalls, **ZION NATIONAL PARK** is Utah's most conventionally beautiful park. On first glance it's also the least "Southwestern," in that its centerpiece, **Zion Canyon**, is a lush oasis that feels far removed from the otherworldly desolation of Canyonlands or the downright weirdness of Bryce. Like California's Yosemite Valley, it's a spectacular gorge, squeezed between mighty walls of rock and echoing to the sound of running water. Also like Yosemite, it's prone to be crowded in summer, though an efficient seasonal shuttle-bus system alleviates traffic problems.

Too many visitors see Zion Canyon as a quick half-day detour off the interstate, as they race between Las Vegas (158 miles southwest) and Salt Lake City (320 miles northeast). Beautiful though the **Scenic Drive** through the canyon may be, Zion deserves much more of your time than that. Even the shortest **hiking trail** within the canyon can help you escape the crowds, while a day-hike will take you away from the deceptive verdure of the valley and up onto the high-desert tablelands beyond. In addition, two less-used roads – **Kolob Canyons Road** and the **Kolob Terrace Road** – lead into remoter sections of the park.

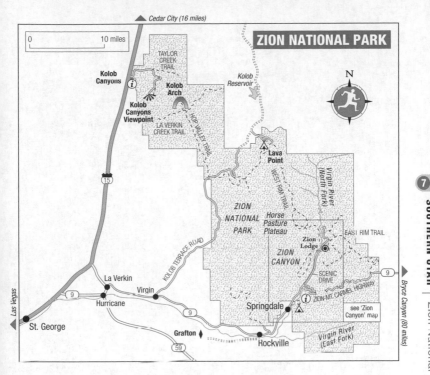

With elevations varying from under 4000ft at the visitor center to almost 9000ft at Kolob Peak, Zion is home to a bewildering array of **flora and fauna**. Its vegetation ranges from the cottonwoods and box elders along the Virgin River to the ponderosa pines and stunted *piñons* that cling to the high sandstone mesas. Desert flowers and cactuses provide unexpected flashes of color in the uplands, as do darting hummingbirds. Resident animals include the bank beaver (so named because it doesn't build dams) and the generally retiring Western rattlesnake.

Summer is by far the busiest **season**. That's despite temperatures in excess of 100°F, and the violent thunderstorms, concentrated in August and a week or so to either side, that bring most of Zion's scant fifteen inches of annual rainfall. If you can, come in April or May to see the spring flowers bloom – though the mosquitoes are also at their peak – or in September and October, to enjoy the fall colors along the river. The park remains open throughout the winter, but daytime highs drop below 40°F in January, while the nights tend to be freezing from November to March.

Zion Canyon

The North Fork of the **Virgin River** has taken thirteen million years to carve **Zion Canyon** into the southern edge of the Markagunt Plateau. For most of the year, the Virgin meanders placidly along the valley floor, en route to the Colorado. After summer thunderstorms, however, run-off from the mesa-tops is channeled down into the canyon, turning it into a torrent that carries as much as 600,000 cubic yards of rock and sand – a good-sized city block – in a single

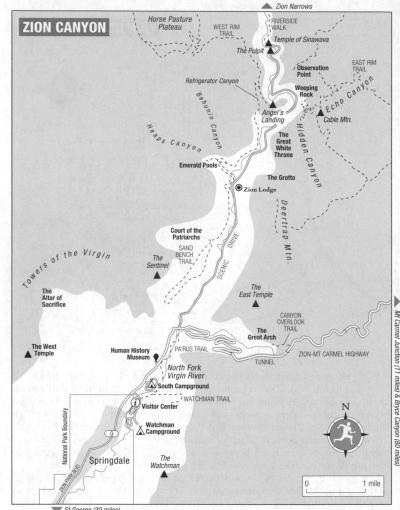

ZION CANYON

Zion Narrows

Horse Pasture
Plateau

WEST RIM
TRAIL

RIVERSIDE
WALK

Temple of Sinawava

The Pulpit

EAST RIM
TRAIL

Observation
Point

Refrigerator Canyon

Weeping
Rock

Echo Canyon

Angel's
Landing

Cable Mtn.

Behunin Canyon

Heaps Canyon

The
Great
White
Throne

Hidden Canyon

Emerald Pools

The Grotto

Zion Lodge

Deertrap Mtn.

Court of the
Patriarchs

SAND
BENCH
TRAIL

SCENIC DRIVE

The
Sentinel

Towers of the Virgin

The
East Temple

The
Altar of
Sacrifice

CANYON
OVERLOOK
TRAIL

The
Great Arch

The West
Temple

Human History
Museum

PA'RUS TRAIL

ZION-MT CARMEL HIGHWAY

TUNNEL

North Fork
Virgin River

South Campground

WATCHMAN TRAIL

Visitor Center

Watchman
Campground

National Park Boundary

9

ZION PARK BLVD

Springdale

The
Watchman

N

St George (30 miles)

0 _____ 1 mile

Mt Carmel Junction (11 miles) & Bryce Canyon (80 miles)

day. Each winter, the canyon walls grow further apart, as water that seeps through the porous sandstone turns to ice and shears mighty chunks off the cliffs.

As you approach from the south, it's abundantly clear that the **Markagunt Plateau** – one of the seven high plateaus that make up the Colorado Plateau in southern Utah, and named for a Paiute word meaning "highland of trees" – constitutes the next rung of the **Grand Staircase** (see p.5). Zion Canyon serves as a handy cross-section to display the different layers of rock. At the lowest level, around the South Entrance, the thick red **Vermilion Cliffs** rise from a barely discernible bed of the even older and darker Moenave and Kayenta strata, deposited at the bottom of swampy seas 200 million years ago. The 2000ft walls of the canyon itself are composed of rusty **Navajo Sandstone**, once a mass of drifting sand dunes.

The first of the colossal peaks that crown the chasm look down from either side of the South Entrance. The **West Temple** is one of two similar mountains here whose summits consist of neat little box-shaped mesas crowned with pine trees, while the **Watchman** stands guard to the east. At this point, the walls are well over a mile apart; officially the canyon doesn't begin for another few miles, but within just ten miles north it dwindles to a mere twenty feet wide.

Although most visitors assume Mormon settlers gave Zion's pinnacles and promontories their portentous names – the **Court of the Patriarchs**, the **Great White Throne**, **Angel's Landing**, and so on – they were coined by a visiting Methodist minister in 1916.

Getting to Zion Canyon

Zion Canyon is 43 miles northeast of St George and sixty miles south of Cedar City, reached by following **Hwy-9** beside the Virgin River for thirty miles east of I-15. Not far beyond the park's South Entrance, just north of Springdale (see p.371), Hwy-9 finally abandons the river, tunneling its way out of the canyon and continuing east to meet US-89. Bryce Canyon, often seen in conjunction with Zion, is 86 miles northeast.

Arrival and information

The **admission charge** for Zion National Park, valid for seven days, is $25 per vehicle, or $12 for motorcyclists, cyclists, and pedestrians. All nationwide passes (see p.41) are sold and accepted. Most visitors pay at the South Entrance kiosks on Hwy-9 north of Springdale, but you can also pay at the highway kiosk that marks the park's East Entrance (daily 8am–5pm).

The park's spacious and partly open-air **visitor center** is set to the right just beyond the South Entrance (daily: late April to late May & early Sept to mid-Oct 8am–6pm; mid-Oct to late April 8am–5pm; late May to early Sept 8am–7pm; ☎435/772-3256, ⊛www.nps.gov/zion). The parking lot alongside the visitor center often fills up by 9am in summer, in which case you'll have to park in Springdale and ride a shuttle bus here (see below). Free handouts include the park newspaper and maps; the bookstore stocks detailed guides; permanent displays explain the park's geology and history; and there's a full timetable of talks, slide shows, and guided hikes.

The former park visitor center, left of the highway a little further on and the first stop on the canyon shuttle bus route (see below), now serves as the **Human History Museum** (same hours as visitor center). While it's not an essential stop, and its photo displays concentrate as much on plants and animals as they do on humans, it does hold some interesting background material.

The **Zion Canyon Field Institute** (☎435/772-3264 or 1-800/635-3959, ⊛zionpark.org) runs hikes, excursions, and lectures in the park, covering topics that range from reptiles to basketry, photography to solar energy, and costing from $25 up to $100 for a full-day class.

Getting around the park

Between late March and the end of October – precise dates vary each year – all visitors to Zion Canyon itself, other than guests staying at *Zion Lodge* (see below), are obliged to leave their vehicles either in Springdale or at the main park visitor center and use the park's network of **shuttle buses**. The **Scenic Drive** within the canyon is accessible to private vehicles during the winter only.

The shuttle buses run on two separate loops. Both are free, and you can get on and off as often as you like. The **Zion Canyon Loop** shuttle, which remains active all year round but is only compulsory between late March and October,

▲ South campground, Zion Canyon

runs between the visitor center and the end of the Scenic Drive, with nine stops including *Zion Lodge*. It operates between 5.45am and 11pm from mid-May until early September, between 6.45am and 10pm in spring and fall, and from dawn until sometime after dusk in winter. The **Springdale Loop** connects Springdale and the visitor center, with nine stops en route, between 5.30am and 11.15pm in summer, and 6.30am and 10.15pm in spring and fall, but closes down in the winter. A short walk connects the different shuttle bus systems at the visitor center; the Springdale buses stop just outside the park, so passengers have to pass through entrance gates on foot to reach the visitor center and the canyon buses.

Hwy-9, the east–west route through the park, remains open all year. However, vehicles measuring over 7ft 10in wide or 11ft 4in high – which includes virtually all RVs – pay $15 on top of the usual park fees to use the **Zion–Mount Carmel tunnel** (see p.377). From mid-April until mid-September, they can only do so between 8am and 8pm; hours vary for the rest of the year. Cyclists are forbidden to ride through the tunnel, but park rangers can arrange for bicycles to be transported by other vehicles.

Zion Canyon practicalities

The only **food** and **lodging** within the canyon is at *Zion Lodge*, an appealing if often overcrowded complex of low-slung wooden buildings set amid well-shaded lawns a couple of miles up the Scenic Drive. **Reservations** for its motel-style rooms, more characterful cabins, and larger suites are handled by Xanterra (reservations ⊕ 303/297-2757, 1-888/297-2757 or 1-888/297-2757, ⓦ www.xanterra.com or www.zionlodge.com; ⊙; property phone ⊕ 435/772-3213). The lodge remains open all year, but rooms in summer should be reserved well in advance.

Whether or not you stay at the lodge, it's well worth stopping to eat in its bright, cool, upstairs **dining room** (⊕ 435/772-7760). The river views will probably linger longer in your mind than its standard breakfasts (daily: summer 6.30–10am; winter 7–10am) and lunches (daily: summer 11.30am–3pm; winter 11am–2pm), both costing $6–9. Dinners are slightly more sophisticated (daily: summer 5.30–9pm; winter 5.30–8pm), featuring entrees such as steak or trout for $16–20. A snack shop near the main entrance (daily: summer 7am–9pm; winter 8am–7pm) serves burgers, sodas, and ice cream.

It's also possible to arrange **horseback rides** from the lodge (March–Oct; daily 3hr rides at 9am & 1.30pm, $75, minimum age 10; daily four 1hr rides $40, minimum age 7; ⊕ 435/679-8665, ⓦ canyonrides.com).

Camping

The **Watchman** and **South campgrounds**, which contain around four hundred sites between them, are close to the visitor center. South, which oddly enough is north of the visitor center, is first-come, first-served, and is open between early March and early Nov only, while Watchman, to the south, stays open year round but accepts reservations between mid-March and Oct only (⊕ 1-877/444-6777 or ⓦ www.recreation.gov). Basic sites at either cost $16 per night, while Watchman also offers sites with electricity for $18, and riverside sites for $20. Arrive early in summer, when they tend to fill by noon daily.

To camp in the **backcountry**, pick up the necessary hiking **permits**, and a copy of the *Zion Backcountry Planner*, from visitor centers. **Commercial campgrounds** nearby include *Zion Canyon Campground* in Springdale (see p.371), and the less appealing *Mukuntuweep Campground* (⊕ 435/648-3011, ⓦ www.xpressweb.com/zionpark; $15) just outside the East Entrance, where there's also a café and a gas station.

Zion Canyon by road

Whether you access Zion Canyon using the park shuttle buses, or visit in winter when you're free to use your own vehicle, your first impressions are going to be garnered from the highway. The main road, **Hwy-9**, passes plenty of dramatic formations as it climbs east toward Bryce, but Zion's most

Zion Canyon may seem like an oasis, but it has never held much of a **human** population. Its earliest inhabitants were probably semi-nomadic hunter-gatherers, who from 500 AD onwards grew crops beside the Virgin River. Known to archeologists as the **Virgin Anasazi**, they are regarded as less sophisticated cousins of the Ancestral Puebloan groups to the east; living in small bands, they never built "cliff palaces" or pueblos. By 1250 AD, drought had driven them out of Zion, leaving isolated pictographs on the canyon walls as their only monument.

During the ensuing centuries, **Paiute Indians** migrated seasonally throughout southern Utah, harvesting the few resources the desert could offer. They saw Zion, however, as the abode of Wai-no-Pits, the evil one, who cursed them with disease, and Kainesava, the God of Fire, whose lightning blazed from its high peaks. When **Mormon missionary** Nephi Johnson arrived in 1858 to explore the Upper Virgin River, the Paiute would lead him no further than Oak Creek, at the canyon entrance.

Isaac Behunin, who set up a log cabin in 1862 where *Zion Lodge* now stands, dubbed the canyon "**Little Zion**" in the hope that it would be a place of refuge for beleaguered Mormons. Some of his fellow farmers were soon taking things too easy; Brigham Young thundered that their indulgence in tobacco and wine made the name "**Not Zion**" more appropriate. In the long run, Zion Canyon proved too narrow to support farming, and its main commercial role was simply as a route through which timber sawn on the high mesas could be shipped out to the plains. Between 1900 and 1930, logs lowered from "Cable Mountain" built the fine homes of such towns as St George.

John Wesley Powell's second Colorado expedition in 1872 (see p.433) had brought the scenery of Zion to national attention, under the Paiute name of "Mukuntuweap Canyon." The canyon itself was set aside in 1909 as Mukuntuweap National Monument; a larger area became Zion National Park in 1919, and the Kolob Canyons district was added in 1956.

In its first full year, 1920, the park attracted fewer than four thousand visitors. Trails and campgrounds remain little changed since their construction during the 1930s, but visitor numbers have since climbed to almost three million per year.

memorable monoliths are ranged on either side of the dead-end **Scenic Drive**, which runs for six miles north alongside the Virgin River.

The Scenic Drive

For half a mile north of the visitor center, Hwy-9 follows the west bank of the river. The highest of the peaks to the left, collectively known as the **Towers of the Virgin**, is the **Altar of Sacrifice**, named somewhat gruesomely for the blood-like streaks of rust that seem to flow from its flat crest.

The highway crosses river just beyond its confluence with **Pine Creek**. Guarded by the **Sentinel** to the west and the **East Temple** to the east, this marks the start of Zion Canyon proper. It's also the site of the Canyon Junction shuttle stop, and the northern trailhead of the **Pa'rus Trail** (see p.380). The **Scenic Drive** branches left on the far side of the bridge, while Hwy-9 heads on east (see below).

From here on north the canyon is so narrow, and the walls so steep, that there's barely room to squeeze in a road. Erosion continues as fast as ever, and the Scenic Drive has repeatedly to be rebuilt after landslides. The first major roadside pull-out comes after 1.7 miles, facing the **Court of the Patriarchs**, where peaks named for Abraham, Isaac, and Joseph stand arrayed around a small canyon west of the river. A mile further on you reach the meadows of **Zion Lodge** (see opposite). In the height of summer, the crowds can be overwhelming, but for most of the year it's a pleasant, shady place to break the day, and it's also the trailhead for the popular **Emerald Pools Trail** (see p.380).

Zion Canyon's one designated picnic spot is the **Grotto**, less than a mile beyond the lodge near the foot of the **West Rim Trail** (see p.381). To one side stands **Red Arch Mountain**, named for a natural archway created in 1880 when a vast chunk of the mountain suddenly collapsed and obliterated a cornfield. To the other, the long western flank of the **Great White Throne** looks from this angle neither white nor especially dramatic.

During the next mile the road passes the trailhead for **Weeping Rock** (see p.383) and the **East Rim Trail** (see p.383), as well as a number of unnamed pull-outs where paths lead down to the river. The best views of all come just under five miles from the start of the Drive, as it completes its long curve around the river's "Big Bend." The lookout here faces the northern aspect of the Great White Throne, framed between the slender neck of **Angels' Landing** (see p.381) to the right and the pipe-like formations of the **Organ** to the left. Glowing at sunset, the throne is utterly majestic.

A mile or so on, the Scenic Drive – and the shuttle-bus route – comes to an end at the large parking lot at the start of the mile-long **Riverside Walk** (see p.383) toward the Narrows. This general area is known as the **Temple of Sinawava**, after a wolfish deity of the Paiute Indians; the most prominent single rock is the **Pulpit**, standing alone near the west bank of the river.

The Zion–Mount Carmel Highway

The side canyon formed by Pine Creek, half a mile north of the visitor center, enables Hwy-9 to continue east, a route known as the **Zion–Mount Carmel Highway**. At first it heads straight for the **East Temple** – topped like its larger twin by a forested mesa – but it's soon forced to start tacking its way up the hillside. At the eastern end of each extravagant switchback comes a better view of the enormous **Great Arch** at the head of the canyon. Measuring 720ft wide by 580ft high, this is not in fact an arch at all, but simply a deep alcove, or what's known as a "blind arch."

Finally the highway burrows into the rock, entering the first and longer of two remarkable **tunnels** blasted through the canyon walls in the 1920s (for traffic regulations, see p.377). Five "windows" punctuate its one-mile length to let in air and light, but you can't stop to admire the views. All the rubble from the excavation tumbled into Pine Creek far below; the river may seem innocuous, but it cleared the whole lot away in the space of a single year.

Easily seen on the enjoyable **Canyon Overlook Trail** (see p.384), the hot dry plateau beyond the eastern end of the main tunnel feels far removed from the lushness of Zion. These pale, smoothly undulating rocks, capped here and there by strange beehives and hoodoos, are the lithified remains of ancient sand dunes. One huge specimen, crisscrossed with stress lines from eons of erosion and resembling some long-abandoned pyramid, is known as the **Checkerboard Mesa**. It looms south of the highway at a clearly marked turn-off five miles beyond the second tunnel, a quarter of a mile short of the park's East Entrance. For accounts of Mount Carmel, Kanab, and points east, see p.387 onwards.

Hiking in Zion Canyon

Every visitor to Zion Canyon should **hike** at least one of its many clearly marked and signposted trails. However, almost all trails except the short Riverside Walk require a stiff climb away from the canyon floor, and with summer temperatures in excess of 100°F and elevations of well over 6000ft, it's all too easy to overdo things. Carry plenty of food and drink, and don't imagine that because you have no trouble walking five miles at home you can do it here, straight up a cliff. Water is available on most trails – although not until around five miles along the West or East Rim trails – but must be purified before use. For more detailed advice on desert hiking, see Basics.

As for specific **routes**, avoid the sun by hiking the east side of the canyon in the morning and the west in the afternoon. If you're reasonably fit and have just one day, the best combination is probably an hour or two along the **Riverside Walk** and a longer climb either to **Angels Landing** on the West Rim Trail or **Hidden Canyon** on the East Rim Trail.

All the trails detailed below set off from either Hwy-9 or the Scenic Drive, but some of the longer ones leave the canyon altogether and end up on backcountry dirt roads. If you're planning a one-way hike, look at the **shuttle board** in the visitor center, to see if you can swap vehicles with hikers coming in the opposite direction. Both *Zion Lodge* and the Zion Adventure Company (see p.382) also operate commercial **hiker shuttle services**.

Hiking **permits** are required for all overnight trips, and all hikes that require technical equipment, most obviously the **Zion Narrows** (see p.382). They cost $10 for one or two people, $15 for three to seven, and $20 for eight up to the group maximum of twelve. You can pick them up at any visitor center the day before you hike, and reserve in advance via the park website; at the very busiest periods, you may have to enter an online **lottery** to make a reservation.

Watchman Trail

Just inside the South Entrance, a right turning leads across the river to the *Watchman* campground (see p.377) and the start of the **Watchman Trail**. This steep mile-long climb switchbacks up a side canyon below Bridge Mountain, then heads back south to loop around a flat promontory below the Watchman itself. Thankfully, it doesn't go right to the top, but its views up the canyon, as well as across to the West Temple and back down to Springdale, tucked among the trees, are a good way to get your bearings when you first arrive. Until around 10am, the canyon walls keep most of the route in shade; later on, it's liable to be baking hot. Allow around two hours to complete the entire two-mile round-trip hike.

Pa'rus Trail

The gentle, paved **Pa'rus Trail**, also open to cyclists, repeatedly crisscrosses the Virgin River on a two-mile route that connects the two campgrounds either side of the visitor center with the shuttle bus stop at Canyon Junction. While it lacks the glamour or rewarding destinations of other, more demanding trails in the park, it's a truly delightful stroll, especially enjoyable around sunset at the end of a hard day.

Emerald Pools Trail

The **Emerald Pools Trail**, which starts conveniently from *Zion Lodge*, is every bit as pretty as the name implies. It's also suitable for walkers of all levels, as the lowest of the three pools can be seen on a gentle round-trip stroll of little more than a mile, while the highest makes a good objective for a more energetic hike.

On the far side of the footbridge that crosses the Virgin River from the lodge, the pink-paved trail to the right is the direct route to the **lower pool**. After an easy climb through the forest, with views straight up the main canyon, it cuts left into Heaps Canyon, and soon reaches a huge overhang of red rock, streaked black by a broad cascade of water. The almost constant flow collects in pools that tend be muddy red rather than emerald green; the overhang is deep enough for the trail to circle inside them, running behind the waterfall.

From this point, the trail becomes confusing, with countless possible routes made by lost or blundering hikers. If you're pressed for time, head back the way you came; alternatively, continue straight ahead, along the shelf on the canyon wall, and in just over half a mile you'll drop back to cross the river at the Grotto picnic area, half a mile north of *Zion Lodge*.

Most hikers head instead for the **higher pools**, by following a narrow path through a cleft in the gigantic split boulder to the left. Having first doubled back to the top of the waterfall, where the stream bubbles out of the woods to spill across a lip of slickrock, take the spur trail to the right on the far side.

A hot, hard climb of not much more than five minutes is rewarded by a delightfully cool seep-fed pool at the foot of the monumental outer walls of the canyon. Climbing any higher is out of the question, but this is a good place to linger, with a small sandy "beach" and plenty of shade. Once back on the main trail, head right while still above the main falls to complete a loop back to the lodge, which should take a total of two to three hours.

Angel's Landing and the West Rim Trail

Serious hikers and backpackers rate the **West Rim Trail** as Zion's most compelling challenge. Even if you have nothing to prove, its views and variety make it well worth attempting, but it's not to be undertaken lightly. The first couple of miles involve a grueling 1500ft climb out of Zion Canyon, while to reach the obvious day-hike destination, **Angel's Landing** – a five-mile round-trip from the valley floor that takes a good four hours – you have to brave a terrifying knife-edge ridge.

The trail starts across the river from the Grotto picnic area, half a mile north of the lodge. As it winds ever more steeply toward the sheer canyon wall, it seems no onward route could possibly exist, but in the end it switchbacks several times and cuts back into a crack in the rock. Unless you've made a very early start, you'll have been out in the sun for a long time by now, and the cool shade of this narrow crevice – **Refrigerator Canyon** – comes as a merciful relief.

However, things soon get worse; beyond the brief flat stretch of the canyon you're confronted by a severe set of switchbacks known as **Walter's Wiggles**. Constructed during the 1920s, these serve as a ladder up an otherwise impassable cliff. At the top lies **Scout Lookout**, a tranquil patch of sand with views up and down Zion Canyon and a population of scavenging chipmunks that feast on the remains of countless well-earned picnics.

Daredevil day-hikers are invariably drawn to the spur trail from Scout Lookout to **Angel's Landing**. What you're letting yourself in for is obvious from the outset; the trail sets off along the top of the steep promontory straight ahead, with awesome drop-offs to either side, and only token stretches of metal chain offer the illusion of security. If you think you're the brave one, take a look to see if there are any climbers scaling the sheer rock face on your left. Your goal is a knee-shaking half-mile on, with a quarter-mile drop to the canyon floor at your feet and the Great White Throne towering a further thousand feet above you on the far side of the river.

Beyond Scout Lookout, the West Rim Trail climbs steadily out of the canyon. After crossing an expanse of slickrock, perilously close to the rim, it descends into a spectacular high-country valley. This is another side of Zion altogether, rimmed with white cliffs, "checkerboarded" by cross-bed hatching, and scattered with rounded outcrops of layered sandstone. For a couple of miles, the trail picks its way gingerly across the valley and up the far side, twice crossing streambeds that nurture forest glades. Finally it runs into the monumental wall of red sandstone that marks the head of **Behunin Canyon**, a huge side canyon off Zion Canyon (itself by now way out of view). Doubling

Hiking the Zion Narrows

Hiking the **Zion Narrows** – the slender gorge through which the Virgin River enters Zion Canyon from the north – has acquired the reputation of being *the* thing every Zion visitor simply must do. Don't believe the hype. It's a very demanding **wilderness experience**, much more suitable for devotees of extreme sports than for casual hikers.

A ravishing "slot canyon" squeezed between mighty sandstone cliffs and interspersed with fertile grottoes, the Narrows is undeniably spectacular. However, you can only trek its full length by following the river downstream from a remote trailhead that's only accessible in a **four-wheel-drive vehicle**. For at least ten of the sixteen miles of hiking from there, you can expect to be wading thigh- or even shoulder-deep in **cold, fast-flowing water**, struggling with every step to find a foothold on the slippery rounded boulders of the streambed. While it's just possible to complete the whole hike in a single, grueling day – the average **hiking time** is twelve hours – it's more realistic to plan to camp overnight along the way. Specialist **equipment** is essential, in the form of waterproof, super-grip footwear, neoprene socks, and a walking stick or two, complemented in the cooler months by a drysuit. It's not a question of whether, but of how often, you'll fall over, so you'll also need zip-lock plastic bags for everything you carry, and since the water isn't drinkable, you'll have to lug that along too. Though it doesn't have the same kudos among the adventure-sports fraternity, you can also sample the Narrows as a **day-hike** by pushing your way upstream, against the current, from the end of the Riverside Walk, and turning back when you've had enough. However, you'll still need all the gear – don't even dream of setting off without it.

For anything beyond a short day-hike, you have to have a **permit** to hike the Narrows, as detailed on p.380. The park service issues a maximum of eighty such permits per day, of which around half can be reserved in advance, while the rest are available first-come, first-served the day before. Making a reservation does not necessarily mean you'll actually be allowed to hike; the Narrows is always liable to be closed due to flash floods or wildfires. In principle, the **best times to hike** are in June or from September until early October. July and August see frequent thunderstorms, so the risk of flash floods is at its highest. In addition, the road to the trailhead is often closed altogether between December and April.

The Narrows is just one among many wonderful hikes on offer in the park, most of which don't require nearly so much planning, expertise, or expense. According to park rangers, its current popularity is largely because it's so heavily promoted by commercial companies. As the Narrows lie inside the national park, operators can't offer guided trips, but they do rent **equipment** and run **shuttle services**. In Springfield, both Zion Adventure Company, 868 Zion Park Blvd (☎435/772-0990, ⓦzionadventures.com), and Zion Rock and Mountain Guides, 1458 Zion Park Blvd (☎435/772-3303, ⓦwww.zionrockguides.com), charge around $17 for one day, or $26 overnight, for the basic summer package of boots, socks and staff, while between October and May, when you need a drysuit as well, it costs $39 for one day, $54 overnight. Both also run shuttles to the trailhead at Chamberlain's Ranch, leaving daily at 6.30am and 9.30am in summer, and less frequently at other times, for $30. If you have your own 4WD vehicle, you can get there by turning left 1.7 miles east of the East Entrance (just east of milepost 46 on Hwy-9), and then following North Fork Road, which in due course becomes a rough dirt track, for around seventeen miles north. The total thirty-mile drive from Zion Canyon takes about ninety minutes.

back, it clings to the cliff face on a long exposed switchback that comes out atop **Horse Pasture Plateau**.

Just to set foot on Horse Pasture Plateau is a stiff target for a day-hike from the floor of Zion Canyon, a total round-trip of something over eleven miles. In the full heat of summer even that would be too much to take on, but the trail continues north for another ten miles, to **Lava Point** off the Kolob Terrace Road (see p.384), with plenty of optional scenic detours en route. This is Zion's most popular backpacking trip, usually done as a two-day expedition, starting from Lava Point and working down, and camping near the southern edge of Horse Pasture Plateau. As with any such overnight hike, a backcountry camping permit is required; see p.380.

Riverside Walk

Not least because it involves no climbing, the mile-long **Riverside Walk** at the end of the Scenic Drive is Zion's best-loved trail. Having watched the canyon walls converge ever closer, the urge to find out what happens beyond the end of the road is irresistible. You may well have more company than you'd prefer, but the views from the gentle paved footpath are too beautiful for that to matter. While it's easy enough to complete the round-trip in under an hour, you'll enjoy it more if you allow much longer.

Walls of deep red sandstone soar to either side of the river, which is flanked by shimmering cottonwoods that turn a rich gold in the fall. There are even patches of low-lying "desert swamp," where bullfrogs bellow in the rushes and willows thrust from the mud.

Riverside Walk ends where the Virgin emerges from **the Narrows**, overlooked by the mighty **Mountain of Mystery**. For eight miles upstream from this sandy little beach, the river fills the entire gorge, often less than twenty feet wide and channeled between vertical cliffs almost a thousand feet high. As explained in the box opposite, it's possible to wade upstream, against the current, to see the Narrows for yourself, while if you arrive towards sunset, you'll also doubtless encounter plenty of exhausted backpackers who have hiked here sixteen miles downstream, from Chamberlain's Ranch.

Weeping Rock

As one of Zion Canyon's easiest short walks, the half-mile round-trip hike to **Weeping Rock** is prone to be overcrowded in summer. Eaten from the canyon wall by a perennial spring, this damp alcove is filled with ferns and tiny flowers; while it comes as a surprise in the desert, however, it's not as beautiful as you may be led to expect. The paved trail up starts from the parking lot at the mouth of Echo Canyon, halfway between *Zion Lodge* and the end of the road.

Hidden Canyon and the East Rim Trail

Rewarding hikes of almost any length can be enjoyed by taking the **East Rim Trail**, which sets off from the Weeping Rock trailhead (see above) but branches right rather than left on the far side of Echo Canyon Creek. Only backpackers who camp overnight on the mesa-top attempt its full 10.5-mile length, and they normally prefer to start from the far end, near the park's East Entrance. However, the strenuous two-mile climb out of Zion Canyon is its most exhilarating segment, and offers several spur trails for day-hikers.

After half an hour of ascending along a cement pathway, enjoying ever-improving views of Weeping Rock, the East Rim Trail reaches a stiff set of switchbacks. By the time you reach the top of those, you've climbed about half a mile up the face of Cable Mountain, but you're still only halfway up to the mesa. A stone bench here makes a good place to ponder the decision whether to keep on going, or head instead for **Hidden Canyon**, a "hanging canyon" that has yet to cut its way down to the floor of Zion. A good goal for a half-day hike, it's a three-mile, three-hour roundtrip from the Scenic Drive. To reach it, follow a spur trail for a further half-mile, beyond a brief stretch of forest and a hair-raising segment, clinging to a wall of rock, which is enough to deter most would-be canyoneers. The broad "lip" of the canyon, perched 700ft above Zion, turns into a waterfall after heavy rain, while the rounded holes scoured into the slickrock fill with water and life. Strictly speaking, the trail ends here; it's just about feasible to press on into the canyon, but only expert rock climbers have any hope of approaching its head.

If Hidden Canyon sounds too intimidating, you may prefer to keep on switch-backing up the East Rim Trail beyond the Hidden Canyon turn-off. A mile or so further on, deep in wafer-thin Echo Canyon – a "slot canyon" with beautiful walls – the **East Mesa Trail** climbs steeply off to the left. A two-mile walk away through the woods on top of the plateau, **Observation Point** commands views all the way down Zion Canyon. The massive cliffs of Cable Mountain and the Great White Throne stare you full in the face, while Angels Landing towers proudly on the far side. To be on the safe side, allow six hours for the full seven-mile round-trip hike this far, though you may do it in less.

Assuming you stay on the **East Rim Trail** rather than taking the East Mesa Trail, it takes a good mile or more to drag yourself up out of Echo Canyon, and there may be streams to negotiate en route. Atop the mesa, walking becomes much easier, as the trails simply follow former logging roads. **Stave Spring**, the only perennial water source on the East Rim Trail, is roughly halfway between Zion Canyon, five miles west, and the East Entrance, slightly further southeast. Overnight campers can head southwest at this point, along a trail that soon forks to the summits of **Cable Mountain** – where you can take a closer look at the century-old workings that hauled timber down into Zion (see p.378) – or Deertrap Mountain. Either hike is a six-mile detour from Stave Spring.

Canyon Overlook Trail

Alongside the ranger station at the eastern end of the long tunnel on the Zion–Mount Carmel highway (see p.379), steps cut into the rock mark the start of the **Canyon Overlook Trail**. So long as you don't mind edging along the brink of a precipice – at one point the trail consists of wooden planks braced against the cliff face – this offers a fascinating variety of terrain in the space of just half a mile. It's also the only trail described here for which you can access the trailhead in your own vehicle year-round – though there's so little parking that you may find that makes little difference. The scenery en route ranges from fern-filled grottoes fed by seeping water to a bare slickrock mesa topped by tiny hoodoos.

The trail ends at a railed viewing area at the head of Pine Creek Canyon; though you can't see it, you're directly above the Great Arch. Only one of the tunnel's five "windows" is visible in the rock wall to your left, but the road emerges below to zigzag into the valley. Straight ahead is the west wall of Zion Canyon; a helpful sign labels the peaks ranged along the far side of the river, from the ruddy tree-capped West Temple to the paler Sentinel. Walking the full length of the trail and returning to the road typically takes around an hour, though you could scurry it in half that.

Kolob Terrace Road

The only road access to the central uplands of Zion National Park is along **Kolob Terrace Road**, which branches inconspicuously north from Hwy-9 at tiny **Virgin**, fifteen miles west of the park's South Entrance (see p.371). Especially in its earlier stages, it's a dramatic drive, but unless you have a high-clearance 4WD vehicle, you won't manage the full 43 miles to meet I-15 just south of Cedar City. Ordinary cars have to turn back after just over twenty miles, so only long-distance hikers or tourists with a spare afternoon tend to come this way. In addition, the entire road is closed to all traffic in winter.

The road starts by climbing through a dry desert valley, heading for two pyramidal mountains that dwarf the cliffs on the horizon. It reaches Zion after just over seven miles, only to exit almost immediately, and then dips repeatedly in and out of the park. As it next re-enters the park, you get superb views north across **Hop Valley** to the russet and white pinnacle of **Burnt Mountain**. Keen backpackers can hike to Kolob Arch from here along the **Hop Valley Trail**, but it's not as easy as it looks; you have to plow through thick sand for most of the way, so the fifteen-mile hike is even more difficult than the route described overleaf.

Soon after you leave the park yet again, twenty miles up from the highway, a dirt road to the right leads 1.7 miles to **Lava Point**, back within the park. As well as being the trailhead for the West Rim Trail, which takes fourteen miles to drop down into Zion Canyon (see p.383), this is a superb vantage point in its own right. Poised four thousand feet higher than the visitor center, it overlooks a panorama that stretches north to Cedar Breaks and southeast to the Kaibab Mountains, with the monoliths of Zion Canyon mere incidental details in the foreground. There's a **picnic area** and a free, first-come, first-served, six-site primitive **campground** with no water nearby (June to mid-Oct only).

Kolob Canyons

Located just off I-15, twenty miles south of Cedar City, the **Kolob Canyons** have formed part of Zion National Park since 1956. Although easier to reach than Zion Canyon, they receive far fewer visitors. In all honesty, they're less immediately impressive than Zion Canyon, and you'll only get the most out of the area if you can spare the time and energy to **hike**. If you stay in your car, you can drive to the end of the five-mile road, admire the view of the red-rock canyons, and be back on the interstate within the hour, wondering what the fuss is about.

Information on the Kolob Canyons can be picked up from the small **visitor center** at exit 40 off I-15 (daily: late April to mid-Oct 8am–5pm; mid-Oct to late April 8am–4.30pm; ☏435/586-9548). As well as providing free hiking advice, rangers also allot 24 numbered backcountry **campsites** ($5). No gas or food is available.

Beyond the visitor center, **Kolob Canyons Road** twists alongside Taylor Creek and then up through Lee Pass, with countless trailheads and roadside viewpoints en route. Its final parking lot faces across the riverbed to a succession of narrow, red-walled **"finger" canyons** cut into the west rim of the Markagunt Plateau. Each was carved by a separate tiny stream; one, Hanging Valley, is interrupted by a sheer 1500ft cliff, stranding an isolated patch of thick forest far above the valley floor. In the distance, you may just be able to make out the West Temple, above Zion Canyon.

Footpaths on the far side of the lot lead to a picnic spot in the woods. From here, the half-mile **Timber Creek Overlook** trail runs through low trees along the top of the ridge, to end at a rocky promontory with views over the endless rolling forests.

Hiking the Kolob Canyons

The two main **hiking trails** in the Kolob Canyons leave from earlier along Kolob Canyons Road. Starting two miles from the visitor center, **Taylor Creek Trail** follows the Middle Fork of Taylor Creek on a five-mile round-trip to **Double Arch Alcove**, passing long-abandoned cabins built by early homesteaders. The trail grows progressively less distinct before it culminates by climbing into the lush hollow in the canyon wall that lies beneath the Double Arch itself. The entire round-trip takes around four hours.

The **Kolob Arch Trail**, one of Zion's very finest trails, leads down from Lees Pass along the drainage of Timber Creek. At fourteen miles for the round-trip, it only makes an appropriate day-hike for confident, experienced desert hikers. It can be muddy going, but at least there's usually plenty of water en route (which must be purified before drinking). The first couple of miles, heading south, feature superb close-up views of the finger canyons; you then veer east to meet **La Verkin Creek** just above a waterfall. The goal for most hikers is **Kolob Arch**, seven miles along, which may or may not be the world's longest natural rock span. Like Landscape Arch, in Arches National Park (see p.451), it's approximately 300ft across; no one agrees how to measure arches any more precisely, so they're generally considered equals. Camping somewhere nearby (by prior arrangement at the visitor center) makes for a less grueling hike and gives you the option of exploring the remote regions that lie farther along La Verkin Creek.

Cedar City

If you're heading **north** from St George or the Zion area, the most direct route is to follow I-15 northeast. In the course of fifty miles, it climbs three thousand feet, passing between the Pine Valley Mountains to the west and the Hurricane Cliffs to the east.

CEDAR CITY, 53 miles northeast of St George, is now half its size. Like its upstart rival, it too was founded in Mormon Utah's precarious early years, as the church bid for self-sufficiency. The Mormons urgently needed **iron**, so when scouting parties discovered iron ore in southern Utah, the **Iron Mission** was dispatched to establish Cedar City in November 1851. Most of its first inhabitants were British miners; they soon succeeded in smelting iron from the hills to the west, but the venture ultimately failed, and ore mined locally has been shipped out for processing ever since.

There's little to see in Cedar City these days. It's not a place you're likely to want to tour on foot, despite the lure of historical markers detailing the former locations of the town's social hall, hospital, brick yard, and flour mill. Local history is recounted at **Iron Mission State Park**, on the main highway a mile or so north of downtown (daily: June to early Sept 9am–7pm; early Sept to May 9am–5pm; $3). Apart from rusty nuggets, the warehouse-like museum is filled with nineteenth-century horse-drawn vehicles, including wagons, sleighs, and hearses.

Tourists do arrive in droves during the summer, however, drawn by the annual **Utah Shakespeare Festival**, a semi-professional event held on the campus of the Southern Utah State University since 1962. Running from late June to the end of October, it usually features nine or so productions, with three or four Shakespeare plays among assorted others (reservations on ☎435/586-7878 or 1-800/752-9849, ⓦbard.org).

Practicalities

A large **visitor center** stands at 581 N Main St (summer Mon–Fri 8am–7pm, Sat 9am–1pm; winter Mon–Fri 8am–5pm; ☎435/586-5124 or 1-800/354-4849, ⓦwww.scenicsouthernutah.com). **Main Street** is handy for food and

lodging; motels with pools include two *Best Western*s, the *El Rey Inn* at no. 80 S
(☎435/586-6518, ⦿www.bwelrey.com; ❹), and the smart *Town and Country
Inn* at no. 189 N (☎435/586-9900, ⦿www.bwtowncountry.com; ❹). *Sullivan's*
at no. 301 S (☎435/586-6761) is part steakhouse, part coffee-shop, while *The
Grind Coffee House*, 19 N Main St (☎435/867-5333), is a busy, very central local
rendezvous, serving pastries and sandwiches as well as coffee, and putting on
regular live music.

Cedar Breaks National Monument

Cedar City stands at an elevation of 5800ft, but the densely wooded plateau to
the east rises a further five thousand feet. **Hwy-14**, the most direct route to
Bryce Canyon, climbs steadily onto the plateau from the narrow gorge east of
town. The scenery along the way is rarely short of spectacular, with views that
stretch south to encompass all of Zion National Park.

Fifteen miles along, shortly after the highway enters the **Dixie National
Forest**, the pink, white, and orange rocks of **CEDAR BREAKS NATIONAL
MONUMENT** stand immediately below the forest that tops the high ridge to
your left. Cedar Breaks is a sort of pocket version of Bryce Canyon (see p.393),
where erosive forces have scooped a natural amphitheater into the hillside and
filled it with brilliantly colored limestone formations. While it lacks Bryce's
opportunities for hiking, it's well worth seeing if you're in the area.

The road through the monument, **Hwy-148**, branches north from Hwy-14
nineteen miles out of Cedar City. When it's clear – it's usually snowbound between
late October and mid-May – you can choose between four similar cliff-edge
viewpoints. The southernmost, **Point Supreme**, is the best, with pinnacles rising
from the orange canyon floor at your feet and sweeping views to the south and
west. The small **visitor center** just behind is only staffed in summer (May–Oct
daily 8am–6pm; ☎435/586-9451, ⦿www.nps.gov/cebr); if you make it here in
spring or fall, you can visit without paying the usual $4-per-person fee. Overnight
temperatures only rise high enough to make the adjoining **campground** ($14) an
appealing proposition between July and September.

You can hike for short distances along the rim at both Point Supreme and
Chessmen Ridge, a mile or so north, but no trails descend into the formations.

East from Zion: US-89

As soon as you leave Zion National Park via its eastern entrance (see p.379),
you're out in flat, open ranching country. Eleven nondescript miles further on,
Hwy-9 meets **US-89** at Mount Carmel Junction. Turn **north** there, and once
across a mountainous ridge you'll find yourself driving up the broad **Long
Valley**, where the **Sevier River** cuts between the Markagunt and Paunsaugunt
plateaus. After just over forty pretty but uneventful miles, punctuated by the
occasional tiny Mormon settlement, you can either keep straight on toward Salt
Lake City or veer east toward Bryce Canyon and the other national parks.

The only real point in heading **south** on US-89 is to reach Arizona, with the
North Rim of the Grand Canyon (see p.355) almost exactly a hundred miles
away. A century ago, when Mormons from Arizona would come this way to be
married in the temple at St George, this route was known as the **Honeymoon
Trail**. The largest town along the highway, **Kanab**, retains a strong Mormon
identity, but it also has a back-of-beyond frontier feel to it and makes a good
overnight stop.

Mount Carmel Junction

The eastward progress of Hwy-9 stops when a north–south wall of red cliffs rears up on the far side of the Virgin River. It's a bucolic spot, with cottonwoods lining the river and horses grazing in the meadows to the north. Unless you're ready to stop for the night, however, there's little reason to get out of the car.

MOUNT CARMEL JUNCTION, where Hwy-9 intersects with US-89, consists of a couple of fairly upscale and reliable **motels**, both with licensed **restaurants**. The *Best Western East Zion Thunderbird Lodge* (☏435/648-2203 or 1-888/848-6358, ⓦzionnational-park.com; ❺), which boasts a pool, spa, and even half a golf course, has a considerable edge over the much plainer *Golden Hills* (☏435/648-2268 or 1-800/648-2268, ⓦgoldenhillsmotel.com; ❸).

Coral Pink Sand Dunes State Park

Few areas in the Southwest conform so exactly to the popular notion of a desert – graceful dunes of fine sand, their parallel crests sweeping toward the horizon – as **CORAL PINK SAND DUNES STATE PARK** (daily 24hr; $5 per vehicle; ☏435/648-2800). This pseudo-Saharan landscape, a dozen miles south of Mount Carmel Junction, is reached by two separate paved roads that leave US-89 four and nine miles southeast of town respectively.

The only dune field in the Colorado Plateau lies at the foot of a seven-mile bluff of the Vermilion Cliffs, which here unusually face the northwest. Its sand grains are eroded from Navajo sandstone, itself originally deposited in the form of dunes.

Hikers who launch themselves from the boardwalk near the entrance station usually find that a few minutes of wading knee-deep in sand sates their *Lawrence of Arabia* fantasies. However, in marked contrast to Utah's federal parks, **off-road vehicles** are positively encouraged. The park was created in response to campaigns by local off-road enthusiasts, and plays host to countless formal and informal **dune buggy races**, most notably each July 4.

▲ Coral Pink Sand Dunes State Park

The well-shaded **campground** ($15) remains open all year, though it only has water in summer. Spending a night here offers the enticing prospect of seeing not only kangaroo rats but, more to the point, the snakes that prey on them. The tiny rats are named for their squatting postures, and the snakes are not a danger to humans.

Kanab

Until new roads were pushed through the region in the 1950s, **KANAB**, seventeen miles southeast of Mount Carmel Junction and just two miles north of the Arizona state line, was renowned as the most inaccessible town in the US. Now it's a significant tourist rest-stop simply because it lies halfway between the Grand Canyon, eighty miles southeast, and Bryce Canyon, 83 miles northeast.

Kanab started life in 1864 as **Fort Kanab**, a frontier outpost so prone to Indian attacks that it was abandoned after just two years. Jacob Hamblin founded the town itself in 1870 as a God-fearing ranching community with a sideline in harboring Mormons who fell afoul of the federal government, among them several perpetrators of the Mountain Meadows Massacre. Pulp novelist Zane Grey later cultivated that lawless image, setting many of his Westerns nearby. Kanab's rugged surroundings also drew Western film greats, from Tom Mix, who filmed *Deadwood Coach* here in 1924, to Clint Eastwood, who swept into town with *The Outlaw Josey Wales* in 1976. The town soon earned the nickname "Utah's Little Hollywood."

With ranching in decline, and the prospect of large-scale coal mining on the **Kaiparowits Plateau** to the northeast having been thwarted by the establishment of Grand Staircase–Escalante National Monument in 1976, Kanab now survives by catering to tourists. US-89 is lined with an above-par assortment of motels and restaurants, with the greatest concentration where it briefly doglegs to run east–west along **Center Street**. A few blocks south, US-89 proper branches off east toward Page, while US-89A continues south into Arizona. For an account of **Fredonia**, seven miles south, and the route to the Grand Canyon, see p.360.

Apart from a few large Western-themed souvenir stores, such as Denny's Wigwam, opposite *Parry Lodge* at 78 E Center St (☏435/644-2452), there's almost nothing to do in Kanab, though hikers may enjoy the views from the **Squaw Trail**, which climbs the escarpment just north of town.

Information and tours

Kanab's large **visitor center** stands just south of Center Street at 78 S 100 East (March–Oct Mon–Fri 9am–7pm, Sat & Sun 9am–5pm; Nov–Feb Mon–Fri 9am–5pm; ☏435/644-5033 or 1-800/733-5263, ⊛www.kaneutah.com). The **BLM** Field Office, 745 E Hwy-89 (mid-March to mid-Nov daily 8am–4.30pm; mid-Nov to mid-March Mon–Fri 8am–4.30pm; ☏435/644-4600, ⊛www.ut .blm.gov), provides information on nearby public lands and current driving conditions.

Accommodation

Kanab holds several good-value budget **motels**, so don't feel compelled to pay extra for a fancier name. All are within easy walking distance of downtown.

Aiken's Lodge 74 W Center St ☏435/644-2625, ⊛aikenslodge.com. This low-slung and not desperately pretty option is nonetheless the ideal budget motel: crisp and clean, right in the heart of town, and with its own pool. ❸

Kanab Quality Inn 815 E AZ-99 ☏435/644-8888 or 1-800/574-4061, ⊛hikanabutah.com. Large new motel, isolated atop a bluff on the eastern edge of town, but with the best rooms in Kanab, plus a free breakfast bar. ❹

Parry Lodge 89 E Center St ☎435/644-2601 or 1-888/289-1722, ⓦparrylodge.com. Opened in 1931, Kanab's oldest motel has an undeniable air of romance. Photos of celebrity guests festoon the lobby and restaurant, while nameplates identify the rooms in which they slept; you can even bathe in John Wayne's extra-large bathtub. *Parry's* isn't *that* great,

though, and some of the newer rooms are dingy and noisy. Rates include a full cooked breakfast. ❹
Shilo Inn 296 W 100 North ☎435/644-2562 or 1-800/222-2244, ⓦwww.shiloinns.com. Large, presentable motel at the north end of town. Some rooms have kitchens, and there's a breakfast buffet, pool, and spa. ❺

Eating

Around twenty **restaurants** cling to the edge of the highway as it passes through Kanab. One or two make the effort to be distinctive, while the others rest safe in the knowledge that however bad they may be, there's precious little choice for a hundred miles in any direction.

Nedra's Too 310 S 100 East ☎435/644-2030. Informal local hangout at the junction of US-89 and US-89A on the south side of town, with a sister restaurant in Fredonia (see p.360). The unifying factor of the Mexican/American menu is the fryer; even the ice cream comes deep-fried. Open daily for all meals.
Parry Lodge 89 E Center St ☎435/644-2601. Attractive dining room where the menu occasionally hints at the healthy, in the form of dishes like poached salmon; unlike most places in Kanab, it

has a license to sell alcohol. Open for all meals in summer, breakfast and dinner only in spring and fall, and closed Nov–March.
Rocking V Café 97 W Center St ☎435/644-8001. This valiant and largely successful bid to improve Kanab's culinary reputation is housed in a former bank, one of the town's oldest buildings. Classic French and Italian dishes for dinner at around $17 per entree; cheaper, lighter lunches. Open daily for lunch and dinner.

East of Kanab: US-89 and Paria Canyon

US-89, which heads due east out of central Kanab, curves northwards into the southern reaches of Grand Staircase-Escalante National Monument (see p.400) as it makes its spectacular 73-mile run to **Page**, Arizona (see p.421). Though not as popular with visitors as the broadly parallel US-89A further south, which allows access to the North Rim of the Grand Canyon, it's still a dramatic drive and has its own potential diversions in the shape of the old **Pahreah** township and the hikes into **Coyote Buttes** and **Paria Canyon**.

Exploring these or any other off-highway areas requires you to drive down dirt roads that become very treacherous in bad weather, while even the shortest hike leads swiftly into remote backcountry. It is therefore essential to pick up detailed, current advice on conditions, either at the BLM office in Kanab or at the BLM's **Paria Contact Station**, 43 miles east (March to mid-Nov daily 8am–5pm; no phone).

Pahreah

Around 35 miles east of Kanab, close to the northernmost point along US-89's sweep through Grand Staircase-Escalante National Monument, an obelisk on the north side of the highway commemorates the founding of the town of **Pahreah** nearby, in 1865. Though initially threatened by Indian raids, Pahreah kept going as a farming community until the 1930s, when it was finally abandoned after repeated floods.

A dirt road leads down from the obelisk toward the actual town site, dropping steeply through some truly stunning badlands, where the rounded hillocks and cliffs alike are striped with gray and bluish clays as well as red sandstone. Four miles down it passes what little remains of the **Paria Movie Set**, used for *The Outlaw Josey Wales* in 1976. The set was dismantled in 1999 after flood damage rendered it unsafe, and now just two very new-looking reconstructions flank the road. Beyond that lies the genuine old town cemetery, while the **Paria River** itself is 5.6 miles from the highway. The whole area is so overgrown with tamarisk and young cottonwood trees that it's all but impossible to find a trace of the settlement, but it's a remote and attractive enough spot to spend a few minutes looking.

Coyote Buttes

Five miles on from Pahreah, between mile posts 25 and 26, a conspicuous but unmarked dirt road leads south from the highway, along a high ridge, toward the **Coyote Buttes** area. Since 2000, this has formed part of **Vermilion Cliffs National Monument**, but despite that enhanced status it remains relatively untrampled by human feet. Its guardians, the BLM, are so determined to keep it that way that hiking is rigidly controlled. Day-hikers who stay within the upper reaches of Wire Pass, Buckskin Gulch, and Paria Canyon do not require **permits**, though they still must pay $5 per person per day. For overnight stays in those areas, and for day-hikes as well as overnight backpacking trips further afield, permits are essential – and with just twenty issued per day for the whole region, ten of them for Coyote Buttes North ($7 per person per day) and ten for Coyote Buttes South ($5), they're very hard to come by. **Reservations** can be made up to four months in advance, either at a BLM office in the area, via the Paria Canyon Project on ☏ 435/688-3246, or online at ⊕ www.blm.gov /az/paria. On the first day of each month, permits become available for the fourth month ahead; thus March 1 is the date on which June permits are first sold. It's not unusual for all permits to sell out within an hour.

What everyone is so eager to see is a rock formation known as **The Wave**, an extraordinary, disorienting ripple of sculpted sandstone atop a hard-to-find prominence known as **Top Rock**, just south of the Arizona–Utah state line in the north section of the buttes. As there's no fixed trail, you'll need good advice to complete the seven-mile round-trip hike in a single day. The BLM requests that specific instructions not be published, in order to discourage unauthorized or poorly equipped hikers; if you're lucky enough to get the necessary reservation, they'll provide you with a detailed map. Both the Coyote Buttes and Buckskin Gulch routes start from the **Wire Pass Trailhead**, reached by leaving US-89 between mile markers 25 and 26 and just over eight miles south into the wilderness. The closest BLM office, the **Paria Contact Station** (daily 8.30am–4.15pm; ☏ 435/644-4628), is four miles east of the highway turn-off; if you're approaching from Page, remember it's an hour later here in Utah than it is in Arizona.

Paria Canyon

The same restrictions on backpacker permits described for Coyote Buttes above also apply to hikers intending to make the four- to six-day trek down **Paria Canyon**, which ends at the start of the Grand Canyon at Lees Ferry, Arizona (see p.354). While it's possible to access the route by first hiking down Buckskin Gulch from the Wire Pass Trailhead mentioned above, most hikers start at the **White House Trailhead**, two miles south of US-89 just east of the Paria Contact Station (see above). A basic campground near the trailhead charges $5 per night.

North from Mount Carmel: Orderville

If instead of heading south from Mount Carmel (see p.388) via Kanab, you turn **north** on US-89, you'll arrive at **ORDERVILLE** within four miles. Despite its historical significance as the longest-lasting of several experiments in communitarian living organized by the **United Order**, a nineteenth-century Mormon group that believed all property should be held in common, modern

Orderville is not worth an extended stay. Aside from two gas stations and a couple of shabby motels it has little to attract passing tourists.

Glendale

Five miles beyond Orderville, the almost equally insignificant hamlet of **GLENDALE** nestles amid a cluster of apple orchards. A white clapboard house that looks much like the rest – complete with a large upstairs veranda – serves as the *Smith Hotel*, 295 N Main St (☎435/648-2156 or 1-800/528-3558, ⓦhistoricsmithhotel.com; ❸), with seven very pleasant en-suite **B&B** rooms. Alongside, the *Buffalo Bistro*, 305 N Main St (closed Tues & Wed; ☎435/648-2778), serves well-prepared steaks and burgers for lunch and dinner, with fresh vegetables and great desserts.

Hatch

Long Valley steadily dries out north of Glendale, so travelers from Cedar City who pick up US-89 at the east end of Hwy-14 – see p.387 – encounter further upland forests rather than farmland.

At 7000ft up, little **HATCH**, 25 miles on, makes a cool overnight stop in summer, but that's the only time its handful of motels are at all busy. The *Riverside Resort & RV Park*, a mile north of town at 594 N Hwy-89 (☎435/735-4223 or 1-800/824-5651, ⓦwww.riversideresort-utah.com; ❸), has a dozen surprisingly nice rooms and suites, plus **camping** facilities for $18 per night, while the somewhat smarter *Bryce–Zion Midway Resort*, 244 S Hwy-89 (☎435/735-4199 or 1-888/299-3531; ❹), offers a choice of cabins or motel rooms, and also a decent **restaurant** serving the usual steak, chicken, and pasta dishes.

Red Canyon and the road to Bryce

The only road in a hundred miles that manages to climb through the wild country east of US-89 is **Hwy-12**, which was blasted into the rocks ten miles north of Hatch to provide a route to **Bryce Canyon** and beyond. Another seven miles' drive from the intersection of Hwy-12 and US-89 brings you to the town of Panguitch (see opposite), but there's accommodation right at the intersection of US-89 and Hwy-12. *Harold's Place* (closed Nov to April; ☎435/676-2350 or 676-8886, ⓦwww.haroldsplace.net; ❸) offers twenty log cabins, two of which sleep six people, plus motel rooms in a separate inn.

Hwy-12 climbs away from US-89 by way of **Red Canyon**. For information on this small precursor of the joys ahead, call in at the Dixie National Forest **visitor center** (☎435/676-8815), a few miles along on the left. This parking lot marks the start of the short Pink Ledges **hiking trail**; longer trails leave from the Forest Service's first-come, first-served *Red Canyon* **campground** ($12, no showers), half a mile further on. Immediately beyond that, the highway tunnels through two artificial red-rock arches, before topping out on top of the Paunsaugunt Plateau, with another ten miles to go before Bryce.

Panguitch

The spruce, squeaky-clean and oddly endearing Mormon town of **PANGUITCH** – 24 miles from Bryce, and fifty from Mount Carmel Junction – was established in 1864 and named for no good reason after the Paiute term for "Big Fish." After an uncertain start, Panguitch became, and remains, the largest town along the Upper Sevier Valley. That was originally due in part to the brick factory responsible for the distinguished brick homes that still adorn its streets, but Panguitch today depends heavily on tourism for its bread and butter. It's a bit too chilly to linger in the off-season, but in summer, the pumps at the eight local gas stations rarely stop spinning (one, Todd's Truck Stop, stays open 24hr), and twenty-odd budget motels and restaurants are kept busy.

Practicalities

Panguitch's **visitor center**, at 55 S Main St (daily May–Oct 9am–5pm; ☎435/676-1160 or 1-800/444-6869, ⓦwww.brycecanyoncountry.com), stocks a **walking tour** of the town's historic homes. You'd have to be more than a little weird, however, to spend your morning doing that rather than setting off into the wondrous deserts. The same management operates the two best **accommodation** options, the *Marianna Inn Motel*, 699 N Main St (☎435/676-8844, ⓦmariannainn.com; ❹), a scrupulously clean, well-run budget motel on the northern edge of town, and the central, nicely restored *Panguitch Inn*, 50 N Main St ☎435/676-8871, ⓦwww.panguitchinn.com; ❹). The half-dozen local **restaurants** are consistently hum-drum, though the moderately priced barbecued meats and huge fruit pies in the Victorian-era **Cowboy's Smokehouse Bar-B-Q**, 95 N Main St (closed Sun; ☎435/676-8030), are hard to resist. If you just want a sandwich, there's a *Subway* near the north end of town.

Bryce Canyon National Park

Few more freakish landscapes can exist than those confined within **BRYCE CANYON NATIONAL PARK**. From the park's rim road, visitors gaze down on a throng of red, yellow, and orange pinnacles of rock, eating like the flames of a forest fire into the thickly wooded plateau. You can hike down into the inferno and thread your way between the top-heavy towers, to explore a barren desert that's aglow with almost psychedelic colors.

Paiute Indians, who hunted in the vicinity, had an elegantly precise word for the landscape: *Unkatimpe-wa-Wince-Pockich*, "red rocks standing like men in a bowl-shaped recess." The current name comes from the Mormon settler **Ebenezer Bryce**, who established a short-lived homestead nearby in 1874 and memorably declared this was "a helluva place to lose a cow." In fact, however, "Bryce's Canyon" is not a canyon at all but a row of crescent-shaped amphitheaters, hollowed into a twenty-mile stretch along the eastern edge of the **Paunsaugunt Plateau**. At up to 9000ft above sea level, this marks the final and most spectacular rung of the Grand Staircase's ascent of southern Utah (see p.5). Between sixty and forty million years ago, the **Pink Cliffs** were deposited in layers of varying thickness and strength on the beds of shallow lakes. Some are limestone, some siltstone; all were dyed and stained with combinations of red, white, orange, blue, or yellow by different concentrations of minerals, especially iron.

Conditions at Bryce are perfect for rapid erosion, with ice forming overnight and thawing in the morning over 200 times per year. Water seeps into cracks in the ground, then expands as it freezes, to wedge the cracks ever wider. Spurs emerge from the cliff-face as it recedes, then dwindle to slender fins and eventually break into separate standing columns. When the topmost rock of a column is hard enough, lower levels erode away beneath it at a much faster rate. A mighty boulder left precariously perched on a tall, narrow pillar is known as a **hoodoo**. At Bryce, thousands upon thousands of hoodoos are crammed into each successive amphitheater, to form a menagerie of multihued, contorted stone shapes. The best known, and most precarious, is **Thor's Hammer**, near Sunset Point.

Since it became a national park in the 1920s – with irregular boundaries designed to minimize the impact on local ranchers – Bryce Canyon has deservedly ranked as a must-see attraction for any visitor to Utah. If you're at all stretched for time, however, this is one park that you can realistically hope to see in a single day, or even an afternoon. Just be sure that you do at least get out of your car and **hike** into the technicolor ravines – far more vivid than the Grand Canyon, as well as much more human in scale. Most visitors pass through between June and August, but the park is, if anything, even more inspiring in the stillness of winter, when the hoodoos rear their heads from a blanket of **snow**.

Getting to Bryce

Bryce Canyon is around a two hours' drive (86 miles northeast) from Zion Canyon, and something over three hours from Capitol Reef, 120 miles further northeast. The only approach is along **Hwy-12**, which runs within the northern boundaries of the park on its way across southwest Utah. However, you won't see the rock formations – or be liable for the entrance fee – unless you turn south off the main highway thirteen miles east of US-89 (a total of twenty miles southeast of Panguitch), or eight miles northwest of Tropic (see p.399). **Hwy-63** reaches the park entrance station after a further three miles, then traces the rim of the Paunsaugunt Plateau for eighteen miles before coming to a dead end at Rainbow Point.

No public **buses** serve Bryce, but charter and sight-seeing flights from elsewhere in the Southwest land at **Bryce Canyon Airport** on Hwy-12, although to no fixed schedule; call ☎435/834-5239 for current details. Oddly enough, this is one of the oldest airports in the US, with pine-log hangars built by the WPA in the 1930s. Once on the ground, rent a car from, or join a tour with, Bryce Canyon Scenic Tours (see below).

Finally, keen **hikers** should note that it's possible to avoid the crowds by walking into the park from **Tropic** (see p.399).

Arrival and information

The **entrance fee** to Bryce, payable at kiosks on the park boundary on Hwy-63, is $25 per vehicle, per week; the national park passes detailed on p.41 are both sold and accepted. Although the park runs **free shuttle buses** to reduce traffic congestion, visitors can still drive to all the scenic overlooks year round. Buses operate between 9am and 6pm daily from late May until late September, along a route that connects the *Ruby's Inn* complex, just south of the intersection of Hwy-12 and Hwy-63, with the overlooks in Bryce Amphitheater. If that's as far as you want to go – and for most people, even enthusiastic hikers, it's entirely sufficient – then there's no reason to use your own car. No buses go as far south as Rainbow Point, however.

The logical first stop for drivers and shuttle passengers alike is the **visitor center**, a short way beyond the park entrance (daily: May–Sept 8am–8pm; April & Oct 8am–6pm; Nov–March 8am–4.30pm; ☎435/834-5322, ⓦwww.nps.gov/brca). A valuable source of information on current weather and hiking conditions, this is also the place to pick up backcountry permits (see p.397).

Canyon Trail Rides, contactable via the desk at *Bryce Canyon Lodge* (☎435/679-8665, ⓦcanyonrides.com), arranges **horseback rides** into the canyon (2hr rides starting at 9am & 2pm, minimum age 7, $50; half-day rides at 8am & 1pm, minimum age 10, $75), as does Scenic Rim Trail Rides, based at *Ruby's* (☎435/679-8761 or 1-800/679-5859, ⓦwww.brycecanyonhorseback.com), at similar prices.

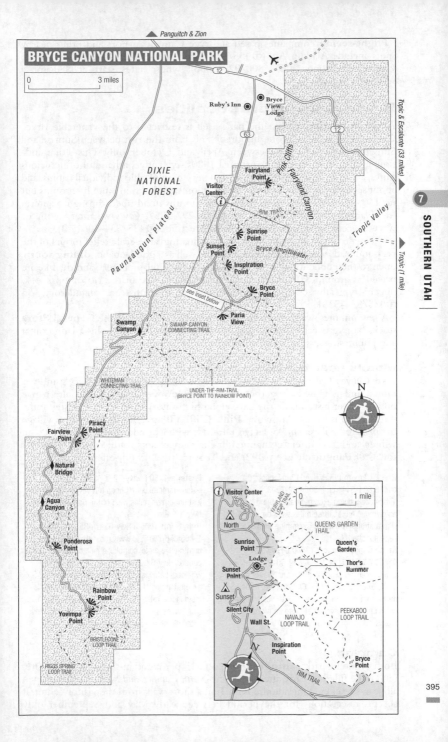

BRYCE CANYON NATIONAL PARK

0   3 miles

▲ *Panguitch & Zion*

12

Ruby's Inn ◉

◉ Bryce View Lodge

63

Tropic & Escalante (33 miles) ▶

12

DIXIE NATIONAL FOREST

Fairland Point

Pink Cliffs

Fairyland Canyon

Visitor Center
ⓘ

RIM TRAIL

Tropic Valley

▶ *Tropic (1 mile)*

Sunrise Point

Sunset Point

Bryce Amphitheater

Inspiration Point

Paunsaugunt Plateau

Bryce Point

see inset below

Paria View

Swamp Canyon

SWAMP CANYON CONNECTING TRAIL

WHITEMAN CONNECTING TRAIL

UNDER-THE-RIM-TRAIL
(BRYCE POINT TO RAINBOW POINT)

N

Piracy Point

Fairview Point

Natural Bridge

Agua Canyon

Ponderosa Point

Rainbow Point

Yovimpa Point

BRISTLECONE LOOP TRAIL

RIGGS SPRING LOOP TRAIL

ⓘ Visitor Center

0   1 mile

FAIRLAND LOOP TRAIL

⛺ North

QUEENS GARDEN TRAIL

Sunrise Point

Queen's Garden

Lodge ◉

Thor's Hammer

Sunset Point

⛺ Sunset

Silent City

Wall St.

NAVAJO LOOP TRAIL

PEEKABOO LOOP TRAIL

Inspiration Point

N

Bryce Point

RIM TRAIL

Flight-seeing companies based at Bryce Canyon Airport and other nearby spots include Aladdin Air (☎435/834-5555 or 1-800/914-3215) and Bryce Canyon Helicopters (☎1-800/979-5050), whose rates start at $80 for a seventeen-minute flight.

Bryce Canyon practicalities

Accommodation within the park itself is restricted to the venerable Bryce Canyon Lodge, located one hundred yards from the rim between Sunrise and Sunset points, and open between April and October only. This stone-and-timber affair, furnished in its original 1920s style, offers a handful of luxurious suites, a row or two of rough-hewn but very comfortable individual cabins, and about seventy relatively ordinary motel rooms. All have en-suite bathrooms but no TVs, and tend to be reserved several months in advance, through Xanterra (reservations ☎303/297-2757 or 1-888/297-2757, ⓦwww.xanterra.com or www.brycecanyonlodge.com; property direct line ☎435/834-5361; ➐).

The main lobby of the *Lodge* holds a fascinating large-scale relief model of the park and leads to several souvenir stores as well as a good-quality **dining room**, open to the public for all meals. Lunchtime quesadillas, burgers, and the like are priced at around $10, and richer dinner entrees like prime rib or pork osso bucco typically cost $19–25. Dinner reservations are mandatory, on ☎435/834-5361.

A few minutes' walk away, slightly north of Sunrise Point, the **General Store** stocks basic groceries, snacks, and camping equipment and holds a laundromat and public showers.

Motels near the park

Bryce Canyon Lodge can only accommodate a tiny proportion of Bryce's summer influx, and is closed altogether in winter. However, half a dozen alternative options loiter just outside the park along highways 12 and 63; the cluster at the intersection is loosely known as **Pink Cliffs Village**, though there's no village to speak of. All remain open year-round, with considerably reduced rates in winter, and have their own unenthralling restaurants. Otherwise, the nearby towns of **Panguitch** (see p.392) and **Tropic** (p.399) both offer motels.

Bryce Canyon Pines Hwy-12 milepost 10 ☎435/834-5441 or 1-800/892-7923, ⓦbrycecanyonmotel.com. Reasonable if anonymous motel, three miles west on Hwy-12, with a strangely shallow swimming pool in a separate shed. ➎

Bryce Canyon Resort 13500 E Hwy-12 ☎435/834-5351 or 1-866/834-0043, ⓦbrycecanyonresort.com. Simple budget motel at the intersection in Pink Cliffs Village, three miles from the park entrance, with basic summer-only cabins and somewhat more comfortable rooms. ➏

Foster's 1150 E Hwy-12 ☎435/834-5227, ⓦfostersmotel.com. Cheap but very shabby motel, just under two miles west of the park turn-off on Hwy-12. ➌

Ruby's Inn 1000 S Hwy-63 ☎435/834-5341 or 1-866/866-6616, ⓦwww.rubysinn.com. Large, unattractive motel complex a mile or so outside the park on Hwy-63. Fifty of the 368 rooms feature whirlpool baths, and there's a heated indoor swimming pool. Paying extra to be housed in the main lodge, rather than one of the outlying sections, only makes sense in the depths of winter. The food in the dining room is consistently atrocious. ➏

Camping

Both of the in-park **campgrounds** cost $15 per night; in summer, all 216 sites tend to be filled by early afternoon. The *North Campground*, which remains open all year, stretches alongside the Rim Trail a short walk from the visitor center. It accepts reservations for the period between early May and September only

(☎1-877/444-6777, ⓦwww.recreation.gov). *Sunset Campground*, a mile or so south, across the highway from the lodge near Sunset Point, operates between May and mid-October, on a first-come, first-served basis. Neither campground offers RV hookups, and the closest showers are by the General Store.

Backcountry campers can choose from several designated sites, all south of Bryce Point below the rim and well away from the main trails. Pick up a $5 permit at the visitor center, and take lots of water.

The nearest **commercial campground** to the park is the slightly more deluxe area adjoining *Ruby's Inn*, a mile north (see above; also ⓦbrycecanyon campgrounds.com; $24 per site), which also caters to RVs. If your heart is set on a night in the woods, head instead for the roadside campground at **Red Canyon**, ten miles west on Hwy-12 (see p.392).

▲ On the trail in Wall Street, Bryce Canyon

Seeing the park

Most visitor activity at Bryce is concentrated around **Bryce Amphitheater**, the largest and most accessible of the indentations in the Pink Cliffs. Whether you park your own car off the loop road that leaves Hwy-63 half a mile south of the visitor center, or get dropped off by the shuttle bus, a brief walk will bring you to the brink of the crescent-shaped depression.

Where along the Rim Trail you get your first blast of the incandescent rocks makes little difference. Of the two official overlooks, around five hundred yards apart, **Sunrise Point** to the north attracts fewer of the tour-bus crowds than **Sunset Point** to the south. Neither name is particularly appropriate; both face east, so you won't see the sun set, while the best place to catch the dawn is **Bryce Point**, a mile or so further south. Here at the southernmost tip of the amphitheater, you can look back west as the first rays of the sun strike the toy soldiers below. Although dawn and dusk are the prime times to **take photos** at Bryce, the views to the east and north are astonishing at any time of day, ranging as much as a hundred miles to encompass the Aquarius Plateau and the Henry Mountains.

Beyond Bryce Amphitheater, Hwy-63 – also known as the **Scenic Drive** – meanders south for another fifteen miles. It's a slow drive, passing a succession of substantially similar viewpoints; no one stops at them all, though each has its merits. Look out in particular for the **Natural Bridge**, which spans a steep gully approximately halfway along the route. Suspended far above the forest, it doesn't cross running water, so technically it's not a bridge but an 85ft arch.

Hwy-63 climbs steadily as it continues south, until finally the ridge it's following narrows to a slender neck, and the road is forced to end at the highest viewpoint of all, **Rainbow Point**. Both this and nearby **Yovimpa Point** command sweeping views south, to Navajo Mountain and the Kaibab forest that fringes the Grand Canyon.

As you leave the park, bear in mind that **Fairyland Point**, reached via a separate turn-off north of the visitor center, is one of Bryce's quietest yet most scenic viewpoints.

Hiking

The **Rim Trail** follows the lip of the plateau for just over five miles, skirting Bryce Amphitheater between Sunrise and Sunset points, and extending both north and south. Die-hard backpackers can continue beyond its southern limit, at Bryce Point, all the way to Rainbow Point, 22.6 miles on, along the **Under-the-Rim Trail** (which has designated camping spots). By far the most popular trails in the park, however, are those that drop into **Bryce Amphitheater** itself. With several alternative routes to the bottom, and a choice of connections once you're there, you can tailor a hike to suit whatever time you have, from a couple of hours to a full day.

The basic experience is much the same whichever trail you take. The rock stratum that has eroded to form the hoodoos, just below the rim, averages from 300 to 500ft thick, so hiking consists of descending between them until you reach the flatter pine forest beyond, walking through the woods, and then climbing back up again. At an elevation of almost two miles, even a brief hike involves considerable effort; you'll need good footwear and plenty of water.

For a concentrated burst of Bryce at its best, the **Navajo Loop Trail** is ideal. The shortest and busiest trail of all, it plummets abruptly from Sunset Point into formations known as the **Silent City**, then circles back up to complete a hike of 1.4 miles. Allow two hours to enjoy the whole roundtrip without exhausting yourself. Taking the trail's steeper right-hand branch as you set off makes for an easier hike, and also brings you, by way of precipitous switchbacks, straight into the cool crevice of **Wall Street**. In places, this awe-inspiring gulf of orange rock is less than twenty feet wide, but it's too deep for the 800-year-old Douglas firs that grow from its sandy floor to poke their heads above the cliffs.

Beyond Wall Street, you swiftly reach a small sandy wash. The return leg of the Navajo Loop Trail starts a short way to the left and follows a slightly gentler incline back to Sunset Point, passing **Thor's Hammer** and other humongous hoodoos en route. Alternatively, continue northwards on the level footpath just above the wash, pausing perhaps to rest in the shade of the pines and junipers. The basin known as the **Queen's Garden** is somewhere over a mile along. Named for an almost translucent fin that's topped by a rocky pile bearing a vague resemblance to Queen Victoria, it's connected by a mile-long trail up the hillside to **Sunrise Point**. During its climb, the path cuts repeatedly through limestone fins and spurs, with each tunnel framing yet another irresistible photograph. Most of the horseback expeditions in the park – see p.394 – pass this way. Dwarfed beneath the ludicrous, multicolored spires and turrets, the horses make an especially surreal spectacle.

East of Bryce

By continuing east from Bryce Canyon, you're leaving civilization firmly behind. This central region of southern Utah is almost entirely given over to wilderness, and there's barely time to draw breath after Bryce before you plunge into Grand Staircase–Escalante National Monument. A few tiny communities cling to the fringes, however, and **Tropic** offers a few creature comforts as you brace yourself for what lies ahead.

Tropic

The first community east of Bryce along Hwy-12 is **TROPIC**, eight miles from the park turn-off. Among the migrants from Panguitch who settled this tiny hamlet in the 1880s – naming it for its allegedly superior climate – was Ebenezer Bryce himself (see p.393). His restored log cabin is now the center-piece of the *Pioneer Village* motel.

Tropic may turn its back on the flamboyance of Bryce Canyon, ranged along the ridge above it, but it has little appeal of its own; the main street consists of a row of motels and fast-food joints, and strolling around the center is unrewarding. However, the unmarked road that leads west from Bryce's log cabin reaches the park boundary in a couple of miles, from where it's a further two-mile hike up to the main formations.

Accommodation

You don't gain much by staying in Tropic rather than the motels closer to the park, but it does have a reasonable range of **accommodation**. However, few of the motels have facilities – for example pools - that might entice you to hang around during the day.

Bryce Canyon Inn 21 N Main St ☎435/679-8502 or 1-800/592-1468, ⓦbrycecanyoninn.com. Standard motel rooms, plus 18 large new log cabins, available in summer only. ❸
Bryce Pioneer Village 80 St Main S ☎435/679-8546 or 1-866/657-8414, ⓦwww.bpvillage.com.

Complex of dull but adequate motel rooms, with showers not baths, and more atmospheric individual cabins, transplanted from the park and equipped with two double beds as well as either baths or showers. ❸–❹

Bryce Point B&B 61 North 400 West ☎435/679-8629 or 1-888/200-4211, ⍟brycepointbb.com. Cheerful family-run B&B attached to a private house; all of the five large rooms have picture windows facing Bryce Canyon, plus their own baths and TVs, and there's also a shared deck with hot tub. ❹

Buffalo Sage B&B 980 N Hwy-12 ☎435/679-8443 or 1-866/232-5711, ⍟buffalosage.com.

Modern, purpose-built B&B perched on a bluff at the northwest end of town and enjoying great views from a wraparound deck. Four comfortable, en-suite, nonsmoking rooms. ❺

Grand Staircase Inn 105 N Kodachrome Drive, Cannonville ☎435/679-8400 or 1-877/472-6346, ⍟grandstaircaseinn.com. Simple but adequate highway motel five miles south of Tropic, attached to a grocery store and gas station. ❸

Eating

No one would make a special trip to eat in Tropic's limited array of restaurants, but once you're here it's not worth driving anywhere else either.

Doug's Place 141 N Main St ☎435/679-8632. Bustling diner attached to a large convenience store, which gets really busy at breakfast time and doesn't make all that romantic a rendezvous for its

conventional meat-and-potatoes dinners.

The Pizza Place Hwy-12 ☎435/679-8888. Quick, functional pizza joint, which also does take-outs and deliveries.

Kodachrome Basin State Park

At the village of Cannonville, five miles south of Tropic, Hwy-12 veers east across the Paria River. If you choose to continue south along Paria Valley instead, on Cottonwood Canyon Road, the pavement runs out after eight more miles at **KODACHROME BASIN STATE PARK**. This assortment of contorted rocky columns, tucked beneath the cliffs that climb to Kaiparowits Peak, was named by a *National Geographic* photographer in 1948 in honor of the latest Kodak film; he felt the area's existing name of Thorny Pasture was too prosaic.

By the standards of Utah's national parks, however, Kodachrome Basin is not especially worth making an effort to see. Its main focus is a unique geological phenomenon, not found anywhere else on earth: its 67 **sand pipes**. Each of these misshapen pillars was formed as an underground geyser, created by an earthquake, which was then blocked with tough calcite sediment. When the softer rock that surrounded them eroded away, they were left towering as high as 150ft above the scrubby plain.

After paying the $6-per-vehicle day-use **fee** at the park entrance station (open 24hr, ☎435/679-8562), follow the road for a couple of miles to the left to reach the park's attractive **campground** ($16; reserve on ☎1-800/322-3770). Various trailheads along the way mark the start of short hikes among the formations. Alternatively, the unpaved road that forks right from the entrance station ends after a little over a mile at the trailhead for **Shakespeare Arch**. A pleasant quarter-mile walk brings you to a small high natural arch, from where you can get good views across the valley to the Pink Cliffs of Bryce Canyon.

Grand Staircase–Escalante National Monument

Created by a controversial presidential decree in 1996, **GRAND STAIRCASE-ESCALANTE NATIONAL MONUMENT** is, at 1.9 million acres, the largest US national monument outside Alaska. Though its staggering landscape unquestionably merits such recognition, it's not so much a homogenous entity as the final piece in a jigsaw puzzle, placing the leftover lands between Bryce,

The first proposal to create **Escalante National Monument** was submitted to Franklin Roosevelt in 1940 by Secretary of the Interior Harold Ickes. Its boundaries would have enclosed 4.5 million acres, stretching from Lees Ferry as far as Moab and Green River, and taken in 280 miles of the Colorado River, 150 miles of the Green River, and 70 miles of the San Juan. That vast area was then crossed by just one road, and no bridge spanned the Colorado. Although Roosevelt saw himself as an environmentalist, the greenery of the Hudson River Valley was far more to his taste than the red rocks of the West. In the face of vociferous Mormon opposition in Utah, not to mention the coming of war, the idea was quietly dropped.

When Canyonlands National Park was created in the 1960s (see p.435), it included only a small proportion of Ickes' suggested tract. Glen Canyon on the Colorado River was by now submerged beneath Lake Powell (see p.422), while the **Kaiparowits Plateau**, which stretches south of Escalante all the way to the lake, remained outside federal protection. That was thanks to pressure from economic interests in southern Utah, acutely aware that what they call Fifty-Mile Mountain stands on top of the world's largest known deposits of **coal**.

Rumors surrounded plans to mine the Kaiparowits Plateau for well over fifty years. The closest any came to fruition was in the 1970s, when the Southern California Edison Company announced its intention to open a 6000-acre mine, complete with new roads and an on-site electricity generating plant. Controversy over the scheme pitted its supporters, the so-called **Sagebrush Rebels** – an informal grouping of Utah's Mormon-dominated business elite, plus the workers whose livelihoods were at stake – against environmentalists from across the nation. Although its abandonment in 1976 was largely due to a slackening of demand for electricity, communities such as Kanab, desperate for jobs, took out their anger by burning effigies of green activists in the streets.

In 1980, a study commissioned by Congress showed that almost 400,000 acres on the Kaiparowits Plateau had already been logged to clear the way for mines. Much of that timber was processed at a mill in Escalante, and when green opposition resulted in a moratorium on tree-felling, Escalante too witnessed its own share of public "hangings."

Hopes that mining money might revitalize Escalante rose once more in the mid-1990s, with the news that a Dutch conglomerate was considering strip-mining the Kaiparowits. By now, however, the pro-mining lobby was merely a vociferous minority, and President Clinton decided that delighting environmentalists in every state was more important than appeasing the business community in Utah. In September 1996 he therefore declared the creation of the **Grand Staircase–Escalante National Monument**.

Utah legislators promptly condemned it as "the mother of all land grabs," and the ropes came out once again, this time to "hang" both Clinton and his Interior Secretary Bruce Babbitt. However, the move was welcomed in the rest of the nation, and now that the die has been cast, even Escalante seems to have accepted it. After years of insisting that they'd rather be farming, logging, and mining than running motels, the predominantly Mormon local population does at least seem to have been guaranteed a secure economic future, even if it's not quite the one they anticipated.

Capitol Reef, the Dixie National Forest, and the Glen Canyon NRA under federal control. From the Aquarius Plateau in the north (as the highest segment of the Colorado Plateau, the top rung of the "staircase") to Lake Powell in the south, only the farming valleys around towns such as Tropic, Escalante, and Boulder remain in private ownership.

Although **Hwy-12** dips in and out of its northern flanks, **US-89** runs briefly through its southern extremities, and the rudimentary **Burr Trail** leads into

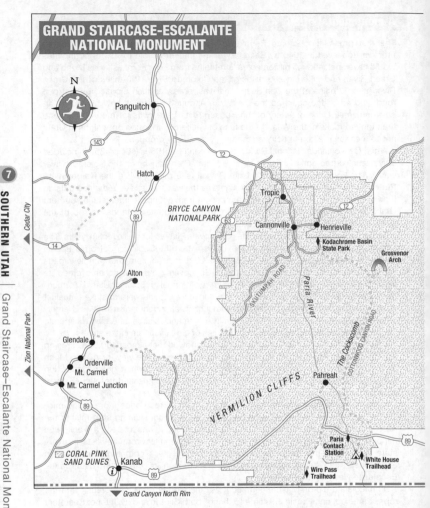

GRAND STAIRCASE-ESCALANTE
NATIONAL MONUMENT

N

Panguitch

143

Hatch

89

BRYCE CANYON
NATIONAL PARK

Tropic

12

63

Cannonville

Henrieville

Kodachrome Basin
State Park

Grosvenor
Arch

Alton

SKUTUMPAH ROAD

Paria River

The Cockscomb

COTTONWOOD CANYON ROAD

Glendale

Orderville
Mt. Carmel

Mt. Carmel Junction

89

VERMILION CLIFFS

Pahreah

89

CORAL PINK
SAND DUNES

Kanab

Paria
Contact
Station

White House
Trailhead

89

Wire Pass
Trailhead

Grand Canyon North Rim

Capitol Reef from its eastern end (see p.417), no paved roads cross this magnificent wilderness. True, dirt tracks provide limited access to the backcountry, but even they don't begin to penetrate the extraordinary canyon country at its heart, and all are in any case rendered impassable by poor weather. What's more, there's only one maintained hiking trail in the whole huge expanse.

Created to "maintain the unspoiled nature" of the region, rather than "develop" it for tourism, Grand Staircase–Escalante was the first national park or monument to be administered not by the National Park Service but by the Bureau of Land Management. No new paved roads have been built, and all facilities are located in existing towns, primarily **Escalante** itself.

Most of the million visitors who pass this way each year arrive with little idea of what to do other than simply drive the hundred-mile stretch of **Hwy-12** between Bryce Canyon and Capitol Reef. Only completed in 1980, thanks to the difficulty of the terrain and the lack of towns en route, this is

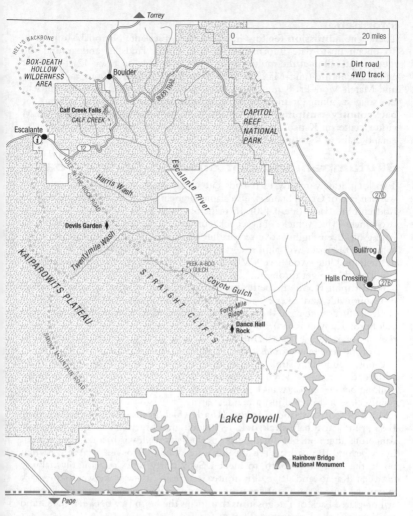

indisputably the most scenic of southern Utah's fifteen or so designated "Scenic Byways." Although no driver could fail to be awed by the highway's ever-changing panoply of red-rock canyons, crystal-clear rivers, and shimmering oases, it's well worth taking the time to get out of your car and explore at least a little on foot.

The **Escalante River**, which drains this whole region, was the last river to be named, let alone explored, in the continental US, and to this day most maps show the area as a vast blank. However, the back roads and trails have begun to bustle with venturesome tourists. Visitors now tend to stay two or three nights rather than just one, spending perhaps one day exploring the remarkable **slot canyons** along rugged **Hole-in-the-Rock Road**, and another in and around delightful **Calf Creek**. For backpackers, the options are all but infinite, though the sandstone bridges and arches on the lower reaches of **Coyote Gulch** and the Escalante River itself are the prime attraction.

Information

There is no **admission fee** for Grand Staircase–Escalante National Monument. To obtain up-to-date information on the public lands in and around the monument, call in at the multi-agency **visitor center** on Hwy-12 at the west end of **Escalante** (mid-March to mid-Nov daily 7.30am–5.30pm; mid-Nov to mid-March Mon–Fri 8am–4.30pm; ✆ 435/826-5499), where the helpful staff can suggest hiking or mountain-biking itineraries and issue free permits for **backcountry camping**. You can also pick up information from the **BLM** visitor center in Kanab (see p.389), or **online** at ⓦ www.blm.gov/ut/st/en/fo /grand_staircase-escalante.html.

Skutumpah and Cottonwood Canyon roads

Two long, lonely, mostly dirt roads cut north–south trajectories through the western end of Grand Staircase–Escalante, branching off from the paved road to Kodachrome Basin (see p.400). In principle, both can be traveled in ordinary, two-wheel-drive vehicles, but check current conditions with rangers before setting off. Even slightly adverse weather can make the going impossible, while in winter the roads will almost certainly be not only impassable, but potential death-traps. Unless you have 4WD, don't base your itinerary on the assumption you'll be able to get through.

Skutumpah Road, the better maintained of the two, starts three miles south of Cannonville and takes 52 miles to reach US-89, nine miles east of Kanab. Both the first sixteen and the last sixteen of those miles are paved (the latter part as Johnson Canyon Road), but that still leaves twenty difficult unpaved miles, as the road picks its way across **Bull Valley Gorge** and through the **White Cliffs**. One of the best hikes comes early on, before the terrain becomes difficult: the five-mile round-trip stroll though the narrows of **Willis Creek**. From the **trailhead**, six miles down Skutumpah Road, it only takes a few minutes' walking before canyon walls begin to climb to either side of the wash, and they swiftly close in to stand just a few feet apart.

Much of **Cottonwood Canyon Road**, which heads east from Kodachrome Basin, runs across bare **slickrock**. Its graded gravel surface becomes extremely dangerous after rain, but during drier periods, it's well worth continuing for ten miles beyond the park to see the intricate double **Grosvenor Arch**. At that point, the road turns south, to meet **US-89** thirty miles on, roughly halfway between Kanab and Page. En route it threads its way between the dark pyramidal fins of the **Cockscomb**, a bizarre geological oddity resembling the armor-plated back of a stegosaurus that forms the boundary between the Grand Staircase and the Kaiparowits Plateau.

Escalante

Hwy-12 climbs northeast from Cannonville, passing through the speck that is **Henrieville** and then ascending the clay cliffs known as "The Blues." Once atop the cliffs you're confronted by the unexpected sight of the high but fertile **Upper Valley**, kept well watered by snowmelt from the Aquarius Plateau.

Mormon militiamen who pursued Indian raiders through the Upper Valley in 1866 noted the rich meadowland beyond, and dubbed the region "Potato Valley" in honor of its abundant wild sweet potatoes. Within ten years, several returned to establish a ranching and farming community. They called it **ESCALANTE**, despite the fact that the Spanish explorer-priest Fray Silvestre de Escalante (see p.504) never came within a hundred miles of here.

Life was harsh during Escalante's early years; the pioneers spent their first winter huddled in primitive dugouts. Then came a period of deceptive ease, as their sheep and cattle multiplied on the open range. By 1910, however, the native grasses on which they grazed were gone forever. The land has never recovered, and Escalante has remained frozen at much the same size and appearance ever since.

Escalante is a neat enough little town, with its main street gently sloping down from west to east and a couple of blocks of four-square brick and timber homes to either side. It's also a screamingly dull place to spend the night, though the wilderness that stretches away in every direction more than makes up for that.

Information

A summer-only kiosk at 100 E Main St (mid-May to mid-Sept daily 10am–6pm; ☎435/826-4810, ⓦwww.escalante-cc.com), next to the *Padre Motel*, handles inquiries about Escalante itself. For information on hiking and camping in the region, head for the **visitor center** of the Grand Staircase–Escalante National Monument, at 755 W Main St (see opposite).

Accommodation

Escalante's half-dozen tiny **motels** are outclassed by the more sizeable *Prospector Inn*. Public **campgrounds** nearby include those at Escalante State Park nearby and Calf Creek (see p.411).

Bunkhouse Motel Escalante Outfitters, 310 W Main St ☎435/826-4266 or 1-866/455-0041, ⓦescalanteoutfitters.com. Hikers' and campers' supply store where each of the seven attractive little log cabins out back has heating but no water, phone, or TV. They share use of a bathhouse. There's also tent and RV camping. ❸

Canyons Bed & Breakfast 15 South 100 East ☎435/826-4747 or 1-866/526-5667, ⓦcanyonsbnb.com. Behind this ordinary town house you'll find five attractive en-suite guest rooms, each with its own little patio. Rates include a high-quality organic breakfast. ❺

Circle D Motel 475 W Main St ☎435/826-4297, ⓦwww.escalantecircledmotel.com. Basic old-style motel, perched at the west end of town, with assorted rooms arrayed a long wooden veranda; ask for one of the newer ones. ❷

Escalante's Grand Staircase B&B 280 W Main St ☎435/826-4890, ⓦwww.escalantebnb.com. B&B-cum-motel, with eight spacious, bright and cheerful rooms. ❻

Prospector Inn 380 W Main St ☎435/826-4653, ⓦwww.prospectorinn.com. Escalante's largest and most modern motel offers spacious, comfortable and good-value twin-bedded rooms. ❸

Eating

Restaurants struggle to survive in Escalante, so it holds just a handful of nondescript diners, where it's hard to stretch a night on the town much beyond twelve and a half minutes.

Circle D Restaurant 425 W Main St ☎435/826-4550. Dull diner/steakhouse, with a Mexican flavor and a few vegetarian alternatives. Open for all meals daily in summer but closed for much of the winter.

Esca-Latte Escalante Outfitters, 310 W Main St ☎435/826-4266. Small-scale espresso bar in outfitters' store, which serves light snacks and pizzas as well as coffee and smoothies, and has the only liquor store in a 160-mile stretch of highway. Summer daily 8am–10pm; winter Tues–Sat 8am–6pm.

Prospector Restaurant 400 West 50 North ☎435/826-4658. Ordinary diner, tucked away from the highway behind the *Prospector Inn*. Mexican specialties such as quesadillas or a combo plate for around $10, and steaks and ribs for up to $20. Open daily for all meals, all year.

Hell's Backbone

While Hwy-12 is by far the quickest route between Escalante and Boulder, summer thrill-seekers can choose instead to take a two-hour, forty-mile trip across the top of the Aquarius Plateau, along the old "Upper Road." Turn north on the 300 East block in Escalante, and the paved **Forest Road 153** heads up Pine Creek Canyon, to reach the appealing mountain-set **Posey Lake** fourteen miles on.

Turn east at the lake, onto Hell's Backbone Road, and the fun begins. Having crawled up the flanks of the 10,000ft Roger Peak, this dirt track teeters along the slender ridge known as **Hell's Backbone**, with sheer drops down to Sand Creek on one side and Death Hollow on the other. The best views come at the hair-raising bridge halfway along. The bizarrely named **Box-Death Hollow Wilderness** far below can only be penetrated on foot and is southern Utah's most difficult hiking region. Tracing its full length necessitates eighteen miles of wading in ice-cold water and takes between four and seven days; don't even consider setting off without talking to the rangers at the visitor center in Escalante.

For the last ten miles, as it descends through the woods to Boulder, Hell's Backbone Road is paved, but the backcountry section is usually closed by snow between October and late May.

Hole-in-the-Rock Road

These days, **Hole-in-the-Rock Road**, which turns south from Hwy-12 five miles east of Escalante, is emphatically a dead end. More than fifty slow, hard miles from the highway, its progress is blocked by tumbled boulders, high above the waters of Lake Powell. When it was created, however, this was intended to become the most direct route across southern Utah.

In November 1879, the 230 Mormon pioneers of the **San Juan Mission** gathered outside Escalante. Intent on reaching their new home, almost two hundred miles east, they were convinced they'd find a shortcut along the uncharted east flank of the Kaiparowits Plateau and across the Colorado. Even when confronted with the abyss of Glen Canyon, their faith saw them through. In the space of six weeks, they dynamited a narrow slit in a fifty-foot cliff – the **Hole-in-the-Rock** – until it was wide enough to squeeze through. Despite snow and ice, they then used ropes to lower 83 wagons down a precipitous "road" that descended 1800ft to the river. Once there, they ferried the whole lot across the Colorado on makeshift rafts, then repeated the entire process to escape the canyon on the far side. A mere hundred more miles of desert brought them to **Bluff** – see p.467 – which they established on April 6, 1880. All 230 members of the party lived through the trek, joined by three babies born en route.

Hole-in-the-Rock Road has never been paved, but its first forty miles are passable for ordinary vehicles for most of the year, and it's now the most popular route into Grand Staircase–Escalante National Monument. It's a long, slow drive, however – allow three hours to get as far as Dance Hall Rock and back, and carry water and emergency supplies – and despite the build-up it's not nearly as dramatic as Hwy-12. The **hiking trails** that branch away from it do make the effort worthwhile though; the best of which for day-trippers is the loop down to the Peek-A-Boo and Spooky **slot canyons**. Staff at the visitor center in Escalante (see p.404) can provide leaflets and simple maps, but if you're planning anything substantial, buy a proper topographical map.

Devils Garden

For its first five miles, Hole-in-the-Rock Road crosses mundane, level ranching country. It then climbs to reveal a first glimpse of the red rocks of Escalante Canyon away to the east, and the surface changes from gravel to mud. As you continue across a sagebrush-strewn plateau, there's no incentive to get out of your car before **Devils Garden**, twelve miles along. The one official picnic area en route, this small valley, below the highway to the west, is scattered with rounded, clay-ish hoodoos and arches, reminiscent of Goblin Valley (see p.430). Countless trails and footpaths weave among the excrescences; none leads anywhere in particular, but it's a great place to play hide-and-seek.

In winter, after the snow has set in – usually sometime in December – Hole-in-the-Rock Road is normally blocked beyond Devils Garden.

The Slot Canyons of Dry Fork

Apart from crossing the occasional bouncy, sandy wash, Hole-in-the-Rock Road remains uneventful as you continue beyond Devils Garden. Now and then, vistas of the color country open up, and 24 miles along you begin to see rounded slickrock domes perched above the canyon. Just as the thought of what lies to the east is becoming seriously frustrating, however, you finally get the chance to see what's down there.

Head east on **Dry Fork Road**, 26 miles (or something over 45min) along Hole-in-the-Rock Road, and after five hair-raising minutes you'll come to a makeshift parking lot on the edge of a shallow canyon. A steep, sandy, and rather hard-to-follow trail takes roughly twenty minutes to switchback down from here into the Dry Fork of Coyote Gulch, where you'll find a couple of Utah's most accessible **slot canyons**. Scoured by fierce desert storms, these kind of impossibly slender and delicate canyons have become hugely popular tourist destinations in the last few years, mainly because they look so utterly gorgeous in photographs. In real life, they're breathtaking, but they're also very dangerous. If there's the slightest threat of rain anywhere nearby, don't go in – and as if that weren't enough, they're also home to midget rattlesnakes.

The first of the pair, **Peek-a-Boo Gulch**, is the gem. Although it's facing you as soon you reach the canyon floor, you might not recognize it. It's *not* the sandy-bottomed canyon heading off to your left, which may be narrow but isn't quite narrow enough to count as a "slot." Peek-A-Boo instead is on the far side, with its mouth at first glance appearing to be blocked by a "chimney" of slickrock. Just to enter it, you have to haul yourself up a couple of chest high ledges, which serve as a foretaste of several more to come. Exploring is irresistible, however, as each twist and turn reveals some new arch, bridge, or tunnel to scramble through or over. The walls to either side are never all that high, and it doesn't take long to get all the way through, but the elegant swirls and patterns in the storm-gouged rock make it a constant delight.

Spooky Gulch, another fifteen minutes' walk down Dry Fork, is by contrast downright intimidating. It starts narrow and just keeps on getting narrower and darker. To keep going at all, you have to crawl early on beneath a big fallen boulder, and after that it becomes a very tight squeeze indeed. Soon it's only possible to walk sideways, with serious pressure on your rib cage and back, and a sandpaper-like rasping at your clothes.

Another slot canyon, **Brimstone Gulch**, lies further still along Dry Fork. However, penetrating it is only possible using technical climbing gear, and even to reach it you have to negotiate a huge boulder that's very difficult indeed to get back up again.

Coyote Gulch

Shortly after Dry Fork, the surface of Hole-in-the-Rock Road becomes sandier and more uneven, and progress is that much slower. A mile or so after the solitary finger of **Chimney Rock** appears on the edge of the mesa, and a total of 33.5 miles from the highway, a parking lot on the right signals your arrival at **Hurricane Wash**. This is the starting point for the monument's most popular **backpacking** route, the three- to four-day round-trip hike down through **Coyote Gulch** to the Escalante River. If you plan to attempt it, get someone at the monument visitor center in Escalante to talk you through the route before you set off.

Strictly speaking, the trail proper begins a quarter-mile down a dirt track to the left of Hole-in-the-Rock Road, but even if your vehicle can get that far, there probably won't be space to park. From there, it's five miles' walk along the sandy but ever-narrowing bed of Hurricane Wash before you reach Coyote Gulch, and then a further eight miles until that meets the Escalante in turn.

Coyote Gulch itself is a spellbinding creek, cutting through a slickrock canyon that's lined with gorgeous sandstone bridges and arches, and punctuated by dramatic waterfalls. Most of it actually lies within the Glen Canyon NRA, but this is the only way to reach it on land. When Lake Powell is at its maximum high-water level, the lake extends all the way up the canyon of the Escalante to its confluence with Coyote Gulch, which means there's no scope for hikers to see, let alone explore, the Escalante River itself. However, in recent years, as described on p.421, the lake waters have remained considerably lower than that. In early 2009, for example, when the surface of the lake was a little above 3600 feet, eight miles of the Escalante River were exposed below the Coyote Gulch confluence, making it possible to hike to long-submerged side canyons as well as beside the river.

Starting from Hurricane Wash, there isn't time to hike to any significant features of Coyote Gulch and back within a single day. However, it is possible to snatch a glimpse on a **day-hike** from the end of **Forty-Mile Ridge**, an almost pure-sand "road" that leaves Hole-in-the-Rock Road another couple of miles further on. The first snag is that if you don't have 4WD, you'll probably only be able to drive the first five miles of Forty-Mile Ridge, and thus face an extra two-mile hike to reach the trailhead at its far end. The second snag is that the trail itself enters Coyote Gulch, two miles along, through the **Crack in the Wall**, an incredibly tight squeeze between sandstone boulders perched above a towering cliff that is every bit as alarming as its name suggests. And the final snag: it's much more difficult coming back the other way, so never climb down unless you're certain you can climb up again.

Assuming you can cope with these obstacles, the rewards are tremendous. Before you drop down into the gulch, you cross some fabulous slickrock slopes with colossal views out over the wilderness. Once there, Cliff Arch, Coyote Natural Bridge, and the huge Jacob Hamblin Arch all lie within reach.

Dance Hall Rock

Under normal conditions, two-wheel-drive vehicles should go no further along Hole-in-the-Rock Road than **Dance Hall Rock**, a mile beyond Forty-Mile Ridge and 36 miles from the highway. The 1879 Mormon party (see p.406) camped alongside this superb natural amphitheater while they worked out how to get across the Colorado, creating evening entertainment to keep up their spirits. An easy walk from the roadway enables you to tread the same stage, and it's also worth exploring the rolling slickrock hills immediately behind. In a couple of places, natural tanks have been scooped deep into the rock, each sheltering a solitary tree on its sandy floor.

The Hole-in-the-Rock

Beyond Dance Hall Rock, the gravel surface gives way to bare slickrock, only negotiable in high-clearance vehicles. The original **Hole-in-the-Rock** lies just

▲ Driving along Highway 12

past the last parking lot, fifteen miles on. Keen hikers can scramble over the rocks that block it and pick their way down to the lake, which depending on its current level, obliterates some or all of the lowermost thousand feet of the pioneers' primitive pathway.

The Upper Escalante River

While driving Hole-in-the-Rock Road certainly offers the thrill of venturing into the back of beyond, several wonderful hikes start right alongside Hwy-12. If your time is at all limited and you'd rather spend it on the trails than behind the wheel, there's a lot to be said for staying on the main road until it reaches the **Escalante River**. The first sighting of the Escalante system comes from a roadside lookout at an extravagant curve five miles on from the Hole-in-the-Rock turn-off.

Immediately below the lookout, perched on a rocky eminence near mile marker 74, the solitary *Kiva Koffeehouse* provides an ideal opportunity to get your bearings (April–Oct daily except Tues 8.30am–4.30pm; closed Nov–March; ☎ 435/826-4550, ⓦ www.kivakoffeehouse.com; ❼).Through panoramic windows or from the flowery patio, you can enjoy fabulous views along the river while enjoying simple snacks such as granola, sandwiches, or enchiladas. A separate cottage nearby holds two guest rooms, named Sunset and Sunrise for obvious reasons.

From here, the highway takes five more miles to drop down to the river itself, which it crosses on a low bridge that's designed to allow floodwaters to flow harmlessly over. Immediately on the far side, a parking lot serves as the trailhead for exhilarating hikes both up- and downstream.

While this can be the starting point for major **backpacking** trips in either direction – Escalante town is two days' walk upstream, while Lake Powell lies at least ten days' hike downstream – intriguing natural features much closer at hand serve as obvious **day-hike** destinations. Whichever way you go, trailside notices announce "Yup, You Gotta Get Wet;" be prepared to ford the river several times. If you're just going a short distance there's no great need to keep pulling your boots on and off – the riverbank is sandy enough to walk barefoot. That said, the whole concept loses its appeal in winter, when the river can freeze right over.

Upstream: Escalante Natural Bridge

The shorter of the two potential day-hikes from Hwy-12 heads **upstream** for just 1.6 miles, as far as **Escalante Natural Bridge**. Having started by following the river away from the highway bridge, you're soon obliged to wade over to its south bank. The canyon here is broad and open, and the trail gentle. Once you've crossed the river four times, so you're now back on its northern side, you'll see the bridge open up on its southern wall. Although it's 100ft wide and 130ft high, it spans a mere trickle, dribbling down from a little side canyon.

Downstream: Maverick Bridge and Phipps Arch

The trail **downstream** from Hwy-12, accessed by walking beneath the road bridge then crossing a footbridge over Calf Creek, is slightly heavier going. Much of the valley floor belongs to private farmers, so you have to scramble and dodge to stay outside their fences, but it's still a lovely walk.

The best day-hike in this direction is twice as long as its upstream equivalent, at nearly seven miles for the round trip. The route leaves the Escalante 1.6 miles along, heading south into sandy **Phipps Wash**. There are no signs or marked trail, so look for footprints and carry a good map. After another half mile, you'll see two prominent knobs of Navajo sandstone atop the canyon wall to your right. A hundred yards before you reach the larger of the two, head right again, up a sandy slope into a side canyon. One hundred yards along, pick your way onto a ledge on your left to avoid a deep sink hole; another hundred yards after that, you'll come to **Maverick Bridge**, spanning the wash in front of another round cavity.

Back on Phipps Wash, keep going south for half a mile until another side canyon opens up to your left. Now things get difficult; to reach the stark, mesa-top **Phipps Arch**, you have to scramble up a steep slickrock ledge, and there's no way of knowing whether you've got the right one until you're up there. The views are so good it doesn't really matter in the end, but make sure you keep track of how to get down again.

Calf Creek Falls

One of the very best **day-hikes** Utah has to offer starts sixteen miles from Escalante. A mile or so north of the Escalante River bridge on Hwy-12, look out on your left for the parking lot at **Calf Creek**. There's a nice little **campground** right here, with minimal facilities ($7 per night), but most visitors simply come for the day to enjoy the magnificent six-mile round-trip walk to the 125ft **Lower Calf Creek Falls**. Summer sun and deep sand can make it more effort than you might expect – allow three to four hours – but this would be a lovely canyon hike even if it didn't culminate with the falls. A day-use fee of $2 is charged.

The clearly marked trail heads upstream between the high red walls of Calf Creek Canyon, following a perennial creek, interrupted by beaver ponds, that feeds a lush riparian environment. Fremont pictographs testify to a long-standing human presence. It takes around ninety minutes to reach the falls themselves, which are absolutely stupendous. Spilling over the pouting lip of a crevice in the center of a vast sandstone amphitheater, they spread over a mossy slope of golden stone, iridescent with permanent rainbows. The (utterly freezing) water that collects in the pool below is fringed by a shaded beach where you can rest before you hike back out again.

The **Upper Calf Creek Falls** do exist, but you can't reach them from here. Instead, you start from a trailhead another six miles along Hwy-12, and make your way for a mile across exposed open slickrock in search of the stream. The slope can seem intimidating, but with good boots it's not too hard, and the views are amazing. Eventually, the trail forks; one strand goes to the top of the 50ft falls, the other to the bottom, where once again a lovely pool awaits.

Boulder

BOULDER, thirty miles beyond Escalante, is not so much a town as a group of farms scattered across a pleasant high-mountain valley. Cattle ranching in this remote spot started in 1889, and in the fifty years it took for it to be connected by road with the outside world, it acquired a reputation as Utah's own little Shangri-La. Now that it's just another stop on the highway, what magic it may once have had has largely gone.

As the western terminus of the controversial **Burr Trail** – see p.417 – Boulder makes an ideal launching point for explorations into the backcountry of Capitol Reef, but few visitors spend much time in the valley itself. On a shallow knoll beside Hwy-12 in the heart of town, the small **Anasazi State Park** holds the excavated remains of an ancient pueblo (daily: mid-May to mid-Sept 8am–6pm; mid-Sept to mid-May 9am–5pm; $4). Its 83 rooms were occupied by the Kayenta Anasazi, an Ancestral Puebloan subgroup, from 1129 AD until 1169 AD, when the complex was destroyed by fire. A six-room replica at the end of the short ruins trail illustrates their daily life, farming along Boulder Creek.

Practicalities

Boulder offers pretty minimal facilities for visitors, though the modern *Boulder Mountain Lodge*, where Hwy-12 meets the Burr Trail (☎435/335-7460 or 1-800/556-3446, ⓦboulder-utah.com; ❹), has twenty comfortable rooms and a reasonable restaurant. There's an **information kiosk**, open erratic hours in season, outside the *Burr Trail Grill* diner nearby (☎435/335-7432).

Otherwise, *Pole's Place*, opposite the state park at 465 N Hwy-12 (☎435/335-7422 or 1-800/730-7422, ⓦboulderutah.com/polesplace; closed Dec–Feb; ❸), is a simple but adequate **motel** with its own café and store.

The least expensive rooms don't have a bathroom but access to a locked bathroom cabin outdoors. The best place to **eat** lies a short distance along the Burr Trail: the spruce, spotless, timber-built *Boulder Mesa Restaurant*, 155 E Burr Trail Rd (⚒ ☏ 435/335-7447), open daily for all meals until 8pm. Everything from cooked breakfasts and smoothies to sandwiches, burgers, and fried chicken is meticulously prepared and presented, and the prices are low.

North to Capitol Reef

Although Hwy-12 leaves Grand Staircase–Escalante for good as it heads north of Boulder, the scenery remains every bit as sublime. The 35-mile link between Boulder and Torrey, across the eastern segment of the Aquarius Plateau, also known as **Boulder Mountain**, takes around an hour to drive. Once Hwy-12 has climbed out of Boulder Valley, successive roadside lookouts survey fabulous vistas to the east, across a sea of gold and red sandstone outcrops to the Waterpocket Fold and beyond.

Primitive Forest Service **campgrounds** en route (☏ 435/425-3702; $9), include those at **Oak Creek**, fifteen miles along, and a little further on at **Pleasant Creek**, where a ranger station can provide full details.

Torrey

Poised at the intersection of highways 12 and 24, eleven miles west of Capitol Reef National Park, **TORREY** has thrown its lot in firmly with the tourist trade. Quietly prospering while so many of its neighbors have faltered, it still consists of little more than one tree-lined central avenue plus a handful of slightly stark brick motels on a ridge to the west, all surrounded by golden meadows grazed by contented cows. However, for visitors who see their evenings as opportunities to meet other travelers, Torrey is the most exciting prospect for at least a hundred miles.

Accommodation

Torrey holds several hundred **motel** rooms, with rates that range across the full spectrum. If you'd rather **camp**, there are a few private campgrounds in town, but the public sites along Hwy-12 (see opposite) or in the national park (see p.416) are far more attractive.

Austin's Chuck Wagon Motel 12 W Main St ☏ 435/425-3335 or 1-800/863-3288, ⊛ www .austinschuckwagonmotel.com. Well-kept two-story "log cabin" motel, beside a tiny church in the town center. Closed Dec–Feb. ❸

Best Western Capitol Reef Resort 2600 E Hwy-24 ☏ 435/425-3761 or 1-888/610-9600, ⊛ www.bestwestern.com/capitolreefresort. Well-equipped modern motel-style hotel, three miles east of Torrey, with great views and a good pool. ❹

Capitol Reef Inn & Cafe 360 W Main St ☏ 435/425-3271, ⊛ capitolreefinn.com. Long-established but crisply maintained little motel, just off the highway in the heart of town, looking south

to Boulder Mountain. On-site restaurant (see below) and small bookstore. ❸

Rim Rock Inn 2523 E Hwy-24 ☏ 435/425-3398 or 1-888/447-4676, ⊛ therimrock.net. New, wood-built hotel, across the highway from the *Best Western* three miles east of Torrey, and offering cheaper rooms and a better restaurant. ❸

Skyridge B&B 950 E Hwy-24 ☏ 435/425-3222 or 1-800/448-6990, ⊛ skyridgeinn.com. Six nonsmoking en-suite B&B rooms – three of which have hot tubs – in tasteful, imaginatively furnished modern home with expansive grounds. It's on the way toward central Torrey from the intersection of highways 12 and 24. ❺

Eating

Whether it's the pressure of competition or just a little local pride, the **restaurants** and **diners** of Torrey make more effort to please than you may have come to expect of southern Utah.

Café Diablo 599 W Main St ☎435/425-3070. Surprisingly inventive dinner-only restaurant, offering a slight Southwestern twist to meats and fish, and even "free-range rattlesnake patties," served with aioli. Open mid-April to Oct only, daily 5–10pm.

Capitol Reef Inn & Cafe 360 W Main St ☎435/425-3271. Bright café that serves some of Torrey's best food, using fresh ingredients like just-caught local trout. The amazing ten-vegetable salad can form part of a real vegetarian feast, with sumptuous banana pies to follow. Avoid the coffee, though. April–Oct only, daily 7am–9pm.

Rim Rock Inn 2523 E Hwy-24 ☎435/425-3398. Dinner-only hotel restaurant that serves better food than its rustic log-cabin decor might suggest. The $18 chicken *molé* is recommended, while the menu ranges from cheaper burgers and pasta dishes up to $30 steaks. Daily 5.30–9pm.

Robbers Roost 185 W Main St ☎435/425-3265. Rustic central bookstore, complete with hammocks and a wooden deck, that's an invaluable resource for information on the parklands, and also serves great coffee. Mon–Sat 8am–4pm, Sun 1–4pm.

Capitol Reef National Park

CAPITOL REEF NATIONAL PARK, the second largest of Utah's five national parks, is also the least visited. Life might be different if it bore the name originally proposed by locals – **Wayne Wonderland**, this being Wayne County. As it is, that word "reef" seems to confuse visitors. It refers to the fact that the hundred-mile rock wall thrust up by the **Waterpocket Fold** presented an almost impenetrable obstacle to nineteenth-century travelers, who therefore likened it to a reef on the ocean. Add the resemblance of the rounded "knobs" of white sandstone that top its central section to the US Capitol in Washington, and you have "Capitol Reef."

Capitol Reef is very much of a piece with the Southwest's other national parks. Within its 378 square miles lie hidden canyons, verdant valleys, and strange rock formations whose colors are drawn from an extravagant palette of golds and greens, reds and whites. Despite stretching for over a hundred miles north to south, the park is often less than ten miles wide. The one east–west highway, **Hwy-24**, crosses it in under twenty miles, following the gorge of the Fremont River. It's an impressive drive, but that's nothing rare in southern Utah, and unless you time your arrival from the west to coincide with the daily magnificent sunset, you could easily pass straight through. Only if you take the time to explore will you get a sense of the magic of the place, and why it fully deserves its national-park status.

Even a couple of hours is enough to admire the western cliffs from the dead-end **Scenic Drive**, south of the park headquarters at **Fruita**. Given half a day or more, you could venture all the way south to Lake Powell on the unpaved **Notom–Bullfrog Road**, tracing the eastern flank of the Waterpocket Fold, or loop back westward via the **Burr Trail**, halfway along. With **hiking trails** of all lengths and levels setting off into the wilderness, it would be easy to spend a week in this one park.

The best **seasons** to visit Capitol Reef are spring, when the fruit trees blossom and the wild flowers bloom, or fall, when the crowds have gone, the cottonwoods change color, and hiking conditions are at their peak. Midsummer temperatures can reach 100°F, and August in particular is prone to flash-flooding, but so long as you set your sights appropriately low – say, to lazing on your back in the orchards, eating fresh fruit – a summer visit is not such a bad idea.

A history of Capitol Reef

Although traces of human occupation date back ten thousand years, Capitol Reef's first known inhabitants were the **Fremont Anasazi**. This Ancestral Puebloan subgroup farmed along the Fremont River from 700 AD until 1300 AD, when climate changes forced them to move on. Archeologists distinguish them from their more sophisticated cousins to the southeast by the fact that they lived in pit houses dug into the hillsides, and didn't keep domesticated dogs or turkeys. The most enduring signs of their presence are the intriguing **petroglyphs** still to be seen on the canyon walls.

After many centuries when only the occasional Paiute hunter passed this way, a small group of Mormons established a permanent settlement in 1878. Their riverside orchards transformed the landscape, and when the post office insisted they gave their community a proper name, a few years later, **Fruita** seemed the perfect choice. The population never rose above fifty, however, and it was soon suggested that the region had more future as a park than a home. The immediate vicinity of Fruita became Capitol Reef National Monument in 1937, and that was upgraded to national park status when it was enlarged to include the entire Waterpocket Fold in 1971. Former Fruita townspeople and their heirs are still entitled to graze cattle within the park, but ranching is slowly being phased out.

Arrival and information

The defunct village of **Fruita**, at the heart of the park, ranges for a mile or so around the intersection of Hwy-24 and the Scenic Drive, eleven miles east of Torrey. Bryce Canyon is 120 miles southwest, the I-70 town of Green River a hundred miles northeast; no public transport passes this way.

The **visitor center**, right at the road junction (daily: summer 8am–7pm; spring & fall 8am–5pm; winter 8am–4.30pm; ☎435/425-3791, ⓦwww.nps .gov/care), stocks free handouts on local geology and history. For information on the surrounding area, contact Capitol Reef Country Travel Council (☎435/425-3365 or 1-800/858-7951, ⓦcapitolreef.org).

Only visitors who embark on the Scenic Drive, south of the visitor center and campground, are liable for the **admission fee** of $5 per vehicle. There are no motels or lodges inside the park; the closest **accommodation** is in Torrey (see p.412). Torrey-based operators include Hondoo Rivers & Trails,

---

The geology of Capitol Reef

The **Waterpocket Fold**, which slopes from north to south for the full hundred-mile length of Capitol Reef National Park, is what geologists call a **monocline**, created when layers of sedimentary rock buckled under pressure sixty million years ago. Within the last ten million years, it has in turn been lifted a mile or so above sea level by the general raising of the Colorado Plateau. Most of the original fold has long since eroded away; the reef itself is just the rump. Its western face consists of a long, jagged cliff of hard rock; it rises more gently from the east, in multicolored waves of sandstone that the Navajo called the "Land of the Sleeping Rainbow."

Here and there, the fold is pierced right through by deeply incised canyons. Often hundreds of feet deep but less than twenty feet wide, these slender gorges were mostly blocked by fallen rocks until Mormon pioneers cleared a way through. After summer thunderstorms, rainwater can cascade through the canyons in fearsome flash floods. At other times, it collects in depressions worn into the rock – the "**water-pockets**" for which the whole mighty edifice is named.

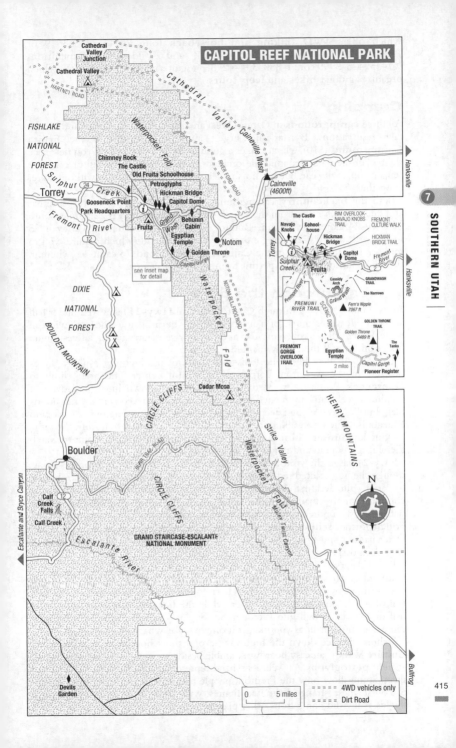

CAPITOL REEF NATIONAL PARK

Cathedral Valley Junction

Cathedral Valley

HARTNET ROAD

FISHLAKE

NATIONAL

FOREST

Cathedral Valley Caineville Wash

RIVER FORD ROAD

24

Caineville
(4600ft)

Hanksville

Sulphur

Creek

Torrey

24

Waterpocket Fold

Chimney Rock
The Castle
Old Fruita Schoolhouse
Petroglyphs
Hickman Bridge
Capitol Dome
Gooseneck Point
Park Headquarters
i
Fruita
Behunin Cabin
Egyptian Temple
Golden Throne

Fremont River

12

Grand Wash

Capitol Gorge

see inset map
for detail

Notom

DIXIE

NATIONAL

FOREST

BOULDER MOUNTAIN

Waterpocket Fold

NOTOM-BULLFROG ROAD

Cedar Mesa

CIRCLE CLIFFS

Boulder

Calf
Creek
Falls

Call Creek

BURR TRAIL ROAD

CIRCLE CLIFFS

12

Escalante River

GRAND STAIRCASE-ESCALANTE
NATIONAL MONUMENT

Escalante and Bryce Canyon

Devils
Garden

Strike Valley

Waterpocket Fold

Muley Twist Canyon

HENRY MOUNTAINS

Bullfrog

N

Inset map

The Castle
Navajo Knobs
Schoolhouse
RIM OVERLOOK-
NAVAJO KNOBS
TRAIL
FREMONT
CULTURE WALK
HICKMAN
BRIDGE TRAIL
Hickman Bridge
Capitol Dome
Torrey
i
Sulphur Creek
Fruita
Fremont River
Cassidy Arch
GRANDWASH
TRAIL
The Narrows
Fremont River
Hanksville
FREMONT
RIVER TRAIL
Fern's Nipple
7067 ft
Grand Wash
GOLDEN THRONE
TRAIL
Golden Throne
6489 ft
The Tanks
FREMONT
GORGE
OVERLOOK
TRAIL
Egyptian Temple
Capitol Gorge
Pioneer Register
0   2 miles

0   5 miles

===== 4WD vehicles only
===== Dirt Road

which offers **4WD**, **hiking** and **horseback** tours (☏435/425-3519 or 1-800/332-2696, ⓦwww.hondoo.com), and Wild Hare Expeditions (☏435/425-3999 or 1-888/304-4273, ⓦscinternet.net/~thehare/), which organizes guided **hikes** and **jeep tours**.

Camping

All three **campgrounds** in Capitol Reef are first-come, first-served and do not take reservations. By far the largest and most popular is the **Fruita Campground** ($10), which makes a good overnight stop even if you never see the rest of the park. Set amid the orchards, a mile south of the visitor center, it remains open all year, but has no showers and in winter can be without water altogether.

Both the **backcountry** campgrounds – much smaller and more primitive, and free – are 35 miles from the visitor center. **Cedar Mesa** is 22.5 miles south of Hwy-24 along the Notom–Bullfrog Road, while **Cathedral Valley** is 25 miles north of Hwy-24 along either the Hartnet Road (which requires you to ford the Fremont River) or the **Caineville Wash Road**. To camp elsewhere in the backcountry, get a free permit from the visitor center.

Driving through the park

At its simplest, driving through Capitol Reef on **Hwy-24** takes well under half an hour. However much of a hurry you may be in, pause once or twice en route. Rather than a token pit stop at the visitor center, try taking a five-minute hike from one of the clearly marked trailheads.

The first of these lies a short distance south of the highway, roughly three-quarters of the way from Torrey to the visitor center. The brief climb to **Gooseneck Point** is rewarded with a 500ft view down into the canyon of Sulphur Creek, an "entrenched meander" that once curved across a flat flood-plain but has been etched deep into solid rock by the uplifting of the Colorado Plateau. Reached by walking ten minutes along a different trail from the same parking lot, **Sunset Point** is as you'd expect a fabulous vantage point to watch the cliffs glow gold and red as the sun goes down.

Hwy-24 passes the visitor center on the right a couple of miles further along, though the huge, fluted red-rock butte known as the **Castle** to the left is bound to catch your eye first. Whether you fork right to join the Scenic Drive, or continue on the main highway, you'll reach the heart of **FRUITA** village within a few hundred yards, where Sulphur Creek meets the **Fremont River**. Fruita's former **schoolhouse**, just north of the highway, was built in 1896, and hasn't had a pupil since 1941; park rangers, not a Mormon schoolmarm, keep it spick-and-span.

The village's old **orchards** are Capitol Reef's crowning glory. A waxy, luxuriant green against the towering red cliffs, they hold almost three thousand trees planted by the pioneers. The cherries and peaches **blossom** in the first half of April, the apples slightly later, while the **harvest** lasts from the second half of June until well into October. So long as you stay in the orchards, you can eat as much fruit as you like; you only pay for what you take away.

A short distance down the highway beyond the schoolhouse, the **Fremont Culture Walk** is an easy boardwalk amble beside a canyon wall crammed with ancient **petroglyphs**. As well as stylized representations of goats and Bighorn sheep, some show how the Fremont people may have seen themselves – unless of course these strange helmeted figures, with triangular bodies and massive shields, really did come from other planets.

Hwy-24 crosses the Fremont two miles east of the visitor center, near the start of the longer **Hickman Bridge Trail** (see p.419). Only beyond this point does **Capitol Dome**, high above the north bank another half-mile ahead, resolve itself into a dome; so far you've seen it from the side, as a slender fin. By now Fremont Canyon is at its deepest, and it's joined within the next couple of miles by **Chimney Rock Canyon** from the north and **Grand Wash** from the south (see p.419). A mile past Grand Wash stands the sandstone cabin of one of Fruita's earliest settlers, **Elijah Behunin**, with the eastern boundary of the park another 2.5 miles down the road.

The Scenic Drive

Other than Hwy-24, the only paved road in Capitol Reef is the **Scenic Drive**, which parallels the golden cliffs of the Waterpocket Fold for twelve miles south from the visitor center. The first couple of miles lead through Fruita, where a cluster of restored barns and houses serve as homes for park employees, while overnight visitors camp out in the orchards.

Beyond the village, and the fee station where your $5 admission charge is collected, the road undulates through the desert, dipping into dry sandy washes and then climbing scrubby rolling hillocks. Successive individual pinnacles, such as **Fern's Nipple** and the **Egyptian Temple**, line the crest of the red-rock battlements to the east. Until Hwy-24 was pushed through Fremont Canyon in 1962, this unlikely route was southern Utah's main east–west thoroughfare. It now ends at a large parking lot, facing a crack in the cliffs that marks the start of **Capitol Gorge**. For a century, traffic squeezed its way between the narrow walls beyond, but now the gravel continuation known as the Capitol Gorge Road peters out just over two miles in. Hikers however can keep going on foot, to see the Pioneer Register where early wagon-drivers carved their names (see p.419).

The Notom–Bullfrog Road

If you'd rather survey the Waterpocket Fold from the comfort of your car than sweat it out along the long drive south along the **Notom–Bullfrog Road** is Capitol Reef's best option. Just be sure to stock up on gas and water; you'll have to drive at least seventy miles to find any facilities.

The road leaves Hwy-24 nine miles east of the visitor center, not far outside the park. Only its first four miles are paved, as far as the tiny but well-irrigated settlement of **NOTOM**, now home to half a dozen ranchers. Thereafter, its rough surface repeatedly ripples into a "washboard" as it follows a dry-as-dust bench above Sandy Creek, with the eerie badlands of the Waterpocket Fold to the west and the volcanic **Henry Mountains** to the east.

Ordinary vehicles should have no problem negotiating the full length of the Notom–Bullfrog Road, which re-enters the park twenty miles along and then leaves it again in the southeast corner fifteen miles on. Seventy miles from the highway, after a final 25-mile segment where you find yourself constantly stopping to swoon at the turquoise expanse of Lake Powell on the southern horizon, you come to the modern marina at **Bullfrog** (see p.428).

The Burr Trail

Most drivers who set off south on the Notom–Bullfrog Road don't make it to Bullfrog but complete a loop around the Waterpocket Fold by branching onto the **Burr Trail**. The only road actually to cross the fold, rather than slice through it, it does so via a fearsome set of switchbacks that climb west from the Notom–Bullfrog Road, roughly halfway down.

The Burr Trail began life as a rutted wagon trail, which was upgraded by uranium prospectors in the 1940s and 1950s. The four miles within the national park are still unpaved, but the remaining thirty, running west to Boulder on Hwy-24, were paved during the late 1980s. Wilderness advocates argued that increased road use would irreparably damage one of Utah's least-spoiled regions; Garfield County authorities, keen to grab a piece of the Capitol Reef action from their Wayne County neighbors, went ahead anyway. From their point of view, they were just in time; the area now belongs to Grand Staircase–Escalante National Monument, so there'll be no further road construction.

If all that leaves you feeling too guilty to take the Burr Trail, you're missing out. The panorama that unfolds as you ascend the switchbacks and head west is out of this world. Looking back across the Notom–Bullfrog Road, you see the top of Swap Mesa and the stark Henry Mountains. Just past the topmost ridge, the Upper and Lower sections of **Muley Twist Canyon** stretch to north and south through the heart of the Fold. Both make excellent multi-day backpacking expeditions, starting from near the highway. As you leave the park and enter the national monument (where the pavement begins), an extraordinary procession of reefs marches south, with the white canyons of the Waterpocket Fold in the foreground and four or five craggy red cliff-faces beyond, leading on to Lake Powell.

The oval plain just west of the park, ringed by the Circle Cliffs, was described by the nineteenth-century geologist Clarence Dutton as "a spot which is about as desolate as any on earth." The Burr Trail leaves it by way of the deep **Long Canyon**, then struggles on to reach Hwy-24 immediately south of Boulder (see p.411).

Cathedral Valley

Capitol Reef's least accessible section is **Cathedral Valley**, north of Hwy-24. Like the Notom–Bullfrog Road, it parallels the eastern side of the Waterpocket Fold, but the territory here is much more forbidding than the sagebrush plain to the south. In among the heavily eroded red, blue, and gray hills lie deep canyons and primeval gardens, populated by strange stone monoliths. Unless you have your own 4WD or high-clearance vehicle, you'll only see it by joining a guided 4WD tour (see p.416).

Two roads run north into the backcountry from Hwy-24, 11.5 and 18.6 miles east of the visitor center. The first, **River Ford Road**, traverses the Fremont River by means of a crude ford a few hundred yards along. If you're planning a loop drive, come this way first – it's not safe to cross when the water's more than a couple of feet deep, and you wouldn't want to find that out at the end of a sixty-mile drive. The second route, the **Caineville Wash Road**, meets the first – by now Hartnet Road – at the far end of Cathedral Valley. Several more dirt roads leave the park at this northern extremity, connecting with I-70 to the north or joining Hwy-72 above Loa to the west.

Hiking in Capitol Reef

You probably won't drive far in Capitol Reef before you feel the backcountry beckoning. Choosing which of the many, mostly short, **trails** to hike is largely a matter of whether you feel up to climbing; only a few, such as the walks through the Capitol Gorge or Grand Wash, remain on level ground, while the rest demand mountain-goat-style scrambling up the slickrock.

If you do choose to stick to the canyon floors, bear in mind the danger of **flash floods** after rain, and don't pause where there's no clear escape route.

Grand Wash

The busiest Capitol Reef trail connects the Scenic Drive with Hwy-24, along the gravelly bed of the **Grand Wash**. Both trailheads are four miles from the visitor center, one at the end of the unpaved Grand Wash Road, which leaves the Scenic Drive a mile past Fruita, and the other on the south bank of the highway a mile or two beyond Capitol Dome.

As a one-way walk, the **Grand Wash trail** is just over two miles long and takes around an hour, but unless you arrange a pick-up at the far end you'll have to double back. In the half-mile stretch known as **The Narrows**, the vertiginous 800ft canyon walls close in to a mere sixteen feet apart. **Butch Cassidy** and his gang are said to have used the tangle of side canyons that lead off Grand Wash as hideouts, but there's no evidence that Butch ever saw **Cassidy Arch**, reached by a short steep climb from near the southeast end of the trail.

Capitol Gorge

The **Capitol Gorge trail**, reached by driving the full length of the Scenic Drive, is every bit as claustrophobic as the Grand Wash. It's a short and easy walk, providing you spare yourself an extra 4.6-mile round-trip by parking not at the foot of the Scenic Drive but at the end of the gravel road beyond, which is where you'll find the trailhead.

In the space of a mile, the trail inches all the way through a crack in the Waterpocket Fold, though hikers have to turn back when they reach the private land on the far side. From 1871 onwards, this "**Blue Dugway**" was a major trans-Utah thoroughfare, as the painstaking inscriptions on the **Pioneer Register**, carved into the canyon wall halfway along, will testify.

A couple of twists of the canyon past the Register, side canyons start to open up to both left and right. Not far along, after two or so sets, a sign on the left reads "Tanks 0.2." Climb up the cairned trail here and within a few hundred yards you'll reach a succession of circular clifftop "tanks." Early travelers would break off from the laborious haul through the gorge, in the hope of finding fresh water in such clifftop "**waterpockets**."

A separate two-mile (one-hour) trail from the Capitol Gorge trailhead launches itself straight up the hillside to the north. The slickrock flatlands that cap the Waterpocket Fold enjoy huge views to Boulder Mountain in the east and the Henry Mountains in the west. The dominant feature up here, however, is the glowing Navajo-sandstone butte of the **Golden Throne**, at the foot of which the trail ends.

Hickman Bridge

While not the easiest of Hwy-24's roadside trails – the Fremont Culture Walk, detailed on p.416, is far less demanding – the **Hickman Bridge Trail** makes a supremely rewarding two-mile, two-hour hike. Setting off along the north bank of the Fremont River, two miles east of the visitor center, it meanders briefly through the cottonwoods before climbing a brisk stairway out of the canyon to the shadeless heights up top.

Once you've marveled at Capitol Dome, off to the east, fork left at the junction ahead. Pockmarked black boulders strewn on all sides, incongruous against the red, pink, and cream sandstone, testify to ancient lava flows. Three-quarters of a mile along, the path loops around and through the arching span of **Hickman Bridge**. A hundred feet high, a hundred feet wide, it's a genuine natural bridge, worn through the rock by a side channel eager to reach the Fremont below. The rocky chaos beneath somehow complements the grace of the bridge itself.

Taking the right rather than the left fork at the junction lets you in for a nine-mile round-trip on the **Rim Overlook Trail**. Highlights include a towering overview of the orchards of Fruita, and the **Navajo Knobs** at its furthermost point.

Lake Powell

Until the early 1960s, it was all but impossible to travel between southwest and southeast Utah. In the unseen heart of the endless desert, the mighty Colorado River churned its way toward the Pacific through a succession of yawning canyons. Here and there boatmen might ferry the occasional passenger across, and a few adventurous souls even rafted down the river itself, but there was no highway for two hundred miles north of Arizona.

Now the Colorado has gone, submerged beneath the huge, docile **Lake Powell**. For many people – especially those who knew the sublime **Glen Canyon** that it destroyed – the new lake is a loathsome abomination. Many more see it as a thing of beauty, and Lake Powell has become Utah's number-one tourist attraction, drawing four million visitors per year – by tradition, over half a million on Labor Day alone – and matched in popularity in the Southwest only by the Grand Canyon. It is, undeniably, an extraordinary spectacle, its turquoise waters rippling against its stark red-rock rim and cradling islands that once were buttes and mesas. No one could ever mistake this for a natural landscape, however, and you don't have to be an out-and-out environmentalist to be disturbed by the transformation of America's last great wilderness into a playground. The concessionaires of the **Glen Canyon National Recreational Area** invite you to "think of Lake Powell as a 160,000-acre bathtub and consider our boats, floats, boards, and tubes as your toys." Beyond the unappealing rhetoric, there's some truth in what they say; granted that the lake exists, if you're going to come here at all, the best way to enjoy your visit is to get out on the water.

▲ Houseboat on Lake Powell

Lake Powell's success as a wet'n'wild theme park has been a surprise spin-off from its real purpose. Glen Canyon Dam was constructed to regulate the flow of water along the Colorado River. Half is kept back to irrigate the deserts of the plateau, while the rest gushes through its turbines, generating electricity as it makes for Arizona and California. Demand is so precisely monitored that the level of the lake fluctuates according to whether it's dinnertime in Phoenix. Hence its closest resemblance to a bathtub – the scummy dirty-bath tidemark that sullies the sandstone around its edge.

The whole vast system cost $300 million to build. When full, Lake Powell is 550ft deep at the dam and holds enough water to cover all of Arizona five inches deep. It stretches back up 186 miles of the Colorado River and 72 miles of the San Juan River, as well as inundating 96 side canyons formed by rivers such as the Escalante and the Dirty Devil. The total shoreline of 1960 miles is longer than the entire US Pacific coast. Despite the searing sun, the lake is officially claimed to lose a mere 2.5 percent of its volume each year to evaporation.

The fullest the lake has ever been was in 1983, when water flowed over the top of the dam, and an emergency release had to be instigated. As recently as 1999, the level was just four feet below the maximum, but drought set in from 2000 onwards, and by 2005 the waters had dropped 146 feet, with the reservoir a mere one-third full. That was enough for Glen Canyon to begin to reappear, and backpackers flocked to marvel at such long-submerged wonders as the Cathedral in the Desert. The lower reaches of the Escalante River sprang back to life; the banks were host once more to 25-foot trees, while the thick layer of sediment deposited on the lake bed steadily washed away. Levels have risen somewhat since then, but as this book went to press the lake was only half full, still almost 100 feet down.

Five of Lake Powell's six **marinas** are accessible by road. Two are south of the state line in Arizona: the largest, **Wahweap**, lies just west of the dam itself and the purpose-built town of **Page**, while the newest, **Antelope Point**, is on Navajo land immediately east of Page. The remaining four are in Utah. **Bullfrog** and **Hall's Crossing**, two-thirds of the way northeast up the lake from the dam, are connected by a ferry service that makes it possible to drive between Capitol Reef National Park and Natural Bridges National Monument. **Hite** is in theory at the northeast limit of the lake, though low water levels have left it stranded high and dry, and it's not currently in operation. The sixth and final marina, **Dangling Rope**, is a refueling station that can only be reached by boat.

There's surprisingly little accommodation on land; it's assumed you'll want to join the armada out on the water, either in your own vessel or in a rented **houseboat**. For a quick taste, you can join a **guided tour** at either Wahweap or Bullfrog – the trips to **Rainbow Bridge** are by far the most popular – or take the **ferry** between Bullfrog and Hall's Crossing.

Page

Home to almost ten thousand people, **PAGE** – which is actually just south of the state line in Arizona but is the only town of any size on the periphery of Lake Powell – is now the largest community in a 720-mile stretch of the Colorado River. Before Glen Canyon Dam was constructed four miles west, this all but barren mesa belonged to the Navajo Nation. Thanks to a small spring, however, it made the best site to house the dam's workforce. The Navajo agreed to swap it for a similar-sized chunk of desert between Bluff and Hatch in southeast Utah, a new road was blasted through the Echo Cliffs, and the town was born on Thanksgiving Day 1958.

The western half of the United States would sustain a population greater than that of our whole country today if the waters that now run to waste were saved and used for irrigation.

President Theodore Roosevelt, State of the Union address, 1901

The twentieth-century growth of the American West was largely the story of the "taming" of the **Colorado River**. If the Colorado were to run dry, Los Angeles, Las Vegas, and Phoenix would die, and the exodus from the Southwest would dwarf anything from the Dustbowl era.

In terms of volume, the Colorado does not rank among the top 25 rivers in the US. However, the sheer aggression with which it hurtles from 13,000ft up in the Rockies makes it the fastest and fiercest of them all. That's why it's responsible for so many magnificent canyons; and that's also why civil engineers can't bear to leave it alone. They yearn to harness its energy with hydroelectric dams and divert its flow to irrigate the desert.

Early in the twentieth century, the sparsely populated southwestern states began to fear that southern California's ever-increasing thirst might drain them dry. 1922's **Colorado River Compact** divided the river between an **Upper Basin**, consisting of Utah, Wyoming, Colorado, and New Mexico, and a **Lower Basin** – Arizona, Nevada, and California. Each basin was to receive 7.5 million acre-feet of the estimated annual flow of 16.8 million, with the dregs left over for Mexico. This was the first of fifteen such agreements in fifty years, largely because the estimates were wrong; the long-term average is thought to be more like 13.9 million acre-feet.

The task of distributing the water fell to a new federal agency, the **Bureau of Reclamation**. Its engineers saw their mission as being to "reclaim" the West to the way it ought to be; the main tool at their disposal was the **dam**. They began in 1935, by damming Black Canyon, on the doorstep of California, with the **Hoover Dam** (see p.484). That project inspired a dam-building spree, in the US and all over world. The Bureau's subsequent plans for the Colorado Plateau were clear from the subtitle of one report: *A Natural Menace Becomes A Natural Resource*. Proposals included damming the Green River in northwest Colorado, the San Juan in New Mexico, and the Colorado itself in both Bridge Canyon in Arizona and Utah's Glen Canyon.

Almost a century earlier, in 1869, John Wesley Powell had been entranced by the idyllic canyon that stretched southwest from the confluence of the Green and Colorado rivers: "A curious ensemble of wonderful features – carved walls, royal arches, glens, alcove gulches, mounds, and monuments ... We decide to call it **Glen Canyon**." Those few river-runners who had seen it since knew it as a cool, tranquil haven, bursting with luxuriant vegetation and desert wildlife, and a far cry from the cataract-filled canyons both up- and downstream. Theirs were lone voices in the wilderness, however; too little known to receive federal protection, Glen Canyon's remoteness was to work against it.

The environmental movement was in its infancy in the 1950s, and its strategy concentrated on defending national parks. The Green River dam-site being within Dinosaur National Monument, **David Brower**, the executive director of the Sierra Club, told Congress that damming Glen Canyon was a far better idea. Conservationists prided themselves on a job well done when it was decided to dam the Green

At first, Page seemed destined to wither away once the dam was completed. Ironically, it gained a new lease of life when Congress decided that instead of building more dams, the Southwest could meet its power needs by burning coal instead. The **Navajo Generating Station**, which creates electricity using coal from Black Mesa and pumps water from Lake Powell to Phoenix, went up four miles southeast of town, and has kept Page in work ever since.

River outside Dinosaur, at Flaming Gorge to the northwest, and to go ahead with damming Glen Canyon. The one concession to "the abominable nature lovers," as one Utah senator termed them, was that water would not be allowed to encroach upon Rainbow Bridge National Monument.

President Eisenhower triggered the first blast at the dam-site in September 1956. Meanwhile, with Glen Canyon doomed but not yet drowned, archeologists, artists, and photographers set out to chronicle its disappearing treasures. These included the glowing, fern-dripping alcove known as the **Cathedral in the Desert**, and the **Crossing of the Fathers**, where the Spanish priests Domínguez and Escalante forded the river in 1776.

On January 21, 1963, the same day that the Colorado River was brought to a halt, President Kennedy's Secretary of the Interior, Stewart Udall – great-grandson of John D. Lee, of Lees Ferry (see p.354) – announced plans to build two further dams within the Grand Canyon. By now, the Sierra Club had realized its mistake; and it promptly made another. This time it argued for building coal-burning power stations instead of hydroelectric dams. The Navajo, thinking nuclear power might soon render its mineral resources worthless, decided to cash in by permitting the strip-mining of Black Mesa (see p.64), and the hideously polluting Navajo Generating Station was constructed outside Page.

It took seventeen more years for Lake Powell to fill to the brim, on June 22, 1980. By now, David Brower, who left the Sierra Club to found Friends of the Earth in 1969, was describing his support for Glen Canyon Dam as "the greatest sin I have ever committed." Shortly before his death, in 2000, the 87-year-old "Archdruid" hosted a "Day of Action Against Dams" at the dam site, and called for Lake Powell to be drained so the canyon could regenerate. One original argument for the dam had been that the Colorado would otherwise fill **Lake Mead**, behind the Hoover Dam, with silt within a few years; Brower argued that the floodgates at Glen Canyon should remain open until that really does happen, perhaps two hundred years from now. Other activists went further. In *The Monkey-Wrench Gang*, Edward Abbey fantasized about dynamiting the dam, and he was among the demonstrators who in 1981 signaled the birth of the **Earth First!** movement by suspending a 300ft strip of plastic down its face to simulate an almighty crack. To some extent, the argument has been won; no major dam has been built since the 1960s, and the general consensus is that Glen Canyon Dam will be the last.

The debate over the future of Lake Powell was given an extra spin by the **droughts** of the early twenty-first century (see p.421), which threatened to restore Glen Canyon by default, and demonstrated how rapidly flora and fauna could re-establish themselves. Some argued that the lake would never refill, others that this latest dry spell was typical of long-term weather patterns, and showed precisely why the dam was necessary. In any case, though drought may be a natural phenomenon, the level of the lake is dictated by political decisions, and specifically the amount of water released to the Lower Basin states. "Interim guidelines" were agreed in 2007 to modify the Colorado River Compact, and set specific distribution figures dependent on the varying level of Lake Mead, but during his unsuccessful presidential campaign in 2008 Arizona senator John McCain called for the whole issue to be renegotiated once again, and the future seems as uncertain as ever.

Arrival and information

Page's helpful **visitor center** is at 608 Elm St (April–June Mon–Sat 8am–6pm; July–Oct 7am–7pm; Nov–March Mon–Fri 8am–5pm; ☎928/645-2741 or 1-888/261-7243, ⓦwww.pagelakepowelltourism.com). Several other offices that purport to be information centers are in fact tour operators offering trips to Antelope Canyon (see p.424).

Accommodation

While no one would choose to spend much time in Page itself, Lake Powell is enough of an attraction to keep its **motels** busy for most of the year, and charge surprisingly high rates.

Best Western Arizona Inn 716 Rim View Drive ☎928/645-2466 or 1-800/826-2718, ⓦwww .bestwesternarizona.com. Standard upmarket motel on the outskirts of Page, commanding a massive desert panorama from the poolside. **④**

Courtyard by Marriott 600 Clubhouse Drive ☎928/645-5000 or 1-877/905-4495, ⓦwww .courtyard.com/pgacy. Page's most incongruous splash of luxury – a 153-room resort, complete with golf course – is below the mesa in view of the dam. **⑥**

Holiday Inn Express 751 S Navajo Drive ☎928/645-9000 or 1-800/465-4329, ⓦwww.hiexpress.com. Good-quality chain motel, with a pool and free continental breakfast. **⑤**

LuLu's Sleep Ezze Motel 208 N Lake Powell Blvd ☎928/608-0273 or 1-800/553-6211. Tiny, very welcoming little motel in central Page, with simple but nice rooms. **③**

Downtown Page

The view as you descend toward Page is utterly surreal. The three power plant chimneys stand silhouetted amid sandstone outcrops, while lines of pylons march off across the desert and the misty hump of Navajo Mountain rises in the distance. As you approach, the waters of Lake Powell emerge from the haze, with drowned buttes poking their heads here and there above the surface.

Page itself, on the other hand, resembles a dull suburban mall writ large; if it has a redeeming feature, you'll have a hard time finding it. Permanent structures have replaced most of its original trailer homes, but the only sight of any interest is the **John Wesley Powell Memorial Museum**, 6 N Lake Powell Blvd (Mon–Fri 9am–5pm; $5; ⓦpowellmuseum.org). As well as charting the exploits of the first man to raft down the Colorado (see p.433), the museum celebrates later river runners and recounts Page's own brief history. It also holds a locally excavated plesiosaur fossil and an amazing collection of fluorescent rocks.

Antelope Canyon

A couple of miles southeast of Page on AZ-98, mile marker 299 marks the trailhead for **Antelope Canyon**, Arizona's most famous, and irresistably, astonishingly beautiful, **slot canyon**. The canyon actually comprises two separate sections, on either side of the highway, and both are on Navajo land.

Immediately north of the highway, **Lower Antelope Canyon** achieved worldwide notoriety in 1997, when the tragic deaths of eleven hikers in a flash flood proved just how dangerous such places can be. In the last few years, the Navajo have realized what an invaluable tourism asset Antelope Canyon represents, and they now control all access (March–Oct daily 8am–5pm; ☎928/698-3347, ⓦwww.navajonationparks.org/htm/antelopecanyon.htm).

In summer, tourists can visit both sections of the canyon simply by turning up at the parking lot. However, not only is there a $6 entry fee, but you also have to pay an outrageous $15 for a "guide" service that consists either of pointing you to the entrance of Lower Antelope or driving you in a shuttle van down to **Upper Antelope Canyon**, a matter of perhaps two miles.

You're deposited just outside a slender, unprepossessing crack in a red sandstone wall. Stepping inside is like entering both a cathedral, in that you find yourself in a majestic chamber adorned with delicate glowing colors, and a pinball machine, in that you can just imagine that any second some mighty and unavoidable boulder will come thundering down the narrow passageway. Walking the full length of the canyon and back takes barely twenty minutes, even with frequent pauses to admire the interlacing fins of multihued rock that swirl overhead, in places to a height of 120ft. A flash flood is capable of filling the slot to the brim with water and spilling over the top; once such a flood recedes, on the other hand, it leaves the canyon floor scrubbed bare of its usual eight-foot layer of fine soft sand.

Be warned that while Antelope Canyon is every bit as beautiful as photos suggest, it offers little of the wilderness feel of other desert highlights. It's both short and narrow enough to feel *very* crowded at busy times, and as the main priority for all visitors is to take photographs, it can feel like a working set rather than a place to contemplate beauty.

Given the high cost of an unaccompanied visit, you may prefer to join a guided **tour** from Page that typically costs about $30 for a one-hour trip and up to $50 for a longer photography tour. Several competing companies have offices in central Page. Highly recommended for his personalized small-group excursions is the affable, self-styled Chief Tsosie of Antelope Slot Canyon Tours, 55 S Lake Powell Blvd (℡928/645-5594, ⓦantelopeslotcanyon.com), which also leads day-trips to lesser-known canyons and overlooks, while Overland Canyon Tours, 48 S Lake Powell Blvd (℡928/608-4072, ⓦoverland canyontours.com), offers extended trips into the backcountry.

Horseshoe Bend

An easy self-guided hike not far south of Page leads to an amazing view of **Horseshoe Bend**, where the Colorado River makes an extravagant 180-degree turn in the depths of Marble Canyon, roughly halfway through its short course between Glen Canyon Dam and the official start of the Grand Canyon at Lees Ferry.

To reach the overlook, drive south on US-89 and turn west on the dirt road just past mile marker 545, exactly 2.6 miles south of the Wal-Mart in Page. The road leads to a parking lot at the foot of a small sandy hill. Climb the railed path to the top of that hill, then down another 0.4 mile to the lip of the gorge. The river itself is only visible from the very edge, which is unrailed, windy, and

▲ Horseshoe Bend

pretty hair-raising. The huge curving sweep far below barely fits into the widest-angled lens. Be sure to carry water and allow about an hour for the exposed round-trip hike.

Eating

With the arguable exception of a couple of plain hotel dining rooms, Page offers a poor choice of restaurants; a *KFC* across from the visitor center is as good a bet as anything else.

Beans Gourmet Coffee House Dam Plaza, 644 N Navajo Drive ☎928/645-6858. Espressos and light snacks, plus picnic lunches to go. Daily 7am–6pm.
Bella Napoli 809 N Navajo Drive ☎928/645-2706. All-you-can-eat Italian buffets (soup, salad, pizza, and pasta) for lunch ($8) and dinner ($12), plus a full menu. Daily 11am–2pm & 5pm onward.

Dam Bar & Grille Dam Plaza, 644 N Navajo Drive ☎928/645-2161. Themed diner and bar, appealingly designed to echo the days when Page was populated solely by dam-building hardhats. Steak and pasta entrees for around $18. Daily 3–11pm.

Glen Canyon Dam

Glen Canyon Dam plugs **Marble Canyon** (see p.353) not at its narrowest point, but at its northern end, just downstream from Wahweap Creek. As US-89 crosses Glen Canyon Bridge four miles outside of Page, the vast curve of the dam is to the north, while Marble Canyon drops 700ft below you.

You can't stop on the bridge, so if you want a better look, call in at the ultra-modern **Carl Hayden Visitor Center** (daily: March–Oct 8am–6pm; Nov–Feb 8.30am–4.30pm; ☎928/608-6404, ⓦwww.nps.gov/glca) on the west bank, which doubles as the main source of information on the **Glen Canyon National Recreational Area**. Free **tours** of the actual dam take 45 minutes to drop via two elevators first to the walkway along the top, and then a further 500ft to the generating station at the bottom. Beneath the roar of the 1.3-million kilowatt turbines, a digital counter steadily ticks off the billions of dollars earned thus far by the sale of power.

Just before the bridge, a spur road on the east bank tunnels down through the cliffs to the river; rafters use it as an access point for the gloriously lazy fifteen-mile **float trip** down to Lees Ferry. There's no whitewater along the way, and strictly speaking you never enter the Grand Canyon, but it's still a very pleasant drift between imposing high-canyon cliffs. The trips are run by Colorado River Discovery, 130 Sixth Ave, Page (daily: May–Sept 7.30am & 1pm; March, April, Oct & Nov 11am; $80 adults, $70 ages 4–11; ☎928/645-9175 or 1-888/522-6644, ⓦwww.raftthecanyon.com). You're expected to bring your own drinks and picnic lunch.

Wahweap

Unlike Page, **WAHWEAP**, a couple of miles west of Glen Canyon Dam, has never become a town. Lake Powell's principal **marina** has, however, grown steadily since it was established in 1963, coordinating most of the boat rental and tour business and also offering several hundred motel rooms.

To the fury of the federal authorities, the first man to appreciate Wahweap's potential did so long before the dam was ever built. Art Greene, the owner of the *Marble Canyon Lodge* (see p.354), ran boat trips upriver to Rainbow Bridge from the 1940s onwards; when he got wind of plans to dam Glen Canyon, he shrewdly leased the land at the mouth of Wahweap Creek at a knockdown rate. Knowing it made the perfect site for a marina, Greene refused to budge, and wound up making a killing as official concessionaire.

Practicalities

Only half the rooms in the plush *Lake Powell Resort* (T928/645-2433 or 1-888/896-3829, Wlakepowell.com; ❻) overlook Lake Powell. Its *Rainbow Room* restaurant, however, provides huge lakeside windows and serves good food daily for all meals, with prices kept relatively low to cater to the many tour groups that pass through. The same management also operates an adjacent first-come, first-served **campground** ($19), as well as an **RV park** (April–Oct $34; Nov–March $19).

Boat tours from Wahweap

In addition to the **Rainbow Bridge** trips detailed below, Lake Powell Resorts and Marinas (see box above) runs boat tours from Wahweap that range from ninety-minute water-only Antelope Canyon excursions ($34 adults, $22 under age 12) to a dinner cruise (daily June–Oct, $99).

Rainbow Bridge National Monument

Millions of tourists have Lake Powell to thank for providing access to the **world's largest natural bridge**, the magnificent **RAINBOW BRIDGE NATIONAL MONUMENT**. The Navajo, seeing this formerly sacred site swarming with visitors, are far less enthusiastic, though at least the height of Glen Canyon Dam, and thus the level of the lake, was mandated to ensure that Rainbow Bridge was not drowned – unlike the nearby and equally revered confluence of the Colorado and San Juan rivers.

Both the Navajo and the Paiute knew of Rainbow Bridge before the first university-sponsored expedition reached it in 1909. Within a year, it was declared a national monument, but it remained far off any beaten track until the coming of Lake Powell. The bridge now lies a couple of miles down **Forbidding Canyon**, a side canyon located around fifty miles by water from the dam.

Tours from **Wahweap** operate year-round (April–Oct daily 8am & 10am; Nov–March Sat 9am; adults $144, under-13s $89; T928/645-2433 or 1-888/896-3829, Wlakepowell.com). These schedules are open to considerable variation, as the length of the trip depends on the level of the lake. What used to be a half-day excursion has become an eight-hour one in recent years because certain deep-water channels are no longer navigable. It's possible that the waters may rise again sufficiently for the tour boats to make two round-trips in a single day. For much of the year, the tours are booked well in advance, so reserve your boat trip before you finalize your accommodation.

Even with the water low, Lake Powell remains a broad expanse, spread beneath a huge sky. When you reach Forbidding Canyon, on the other hand, you enter another world; it's a beautiful high-walled slot canyon that twists mysteriously away from the lake proper. Eventually, the tour boats moor at a floating jetty, the precise location of which varies. A walk from here that's currently over a mile leads to the astonishing sandstone gateway of the bridge, climbing nearly 300ft high. It's also almost 300ft wide, with Navajo Mountain visible through its superbly smooth curve. The upper section, including the forty-foot-thick span, is composed of Navajo sandstone, while the base belongs to the harder Kayenta formation, not so easily cut by flowing water. When the lake is full, the bridge spans open water, but these days the former streambed is usually dry. What were once waterfalls nearby have also been exposed; what a spot this must have been. The Park Service asks visitors to consider not walking right up to, or beneath, the bridge itself, out of respect for Navajo spiritual traditions. Almost everyone goes anyway.

With a great deal more difficulty, Rainbow Bridge can also be reached on **foot**. Two fourteen-mile trails start respectively 38 and 42 miles up Arrowhead Hwy-16, which runs north from Hwy-98 from a junction 57 miles southeast of Page. They loop to either side of Navajo Mountain, then join for the last half-mile. Only experienced canyoneers should attempt this hike, having obtained **permits** from Navajo Nation Parks & Recreation ($5, plus $5 per person per night; ☎928/871-6647, ⓦnavajonationparks.org). The Glen Canyon Natural History Association (ⓦglencanyonnha.org) can provide up-to-date details on the two alternative routes.

Bullfrog

The marina at **BULLFROG** is slapped atop the slickrock on the west side of Lake Powell, seventy miles upstream from Wahweap, or seventy miles southeast of Capitol Reef National Park on the Notom–Bullfrog Road (see p.417). It's the focus of a small community that now proudly boasts its own high school, as well as a Glen Canyon NRA **visitor center**, open in summer only (May–Oct daily 8am–5pm; ☎435/684-7400, ⓦwww.nps.gov/glca).

A houseboat on stilts above the road serves as a sign for the *Defiance House Lodge* (☎435/684-3000 or 1-800/528-6154, ⓦlakepowell.com; ⓺). The best place to enjoy the big lake views from this pricey mesa-top **motel** is its *Anasazi* restaurant, even though the food itself is indifferent. The park concessionaires also have some fully furnished but deeply unatmospheric "**family units**"

The Lake Powell Ferry

The ferry crossing between Bullfrog and Hall's Crossing takes 25 minutes. In recent years the timetable has run as follows:

	From Hall's Crossing	From Bullfrog
April to mid-May	8am, 10am, noon, & 2pm	9am, 11am, 1pm, & 3pm
mid-May to mid-Sept	8am, 10am, noon, 2pm, 4pm, & 6pm	9am, 11am, 1pm, 3pm, 5pm, & 7pm
mid-Sept to Oct	8am, 10am, noon, 2pm, & 4pm	9am, 11am, 1pm, 3pm, & 5pm
Nov–March	8am & 2pm	9am & 3pm

Fares: Foot passengers $5, bicycles $5, motorcycles $10, ordinary cars $20. Increased rates for larger vehicles.

Ferry service is frequently suspended for repairs in winter; contact Glen Canyon visitor centers for current information and up-to-date schedules (☎435/634-3088 or ⓦwww.nps.gov/glca).

(similar to trailers) for rent (●). A year-round first-come, first-served **campground** charges $20 per night (☎ 435/684-3000).

Hall's Crossing

HALL'S CROSSING, on the east shore of Lake Powell, now plays second fiddle to its larger neighbor Bullfrog to the west. As the name suggests, it was the base of a river ferry operator long before the lake existed. **Charles Hall** started out by building his own boat at Hole-in-the-Rock, 35 miles downstream (see p.408), in 1870. Business there was so bad that he moved here in 1881, only to give up altogether when the transcontinental railroad rendered his service redundant. Hall charged $5 per wagon and 75¢ per passenger; the going rate these days for a family car is $20 (see box opposite).

The GNRA Ranger Station above Hall's Crossing marina is rarely staffed; call ☎ 1-800/582-4351 in emergencies. **Accommodation** possibilities are limited to family units in a glorified trailer park (phone number and rates as for Bullfrog), or an $20-per-night first-come, first-served **campground** (☎ 435/684-7000). If you're looking for a **meal**, you can either take your pick from a small assortment of Twinkies on sale at the local gas station, or a marginally wider range of groceries at the marina store. There's nothing at all at the **ferry ramp**, just over a mile beyond the marina.

When they finally get around to colonizing Mars, the first settlement should look much like the airstrip on top of the bare red mesa that rises above Hall's Crossing. Hwy-276 to the east makes an exhilarating drive, dropping down the **Clay Cliffs** with views across the red plains to Monument Valley, and running for forty empty miles to meet Hwy-95 near Natural Bridges (see p.465).

Ticaboo

Hwy-276 sets off bravely into the desert northwest of Bullfrog, passing a series of unlikely looking warehouses used to store boats during the winter. Twelve miles up, well past the turning to Notom (see p.417) and only a few miles short of the red-tinged peak that marks the southernmost point of the Henry Mountains, the grandiose resort development of **TICABOO** stands to the left of the highway. An optimistic venture that still hasn't quite paid off, Ticaboo consists merely of the comfortable *Ticaboo Lodge* (☎ 435/788-2110 or 1-888/802-2293, Ⓦ ticaboo .com; ●), a convenience store but no restaurant, and a Conoco gas station.

Hite

Lake Powell's northernmost marina, at **HITE**, is reached via **Hwy-95**, which branches off Hwy-24 halfway between Capitol Reef and I-70 to run for 122 miles southeast to Blanding. The only highway to cross the Colorado between the Glen Canyon Dam and Moab, Hwy-95's most dramatic segment is the twenty-mile stretch as it approaches the river from the west, rattling along beside the North Wash.

At the mouth of the North Wash canyon, the highway climbs to the windswept hilltop that holds **Hite Overlook**. You'll almost certainly be confronted here by the fact that while Hite remains accessible by road, it's no longer on the lake. An ongoing drought let Lake Powell recede out of sight several years ago; it's just possible the waters will have returned by the time you read this, but don't bet on it.

Hite has always felt like something of a God-forsaken spot, and even more so these days that it's lake-forsaken as well. Beyond the overlook, Hwy-95 loops north to cross first the Dirty Devil River and then the Colorado. Reaching the ramshackle **Hite Marina** itself involves a detour of a couple of miles on the far side. At the time of writing, no boats could reach Hite, so all the marina facilities were shut. There's still a small gas station and a grocery store (open 11am–2pm only), and it's even possible to rent a **"family unit"** (same phone number and rates as for Bullfrog), though that would be a seriously bad idea. There's also primitive camping alongside the marina if you absolutely have to spend the night (☎435/684-7400).

Between Capitol Reef and Canyonlands

No direct route crosses the tract of craggy sandstone and eroded clay that stretches for a hundred miles east of Capitol Reef. Travelers making the circuit of Utah's parks are obliged to make a giant detour to the north or south, either crossing Lake Powell at Hite or taking **Hwy-24** up to meet I-70 and then looping back down to Moab – a total drive of around 150 miles.

The scenery along Hwy-24 is consistently awesome, beginning with the **badlands** twenty miles beyond Capitol Reef, where the 1500ft **Factory Butte** rises above corrugated humps of grayish-blue clay reminiscent of Arizona's Painted Desert (see p.278). Only small sections of the backcountry are at all accessible, however, and the town of **Green River** on the interstate is the only town of any size the whole way to Moab.

Hanksville

Forty miles from the Capitol Reef visitor center, Hwy-24 turns sharply north toward the interstate, while Hwy-95 runs south toward Lake Powell. The tiny farming community of **HANKSVILLE** stands at the intersection, a few miles south of the confluence where the Fremont and Muddy rivers join to form the Dirty Devil.

Hanksville is only a dot on the map, but with the next dot a good fifty miles away in any direction, it draws in enough weary drivers to keep it ticking. Its handful of basic accommodation options include the friendly *Joy's*, 296 S Center St (☎435/542-3252; ❸; closed Nov–March), a three-room **B&B** open to couples only, and a small family-run **motel**, the *Whispering Sands*, 140 S Hwy-95 (☎435/542-3238, ⓦwww.whisperingsandsmotel.com; ❹). There's also a large commercial **campground**, the *Red Rock*, at 226 East 100 North (mid-March to Oct, $18; ☎435/542-3235, ⓦredrockcampground.net), which has a decent restaurant. Poised on a low bluff close to the intersection, *Blondie's Eatery*, 3 N Hwy-95 (☎435/542-3255), is better than it looks, serving steak and eggs for around $8.

A couple of solitary structures also interrupt the badlands west of Hanksville. The *Caineville Cove Inn*, at mile marker 99 on Hwy-24 (☎435/456-9900, ⓦcainevillecove.com; ❸), is a small but comfortable motel with a swimming pool, while the *Luna Mesa Oasis*, two miles on at mile marker 101 (April–Oct; closed Sun; ☎435/456-9122; ❶–❷), is an inexpensive Mexican restaurant.

Goblin Valley State Park

Utah's quirkiest park, **GOBLIN VALLEY STATE PARK**, nestles at the foot of the San Rafael Reef, a short distance west of Hwy-24 just over twenty miles north of Hanksville. This small patch of barren desert became a park for the simple reason that its clay-like rock formations are **funny**. The man who first noticed them, in the 1940s, called it Mushroom Valley, but "goblin" is as good a name as any. In the 1999 movie *Galaxy Quest*, Goblin Valley doubles believably as an alien planet, with its rocks coming to life in one fabulous sequence.

To reach the park, branch west from Hwy-24 near mile post 137 – half a mile north of the dirt road that leads to **Horseshoe Canyon**; see p.440 – and drive for five miles along Temple Mountain Road, then turn south onto a seven-mile paved spur road. Past the entrance kiosk ($7 day-use fee, open 24hr; ☎435/564-3633), the road ends beside a sheltered overlook, poised above a slim valley whose sandy floor is completely devoid of vegetation. It's filled instead with parallel fins of pale Entrada sandstone, each topped by a ridge that's indented with weird eroded figures. Some hoodoos also stand alone, while larger buttes and columns loom around the periphery.

A couple of formal trails lead down into the valley, but no one bothers to follow them, preferring to slither at random from one misshapen masterpiece to the next. Once you're on the valley floor, a typical monster in the maze will rise a few feet over your head; some really do look like goblins, complete with eyes and ears.

Away from the main valley, but still engulfed by stunted sandstone sprites, the park has a well-equipped **campground** with running water, toilets, and showers, open year-round ($16; reservations on ☎1-800/322 3770).

The San Rafael Swell

The **San Rafael Swell**, fronted by the "reef" that soars immediately northwest of Goblin Valley, is one of southern Utah's least known but most tantalizing wilderness areas. With so many mapped and tamed parklands in the region, offering such instant and abundant rewards, few out-of-state visitors add this difficult, mountainous terrain to their itineraries. A glimpse of it from I-70, as the interstate plunges east down its craggy foothills toward Green River, usually suffices.

In the past, most of the swell was only safely accessible in 4WD vehicles. Now a significant number of dirt roads have been upgraded, and local tourist authorities have produced lavish booklets and maps of possible driving tours. If you're driving an ordinary two-wheel-drive vehicle, it's still essential to enquire locally, in Green River or Goblin Valley, before attempting to explore on your own. Conditions vary month to month; many roads become impassable every winter, and are only fit for conventional use in early summer, when the latest winter's has been repaired.

A couple of highlights are detailed below; others, for which you're more likely to need 4WD, include **Little Wild Horse Canyon**, a slot canyon that cuts into the reef roughly seven sandy miles west of Goblin Valley, and the swell's highest point, the **San Rafael Knob**, a four-hour round-trip hike from the end of Copper Globe Road, which heads south from I-70 at exit 114.

Black Dragon Canyon

The most accessible part of the San Rafael Swell, spectacular **Black Dragon Canyon**, lies immediately north of I-70 three miles west of Hwy-24, and a total of seventeen miles west of Green River. You can only approach it from the interstate's westbound lane. Pull directly off the highway just past milepost 147, and go through the gate, closing it behind you. Drive straight ahead for a mile on a dirt road, ignoring a possible west turn, then follow the sign west, and park when the road surface deteriorates. From there, a short walk leads into the towering, golden-walled canyon itself. The prime goal is a group of dramatic Barrier Canyon-style **pictographs** (see p.441), on the north side a quarter-mile along. If that's all you have time for, you can easily be back on the interstate within an hour of leaving it.

Alternatively, with a good map, you can make a day of it by hiking the full length of the canyon, which is barely two miles long, then climbing north over a pass and back down again to meet the San Rafael River, which will lead you back to where you left your car. That demanding fifteen-mile loop will take at least seven hours to complete.

Heart of Sinbad Road
The 24-mile **Heart of Sinbad Road** runs from the end of Temple Mountain Road – the spur road off Hwy-24 that leads to Goblin Valley (see opposite) – up to exit 131 off I-70, 33 miles west of Green River. Unpaved, but usually good enough for ordinary vehicles, it provides access to many remote and fascinating areas of the San Rafael Swell. There's no room here to describe them all; pick up a brochure in Green River and choose for yourself.

Green River

Hwy-24 joins I-70 44 miles north of Hanksville, just as the interstate completes a dramatic descent from the uplands of the San Rafael Swell to slope gently east through a landscape of soaring buttes. Within a few miles, a ribbon of green vegetation becomes visible ahead, cutting through the desert at the bottom of a long broad valley – the line of the **Green River**. To the north stand the forbidding **Uintah Mountains**, while to the south the stream burrows into a labyrinth of twisting canyons, so this is the best place to ford the river for hundreds of miles.

The town of **GREEN RIVER** has long straddled crucial cross-country routes. For east–west travelers, it remains the major way-station between Colorado and Utah, while river-runners from John Wesley Powell onwards have launched themselves south from here toward the Colorado.

While Green River is a welcome oasis, however – fertile enough to be the "melon-growing capital of east Utah" – it still amounts to little more than a strip of motels, gas stations, and fast-food outlets. Given a sensible reluctance to erect permanent structures too close to the river, there's a gap where you might expect downtown to be; most of the built-up strip lies to the west.

The east bank of the river, however, holds the well laid-out **John Wesley Powell River History Museum**, at 1765 E Main St (daily: April–Oct 8am–8pm; Nov–March 9am–5pm; $4; ⓦjohnwesleypowell.com). This recounts the epic journeys of the Canyonlands region's first true explorer, whose second voyage started at Green River on May 22, 1871. Powell made that trip partly because he lost the notes from his first, so the second time around he ensured his every movement was fully recorded, in photos that now make marvellously evocative viewing. A multimedia show and several rooms of exhibits cover later developments in river navigation, ranging from steamers – none managed more than a handful of voyages – up to the army-surplus rubber inflatables that triggered the postwar boom in whitewater rafting. Glance out of the panoramic windows, and you'll see that the river here is not green at all, but a dark muddy brown.

Arrival and information
The Powell museum at 1765 E Main St doubles as Green River's friendly **visitor center** (hours as above; ⓣ435/564-3427, ⓦgreenriverutah.com), which can advise you on driving local backcountry roads. Amtrak's *California Zephyr* calls at the train station at 250 S Broadway daily, heading east toward Denver at 8.59am and west toward Salt Lake City at 5.58pm, while Greyhound **buses** between Denver and points west stop at the *Rodeway Inn*, 525 E Main St (ⓣ435/564-3521).

Until **John Wesley Powell** led the first expedition to float down the full length of the Green and Colorado rivers, the Colorado Plateau was a vast blank at the heart of maps of the American West. No one knew how the mountains and waterways of the region fitted together, or whether falls larger than Niagara might prevent river traffic completely.

Born in Ohio in 1834, the son of a traveling preacher, Powell spent his youth making solo forays along the Ohio, Mississippi, and Illinois rivers. He lost his right arm fighting for the Union at Shiloh, where he formed a lasting friendship with future president Ulysses Grant. Once the Civil War was over, the veteran major headed west to explore the Colorado Plateau.

Powell, his brother Walter, and a volunteer crew of eight frontier types set off in four flat-bottomed wooden boats from Green River, Wyoming, on **May 24, 1869**. Powell was lashed to an upright wooden chair in the leading vessel. Not long after entering the Uintah Mountains, by way of **Flaming Gorge**, one boat was smashed to smithereens in Lodore Canyon. They then whisked through Green River, Utah, and plunged into the desert, encountering their biggest challenge so far in the shape of **Cataract Canyon**, soon after the Green met the Grand to form the Colorado. Wherever possible, they carried their boats around the fiercest rapids, and with prodigious energy Powell repeatedly climbed out of the canyon to get his bearings. After several terrifying days, they burst out of the gorge, for an idyllic period of respite in **Glen Canyon**.

Three members of the party became demoralized in the depths of the **Grand Canyon**, when the blackness of the walls to either side seemed to presage further ferocious rapids ahead. They decided to hike their way out, only to be murdered mysteriously – some say by suspicious Mormons, others by Shivwits Indians. Powell, however, made it through the remainder of the canyon with unexpected ease; it took him merely one more day to reach the **Grand Wash Cliffs**, at the confluence of the Colorado and Virgin rivers (now beneath Lake Mead) on August 30. Two of his crew continued all the way to the Pacific, but Powell and his brother left the river, after almost a hundred days afloat.

Now a national celebrity, Powell returned for a better-funded and more leisurely trip two years later. Starting this time from Green River, Utah, he documented his experiences in much greater detail, and used them as the basis of a bestselling book. During the voyage, he left the canyon at every opportunity, and even returned to Washington DC for the winter, while his crew holed up in Kanab.

In later years, Powell became director of the Smithsonian Institution's **Bureau of Ethnology** in Washington, DC, and of the **US Geologic Survey**. His forceful opinions as to how the federal government should administer the limited resources of the West – and especially its water – are now regarded as prophetic. Refusing to accept the then-current adage that "rain follows the plow," he argued that state boundaries should be drawn along natural watersheds, to prevent water issues from bedeviling the region's political future. His advocacy of federally funded water projects led the bureaucrats to name **Lake Powell** in his honor, but one can't help imagining that Powell himself would prefer Glen Canyon as it was in the beginning.

Companies running **rafting trips** from Green River include Moki Mac River Expeditions (☎435/564-3361 or 1-800/284-7280, ⊛www.mokimac .com) and Holiday Expeditions (☎435/564-3273 or 1-800/624-6323, ⊛www.bikeraft.com). Every Memorial Day, hundreds of boats set out on weekend-long convoy trips that cruise down to the Colorado confluence and then chug back upriver to Moab.

7

SOUTHERN UTAH | Between Capitol Reef and Canyonlands

The Green River

But for political shenanigans in the 1920s, the **Green River** might rank among the world's most famous rivers. It starts by flowing north to loop around the Wind River Mountains of central Wyoming, then heads south into Utah, briefly ducks into the northwest corner of Colorado, and then crosses Utah to meet the **Colorado River** after a 730-mile journey.

The Green River was first identified by Fray Alonzo de Posada in 1686 as the boundary between the territories of the Ute and the Comanche. Until 1859, when Captain J.N. Mancomb discovered the confluence deep in the heart of the canyonlands, no one knew that it flowed into the Colorado. The **Colorado River** had been named by the Spanish founder of New Mexico, Juan de Oñate, in 1606, while French trappers in what's now Colorado stumbled across what they named the **Grand River** a century later.

The trouble is, at the confluence the Colorado has flowed a mere 430 miles from the Rockies of central Colorado. As geographical convention dictates that the principal course of a river is its longest, the Green River should be regarded as the main course of the Colorado River, and their entire combined course should bear the same name. Either the Green should become the Colorado, or the Colorado below the confluence should become the Green – in which case the Grand Canyon should arguably be called the Green Canyon, which doesn't bear thinking about.

The news that the "Colorado River" did not originate in Colorado, as had always been assumed, mortified Colorado's legislators. In the 1920s, they simply defied convention and renamed the Grand the Colorado, which fortunately dovetailed with a vote in conservative Utah against changing the name of the Green River.

Accommodation

Although Green River is not much of a destination in its own right, it has around five hundred **motel** rooms. They tend to fill by early evening in summer, partly with the overspill from Moab and partly with long-distance interstate travelers. The best **camping** is at the attractive waterfront Green River State Park, south of Main Street, on the river's west bank ($16; ☎435/564-3633, for summer reservations, costing $8 extra, call ☎1-800/322-3770).

Best Western River Terrace 1740 E Main St ☎435/564-3401 or 1-800/780-7234, ⊛www.bestwesternutah.com. High-quality motel, often filled by tour groups, with a pool, river views, and adjacent restaurant. ❹

Holiday Inn Express 1845 E Main St ☎435/564-4439 or 1-800/465-4329, ⊛www.ichotelsgroup.com. Crisp, clean chain motel, next door to the museum and visitor center, with an indoor pool, laundry, and free breakfast. ❺

Super 8 1248 E Main St ☎435/564-8888 or 1-800/800-8000, ⊛www.super8.com. Reliable budget motel, perched on a slight elevation at the east end of town. ❸

Eating

As well as the usual fast-food places and a couple of local cafés, a handful of Green River's motels have their own restaurants.

Ben's Cafe 115 E Main St ☎435/564-3352. Friendly if grungy diner toward the west end of town, where almost nothing on the menu costs over $10. Open daily for all meals.

Green River Coffee Co 25 E Main St ☎435/564-3411. Lively local coffee bar, just south of the main drag a mile or so west of the river. Mon–Thurs 6am–2pm, Fri–Sun 6am–5pm.

Tamarisk Restaurant 870 E Main St ☎435/564-8109. Brisk, busy restaurant, overlooking the river opposite the museum; the menu is wide-ranging and cheap, with most full dinners costing under $10, but the salad bar is atrocious. Open daily for breakfast, lunch, and dinner.

Canyonlands National Park

CANYONLANDS NATIONAL PARK, the largest and most mag[nificent of] Utah's national parks, is as hard to define as it is to map. Its closest [counterpart,] the Grand Canyon, is simply an almighty crack in an otherwise rel[atively level] plain; the Canyonlands area is a bewildering tangle of canyons, plateaus, fissures, and faults, scattered with buttes and monoliths, pierced by arches and caverns, and penetrated only by a paltry handful of dead-end roads.

The 527 square miles of the park are just the core of a much larger wilderness that stretches to the horizon in every direction. To nineteenth-century explorers, this was the epitome of useless desolation; only since uranium prospectors blazed crude trails across the trackless wastes in the 1950s has it become at all widely known. Even after Canyonlands park was created in 1964, it took a couple of decades before tourists arrived in appreciable numbers.

Canyonlands focuses upon the Y-shaped confluence of the Green and Colorado rivers, buried deep in the desert forty miles southwest of Moab. There's only one spot from which you can see the rivers meet, however, and that's a five-mile hike from the nearest road. With no way to get down to the rivers, let alone cross them, the park therefore splits into three major sections. The **Needles**, east of the Colorado, is a red-rock wonderland of sandstone pinnacles and hidden meadows that's a favorite with hardy hikers and 4WD enthusiasts, while the **Maze**, west of both the Colorado and the Green, is a virtually inaccessible labyrinth of tortuous, waterless canyons that presents a stiff challenge even to expert climbers and backpackers. In the wedge of the "Y" between the two, the high, dry mesa of the **Island In The Sky** commands astonishing views across the whole park and beyond, seen from overlooks that can easily be toured by car. Getting from any one of these sections to the others involves a drive of at least a hundred miles. The Needles and the Island In The

---

Canyonlands fees and permits

The **entry fee** for Canyonlands National Park – $10 per vehicle, $5 for cyclists or hikers – is valid for seven days in all sections of the park. All the usual passes (see p.41) are sold and accepted.

Only limited numbers of visitors are allowed to spend a night or more in the **backcountry**, and all such groups are required to have **permits**. **Backpacking** permits, covering a maximum party of seven persons in the Needles and Island In The Sky districts, or five persons in the Maze, cost $15. Permits for **four-wheel-drive** or **mountain biking** expeditions that involve backcountry camping, issued for groups of up to three vehicles with a total of fifteen people in the Island In The Sky, ten in the Needles, or nine in the Maze, are $30. **Day-use** permits, costing $5, are also required for bikes and 4WD vehicles that enter Horse or Lavender canyons in the Needles district.

Though not compulsory, **reservations** are essential for the most popular areas, especially in spring and fall. They must be purchased at least two weeks in advance, and are issued for dates throughout each calendar year from the second Monday of July in the previous year. Permits must be picked up in person – with every member of the group present – from the appropriate park visitor center, at least one hour before it closes.

Reservations can only be made by mail or fax (**NPS Reservations Office**, 2282 S West Resource Blvd, Moab UT 84532-8000, Ⓕ435/259-4285); for more information call Ⓣ435/259-4351 (Mon–Fri 8am–4pm); contact a park visitor center, or see the official **park website** Ⓦ www.nps.gov/cany.

.y are reached via long approach roads that leave US-191 north and south of Moab respectively; the Maze is an endless jolting ride on dirt tracks from either Hwy-24 or the town of Green River.

The **rivers** themselves count as Canyonlands' fourth major component. A **rafting** expedition from Moab, with the operators detailed on p.458, is the best way to experience the eerie stillness of the deep canyons, at once exhilarating and supremely restful. However, since there's no way out before Lake Powell, you'll need to set aside several days, and several hundred dollars – and be prepared to face the intense whitewater rapids of **Cataract Canyon**, just beyond the confluence.

One final subsection of the park, **Horseshoe Canyon** in the west, was added in 1971 to preserve the Southwest's finest collection of ancient **rock art**.

With no lodging and little camping in the park, you'll probably need to make repeated visits on successive days, while as there's no loop road to whisk you through it, it takes a full day to have even a cursory look at a single segment. If you're among the many visitors who find the conditions too grueling to spend much time out of your car – summer temperatures regularly exceed 100°F, and most trails have no water and little shade – then the Island In The Sky is the most immediately rewarding option. On the other hand, if you fancy a long day-hike you'd do better to set off into the Needles.

The largest selection of **motels** near Canyonlands is in Moab (see p.455), while park **campgrounds** are detailed on p.439, and p.446. Operators that run **tours** into the Canyonlands backcountry are listed on p.458.

The Island In The Sky

It's not obvious from most maps, but like the Colorado River confluence over which it looms, the mesa known as the **Island In The Sky** is itself shaped

The geology of Canyonlands

In a land with so little water, the sheer *effort* that went into creating the splendor of Canyonlands is almost impossible to conceive. As you look out from the park's highest point, atop the Island In The Sky, the cliffs drop away a thousand feet, with the rivers a thousand feet below that. For a hundred miles south, successive plateaus, benches, and tablelands diminish into the distance, studded with the occasional butte. And yet twelve million years ago, this entire landscape was one vast plain, level with where you're standing. Bit by bit, at the rate of two inches every thousand years, the topsoil has crumbled to silt and been carried away by the rivers. Most was deposited at the edge of the Pacific, but now it's gradually filling up Lake Powell instead.

Canyonlands was not literally carved by the rivers, however. Both the Green and the Colorado began life as gentle streams. In the last twelve million years, as the Colorado Plateau pushed up, they have remained in their original courses, ever more deeply entrenched into the earth. Meanwhile, ice produced in a ceaseless cycle of freezes and thaws has chiseled away at the rocks that surround them, tumbling boulders into the water to be swept away.

Canyonlands is unique in that it rests on a mile-thick bed of **salt**, deposited on the bottom of an ancient sea three hundred million years ago. That salt was covered by subsequent layers of sediment, themselves interspersed with further deposits of salt. Under the pressure of thousands of feet of harder rock, the salt layers are squeezed like toothpaste until they flow far underground, then bubble up toward the surface. As they do so, they push up fins and spurs of rock that crack and split to create phenomena such as the Needles, or they may hit ground water and dissolve, leaving gaping caverns behind.

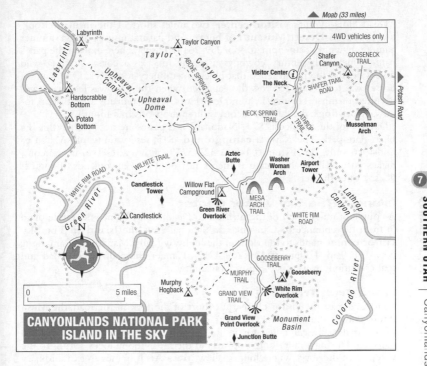

CANYONLANDS NATIONAL PARK
ISLAND IN THE SKY

like a "Y." After a steady climb of around 25 miles, **Hwy-313**, which heads southwest from US-191 eight miles north of Moab, enters the park across the slender **Neck** that forms the right-hand fork of the Y. It then branches to the northwest, to run as far as the crater of **Upheaval Dome**, and to the south, where it ends at the overwhelming **Grand View Point**.

Most Island In The Sky visitors simply drive from one overlook to the next. Some also walk one or two of the short, easy trails that cross its thin capping of Kayenta sandstone, to gaze over the brink of the sheer Wingate cliffs that hold it up. It is also possible, however – either in a sturdy 4WD vehicle, or by some very strenuous hiking – to make your way down to the pale plateau of the **White Rim**, prominent a thousand feet below.

Note that whatever certain inaccurate maps may suggest, ordinary vehicles **cannot** reach the Island In The Sky from Moab by way of Hwy-279, the Potash Road.

Dead Horse Point State Park

Shortly before the national-park boundary, twenty miles in from US-191, a turning to the east leads in four miles to the smaller but equally breathtaking **Dead Horse Point State Park**. This miniature version of the Island In The Sky stands at the tip of another narrow mesa, poised two thousand feet above a stupendous "gooseneck" loop in the Colorado. Off to the east, the turquoise ponds of Moab's potash plant (see p.457) make a garish contrast with the red rocks, while the Anticline Overlook (see p.461) stands guard above the far side of Meander Canyon.

Dead Horse Point's **visitor center**, two miles short of the main overlook, incorporates a **Desert Museum** of human and natural history (daily: summer 8am–6pm; winter 8am–5pm; ☎435/259-2614). Displays here explain the park's name: nineteenth-century cowboys used the mesa as a corral, herding wild horses behind the piñon fence that blocked its ninety-foot neck. One band of horses was too scared to cross the gap even when the gate was left open, and perished of thirst. For that matter, Dead Horse Point remains a death trap for unwary pet **dogs**; the current record is three drop-offs in a month.

Day-use of the park costs $7 – National Parks passes are not valid, as this is a Utah state park. The *Kayenta* **campground** ($15, reservations mid-March to mid-Oct only, $8 extra; ☎1-800/322-3770, ⓦwww.reserveamerica.com) makes an excellent alternative if there's no room in Canyonlands, though it doesn't offer showers.

Island In The Sky Visitor Center

A couple of miles south of the turn-off to Dead Horse Point, and a mile or so in from the entrance to Canyonlands National Park, the **Island In The Sky visitor center** stands to the right of the highway (daily: March–Oct 8am–6pm; Nov–Feb 9am–4.30pm; ☎435/259-4712). Rangers have details on road and trail conditions as well as campsite availability.

Mesa Arch Trail

Four miles past the visitor center, just short of the fork in the road, the **Mesa Arch Trail** is the Island In The Sky's best short hike. It's more of a walkway than a trail really, cemented for its full length and equipped with occasional stairways. During a mile-long loop around the mesa-top hillocks, it runs to the very rim of the abyss, where long, shallow **Mesa Arch** frames an extraordinary view of the La Sal Mountains, 35 miles northeast. Admiring Washer Woman Arch and Monster Tower, closer at hand, it would be easy to stumble right through the gap – there's no barrier.

Grand View Point Overlook

Grand View Point Overlook, at the southern end of the road, is the Island In The Sky's definitive vantage point, and an agoraphobe's nightmare. It commands a hundred-mile prospect of layer upon layer of naked sandstone, here stacked thousands of feet high, there fractured into bottomless canyons.

The most conspicuous feature is the plateau formed by the **White Rim** layer, a thousand feet below, whose faint smattering of grass is crisscrossed by abandoned mining trails and ends at the White Rim itself. That peters out in the mass of white-capped red-rock pillars known as **Monument Basin**, where the **Totem Pole** may be 305ft tall but looks the size of a pencil. Neither river can be seen; the Colorado River is tucked out of sight another thousand feet down, while the equivalent canyon of the Green River is hidden by the twin buttes to the west. Everything is mirrored by an identical chaos on the far side, however, rising toward the snowcapped peaks of the **Abajo Mountains**, forty miles south.

A stroll along the **Grand View Trail**, a two-mile roundtrip that heads across a lovely level shelf just below and to the right of the overlook, enables you to contemplate the whole jigsaw puzzle from countless additional angles. Every now and then, you may spot the silhouette of the Needles, far to the south.

By the middle of each day, the entire landscape takes on a hazy pallor; for the best **photographs**, you'd ideally be at the national-park overlooks early in the morning, and Dead Horse Point at sunset.

Green River Overlook and Willow Flat campground

A couple of hundred yards north of the fork in the park road, a paved 1.2-mile spur road leads to the **Green River Overlook**. The clearer, flatter expanse of the White Rim that spreads below is pierced by the green-trimmed meandering course of the river itself, as it flows through placid **Stillwater Canyon**. At this very spot, in the Biblical epic *The Greatest Story Ever Told*, Max von Sydow (aka Jesus) delivered the Sermon on the Mount to an audience of Moab Rotarians bedecked in false beards and tea towels.

The Island In The Sky's only developed **campground**, the waterless, twelve-site, first-come, first-served *Willow Flat* ($10), is just back from the overlook.

Upheaval Dome

The park road ends five miles north of the fork at the geological oddity of **Upheaval Dome**. This jagged 1500ft-deep crater is a highlight of air tours (see p.459), but from close up, at the end of the steep ten-minute climb from the parking lot, it's a disappointment. Elaborate theories that explained the prongs of pale stone bursting from its darkest depths as the product of undulating subterranean salt have recently been abandoned in favor of the simpler notion of a sixty-million-year-old **meteor strike**.

Over the Edge: the White Rim Road

The reason the Island In The Sky is accessible at all, and that crude dirt tracks strike off into the wilderness everywhere you look, is that this region was a prime target for freelance **uranium prospectors** in the 1950s (see p.453). They knew uranium is often found in the gray-green rocks of the **Chinle formation**, which here forms the talus slopes at the bottom of the Wingate-sandstone cliffs, not far above the White Rim.

The rough-and-ready hundred-mile **White Rim Road**, scraped by would-be miners at the base of the cliffs, is now most often explored on three- or four-day **4WD expeditions**, with overnight stops at primitive campgrounds en route (by permit only; see p.435). Only the hair-raising **Shafer Trail Road**, which drops just south of the visitor center, connects the mesa-top with the White Rim; otherwise drivers join the White Rim

▲ Green River Overlook

Road by means of the **Potash Road** from Moab (see p.457), or along **Mineral Bottom Road**, which runs west from Hwy-313 a couple of miles north of the Dead Horse Point turn-off. None of these routes should be attempted in ordinary vehicles.

Hikers can, however, clamber between the Island In The Sky and the White Rim along various trails. All are too demanding for a round-trip day-hike down to the White Rim – let alone to either river – to be a good idea. Register with the Park Service before you set off on a multi-day trip. Options include the **Lathrop Trail**, an utterly exhausting nine-mile route all the way to the Colorado, passing close to abandoned but potentially toxic uranium mines; the **Upheaval Canyon Trail**, which drops down to the Green River from the far side of Upheaval Dome; and the **Shafer Trail Road** itself.

Horseshoe Canyon

Remote **Horseshoe Canyon**, a detached chunk of Canyonlands National Park located well northwest of its main body, is home to the most extraordinary **rock art** in North America. No one now knows the meaning of the mysterious, haunting figures that line the sandstone walls of the **Great Gallery**; although to the modern eye they suggest an astonishing sophistication, they are among the **oldest** such images to survive.

Even if you're not a rock-art enthusiast, the six-mile round-trip **hike** down to the gallery – there's no road access – is one of Utah's most beautiful. With either forty miles of dirt road to negotiate south of Green River, or 32 miles southeast from Hwy-24, before the trail even starts, few visitors come this way, so you may well get the gorgeous red-rock canyon, rustling with wildlife, to yourself.

The San Rafael Desert: the road to Horseshoe Canyon and the Maze

Unless the weather has been dreadful – check at the Green River visitor center (see p.432) – ordinary vehicles should have no problem driving to Horseshoe Canyon. Of the two alternative routes, the one that starts from **Green River** is more convenient if you want to sleep in a motel the night before, but it's marginally more likely to be impassable. Assuming it's clear, follow signs for the airport from the town center until you cross the railroad tracks. Once the surface has turned to gravel, fork left at a BLM sign pointing toward the San Rafael River.

After an initial flat section, the road pushes through painted-desert badlands formed by the fossil-rich Morrison Formation, then winds down to a glorious panorama of Monument Valley-style buttes. It crosses the **San Rafael River** on a rickety wooden bridge after nineteen miles, then climbs again to offer views that stretch west to the Henry Mountains and east to the La Sals.

Just over forty miles south of Green River, beyond **Antelope Valley** – home to one of Utah's few surviving herds of pronghorn antelope – an easily missed spur road branches off east. The **Horseshoe Canyon trailhead** is at its far end, at the edge of the plateau two miles along.

As the road veers west, a junction 5.5 miles past the Horseshoe Canyon turn-off marks the start of the 21-mile drive south to **Hans Flat Ranger Station**, the main point of access for the Maze (see p.442). Keep going west, and a total of 32 miles from Horseshoe Canyon – at best, around an hour's driving – you'll finally meet **Hwy-24**, just south of Goblin Valley (see p.430). This last stretch crosses Sweetwater Reef before dropping into the **San Rafael Desert**, where it insinuates itself between two impressive buttes known as Little Flat Top and Big Flat Top.

Camera! Drive! Action!

Many travelers are inspired to visit the Southwest not by some worthy documentary or picture-spread, but by the stunning visual iconography of a Hollywood movie. The dramatic desert scenery is perfect for a road trip, whether you drive an open-top convertible, as in *Thelma and Louise* (1991), or a mighty Harley Davidson, as in *Easy Rider* (1969). To immerse yourself fully in the often surreal landscapes, be sure at some point to leave your vehicle and set off on foot; the region's ten national parks provide infinite opportunities to scout out locations and put yourself in a starring role.

Easy Rider ▲

The open road

In a land all but devoid of public transport, planning your own road trip is not just a romantic adventure but a practical necessity. And you can create a truly superb itinerary simply by following in the footsteps of the movie crews. Thelma and Louise, for example, spent most of their time in southeast Utah, cruising beneath the sandstone formations of Arches National Park and making their climactic leap at what's now known as Thelma and Louise Point in Canyonlands (under the impression it was the Grand Canyon). The hog-ridin' hippies of *Easy Rider*, on the other hand, smoked grass in Monument Valley, picked up a hitchhiker near Flagstaff, and hung out at Taos Pueblo before heading on to New Orleans.

Route 66 ▲

San Juan Skyway ▼

Scenic drives

The most famous road-trip in the US, **Route 66**, crosses northern New Mexico and Arizona. While its fading neon signs, run-down motels, and dusty diners evoke bygone days, for sheer scenic beauty the Southwest holds plenty of even more appealing driving routes.

Hwy-12, southern Utah. A magnificent drive, skirting the remote Grand Staircase-Escalante wilderness on its way from Bryce Canyon to Capitol Reef. See p.402.

San Juan Skyway, southwest Colorado. A mountain-top loop through the Rockies, connecting Wild West mining towns with vibrant ski resorts. See p.94.

Road between the Rims, northern Arizona. The Grand Canyon is just 11 miles across, but this 215-mile highway is the only route between the North and South rims. See p.353.

The High Road, northern New Mexico. Enjoy the slow route from Santa Fe to Taos, exploring time-forgotten Hispanic villages in the Sangre de Cristo mountains. See p.156.

The Wild West

Director John Ford shot seven movies in **Monument Valley**, including *Stagecoach* (1939) and *The Searchers* (1956), while its magnificent buttes and stark silhouettes also star in *Back to the Future III* (1989) and *Forrest Gump* (1994).

Real-life Southwestern gunfights and jailbreaks have inspired many a movie, and towns like Tombstone, Arizona – immortalized in *Gunfight at the OK Corral* (1957) and the later, more satisfying *Tombstone* (1994) – and Lincoln, New Mexico – as evoked in Sam Peckinpah's *Pat Garrett and Billy the Kid* (1973) – make memorable destinations. Two more lovable outlaws, in *Butch Cassidy and the Sundance Kid* (1969), were filmed near Utah's Zion Canyon, though they ventured east to Colorado to hold up the Durango & Silverton Railroad.

Out of this world

The other-worldly Southwestern landscape also lends itself to being cast in **science fiction** movies. *Planet of the Apes* (1967) was filmed at Lake Powell, White Sands stood in for David Bowie's waterless home planet in *The Man Who Fell to Earth* (1976) and Utah's Goblin Valley was a hostile alien desertscape in *Galaxy Quest* (1999). The desiccated, aeons-old deserts can represent the **remote past** as well. In *The Greatest Story Ever Told* (1965), Max von Sydow as Jesus delivered the Sermon on the Mount to a crowd of Moab extras at Green River Overlook in Canyonlands.

▲ Tombstone

▼ Goblin Valley State Park

▼ Green River Overlook

Canyonlands Needles District ▲

Hiking on the South Kaibab Trail ▼

The dusty trail

Touring the Southwest's ten **national parks** is a sure-fire way to see the desert at its filmic best. Arizona's three parks include the awesome Grand Canyon, Petrified Forest, and the cactus-studded hills of Saguaro. Mesa Verde's "cliff dwellings" are in southwest Colorado, while Carlsbad Caverns lies beneath a mountain in southeast New Mexico. Southern Utah holds an amazing five – Zion, Bryce Canyon, Capitol Reef, Canyonlands, and Arches.

Almost all the parks offer **hiking trails** where you can escape the crowds and enjoy genuine wilderness. Don't underestimate the physical challenges, however. Talk to park rangers before attempting long trails, and read the Basics chapter in this book.

Top ten trails

The following trails, in ascending order of length, represent ten of the very best the Southwest has to offer.

▶▶ **Mesa Arch Trail** Canyonlands, one hour; p.438

▶▶ **Canyon Overlook Trail**, Zion one hour; p.384

▶▶ **Navajo Loop Trail** Bryce Canyon two hours; p.398

▶▶ **Delicate Arch Trail** Arches, two hours; p.450

▶▶ **Hickman Bridge Trail** Capitol Reef, two hours; p.419

▶▶ **Horseshoe Canyon** Canyonlands five hours; p.440

▶▶ **Chesler Park Loop Trail** Canyonlands, one day; p.445

▶▶ **North Kaibab Trail to Rainbow Falls** Grand Canyon, one day; p.359

▶▶ **West Rim Trail** Zion, one day; p.381

▶▶ **South Kaibab/Bright Angel trails** Grand Canyon, two days; p.342

The rock art of Horseshoe Canyon

At the time it was first studied, Horseshoe Canyon was called **Barrier Canyon**, and that name still defines the style of art for which it's famous. Such art is characterized by anthropomorphic figures, roughly life-sized but weirdly elongated, and often lacking both arms and legs. Those that have eyes have large round ones, or simply empty sockets, and many seem draped in stylized robes; for most visitors to this lonely desert backwater, the cumulative effect is to suggest ghosts or spirits from another, different time.

While spear points found in Horseshoe Canyon date back twelve thousand years, archeologists believe the pictographs were produced by people of the **Archaic** culture, which flourished between 7500 BC and 500 AD. At the start of that period, the climate was much wetter, and the canyon held lakes, ponds, and plentiful game. When conditions dried out, it was briefly abandoned, but then reoccupied.

Life was now far more difficult, and **shamanistic rituals** attempted to ensure successful hunting. These involved the creation first of clay statuettes, from 5000 BC onwards, and later of figurines made from split willow-twigs. Many represent what seem to be deities or shamans as well as animals; and the Great Gallery pictographs are thought to depict those same entities.

As for **technique**, the Great Gallery is very literally rock art. To produce the paint, different colored rocks were ground up, dissolved in water, and bonded with saliva produced by chewing seeds. The red is hematite, heavy with rust; the white is gypsum or chalk; even the blue comes from a local stratum. Some figures were produced with brushes, others by blowing or flicking paint at a stencil. Digital manipulation of photos of the images reveals not only faded colors but even different layers, so archeologists can see how specific figures were changed and redrawn over the centuries.

Experts estimate the gallery to be between 1600 and 6000 years old. Certain sites seem to have been rendered inaccessible by rockfalls that occurred a very long time ago indeed. All that's certain is that none dates from later than 400 AD, when the Archaic people acquired the bow and arrow – not shown in any Great Gallery images – and began to transform into the **Fremont** culture. Fremont art, as seen elsewhere in Utah as well as here in Horseshoe Canyon, has its own very distinct style.

Note that if you're heading east from Capitol Reef, it's much quicker to reverse the route described above; just be sure you have enough gas.

The hike to the canyon

At certain times of year, but recently only between mid-September and mid-October, rangers lead six-hour **guided hikes** into Horseshoe Canyon, starting at 9am on Sat & Sun; call ☏435/259-2652 to check. Otherwise, it's easy enough to make the trek on your own, but be sure to allow at least five hours for the round-trip; start early, or sit out the midday sun down in the canyon.

The route picks its way down from the trailhead described above, marked by cairns as it crosses patches of deep sand alternating with slickrock. Once you reach the bottom, after perhaps half an hour, follow the sandy wash to your right. Stay initially on its left bank, and within ten minutes you should spot the first rock-art site, the **High Gallery**, above the talus on the canyon's left wall. It's not easy to see detail here, though, so you'll soon be ready to press on.

All the remaining sites lie across the wash on the right wall. The first, the **Horseshoe Shelter**, nestles beneath an overhanging cliff a hundred yards further on. When Harvard archeologists excavated this site in 1930, it held several rooms; all that remains is a vivid band of **pictographs** in the palest stratum of the rock, which was above the roofs of the shelters and is thus now out of reach. The animals, squiggles, and triangular figures – many with strange protuberances on their heads – date from the Fremont era, but the scattering of ghostly footless figures are in the earlier Barrier Canyon style.

Another twenty-minutes' walk on, beyond several twists and turns in the canyon walls, climb up into a massive pale sandstone alcove, where a red-and-white band of rock holds another small collection of pictographs.

Eventually, after twenty more minutes, you round the final bend to be confronted by the **Great Gallery**, suddenly apparent beneath a lesser overhang. It's a breathtaking moment. Framed between the cottonwoods, a long row of dark, hollow-eyed, other-worldly entities stands stark against the pale rock. Though the details grow clearer the closer you get, somehow a sense of vast, alien distance remains.

Apart from a couple of well-shaded stone benches, and pit toilets nearby, there are no facilities for visitors. Look out, however, for two army-issue metal boxes, marked PLEASE OPEN ME: one holds a set of powerful binoculars, the other copies of relevant academic papers.

No **camping** is permitted in Horseshoe Canyon itself, but there's a basic site beside the parking lot at the trailhead.

The Maze

The name of Canyonlands' **Maze** district is no exaggeration. This brainteaser of convoluted canyons and barren desert washes, west of the Green and Colorado rivers, must be the least explored region of the US. If you're determined to get away from it all, the Maze is the place for you; getting back to it all when you've finished is more of a problem.

Somewhere in the heart of the Maze is the legendary **Robbers Roost**, a canyon fastness used as a hideout by nineteenth-century cattle rustlers and bandits like **Butch Cassidy** and his Wild Bunch. They'd escape the long arm of the law by riding the Outlaw Trail up from the Green River near Mineral Bottom; lacking their familiarity with the terrain, pursuing posses had to turn back defeated. No roads entered the region until uranium prospectors bulldozed their way in during the 1950s.

Even today, you'll need a high-clearance 4WD vehicle to get any further than **Hans Flat Ranger Station**, also referred to as the **Maze Visitor Center** (daily 8am–4.30pm; ☎ 435/259-2652), which stands 21 miles south of the road through the San Rafael Desert to Horseshoe Canyon, described on p.440. That makes it 46 miles east of Hwy-24 and 66 miles south of Green River. An even worse sixty-mile dirt track also runs south, to connect it with Hite on Lake Powell. Though technically the ranger station is in Glen Canyon NRA, it's the main source of information for hikers and drivers setting off into the Maze.

The **jeep roads** beyond Hans Flat take another twenty or thirty miles to jostle and switchback into the actual Maze. One route in ends at the **Maze Overlook**, another at **Doll House Butte**, which marks the far end of the **Land of Standing Rocks**, above the west bank of Cataract Canyon and straight across from the Needles.

Having come this far, most backpackers launch themselves into the wilderness for days or weeks at a time. There are few formal trails, but favored destinations include **Pictograph Canyon**, not far beneath the Maze Overlook, where Barrier Canyon-style pictographs (see p.441) seem to record the moment when the Archaic people first acquired agriculture. However, unless you're extremely self-sufficient, a workhorse when it comes to carrying vast quantities of water, and a fearless, fully equipped rock-climber, you're never going to see them.

The Needles

Thanks to its intricate tracery of backcountry trails that offer the chance to engage with the landscape as opposed to merely marveling from a distance, the **Needles** district is Canyonlands National Park's most satisfying segment for hikers, bikers, and 4WD drivers. While it has its share of long-range vistas – including the park's only **Confluence Overlook** – the Needles is noted primarily for its namesake thickets of candy-striped **sandstone pillars**. Clustered on scrubby rock outcrops, concealing pockets of incongruous grassland, these intriguing formations can be explored on brief forays or multi-day backpacking expeditions.

The **Needles** area is a very long way from civilization, at the far end of the stunning **Hwy-211**, a total of 75 miles from Moab and fifty from Monticello. If you're planning a number of successive day-hikes, it makes sense to camp overnight, so reserve a spot at *Squaw Flat* or in a backcountry site as soon as you know you're coming (see p.435). Note incidentally that, confusingly enough, the **Needles Overlook** is not in the national park at all, but in the BLM's Canyon Rims area; see p.460.

Ordinary mortals, as opposed to obsessive canyoneers, should also be warned that even casual **hiking** in the Needles may be the hardest thing you've ever done. Carry a good map and at least four pints of water per person, stick to the trails, and above all be very careful how far you climb – it's much easier to go up than it is to come down, and you run the risk of getting "rim-rocked."

The road to the Needles: Squaw Flats Scenic Byway

The 35-mile **Hwy-211** – also known as the **Squaw Flats Scenic Byway** – heads west of US-191 forty miles south of Moab. You can't miss the turning; it's marked by a colossal butte immediately opposite, which, if you happen to be hungry, may well seem to resemble a giant brioche.

As it winds lazily into the park, between cottonwood-lined **Indian Creek** stream and canyon walls of rich red sandstone, and overlooked by the twin castellated **Sixshooter Peaks**, the byway seems to carry you back a century, into the unspoiled Wild West. Much of the route lies through open grazing country, making this one of the few spots in the Southwest where you're still likely to see genuine **cowboys** riding the range. The Dugout Ranch, halfway along, was established in 1885, and later amalgamated with its neighbors to form the Indian Creek Cattle Company, Utah's largest cattle outfit.

Newspaper Rock

Newspaper Rock Recreation Site, next to Hwy-211 twelve miles west of US-191, preserves a panel of black desert varnish that's inscribed, like some prehistoric newspaper, with literally hundreds of **petroglyphs**. For ancient peoples, this made a perfect site to create conspicuous and enduring images, sheltered by a protective rock lintel beneath a hillock at a narrow bend in the valley immediately north of the Abajo Mountains. Besides abstract designs, images include helmeted human figures, buffalo, and bighorn sheep, plus lots of six-toed footprints and what look like bear pawprints. Some are probably symbols left by clans who performed particular ceremonies here, or simply passed by. With the obvious exception of recent graffiti, it's hard to say when they were executed, but you have to suspect that most are not in fact all that old; nineteenth-century Ute are thought to be responsible for the mounted riders, shown hunting with bows and arrows.

The riverside woods across the road from the rock hold a lovely if basic **campground**, free but waterless. A short way further west, Hwy-211 meets the mountain road from Monticello that's described on p.462.

▲ Petroglyphs at Newspaper Rock

The Needles Outpost

Up a short spur road just outside the park boundary, the privately owned **Needles Outpost** (March–Nov daily 8am–7pm; ☎435/979-4007, ⓦcanyon landsneedlesoutpost.com) is a summer-only grocery store and gas station that has its own small **campground** ($20). Showers cost $3 extra, or $7 if you're not staying overnight.

Driving into the Needles

Rangers at the **Needles visitor center**, a mile inside the park (daily: March–Oct 8am–5pm; Nov–Feb 9am–4.30pm; ☎435/259-4711), can provide up-to-date hiking information. They issue 34 **backpacking permits** per night, each for a group of up to seven people; in high season, if you don't have a reservation (see p.435) the chances are none will be available. Day-hikers don't need permits.

Roughly three miles along from the visitor center, a left turning leads to the first-come, first-served, *Squaw Flat* **campground**, where space is at an absolute premium in spring and fall ($15). Ordinary vehicles can continue beyond the campground, on an uneven dirt road, for three more miles to **Elephant Hill**.

The main park road presses on past the Squaw Flat turn-off for another four miles, ending where the **Big Spring Canyon Overlook** confronts an array of mushroom-shaped hoodoos.

Short Hikes in the Needles

The best hiking in the Needles is unquestionably on the Chesler Park and Confluence Overlook trails detailed below, If you're pressed for time, however, several shorter trails set off from close to the main park road. A mile south of the visitor center, the **Cave Spring Trail** is an enjoyable 25-minute hike that begins by leading under a group of overhangs. One holds a remarkably preserved old cowboy camp, another shelters assorted petroglyphs. Two short ladders then climb to the top of a low mesa, where you walk back to your car across the slickrock.

Another two miles west, the half-mile **Pothole Point Trail** is an easy stroll to the top of the roadside ridge. Half a mile on from there, the 2.5-mile, two-hour **Slickrock Trail** is much more challenging. While the trail itself is not technically difficult, if you're on it at all that's probably because you didn't get here early enough to tackle anything longer, in which case you'll be exposed to the full heat of the midday sun. Its shadeless route nonetheless provides a tremendous orientation to the region, following a cairn-marked footpath from one sandstone knoll to the next, each with its own long-distance mountain-and-mesa views.

The Chesler Park Loop Trail

Chesler Park, the high grassy meadow whose stubby sandstone pinnacles gave the Needles its name, makes a great destination for a long day-hike. Simply to reach it requires a six-mile round-trip trek from Elephant Hill, or a ten-mile one from Squaw Flat campground, while looping around the "park" itself adds another five miles. Allow seven hours for the complete hike from Elephant Hill, even longer if you start from Squaw Flat.

As you climb across the cairned stretches of slickrock that rise from both Elephant Hill and Squaw Flat, look north for sweeping views to the Island In The Sky, with the White Rim etched beneath it. The two trails meet half an hour up from Elephant Hill, then dip west to cross the wash that runs through **Elephant Canyon** – it may look dry, but there's usually water flowing beneath the sand – before the final ascent to Chesler Park.

For the most part, the **Chesler Park Loop Trail** undulates around the edge of the 600-acre clearing, on the slopes below the red-and-white barber-pole Needles. On the eastern flank, however, it runs straight across the lavender-tinted grassland, while in the far southwestern corner it disappears into an extraordinary mini-canyon whose blackened walls are seldom even three feet apart. This claustrophobic segment, the mile-long **Joint Trail**, is the highlight of the trip. A ledge perched above its eastern end, a 500ft detour off the main trail, provides a superb overview of Chesler Park. Through a gap to the west, the gigantic Doll House Butte (see p.442), across the Colorado, can also be glimpsed. If you have a 4WD vehicle, you can join the Chesler Park Loop near the Joint Trail, and walk the loop alone as a five-mile hike.

As an alternative to circling Chesler Park, consider following the spur trail that branches south along Elephant Canyon. It takes just over three miles of steady climbing to reach **Druid Arch**, named for its resemblance to the rough-hewn monuments of Stonehenge.

Several more trails connect Chesler Park and Elephant Canyon with Squaw Flat, including routes through **Squaw Canyon** and the upper reaches of **Big Spring Canyon**. Backcountry **camping** is only allowed at specific sites along the jeep road that runs west and north of Chesler Park, of which the closest to the main trails is at Devils Kitchen Camp – and you'd be lucky to get a permit (see p.435).

The Confluence Overlook Trail

According to writer Edward Abbey, the local business community only agreed to the creation of Canyonlands park in 1964 on the understanding that its different parts would be linked by a loop drive, of which the focus would be the **Confluence Overlook**. It was even anticipated that this would be the site of a Junction Dam, which would create an even larger lake than Lake Powell. In the absence of either road or dam, the demanding but utterly magnificent eleven-mile round-trip hike from **Big Spring Canyon Overlook**, which takes a good seven hours, remains the only way to see the spot where the Green River meets the Colorado.

The trail starts with a steep drop down into Big Spring Canyon, then laboriously climbs out again. After twenty exhausting minutes you emerge through a natural portal between two huge nodules to be greeted by long-distance views of the red-rock wilderness ahead – and cool shade closer at hand. A short metal ladder brings you out onto a level plateau, but you're soon descending again into **Elephant Canyon**, at this point several miles north of, and considerably broader than, the segment near Chesler Park (see above). Each time you climb back onto the slickrock mesa-top, new views open up, either south to the Needles or north to Junction Butte beneath the Island In The Sky.

Clambering from rock to rock beyond Elephant Canyon, you pass through several lifeless valleys known as **grabens**, from the German for "ditches." These were created 55,000 years ago, when shifting underground salt beds caused landslides. At times, the scrambling is hard going, and you have to haul yourself up onto head-high ledges, but it always stops short of actual rock climbing. Finally, after a half-mile section of jeep road – 4WD drivers can get this far via a nine-mile drive from Elephant Hill – you teeter out to the edge of the plateau and see the confluence for the first time.

A thousand feet below the **Confluence Overlook**, the Green River flows in from the west, and the Colorado from the northeast. They're never the same color. Sometimes the Green really is a pale green, and the Colorado almost red, tinted with dissolved red sandstone; at other times the Green is more of a yellow, and the Colorado a muddy chocolate. In any case, the two hues remain distinct

for the first mile or two after the rivers combine, intermeshing lik
they flow parallel but separate toward fearsome Cataract Canyon.

Arches National Park

ARCHES NATIONAL PARK seems to have become the national park for
people who aren't quite sure whether they like national parks. It's not too hard
to get to, just five miles north of Moab; it's not too big, with just twenty miles
of paved roads; and it has a catchy name, to tell you what to expect. Nearly a
million visitors a year drive in, tick off however many arches they feel they have
time for, and drive on to their next destination.

Thanks to *Desert Solitaire*, **Edward Abbey's** lyrical evocation of his year as an
Arches ranger, the park is also dear to environmentalists and wilderness enthusiasts. The irony is that when Abbey was here, during the 1950s, there was no
road into the body of the park, and the only way to explore it was to blaze your
own trails. Now you can cruise round in a couple of hours, and barely step out
of your vehicle.

For all that, Arches remains very much worth visiting. The **Colorado River**
here is literally peripheral, running unseen along the park's southern boundary.
The emphasis instead is on the stark, strangely disjointed **sandstone scenery**
of the higher ground to the north. As at Canyonlands, these rocks rest on an
unstable layer of salt. Salt Valley, which slopes down across the park toward the
Colorado, was formed by the collapse of an underground salt dome. That
massive subsidence left high ridges to either side, which cracked along vertical
fault lines to create long parallel "fins" of orange-pink Entrada sandstone.

Over the eons, water collects in pores in the fins and scours them into
potholes; piece by piece, the stone flakes away, until a hole is worn right
through. Estimates of how many such "**arches**" the park holds vary from the
eighty or so named on maps to the official count of over two thousand. No one
has bothered to define whether a "window" is a type of arch or just another
word for one, but it's agreed that an arch or window has to be at least three feet
wide. Both are distinct from "bridges," which span running water.

To Abbey, the arches themselves were a "small and inessential" feature of the
landscape. Unless you're a real obsessive, the appeal of hunting down arch after
arch soon palls. The park's short, straightforward **hiking trails** are enjoyable in
their own right, however, so you're bound to see a good number of arches along
the way. **Delicate Arch** is by far the most impressive, in that it's a free-standing
crescent of rock. Most of the rest are just holes, though **Landscape Arch** is
such a big one it would be a shame not to see it.

Apart from one solitary cabin, testament to a failed attempt at cattle ranching,
very few traces of human occupation remain in this forbidding desert. It became
a national monument after the Klondike Bluffs area was found by a wandering
prospector in the 1920s, and was enlarged into a national park in 1971.

Most visitors now arrive in **mid-summer**, despite blazing temperatures that
can reach 110°F. Hiking conditions are much more bearable in spring – when
the wild flowers blossom – or fall.

Arrival and information

Arches National Park has just one **entrance**, east of US-191 just over two miles
across the Colorado River from Moab. The **admission charge**, valid for seven
days, is $10 per vehicle, or $5 for motorcyclists, cyclists, and pedestrians. All the
passes detailed on p.41 are sold and accepted.

In what was universally seen as a final, gratuitous slap in the face for environmentalists, **President George W. Bush** chose to end his presidency by opening up 77 tracts of BLM-managed Utah wilderness, several of them within sight of Arches National Park, to **oil and mineral exploitation**. Although the leases duly went up for auction in Salt Lake City in December 2008, the whole process was so rushed that the sales were suspended by a federal judge in January 2009, in order for the appropriate environmental reviews to take place. In a further remarkable twist, Utah activist Tim DeChristopher threw the auction into chaos by bidding successfully for twelve separate parcels. He didn't have a penny of the almost two million dollars asking price, but subsequently managed to raise enough from online contributors to put down a deposit. What ultimately becomes of the lands is regarded as a test case for the future of Utah's wilderness.

The fancy **visitor center** (daily: early March to Oct 7.30am–6.30pm; Nov to early March 8am–4.30pm; ☎435/719-2299, ⓦ www.nps.gov/arch) stands at the base of a long, tall escarpment, that conceals the bulk of the park from the highway. While it's bursting with the latest technology, its huge model arches are much more show than tell, and there's little information of any substance to be found. Rangers issue backcountry permits (see p.435), and provide hiking advice.

Note that each **parking lot** along the road is designed to hold a specific number of vehicles, to limit hiker number on any one trail. Park illegally, and there's a $25 on-the-spot fine. No vehicles, or bikes, are allowed on the trails, but there are a few **4WD** roads.

Camping

Rangers at the visitor center will know whether there's room at Arches' only **campground**, at the far end of the road across from the **Devil's Garden** trailhead ($20; no showers; water only available mid–March to Oct). The campground remains open all year; 24 of its 52 sites are always first-come, first-served, and throughout the summer, all are usually taken by early morning. The remaining 28 can be reserved in summer only, between four and 180 days in advance (☎518/885-3639 or 1-877/444-6777, ⓦ www.recreation.gov). The nearest **motels** are in Moab; see p.455.

If you pick up a free **permit** at the visitor center, you can camp anywhere in the **backcountry** that's out of sight of roads, trails, and named arches. In practice, Arches sees little overnight backpacking, as most people do all the hiking they want within a day.

Park Avenue and Courthouse Towers

Beyond the visitor center, the park road begins its eighteen-mile journey north to Devil's Garden with a steep climb up the cliffs, offering views across to Moab. A parking lot at the top, a mile along, marks the start of the simple one-mile walk down **Park Avenue**. The trail follows the rocky bed of a dry wash, named for the "skyscrapers" that top the high ridges to either side. It ends amid a group of chunky monoliths known as the **Courthouse Towers**; any arches there may once have been have long since fallen.

Unless you arrange to be met at the northern of its two trailheads, you'll have to walk Park Avenue as a two-mile round-trip. The road in between the two passes the **La Sal Mountains Viewpoint**, which offers the first glimpse of the peaks to the east.

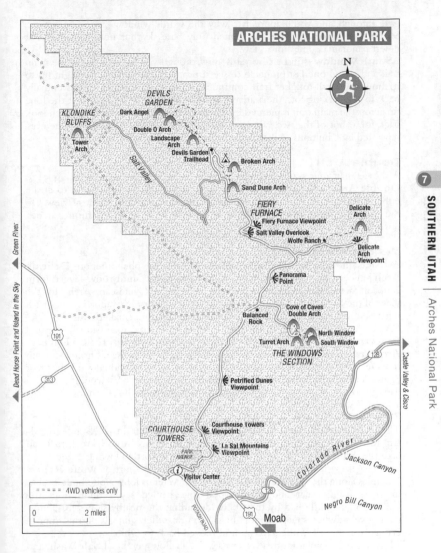

The Windows Section

In the heart of the park, almost ten miles up from the visitor center, the fifty-foot **Balanced Rock** rests precariously on its slanted pedestal. Immediately beyond, a spur road to the right leads in three miles to the **Windows Section**. Several fine arches can be admired from the parking lot at the end, the largest in the park, which is also the starting point for a couple of very popular short trails.

North and South Windows

The busy one-mile loop trail to the North and South Windows ambles gently upwards for a couple of hundred yards toward **North Window**, the only one of the pair visible from the road. Take the steeper spur trail that leads right up to it, gaze through, and you'll appreciate why the word "window" is so appropriate. So far the gaping aperture has framed only blue sky, but now a magnificent desert panorama comes into view.

South Window is just a few yards away, though you have to rejoin the main trail and round one last pinnacle to see it properly. You can't climb right up to it, though a much rougher trail continues around the back and leads eventually back to the parking lot. Alternatively, you'll have noticed by now that the lone fin across the main trail is pierced by **Turret Arch**. Wander over there, then look back for a shot of the two windows side by side – a pair of dazzling blue eyes, separated by a bulbous snub nose.

Double Arch

A shorter, half-mile trail leads from further around the Windows parking lot to **Double Arch**, where the roof of a wedge-shaped arch has fallen in to create either a skylight, or two separate arches, depending on your point of view. On the far side, the **Cove of Caves** is packed with incipient future arches, burrowing into the cliffs.

Delicate Arch

As befits the state's single most remarkable natural phenomenon, **Delicate Arch** has become a symbol of Utah. Oddly enough, its sturdy bow-legged form is not in fact all that delicate. It was originally called "Landscape Arch," for the view of the La Sal Mountains it so neatly frames, and only swapped names with what is now Landscape Arch (see opposite) due to a mapmaker's mistake.

A side road toward Delicate Arch leaves the park road shortly beyond **Panorama Point**. The arch itself can only be reached via the grueling **Delicate Arch Trail**. If you lack the time or energy for that, you can see it from afar from the **Delicate Arch Viewpoint**, at the end of a level hundred-yard trail that begins a mile further on. For **photographs**, Delicate Arch Viewpoint is best in early morning, while the Delicate Arch Trail is better in the afternoon.

The Delicate Arch Trail

The **Delicate Arch Trail** may be just 1.5 miles long, but the three-mile round-trip to the arch and back involves a steep climb across bare slickrock that can take the wind out of the hardiest hiker's sails; it's worth allowing a good two hours to enjoy it without rushing. The trail starts just short of **Wolfe Ranch**, 1.2 miles along the spur road, where Civil War veteran John Wolfe built a cabin in 1906, using cedar and cottonwood logs hauled seven miles from the Colorado. His cattle had by then been denuding the nearby slopes for almost twenty years; when sheep-farmers began to graze their animals on this impoverished soil as well, Wolfe gave up and moved back to Ohio.

Beyond the cabin, a footbridge crosses the shallow perennial **Salt Wash**, and the trail begins its determined ascent. Considering that fewer than ten inches of rain fall here each year, the terrain is surprisingly varied, from the scrubby riverbanks, choked with tamarisk, by way of a small-scale piñon-juniper forest, up to the naked rock three-quarters of a mile up. An alcove off to the left, just below the hill top, cherishes "**hanging gardens**" of rushes and even orchids, fed by a spring that stains the rocks.

It's easy to lose the sparsely cairned trail at the top of the mesa; the trick is to follow a narrow ledge in the rock that leads around the back of a high fin. Suddenly, from a viewing area neatly fenced off by a natural rock parapet, you're confronted by the full glory of **Delicate Arch**. Standing in superb isolation on the high lip of a canyon, it looks taller than its 45 feet. Quite how much closer

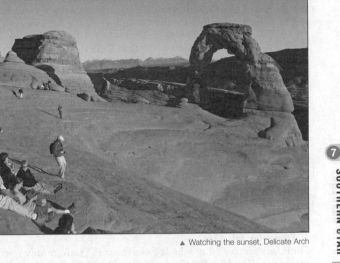
▲ Watching the sunset, Delicate Arch

you dare to approach depends on your confidence walking across the steeply inclined slickrock. There's no physical reason to stop you from standing right under it; lots of people do.

Delicate Arch is deservedly the most popular place in the park from which to see the **sunset**. Be sure to arrive at the trailhead at least an hour before the sun is due to go down, and longer in busy periods, when parking is at a premium. The sumptuous red glow of the arch deepens right until the final moment, so it's worth staying up there as long as you can – which means you'll be glad of a **flashlight** for the hike back down again.

The Fiery Furnace

An uninspiring overlook three miles on from the Wolfe Ranch turn-off gives little idea of the labyrinthine complexity of the **Fiery Furnace**. Named not for any exceptional heat but for its golden late-afternoon glow, this warren of high walled dead-end gullies and parallel fins is so disorientating, and so fragile, that you're strongly advised to enter it on a ranger-led **guided hike**. These take place daily in high season between mid-June and mid-September at 10am and 4pm, and at 10am and 2pm in spring and fall. Numbers are restricted, so register at the visitor center as soon as you arrive, and pay the **fee** of $10 for adults, $5 for ages 7 to 12. The hikes are fascinating, but don't involve walking all that far; most of the time is spent standing still, while the ranger explains the rock formations and signs of life along the way. Even if you hike into the Furnace without a guide, you need to register at the visitor center, and pay $1. No backcountry camping is permitted.

Devil's Garden

The park's largest concentration of arches is found in the **Devil's Garden**, beyond the far end of the road eighteen miles up from the visitor center. The prime target here is the 300ft **Landscape Arch**, reached by a graveled, reasonably level one-mile trail. This slender span is so frail that hikers are not allowed up to or through the arch itself; as mentioned opposite, what's now Landscape Arch was originally Delicate Arch, and vice versa. A sixty-foot-long slab dropped off it in 1991, and lesser rockfalls happen all the time, such as the one that destroyed nearby **Wall Arch** in August 2008. Arch aficionados will probably still be debating whether Landscape Arch or Kolob Arch in Zion National Park (see p.386) is the world's longest arch when it finally disintegrates. Landscape Arch is much harder to photograph than Delicate Arch, especially when the sun is behind it in the afternoon; try to come as early in the day as you can.

If your appetite for high-desert hiking has been whetted, press on beyond Landscape Arch on a trail that immediately becomes far cruder. After another mile – during which one hundred-yard section obliges you to totter along the top of a narrow sandstone fin – you round a corner to see **Double O Arch** on the skyline. At first, only its large upper oval is visible; as you approach, you'll see the much smaller ring beneath it as well. The pallid alkali wastelands that stretch away to the east were once prime uranium territory, and one heavily polluted section is still known as the "**Poison Strip**."

The four-mile round-trip hike to Double O Arch also leads past half a dozen other named arches and assorted minor pinpricks and peepholes. Real gluttons for punishment can turn it into a seven-mile loop, by circling back on the Primitive Loop Trail, but that route is every bit as demanding as its name implies.

Klondike Bluffs

For hikers keen to escape the crowds, the park's most readily rewarding destination is the **Klondike Bluffs** area, reached by a narrow but good-condition road that branches west from the main road a mile or so south of Devil's Garden. After seven miles, take the second of two all but adjacent left turns, and park at the end another mile along. The wonderful **Tower Arch Trail**, a two-mile, two-hour round trip hike, sets off straight up the steep bluff ahead of you. The arch itself, at the far end, is totally stupendous, an enormous graceful arc topped by a giant hoodoo, but the high-desert landscape en route, overlooked by the so-called **Marching Men**, orange monoliths reminiscent of Canyonlands' Needles district, is equally enjoyable.

Moab

Boom-and-bust cycles are a recurring theme in Western history, but few communities have experienced such a rollercoaster ride as **MOAB**. Within the last sixty years, it has gone from an insignificant backwater in the 1940s to being celebrated as "The Richest Town in the USA" during the 1950s, before slumping into depression in the 1980s only to re-emerge, almost against its will, as the Southwest's number-one adventure-vacation destination.

Through it all, Moab has never been a large town – its population remains well short of ten thousand – and neither is it, in itself, a particularly attractive one. The **setting** is what matters. With two national parks on its doorstep, plus millions more acres of public land, Moab is an ideal base for **outdoors enthusiasts**. The first to turn up were **jeep** drivers, taking advantage of the remote dirt roads cleared by the uranium prospectors. Then the **whitewater rafting** companies moved in, and the town swiftly became a mecca for **mountain bikers**, too, lured by the legendary **Slickrock Bike Trail**. These days, Moab is almost literally bursting, all year, with lycra-clad holidaymakers from all over the world.

Perhaps the main reason Moab has grown so fast is that out-of-state visitors tend to find Utah's rural communities so irredeemably boring. As soon as Moab emerged from the pack, it became a beacon in the desert, attracting tourists ecstatic to find a town that stayed up after dark. While Moab amounts to little more than a five-mile strip of motels, restaurants, and bars, that's enough to make it the only southern Utah town where you can stay for a week and still feel that you haven't seen everything, and everyone, a dozen times.

A history of Moab

Moab stands just south of the Colorado River, at the north end of a long valley created when an underground salt dome collapsed. A similar valley slopes down to the river on its northern side, making this the best place to cross the Colorado in all of Utah. Though Ute Indians passed this way for generations, the site was first recorded by Juan de Rivera in 1765, and a ferry service later helped travelers on the **Old Spanish Trail**. Mormon pioneers named the farming settlement they who established here in the 1870s for the biblical wilderness of Moab, at the edge of Zion.

Until Charlie Steen discovered **uranium** in 1952, the biggest thing to hit Moab was when **Butch Cassidy** hijacked the Colorado ferry on his way home from a bank job. The uranium boom lasted well into the 1970s, but as it dwindled, the local political scene turned very sour. Moab was a major focus of the **Sagebrush Rebellion** (see p.401), which pitted mine-owners and Utah businessmen, together with their fearful workforce, against the burgeoning national coalition of **environmentalists** and the federal government. Grand

Charlie Steen: the Uranium King

In the early 1950s, as the Cold War gathered steam and nuclear power stations seemed to hold infinite promise, the US government offered a $10,000 reward to anyone who discovered a mineable domestic uranium deposit – even on public land – and guaranteed to buy whatever it produced for the next ten years.

Freelance prospectors converged on the Colorado Plateau, where uranium had been found and mined as early as 1912. Their war-surplus jeeps piled with provisions, they set off into Utah's uncharted backcountry, waving their Geiger counters at any likely-looking rocks. Most knew which strata offered the best odds, and searched for places along the cliffs and canyon walls where they might be exposed.

Charlie Steen, a geologist from Texas, was mocked for insisting that he could find uranium by **drilling**. Projecting the angle of the canyonlands' crazily tilted slopes deep underground, he'd calculate where the precious mineral might have accumulated atop layers of harder rock. Concentrating on the **Lisbon Valley**, thirty miles southeast of Moab, he staked out countless claims and gave each a Spanish name.

In July 1952, the 31-year-old Steen broke his last drill bit in a 200ft bore on the **Mi Vida** ("my life") claim. Driving back to his trailer home in despair, he pulled into a gas station in Cisco, Utah. The attendant offered to test the final plug of rock on Steen's pick-up; his Geiger counter went straight off the scale.

Following his $60-million strike, Steen opened a processing mill in Moab that became Grand County's largest employer. As the "**Uranium King,**" he built himself a hilltop mansion above town and threw a lavish annual party for all its citizens. He'd circle above Moab at night in his own plane, since TV reception was better at that altitude, and was even a celebrity guest on *I Love Lucy*. In quick succession, he was elected to the Utah senate, then resigned after failing to change the state's liquor laws. Selling Mi Vida, he moved to Nevada, only to fritter his entire fortune away, losing $250,000, for example, on a pickle factory.

By the early 1970s, Steen was back in Utah, once more searching the canyon country as a penniless prospector. This time he traveled in disguise under a false name, in order both to avoid media attention and to protect any discoveries he might make. Success eluded him, however, and he eventually conceded defeat and moved to Colorado, where he died in 2006.

County commissioners repeatedly defied federal legislation by smashing bulldozers into neighboring **Negro Bill Canyon** – named for a local character and administered by the BLM – in the hope of opening it and other protected wilderness areas for mineral exploitation.

While they may have won the bitter **Bulldozer Wars** – Ronald Reagan came to power proclaiming that he too was a "Sagebrush Rebel" – Utah's conservatives were no match for the world economy. When the uranium market crashed

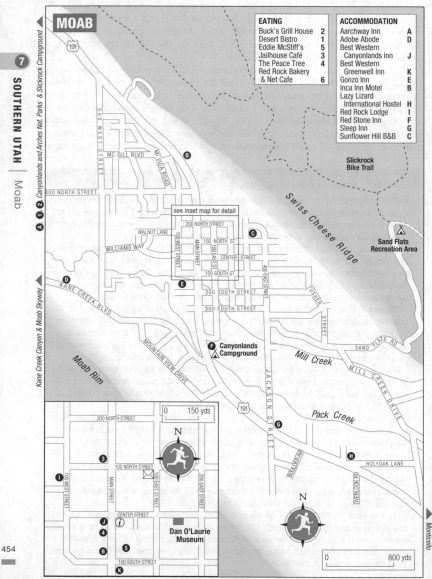

MOAB

EATING	
Buck's Grill House	2
Desert Bistro	1
Eddie McStiff's	5
Jailhouse Café	3
The Peace Tree	4
Red Rock Bakery & Net Cafe	6

ACCOMMODATION	
Aarchway Inn	A
Adobe Abode	D
Best Western Canyonlands Inn	J
Best Western Greenwell Inn	K
Gonzo Inn	E
Inca Inn Motel	B
Lazy Lizard International Hostel	H
Red Rock Lodge	I
Red Stone Inn	F
Sleep Inn	G
Sunflower Hill B&B	C

Slickrock Bike Trail

Swiss Cheese Ridge

Sand Flats Recreation Area

191

500 WEST STREET

MC GILL BLVD

MI VIDA ROAD

400 NORTH STREET

WALNUT LANE

WILLIAMS WAY

KANE CREEK BLVD

MOUNTAIN VIEW DRIVE

see inset map for detail

200 NORTH STREET

100 NORTH ST

100 WEST STREET

MAIN STREET

100 EAST ST

CENTER STREET

100 SOUTH ST

200 SOUTH STREET

300 SOUTH STREET

400 EAST STREET

FISHER STREET

JACKSON STREET

Canyonlands Campground

Mill Creek

SAND FLATS RD

MILL CREEK DRIVE

Pack Creek

191

BOULEVARDE

HOLYOAK LANE

OVERLOOK RD

Moab Rim

Kane Creek Canyon & Moab Skyway

Canyonlands and Arches Nat. Parks & Slickrock Campground

Monticello

0   150 yds

N

200 NORTH STREET

100 NORTH STREET

100 WEST STREET

MAIN STREET

100 EAST STREET

200 EAST STREET

CENTER STREET

Dan O'Laurie Museum

100 SOUTH STREET

N

0   800 yds

in 1980, and the bottom also fell out of oil, coal, and potash, unemployment in Moab rocketed, and the population dwindled.

The wilderness devotees who saw the region's future as resting with **tourism** successfully seized their opportunity. Out of nowhere, Moab became the West's hottest new destination, the desert equivalent of chic mountain hideaways like Aspen and Telluride in Colorado.

Sadly, almost everyone agrees that things have now gone too far. Most of the old-timers have left, driven out by rising real-estate prices and reluctant to swap mining for motel clerking at a third of the wages. Low-impact ecotourism seemed a real possibility when only the select few had even heard of Moab, but the canyonlands are taking as hard a battering from the fat-tire brigade as they ever did from the mining conglomerates. Just to make matters worse, the price of uranium is rising once again. Amid constant rumors that Utah is about to experience another uranium boom, a handful of mines have already reopened.

Getting to Moab

No scheduled **buses** connect Moab with the outside world, but Bighorn Express (℡801/417-5191 or 1-888/655-7433, ⓦbighornexpress.com) runs a daily **shuttle service** between Salt Lake City and Moab ($75 one-way), via the Amtrak station at Green River, and continuing on to Monticello.

Taxis in town, including shuttle services for bikers, rafters, and hikers, are operated by Coyote Shuttle (℡435/259-8656, ⓦcoyoteshuttle.com) and Roadrunner Shuttle (℡435/259-9402, ⓦroadrunnershuttle.com).

Information

Moab's superb **visitor center**, in the heart of town at Center and Main (daily: March to mid-May & late Sept to Oct 9am–1pm & 2–5pm; mid May to late Sept 8am–9pm; Nov–Feb 9am–noon & 1–5pm; ℡435/259-8825 or 1-800/635-6622, ⓦdiscovermoab.com), carries brochures and maps for the nearby parks and public lands. Its website has a full calendar of local events and festivals.

Accommodation

If you've already been in Utah for a while when you reach Moab, its glittering neon **motel** signs may well come as a surprise. On many nights between mid-March and October, all the 1500-plus rooms in the town's thirty-plus motels are taken, so **reservations** are strongly recommended. In winter, **room rates** can drop as low as $40 per night, but you'd be lucky to find anything much below $80 in high season.

Moab's dozen commercial **campgrounds** can be a godsend, considering the dearth of sites in the national parks – Canyonlands options are described on p.439, and p.446, and the one in Arches on p.448 – but they do tend to be dominated by family parties.

Hotels, motels, and hostels

Aarchway Inn 1551 N Hwy-191 ℡435/259-2599 or 1-800/341-9359, ⓦwww.aarchwayinn.com. Large, well-equipped motel with a nice pool, not far from the Colorado River at the north end of town. ⑥

Best Western Canyonlands Inn 16 S Main St ℡435/259-2300 or 1-800/649-5191, ⓦcanyonlandsinn.com. Standard, dependable *Best Western*, across from the visitor center. ⑥

Best Western Greenwell Inn 105 S Main St ℡435/259-6151 or 1-800/780-7234, ⓦbestwesternmoab.com. Central, modern hotel that offers spacious good-value rooms with tasteful furnishings and fittings. ⑤

Gonzo Inn 100 W 200 South ℡435/259-2515 or 1-800/791-4044, ⓦwww.gonzoinn.com. Luxurious if rather self-consciously hip 43-room inn – or "funky place to crash," if you prefer – complete with kitsch-retro furnishings, quirky artworks, and an espresso bar. ⑥

Inca Inn Motel 570 N Main St ☎435/259-7261 or 1-866/462-2466, ⓦ www.incainn.com. Clean, minimally equipped but adequate budget motel, with pool. ❸

Lazy Lizard International Hostel 1213 S Hwy-191 ☎435/259-6057, ⓦ lazylizardhostel.com. Amiable, very laid-back independent hostel, a mile south of the center, with $10 beds in six-person dorms, $7 camping, and private cabins for $30-plus, plus hot tub, kitchen, and internet access. ❶

Pack Creek Ranch PO Box 1270, Moab UT 84532 ☎435/259-5505 or 1-888/679-6622, ⓦ packcreekranch.com. Large guest ranch, with individual cabins and cottages capable of holding from two to twelve guests, plus assorted pools and tubs, twenty miles southeast of town, just off the lower reaches of the La Sal Mountain Loop Road (see p.460). Horseback trail rides available April–Oct. ❹

Red Cliffs Lodge Mile 14, Hwy-128 ☎435/259-2002 or 1-866/812-2002, ⓦ redcliffslodge.com. Luxury resort occupying a beautifully verdant location beside the Colorado sixteen miles northeast of town. As well as seventy Western-themed suites, it holds two restaurants, stables, a large pool, and even a winery. ❼

Red Rock Lodge 51 North 100 West ☎435/259-5431 or 1-877/207-9708, ⓦ www.red-rocklodge .com. Though entirely lacking the flair of Moab's fancier inns, this simple traditional motel offers clean rooms in a supremely central location. ❸

Red Stone Inn 535 S Main St ☎435/259-3500 or 1-800/772-1972, ⓦ moabredstone.com. Bargain-rate modern motel, a few blocks south of the center, with plain good-value rooms and use of a nearby pool. ❹

Sleep Inn 1051 S Main St ☎435/259-4655 or 1-877/424-6423, ⓦ www.moab-utah.com /sleepinn. Comfortable chain motel, with a pool and

an indoor spa, whose location a mile south of downtown means it offers competitive rates. ❺

B&Bs

Adobe Abode 778 W Kane Creek Blvd ☎435/259-7716, ⓦ www.adobeabodemoab.com. Attractive, low-slung, Pueblo-style home, which despite being a few hundred yards from downtown Moab feels like it's way out in the desert. All its six B&B rooms are comfortable and tastefully furnished, and the breakfasts are superb. ❺

Castle Valley Inn 424 Amber Lane, Castle Valley ☎435/259-6012 or 1-888/466-6012, ⓦ castle valleyinn.com. Large, beautifully furnished B&B, set in spacious grounds in magnificent Castle Valley, twenty miles east of town (see p.459). Five en-suite rooms and three separate bungalows. ❹–❼

Sunflower Hill B&B 185 North 300 East ☎435/259-2974 or 1-800/662-2786, ⓦ sunflowerhill.com. Antique-furnished former farmhouse, now a twelve-room B&B, away from the bustle on a dead-end side street. All units are en suite, some are in separate cottages, and there's a pool. ❼

Campgrounds

Canyonlands Campground 555 S Main St ☎435/259-6848 or 1-800/522-6848, ⓦ canyon landsrv.com. Large, year-round site in the heart of town, catering mainly to RVs but equipped with tent sites from $20 per night.

Sand Flats Recreation Area 1924 S Roadrunner Hill ☎435/259-6111, ⓦ www.utah.com /playgrounds/sand_flats.htm. Barely developed BLM campground, intended primarily for mountain bikers and costing $10 per night, along the top of the mesa to the east of town near the Slickrock Bike Trail.

Slickrock Campground 1301 N-Hwy 191 ☎435/259-7660 or 1-800/448-8873, ⓦ slickrock campground.com. Moab's largest site, a mile north of town, is a pleasant and well-shaded spot, charging $22 per tent per night, and offering a pool and hot tub, plus a store.

The Town

Main Street, the broad five-mile section of **US-191** that sweeps through the center of Moab, is lined with gas stations, diners, motels, and other businesses. For two blocks north and south of **Center Street**, which crosses it at the visitor center in the middle, window-shopping pedestrians stroll the sidewalk and browse the menus. Elsewhere, everybody either drives or cycles. Squeezed between Swiss Cheese Ridge to the east and the Moab Rim to the west, the town has little room to expand, but you can still see a few pioneer homes, and the occasional apple orchard, if you venture down the side streets.

Local history is enjoyably recalled at the **Dan O'Laurie Museum**, also known as the Canyon Country Museum, at 118 E Center St (April–Oct Mon–Fri 10am–6pm, Sat & Sun noon–6pm; Nov–March Mon–Fri 10am–3pm, Sat & Sun noon–5pm; free). Displays start with a mammoth tusk dredged from the Colorado and a replica petroglyph claimed to show the "Moab mastodon." The usual small-town assortment follows, ranging from an Ancestral Puebloan basket to Moab's first telephone switchboard, plus souvenirs from the uranium days.

Eating

While Moab offers by far the greatest choice of **restaurants** in southern Utah, and for once most places make a serious effort to cater to **vegetarians**. Full menus appear in the *Moab Menu Guide*, available free at local motels (W www .moabhappenings.com/menuguide.htm). There's also no problem getting a **drink** – Moab even has two pubs and its own winery. Several bike shops have espresso counters for early-morning customers.

Amid much local controversy, certain restaurateurs have taken to adding a fifteen percent **service charge** to all checks. Be sure you don't end up paying twice.

Buck's Grill House 1393 N Hwy-191 ☎435/259-5201. Belying its stockade-like exterior, this dinner-only "American Western Food" joint is actually a sophisticated affair, serving rich, classy Southwestern food, such as artichoke ceviche or duck tamales, at very reasonable prices. No entree costs over $20. Daily 5.30–9.30pm.

Desert Bistro 1266 N Main St ☎435/259-0756. Top-notch dinner-only restaurant, set in a ranch home with a patio that's perfect for summer nights. On the modern Mediterranean-influenced bistro menu, entrees like venison medallions or smoked rabbit *agnolotti* cost up to $38. Daily 5.30–10pm.

Eddie McStiff's 57 S Main St ☎435/259-2337. Central pub, next to the visitor center, where interesting beers include raspberry and blueberry. The restaurant serves a varied menu, with inexpensive salads, fancy Southwestern pizzas (with toppings like sundried tomatoes and jalapeño peppers) from $13, plus pasta and steak dinners, but the service can leave a lot to be desired. Lunch and dinner daily.

Jailhouse Café 101 N Main St ☎435/259-3900. Very popular central café, open for breakfast only. Indoor and outdoor seating year-round, and great specials like ginger pancakes and eggs Benedict, for around $11. Daily except Tues 7am–noon.

The Peace Tree 20 S Main St ☎435/259-8503. Very central juice bar and café that serves good sandwiches, wraps, and smoothies to take out or eat on the small outdoor patio. Daily 8am–6.30pm.

Red Rock Bakery & Net Cafe 74 S Main St ☎435/259-5941. Small café-bakery opposite the visitor center, with wi-fi. Daily 7am until dusk.

Around Moab

Although most visitors head straight for the national parks, several lesser-known areas in the Moab region are well worth exploring. Both upstream and downstream, minor roads run alongside the **Colorado River**, while the **La Sal Mountains** to the east make a snowy contrast to the aridity of the desert.

The Potash Road

The dead-end **Potash Road**, Hwy-279, which doubles back southwest along the Colorado's west bank from just north of the bridge on US-191, passes several intriguing **rock art** sites and provides a great close-up view of the river. In this stretch the Colorado is broad and lazy, tinted the same reddish brown as the Navajo sandstone cliffs that tower above it. These cliffs are often busy with **rock climbers**; to rent equipment or join a guided climb, contact Pagan Mountaineering (☎435/259-1117, W www.paganmountaineering.com).

Seven miles down the road, you reach a group of **petroglyphs** a dozen feet up on the canyon wall to the right. Scraped into the dark "desert varnish" by

As southern Utah's main center for wilderness activities, Moab is filled with companies that specialize in guiding and equipping adventurous travelers. The visitor center supplies free route maps for bikers and 4WD drivers, plus lists of tour operators and rental outlets, online at ⓦwww.discovermoab.com/tour.htm. The National Park Service keeps a similar list at ⓦwww.nps.gov/cany/planyourvisit/guidedtrips.htm.

Colorado River trips

Virtually everyone who goes **rafting** on the Colorado River does so with one of Moab's **river-running operators**. Motorized half- and one-day Colorado River trips start at around $45; multi-day expeditions, and day-trip combinations such as jeep-and-raft or horse-and-raft, are also available. **Shorter** trips start northwest of Moab, near Fisher Towers, and arrive near town in the afternoon; many companies give passengers the chance to float quieter stretches in two-person kayaks. While there are enough stretches of small-scale whitewater to whet the appetites of first-timers, a little romance is lost by the fact that the road runs alongside the river for much of the way. **Longer** (2–7 day) trips head through **Cataract Canyon** and other wild Canyonlands spots. **Oar-powered rafts** are slower but much quieter, and less expensive. Expect to pay anything from $950 upwards for a five-day trip, depending on whether you're prepared to lift a finger to help.

Operators include Worldwide River Expeditions (☏435/259-7515 or 1-800/231-2769, ⓦwww.worldwideriver.com), Adrift Adventures (☏435/259-8594 or 1-800/874-4483, ⓦwww.adrift.net), and Tag-a-Long Expeditions (☏435/259-8946 or 1-800/453-3292, ⓦwww.tagalong.com).

Mountain biking

While the Moab area is ideally suited to **mountain biking**, only experienced riders should attempt its most famous route, the **Slickrock Bike Trail**, in the **Sand Flats Recreation Area**. Laid out as a motorbike trail in 1969, this challenging ten-mile loop

▲ Mountain biking, the Slickrock Bike Trail

explores the sandstone knobs east of Moab, skirting the rim of Negro Bill Canyon. Following the white dotted line around this exposed expanse of lithified red dunes, up steep inclines and along narrow ledges, takes at least four hours. Be sure to allow enough daylight, and carry two gallons of water – far more than you can take in bike bottles alone.

To reach the trail, climb Salt Flats Road up from Millcreek Drive, which branches off 400 East Street four blocks south of Center Street. There's a fee of $5 per vehicle or $2 per person. Several Moab companies, including Roadrunner Shuttle (☎435/259-9402, ⓦroadrunnershuttle.com), offers a shuttle service to carry cyclists up to this and other trails. If you're looking for an easier ride, try the red-rock side canyons east and west of Moab, such as **Kane Creek**.

Among Moab **bike shops** offering daily rental and guided tours, including trips into Canyonlands National Park, are Rim Tours (☎435/259-5223 or 1-800/626-7335, ⓦwww.rimtours.com) and Poison Spider (☎435/259-7882 or 1-800/635-1792, ⓦwww.poisonspiderbicycles.com).

Jeep tours and rentals

Most of the thousands of miles of **jeep trails** around Moab were built by miners and haven't been maintained since. Collect a free map and guide at the visitor center, and rent a four-wheel-drive jeep or pickup truck for around $115 per day from Canyonlands Jeep Adventures at 225 S Main St (☎435/259-4413, ⓦwww.moab-utah.com/canyon landsjeep). Tag-a-Long Expeditions, see above, offers **guided jeep tours** from $80.

Scenic flights

From a small airfield twenty miles north of Moab on US-91, Redtail Aviation (☎435/259-7421 or 1-800/842-9251, ⓦwww.redtailaviation.com) and Slickrock Air Guides (☎435/259-6216, ⓦwww.slickrockairguides.com) run unforgettable **flights** over the Canyonlands area, starting at $135 per person for one hour.

Fremont Indians, between 700 and 1300 AD, they depict animals and anthropomorphic figures, including a chain of linked humans resembling paper dolls.

A mile further on, two mounted metal tubes tucked among the roadside bushes point to a group of barely discernible **dinosaur tracks**. More petroglyphs can also be seen, this time higher on the cliffs.

Just beyond the frankly unremarkable **Jug Handle Arch**, seven miles on and seventeen miles from US-191, the valley floor widens. The road officially ends here, at the ugly green plant where Moab Salt produces salt and **potash** (potassium carbonate), accompanied by billowing clouds of white smoke. How much further you choose to drive will probably depend on whether you own the vehicle you're driving. The surface is paved for another 1.3 miles, while 1.7 bumpy miles beyond that you get your first glimpse of the 23 vinyl-lined **evaporation ponds** where the potash is prepared. Dyed a lurid bluish-turquoise to speed evaporation, they're a real eyesore, clearly visible from Dead Horse Point far above (see p.437).

Only **4WD** vehicles can continue past the ponds and the nearby boat-launch ramp. *Thelma and Louise* freeze-framed their way into the final credits from the mesa-top a few miles further up, and in due course the Potash Road meets up with the White Rim Road in Canyonlands (see p.439).

Castle Valley and the La Sal Mountains

Turning northeast off US-191 just south of the bridge takes you onto **Hwy-128**, which follows the Colorado's east bank for 35 miles, then crosses the river to meet **I-70** ten miles further up. In summer, this superbly scenic section of the river is busy with one-day rafting trips. Roughly twenty miles along, the three-pronged red butte of **Fisher Towers** rises to the right of the road. These were originally "Fissure Towers," there was no "Fisher."

For an excellent sixty-mile **loop trip** back to Moab – which takes something over two hours to complete in summer, and is usually closed by snow between November and April – turn right, southeast, fifteen miles along the river road, onto Castle Valley Road. **Castle Valley** is a verdant cleft that boasts some quintessentially Western scenery, with red sandstone walls and buttes such as the **Priest and Nuns** to the east and high dark hills to the west. At its far southern end, eleven miles along, another right turn sets you climbing up the volcanic 10,000ft **La Sal Mountains**. A handful of narrow squeezes and hairpins later, you reach a vantage point commanding views across the Colorado to Arches and Canyonlands. Beyond that, the road runs through the high mountain landscape of the **Manti–La Sal National Forest**, a feast of color in late fall. A few campgrounds are tucked into the woods, but you won't see another building before the road eventually drops back toward Moab Valley.

It's equally easy to drive this loop in the opposite direction – for morning starts, drive south from Moab to keep the sun behind you for most of the way.

Hole N" The Rock

The peculiarly punctuated **Hole N" The Rock**, 15 miles south of Moab on US-191 (daily 9am–5pm; $5; ⓦtheholeintherock.com), is a classic piece of 1950s Americana. Having started out with a roadside diner at the foot of a cliff, Albert Christensen and his wife Gladys ended up hollowing an entire home deep into the red sandstone. Albert was a dreadful taxidermist – his unfortunate donkey Henry has to be seen to be believed – and painter – cross-eyed Christs a specialty – but his cool, well-lit house is a masterpiece. He died in 1957, without completing the spiral staircase that was planned to lead 65ft up to a roof-top patio. In the fine tradition of the jewelry that Gladys made from broken beer bottles, the gift store is stocked with home-spun souvenirs. Don't confuse the Hole N" The Rock with the Hole-in-the-Rock pioneer river crossing near Escalante, incidentally; see p.408.

Canyon Rims Recreation Area

The vast and almost completely empty mesa, west of US-191, that separates Moab from the Needles district of Canyonlands National Park (see p.435), is largely taken up by the BLM-run **Canyon Rims Recreation Area**. Not much recreation goes on up here, although it has the usual 4WD-only roads and a scattering of hiking trails; there are also two basic year-round **campgrounds**, *Hatch Point* near the far end, and *Windwhistle* closer to the highway (water at both mid-April to mid-Oct only; $12; ☎435/259-6111).

Only consider visiting the two main overlooks if you have a lot of time to spare – it involves a two-and-a-half-hour detour from the highway – or if you're not going to the Needles district, in which case the **Needles Overlook** provides a (relatively) quick overview as dramatic as any in Canyonlands itself.

The Needles Overlook

The paved road into Canyon Rims leaves US-191 32 miles south of Moab. Its dreary 22-mile course westwards comes to an abrupt halt at the windswept **Needles Overlook**, where a short railed footpath gives eagle's-eye views across the canyonlands. Specific landmarks are hard to pick out amid the orange sandstone ledges that spread below, but looking south you should spot the twin

Sixshooter Peaks and Hwy-211 winding alongside Indian Creek toward the Needles district (see p.443). Further west, the Needles themselves poke from the hillocks, while the Colorado loops from the north toward its confluence with the Green River.

The Anticline Overlook

Fifteen miles in from US-191, or seven miles short of the Needles Overlook, forking right onto an even, broad gravel road commits you to the 25-minute drive across the tumbleweed-strewn sagebrush desert to the **Anticline Overlook**. You probably won't pass another vehicle before the final parking lot, from which a five-minute walk leads to a high promontory that faces the potash ponds (see opposite) and **Dead Horse Point** across the Colorado.

Some people call this the Anti-climax Overlook, disappointed to realize that they've driven almost all the way back to Moab. As you'll see if you follow the fence around the headland, only **Kane Creek Canyon** – where the creek is a tiny green sliver in the red wasteland – intervenes. You'll almost certainly hear motorbikes scrambling across the slickrock of the Moab Rim on the far side. To the northeast, silhouetted above a brief stretch of the Colorado, you also get a remarkable view of the fins of **Arches National Park**, where the line of sight passes straight through the South Window.

Southeast Utah

It may lack big name national parks, but Utah's **southeast corner** is every bit as scenic as the neighboring regions. The desert here is so unforgiving that only a handful of widely separated settlements cling to life, and large tracts remain entirely without roads.

Culturally as well as geographically, southeast Utah has much in common with the Four Corners area. The **Ancestral Puebloans** were here in force, as countless abandoned pueblos testify. While they moved off to the south and east around 1250 AD, even now almost half the population of **San Juan County**, which covers the bulk of the region and is larger than several states, is Native American. A few are Utes, but most are **Navajo**, many of them descended from families who hid here during the 1860s to escape the Long Walk (see p.517).

The first **Mormons** to reach this far-flung corner were the Hole-in-the-Rock pioneers (see p.406), who established **Bluff** in 1880 and went on to found **Blanding** and **Monticello** as well. All those towns make viable bases, but the real attraction, as ever, is the landscape, with hikers heading for **Natural Bridges National Monument**, more ambitious backpackers for **Grand Gulch**, and drivers rattling across the desert to the unbelievable **Muley Point**, **Goosenecks State Reserve**, and the **Valley of the Gods**.

Monticello

The first fifty miles of US-191 south of Moab are so desolate that it comes as a major shock, on climbing some straggling foothills, to find yourself confronted by plowed green fields. To Mormon pioneers, this terrain resembled Thomas Jefferson's country home in Virginia – hence the name of **MONTI-CELLO** (pronounced "monti-sello"), six miles further on. Farming has never been all that easy here, however, and the economy has only recently been steadied by tourism.

The normal route to Canyonlands's Needles District, fifty miles northwest, is to take Hwy-211 west from US-191, 22 miles north of town. In summer, it's also possible to take a very different approach, through the volcanic **Abajo Mountains**, which rise west of town to over 11,000ft. The straightforward road up, reached by turning left onto Abajo Drive from the west end of 200 South, passes through some lovely quasi-Alpine meadows where you may spot browsing deer. You then veer north and drop down a much rougher track, to meet Hwy-211 near Newspaper Rock (see p.444).

To the east of Monticello, US-491 (previously infamous as **US-666**; see p.99) heads off to Colorado through what looks like a segment of the Great Plains that has wandered astray, complete with grain silos and fields of wheat and beans.

Arrival and information

Monticello's **visitor center** – also a small museum of frontier life – is at 232 S Main St (daily except Tues 9am–6pm; ☎435/587-3235 or 1-800/574-4386, ⓦsoutheastutah.org). Bighorn Express (☎801/328-9920 or 1-888/655-7433, ⓦbighornexpress.com) offers a **shuttle service** to and from Moab and Salt Lake City.

Accommodation

Monticello is a much less lively place to spend the night than Moab, but it does contain a few reasonable **motels**.

Best Western Wayside Inn 197 E Central Ave ☎435/587-2261 or 1-800/633-9700, ⓦbestwesternmonticelloutah.com. Comfortable motel, with pool and spa, a few yards down US-491 toward Colorado. ❸

Canyonlands Motor Inn 197 N Main St ☎435/587-2266 or 1-866/747-7629, ⓦcanyonlandsutah.com. Run-of-the-mill roadside motel, on the north side of town; adequate rooms at reasonable rates. ❸

Days Inn 549 N Main St ☎435/587-2458 or 1-800/325-2525, ⓦwww.daysinn.com. The biggest, smartest motel around, on the brow of the hill at the north end of town. ❹

Eating

Like any self-respecting farming town, Monticello abounds in wholesome if unexciting **diners**, plus a few fast-food outlets.

MD Ranch Cookhouse 380 S Main St ☎435/587-3299. Attractive timber-built restaurant, with heavy wooden furniture and a gift store, that's a bright, efficient oasis in such a quiet town. Grilled breakfasts and sandwich lunches, but the real *raison d'être* is big steak dinners, like the $19 New York steak, served with "Them Taters," an extraordinary concoction cooked in a Dutch Oven and containing mushroom soup, chiles, and bacon.

They also have fish, shrimp, ribs, and veggie burgers. Live music Fri & Sat.

The Peace Tree 518 N Main St ☎435/587-5063. Espresso coffees, smoothies, and fresh pastries from 8am, on the open-air terrace of a gift store. Closed Wed in Oct & April, closed completely Dec–March.

Wagon Wheel Pizza 164 S Main St ☎435/587-2766. Home-made pizzas of all sizes and one shape, plus deli sandwiches.

Blanding

BLANDING, just over twenty miles southwest of Monticello, was established as "Grayson" in 1905, when a new irrigation channel brought water to this site from the Abajo Mountains. In 1915, **Thomas Bicknell**, an East Coast millionaire, offered to give a library to any Utah town that would change its name to his own. Two jumped in; Thurber, near Torrey, became Bicknell, while Grayson took his wife's maiden name, Blanding. Each got a new library, though it's said they didn't get as many books as they'd expected.

Having skirted the Abajos, US-191 runs due west as it enters Blanding, and at the four-way stop in the center of town, makes a sharp dogleg turn south. That brief pause is as much time as most travelers give Blanding, whose broad avenues seldom display much sign of life. However, head north at the central junction, then west, and you'll come to the interesting **Edge of the Cedars State Park**, 660 West 400 North (daily: mid-April to mid-Sept 9am–6pm; mid-Sept to mid-April 9am–5pm; $5; ☎435/678-2238). Displays in its excellent museum range from the Ancestral Puebloans to the Anglos. In a town with a notorious reputation for illegal pot-hunting by profit-seeking amateurs – or "Moki poachers" – it emphasizes the importance of proper archeology. Some of the Ancestral Puebloan artifacts are truly remarkable, including pots and pendants, stylish wooden plates, and a complete loom dated to 1150 AD. Outside, a footpath leads around a pueblo occupied between 700 and 1220 AD. In the only excavated section, visitors can climb down a ladder into a musty, haunting *kiva*.

Arrival and information

Blanding's large new **visitor center** is at the north end of town, at 12 N Grayson Parkway (Mon–Sat 8am–7pm; ☎435/678-3662, ⓦblandingutah.org). No public transportation serves the town.

Accommodation

Traffic between Lake Powell to the west and Moab to the north keeps Blanding's **motels** busy enough in summer, but they're not a very inspiring bunch.

Abajo Haven Guest Ranch 5440 N Cedar Edge Lane ☎435/979-3126, ⓦwww.abajohaven.com. Comfortable, wonderfully rural rental cabins, six miles north of Blanding, each with one double and two single beds. Barbecue dinners available. ❸

Four Corners Inn 131 E Center St ☎435/678-3257 or 1-800-574-3150, ⓦfourcornersinn.com. Large, modern, two story motel, just after the highway doglegs to the right, with some kitchenettes and free continental breakfasts. ❹

Sunset Inn 88 W Center St ☎435/678-3323. Surprisingly comfortable, albeit very basic, very central motel with rock-bottom rates. ❶

Super 8 755 S Main St ☎435/678-3880 or 1-877/888-8981, ⓦwww.super8.com. Spick-and-span chain motel at the south end of town, with a strict nonsmoking policy. ❹

Eating

Eating in Blanding is indeed bland eating.

Homestead Steak House 121 E Center St ☎435/678-3456. Ribs, burgers, chicken, and steaks, served for lunch and dinner in the throbbing epicenter of downtown Blanding.

Old Tymer 736 S Main St ☎435/678-2122. Conventional tourist diner, at the south end of town. Open daily for all meals.

The Peace Tree 164 N Grayson Parkway ☎435/678-3969. Espresso coffees, smoothies, and fresh pastries, plus wraps and salads for $8.50. Mon–Fri 7am–5pm, Sat 8am–3pm.

West of Blanding

A mile or so south of Blanding, at a junction marked only by a solitary gas station, **Hwy-95** heads west from US-191, to embark on a magnificent 120-mile trans-Utah journey to Hanksville. Until it was completed in 1976 – hence its other name, the **Bicentennial Highway** – east–west travel was effectively barred by the massive monocline of **Comb Ridge**, ten miles west of Blanding. To the Navajo, this thousand-foot wall of red rock, stretching eighty miles from north to south, was the backbone of the earth, as well as one of four "arrowheads" protecting their homeland. To Mormon pioneers, it was a definitive "reef" (see p.413). To the modern highway builders, it was an obstacle they simply had to blast their way through.

No towns interrupt Hwy-95 apart from the speck that is **Hite**, 87 miles along at Lake Powell (see p.420). Several side canyons off Hwy-95 bear traces of an Ancestral Puebloan presence, while the cattle ranchers who tried their hands here a century ago were succeeded by uranium miners in the 1950s.

The Butler Wash Ruins

Ten miles west of the highway intersection, a short spur road climbs west of Hwy-95 to the parking lot for the **Butler Wash Ruins**, a stimulating Ancestral Puebloan site located on BLM land (24hr; free). A ten-minute hike, much of it up steep bare rock, leads to an overlook into a side canyon just short of the crest of Comb Ridge. The ruins are in the topmost of three natural rock alcoves; a long stone ledge to the left leads down to the fertile wash where the inhabitants farmed. The complex includes one Kayenta-style square *kiva* and three Mesa Verde-style round *kivas*.

Comb Ridge

Immediately beyond Butler Wash, Hwy-95 picks its way down the intense red wall of **Comb Ridge** to a cottonwood-rich valley, watered by **Comb Wash**. Confronted by the ridge on their endless journey east, the Hole-in-the-Rock party decided to head south at this point, which explains why they ended up at Bluff (see p.467). Don't copy them, however; a tempting dirt road does branch south from the highway beside the stream, with a nice little campground a short way along, but it soon succumbs to deep drifts of sand no ordinary vehicle could hope to overcome.

Mule Canyon

Seven miles west of Comb Wash, after Hwy-95 has clambered back up onto the plateau, a dirt road to the north, signed for Texas Flat, leads to two separate trailheads for **Mule Canyon**. The northern sides of each of this shallow canyon's two forks hold several small, well-preserved Ancestral Puebloan **cliff dwellings**. Both forks are around six miles long, but the most interesting ruins are roughly one mile and three miles along the South Fork, so a six-mile dayhike is enough for most visitors. In itself, it's not a difficult walk, but as few hikers pass this way it's important to be prepared for all eventualities. Ask for advice at Kane Gulch Ranger Station (see p.466).

A separate paved turnoff, half a mile along from the Texas Flat road, leads in a few yards to **Mule Canyon Ruin**, a partly restored Ancestral Puebloan pueblo dating from 1000 AD. This small site, a bit too near the highway to be very evocative, is similar to Boulder's Anasazi State Park (see p.411). Its most conspicuous features – a round *kiva* now roofed over for preservation, and a two-story masonry tower – are connected by an underground tunnel, perhaps used for surprise appearances during religious ceremonies.

Through the Bear's Ears

Before Hwy-95 was constructed, the main road west of Blanding – and the principal access to Natural Bridges (see below) – was a dirt track that climbed across the southern fringes of the Abajo Mountains. In reasonable weather, ordinary vehicles can still follow this attractive route, by turning north from Hwy-95 seven miles from the intersection. The 32-mile detour takes well over an hour.

After a cool, pleasant drive through mountain-top woodlands, the road crosses a razorback ridge above Arch Canyon to descend between two rounded outcrops known as the **Bear's Ears**. This prominent landmark is regarded by the Navajo as the embodiment of a bear, guarding the northern limits of their territory. The road eventually switchbacks down a sheer red cliff to join the approach road into Natural Bridges.

Natural Bridges National Monument

Three of the world's largest natural bridges span the streambeds of the small, unspectacular White and Armstrong canyons, which cut through the white sandstone of **Cedar Mesa** southwest of the Abajo Mountains. **NATURAL BRIDGES NATIONAL MONUMENT** was the loneliest of spots when prospector Cass Hite stumbled across it in the 1880s, and remained all but inaccessible when it became Utah's first federal park in 1908. It's now easily accessed by a four-mile spur road off Hwy-95, forty miles west of Blanding.

Originally dubbed Edwin, Augusta, and Caroline, the bridges were given Hopi names when it was realized that much of the rock art on the canyon walls represented Hopi clan symbols. This was one of the many places that the Ancestral Puebloan ancestors of the Hopi passed through during their migrations, departing around 1270 AD after a stay of perhaps six hundred years.

Each bridge can be seen from overlooks along the one-way, nine-mile **Bridge View Drive** that loops through the monument. With considerably more effort, you can clamber down into the canyons for closer inspection, and also follow the stream from one to the next for a potential hike of up to nine miles.

Practicalities

Admission to Natural Bridges costs $6 per vehicle or $3 per person; the gates to the loop drive open between dawn and dusk daily. The **visitor center** stocks free trail guides and other background material (daily 9am–5.30pm; ☎435/692-1234, ⓦwww.nps.gov/nabr), and excellent displays explain how the bridges were formed. The visitor center holds the only public **payphone** in the 122 miles between Hanksville and Blanding, and is also the only source of water for the first-come, first-served, **campground** nearby ($10). The nearest **motels** are in Blanding.

Bridge View Drive

The first and largest bridge, **Sipapu Bridge**, was named for the "hole" through which the Hopi emerged into this world. Standing at 220ft high by 268ft wide, it is surpassed only by Rainbow Bridge (see p.427). Although the roadside overlook provides a good straight-on view as it thrusts from a tangle of rocks, you'll only really appreciate Sipapu's size if you hike down from the trailhead half a mile further on. The monument's most difficult trail involves three short ladders, two metal staircases, and a couple of stretches of slickrock with steep drop-offs. A ledge halfway down offers the best photos; by the time you're amid the trees directly beneath it, it's too big to fit in most viewfinders.

The next roadside parking lot is the start of a half-mile mesa-top trail that leads to a vantage point above **Horsecollar Ruin**. This small Ancestral Puebloan site, tucked into an alcove low on the canyon walls, is not visible from below.

Kachina Bridge, the next stop, is much thicker than Sipapu, being more of a tunnel beneath a broad span of desert-varnish-stained sandstone. Seen from the overlook, it's far less distinct, with rocks rather than sunlight visible through the gap. On the trail down, railings guide you across the slickrock, and there's a crude staircase made from sandstone slabs. The stream at the bottom is lined by splendid cottonwoods, while pictographs near the base of the bridge resemble the *kachinas* of Hopi religion (see p.78).

Natural bridges are short-lived phenomena. Even the oldest in the monument – **Owachomo**, two miles beyond Kachina by road – is a mere five thousand years old, and it's unlikely to last much longer. Though 180ft across, it tapers to just nine feet thick. It now stands slightly to one side of the streambed of Armstrong Canyon, reached by an easy half-mile round-trip hike down from the overlook.

The **streambed trail** that connects the three bridges makes a delightful walk, meandering along the sandy wash beneath the trees. However, unless you double back, returning to your starting point involves a long hike across the mesa top, which is not as flat as you'd imagine and offers very little shade; allow five hours for the full 8.6-mile walk. One idea would be to start from Owachomo or Kachina and hike back toward Sipapu, hoping you'll meet up with someone who can give you a ride back to your vehicle.

Grand Gulch Primitive Area

If you share a passion for archeology with the stamina for long-distance hiking, an expedition into the **GRAND GULCH PRIMITIVE AREA**, south of Natural Bridges, can make you feel like a real-life Indiana Jones. Every twist and turn of this deep, dramatic gorge seems to be filled with relics of its thousand-year occupation by the Ancestral Puebloans, although they abandoned the canyon six centuries before it was named by the Hole-in-the-Rock pioneers.

Grand Gulch gouges across Cedar Mesa for just over fifty miles, dropping 2700ft to meet the San Juan River. There's no access for vehicles; the only path in starts from **Kane Gulch Ranger Station** (March to mid-June, plus Sept & Oct, daily 8am–noon; no phone), five miles south of the point where Hwy-261 leaves Hwy-95, two miles east of the Natural Bridges turn-off. Typical backpacking expeditions last as long as a week, and you can only camp overnight in the gulch with a $5 permit, obtainable between three months and two days in advance from the BLM office at 365 N Main Street in Monticello (see p.461; ☎435/587-1510, ⊛www.blm.gov/utah/monticello). So long as your group consists of fewer than eight people, you should be able to pick up a permit at the ranger station on the day you set off. In any case, register there before you set off, even if you're just day-hiking, for which a fee of $2 is levied.

The trail begins by dropping steadily down Kane Gulch, a side canyon that deepens as it goes, and joins Grand Gulch proper four miles along. **Junction Ruin** here, the largest ruin in the canyon system, makes a popular day-hike destination, though **Turkey Pen Ruin**, at 4.7 miles, and **Stimper Arch** just beyond, are also within round-trip reach. If you're making a longer trip, it's possible to leave Grand Gulch via **Bullet Canyon** to the east – in which case a total hike of 23 miles brings you back to Hwy-261 roughly seven miles south of the ranger station – or **Collins Canyon** to the west further along – a 38-mile hike that ends at a dirt road south of Hwy-276. For either route, you'll need a car shuttle to get back to your vehicle, but that's probably easier to arrange than fixing for someone to meet you by boat on the San Juan, the only way out if you hike all the way to the end of Grand Gulch. Most visitors find it simpler just to double back at some point en route.

Kane Gulch Ranger Station can also provide details on day-hikes that head **east** from Hwy-261, into remote side canyons on Cedar Mesa. Road conditions are often treacherous, so don't set off without up-to-the-minute advice.

Muley Point

South of Kane Gulch, Hwy-261 crosses Cedar Mesa for its remaining seventeen miles. Before you take the plunge on the **Moki Dugway**, **MULEY POINT**, exactly five miles west of its top along a red-dirt road, is an absolute must-see. Note that the turn-off is signposted, but the sign is only conspicuous if you're coming from the north, and that the lesser viewpoint 3.9 miles along is *not* Muley Point.

When they finally get around to declaring all of southern Utah to be one vast national park, Muley Point will surely be the centerpiece. Quite simply, these are among the most stupendous views in the world (though they're at their finest in the morning, when the sun is behind you). You're now at the southernmost tip of Cedar Mesa and the eastern extremity of Glen Canyon NRA. Far below, the San Juan River goosenecks its way west, while the Navajo Nation stretches off on the far side. Features on the horizon include Monument Valley in all its glory, the Sleeping Ute in Colorado, Navajo Mountain, and the cliffs above the west shore of Lake Powell.

The Moki Dugway

Hwy-261 doesn't stand on ceremony when it needs to get down off Cedar Mesa; it just plummets over the edge. The **MOKI DUGWAY**, which drops 1100ft in little more than two miles, is an exhilarating switchback ride, much of it still on a "washboard" strip of gravel, although it feels a whole lot safer now that most of its many hairpin bends are paved. This ancient trail was originally improved by mining companies during the 1950s; you'll just have to hope you don't meet a truck-load of uranium coming the other way. If you have the nerve, the pullouts for vehicles to pass make great viewpoints, but it's best to do all your sightseeing at the top. Soon after the pavement resumes at the bottom of the Moki Dugway, another dirt road marks the western end of the **Valley of the Gods**; see p.469.

Goosenecks State Reserve

Just before Hwy-261 meets US-163, six miles from the foot of the Moki Dugway and five miles north of Mexican Hat, the inconspicuous **Hwy-316** branches away west, to end 3.5 miles along at the extraordinary **GOOSENECKS STATE RESERVE**. Although the railed viewing area here stands a thousand feet below Cedar Mesa, the **San Juan River** is still another thousand feet down.

The river is an amazing sight, looping between huge pyramidal buttes in a textbook example of what geologists call an "entrenched meander." Its serpentine coils – once meanders on a muddy plain, later fixed in stone by the uplifting of the Colorado Plateau – are so extravagant that it flows six miles while advancing little more than one mile west. Above the distant sliver of riverbank greenery, alternate layers of gray limestone and red sandstone stripe the cliffs, while Monument Valley once again stands out on the skyline.

Goosenecks State Reserve has no visitor center and no opening hours, and charges no fee.

Bluff

BLUFF, a pretty little riverside settlement whose somewhat humdrum existence belies the extraordinary efforts its founders made to get here, lies 23 miles south of Blanding on US-191. The 230 **Hole-in-the-Rock** pioneers who reached this site on April 6, 1880, had trekked right across the heart of

Utah, literally blasting their way through the canyons of the Colorado; for the full story, see p.406.

Once they arrived, they settled down to a life of ranching and agriculture, made difficult by the San Juan River's propensity to flood. The back streets still hold a dozen or so of their original sturdy homes, making Bluff the region's least spoiled, most authentic town. Its setting is consistently stunning, from the red-rock pinnacles known as the **Navajo Twins**, which mark the mouth of the narrow **Cow Canyon** gorge through which US-191 drops in from the north, to the cottonwoods that line the San Juan River, glinting against the sheer red bluff that rises on the far side. **Ancestral Puebloan** remains abound, including petroglyphs along Hwy-163 to the east, and the unexcavated mound, thought to conceal a buried pueblo, beside the town cemetery on a hillock just north of the center.

Information and tours

Bluff doesn't have a **visitor center**, but local information is available at ⓦsoutheastutah.org. In late October, it plays host to the three-day **Utah Navajo Fair** (see p.60).

The town is a center for **river-running** on the San Juan, with rafts putting in at **Sand Island Recreation Area**, three miles west. The chief local operator, Wild Rivers Expeditions (☏435/672-2365 or 1-800/422-7654, ⓦwww.riversandruins.com), runs one-day float trips to Mexican Hat (adults $165, under-13s $123), plus assorted longer voyages. In addition, **Far Out Expeditions** (☏435/672-2294, ⓦfaroutexpeditions.com) runs all-day 4WD tours of Monument Valley, for around $165 per person in groups of three or more, and half-day trips to canyons and archeological sites closer at hand.

Accommodation

Bluff may not be the fanciest place in the world, but its genuine small-town feel makes it a nicer prospect than any of its neighbors. It's also a handy overnight stop for **Hovenweep National Monument**, forty miles northwest; see p.82.

Calf Canyon B&B Seventh East at Black Locust ☏435/672-2470 or 1-888/922-2470, ⓦcalfcanyon.com. Spacious three-room B&B, set in an imposing Victorian family home, on the northeast side of town. Closed Nov–March. ❻

Desert Rose Inn 701 W US-191 ☏435/672-2303 or 1-888/475-7673, ⓦdesertroseinn.com. Modern timber-built motel at the west end of town, with thirty attractively designed and well-furnished rooms plus individual cabins of similar standard. ❹

Far Out Guest House 700 East & Mulberry ☏435/672-2294, ⓦwww.faroutexpeditions.com. Historic home that holds two guestrooms, each of which has six beds and can be rented by groups of up to six people at progressively increasing rates. Most visitors are here to take one of Far Out's tours, detailed above. ❹

Kokopelli Inn 160 E US-191 ☏435/672-2322, ⓦkokoinn.com. Friendly, quiet roadside motel, adjoining a gas station and grocery with a deli counter. ❸

Recapture Lodge PO Box 309, US-191 ☏435/672-2281, ⓦrecapturelodge.com. Pleasantly rural wooden motel, reaching back toward the river, with a pool; also a few rooms in two old pioneer homes. The owners also offer a shuttle service, including to Monument Valley expeditions. ❸

Eating

Bluff has just enough **restaurants** to keep visitors happy, though they're too spread out to walk from one to the next comparing menus.

Comb Ridge Coffee US-191 ☏435/672-9931. Espressos and pastries in a buzzy gallery setting, opposite the *Desert Rose*. Daily except Mon 7am–3pm.

Cottonwood Steakhouse US-191 ☏435/672-2282. Open-air barbecue at the west end of town, with wooden tables arranged around a giant cottonwood. A great place to enjoy beer and steaks (priced at up to $25) beneath the stars; although the menu's a bit short if you're not a beef-eater. One corner of the pseudo-Western stockade serves as Fort Crapper. Dinner only, from 5pm in spring and fall, 6pm in summer. Closed Nov–March.

Twin Rocks Cafe Navajo Twins Drive ☎435/672-2341. Glass-fronted diner, set against the rocks north of town, just west of US-191. Breakfast bagels and muffins, then salads and sandwiches, and chicken or fajita dinners for around $10. The adjoining *Trading Post* is well worth exploring. Summer daily 7am–10pm; winter Mon–Sat 8am–9pm.

The Valley of the Gods

Bluff is very much at the edge of the desert; driving west you soon descend the southern end of **Comb Ridge** (see p.464) into vintage red-rock badlands, with the buttes of Monument Valley silhouetted above the horizon.

Similar, smaller-scale monoliths can be toured closer at hand, with no admission fees, in the **VALLEY OF THE GODS**. This "garden" of isolated sandstone columns – said by the Navajo to be petrified warriors – holds no fixed hiking trails. Drivers can see it all from a winding **seventeen-mile dirt road**, which leaves US-163 on the far side of Lime Creek, roughly eighteen miles west of Bluff, and meets Hwy-261 near the foot of the Moki Dugway (see p.467), 10.6 miles northwest of Mexican Hat.

It's a rough road, which becomes impassable when wet, but if you don't mind a few bangs on the bottom as you cross dry stony washes you should be able to make it in a rental car. The east side holds the best "monuments," and the most difficult terrain, but there's something to be said for driving in from the west, which offers great views all the way along.

The only building en route is the *Valley of the Gods B&B* (☎970/749-1164, ⓦzippitydodah.com/vog; ⑤), which squats in superb isolation half a mile in from the west. All of its four rooms have baths, dinner is served by prior arrangement, and the owners can also fix backcountry **tours**.

Mexican Hat

MEXICAN HAT, the last stop in southeastern Utah before the start of the Navajo Indian reservation across the San Juan River, is an appealingly dusty outpost that has never amounted to a town. Having sprung into being in 1901, following false reports that gold had been discovered nearby, it was kept going by a genuine oil strike in 1908 and the uranium boom of the 1950s. It now makes a convenient base for **Monument Valley**, twenty miles south (see p.65).

Mexican Hat Rock, the sandstone sombrero for which the settlement was named, looks down on the San Juan a mile north. The highway passes a few hundred yards west, but a gravel road permits closer inspection. It's at its best in the afternoon, when the sun strikes the amazing zigzag striations of the gray and white cliffs across the river. This pattern, known as the **Navajo Blanket**, is said to show the skin markings of a giant bullsnake that lives in the river below, and carved out the "goosenecks" to the west (see p.467).

Practicalities

All Mexican Hat's four **motels**, except the budget *Canyonlands*, have their own inexpensive restaurants and stores and are substantially the same. There are virtually no other buildings around.

Canyonlands Motel US-163 ☎435/683-2230. Very basic ten-room motel, on the higher side of the highway next to the Texaco gas station, and open in summer only. ❸

▲ Mexican Hat Rock

Hat Rock Inn US-163 ☎435/683-2221,
🌐hatrockinn.com. Modern, timber-built motel, 100
yards up from the river, with good quality rooms
and its own Mexican restaurant, the *Hat Rock Café*.
Trail rides and jeep tours available. Closed mid-Nov
to Feb. ④

Mexican Hat Lodge US-163 ☎435/683-2222,
🌐www.mexicanhat.net. Mexican Hat's northernmost motel – a former dance hall – has a pool

and a nice open-air steakhouse. Closed
Nov–Jan. ④

San Juan Inn US-163 ☎435/535-2210 or
1-800/447-2022, 🌐sanjuaninn.net. Solid, long-
established motel perched fifty feet above the north
bank of the San Juan, beside the highway bridge.
The *Olde Bridge Grill* serves a full menu from 7am
daily, ranging from Navajo tacos to steaks, plus
cold beers. ④

Las Vegas

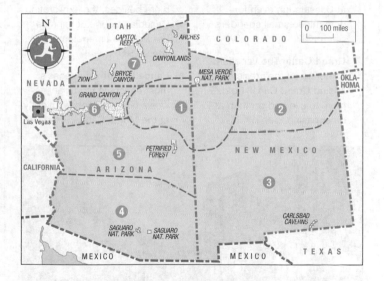

CHAPTER 8

Highlights

✳ **Luxor** Bursting with Egyptian motifs and attractions, this giant, smoked-glass pyramid is irresistible for all ages. See p.480

✳ **New York–New York** A loving re-creation of the Big Apple in the heart of the Big Cheese. See p.481

✳ **The Forum** "Living statues" and fake sky make the mall at Caesars fun even for determined small spenders. See p.482

✳ **Grand Canal** The Venetian, centering on the irresistibly absurd Grand Canal, holds more to see and do than any other casino. See p.482

✳ **Big Shot** The city's craziest thrill ride: free fall from the top of the Stratosphere. See p.483

✳ **The Buffet at Bellagio** Quantity and quality; you pay a bit extra, but Bellagio's buffet is out of this world. See p.485

✳ **Cirque de Soleil** With Love, O, Mystère, and Ká, plus more besides, the exhilarating Canadian troupe dominates Las Vegas's entertainment scene. See p.489

✳ **Lance Burton** Las Vegas's most engaging magician wows family audiences nightly at the Monte Carlo. See p.490

▲ Grand Canal, *The Venetian*

Las Vegas

Little emphasis is placed on the gambling clubs and divorce facilities – though they are attractions to many visitors – and much is being done to build up the cultural attractions. No cheap and easily parodied slogans have been adopted to publicize the city, no attempt has been made to introduce pseudo-romantic architectural themes or to give artificial glamour or gaiety. Las Vegas is itself – natural and therefore very appealing to people with a wide variety of interests.

WPA Guidebook to Nevada, 1940

himmering from the desert haze of Nevada like a latter-day El Dorado, **LAS VEGAS** is the most dynamic, spectacular city on earth. At the start of the twentieth century, it didn't even exist; now it's home to over one million people, with such a stream of newcomers that it needs a new school every month. Boasting nineteen of the world's twenty-five largest hotels, it's a monument to architectural exuberance, whose flamboyant, no-expense-spared **casinos** lure in thirty-seven million tourists each year.

Las Vegas has been stockpiling superlatives since the 1950s, but never rests on its laurels for a moment. Many first-time visitors expect the city to be kitsch, but the casino owners are far too canny to be sentimental about the old days. Yes, there are a few Elvis impersonators around, but what characterizes the city far more is its endless quest for **novelty**. Long before they lose their sparkle, yesterday's showpieces are blasted into rubble, to make way for ever more extravagant replacements. Around twenty years ago, when the fashion was for fantasy, Arthurian castles and Egyptian pyramids mushroomed along the legendary Strip; next came a craze for constructing entire replica cities, like New York, Paris, Monte Carlo, and Venice; and the current trend is for high-end properties that attempt to straddle the line between screaming ostentation and "elegant" sophistication.

While Las Vegas has certainly cleaned up its act since the early days of Mob domination, there's little truth in the notion it's become a **family** destination. Neither is it as consistently **cheap** as it used to be. It's still possible to find good, inexpensive rooms, and the all-you-can-eat buffets offer unbeatable value, but the casino owners have finally discovered that high-rollers happy to lose hundreds of dollars per night don't mind paying premium prices to eat at top-quality restaurants, while the latest developments are budgeting room rates of more like $300 than $30 per night.

Your first hours in Las Vegas are like entering another world, where the religion is luck, the language is money, and time is measured by revolutions of a roulette wheel. Once you're acclimatized, the whole spectacle can be absolutely exhilarating – assuming you haven't pinned your hopes, and your savings, on the pursuit of a fortune. Even so, while Las Vegas is an unmissable destination, it's also one that palls for most visitors after a couple of (hectic) days.

If you've come solely to gamble, there's not much to say beyond the fact that all the casinos are free and open 24 hours per day, with acres of floor space packed with ways to lose money: **million-dollar slots**, video **poker**, **blackjack**, **craps**, **roulette** wheels, and much, much more. The casinos will just love it if you try to play a system; with the odds stacked against you, your best hope of a large win is to bet your entire stake on one single play, and then stop, win or lose.

A history of Las Vegas

Las Vegas has a shorter history than almost any other city in the world. The only US city founded in the twentieth century to boast over a million inhabitants, it's also the only one that has consistently prioritized the need to attract visitors over the quality of life of its own residents.

The name *Las Vegas* – Spanish for "the meadows" – originally applied to natural springs where from 1829 onwards travelers on the Old Spanish Trail would halt. For the rest of the nineteenth century, the Paiute Indians shared the region with Mormon ranchers, and the valley had a population of just thirty in 1900. Things changed in 1905, with the completion of the now-defunct rail link between Salt Lake City and Los Angeles. Las Vegas itself was founded on May 15 that year, when the railroads auctioned off lots around what's now Fremont Street.

Ironically, Nevada was the first state to outlaw gambling, in 1909, but it was made legal once more in 1931, and the workers who built the nearby Hoover Dam flocked to Las Vegas to bet away their pay-packets. Providing abundant cheap electricity and water, the dam amounted to a massive federal subsidy for the infant city. Hotel-casinos such as the daring 65-room *El Rancho* began to appear in the early 1940s, but the Midwest Mafia were the first to appreciate the potential for profit. Mobster Bugsy Siegel raised $7 million to open the *Flamingo* on the Strip in December 1946; early losses forced him to close again in January, and although he swiftly managed to reopen in March, his erstwhile partners were dissatisfied enough with their returns to have him murdered in LA in June.

By the 1950s, Las Vegas was booming. The military had arrived – mushroom clouds from **A-bomb tests** in the deserts were visible from the city, and visitors would drive out with picnics to get a better view – and so too had big guns like **Frank Sinatra**, who debuted at the *Desert Inn* in 1951, and **Liberace**, who received $50,000 to open the *Riviera* in 1955. As the stars gravitated toward the Vegas honeypot, nightclubs across America went out of business, and the city became the nation's undisputed live-entertainment capital.

The beginning of the end for Mob rule in Vegas came in 1966, after reclusive airline tycoon **Howard Hughes** sold TWA for $500 million and moved into the *Desert Inn*. When the owners tired of his nongambling ways, he simply bought the hotel, and his clean-cut image encouraged other entrepreneurs to follow suit. **Elvis** arrived a little later; the young rock'n'roller had bombed at the *New Frontier* in 1956, but started a triumphant five-year stint as a karate-kicking lounge lizard at the *International* (now the *Las Vegas Hilton*) in 1969.

Endless federal swoops and stings drove the Mob out of sight by the 1980s, in time for Vegas to reinvent itself on a surge of junk-bond megadollars. The success of Steve Wynn's *Mirage* in enticing a new generation of visitors, from 1989 onward, spawned a host of imitators. *Excalibur* and the *MGM Grand* were followed by *Luxor* and *New York–New York* and then, as the millennium approached, by the opulent quartet of *Bellagio*, *Mandalay Bay*, the *Venetian*, and *Paris*. Although the 21st century started with shockwaves, when Steve Wynn was forced to sell *Bellagio* and the *Mirage* to the MGM group, and 9/11 triggered a major downturn, Las Vegas

Second only to making your fortune as a reason to visit Las Vegas is the prospect of **getting married**. Over a hundred thousand weddings are performed here each year, many so informal that bride and groom just wind down the window of their car during the ceremony. Though a Vegas wedding has become a byword for tongue-in-cheek chic, however, most marriages are deeply formal affairs. Casinos and independent wedding chapels alike compete to offer elaborate ceremonies with all the trimmings, from white gowns and black limousines to garters and *boutonnières*. Especially busy days include New Year's Eve, which gives American couples the right to file a joint tax return for the preceding year, and Valentine's Day.

Assuming you're at least 18 years old and carrying picture ID, you don't have to be a local resident or take a blood test. Simply turn up at the Clark County Marriage License Bureau, downtown at 201 E Clark Ave (daily 8am–midnight; ☎702/671-0600), and buy a marriage license for $55 cash. You can then walk over to the Clark County Court House at 309 S Third St (daily 8am–10pm), and be married by the Commissioner for Civil Marriages.

Wedding chapels claim to charge as little as $60 for basic ceremonies, but at that sort of rate even the minister is an "extra" costing an additional $50. Reckon on paying at least $200 for the bare minimum, which is liable to be as romantic a process as checking in at a hotel, and to take about as long. The full deluxe service ranges up to whatever you can afford. Novelty options include floating on a gondola in the *Venetian's* Grand Canal (☎702/414-4253), or beside your helicopter at the bottom of the Grand Canyon (Papillon; ☎702/736-7243, ⓦwww.papillon.com).

Graceland Wedding Chapel 619 S Las Vegas Blvd ☎702/382-0091 or 1-800/824-5732, ⓦwww.gracelandchapel.com. Home of the King – Elvis will act as best man, give the bride away, or serenade you, but unfortunately he can't perform the service.

Little Church of the West 4617 Las Vegas Blvd S ☎702/739-7071 or 1-800/821-2452, ⓦwww.littlechurchlv.com. This fifty-year-old chapel has moved progressively down the Strip to its current site south of *Mandalay Bay*. Among the quieter places to exchange Vegas vows – if that's really what you want.

Little White Chapel 1301 S Las Vegas Blvd ☎702/382-5943 or 1-800/545-8111, ⓦwww.alittlewhitechapel.com. The chapel (indeed, little and white) where Bruce Willis and Demi Moore married each other, Michael Jordan and Joan Collins married other people, and Britney Spears married Jason Alexander in 2004. Open all day every day, with drive-in ceremonies in the "Tunnel of Love" if you're in a major hurry.

bounced back. The *Venetian* has gone from strength to strength as the flagship for all that the city does best; Wynn himself opened his biggest casino yet, *Wynn Las Vegas*; and MGM pressed ahead with the colossal CityCenter development even as the storm clouds of the latest recession were appearing on the horizon.

Arrival, information, and getting around

Las Vegas's busy **McCarran International Airport** is a mile east of the southern end of the Strip, and four miles from downtown. Some hotels run free shuttle buses for guests, while Bell Trans (☎702/739-7990, ⓦwww.bell-trans .com) runs **minibuses** to the Strip ($6.50) and downtown ($8). From the airport, a **taxi** to the Strip costs from $15 for the southern end up to $30 for casinos further north, though fares can vary enormously depending on the time taken. Amtrak **trains** don't serve Las Vegas, but Greyhound's long-distance **buses** arrive at 200 S Main St downtown.

Traffic is so bad in Las Vegas that if you've just come to explore the Strip, it's not worth renting a car. Be warned, though, that on summer days it's too hot to walk more than a couple of blocks along the Strip. **Public transport** does exist. The **Las Vegas Monorail** runs along the eastern side of the Strip from the *MGM Grand* to the *Sahara* (Mon–Thurs 7am–2am, Fri–Sun 7am–3am; single trip $5, 1-day pass $12; ⓦwww.lvmonorail.com), but doesn't go to the airport or downtown. Separate, free monorail systems also link *Mandalay Bay* with *Excalibur* via *Luxor*, the *Monte Carlo* with *Bellagio* via *CityCenter*, and the *Mirage* with *TI*. In addition, the city-run, 24-hour **Deuce bus** ($2; ⓦwww .catride.com) connects the Strip with downtown, while the oak-veneered streetcars of the **Las Vegas Strip Trolley** ($2.50; ⓦwww.striptrolley.com) ply the Strip between *Mandalay Bay* and the *Stratosphere*.

The **visitor center** at the Convention Center, 3150 Paradise Rd, is not worth visiting (daily 8am–5pm; ⓣ702/892-7575 or 877/847-4858, ⓦvisitlasvegas .com). You'd do better to buy the daily *Las Vegas Review-Journal*, which always incorporates a four-page guide to the city.

Accommodation

Although Las Vegas has well over 140,000 motel and hotel rooms, it's best to book **accommodation** ahead if you're on a tight budget, or arriving on Friday or Saturday; upwards of two hundred thousand people descend on the city every weekend. Las Vegas hotels no longer offer cheap deals at the drop of a hat. It is true that serious gamblers can get their accommodation free, but to count as "serious" you'd have to commit yourself to gambling several thousand dollars.

Even if you stay in the same room for several days, you'll be charged a different rate for each day, depending on the day of the week, and what's going on in town. The only sure-fire way to get a cut-price room is to **visit during the week** rather than on the weekend. Rates rise enormously on Friday or Saturday, by at least $50 extra in a lower-end property, well over $100 in the big-name casinos. On top of that, many hotels won't accept Saturday arrivals. **Room taxes** add an additional eleven percent downtown, nine percent elsewhere.

The **Las Vegas Convention & Visitors Authority** offers an availability and reservations service on ⓣ1-877/847-4858. It's also worth trying both general **online reservations** websites, and local specialists like *Las Vegas Hotel Reservation Center* (ⓣ702/873-8041 or 1-800/394-7750, ⓦwww.lasvegashotel.com).

The Strip

Bellagio 3600 Las Vegas Blvd S ⓣ702/693-7111 or 1-888/987-6667, ⓦwww.bellagio.com. Extremely luxurious rooms, with plush European furnishings and marble bathrooms, an amazing pool complex, and some great restaurants. ❾

Caesars Palace 3570 Las Vegas Blvd S ⓣ702/731-7222 or 1-866/227-5938, ⓦwww.caesarspalace .com. Right in the heart of the Strip, the older rooms in this epitome of 1960s luxury still burst with pseudo-Roman splendor, while those in the newer Tower are more conventionally elegant. It's just a shame the place is such a colossal, baffling labyrinth, though it does hold top-class restaurants and shops. ❼

Circus Circus 2880 Las Vegas Blvd S ⓣ702/734-0410 or 1-800/634-3450, ⓦwww.circuscircus .com. Venerable Strip hotel popular with budget tour groups. Kids love the theme park and (almost) nonstop circus acts, while adults love the low room rates. Rooms in the motel-like Manor section at the back are pretty grim; pay a little more to stay in one of the Towers instead. ❹

Excalibur Hotel & Casino 3850 Las Vegas Blvd S ⓣ702/597-7700 or 1-877/750-5464, ⓦwww .excaliburcasino.com. The four thousand rooms in this fantastically garish fake castle are nothing special. Few have views to speak of – many face in rather than out – their theming is minimal, and they have showers, not baths. What's more, the whole place tends to be uncomfortably crowded. **4**

The Flamingo 3555 Las Vegas Blvd S ☎702/733-3111 or 1-888/902-9929, ⓦ www.flamingo lasvegas.com. While not quite in Vegas's premier league, Bugsy Siegel's *Flamingo* offers four thousand well-appointed rooms in an extremely central location, plus a great tropical-themed pool complex, complete with real flamingos. **4**

The Imperial Palace 3535 Las Vegas Blvd S ☎702/731-3311 or 1-800/634-6441, ⓦ www .imperialpalace.com. One of the best-value options in the heart of the Strip. Standard rooms are more than adequate, with balconies overlooking the pool, while the irresistible "luv tub" suites, at about $30 extra, offer huge beds, even bigger sunken baths, and mirrors everywhere you can imagine. **4**

🏃 **Luxor Las Vegas** 3900 Las Vegas Blvd S ☎702/262-4444 or 1-877/386-4658, ⓦ www.luxor.com. All two thousand rooms in this vast smoked-glass pyramid have tremendous views – and they're much larger than usual. Unlike the extra two thousand rooms in the *Luxor*'s newer tower next door, however, most have showers, not baths. **4**

Mandalay Bay Resort & Casino 3950 Las Vegas Blvd S ☎702/632-7777 or 1-877/632-7800, ⓦ www.mandalaybay.com. This upscale, young-adult playground is a long way south of the central Strip, but all its luxurious rooms have both bath and walk-in shower, and there's a spectacular wave pool. **7**

MGM Grand 3799 Las Vegas Blvd S ☎702/891-7777 or 1-877/880-0880, ⓦ www.mgmgrand.com. Waiting for any kind of service, especially check-in, in this behemoth – 5044 rooms and counting – can be horrendous, but you get a great standard of accommodation for the price. **6**

The Mirage 3400 Las Vegas Blvd S ☎702/791-7111 or 1-800/627-6667, ⓦ www.mirage.com. The glitzy *Mirage* is not the market leader it used to be, and its smallish rooms are complemented by even smaller bathrooms. Even so, the public areas downstairs remain impressive, the pool complex is nicely laid out, and the weekday rates for staying in one of Las Vegas's most prestigious addresses aren't at all bad. **6**

🏃 **New York–New York Hotel & Casino** 3790 Las Vegas Blvd S ☎1-866/815-4315, ⓦ www.nynyhotelcasino.com. Thanks to sheer attention to detail, this is the most exuberantly enjoyable casino on the Strip – and it's small enough that you're not always shuffling down endless corridors. The rooms are very nice, if a bit cramped, and filled with Art Deco flourishes. **5**

Paris–Las Vegas 3655 Las Vegas Blvd S ☎702/946-7000 or 1-877/796-2096, ⓦ www .parislasvegas.com. If not the absolute pinnacle of luxury, rooms and services at the flamboyant French-themed *Paris* are still pretty good, and for location, views, and ambience it more than holds its own. **8**

Planet Hollywood 3667 Las Vegas Blvd S ☎702/785-5555 or 1-866/517-3263, ⓦ www .planethollywoodresort.com. Some of the nicest mid-rate rooms in town, remodeled with movie memorabilia when the former *Aladdin* became *Planet Hollywood*. They're an awful long way from the self-park garage though. **7**

The Stratosphere Hotel & Casino 2000 Las Vegas Blvd S, Las Vegas NV 89104 ☎702/380-7777 or 1-800/998-6937, ⓦ www.stratosphere hotel.com. Despite its very unfashionable location at the far north end of the Strip, the *Stratosphere* has survived thanks to rock-bottom rates and a steady flow of budget tour groups. No accommodation is in the hundred-story tower, so don't expect amazing views, just large, plain, but good-value rooms, more likely than most to offer last-minute availability. **3**

TI 3300 Las Vegas Blvd S ☎702/894-7111 or 1-800/288-7206, ⓦ treasureisland.com. Formerly known as *Treasure Island*, and no longer geared toward families, *TI* remains a fun and convenient place to stay, though the rooms themselves are relatively small. **5**

The Venetian 3355 Las Vegas Blvd S ☎702/414-1000 or 1-877/883-6423, ⓦ www.venetian.com. Even the standard rooms at this upscale Strip behemoth are split-level suites, with antique-style canopied beds atop raised platforms, plus spacious living rooms, marble bathrooms with walk-in showers, and a mind-blowing array of shops and restaurants at hand. **9**

Wynn Las Vegas 3131 Las Vegas Blvd S ☎702/770-7100 or 1-877/321-9966, ⓦ www .wynnlasvegas.com. Steve Wynn has once again rewritten the Strip's definition of luxury, but the very stylish rooms, most of which offer great views of the "Lake of Dreams," come of course at a substantial price. **0**

Downtown and off the Strip

California Hotel 12 Ogden Ave at First St ☎702/385-1222 or 1-800/634-6505, ⓦ www .thecal.com. Thanks to a long-standing connection with Hawaii, most of the guests in this mid-range, downtown casino are Hawaiian, and Hawaiian food and drink (not as interesting or flavorful as you might imagine) dominate the bars and restaurants. The actual rooms are plain but adequate. **3**

El Cortez Hotel & Casino 600 E Fremont St ☎702/385-5200 or 1-800/634-6703, ⓦelcortez hotelcasino.com. Veteran downtown casino, refreshed by a recent facelift, with cut-price rooms in the main building, and great-value mini-suites in a newer tower. The rudimentary bargain-basement accommodation in *Ogden House* across the street costs just $24 for a private en-suite double. Hotel rooms ❶

Golden Gate Hotel and Casino 1 E Fremont St ☎702/385-1906 or 1-800/426-1906, ⓦwww .goldengatecasino.com. Downtown's oldest joint dates from 1906, when Las Vegas was just a year old. With a hundred retro-furnished rooms – some with flowery windowboxes – it's tiny by Vegas standards, and slightly lower-key than its Fremont Street neighbors. ❺

Hard Rock Hotel & Casino 4475 Paradise Rd ☎702/693-5000 or 1-800/473-7625, ⓦwww .hardrockhotel.com. Over a mile east of the Strip, "the world's only rock'n'roll casino" can't match Las Vegas's showcase giants for size or splendor. Instead, it's a relatively intimate and even chic alternative, with above-average rooms – the French windows actually open – high-class restaurants, a fabulous pool, and the odd big-name rock gig. ❼

Main Street Station 200 N Main St at Ogden ☎702/387-1896 or 1-800/713-8933,

ⓦwww.mainstreetcasino.com. Downtown's best-value option, with four hundred large rooms plus a brewpub and good restaurants. Ask for a room on the south side, rather than next to the freeway. ❹

The Palms 4321 W Flamingo Rd ☎702/942-7777 or 1-866/942-7770, ⓦwww.palms.com. Although it ranks among the hottest casinos in town, thanks to some very fancy nightclubs and restaurants, for ordinary folks who can't get into the exclusive celebrity areas the *Palms* is really just a present-able but rather dull locals casino. So while the rooms are very comfortable, you may not feel it's worth paying premium rates for the inconvenient location a mile west of the Strip. ❼

USA Hostels Las Vegas 1322 E Fremont St ☎702/385-1150 or 1-800/550-8958, ⓦwww .usahostels.com. Former motel, in a slightly forbid-ding neighborhood ten blocks east of downtown. It's much the better of the city's two independent hostels, with dorm beds from $21 and private double rooms from $58. Rates include free breakfast; cheap dinners are also available. There's also a heated swimming pool. The friendly staff arrange city and national-park tours, as well as a weekly clubbing night. ❶–❸

The City

Though the Las Vegas sprawl measures fifteen miles wide by fifteen miles long, most tourists stick to the six-mile stretch of **Las Vegas Boulevard** that includes both the **downtown** area, slightly southeast of the intersection of I-15 and US-95, and the **Strip**, home to the major casinos. In between lie two somewhat seedy miles of gas stations, fast-food drive-ins, and wedding chapels, while the rest of town is largely residential and need barely concern you at all.

The Strip

For its razor-edge finesse in harnessing sheer, magnificent excess to the deadly serious business of making money, there's no place like the **Las Vegas Strip**. It's hard to imagine Las Vegas was once an ordinary city, and Las Vegas Boulevard a dusty thoroughfare scattered with the usual edge-of-town motels. After six decades of capitalism run riot, with every new casino-hotel setting out to surpass anything its neighbors ever dreamed of, the Strip seems to be locked into a hyperactive drive for thrills and glamor, forever discarding its latest toy in its frenzy for the next jackpot.

Each casino is a self-contained fantasyland of high camp and genuine excite-ment, where the action keeps going day and night, and you rapidly lose track of which is which. Even if you do find your way back out onto the streets, the scorching daytime heat is liable to drive you straight back in again; night is the best time to venture out, when the neon's blazing at its brightest.

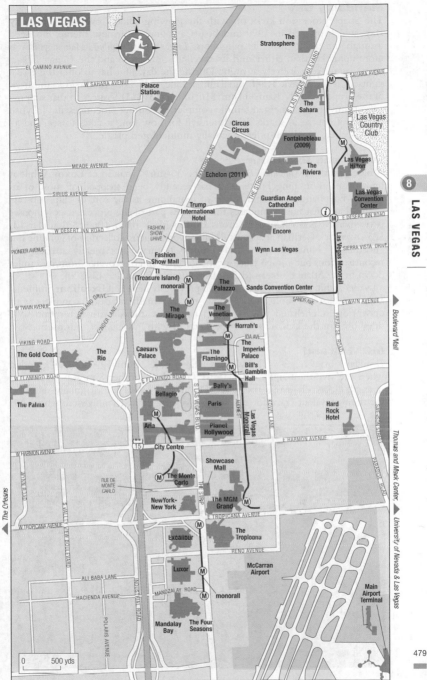

▲ Boulevard Mall

Thomas and Mack Center ▲ University of Nevada & Las Vegas

Mandalay Bay

The Strip's procession kicks off with the glowing, gilded tower of **Mandalay Bay**, which opened in 1999 and boasts a vaguely Burmese theme. Financed through the profits from its neighbors, *Luxor* and *Excalibur*, *Mandalay Bay* is more upmarket than either, and its excellent restaurants and the *House of Blues* music venue keep it lively at night. During the day, all it has to offer the casual sightseer is the **Shark Reef** aquarium, a long walk from the Strip at the back of the property (daily 10am–11pm; $16, under-13s $11). Visitors to that supposedly steamy, half-submerged temple complex encounter crocodiles and jellyfish as well, of course, as sharks. It's expensive for how long it takes to see, and all the so-called "coral" on offer is actually multicolored plastic.

Luxor and Excalibur

A block north of *Mandalay Bay* stands the 36-story pyramid of **Luxor**. While it remains an astonishing building, it has recently been stripped of most of its ancient-Egyptian trappings, in favor of rebranding as the sort of "hip," upscale casino resort that now dominates the Strip. As part of the process, it now houses two expensive permanent exhibitions: **Bodies** (daily 10am–10pm; $31, under-13s $23), maverick German anatomist Gunther Von Hagens' collection of genuine but "plastinated" human corpses, and **Titanic**, featuring not merely artifacts and reconstructions but a huge piece of the doomed liner, recovered from two miles down in the Atlantic Ocean (daily 10am–10pm; $27, under-13s $20).

Luxor's architect, Veldon Simpson, had previously designed **Excalibur**, immediately north. A less-sophisticated mock-up of a medieval castle, complete with drawbridge, crenellated towers, and a basement stuffed with fairground-style sideshows for the kids, it's usually packed out with low-budget tour groups.

MGM Grand

Excalibur's brief reign as the world's largest hotel, from 1990 to 1993, ended when the five-thousand-room **MGM Grand** – another Simpson creation – opened, diagonally across the street. The *MGM Grand* too originally reflected the then-prevalent craze for making Las Vegas a child-friendly destination, but

▲ Elvis impersonator, Imperial Palace

these days its one concession to children is its **Lion Habitat**, a walk-through wooded zoo near the front entrance, where real lions lounge around a ruined temple beneath a naturally lit dome (daily 11am–10pm; free). Bigger than *Luxor* and *Excalibur* combined, the MGM Grand is these days the world's third-largest hotel, ranking second in Las Vegas to the Venetian/Palazzo complex.

New York–New York

Excalibur and the *MGM Grand* are not the only giants facing off across the inter-section of Las Vegas Boulevard and Tropicana Avenue, said to be the busiest traffic junction in the US. The northwest corner, diagonally opposite the veteran *Tropicana*, is occupied by an exuberantly meticulous recreation of the Big Apple, **New York–New York**. This miniature Manhattan – built vertically, like the original, in response to space limitations – boasts a skyline featuring twelve separate skyscrapers and is fronted, of course, by the Statue of Liberty. Unusually, the interior is every bit as carefully realized, with a lovely rendition of Central Park at dusk (not perhaps somewhere you'd choose to be in real life). In one respect, it even surpasses New York itself: for $14, or $25 all day, you can swoop around the whole thing at 65mph on the hair-raising Manhattan Express **roller coaster**.

Planet Hollywood

Planet Hollywood is a remodelled version of the former *Aladdin*, which hit the rocks in 2004. In keeping with the latest generation of casinos, it's all geared towards a young crowd, with a screaming loud decor it calls "Hollywood Hip." The mile-long **Miracle Mile Shops**, wrapped in a figure-eight around the casino and its theater, is looking quite a mess, having attracted some frankly tacky stores, diners, and bars.

CityCenter

The enormous **CityCenter** complex, unveiled in 2009 between the *Monte Carlo* and *Bellagio*, is a bold attempt by MGM-Mirage to reshape Las Vegas' urban landscape. The exciting new theme here is that there is no theme; CityCenter is supposedly the kind of project that might be built in any city. Whether it's a sign Las Vegas has finally come of age, or a disastrous blunder in times of recession remains to be seen. CityCenter consists of the twin, residential **Veer Towers**, each leaning five eye-catching degrees off vertical in opposite directions; three non-gaming hotels, the **Harmon Hotel**, the **Mandarin Oriental**, and the completely condo **Vdara**; the 61-story, 4000-room **Aria** resort and casino; and the **Crystals**, a high-end retail, dining and entertainment "district," topped by a spikey angular roofscape. At the time this book went to press, construction was all but completed, but nothing had yet opened. Almost the only specific feature promised by MGM Mirage was that Aria will host a new Cirque du Soleil show, setting out to do for Elvis Presley what *Love* has done for the Beatles (see p.490).

Paris

Paris was the 1999 handiwork of the same designers as *New York–New York*. With a half-size Eiffel Tower straddling the Arc de Triomphe and the Opera, it all feels a little compressed, but once again the attention to detail is a joy. There's also a fine assortment of top-notch French restaurants. Elevators soar through the roof of the casino and up to the summit of the Eiffel Tower, for stunning views of the city, at their best after dark (daily 9.30am–12.30pm; $10).

Bellagio

Paris' Eiffel Tower was cheekily positioned to enjoy a perfect prospect of **Bellagio**, opposite. In 1998, Steve Wynn unveiled the *Bellagio* as his attempt to build the best hotel in world history. It is undeniably a breathtaking achievement, striving to be somehow more authentic than the original town on Lake Como. The trouble is that *Bellagio* is not in Italy; it's in Las Vegas, and stuffed full of slot machines. The main hotel block, a stately curve of blue and cream pastels, stands aloof from the Strip behind an eight-acre artificial lake in which hundreds of submerged fountains erupt every half-hour in Busby-Berkeley water-ballets, choreographed with booming music and colored lights.

Otherwise, *Bellagio*'s proudest boasts are the **Via Bellagio**, a covered mall of impossibly glamorous designer boutiques, and its opulent **Conservatory**, where a network of flowerbeds beneath a Belle Epoque canopy of copper-framed glass is replanted every few weeks with ornate seasonal displays.

Caesars Palace

Across Flamingo Road from *Bellagio* – this is the intersection where Tupac Shakur was gunned down in 1996 – **Caesars Palace** still encapsulates Las Vegas at its best. Here, a moving walkway delivers you past grand marble staircases that lead nowhere, and full-size replicas of Michelangelo's *David*, into a vast labyrinth of slots and green baize, peopled by strutting half-naked Roman centurions and Cleopatra-cropped waitresses. Above the stores and restaurants of the **Forum**, the blue-domed ceiling dims and glows as it endlessly cycles from dawn to dusk and back again. The mall itself is now three stories tall, but you may have to hurry to see the gloriously kitsch "living statues" who inhabit its various fountains; they seem to be disappearing into the netherworld at an alarming rate.

The Mirage and TI

Night-time crowds jostle for space on the sidewalk outside the glittering **Mirage**, beyond *Caesars*, to watch the recently rebuilt volcano that erupts every fifteen minutes, spewing water and fire into the lagoon below. Although veteran magicians Siegfried and Roy were finally driven into retirement by Roy's near-fatal accident in 2003, their trademark white tigers can still be seen in the *Mirage*'s spacious **Secret Garden & Dolphin Habitat** (Mon–Fri 11am–5.30pm, Sat & Sun 10am–5.30pm; $15, under-10s free).

Next door, a pirate galleon and a British frigate, crewed by actors, continue to do noisy battle outside **TI**, the former *Treasure Island*, though ludicrously enough the sailors these days are no longer gnarled buccaneers but the scantily clad **Sirens of TI** (every 90min after dark; free). *Treasure Island* used to be pirate-themed throughout, but having abandoned all thoughts of appealing to children, its lovingly crafted fripperies have been stripped away.

The Venetian and the Palazzo

Across the Strip from *TI*, the facade of the **Venetian** includes loving facsimiles of six major Venice buildings, as well as the Rialto Bridge and the Bridge of Sighs. The main emphasis in the casino itself is on the **Grand Canal Shoppes**, reached via a stairwell topped by vivid frescoes copied from yet more Venice originals. The ludicrous recreation of the **Grand Canal** at the top, complete with gondolas and singing gondoliers ($15 a ride), is quintessential Las Vegas, and as such utterly irresistible – it's *upstairs*, for God's sake.

When the Venetian first opened, it held two much-publicized outposts of the Guggenheim Museum. Both, sadly, have now closed, leaving just a ridiculously expensive branch of **Madame Tussaud's** waxwork museum (daily 10am–10pm, some seasonal variation; $24, under 13s $14). 2008 did however see the opening of the adjoining **Palazzo**, which can be entered either via the Grand Canal Shoppes or directly from the Strip. Officially, it's regarded as being a resort in its own right, but so far it seems remarkably devoid of any identity, and just feels like a big, bland mall.

Wynn Las Vegas

Wynn Las Vegas, next door to the *Venetian*, was built by Steve Wynn on the site of the vanished *Desert Inn*, using all the fortune he accrued by building and selling the *Mirage* and *Bellagio*. In a nutshell, it's *Bellagio* re-imagined for a younger, hipper and even richer crowd, with a shift away from European elegance in favor of contemporary Asian design. The resort is partly obscured behind an artificial tree-covered mountain; once you find your way inside, you find that's the backdrop for the enormous **Lake of Dreams**, an "environmental theater" in which ethereal sculpted figures emerge from a large expanse of water, in front of a massive waterfall that continually changes color.

The interior of *Wynn Las Vegas* is a riot of color, with spectacular patterns and motifs sprawling all over carpets, mosaics, and tiles, and a central atrium filled with sparkling trees and dazzling flowers. It has all proved profitable enough for the original hotel tower to be joined by a second, taller tower, dubbed **Encore** and clad in the same glossy "Wynn Bronze."

The North Strip: Circus Circus and the Stratosphere

North of *Wynn Las Vegas*, the long-neglected northern segment of the Strip was, until the recession hit, widely expected to be the city's next growth area. Both the veteran *New Frontier* and *Stardust* casinos have been demolished, but it now seems uncertain whether the promised *Echelon* and *Fontainebleau* mega-resorts will materialize.

Instead, the main landmarks here are the family-oriented **Circus Circus**, which holds an indoor theme park, the **Adventuredome** (Mon–Thurs 11am–6pm, Fri & Sat 10am–midnight, Sun 10am–9pm; all-day pass adults $25, kids $15), and the **Stratosphere**, which at 1149ft is the tallest building west of the Mississippi. The outdoor deck near its summit offers amazing panoramas across the city ($14); while three wonderfully demented thrill rides can take you even closer to heaven (Sun–Thurs 10am–midnight, Fri & Sat 10am–2am; $34 all-day rides). Insanity and X-Scream dangle riders over the edge, strapped into individual seats and in a precarious gondola respectively; and the terrifying Big Shot is an open-air couch that shunts to the top of an additional 160-foot spire, then free-falls down again. Half a mile east, at 3000 Paradise Rd, the **Las Vegas Hilton** is, since it closed its **Star Trek Experience** theme ride, no longer worth visiting.

Downtown and the Liberace Museum

As the Strip has evolved from strength to strength, **downtown** Las Vegas, the city's original core, has been neglected. Long known as "Glitter Gulch," it never really was a "downtown" in the conventional sense, having never held many stores or businesses apart from its few compact blocks of lower-key casinos. It is, however, forever attempting to recast itself as a genuine rival to the Strip. In the **Fremont Street Experience**, five entire blocks of its central street have been roofed over to form a "Celestial Vault", studded with over twelve million LED nodules to create a screen that's illuminated in dazzling nightly displays (hourly, sunset–midnight; free).

The only off-Strip museum worth visiting is the **Liberace Museum**, two miles east of the Strip at 1775 E Tropicana Ave (Tues–Sat 10am–5pm, Sun noon–4pm; ⓦ www.liberace.org; $15). Liberace, who died in 1987, started out as a classically trained pianist playing the bars of Milwaukee during the 1940s. His subsequent career is recalled by a yellowing collection of cuttings and

For details of day trips to the Grand Canyon from Las Vegas – or more precisely, to the so-called Grand Canyon West, the nearest part of the canyon – see p.351.

family photos, along with an electric candelabra, bejeweled quail eggs with inlaid pianos, rhinestone-covered fur coats, glittering cars, and more.

Red Rock Canyon

For a taste of Southwestern canyon scenery, and a blast of sunlight and fresh air away from the casinos, head twenty miles west of the Strip along Charleston Boulevard to **Red Rock Canyon National Conservation Area**. This BLM-run park consists of a cactus-strewn desert basin surrounded by stark red cliffs pierced repeatedly by narrow canyons accessible only on foot.

Red Rock Canyon's **visitor center** (daily 8am–4.30pm; ☏702/363-1921, ⓦwww.redrockcanyon.blm.gov), stands at the start of the **Scenic Drive** (daily 7am–dusk; $5 per vehicle). As this thirteen-mile loop road meanders around the edge of the basin, it passes trailheads like the one for the cool, slender **Ice Box Canyon** (a 2.5-mile round-trip hike), and the three-mile **Pine Creek Trail**, which follows a flower-lined creek beyond a ruined former homesite toward a towering, red-capped monolith.

Lake Mead and the Hoover Dam

Many Las Vegas visitors make the pilgrimage to **LAKE MEAD**, the vast reservoir thirty miles southeast of the city that was created by the construction of the Hoover Dam. As with the similarly incongruous Lake Powell (see p.420) it makes a bizarre spectacle – the blue waters a vivid counterpoint to the surrounding desert – but it can get excruciatingly crowded all year round.

Though the Lake Mead National Recreation Area straddles the border between Nevada and Arizona, the best views come from the Nevada side. Even if you don't need details of how to sail, scuba-dive, water-ski, or fish from the marinas along the five-hundred-mile shoreline, call in at the Alan Bible visitor center (daily 8.30am–4.30pm; ☏702/293-8990, ⓦwww.nps.gov/lame), four miles northeast of Boulder City on US-93, to enjoy a sweeping prospect of the whole thing.

Eight miles on, beyond the rocky ridges of the Black Mountains, US-93 reaches the **Hoover Dam** itself. Designed to block the Colorado River and provide low-cost electricity for the cities of the Southwest, it's among the tallest dams ever built (760ft high), and is made of enough concrete to build a two-lane highway from the West Coast to New York. It was completed in 1935, as the first step in the Bureau of Reclamation program that culminated with the Glen Canyon Dam (see p.421). Three levels of visit are possible; you can simply explore the **Hoover Dam Visitor Center** on the Nevada side of the river (daily April–Sept 8.30am–5.45pm; Oct–March 9.15am–4.15pm) for $8, or take a half-hour ($11) or two-hour **guided tour** ($30).

Eating

Restaurants in Las Vegas used to think that visitors wouldn't pay for gourmet food. Casinos laid on pile-'em-high buffets and cheap 24-hour coffeeshops, but the only quality restaurants were well away from the Strip. Things have changed: food has become another element of the entertainment and the major casinos compete to attract superstar chefs to open Vegas outlets. Many tourists now come to the city specifically to dine at fabulous restaurants, without having to reserve a table months in advance or pay sky-high prices. Not that fine dining comes cheap in Las Vegas; it's just that most of the big-name restaurants are less expensive – and less snooty – than they are in their home cities.

The restaurants below form only a tiny proportion of the total. The choice on the Strip in particular is overwhelming, and you'll almost certainly find a good restaurant to suit your tastes and budget in your own hotel. For that reason, the places reviewed here tend toward the higher end of the spectrum; they're the exceptional ones worth making a special effort to reach. Note, too, that in terms of price or quality, let alone convenience, there are few reasons to venture into the rest of the city; good places do exist away from the Strip and downtown, but the best are right where the tourists are.

Buffets

Almost every casino still features an all-you-can-eat **buffet**, open to guests and nonguests alike for every meal. The best buffets of the lot are at high-end casinos like *Bellagio* and *Paris*, where they've raised enough to provide true gourmet feasts. Most buffets however remain locked in the cheaper, more traditional approach; much like a food court in an upmarket mall, you'll get good fast food, but not great cooking. The best of those are neither on the Strip nor downtown, but in casinos like the *Rio* and the Stations chain that depend on locals as well as tourists. By contrast, those at the largest Strip casinos, like *Excalibur* and the *MGM Grand*, are often poor value.

Bistro Buffet *The Palms*, 4321 W Flamingo Rd ☏702/942-7777. Easy to find and afford, the Palms' buffet has rapidly established itself as a local favorite. Food and decor alike are bright and appealing, with a broad spectrum that takes in salads, a little sushi, Mexican and Italian specialties, teriyaki chicken, barbecue beef, and a lot of lovely cakes and pies. Breakfast is $8, lunch $10, and dinner $17.

The Buffet *Bellagio*, 3600 Las Vegas Blvd S ☏702/791-7111. Far and away Las Vegas's best buffet. At 800 items, all prepared fresh in small quantities, the sheer range is extraordinary. At breakfast ($14), in addition to bagels, pastries, and eggs, you can have salmon smoked or baked, fruit fresh or in salads, and omelettes cooked to order. Lunch ($20) can include sushi, dim sum, wild boar ribs, and seared quail, plus fresh focaccia and tasty fruit tarts. At dinner, costing $28 Mon–Thurs & Sun and $36, including champagne, Fri & Sat, the stakes are raised again with lobster claws, fresh oysters, and venison.

Garden Court Buffet *Main Street Station*, 200 N Main St ☏702/387-1896. Downtown's best-value buffet, ranging from fried chicken and corn at the "South to Southwest" station, to tortillas at "Ole," and pork chow mein and oyster tofu at "Pacific Rim." Breakfast is $7, lunch $8, and dinner $11–16.

Le Village Buffet *Paris*, 3655 Las Vegas Blvd S ☏702/946-7000. Rather than incorporating every conceivable cuisine, *Paris's* buffet showcases only delicious French dishes, with great seafood, succulent roast chicken, and super-fresh vegetables. The setting is a little cramped, squeezed into a very Disney-esque French village, but the food is *magnifique*. Breakfast is $15, lunch $18, and dinner $25.

Todai Seafood Buffet Miracle Mile Shops, *Planet Hollywood*, 3663 Las Vegas Blvd S ☏702/892-0021. *Todai* specializes in magnificent all-you-can-eat Japanese spreads. It's seafood heaven, with unlimited sushi and sashimi plus hot entrees, noodles, and barbecued and teriyaki meats. Lunch Mon–Fri $18, Sat & Sun $20; dinner Mon–Thurs $28, Fri–Sun $30.

Restaurants on the Strip

America *New York–New York*, 3790 Las Vegas Blvd S ☏702/740-6451. Cavernous diner, with a vast 3D "map" of the United States curling from the ceiling, and a staggeringly eclectic menu. At any hour of the day or night, there really is something for everyone, and it's all surprisingly good. Daily 24 hours.

Aureole *Mandalay Bay*, 3950 Las Vegas Blvd S ☏702/632-7401. Welcome to wine-lover's heaven, where harnessed "wine angels" swoop around a three-story "wine tower" that holds 10,000 bottles, at prices from $40,000 down to $24. New York chef Charlie Palmer's "progressive American cuisine" is every bit as impressive. Choose between three-course menus at $75 and $85, or the $95 "Celebration Menu," which features seven smaller courses. Standout dishes, all beautifully presented, include the curry-nut crusted tuna, the caramelized Sonoma duck, and the pork chop stuffed with prosciutto and gruyère. Sun–Thurs 6–10.30pm, Fri & Sat 5.30–10.30pm.

Bouchon Venezia Tower, *The Venetian*, 3355 Las Vegas Blvd S ℡ 702/414-6200. Despite its sky-high reputation and exclusive setting, Thomas Keller's spacious French bistro is friendly and affordable. A delicious French onion soup costs $8.50 and a roast chicken with onions and lentils costs $27.50. Breakfast is a Francophile's dream of croissants, pastries, yogurt, and coffee. Sitting outside on the huge piazza is a real joy. Daily 7–10.30am & 5–11pm.

Dos Caminos Mexican Kitchen *The Palazzo*, 3355 Las Vegas Blvd S ℡ 702/577-9600. For flair as well as food, this huge, beautifully designed Mexican restaurant is highly recommended, from the deliciously creamy guacamole onwards. Dinner might start with roasted plantain empanada ($10) followed by avocado-leaf-crusted big-eye tuna ($25); at weekends, lunch is replaced by a well-priced, relaxed brunch. Mon–Thurs 11am–11pm, Fri 11am–midnight, Sat & Sun 10am–midnight.

Fat Burger 3765 Las Vegas Blvd S ℡ 702/736-4733. There's no more to this gleaming, all-American burger joint than meets the eye. Quite simply, you can walk or drive in from the Strip at any time, and get a perfect burger, fries, and shake. Daily 24 hours.

Il Fornaio *New York–New York*, 3790 Las Vegas Blvd S ℡ 702/650-6500. The nicest place to enjoy the atmosphere of the casino, this rural-Italian restaurant is a real joy. Choose from pizzas for around $14, or entrees like seafood linguini ($22) or rotisserie chicken ($19.50). Delicious olive breads, pastries, and espresso coffees are also sold in a separate deli nearby. Daily 7am–midnight.

Mon Ami Gabi *Paris*, 3655 Las Vegas Blvd S ℡ 702/944-4224. The first and the finest casino restaurant to offer open-air seating right on the Strip has the feel of a proper French pavement bistro. At lunch, try the gloriously authentic onion soup ($8), the mussels ($11), or the thin-cut *steak frites* ($20). Dinner features more expensive steak cuts and fish entrees. Mon–Thurs 11.30am–11pm, Fri 11.30am–midnight, Sat 11am–midnight, Sun 11am–11pm.

Olives *Bellagio*, 3600 Las Vegas Blvd S ℡ 702/693-8181. *Bellagio's* best-value gourmet restaurant has a lovely terrace setting, facing the Eiffel Tower across the lake. Even if it is the kind of place that calls a $15 pizza an "individual oven-baked flatbread," the largely Mediterranean menu is uniformly fresh and superb. It's a great spot for lunch, with $11–16 appetizers like beef carpaccio, pasta dishes like butternut squash tortelli ($17), and specials such as a jumbo lump crab cake sandwich ($25). Dinner entrees are pricier, at up to $50. Daily 11am–2.30pm & 5–11.30pm.

Phô at the Coffee Shop *TI*, 3300 Las Vegas Blvd S ℡ 702/894-7111. If you're looking for a simple, cheap and tasty meal, there's no faulting the Strip's only Vietnamese restaurant. Its specialty here is hearty bowls of *phô* soup, available in chicken, beef or vegetable flavors for $10, while rice or vermicelli noodle dishes start at $10.50. Sun–Thurs 11am–11.30pm, Fri & Sat 11am–2.30am.

Red 8 *Wynn Las Vegas*, 3131 Las Vegas Blvd S ℡ 702/770-9966. Airy, relaxed Asian bistro where the food is traditional Southeast Asian, predominantly Chinese, with Malaysian and Mongolian thrown in. Subtle, aromatic flavors abound – dim sum ($6–10) include tasty pan-fried turnip cakes and steamed buns – and you'll also find perfectly executed classics like spicy shredded jellyfish ($9), barbecued duck or pork ($16), or Kung Pao shrimp ($19). Mon–Thurs 11.30am–10pm, Fri 10.30am–1am, Sat 11.30am–1am, Sun 10.30am–10pm.

Restaurants elsewhere

Carluccio's Tivoli Gardens 1775 E Tropicana Ave ℡ 702/795-3236. Upscale Italian restaurant, two miles east of the Strip, with an irresistible angle – it was designed by Liberace himself, whose museum stands next door. The menu is wide ranging and consistently rich, with pizzas and chicken dishes at $11–15, and linguini with mussels for $16, but it's hard to resist Liberace's own personal favorite, the $10 baked lasagna. Daily except Mon 4.30–10.30pm.

The Coffee Shop *Binion's Horseshoe*, 128 E Fremont St ℡ 702/382-1600. Deep in the bowels of the *Horseshoe*, it's the round-the-clock Las Vegas coffee shop of your dreams. The food is American-diner-heaven, with excellent prices for a changing timetable of specials. Breakfast, which works out better value than most buffets, is served 24hr, while a different blue plate special, such as Thursday's chicken pot pie, is dished up daily 11am–10pm for $7.99. Otherwise, typical dinner entrees cost around $10. Daily 24hr.

Mr Lucky's 24/7 *Hard Rock Hotel*, 4455 Paradise Rd ☎702/693-5000. With its open kitchen, faux-fur booths, and subdued tan-and-cream paint-job, the *Hard Rock*'s 24hr coffee shop is a very stylish joint, and the food is well above average too. As well as all the usual breakfast items, it serves burgers, sandwiches, pizzas, and pasta dishes for $9–13, a 16-oz steak for $19, and milkshakes or microbrews for under $5. Daily 24hr.

Nobu *Hard Rock Hotel*, 4455 Paradise Rd ☎702/693-5090. Las Vegas's chic-est celebrity restaurant, run by Japanese–Peruvian chef Nobu Matsuhisa, as seen in New York, LA, and London. The decor is supremely tasteful, and the food is exquisite, though the temptation to order yet another morsel means the prices tend to rocket before your eyes, whether you simply go for the sushi bar or select from the "special cold dishes" (three oysters for $15, or salmon tartar with caviar at $22). Sushi or sashimi dinners start at $30, with set menus from $100. Daily 6–11pm.

Paymon's Mediterranean Cafe and Lounge 4147 S Maryland Pkwy at Flamingo ☎702/731-6030. This highly recommended Middle Eastern restaurant, is simple but also Vegas's best vegetarian option. Salads, pita sandwiches or spinach pie cost $8–10, while dips such as hummus or the eggplant-based *baba ganosh* are $5. Daily 11am–1am.

Bars and clubs

As the perfect fuel to turn a dithering gawker into a diehard gambler, alcohol is very easy to come by in Las Vegas. If you want a drink in a casino, there's no need to look for a bar; instead, a tray-toting waitress will come and find you. All the casinos do have actual **bars** as well, but in terms of enjoying a proper night out, they're just a small part of the picture. The old-fashioned **Las Vegas lounge** has returned in force, whether knowingly retro-styled for 20-something rockers, glammed up as an "ultra-lounge," or lovingly re-created for older visitors looking to recapture the quieter but still somehow deliciously decadent flavor of the Rat-Pack era.

What's even more striking is that Las Vegas has finally come of age as an international **clubbing** capital. No longer are clubbers considered a breed apart from tourists; instead, the success of nightclubs at hipper casinos like the *Hard Rock* and *Mandalay Bay* has prompted all their major rivals to follow suit, often with spectacular results.

As for **live music**, check newspapers like *City Life* and the *Las Vegas Review Journal* to see who's appearing when you're in town.

Bars and lounges

Art Bar 1511 S Main St ☎702/437-2787. Just the kind of bar you hope to find in Las Vegas, but never do – a genuine local downtown dive, peopled by alternative types. DJs and live bands at weekends especially, plus karaoke on Tues. Daily 2pm–6am.

The Beatles Revolution Lounge *Mirage*, 3400 Las Vegas Blvd S ☎702-692-8383, ⓦwww .thebeatlesrevolutionlounge.com. Once you get past the somewhat silly claim that this ultra-lounge truly reflects an artistic collaboration between the Beatles and the Cirque du Soleil, you can enjoy the psychedelic lightshow and fab 1960's decor. DJ sets most nights, live indie bands Tues. Closed Sun.

Liquidity *Luxor*, 3900 Las Vegas Blvd S ☎702/262-4591. Very blue, very modern, water-themed ultra-lounge in the center of *Luxor*, with waterfalls both real and virtual cascading from the ceiling. Daily 24hr.

Nine Fine Irishmen *New York–New York*, 3790 Las Vegas Blvd S ☎702/740-6463. The affinity between New York and all things Irish finds expression in this wood-paneled pub, shipped from Ireland and featuring Irish musicians, singers, and dancers nightly. Sun–Thurs 11am–2.30am, Fri & Sat 11am–3.30am. Cover $5 Wed & Thurs, $10 Fri & Sat.

Parasol Up, Parasol Down *Wynn Las Vegas*, 3131 Las Vegas Blvd S ☎702/770-7000. Matching pair of see-and-be-seen bars, decked out in Wynn's signature psychedic palette and facing the Lake of Dreams; *Up* is at the top of the central staircase, while *Down*, at the bottom, offers additional outdoor seating that's very much in demand. Daily 24hr, no cover.

Triple Seven Brewpub *Main Street Station*, 200 N Main St ☎702/386-4442. Roomy, high-ceilinged downtown brewpub with poor service but great beers and tasty food. Daily 11am–7am.

V Bar *The Venetian*, 3355 Las Vegas Blvd S ☎702/414-3200. The minimalist Oriental styling in this upscale, understated, grown-up bar, towards the back of the *Venetian*, is tempered with warm auspicious reds, and glamorous waitresses glide around dressed in slinky slips. An espresso martini certainly kicks off the evening nicely. Daily 5pm until late, no cover.

Clubs and music venues

Gipsy 4605 Paradise Rd ☎702/731-1919, ⓦgipsylasvegas.com. High-profile gay dance club, where apart from the free cruise nights on Wednesdays, there's normally some form of live entertainment to justify the $5 post-midnight cover charge, with go-go boys performing Friday, and beer busts most nights. The elaborate lost-city decor attracts young ingenues and local celebs. Daily 10pm–6am.

House of Blues *Mandalay Bay*, 3950 Las Vegas Blvd S ☎702/632-7600, ⓦwww.hob.com. The Strip's premier live-music venue, the voodoo-tinged, folk-art-decorated *House of Blues* has a definite but not exclusive emphasis toward blues, R&B, and the like. Typical prices range from around $35 for B-list names up to $100 for stars like Aretha Franklin.

The Joint *Hard Rock Hotel*, 4455 Paradise Rd ☎702/693-5066. The venue of choice for big-name touring rock acts, not least because its affluent baby-boomer profile enables bands like Aerosmith to charge $200 a throw. Tickets to see the Rolling Stones here cost $505 and $1005, but more typically admission for performers such as Elvis Costello ranges between $75 and $125. The cheaper rates are for the much less atmospheric balcony.

LAX *Luxor*, 3900 Las Vegas Blvd S ☎702/262-4529, ⓦwww.laxthenightclub.com. Spread over two stories, and part owned by Christina Aguilera, *Luxor's* outpost of Hollywood's hot LAX nightclub goes for an opulent, opera-house ambience; with

so much attention devoted to the VIP tables, however, ordinary customers can expect both to wait in line a long time, and to feel squashed into random corners, once they do get in. Wed–Sat 10pm–5am. Cover men $30, women $20.

rumjungle *Mandalay Bay*, 3950 Las Vegas Blvd S ☎702/632-7408. Hybrid bar-restaurant-nightclub, where you'll have to wait in line then run a gauntlet of go-go dancers just to get in. Pay $45 for the flame-grilled Brazilian feast, served until 11pm, and you're spared the cover charge. Leopardskin-clad staff serve well-priced cocktails, plus a vast menu of rums, while it's too loud to do anything more than watch the pole dancers above the bar, or join the Latin-tinged action on the (small-ish) dance floor. Mon, Wed, Fri, & Sat 5.30pm–4am, Tues, Thurs, & Sun 5.30pm–2am. Cover (for non-diners only) $20.

Studio 54 *The MGM Grand*, 3799 Las Vegas Blvd S ☎702/891-7254, ⓦwww.studio54lv.com. A three-story, four-dance-floor re-creation of New York's legendary *Studio 54*, complete with surly doormen. A separate upstairs locals' room ensures it's not totally dominated by tourists. Cover men $20, women $10.

Tabú *MGM Grand*, 3799 Las Vegas Blvd S ☎702/891-7183. Still the definitive Las Vegas ultra-lounge; not only do go-go girls dance on the tables, but the tables themselves respond to touch by dancing with swirling colors. Expert and beautiful staff mix any cocktail, while, despite the lack of a proper dance floor, they host themed nights like "Super Slide" (old-school hip-hop) on Thurs. Sun, Mon, & Thurs–Sat 10pm–5am. Cover $20.

Tao *The Venetian*, 3355 Las Vegas Blvd S ☎702/388-8588, ⓦwww.taolasvegas.com. The decor at *Tao*, right at the front of the *Venetian* on the first floor is extremely opulent, and very Asian influenced, with lots of glowing golden Buddhas, and it attracts very big names indeed, with Paris Hilton hosting some nights, Mary J Blige performing at parties, and so on. Lines form early at weekends and not everyone gets in. A rooftop pool section, known as *Tao Beach*, opens in summer only. Thurs–Sat 10pm–5am. Cover Thurs & Fri $20, Sat $30.

Entertainment

There was a time when Las Vegas represented the pinnacle of any show-business career. In the early 1960s, when Frank Sinatra's Rat Pack were shooting the original *Ocean's 11* during the day then singing the night away at the *Sands*, the city could claim to be the capital of the international entertainment industry. Then the world moved on. In the last few years, however, Las Vegas has started

▲ The dancefloor, Studio 54

to come back into its own. One by one, the cheesy, feathers–and–tassels revues have closed down, to be replaced by surprisingly stimulating, postmodern shows by the likes of the now-ubiquitous **Cirque de Soleil** and the **Blue Man Group**. A new generation of big-name stars are taking up the kind of long-term residencies we all thought had vanished with Elvis. **Celine Dion** paved the way at *Caesars'* huge Colosseum, while divas like Cher, Bette Midler, and Elton John have followed in her wake.

The Amazing Johnathan Harmon Theater, Miracle Mile Shops, *Planet Hollywood*, 3667 Las Vegas Blvd S ⊕702/836-0833, ⑩www.amazingj.com. The emphasis on the Amazing Johnathan's unbridled craziness might lead you to expect a crude late-night gross-out, but barring the cartoonish violence he directs against his ditzy blonde assistant "Psychic Tanya," Johnathan's a lovable character. He's basically a comedic magician, with the emphasis on the comedy, meaning that he barely completes a trick all evening. That's probably for the best, anyway, as carefully honed patter and hilarious skits like "Bad Karate Theater" make this one of Las Vegas's funniest shows. Tues–Sat 9pm. $69–80.

Blue Man Group The Venetian, 3355 Las Vegas Blvd S ⊕702/414-7469, ⑩www.blueman.com. The Blue Men Group have lasted over ten years on the Strip where so many other shows – shows with stars, plots, and even words – have failed within months. How? By the synchronized eating of breakfast cereal; by performing live endoscopies on audience members; by catching marshmallows tossed across the stage in their mouths. Although (very funny) deadpan humor is a major component, two further elements keep the crowds happy. First

is the exhilarating music, which besides pieces set to the Sex Pistols and Jefferson Airplane, also includes lots of meaty drumming on industrial tubing from the Men themselves; and second are some truly stunning special effects. It's not for everyone, but breathtaking novelty is a good part of what Las Vegas is all about, and in their own purpose-built theater the Men represent a welcome alternative to the now veteran Cirque du Soleil. Daily 7pm & 10pm. $76.50–126.

Folies Bergere *Tropicana*, 3801 Las Vegas Blvd S ⊕702/739-2411. A fixture at the Tropicana since 1959, the *Folies Bergere* is the longest-running show in the US. While there have been changes over the years, the basic formula remains the same: a mildly "naughty" Parisian revue designed to blow the minds of stout, bearded farmers from Iowa. Showgirls with fixed grins and feathered headdresses – and topless at times during certain performances – high-kick and waltz through a succession of big production numbers. Mon, Wed, Thurs, & Sat 7.30pm & 10pm (topless); Tues & Fri 8.30pm (topless); over-16s only. $42.50–53.50.

Kà *MGM Grand*, 3799 Las Vegas Blvd S ⊕702/891-7777, ⑩www.ka.com.

Las Vegas' fourth Cirque de Soleil production, *Kà*, is an absolute must-see. The most expensive theatrical production ever staged, anywhere, it boasts a quite extraordinary set; the stage floor not only rises, but can swivel and pivot in every direction. At one moment, it can turn into a steep cliff-face to which the performers cling for dear life; at the next, they may simply fall, mid-battle, into the abyss below. *Kà* is much more plot-driven than other Cirque shows, telling a complex saga about two Asian twins separated by enemy kidnappers, allowing more scope for darkness and emotional impact during the succession of truly breathtaking set-pieces. Add in some extraordinary puppetry and sumptuous costumes, and even if you're left unmoved by the story, *Kà* is certain to expand your horizons. Tues–Sat 7pm & 9:30pm. $69–150.

Lance Burton *The Monte Carlo*, 3770 Las Vegas Blvd S ⏀702/730-7160. Las Vegas's best family show, featuring the superb and very charming master magician Lance Burton. As well as traditional but very impressive stunts with playing cards, handkerchiefs, and doves, Burton also features large-scale illusions like the disappearance of an airplane and a narrow escape from hanging. Tues & Sat 7pm & 10pm, Wed–Fri 7pm. $70 & $76.

Legends in Concert *The Imperial Palace*, 3535 Las Vegas Blvd S ⏀702/794-3261. Celebrity-tribute (impersonators) show, with a changing roster that ranges from Dolly Parton to Barry White. For musical prowess, the vocal groups like the Four Tops or the Temptations are unbeatable, while a tongue-in-cheek Elvis clowning through *Viva Las Vegas* makes a fitting finale. Check if they're giving away tickets on the sidewalk before you buy. Mon–Sat 7pm & 10pm. $50, including two drinks; ages 12 and under $35.

Love *The Mirage*, 3400 Las Vegas Blvd S ⏀702/796-9999 or 800/963-9634, Ⓦwww.cirquedusoleil.com. In which the Cirque du Soleil do their stuff to a specially remixed Beatles soundtrack. Intimate at some moments and exuberantly all-embracing at others, *Love* is a beautifully judged and profoundly moving show. Nostalgic and visionary in equal measures, it celebrates the Beatles' achievement while skillfully avoiding anything too literal – the actors don't play specific Beatles, and although characters from their songs appear, they evoke the general mood rather than acting out the lyrics. The costumes, lighting and staging are all magnificent, and some of the set-pieces are astonishing. When all's said

and done, it's a dance show, but if that might normally put you off, don't let it – it's an irresistible evening. Mon & Thurs–Sun 7pm & 9.30pm. $109–165.

Mac King Improv Theater, *Harrah's*, 3475 Las Vegas Blvd S ⏀702/369-5111. This afternoon magic show is one of Las Vegas's best entertainment bargains. Mac King's an endearingly wide-eyed innocent in a plaid suit who specializes in good old close-up magic, using ropes, cards, torn-up $20 bills and the like. His corny patter leaves plenty of room for good-natured improvised gags at the expense of those unwary audience members he lures up on stage. Tues–Sat 1 & 3pm. $25.

Mystère *TI*, 3300 Las Vegas Blvd S ⏀702/796-9999 or 800/963-9634, Ⓦwww.cirquedusoleil.com. The Cirque du Soleil's original Las Vegas show is such a visual feast that it barely matters whether you see its dreamscape symbolism as profound and meaningful or labored and empty. Seen at first as being too "way-out" for Las Vegas, its success redefined the city's approach to entertainment. Above all, it's a showcase of fabulous circus skills, with tumblers, acrobats, trapeze artists, pole climbers, clowns, and strong men, but no animals apart from fantastic costumed apparitions. Sat–Wed 7pm & 9.30pm. $66–105.

O *Bellagio*, 3600 Las Vegas Blvd S ⏀702/796-9999 or 800/963-9634, Ⓦwww.cirquedusoleil.com. Another Cirque du Soleil triumph, and a remarkable testament to what's possible when the budget is barely an issue. Any part of the stage at any time may be submerged to any depth. One moment a performer walks across a particular spot, the next someone dives headfirst into it from the high wire. From the synchronized swimmers onwards, the Cirque display their magnificent skills to maximum advantage. Highlights include a colossal trapeze frame draped like a pirate ship and crewed by fearless acrobats and divers, and footmen flying through the air in swirls of velvet drapery. Wed–Sun 7.30pm & 10.30pm. $103–165.

V – the Ultimate Variety Show V Theatre, *Planet Hollywood*, 3667 Las Vegas Blvd S ⏀702/932-892-7790, Ⓦwww.vtheshow.com. Old-fashioned but enjoyable revue show that gives assorted singers, comedians, jugglers, and the like a few minutes each to prove their worth. If the hilarious Russ Merlin is on the bill, be sure not to miss it. Daily 7pm & 8.30pm. $65, or $85 with dinner.

Contexts

Contexts

History

W hat is now the Southwest USA has been home to Native Americans for about twelve thousand years. Around four hundred years ago, they were joined by a small group of Hispanic colonists, who claimed the region for Spain as New Mexico. After over two hundred years of Spanish rule, it passed briefly into the hands of the newly independent nation of Mexico, before being taken over by the United States, which has now held it for a little over 160 years.

Throughout that long history, the Southwest has been either controlled, or at least heavily influenced, by distant powers. Its best-known ancient peoples, the Ancestral Puebloans and the Hohokam, drew their cultural inspiration from Mexico; the settlers of Santa Fe looked to Madrid and Mexico City for financial and spiritual support; and even today the region owes much to federal funding from Washington.

What makes the history of the Southwest so fascinating is that so many of the different peoples who have migrated into the region are still there, and still interacting with each other. In the words of an anthropologist from Zuni Pueblo, "the Anasazi are alive and well and living in the Rio Grande valley." The Navajo, relative latecomers, form the majority population in the Four Corners region, though they've never displaced the Hopi. Santa Fe remains a visibly Hispanic, Catholic city, while Utah is still over sixty percent Mormon, and Phoenix and Las Vegas typify the Anglo impact.

The Paleo Indians

No trace of human beings in the Americas has been dated any earlier than fourteen thousand years ago, when the true pioneers of North America, nomadic hunter-gatherers from Siberia, first reached Alaska. Thanks to the last ice age, when sea levels were three hundred feet lower than the modern Bering Strait, a **"land-bridge"** – actually a vast plain, measuring six hundred miles north to south – connected Eurasia to America.

At that time, Alaska effectively formed part of Asia rather than North America, being separated by impenetrable glacier fields from Canada. Much like an air lock, the region "opened" in different directions at different times; migrants reaching it from the west, unaware that they were leaving Asia, would at first have found their way blocked to the east. Several generations might have passed, and the connection back to Asia severed, before an eastward passage appeared. This migration was almost certainly spurred not by the urge to explore, but the pursuit of large mammal species, especially the mammoth, that had already become extinct throughout almost all of Eurasia. Imagine therefore the glee of the so-called **Paleo Indians** when they finally encountered America's own indigenous "megafauna," such as mammoths, mastodons, giant ground sloths, and long-horned bison, all of which had evolved without fear of, or protection against, human predation.

It's intriguing to reflect how small the original group of human settlers may have been. A band of a hundred individuals need only have advanced into the virgin continent at a rate of eight miles per year, with an annual population growth of 1.1 percent, to fill North and South America with ten million people within a thousand years.

Between 10,000 BC and 8000 BC, the Southwest was dominated by the so-called **Clovis** culture, whose distinctive flaked-stone spear-points were first identified at Clovis, New Mexico. Living in small groups, constantly on the move, Clovis hunters pursued their prey across large distances. Their weapons have been found poking from the ribs of mammoths, and they seem to have been such successful killers that they drove the indigenous fauna – which included horses – to extinction.

The Archaic culture

As the large animals died out, early Southwesterners had to adapt and became **hunter-gatherers**. Learning where and when particular plants ripened, the people of the **Archaic** or **Desert** culture migrated seasonally within relatively restricted areas – often between canyons or valleys and nearby hillsides – in search of fresh food. Hunting for small mammals such as rabbit and deer was still important, however. The development of shamanistic rituals is demonstrated by the clay statuettes and split-twig figurines, depicting deities as well as animals, that have been found in remote locations in the Grand Canyon and elsewhere. Few traces of their actual homes survive, however; it's thought they lived in caves wherever possible. The most remarkable manifestation of Archaic culture was the mysterious rock art of the **Great Gallery** in Canyonlands National Park (see p.440); they also constructed "intaglios," giant earthworks in the shape of enigmatic figures or snakes, in the deserts of southwest Arizona.

The Archaic era was brought to an end by the infiltration of Mexican influences from the south. The first and most crucial was agriculture. **Corn** – in the shape of tiny fingers of maize, much smaller than today's strains – may have been cultivated in the highlands of southern Mexico as early as 5000 BC. The skill of growing it then spread northwards from group to group, accompanied by the prayers and rituals necessary to ensure a good harvest, and may have reached southern New Mexico around 1500 BC. However, anthropologists have noted a reluctance among hunter-gatherers the world over to give up what they regard as a pleasant lifestyle, which offers individuals food in return for comparatively little effort, plus lots of free time. The Southwest followed that pattern, in that a low level of farming – more like gardening – served at first to supplement the traditional diet. Communities only made the transition to intensive agriculture when forced to by increasing population levels.

The Basketmakers

Southwestern peoples embarked on the large-scale cultivation of crops – corn, together with a more recent arrival, **squash** – from around 100 BC onwards. The first such society was named **Basketmaker II** by early archeologists, who assumed that more primitive "Basketmaker I" sites waited be found. The Basketmakers lived in extended family groups, in shallow **pithouses** – rectangular pits two to six feet deep, with earth-covered roofs that rose above ground level. They hunted using the *atlatl*, a lever-like spear-throwing device. Cooking entailed dropping hot rocks into waterproof yucca-leaf baskets lined with pitch. By now they had also domesticated **dogs**, for hunting, and **turkeys**, for feathers rather than food.

A separate history of the **Hopi** tribe appears on p.511, and of the **Navajo** and **Apache** peoples on p.515.

Pottery spread from Mexico, via the Mimbres region of southwest New Mexico (see p.216), in the first few centuries AD. All pots were made by women, hand-coiling successive strips of rolled clay on top of each other and then smoothing them together. The use of fragile ceramic vessels presupposes a relatively sedentary society but brings great benefits: **beans** are much easier to boil in a pot than a basket, so the Southwest acquired its third great staple food, and basketmaking declined.

Around 500 AD, the so-called **Basketmaker III** culture emerged. As well as corn, squash, and beans, they grew another Mexican import, **cotton** – originally cultivated mainly for its oil-rich edible seeds – and used **bows and arrows**. Sizeable **villages** (what the Spanish later called **pueblos**) started to appear.

Each village soon focused around one specific, larger than usual pithouse, which was probably set aside for public or ritual use. Such buildings are recognizable as the first **kivas** – the ceremonial underground chambers that remain at the heart of Pueblo religion. Each *kiva* was entered from above, via an opening that also served as the smokehole for the central firepit. A bench ran around its circumference, and niches were set into the walls, perhaps to hold ritual objects. A small depression in the floor in front of the firepit, known as the **sipapu**, symbolized the hole through which human beings emerged onto this earth.

The Ancestral Puebloans

By 700 AD, much of the Southwest was populated by the forerunners of modern Pueblo Indians. This book follows archeologists and Pueblo Indians by calling these people "**Ancestral Puebloans**" in preference to the previously common term "**Anasazi**." The Hopi in particular object to that name, which comes from a Navajo word meaning "enemy ancestors," and have championed the use of either their own word for "ancestors," **Hisatsinom**, or the more generally applicable "Ancestral Puebloans."

Between 700 AD and 1300 AD, Ancestral Puebloan civilization spread beyond the **Four Corners** to cover most of what's now northern Arizona and New Mexico, as well as southern Utah and Colorado, the depths of the Grand Canyon, and into southern Nevada. Besides the initial increase in the size and sophistication of villages came a crucial change. Individuals stopped living in pithouses, and instead built surface structures of mud plastered onto a brushwood framework – a style known as wattle-and-daub. However, they continued to dig large subterranean *kivas*, which kept the pithouse form but were exclusively designed for communal or ceremonial use. Many such *kivas* could now be accessed not only through the roof, but also via concealed underground tunnels, which may have enabled costumed priests or dancers to make surprise appearances during rituals.

The Ancestral Puebloans were the first North Americans to use looms to **weave** cotton. In addition to cotton clothes, they made blankets and even socks from yucca leaves interwoven with turkey feathers, and wore yucca sandals. For a time, they flattened and broadened their skulls by binding infant' heads against cradleboards. As you might imagine from their tiny doorways and cramped living quarters, they were small, with women averaging five feet in height and men a few inches more. Life expectancy was thirty or less, although perhaps one in ten reached the age of 50. Adults were plagued by the twin problems of arthritis and loss of teeth. Their teeth were worn away by grit, the result of grinding corn between a hand-tool or *mano* and a flat slab known as a *metate*, both made from sandstone. They also had some medical expertise, using cottonwood bark, which contains the main active ingredient of aspirin, as a painkiller, and the sap from piñon pines as an all-purpose antiseptic.

By the time the Ancestral Puebloans reached their cultural peak in the Four Corners, during the eleventh century, three main subgroups had emerged, centered on Chaco Canyon in what's now northwest New Mexico, Mesa Verde in southwest Colorado, and the Kayenta region of northeast Arizona.

The **Chacoans** seem to have been the most sophisticated of all, as witnessed not only by the architectural complexity of the multistory pueblos of Chaco Canyon, but by the fact that the canyon was so unsuited for large-scale occupation that they must have survived by extracting tribute from surrounding regions. A detailed account of the "Chaco Phenomenon" appears on p.102.

The wealth of Chaco demonstrates that by 1050 AD the Southwest was crisscrossed by extensive **trading routes**. In the absence of pack animals, most trade was in lightweight ritual or ornamental objects rather than the necessities of life. In exchange for **turquoise** from Cerrillos (see p.140), which passed from group to group all the way down to the Aztecs, the Ancestral Puebloans received silver and copper goods from Mexico, sea-shells from the Pacific, and the most prized ceremonial objects of all – live **macaws**.

The decline of Chaco, during the first half of the twelfth century, was mirrored by a general decline in the Ancestral Puebloan population. Following a period of instability and mass migrations, however, Ancestral Puebloan civilization had a majestic final flourish in the Four Corners during the thirteenth century. Not only did they construct the "**cliff dwellings**," squeezed into narrow alcoves high on canyon walls, for which they're now celebrated, but major **towns** also grew up. Colorado's Montezuma Valley was typical in holding eight large pueblo complexes, each home to over a thousand people. The nearby cliff dwellings preserved in **Mesa Verde** National Park (see p.86) were home to a smaller, probably peripheral group; though compellingly beautiful to modern eyes, they represent a relatively minor aspect of Ancestral Puebloan life.

The disappearance of the Ancestral Puebloans

The "**disappearance**" of the Ancestral Puebloans from the entire Four Corners region between 1275 AD and 1300 AD is still widely presented as a great mystery. However, the puzzle has largely been solved. Modern Pueblo peoples are so self-evidently their descendants that it's clear the Ancestral Puebloans migrated away rather than simply dying out. Why they did so is harder to explain. Traditional accounts say that a sustained **drought** forced them to leave, but such droughts were not uncommon, and the region remained capable of producing enough food to support them.

It seems more likely that the drought coincided with a period of cultural upheaval. While archeologists argue as to whether specific Ancestral Puebloan cliff dwellings were intended for defense, the region as a whole was unarguably prone to violent conflict at this time. Recent proof of cannibalism in the Montezuma Valley has shattered notions of Ancestral Puebloan society as being utterly peaceful, and isolated groups appear to have banded together in larger settlements for mutual defense.

The influence of the blood-drenched civilizations of ancient Mexico was also at its height. As described on p.78, the **kachina** religion, which centered on supernatural entities that, at this formative stage, closely paralleled the warring deities of the Aztecs, spread rapidly across the Southwest. Some archeologists even controversially argue that the *kachina* cult was introduced by cannibalistic warrior refugees from the south. In any case, over time, religious emphasis shifted away from blood and sacrifice toward ceremonies designed to bring rain, and thus corn. The drought of the late thirteenth century may have been the first crucial test of, or judgment upon, those rainmaking powers; possibly charismatic religious leaders persuaded their followers that the failure of the harvest was a signal to move on.

In addition, the Ancestral Puebloans had severely depleted their **environment**. The need for fuel and building materials meant that the landscape around their settlements had been stripped bare; the pueblos of Chaco Canyon, for example, used over 200,000 large wooden beams. Cutting down trees not only made the search for firewood increasingly arduous, but led to the process known as *arroyo-cutting*, whereby, once the trees that held their banks together were removed, previously placid streams became savage torrents that destroyed prime riverside farmland. It may be no coincidence that the Four Corners remained all but deserted until the arrival of the Navajo during the sixteenth century (see p.515); it may have taken that long to recover from overexploitation.

The Hohokam

While the Basketmakers and Ancestral Puebloans held sway further north, the deserts of southern Arizona and northern Mexico were home to the equally sophisticated **Hohokam** civilization. This region was not then so barren as it appears today – much of it was covered with grass until it was overgrazed by Spanish cattle – and the Hohokam were primarily **farmers**. They lived in what the Spanish later called **rancherías** – sprawling farming communities, where each separate homestead consisted of a framework of timber, brush-coated with mud. Thousands of such villages, most occupied for many generations, were scattered across the desert, interspersed with larger "towns" that were probably ceremonial and trading centers rather than residential districts. The population was most heavily concentrated in the **Phoenix Basin**, where inhabitants compensated for the lack of rainfall by digging over three hundred miles of irrigation **canals**. Constructed without the use of metal tools, and requiring constant maintenance, these enabled the Hohokam to reap two separate harvests each year, with corn, beans, and squash as the staples.

Whether the Hohokam migrated into the region from central Mexico around 300 BC, as some archeologists believe, or simply evolved from indigenous desert peoples, they were clearly heavily influenced by Mexican culture. Each major town had at least one Mexican-style **ballcourt**, where a ritual game was played with a rubber ball, and a raised-earth **platform mound** – a primitive pyramid – used for religious ceremonies. Like the Ancestral Puebloans, with whom they had little direct contact, the Hohokam traded commodities like cotton and salt for treasured ritual items from the south, such as copper bells, onyx, parrots, and macaws.

During the eleventh century, the Hohokam trading complex known as **Snaketown**, at the confluence of the Gila and Salt rivers, rivaled Chaco as the Southwest's largest settlement. Though Snaketown then declined, the Phoenix Basin became one of the most densely populated areas in North America, with perhaps eighty thousand inhabitants in the thirteenth century. However, the Hohokam **disappeared** at much the same time as the Ancestral Puebloans, around 1350 AD. The very word "Hohokam" means "all used up" in the language of the later **'O'odham** people of southern Arizona, and reflects 'O'odham oral history that the Hohokam drained every possible drop of sustenance from the land. So extensively did they damage the region's delicate ecological balance that their descendants were reduced to an impoverished subsistence lifestyle. In addition, by the end of the seventeenth century the arrival of European **diseases** such as smallpox, measles, and typhus reduced the population of the Phoenix Basin to less than five thousand.

While no modern Native American group claims direct descent from the Hohokam, certain cultural traits endure. The *ranchería* style of dwelling persisted until recently among tribes such as the Yavapai, the Havasupai, and the **'O'odham** themselves. Those peoples also follow an individualistic system of belief, without *kachinas* or *kivas*, and depending on shamans rather than priests, that seems to be in line with what little is known about Hohokam religion.

The Mogollon

Archeologists distinguish a third significant group among the pre-Columbian peoples of the Southwest – the **Mogollon**. Contemporaneous with the Ancestral Puebloans and the Hohokam, and sharing elements of both cultures, the Mogollon occupied an extensive area in what's now west-central New Mexico and east-central Arizona. The Mogollon people lived on the cool plateau above the **Mogollon Rim**, a 200-mile long, 2000ft high escarpment that marks the southern limit of the Colorado Plateau, farming the upland meadows and hunting in the adjacent mountains.

Being so close to Mexico, the Mogollon heartland, which focused on the valleys of the **Gila** and **Mimbres** rivers, was probably the first area of the Southwest to acquire agriculture and pottery. The Mogollon only stopped building pithouses around the eleventh century, and the few pueblos they constructed, such as the one now preserved as Gila Cliff Dwellings (see p.217), were on a small scale. In one respect, however, Mogollon culture was unsurpassed – the extraordinary **pottery** produced by the **Classic Mimbres** people, a Mogollon offshoot described on p.216.

Much like the Four Corners, the entire Mogollon region became **depopulated** during the fourteenth century. As the Mogollon peoples had probably introduced the *kachina* religion to the Southwest, their descendants presumably helped to create modern Pueblo culture. Specific Mogollon-descended pueblos may well have been the hardest hit by the arrival of both the Spaniards and the Apache, however, and if their inhabitants survived at all, they probably fled north as refugees.

The Pueblo world and the Spanish invasion

Although the Ancestral Puebloan era ended with their departure from the Four Corners, their immediate descendants created the Southwest's largest pre-Hispanic communities of all. In particular, the city of **Casas Grandes**, which flourished between 1300 AD and 1400 AD in what's now northern Mexico, consisted of over two thousand rooms and served as a major macaw-breeding center.

However, the most enduring legacy of the Ancestral Puebloans was the emergence of **Pueblo** communities throughout what had previously been under-populated areas of northern New Mexico. Most Mesa Verdeans migrated to the northern reaches of the **Rio Grande** valley, where they founded pueblos such as Taos and Santa Clara; their language, known as Tanoan, evolved into today's Tiwa and Tewa languages. The Chacoans, on the other hand, who spoke the language that became Keresan, moved further south to establish pueblos like Cochiti and Santo Domingo, as well as Ácoma and Zuni to the west.

Other population centers – lesser known now, as they failed to survive the impact of the Spanish – included the **Galisteo Valley**, not far southeast of Santa Fe, which held a dozen large pueblos; the **Chama Valley**; and **Tigüex** near modern Albuquerque.

By the time the Spanish arrived, the Southwest may have held a hundred separate pueblos, with a total population approaching one hundred thousand. New forms of social organization had emerged, and individual pueblos consisted of alliances of either **clans** – each with its own religious or military responsibilities – or **moieties** – the technical term for a society divided into two halves, in which half the pueblo might belong to a *kiva* associated with winter ceremonies, and the other half to one connected with summer. However, pueblos did not have chiefs or leaders in the European sense, and neither was there any tradition of alliances between pueblos. That lack of political unity seriously weakened their ability to resist the Spanish invaders, who turned their attention northwards after completing the conquest of Mexico.

The coming of the Spaniards

The first Spanish expedition to reach what is now the US, led by **Ponce de León**, sailed up the Atlantic Coast in 1513 and named **Florida**. The next Spanish voyage, in 1528, ended in shipwreck in Tampa Bay, but a junior officer, **Alvar Núñez Cabeza de Vaca**, survived. Together with three shipmates, he spent eight years on an extraordinary transcontinental odyssey. Living with various Native American groups – initially held as slaves, later revered as seers – they made their way across Texas, following the Pecos River and the Rio Grande. It's unlikely that they reached modern New Mexico or Arizona, but while staying in the pueblo of the Jumano tribe, somewhere on the Rio Grande, they heard tales of larger pueblos further north, and in northern Mexico they were given emeralds that had been purchased with parrot feathers from a people who lived to the north.

Cabeza de Vaca's eventual arrival in Mexico City in 1536 created a sensation, and the Viceroy of New Spain resolved to investigate his tales of golden cities deep in the desert. After all, it was still less than twenty years since the Spanish had conquered the inconceivably wealthy Aztecs, and subsequent expeditions within New Spain had discovered further riches. One of Cabeza de Vaca's companions had been a black African from Morocco, called **Esteban de Dorantes**. Rather than return to a life of slavery, he volunteered to map the route for a new expedition led by the Franciscan friar **Fray Marcos de Niza**. In 1539, Esteban set off ahead of Fray Marcos, and followed a long-established native trading route north across the Rio San Pedro into what's now Arizona.

A giant of a man, dressed like a shaman in jewelry and feathers and accompanied by two colossal greyhounds, he amazed the native peoples he encountered, and soon acquired a large entourage. Having arranged to send a signal back to Fray Marcos if he discovered anything to rival the marvels of Mexico, he duly did so as he approached the pueblo of **Zuni** (see p.107). Zuni was a major trading center, where the trail from the south met others from the west and east. The Zuni villages were nonetheless simply clusters of adobe houses. Esteban's demands for tribute appearing incompatible with his claims to be a medicine man, the Zuni punished his sacrilegious behavior by killing him, cutting him into strips, and distributing his flesh among their neighbors.

Hearing of Esteban's death, Fray Marcos fled back to Mexico. Although he had probably not even reached Arizona, he announced "this land … is the greatest and best of all that have been discovered." Calling the six Zuni villages the **Seven Cities of Cíbola**, he identified them with the legendary Seven Cities of Antillia, prosperous Christian communities that had long been sought by Spanish explorers.

On February 22, 1540, therefore, a further expedition, led by **Francisco Vásquez de Coronado**, set off into the Southwest from Compostela in northern Mexico. More than three hundred Spanish soldiers, along with hundreds of Indian "allies" and servants and several thousand horses and cattle, marched through Arizona to reach Zuni on July 7. In front of the town of Hawikku, the Zuni drew a line of sacred cornmeal along the ground, and forbade the Spaniards to cross. During the pitched **battle** that ensued – the first ever fought between Europeans and Native Americans – Coronado himself was knocked unconscious, but Spanish weapons prevailed. When the town was taken, its storehouses revealed not gold, but something by now equally precious – food.

Within two weeks, news of the fall of Zuni spread throughout the Southwest. Coronado made his headquarters in the conquered pueblo and dispatched exploratory parties in all directions. One such, under Pedro de Tovar, forced the "warlike" Hopi pueblos to surrender (see p.512) and reached as far as the **Grand Canyon**; another, commanded by Melchor Díaz, crossed the Colorado further south, and thus penetrated modern **California**. A detachment led by Hernando de Alvarado headed east, passing Ácoma Pueblo – "the greatest stronghold ever seen in the world" – and reaching the pueblos of the Rio Grande.

Meanwhile, emissaries from the Pueblo world were traveling to Zuni. Peaceful overtures from two men from **Cicuyé** (now Pecos NHP; see p.131), known to the Spaniards as **Cacique** ("Governor") and **Bigotes** ("Whiskers"), persuaded Coronado to move his expedition east. Camping for the winter beside the Rio Grande, in a region they called **Tigüex**, they commandeered an entire pueblo for a base. This may have been Kuaua, now preserved as Coronado State Monument (see p.138) – it's hard to say, because relations with the Tigüex soon degenerated into full-scale war, and in a bloody succession of sieges and massacres, all the Tigüex pueblos were destroyed.

Coronado remained convinced that gold was somewhere to be found. In the spring of 1541, he decamped northeast to Cicuyé, a prosperous community where Pueblo peoples traded with nomads from the Plains. In what may well have been a deliberate plot, Cacique and Bigotes introduced him to "**the Turk**," a Pawnee captive, who knew of a city far to the east, **Quivira**, that was rich in gold. Details of the Turk's story suggest that he was familiar with the culture of the Mississippi Indians, the leaders of Cicuyé probably hoped that he'd lead the Spaniards into oblivion on the endless Plains.

In the event, the expedition wandered for three fruitless months across what they called "the domain of the cows," in honor of its vast buffalo herds. From the Llano Estacado or "Staked Plains" of **Texas**, where they drove wooden stakes into the ground to avoid losing their way, they veered northeast into **Kansas**, following the Arkansas River along what later became the Santa Fe Trail. They did indeed reach a land known as Quivira, but its inhabitants were nomadic and utterly gold-free buffalo-hunters. At that point, Coronado lost patience; the Turk was garrotted and the Spaniards returned to the Rio Grande. Remarkably, at their furthest east Coronado's party may have come within a hundred miles of Hernando de Soto's even more rapacious military expedition, which having marched up from Florida was then exploring west of the Mississippi. Legend has it that one unfortunate Indian band fleeing Coronado's advance blundered into the de Soto group.

After another beleaguered winter in Tigüex, the Coronado expedition embarked on the long journey back to Mexico, leaving behind a handful of (swiftly martyred) missionaries and many of their Mexican-Indian allies.

The colony of New Mexico

During the fifty years after Coronado's departure, unauthorized Spanish adventurers made occasional forays into the Southwest. Not until 1598, however, was **Don Juan de Oñate** granted royal permission to establish a permanent **colony**. His expedition, consisting of 130 families and two hundred single men, crossed the Rio Grande near modern El Paso on May 1 and took possession of the land as **New Mexico**. Regional geography remaining unknown, the precise boundaries of the colony were not specified, but broadly speaking it extended from the Colorado River in the west to the Pecos River in the east, and included not only what's now New Mexico, but all of Arizona, plus parts of Utah, Colorado, Nevada, and California. The name "Mexico" then referred only to Mexico City – the modern country of Mexico was known as "New Spain" until 1821 – so "New Mexico" was named in the hope that it would match the riches of the Aztecs.

Each pueblo Oñate's party reached as they traveled north had been hurriedly deserted by its inhabitants, fearful of being captured as slaves. Eventually, at the confluence of the Rio Grande and the Chama River near modern Española, the settlers took over the pueblo of Ohkey Owingeh, renamed it San Juan, and made it their **capital**. Like Coronado before him, Oñate sent soldiers to all quarters of his new realm in search of gold; and like Coronado he soon found himself at war. After a group commanded by Oñate's nephew was all but wiped out, he launched a full-scale artillery onslaught on Ácoma Pueblo. Over eight hundred Acomans were killed, and eighty male prisoners had their feet publicly chopped off in the pueblos of the Rio Grande.

By the time Oñate returned to his capital, most of the colonists had given up and returned to Mexico. Oñate himself was recalled to Mexico City in disgrace once Franciscan missionaries reported his cruelty. Meanwhile, however, Captain Pérez de Villagrá had trumpeted Oñate's "achievements" in an epic poem, *Historia de Nueva México*. Villagrá still insisted that New Mexico could become the greatest kingdom in the Spanish empire, and he was sufficiently believed for Madrid to launch another attempt at colonization. **Don Pedro de Peralta** was therefore sent to New Mexico to found a new capital, and the city of **Santa Fe** was duly laid out in 1610.

New Mexico's first Spanish colonists dreamed of emulating their predecessors in Mexico, who had accumulated land and wealth in prodigious quantities. However, it soon became clear that New Mexico was the end of the road, with no access to the ocean and no rich neighbors the Spaniards could either trade with or plunder. Santa Fe never grew into a mighty city, but remained a remote military outpost of crude adobe buildings. Enterprising colonists therefore dispersed up and down the Rio Grande valley, appropriating Pueblo farmlands – and often enslaving Pueblo peoples – to create **ranches** to raise sheep and corn and grow peaches, plums, and cherries. **Wheat** was the most significant new crop. Unlike the traditional triumvirate of corn, beans, and squash, which must be grown entirely in spring and summer, wheat can be planted in December for harvest in June.

At the same time, **Franciscan missionaries** set out to convert the Pueblo Indians to Catholicism. One or two friars would attach themselves to a pueblo, recruit Indian labor to build adobe mission churches, and set about persuading the Pueblos that their *kachina* cults and corn ceremonies were wicked.

Throughout the seventeenth century, Spanish civil and religious authorities in New Mexico were at loggerheads. While deploring violence against the Pueblos, the church demanded the eradication of their beliefs; the military governors preferred not to antagonize the Indians unnecessarily, but felt their authority ultimately rested on the sword.

Quite apart from any specific actions, the very presence of the Spaniards utterly disrupted the region. Settled communities like the Rio Grande villages were especially vulnerable to **epidemic diseases** such as smallpox, measles, and typhus, unknown before the arrival of the Europeans. By 1640, the Pueblo population had dropped from a hundred thousand to around thirty thousand, and more than half of all pueblos had been abandoned. Existing patterns of **trade** across the Southwest had also been shattered, and the Rio Grande valley became a prime target for Native American raiders who coveted Spanish arms and, above all, **horses**. Tribes such as the Navajo and the Apache – see p.516 – turned from wandering nomads into fearsome mounted warriors, and all too often the Pueblo peoples bore the brunt of their attacks.

The Pueblo Revolt

In 1675, as it became ever more obvious that traditional Pueblo beliefs still endured beneath a veneer of Catholicism, the Spanish arrested 47 Pueblo religious leaders. Three were condemned as "witchdoctors" and hanged at Santa Fe; the rest were publicly horsewhipped. One of these, a man called **Po'pay** from San Juan Pueblo, made his way to Taos Pueblo and turned one of its *kivas* into the center of a campaign of resistance. A date was set for a concerted uprising against the Spanish, and knotted strings were sent out to all the pueblos, with the instruction to untie one knot each night until the last signaled the arrival of the great day. Somehow, the plot was betrayed, so the **Pueblo Revolt** began a day early, on August 9, 1680.

For the first and only time in their history, the Pueblos of the northern Rio Grande, plus their cousins in Ácoma, Zuni, and the Hopi mesas, combined in unison; they were even joined by the Navajo and the Apache. Their anger fell especially upon the missionaries; 21 out of New Mexico's 33 priests were murdered, as were 375 men, women, and children out of a total of 2350 Spanish colonists.

After a ten-day **siege of Santa Fe**, the governor, the garrison, and one thousand citizens were allowed to retreat south. They were joined en route by the Christianized majority from Isleta Pueblo – the only modern pueblo not to join the attack – and all the Pueblo peoples who lived south of Albuquerque.

For the next thirteen years, the refugees remained together at what's now Ciudad Juarez, across the Rio Grande from El Paso. Those Indians who had joined the exodus founded Ysleta del Sur and other nearby pueblos, while the former colonists, refused permission to continue any further south, awaited an opportunity to return north.

Back in Santa Fe, the doors and windows of the Palace of the Governors had been sealed and the building turned into a multistory pueblo. Po'pay was nominally in control, but the concept of a central political administration was alien to the Pueblos, and the alliance soon fragmented.

In 1692, the Spanish crowned appoint a new governor of New Mexico, **Don Diego de Vargas**. His exploratory expedition encountered no opposition when it returned to Santa Fe that September. He set off again with a party of colonists the following year; this time they had to fight before they could re-enter the city, in December 1693. The return of the Spanish triggered mass migrations throughout the region. Modern Navajo culture originated from the intermingling of the ancestral Navajo with Pueblo refugees during this period. Further minor insurrections followed, but the **Reconquest** was completed by 1696.

The eighteenth century

Although Hispanic settlers continued to dominate the region for 150 years after the Pueblo Revolt, New Mexico was always a peripheral part of the Spanish empire. Separated from the rest of New Spain by vast tracts of empty desert, the colonists were obliged to be self-sufficient, and found themselves thrown into alliance with the Pueblo peoples to resist the threat of Ute and Comanche attack. The Spaniards and the Pueblos had much in common; the New Mexican landscape was similar to that of Andalucia in Spain, as indeed were its adobe hamlets or *pueblos*. The Pueblos had long been subsistence farmers who traded for rare luxuries with far-off civilizations to the south, and the Hispanic ranchers slotted into the same pattern. There was little intermarriage, although Pueblo communities acquired sizeable populations of *genízaros*, the bastard offspring of captured Plains Indians and their Spanish masters.

In the first half of the eighteenth century, the **French** established their own colony to the east, **Louisiana**. The Spanish responded by setting up missions among the Indians of what now became a separate province of New Spain, **Texas**. As the French and Spanish zones of influence expanded, there were armed clashes; thus a combined force of Spaniards and Pueblos was defeated by a French–Pawnee alliance near North Platte, Nebraska, in 1720.

In general, the French coexisted more amicably with Native Americans than did the Spanish; predominantly traders, eager to acquire beaver and other furs, they were less interested in converting Indians to Christianity. Unlike the Spanish, they were also prepared to supply Indians with **guns**. As a result, the Comanche, Ute, and Apache, equipped with European firearms, consistently raided along the Rio Grande at harvest time, seizing crops and livestock, while the Hispanic villagers, inadequately supplied from Mexico, could only offer minimal resistance with their bows and arrows. The colonists financed the occasional retaliatory expedition by selling Indian captives to work as slaves in the silver mines of Mexico, thereby incurring ever greater Indian hostility.

Louisiana having proved no more profitable to France than was New Mexico to Spain, Louis XV of France simply gave it to Spain in 1762. The Mississippi River now formed the Spanish frontier in North America. Determined to resist encroachment by the infant United States, King Carlos III placed the entire region under his direct control from Spain in 1776. However, far too few Hispanic settlers moved in to make any difference, and in 1802, as the Spanish empire weakened, he handed Louisiana back to Napoleon. Carlos' hope that the French would serve as a buffer against the Yankees was misplaced; Napoleon sold his American territories to the US in the following year, in the **Louisiana Purchase**.

At the end of the century, Santa Fe was home to around two thousand Hispanic citizens, while the Pueblo population had dwindled to perhaps nine thousand, in a mere nineteen pueblos.

The settlement of Arizona

Before the Pueblo Revolt, the Spanish presence in New Mexico was confined to the valley of the Rio Grande and the scattered pueblos to the west. Under the names of **Pimería Alta** and **Papaguería**, what's now southern Arizona was left to peoples the Spaniards called the **Pima** and the **Papago**, known today as the **'O'odham**.

Around 1700, however, **Jesuit** missionaries conceived the notion of constructing a chain of missions all the way from New Spain to California, and built churches in a couple of 'O'odham villages. Hispanic ranchers and prospectors also drifted in. In 1736, a Yaqui Indian created a silver-mining camp, a few miles southwest of modern Nogales, called **Arizonac**. The name came either from the 'O'odham *ali shonak*, meaning "small springs," or from the Basque language of Spain, in which *arritza onac* means "valuable rocky places," and *aritz onac* means "good oaks."

After an 'O'odham rebellion killed several Jesuits, the Spanish installed a military *presidio* (fort) at **Tubac** (see p.254) in 1752, relocated forty miles north to San Agustín de **Tucson** in 1776. Another Indian revolt in 1781, in which 150 settlers were wiped out during mass at **Yuma**, dashed Spanish hopes of establishing a permanent trail to California, and Tucson, like Santa Fe, came to be seen as an insignificant dead-end town. In 1804, when around a thousand Spanish colonists lived in the vicinity, its commander reported, "we have no gold, silver, lead, tin, quicksilver, copper mines, or marble quarries ... the only public work here that is truly worthy of this report is the church at **San Xavier del Bac**" (see p.252).

The end of the Hispanic era

The decline in New Mexico's importance to its Spanish rulers was mirrored by increasing contacts with the rest of North America. In the closing years of the eighteenth century, permanent trails were established both west to California – in the form of the **Old Spanish Trail**, painstakingly mapped across Utah by Franciscan friars **Domínguez** and **Escalante** in 1776 – and east to St Louis, along the **Santa Fe Trail** blazed by French explorer Pedro Vial in 1792. After the Louisiana Purchase, official US expeditions also crossed the Plains, such as **Lewis and Clark**'s trek to the Northwest in 1804 and **Lt. Zebulon Pike**'s incursion into New Mexico in 1807.

Within a few years, the Spanish grip on the New World was finally loosened;, Mexico became an independent nation following a **revolution** in 1821. Although their governors swiftly transferred allegiance to Mexico City, neither

New Mexico nor California saw any advantage in their new status as Mexican territories. As the flow of resources from the south – including the handouts that had started to keep the Apache relatively docile – dwindled, the effect on the New Mexican economy was crippling.

For the authorities in Santa Fe, the only answer seemed to be to increase trade with the US. Traffic along the Santa Fe Trail swiftly turned New Mexico into an entrepôt through which American goods were shipped south into Mexico. No Americans were permitted to live in New Mexico, but freebooting Anglos made their way across the Plains to seek their fortunes in the West. Fur-trapping "**mountain men**" such as **Bill Williams** and **Kit Carson** made extended forays along the region's rivers in pursuit of beavers (known as "hairy banknotes"). **Taos** became renowned for its annual rendezvous, at which Anglo, Hispanic, and Native American traders gathered far from the authority of any government. Northern New Mexico was now also beyond the reach of the Catholic Church; devout Hispanics kept their faith alive by forming sects such as the **Penitentes** (see p.157) and established a tradition of religious folk art that endures to this day.

Meanwhile, enough Yankee newcomers had flocked into **Texas** to outnumber its loyal Mexican subjects. In 1836, after Texas fought to gain independence from Mexico and then voted for annexation by the US, the president of Mexico attempted to hold onto New Mexico by closing down the Santa Fe Trail. It was too late. The doctrine that it was the United States' "**Manifest Destiny**" to extend across the whole continent led the US government first to try to **buy** New Mexico and California, and then, when negotiations failed, to declare **war** on Mexico in 1846. American economic might was neatly illustrated when the US Army of the West took Santa Fe without a fight, in August 1846; the Mexican governor was simply paid $50,000 to leave, together with his garrison.

Territorial days: New Mexico and Arizona

Under the **Treaty of Guadalupe–Hidalgo**, signed in September 1847 after US soldiers had captured Mexico City, the United States took formal possession of New Mexico, Texas, and California – seen as the real prize – in return for $18.25 million. New Mexico, which consisted of all those parts of modern New Mexico and Arizona that lie north of the Gila River, plus areas of Nevada and Utah, was generally regarded as an arid, worthless wasteland.

Ironically, only the discovery of **gold** in California in 1847 gave New Mexico any great value to the US – as a route west. Surveyors mapping possible courses for a southern transcontinental railroad soon realized that the best routes lay on the Mexican side of the border. The Mexican government accepted the least extensive of five suggested land deals, and in June 1854, the $10 million **Gadsden Purchase** gave the US what's now southern Arizona, including Tucson, Tubac, and Tumacácori.

Another 25 years passed before the railroad reached the Southwest, but prospectors trekking to and from California soon began to investigate the region more thoroughly. After gold was found near the confluence of the Gila and Colorado rivers, **miners** fanned out across central Arizona, and reports of rich silver and copper lodes lured ever more migrants in.

Feeling little in common with the Hispanic farming communities of the Rio Grande, the new arrivals argued that the territory was too large to govern as a single unit and should be split in two. Many came originally from the South, and seized upon the start of the **Civil War** in 1861 to declare the formation of the Confederate Territory of **Arizona**, consisting of all the Gadsden Purchase lands. Its capital was Mesilla, in what's now New Mexico. The Confederate cause in the Southwest was short-lived: a Confederate army was turned back by Union forces at **Glorieta Pass** – outside Santa Fe, near modern Pecos – in March 1862. The federal government recognized the existence of Arizona in 1863, but to avoid giving it a built-in Confederate majority drew a north–south boundary rather than an east–west one, and thereby delineated the two modern states.

The Indian wars

In the early years of the Civil War, US Army outposts throughout the Southwest were abandoned when the troops were sent east. That spurred a new era of raiding by the **Apache** and **Navajo**, and the Anglo and Hispanic settlements of southern Arizona in particular became depopulated. By late 1861, only two significant non-Native settlements survived in Arizona; two hundred citizens remained in Tucson, while a band of miners held out at Patagonia.

However, the Army soon returned in greater strength than ever, resolved to eradicate the Indian "menace" once and for all. As detailed on p.517 onwards, Brigadier General James Carleton and Kit Carson drove the **Navajo** into exile in New Mexico in 1865 – they were soon back in Arizona, but never again posed a military threat – while a long cycle of treaties, betrayals, and guerrilla campaigns wore down **Apache** resistance by 1886.

Towards statehood

The increasing subjugation of the region's Native American population opened the way for a large-scale influx of Anglo settlers. During the 1860s, ancient Hohokam canals in the Salt River Valley were cleared to irrigate the new city of **Phoenix**, which swiftly became the capital of Arizona. Mining camps in the mountains, such as **Silver City** in New Mexico and **Tombstone** and **Jerome** in Arizona, turned into fully fledged towns, while massive cattle ranches began to spread across the open desert.

At first, the Anglo newcomers were almost exclusively male and married into Hispanic families. Spanish remained the lingua franca, Catholicism the dominant religion, and silver Mexican pesos the common currency. With the coming of the **railroad**, however, around 1880, things began to change, and north–south links were replaced by commerce oriented toward the east and west. The Southwestern economy became increasingly **extractive**, digging up minerals and depleting natural resources for shipment to distant cities. Where Native Americans and Hispanics had farmed for self-sufficiency, the Anglos sought profit. During the 1880s, huge herds of sheep and cattle were introduced to marginal grasslands that swiftly proved incapable of supporting them.

Toward the end of the nineteenth century, tensions pitted both the large-scale mining and cattle-raising concerns, backed by wealthy eastern corporations and the federal government, against individual prospectors and cowboys. These swiftly became so acute, and so recurrent, that some historians speak of a **Western Civil War of Incorporation**. Many legendary Wild West incidents, like the **Gunfight at the OK Corral** in Tombstone, Arizona (see p.261) and the **Lincoln County War** in New Mexico, which brought Billy the Kid into the public eye (see p.196), stemmed more from behind-the-scenes political maneuvering than from the whims of trigger-happy outlaws.

Besides luring cowboys, miners, and other adventurers to the Southwest, the railroads also created new industries. Communities like Flagstaff and Williams sprang up to exploit the vast ponderosa forests of northern Arizona, while the increased accessibility of the Grand Canyon, publicized by the voyages of John Wesley Powell (see p.433), meant that the first **tourists** began to arrive.

Meanwhile, in New Mexico, Hispanic villagers looked on helplessly as their lands were parceled out to newly arrived Anglo ranchers. New Mexicans had traditionally owned small plots for individual use and shared grazing lands in common, but American courts refused to recognize communal land rights.

To a considerable degree, it was anti-Hispanic Anglo racism that delayed **statehood** for both Arizona and New Mexico. For many years, Republicans in Washington clung to the idea that they should be reunited and admitted as a single state, in the hope that Arizona's larger Anglo population would help to "temper" the Hispanic majority in New Mexico. Arizonans overwhelmingly defeated that proposal in a referendum in 1906 (which passed in New Mexico), and both were finally admitted in 1912 – **New Mexico** in January as the **47th state**, **Arizona** in February as the **48th**, the last of what are now known as the "**Lower 48**."

Utah in the nineteenth century

Until the nineteenth century, the history of what's now the state of Utah forms a minor adjunct to the story of the Southwest as a whole. Its main Ancestral Puebloan groups, the Virgin and the more nomadic Fremont peoples, abandoned southern Utah around the same time their Four Corners brethren moved away. By the time Spanish explorers such as Domínguez and Escalante began to pass through, in search of a route to California, it was the domain of Ute and Paiute Indians. Twelve to thirty thousand of them were present in 1850; most had traditionally been farmers, but they had recently acquired horses and were starting to raid travelers on the newly created Old Spanish Trail, which linked Santa Fe to Los Angeles.

The reports of men like the fur trapper **Jedediah Smith**, who named the Virgin River, and **John C. Frémont**, who mapped much of southwest Utah in the early 1840s, attracted the region's first permanent white settlers. By far the most important of these were the massed ranks of the Church of Jesus Christ of Latter-Day Saints, known to the outside world as the **Mormons**.

The Mormons

The Mormon church was founded by **Joseph Smith**, who was born to a family of itinerant farmers in Sharon, Vermont, on December 23, 1805. Smith was a farmhand in Palmyra, western New York, when he had his first vision of the **Angel Moroni** in 1823. On his third annual visit, Moroni led him to a set of golden plates hidden in a nearby hillside. Only Smith was ever to see them; concealed behind a curtain in his house, he translated them from the "reformed Egyptian" with the aid of two mysterious devices (the Urim and the Thummim), and thus dictated the *Book of Mormon*. Harshly described by Mark Twain as "chloroform in print," this revealed that two Israelite families fled Jerusalem around 600 BC, and sailed east from the Red Sea to the "Promised Land," led by a man named Lehi. His sons later quarreled; Nephi remained loyal and was rewarded by a visit from the risen Christ, while Laman and Lemuel led the dissident, cursed Lamanites, the ancestors of the Native Americans. After a thousand years of conflict, the Lamanites finally defeated the Nephites in a great battle at the hill of Cumorah. The one Nephite survivor – Moroni, son of Mormon – buried the plates close by.

Smith proclaimed his new church on April 6, 1830. He was not unique among contemporary frontier prophets in attracting thousands of followers. His vision of an ordered, communalistic society – clearly rooted in the economic uncertainty of his own life – struck a deep chord with his peers. To their unconverted "**Gentile**" neighbors, on the other hand, leadership by divine revelation smacked of Catholicism, and the Mormons were suspected of owing their loyalty to their church not their country. Their most controversial trait was **polygamy**, or "celestial marriage." Smith denied this to outsiders, pointing to a passage in the *Book Of Mormon* that called polygamy "abominable." In private, however, he declared his disciples to have a sacred duty to marry and produce children, thereby freeing disembodied spirits from limbo by giving them bodily form. Preaching the salvation of the dead, which said that the dead could be baptized by proxy, he argued that Mormon marriage was different to the "until death do us part" Christian sacrament. Church elders had a duty to establish polygamous, patriarchal families that would endure into the afterlife. Smith also became a Mason, and many of his church's rituals were inspired by Masonic practices.

In the face of constant harassment, Smith moved his family to Kirtland, **Ohio** – where they built their first temple – and then on to **Missouri** in 1838. After bloody clashes between slave-holding Gentiles and the Mormon militia, the Sons of Dan, he was captured and sentenced to death, then allowed to escape by sympathetic guards. The Mormons were next given sanctuary by the governor of **Illinois**, who saw them as hard-working potential citizens, and their new settlement of **Nauvoo** swiftly became the largest city in that state, with a population of 25,000.

In 1844, when Joseph Smith announced that he was running for president, the Latter-Day Saints were being attacked not only by their neighbors but also from within. When a group of anti-polygamy dissenters attempted to establish a rival church in Nauvoo and set up their own newspaper, Smith ordered that its presses be destroyed. Together with his brother Hyrum, Smith was arrested and imprisoned in nearby Carthage. A "blackface" mob attacked the jail, and both men were shot.

It was widely assumed that the Mormon Church would disintegrate after Smith's death. However, although one of his sons decamped to Missouri with his own monogamous splinter group, Smith's successor, **Brigham Young**, held the flock together. Young, who was also of Puritan Vermont stock, promised the governor of Illinois in 1845 that the Mormons would abandon Nauvoo, and set about organizing a mass **westward migration**. In the winter of 1846, ten thousand Saints camped near modern Omaha, Nebraska, while Young scouted ahead. Descending the western flank of the Rockies, he declared "This is the place," and in 1847 his followers founded **Salt Lake City**.

At that time, the all but empty wilderness claimed by the Mormons as **Deseret** (a Mormon word meaning "honeybee," to denote industry), or the **Great Basin Kingdom**, still belonged to Mexico. As well as what's now Utah, its putative boundaries included almost all of modern Nevada, most of Arizona and southern California, and sizeable chunks of four other present-day states. Mormon dreams of establishing an independent theocracy, outside the United States, were dashed within a year, when the US government annexed the entire region and the Gold Rush wagon trains began to roll west. The Saints therefore petitioned Congress for Deseret to be granted statehood. Suspicious of its religious underpinnings, Congress instead recognized a smaller area as the **Territory of Utah** in 1850, and appointed Brigham Young as its first governor.

The Mormons embarked on a massive communal effort to irrigate the desert. They were joined over the next decade by thousands more converts recruited by missionaries throughout America and Europe, to reach a total by 1860 of over fifty thousand. Fifteen thousand arrived from England alone, of whom three thousand literally walked across America, pushing their belongings in handcarts ahead of them.

During the 1850s, and especially once Young, who felt no further need for diplomacy, had publicly acknowledged the existence of polygamy in 1852, the federal government came to see the Mormons as a significant threat to the Union. The newly formed Republican party railed against slavery and polygamy in equal measure, as "twin relics of barbarism." Congress decided to appoint a new non-Mormon governor of Utah, and sent him west with a detachment of 2500 soldiers, representing one-sixth of the US army. Salt Lake City was temporarily abandoned, but thanks to the secession of the Confederacy, the anticipated Mormon War never quite happened.

When the **Civil War** in the East cut off supplies of commodities such as cotton, Brigham Young redoubled his commitment to making the Mormons **self-sufficient**. Pioneer parties created "missions" throughout the Southwest, but while many of the small farming communities they established still survive – including **Cedar City** and **St George** in southern Utah – they did little to diminish Utah's economic interdependence with the rest of the US. The advent of the railroads and the arrival in Utah of ever-increasing numbers of non-Mormons – especially miners – exacerbated the situation.

As the Mormons set out to "tame" the wilderness, the **Ute** fought back. Reciprocal raids by Utes and whites escalated into the **Black Hawk War**, waged between 1865 and 1867, following which the Utes were finally confined to reservations in the territory that by now bore their name. In an eerie postscript, the dying Ute leader, Black Hawk, insisted on touring all the towns affected by the war, to apologize in person. With Indian resistance broken, the Mormons spread throughout southern Utah. The "**Hole in the Rock**" party (see p.406), for example, trekked across the central deserts in the winter of 1879–80 to establish **Bluff** in the east. Little now survives from simultaneous Mormon attempts to settle in **northern Arizona**, apart from a few tiny settlements along the **Arizona** Strip (see p.360).

Meanwhile the federal authorities renewed their attacks on polygamy. The **Morrill Anti-Bigamy Act** of 1862, which was upheld by the Supreme Court in 1878, subjected polygamists to disenfranchisement and the confiscation of their property. Utah retaliated by giving women the vote, so Mormon women could consolidate the Church's hold on State power; the **Edmonds–Tucker Act** of 1887 hit back, dissolving the Church and confiscating its assets, and once more disenfranchising women.

After Brigham Young died in 1877, the new Mormon leaders sensed that they'd do better to drop polygamy on their own terms before being forced to do so. Polygamy was therefore formally renounced in 1890 – although a few thousand dissidents still practice it to this day – clearing the way for Utah to become a **state** in **1896**. Mormons were now encouraged to participate in national politics; church authorities even suggested that half should become Democrats and half Republicans.

The modern Southwest

Arizona, New Mexico, and Utah spent most of their first century of statehood battling to secure ever greater quantities of **water**. In the early years, the main objective was to prevent California from grabbing the lion's share of the flow of the Colorado River. Later on, cities like Phoenix fought for federal funds to build grandiose water-diversion schemes. The political machinations behind the construction of the **Hoover Dam** in the 1930s, and the damming of **Glen Canyon** in the 1960s, are chronicled on p.422. Suffice it here to say that with the completion of the **Central Arizona Project** in 1991, John Wesley Powell's nineteenth-century prediction that "All the waters of all the arid lands will eventually be taken from their natural channels" has now all but come true.

While New Mexico at the start of the twentieth century remained as a cluster of farming towns along the Rio Grande Valley – Arizona was prospering on the large-scale exploitation of its mineral wealth. **World War I** saw copper prices leap, and in alliance with state politicians mine-owners easily quashed labor disputes. Arizonan employers could also take cynical advantage of the vast pool of potential workers just across the border to the south. After the Wall Street Crash of 1929, for example – by which time the state was responsible for half of all US copper production – over 500,000 Mexican laborers, now surplus to requirements, were deported.

Though the **Depression** hit hard across the Southwest, the region also benefited from a massive injection of federal cash, in the form of make-work public projects such as dam- and road-building. **World War II** not only renewed demand for copper and other metals but kick-started **urbanization** throughout the Southwest. Partly to make them less vulnerable to attack, defense installations were relocated away from the coasts, presenting **Albuquerque** and **Phoenix** in particular with their first major industrial plants, as well as greatly increased numbers of consumers. A former school in **Los Alamos**, New Mexico, was transformed into the laboratory that developed the atomic bomb – hence, some say, the alien crash-landing at **Roswell** in 1947 (see p.204).

After the war, the defense and other industries stayed on, and the ensuing period of mass migration to the Southwest resulted in an extraordinary population boom. Arizona and New Mexico were home to around 500,000 people each in 1940; Arizona's population has now topped six million, with half that number in the metropolitan Phoenix area alone, while New Mexico is fast approaching two million. Even more striking is the fact that whereas at the start of the twentieth century, Arizona was 84 percent rural, by the end of the century around 90 percent of the population were city-dwellers. **Las Vegas**, Nevada, did not even exist until 1905; it now boasts well over a million inhabitants.

Meanwhile, **southern Utah** has remained sparsely inhabited. Attempts at large-scale ranching in the late 1800s resulted in destructive overgrazing, and the region relied on subsistence farming until the discovery of **uranium** in 1952 (see p.453) triggered a **mining bonanza** that sent prospectors scurrying into every nook and cranny of the wilderness. Local Mormon businessmen of southern Utah lobbied hard for mine and dam projects in the face of growing environmental opposition. Calling themselves the **"Sagebrush Rebels,"** they attracted support from then-President Ronald Reagan, but were ultimately defeated as much by the realities of world commodity markets as by the "tree-huggers" they despised. Since the collapse of mining in the early 1980s, **tourism** has finally been appreciated as a major industry, and towns like **Moab** have developed facilities for travelers smitten by the lure of the desert.

The Hopi

N owhere in the Southwest is the continuity between the pre-Hispanic past and the present more apparent than on the three Hopi mesas, on the southern edge of Arizona's Black Mesa. The Hopi have lived here for at least one thousand years, preserving their culture despite repeated incursions from outsiders, and their history is sufficiently distinct to be worth relating as a separate narrative.

For a guide to visiting the Hopi mesas today, and an account of the *kachina* religion, see p.77.

The origin of the Hopi

According to Hopi mythology, this, the **Fourth World**, is inhabited by the righteous people who escaped the destruction of the Third World by climbing a reed through the dome of the sky. They emerged in the depths of the Grand Canyon, through a hole beside the Little Colorado River known as the *sipapu*. There they were greeted by the terrifying but kindly disposed deity **Maasaw**, who explained the rules of life in this world and despatched them on migratory journeys to the four points of the compass. Their wanderings ended with a return to the **Sacred Circle** and the establishment of the villages on what are now the Hopi mesas.

Both myth and history depict the Hopi as a peripatetic people who became ever more sedentary as they learned agriculture and pottery. Archeologists and Hopi alike recognize a cultural continuity between the Hopi and the ancient peoples of the Southwest. There's no doubt that the earliest occupants of the Hopi mesas migrated here from nearby Kayenta **Anasazi** and Sinagua settlements, but whether they had previously wandered further afield – most obviously, into central America, where the language and beliefs of the **Aztecs** show clear parallels to the Hopi – remains unproven.

Though the Hopi mesas were probably inhabited by around 700 AD, what the Hopi describe as the "**gathering of the clans**" reached its peak between 1100 AD and 1300 AD, and thus coincided with the abandonment of the most famous Ancestral Puebloan sites. One by one, small groups of refugees arrived at the mesas and petitioned for land and the right to settle. Each was required to demonstrate what it could offer those already there, with the crucial factor being the ceremonial power to produce rain. Once allowed to stay, each group – most were probably no more than individual families – was regarded as a separate **clan**.

The Bear clan, said to have come from Mesa Verde, was the first to arrive – which is why it retains precedence to this day – and established the Second Mesa's "mother village," at the foot of the mesa. Originally called Maseeba, this village changed its name to **Shungopavi** when it relocated to the mesa-top several centuries later. Similarly, **Walpi** on First Mesa, when founded by the Snake clan from Hovenweep, stood several hundred yards below its present, highly defensible mesa-top site. **Oraibi**, the "mother village" of Third Mesa, is generally regarded as the oldest Hopi village because it has occupied the same spot since its foundation; beams have been dated to 1260 AD, but some dwellings may be a century or more older.

By 1275 AD, the three mesas held 35 villages. The Fire, Water, and Coyote clans had come from the cliff dwellings of Keet Seel and Betatakin, now in Navajo National Monument; the Flute clan from Canyon de Chelly; the Rabbit clan from the south, perhaps Casas Grandes in Mexico; and others had streamed in from Chaco Canyon and the Sinagua sites of Wupatki and Walnut Canyon. While each village remained autonomous, this disparate community forged a common culture, adopting its own variation of the **kachina** religion as it spread throughout the Southwest (see p.78).

The coming of the Spaniards

Hopi prophecies have long predicted the return of *Pahaana*, the "True White Brother" separated from the Hopi at an early stage of their migrations. Assuming that he finds the Hopi living in purity and righteousness, he will help solve any problems they face and lead them into the Fifth World.

If the Hopi saw *Pahaana* in the first **Spanish** explorers to reach the mesas, their illusions were soon shattered. A detachment of Coronado's expedition led by Lieutenant Pedro de Tovar (see p.500) arrived in 1540. Exactly what happened is uncertain. Alerted by the Zuni, the Hopi greeted the party in the fields, signaling them not to cross a line of sacred cornmeal sprinkled on the earth. According to the official Spanish report, a Franciscan friar, exasperated by the rigmarole, commented, "To tell the truth, I do not know why we came here" – and that was enough to trigger a Spanish onslaught. By the next sentence, the two sides are at peace, and Hopi guides went on to lead a group of Spaniards to the Grand Canyon (see p.321).

During that and subsequent sixteenth-century Spanish incursions, the Hopi took care to make their lands – which the Spanish called **Tusayan** – appear valueless. As a result, the Spanish never bothered to leave either a garrison or any settlers. Franciscan **missionaries** did, however, return in 1629 to build churches in Awatovi, Shungopavi, and Oraibi. The one at Awatovi was on a similar scale to the mission that still survives at Ácoma (see p.110) and required a similar amount of forced Indian labor; others involved the filling-in and "rededication" of existing *kivas*. The missionaries also introduced sheep and cattle, so the Hopi were the first people to raise livestock in Arizona.

The Hopi were enthusiastic participants in the **Pueblo Revolt** of 1680, sacking the churches and killing four priests. Fearing a Spanish return, they welcomed Tewa-speaking Pueblo refugees from the Rio Grande, who founded the First Mesa village of Hano. By now, the **Navajo** – whom the Hopi called *Tasavuh* or "head pounders," as they were said to bash in their captives' skulls with a rock – had entered the picture. They too joined the Pueblo Revolt, but were also starting to crowd the Hopi away from their summer farming and grazing lands, and to raid for animals. During this unsettled period, the villages of Walpi, Shungopavi, and Mishongnovi moved to fortified positions on the mesa tops.

After the Spanish reconquered New Mexico, those Hopi who still regarded themselves as Christians gathered in **Awatovi**. When the other Hopi villages realized the people of Awatovi were willing to invite the missionaries back to stay, they determined to eradicate the Christian menace once and for all. At the end of 1700, the men of Awatovi were betrayed by their headman, who called a predawn meeting in the *kiva*. Warriors from all the other villages pulled up the ladder, rained arrows down on the trapped men, and then set light to the *kiva*; surviving women and children were shared out as booty.

That savage act probably spared the Hopi both internal dissent and missionary interference for the rest of the Spanish and Mexican era. The mesas were, however, increasingly beleaguered by mounted Navajo and Ute war parties and slave raiders from the south.

The Hopi under the United States

By the time the Southwest was acquired by the United States, during the 1840s (see p.505), the Hopi were desperate for protection from the marauding Navajo. Hopi scouts eagerly participated in General Carleton's 1864 round-up which forced the Navajo on the Long Walk to Bosque Redondo (see p.517).

Within a few years, the Navajo were back, reasserting control over their former territory and raiding to replenish their herds. Called to define who "owned" what land, the US government was inadequate to the task. The very concept of a "tribe" was a federal invention; neither Navajo nor Hopi recognized any authority above clan or village level. Moreover, the idea of a reservation only worked if one group or other had exclusive use of an area. Only villages and fields counted as the "possession" of land; hunting grounds were regarded as unoccupied. Because the San Francisco Peaks are sacred to, and used by, both the Navajo and the Hopi, they belong to neither.

The **Moqui Indian reservation**, established in 1882 as a rectangle measuring 70 by 55 miles, did not even include all the Hopi villages. The hundred Hopi at Moenkopi were excluded, while three hundred Navajo lived within the boundaries. As was standard, the decree creating the reservation states that it was intended not only for the Hopi but for "such other Indians as the Secretary of the Interior shall settle thereon." The resultant disputes have simmered ever since.

Outsiders now appeared on the mesas in ever-increasing numbers. Mormon and Mennonite **missionaries** came and went, and **anthropologists** stuck their oars in; Jesse Walter Fewkes called the Hopi "the most primitive aborigines of the United States" in 1891. **Tourists** too came by bus and railroad, with two-thousand-plus turning up for the annual Snake Dances. Century-old images of Hopi ceremonies make it clear why photography was soon barred altogether; crowds and cumbersome equipment made it all but impossible to move. Above all, the federal agents of the **Bureau of Indian Affairs** caused the most grief, ordering haircuts for all Hopi men, for whom long hair is a sign of initiation, and kidnapping Hopi children to attend distant boarding schools, from 1887 onwards. Nineteen elders who protested against compulsory Christian education were imprisoned on Alcatraz in 1894.

The modern era

At the start of the twentieth century, the Hopi were divided between what outsiders perceived as the "**Friendlies**," who if not well disposed toward the federal government at least felt resistance was futile, and the "**Hostiles**," who sought to defend and preserve the old ways. Their differences in fact stemmed largely from tensions between clans, and a breakdown in the allocation of resources and land. The split became explicit at **Oraibi**, where the two factions declared themselves unable to coexist any longer. On September 8, 1906, each lined up behind its leader, with each man's hands on the shoulders of the next, for a "pushing contest." Literally pushed out, the "Hostiles" established their own village of **Hotevilla** nearby.

The dispute at Oraibi politicized the role of each village's ceremonial priest, known as the **kikmongwi**. When the Hopi were obliged to adopt a Tribal Constitution in 1936, the *kikmongwis* were automatically appointed as governors of their village. Part of their function was to endorse members elected to the new **Hopi Tribal Council**. Ever since then, however, many *kikmongwis* have refused to recognize the authority of the tribal council and aligned themselves instead with the **Traditionalists**, the heirs of the "Hostiles."

Paradoxically, the Traditionalists, who regard themselves as the guardians of all that is truly Hopi (and speak of their opponents as the *pensilhoyam*, or "little pencil people"), have raised awareness of the Hopi throughout the world. Rather than waiting for their savior brother figure *Pahaana* to appear, they have embarked on a search for him. The movement started immediately after World War II, when certain Hopi elders announced that following the use of the atomic bomb it was time to reveal teachings and prophecies that were supposed to remain secret until "a gourd of ashes fell from the sky." Since 1948, the Traditionalists have written to every US president, and addressed the United Nations, with a message stressing Hopi sovereignty and religious integrity and the importance of respecting the environment. Among their successes was the recognition of Hopi religion as a "peace religion," which excluded Hopi from military service.

In practical terms, the Traditionalist movement has been a focus for opposition to **mineral leasing**. After the Hopi Constitution's definition of the role of the tribal council as being to *prevent* leasing was illegally overruled by the Secretary of the Interior in 1961, strip mining by the Peabody Company devastated much of Black Mesa (see p.64). Almost all the income the leases earned during the 1960s was invested in an unsuccessful bra factory near Winslow. In the 1980s, the leases were renegotiated on much more favorable terms, including environmental stipulations, and mining became more acceptable to many Hopi. However, Traditionalists resistant to becoming dependent on external agencies, continued to strive through the courts to have the mines closed down, and although they didn't succeed, Black Mesa Mine did indeed cease operations in 2006 (see p.64).

Meanwhile, the **Navajo–Hopi land dispute** has raged on. By 1958, the Navajo living on Hopi lands outnumbered the Hopi by more than two to one, and the Navajo reservation had completely surrounded the Hopi mesas. Much of the impetus to resolve the problem came from the federal authorities and the mineral companies, who could not start mining until definite title to the land was established. Public sympathies, and court rulings, swayed back and forth for decades. A **Joint Use Area** was established in 1958, to be shared equally between the Hopi and the Navajo, but it soon became evident that 98 percent of it was being used by the Navajo alone. In the 1970s, therefore, separate Hopi and Navajo **Partitioned Lands** were defined, stipulating that Hopi living on the Navajo side of the line relocate, and vice versa. More Navajo than Hopi were affected, and the plight of the **Big Mountain** Navajo in particular, who were given five years to move in 1981, made them a national *cause célèbre*.

The most recent solution, the **Navajo–Hopi Land Dispute Settlement Act**, was authored by John McCain and signed by then President Clinton in 1996. It allowed Navajo residents of Hopi land to sign 75-year leases, after which ownership will revert to the Hopi. Dissident Navajo argue that the problem has simply been postponed for another generation.

The Navajo and the Apache

The best-known Native American peoples in the Southwest – mainly on account of their fierce resistance against the US Army in the nineteenth century – are the **Navajo** and the **Apache**. Both are now largely concentrated in Arizona, though both also occupy parts of New Mexico, and the Navajo Nation extends into southern Utah. They are also relative newcomers, having moved into their current territories – with just as devastating an impact – around the time that the Spaniards arrived.

Although the Navajo and the Apache are now distinct peoples, their languages are, with patience, mutually comprehensible, and their paths only diverged within the last five hundred years. Both are descended from **Athabascan** peoples, whose Asian ancestors crossed into Alaska seven or eight thousand years ago, long after the New World's first migrants. Other Athabascans remained in the north, becoming the **Dene** peoples of Alaska and northwest Canada, and the **Na** of the northwest US, who included the Haid and Tlingit. At some point, however, the ancestral Navajo and Apache migrated south, hauling their possessions on dog-sleds as they pursued bison down the eastern flanks of the Rockies.

Estimates of when they reached the Southwest – somewhere on the edge of the Plains, east of the Rio Grande range from 575 to 1525 AD, with the most likely date being 1250 to 1300 AD. Like nomads the world over, they traded the fruits of their hunting and gathering, especially buffalo hides, for the agricultural produce of more settled communities like the Rio Grande pueblos. Chroniclers traveling with Coronado in 1540 (see p.500), drew no distinction between the Navajo and the Apache, referring to both as *Querecho*. However, by the time the Spanish returned at the end of the century, the Navajo, who called themselves the *Diné*, had separated from the Apache, or *Ndee*.

The Navajo

It used to be thought that it was the arrival of the warlike Navajo in the Four Corners that forced the Ancestral Puebloans to leave at the end of the thirteenth century (see p.497). In fact, however, the Navajo only moved west to occupy the now-empty San Juan Basin well after the Ancestral Puebloans had gone. Some even suggest that the Ancestral Puebloans ejected the Navajo, arguing that when the inhabitants of Chaco Canyon and Mesa Verde headed east to establish pueblos along the Rio Grande, they displaced the ancestors of today's Navajo from their riverside homes.

During the late sixteenth century, a region centered on Largo Canyon, east of modern Farmington – still the core of Navajo territory – became known as the **Dinétah**, meaning "Among the People." The *Diné* defined their new realm as lying between four **sacred mountains**: Blanca Peak, or *Sis Naajini*, away to the east in Colorado; Hesperus Peak (*Dibé Nitsaa*), also in Colorado but to the north, near modern Durango; Mount Taylor (*Tsoodzil*), further south in New Mexico; and the San Francisco Peaks (*Dook'o'ooslííd*) near what is now Flagstaff, Arizona. Legends grew up detailing how First Man and First Woman lived near **Huerfano Mountain**. They found a baby on **Gobernador Knob** whom they named Changing Woman, who in turn gave birth to the Navajo Twins, Monster Slayer and Child Born for Water.

The Lords of the World

By the 1580s, the Navajo were impinging upon the pueblos of Ácoma, Zuni, and Hopi. Their expansion was given a huge boost when a permanent Spanish presence enabled them to acquire **horses**. From 1606 onwards, the Navajo embarked on a cycle of raiding Hispanic and Pueblo settlements along the Rio Grande, seizing livestock, new crops, and metal wares. In the Tewa language, spoken in many pueblos, *apache* means "strangers" or "enemies," and *nabaj* means "big planted fields." The first Spanish mention of the "**Apaches de Nabajú**" appeared in 1626, and the name was soon truncated to "Navajo."

The Navajo and Pueblo peoples were not always at war, however. Some Navajo joined the 1680 **Pueblo Revolt** (see p.502), which briefly expelled the Spanish from the Southwest. When the Spanish reconquered the region a dozen years later, many Pueblo peoples escaped their revenge by retreating to live with the Navajo. As detailed on p.101, modern Navajo culture, a hybrid of Athabascan and Pueblo elements, was forged in the remote "**Pueblitos of Dinétah**," in Largo and Gobernador canyons.

While any explicit Pueblo-Navajo alliance soon foundered, the Navajo had by the eighteenth century acquired such Pueblo skills as pottery and weaving, as well as Pueblo-influenced social and religious structures. Obtaining horses vastly increased their mobility, while their large flocks of **sheep** enabled them to live well on what had previously been marginal lands. They therefore expanded westwards to cover a much greater area, occupying most of northeast Arizona and encircling the Hopi.

To contemporary Spaniards, the Navajo were **Los Dueños del Mundo**, the "Lords of the World" – feared horsemen with a solid economic base in their own lands who still plundered the pueblos at will. For most of the eighteenth century, however, the Navajo and the Hispanic settlers of New Mexico were nominally at peace, united in resisting incursions by the **Utes** and **Comanches** of the north. Then the Navajo realized that the Spanish were tacitly encouraging **Ute** and **Comanche** raiders, and buying their Navajo captives as slaves. After 1786, when the Spanish signed a formal treaty with the Comanche, they were at constant war with the Navajo.

With conversion to Christianity as an excuse, Navajo women and children were shipped into slavery in Mexico; the Navajo replenished their numbers by carrying off Pueblo villagers. Certain mission settlements had to be abandoned in the face of Navajo attacks. By and large, the Navajo heartlands remained impregnable, although **Lieutenant Narbona**'s party of 1805 penetrated the Canyon de Chelly and massacred over a hundred Navajo (see p.70).

War with the United States

Mexican independence in 1821 did nothing to diminish the conflict, and the Navajo and the Hispanic settlers of New Mexico were still at loggerheads when the US Army took control of the Southwest in 1846. To Navajo amazement, the American invaders expected them to make peace with their old enemies, on the basis that the New Mexicans were now themselves considered to be Americans.

A major factor in the American failure to sign and keep treaties with the Navajo was the fact that the Navajo were not a single homogenous group. They did not have "chiefs", let alone a single paramount chief. No Navajo could speak for much more than his immediate family, or felt bound by a pact signed by another without his knowledge or consent. Even so, the Navajo remained broadly at peace with the Americans until a widely respected elder – who, confusingly, had taken the name **Narbona** – was murdered and scalped by US soldiers, under a flag of truce, in 1849. For the next fifteen years, Narbona's son-in-law, **Manuelito**, fought a running war with the US cavalry. New Mexican slave raiders, meanwhile, continued to steal Navajo children.

In 1863, **General James Carleton** resolved that the Navajo should be removed from their lands altogether, partly so that they might "become an agricultural people and cease to be nomads" and partly to allow New Mexicans to expand beyond the Rio Grande valley and seize whatever agricultural and mineral wealth the *Dinétah* might hold. A scorched-earth campaign led by veteran scout **Kit Carson** culminated in 1864 with the destruction of the *hogans*, fields, and peach orchards of Canyon de Chelly. As the starving Navajo surrendered, they were sent to "Fair Carletonia," the **Bosque Redondo reservation** at Fort Sumner in eastern New Mexico (see p.194).

Nine thousand Navajo made the **Long Walk** of 370 miles to Bosque Redondo, where three thousand of them died. The reservation was utterly unsuitable for agriculture; far from being self-supporting, it became a burden on the federal government. Carleton was dismissed, and in 1868, after four years, twelve Navajo leaders – including **Barboncito**, who pleaded "I hope to God you will not ask me to go to any other country except my own" – signed a treaty that allowed them to return home.

The Navajo Nation

By treating the Navajo as an independent people, the 1868 treaty (or "Old Paper") formed the basis of the Navajo Indian reservation – which the Navajo call the **Navajo Nation** – as it endures to this day. The original reservation of 1868 was, however, just a small rectangle of northeast Arizona and northwest New Mexico, which included Canyon de Chelly and Shiprock but not Window Rock. Here the survivors of Fort Sumner rejoined those Navajo who had evaded capture in the backcountry; some had hidden near **Navajo Mountain**, and now regarded it too as a sacred peak.

During the twentieth century, the Navajo **population** grew at a phenomenal rate, from 20,000 in 1900 to approaching 350,000 today. Similarly, the reservation expanded from six thousand to 27,000 square miles. A formal Navajo **government** was only established in 1923, when the major oil companies needed

Navajo clans

The basis of Navajo society and family life is the **clan** system. Each Navajo child is born "to" its mother's clan, and born "for" its father's clan. Navajo identify themselves to each other by the clans of their parents, and no one is supposed to marry a member of either their mother's or father's clan. Traditionally, all clan members were responsible for each other's crimes or debts.

Originally, there were just four clans, each descended from one of the four pairs of men and women created in the west by Changing Woman. There are now more like sixty, with each new clan having arisen when a woman from another tribe, or another place, has married into the Navajo. While certain clan names identify the descendants of Zuni, Mescalero, Mexican, Ute, and Jemez newcomers, most hark back to specific locations on the reservation, mythical incidents, or other attributes – the Turning Mountain Clan, Salt Clan, the People That Have Fits Clan, the Rock-Extends-into-Water Clan, and so on.

someone who could sign leases allowing them to exploit the reservation's newly discovered oil reserves. The **chapter** system of local administration was set up soon afterwards, and Window Rock became tribal headquarters in 1927.

The most traumatic event of the twentieth century was the 1933 **stock reduction**, when the federal authorities killed off a million sheep and goats and reduced the total Navajo herd to half a million animals. They argued that overgrazing was washing silt into the Colorado that threatened the new Hoover Dam; the effect was to force a change away from pastoralism toward wage labor.

Since World War II, the Navajo Nation has continued to modernize, acquiring its first paved road in 1947 and the first college ever built on an Indian reservation, Tsaile's Navajo Community College, in 1969. While many families still manage to live a traditional Navajo lifestyle, the exploitation of **mineral** resources has brought the greatest change. Mines and generating stations have appeared across the region, often just outside the reservation but still dependent on Indian labor. Many projects have been deeply controversial. The **Four Corners plant** near Farmington has been described as the single worst source of pollution in the US, while the Peabody Company's strip-mining of **Black Mesa** to feed the **Navajo Generating Station** at Page is widely regarded as an environmental tragedy. In 1979, **Church Rock**, northeast of Gallup, was the scene of the worst contamination in US nuclear history, when a dam burst at the United Nuclear Corporation mill released almost a hundred million gallons of radioactive water and a thousand tons of radioactive mud.

In 1975, Tribal Chairman **Peter MacDonald** (subsequently jailed for corruption) helped set up the Council of Energy Resource Tribes, which he described as a "domestic OPEC." While the mineral leases of the 1950s and 1960s paid pitifully low returns, more lucrative agreements have now strengthened the Navajo economy. Navajo opposition to the principle of mineral exploitation has also grown however, as its long-term effects become apparent. Many feel that the long-running **Navajo–Hopi land dispute** (see p.514) has been manipulated by federal politicians and mineral companies for their own ends.

The Apache

Around 1600 AD, as the Navajo began to incorporate Pueblo elements and become an entirely distinct people, the **Apache** fragmented into several separate groups. The **Western** Apache occupied the mountains of central Arizona; the **Jicarilla**, regions of northwest New Mexico between the Chama Valley and the Four Corners; and the **Lipan** moved east onto the plains of west Texas. At the same time, in southern New Mexico, the **Mescalero** started to range east of the Rio Grande, while the **Chiricahua** spread west as far as what's now southern Arizona.

These groups were not the "tribes" outsiders like to imagine. Apache lived in nomadic, clan-based societies of between thirty and two hundred people, each with its own "chief." A chief's primary responsibility was to ensure his band got enough food; his authority collapsed in the event of failure. Most groups raised a few seasonal crops, but supported themselves above all by **raiding**, not only against settled Pueblo communities, but against the Navajo, and even each other.

The coming of the Spaniards gave the Apache **horses** for the first time. At first, they stole them solely to eat, but once they learned to ride they swiftly adapted to a calendar of raiding the Rio Grande villages at harvest time, while allowing them to continue unmolested for the rest of the year. It was beneath

Apache dignity even to breed their own horses, let alone sheep like the Navajo; they simply stole livestock as they needed it.

The colonists of New Mexico, who remained confined throughout Spanish and Mexican rule to a fragile ribbon of riverside land, called the huge Apache-dominated territories that surrounded them **Apachería**. Since the Apache never united to engage in formal warfare – no Apache war party in history exceeded two hundred warriors – it was impossible to take concerted action against them. In the first half of the eighteenth century, the Apache were nonetheless forced to consolidate into smaller and more mountainous areas, as the even more aggressive mounted **Comanche** warriors swept in across the Plains with ever-increasing regularity.

Later in the eighteenth century, the Spaniards managed to pacify the Apache by establishing *presidios* or forts that supplied them with food, alcohol, and even guns that were adequate for hunting but not war. When Mexico became independent, however, in 1821, the new administration could no longer afford such subsidies. Instead it placed a bounty of $100 on each Apache scalp – male or female, young or old – brought into the *presidios*.

The Apache Wars

To the US government, which took over New Mexico in the 1840s, the Apache way of life was anathema. As a group of Mescalero Apache acknowledged to a US Army quartermaster in 1850, "We must steal from somebody … if you will not permit us to rob the Mexicans, we must steal from you or fight you." In total, the Southwest held between six and eight thousand Apache. By far the strongest resistance came from a group of just over a thousand, the **Chiricahua**, led by a chief known as **Cochise**, meaning "Oak."

Conflict between the US Army and the Apache flared into war in 1861, when Cochise agreed to meet Lt. George Bascom in southeast Arizona, and found himself falsely accused of kidnapping a child. Although Cochise managed to escape into the Dragoon Mountains, his brother and two nephews were hanged. Cochise then rampaged across Arizona, killing miners, prospectors, stagecoach passengers, and soldiers. As Anglos packed up and fled the territory, he imagined he had driven them out forever. Little did he realize that his campaign had coincided with the start of the **Civil War**, so all US forces had been withdrawn east.

Within a year, the Union army was back, led by General James Carleton (see p.517). His Apache policy was simple, though directed at first against the Mescalero rather than the Chiricahua: "All Indian men of that tribe are to be killed whenever and wherever you can find them." During the winter of 1862–63, the Mescaleros were rounded onto the **Bosque Redondo** reservation in eastern New Mexico, where they were soon joined by the Navajo (see p.194).

In 1862, Cochise's group had linked up with another Chiricahua band, the **Warm Springs** Apache of New Mexico, under the veteran **Mangas Coloradas**. The treacherous murder of Mangas Coloradas the following year, by US soldiers at Pinos Altos, where he had been invited for peace negotiations, hardened Chiricahua resolve. Over the next ten years, the US Army spent $38 million on campaigns that killed a total of a hundred Apache; the Apache meanwhile accounted for over a thousand Americans.

During this period, the name of **Geronimo** became widely feared. He was born around 1823 into the Bedonkohe subgroup of the Chiricahua Apache, near New Mexico's Gila cliff dwellings (see p.217). Named Goyahkla, "One Who Yawns," he reached adulthood without seeing a white American. After his mother, wife, and three children were killed by Mexican soldiers at Janos in northern Mexico, in 1851, he sought revenge in repeated raids on Mexico. Somehow, the Mexican battle-cry to St Jerome, "Geronimo," became the name he used for the rest of his life. Although he became a respected healer and medicine man, he was never, strictly speaking, a "chief."

In the **Camp Grant Massacre** of 1871, a Tucson-based alliance of Tohono 'O'odham Indians, Hispanics, and Anglos massacred 144 Apache – of whom no more than eight were men – supposedly under the protection of the US Army in Aravaipa Canyon, Arizona (see p.238). A public outcry back East led President Grant to adopt a new policy toward the Apache, under which the **White Mountain** (also known as the Fort Apache Indian Reservation; see p.282) and **San Carlos** (see p.238) **reservations** were established in 1872.

Any Apache who failed to present themselves at the reservations, however, were deemed renegades. **General George Crook**, ordered to hunt them down, adopted the scorched-earth strategy of "total war," developed during the Civil War. Employing White Mountain Apache scouts, on the basis that the best person to track an Apache was another Apache, he "overhauled" the Tonto Basin during the winter of 1872–73, killing five hundred Apache.

Following an uneasy truce, the Chiricahua were granted their own reservation, a small square of fifty miles in each direction that centered on what's now Chiricahua National Monument (see p.265). Within three years, however, renewed cross-border raiding after the 1874 death of Cochise caused the reservation to be disbanded. The Chiricahua were moved onto the San Carlos reservation, although they traditionally regarded the San Carlos Apache as "Bi-ni-e-Dine," or "brainless people."

In 1877, another Chiricahua leader, **Victorio**, assembled a five-hundred-strong band of Apache from the many different groups who hated life at San Carlos. A lengthy guerrilla campaign across New Mexico and West Texas resulted in a thousand more Anglo deaths before the Chiricahua were driven into Mexico and killed in Chihuahua in October 1880. The few survivors were sold into slavery.

Geronimo, who had not joined Victorio, now became the focus for dissident Apache. During the 1880s, he repeatedly burst out of the reservation and onto the warpath, with a dwindling band of followers each time. The first time was in 1881, when he passed within a few miles of Tombstone and was pursued by Wyatt Earp and his brothers. In 1883, General Crook tracked him down in the Sierra Madre in northern Mexico, and was briefly captured by the Apache before Geronimo chose instead to surrender to him.

Geronimo fled the reservation again in 1885 and surrendered to Crook once more in Mexico in 1886, on the understanding that he'd be exiled to the eastern United States for not more than two years. Before Crook could get him back to San Carlos, Geronimo got drunk and escaped yet again. Crook resigned his command, to be replaced by **General Nelson Miles**.

The Chiricahua's final five-month guerrilla campaign, in the summer of 1886, pitted 37 Apache, of whom eighteen were warriors, against five thousand soldiers, a quarter of the entire US Army. General Miles eventually managed to contact Geronimo in Mexico, and falsely told him that all the Chiricahua who remained on the reservation had been shipped to **Florida**. In despair, Geronimo **surrendered** for the fourth and final time in Skeleton Canyon, Arizona on September 3, 1886. The general's lie now became the truth. Geronimo and five hundred Chiricahua – along with the Apache scouts who had fought alongside the US Army – were indeed sent to Florida. Men and women were segregated in separate camps. In time, the Chiricahua were reunited on reservations in first

Alabama, and then Oklahoma, but Geronimo never returned to the Southwest. Among many public appearances in his later years, he rode at the head of Teddy Roosevelt's inaugural procession in 1905; he died in 1909.

In 1913, the 261 surviving Chiricahua were allowed to choose between remaining in Oklahoma or joining the Mescalero Apache in New Mexico; around two-thirds made the trip. It's thought that the Army never did round up perhaps ten Chiricahua, who stayed hidden in Mexico; free Apache were reported still to be fighting in the Sierra Madre as late as the 1930s.

The Apache today

Around twenty thousand Apache now live in the Southwest. Their largest two reservations are in Arizona: the **Fort Apache** Reservation (see p.282), which has the third highest population of all Native American reservations in the US, and the neighboring **San Carlos** Reservation (see p.238). The **Jicarilla** still live in northwest New Mexico, concentrated around Dulce (see p.174).

Visitors are most likely to come into contact with the **Mescalero Apache**, who share their lands with the descendants of the last Chiricahua in the mountains of southeast New Mexico. Among ventures here that have brought them a rare degree of economic security are the Ski Apache **ski resort** (see p.200), which the tribe bought for $1.5 million in 1962 and features the luxurious *Inn of the Mountain Gods* hotel/casino. More controversially, the Mescalero have also signed an agreement permitting the storage of high-level nuclear waste adjacent to the reservation.

Books

The following books proved useful, interesting, or entertaining during the research for this guide. A large proportion are only sold in bookstores in the Southwest itself, though they can usually be obtained online.

History and archeology

Richard Abanes *One Nation Under Gods*. Polemic but fascinating account of Mormon history from an unyielding Christian perspective, which documents some very murky goings-on during the nineteenth century.

Donald A Barclay, James H Maguire, and Peter Wild (eds) *Into the Wilderness Dream*. Gripping collection of Western exploration narratives written between 1500 and 1800; thanks to numerous little-known gems, the best of many such anthologies.

Pedro de Castañeda *The Journey of Coronado*. An invaluable historic document – the eyewitness journals of a Spaniard who accompanied Coronado into the Southwest in 1540.

Fray Angélico Chávez *My Penitente Land*. Inspirational history of Hispanic New Mexico, written by a Franciscan friar, which stresses the parallels between the New Mexican landscape and pastoral lifestyle – and soul – and both Spain and ancient Palestine.

Richard Flint *No Settlement, No Conquest*. Published in 2008, a satisfying and accessible overview of current knowledge about Coronado's epochal expedition, from an author who's written and edited several more academic volumes.

Jack D. Forbes *Apache, Navajo, and Spaniard*. An unsettling but thoroughly documented account of seventeenth-century frontier conflicts, which challenges much

received wisdom by suggesting, for example, that the Ancestral Puebloans violently displaced the Navajo along the Rio Grande.

Pat Garrett *The Authentic Life of Billy, the Kid*. "I have known the Kid personally since and during the continuance of what was known as the Lincoln County War, up to the moment of his death, of which I was the unfortunate instrument" – irresistible Western history, straight from the horse's mouth.

Rick Hendricks and John P Wilson (eds) *The Navajos in 1705*. The little-known campaign diary of Spanish soldier Roque Madrid provides the first eyewitness account of the Navajo in the Four Corners.

Paul Horgan *Great River: The Rio Grande in North American History*. Horgan's monumental study of New Mexican history makes weighty reading; his more accessible *The Centuries of Santa Fe* is a lightly fictionalized set of biographies drawn from different periods of history.

John D Lee *Mormonism Unveiled*. In his "Life and Confession," John Lee, of Lees Ferry fame, doesn't quite tell all he knows – like where he buried the gold – but there's a lot of eye-opening material in here.

Clyde A. Milner II, Carol A. O'Connor, and Martha A. Sandweiss *The Oxford History of the American West*. Fascinating essays on Western history, covering topics ranging from myths and movies to art and religion.

David Grant Noble *New Light on Chaco Canyon.* An informative overview of research into New Mexico's most important Ancestral Puebloan site.

Stephen Plog *Ancient Peoples of the Southwest.* Much the best single-volume history of the pre-Hispanic Southwest, packed with diagrams and color photographs.

Carroll L. Riley *The Kachina and the Cross.* A history of the early relations between Pueblo peoples and Hispanic colonists, highlighting how they grudgingly came to share the land of New Mexico. The same author's *Rio del Norte* traces the story of the upper Rio Grande valley from prehistoric times to the Pueblo Revolt, while his *Becoming Aztlan* explores links between the ancient Southwest and Mexico.

Joe S. Sando and Herman Agoyo (eds) *Po'pay: Leader of the First American Revolution.* A remarkable collection of essays by Pueblo Indians on the history of the Pueblo Revolt and its charismatic leader.

Thomas E. Sheridan *Arizona – A History.* Stimulating reassessment of 11,000 years of Arizona history.

Alex Shoumatoff *Legends of the American.* Anecdotal, and entertaining first-person survey of several centuries of Southwestern history.

Richard White *It's Your Misfortune and None of My Own.* Dense, authoritative, and all-embracing history of the American West, which debunks romanticization of the rugged pioneer by stressing the role of the federal government.

Charles Wilkinson *Fire on the Plateau.* This authoritative examination of the recent history of the Colorado Plateau is good on environmental and legal issues, but a bit heavy on personal reminiscence.

Native Americans

Between Sacred Mountains. Superb overview of Navajo history, culture, and politics, written by Navajo teachers and parents as a sourcebook for Navajo students.

Richard O. Clemmer *Roads in the Sky* (Westview). A history of the Hopi, with an emphasis on the twentieth century and the role of prophecy.

Nancy Yaw Davis *The Zuni Enigma.* An intriguing if ultimately unconvincing elaboration of the author's theory that a wandering group of Japanese pilgrims joined the Zuni tribe during the thirteenth century.

Angie Debo *Geronimo.* Gripping full-length biography of the Apache medicine man who led the last Native American uprising against the US Army.

Paula Richardson Fleming and Judith Lynn Luskey *The Shadow Catchers.* A history of nineteenth-century photographers of Native Americans, with some stunning images of the Hopi and Navajo.

Robert H. Keller and Michael F. Turek *American Indians and National Parks.* What happens when the federal park system appropriates land from its former indigenous inhabitants; Mesa Verde, Rainbow Bridge, and the Grand Canyon are among examples considered in detail.

Raymond Friday Locke *The Book of the Navajo.* Comprehensive history of the Navajo, from their mythic origins to the present day.

Jerry Mander *In the Absence of the Sacred.* Stimulating diatribe that pits the endurance of Native American values – with much discussion of the Hopi and Navajo – against the shortcomings of modern technology.

Robert S. McPherson *Sacred Land Sacred View*. Intriguing anthropological account of how the Navajo perceive the Four Corners region.

🏃 **David Roberts** *Once They Moved Like The Wind*. Excellent, fast-moving history of the Apache.

Polly Schaafsma (ed) *Kachinas in the Pueblo World*. Well-illustrated survey of the *kachina* cult in the Southwest (see p.178).

Stephen Trimble *The People*. Superb introduction to all the Native American groups of the Southwest, bringing the history up to the late twentieth century via contemporary interviews.

Frank Waters *The Book of the Hopi*. As authoritative an account of Hopi religion as it's possible to find, though it's said that Waters' informants were not themselves initiated into all the secrets of the *kiva*.

Travel

Edward Dolnick *Down The Great Unknown*. Deft retelling of the saga of John Wesley Powell's first Grand Canyon voyage that takes great pains to make it all intelligible to modern readers, with the analogies flowing thick and fast.

Colin Fletcher *The Man Who Walked Through Time*. Enjoyable account by the first man to hike the full length of the Grand Canyon.

Susan Shelby Magoffin *Down the Santa Fe Trail and into Mexico*. Absorbing first-person account by a trader's wife who reached Santa Fe in August 1846 in time to witness the Yankee takeover of New Mexico.

John Wesley Powell *The Exploration of the Colorado River and Its Canyons*. Powell is said to have adapted the details of his first epic journey down the Colorado – see p.433 – for public consumption, but his journals still make exhilarating reading.

Douglas Preston *Cities of Gold*. Long but very readable account of a horseback journey in the steps of Coronado, which throws a lot of light on history both ancient and modern.

David Roberts *In Search of the Old Ones*. An engaging chronicle of one man's obsession with Southwestern archeology.

🏃 **Mark Twain** *Roughing It*. This rollicking account of Twain's peregrinations across the nineteenth-century West may well be the greatest story ever told, though only his account of the Mormons is of much relevance here.

Ted J. Warner (ed) *The Domínguez-Escalante Journal*. The extraordinary diary of the two Franciscan friars who crossed Utah in 1776 in search of a new route to California, and came back via the Grand Canyon.

The contemporary Southwest

Christina Brinkley *Winner Takes All*. The bang-up-to-date story of how billionaires Steve Wynn and Kirk Kerkorian are battling to shape modern Las Vegas.

Alan Hess *Viva Las Vegas*. A beautifully illustrated survey of Las Vegas's

architectural history, throwing fascinating sidelights on the development of the city.

Shawn Levy *Rat Pack Confidential*. Enjoyable hymn to the "last great showbiz party," when Las Vegas prostrated itself at the feet of Frank Sinatra and the boys.

Scott Norris (ed) *Discovered Country.* Essays on the impact of tourism on the Southwest, with some interesting material on the repackaging of Native American culture for Anglo consumption.

William E. Riebsame (ed) *Atlas of the New West.* Absorbing, well-illustrated compendium of changes and developments in the contemporary West.

Debra Rosenthal *At the Heart of the Bomb.* Intriguing reportage of what really goes on in New Mexico's vast defense laboratories.

Hal K. Rothman *Devil's Bargains: Tourism in the Twentieth-Century American West.* Thought-provoking assessment of how tourism has shaped the modern West, which overturns many a cozy historical myth about places such as Santa Fe and Las Vegas.

Jim Stiles *Brave New World.* An idiosyncratic Moab writer lays out how tourism, though supposedly environmentally aware, has served southeast Utah no better than did mining and ranching.

Hunter S. Thompson *Fear and Loathing in Las Vegas.* Classic account of a drug-crazed journalist's lost weekend in early-1970s Vegas; what's really striking is how much further over the top Las Vegas has gone since then.

Mike Tronnes (ed) *Literary Las Vegas.* Sin City, Nevada, as seen by Tom Wolfe, Joan Didion, Noel Coward, and others.

Mike Weatherford *Cult Vegas.* Local entertainment columnist runs a loving eye over Las Vegas's music and movie scene; both Elvis and Sinatra get their own chapters.

Chris Wilson *The Myth of Santa Fe.* Eye-opening and very detailed account of how the Santa Fe known to tourists today is largely a twentieth-century concoction.

Environment and natural history

Edward Abbey *Desert Solitaire.* Abbey's classic evocation of his year as a ranger at Arches National Park was the first of his many volumes championing the wildernesses of the Southwest.

Donald L. Baars *A Traveler's Guide to the Geology of the Colorado Plateau.* Among the more readily comprehensible explanations of the geology of the Four Corners.

Philip L. Fradkin *A River No More* (University of California Press). The story of the Colorado River, from John Wesley Powell to the water-management issues of today.

Michael P. Ghiglieri and Thomas M. Myers *Over The Edge: Death in Grand Canyon.* In their bid to account for the demise of every single person known to have died within the Grand Canyon, the authors transcend the merely morbid to throw fascinating light on every aspect of the canyon's history, and provide masses of useful advice on how to avoid becoming another fatality. The morbid stuff's good, too.

Russel Martin *A Story That Stands Like A Dam* (Henry Holt, US only). Meticulously chronicled indictment of the West's last great dam, which inundated Glen Canyon in the 1960s.

Lisa Michaels *Grand Ambition.* Gripping novelistic reconstruction of a true-life romantic mystery; just what did happen to honeymooners Glen and Bessie Hyde in the winter of 1928, when they tried to row down the Grand Canyon?

Barbara J. Morehouse *A Place Called Grand Canyon*. Fascinating academic analysis of how the Grand Canyon has been defined and exploited.

John A. Murray *Cinema Southwest*. A critical, well illustrated overview of the long history of movies filmed in the Southwest, with plenty of location information.

🏃 **Marc Reisner** *Cadillac Desert*. The damning saga of the twentieth-century damming of the West.

Raye C. Ringholz *Uranium Frenzy*. Lively account of the 1950s uranium boom on the Colorado Plateau, with plenty of hard-hitting material on the health consequences for the miners.

🏃 **Jeremy Schmidt** *Grand Canyon National Park – A Natural History Guide*. A superb single-volume account of the Grand Canyon's environment, ecology, and geological origins.

Bette L. Stanton *Where God Put The West*. Photo-packed history of moviemaking in Monument Valley and Moab.

Ann Zwinger *Wind in the Rock*. An inveterate canyoneer's account of the natural history of southeast Utah.

Fiction

Edward Abbey *The Monkey Wrench Gang*. Classic wishful thinking from the wilderness advocate, this fast-paced novel centers on plans by environmental saboteurs to destroy the Glen Canyon dam.

🏃 **Willa Cather** *Death Comes for the Archbishop*. Not as sensational as the title implies, but a magnificent evocation of the landscapes and cultures of nineteenth-century New Mexico. Cather's *The Professor's House* features an extended account of the discovery of Ancestral Puebloan remains on a remote New Mexican mesa.

Natalie Goldberg *Banana Rose*. Taos-based creative-writing guru – her *Wild Mind* and *Writing Down the Bones* have inspired countless would-be writers – practices what she preaches in this evocative novel, set partly in New Mexico.

Zane Grey *Riders of the Purple Sage*. Gloriously purple prose, first published in 1912, from the doyen of Western writers.

Tony Hillerman *A Thief of Time*, *The Dark Wind*, and several others.

The late Tony Hillerman wrote around a dozen entertaining, intricately plotted detective novels set on and around the Navajo Nation, all packed with fascinating detail about Navajo, Hopi, and Zuni culture and beliefs.

🏃 **Barbara Kingsolver** *Pigs in Heaven*. A magnificent evocation of tensions and realities in the contemporary Southwest, by a Tucson-based writer who ranks among America's finest prose stylists.

Cormac McCarthy *Blood Meridian*. A disturbing portrayal of the West in all its bloody reality – the scenes at Yuma Crossing are horrendous – if a tad macho for some tastes.

N. Scott Momaday *House Made of Dawn Time*. Pulitzer Prize-winning novel, written by a Kiowa Indian, about the spiritual crisis of a young Pueblo Indian.

John Nichols *The Milagro Beanfield War*. Thanks to the Robert Redford movie, this entertaining saga of a water-rights rebellion by dispossessed Hispanic villagers in northern New Mexico is the best known of

Nichols' *New Mexico* trilogy (the others are *The Magic Journey* and *The Nirvana Blues*).

🏃 **Michael Ondaatje** *The Collected Works of Billy the Kid*. Slim volume of poetry and contemporary accounts which add up to an evocative picture of New Mexico's most famous tearaway.

Simon J. Ortiz *Men on the Moon*. Evocative contemporary short stories by an Ácoma Indian poet.

Leslie Marmon Silko *Almanac of the Dead*. Epic novel, by a Laguna Pueblo Indian, of a Native American mother searching for her lost child on the fringes of the Tucson underworld; look out also for Silko's *Ceremony*.

Glossary

adobe Construction material, consisting of bricks of mud, sand, and grass or straw, and by extension a building itself; see p.117.

Anasazi Term formerly used for the ancient people of the Four Corners region; see p.495.

anticline Geological term for a dome or ridge shoved upwards by subterranean bulging.

arroyo Flat, often dry desert streambed.

atlatl Spear-throwing device – a sort of detachable, lever-like handle that gave extra power and accuracy – used by ancient Native Americans.

backcountry Term used particularly in national parks to signify wilderness areas that cannot be reached by road (as opposed, occasionally, to frontcountry).

bulto or **santo bulto** Carved wooden statue of a saint, characteristic of Hispanic New Mexico.

butte A flat-topped outcrop of rock that's taller than it is wide, usually formed by the erosion of a larger mesa.

casita Cottage, now applied mainly to individual guest accommodations in upmarket B&Bs.

cuesta Long sloping mesa terminated by an abrupt bluff.

desert varnish A natural veneer, caused by leaching minerals, that accretes on exposed rock faces and makes an ideal surface on which to etch petroglyphs.

genízaros In colonial New Mexico, the mixed-race offspring of captured Plains Indians and their Spanish masters.

graben narrow valleys created by the erosion of underground salt beds, from the German for "ditches".

Grand Staircase Topographical feature of southwest Utah, stretching from the Grand Canyon to Bryce Canyon; see p.5.

Great House Archeological term for a defensively oriented, multistory ancient pueblo with hundreds of rooms, as seen at Chaco Canyon; see p.102.

Great Kiva Archeological term for a *kiva* that was used by an entire community rather than an individual clan or family.

heishi Necklace of threaded disks, usually cut from seashells, as made originally by Ancestral Puebloans and now by Santo Domingo Pueblo.

Hisatsinom The Hopi name for their Ancestral Puebloan forebears.

hogan Navajo dwelling; see p.74.

Hohokam Ancient people of southern Arizona; see p.497.

hoodoo Natural sandstone formation in which a boulder is left balanced on a slender pillar, as at Bryce Canyon; see p.393.

kachina (also spelled **katsina**) "Spirit messengers," central to the religions of the Hopi and other Pueblo Indians; see p.78.

kiva chamber used for religious ceremonies by Pueblo Indians, usually located underground.

latilla Light pole used in the roof construction of adobe buildings.

LDS Abbreviation to denote the Latter-Day Saints, or Mormons.

mano Handheld stone traditionally used to grind and crush seeds.

mesa From the Spanish for "table;" a large, broad flat-topped outcrop of rock.

metate Stone slab or trough, used with a *mano* for grinding seeds.

Mimbres Ancient people of southern New Mexico, renowned for their pottery; see p.216.

Moki or **Moqui** The former name for the Hopi people of northern Arizona.

monocline an abrupt irregularity in the usual stratification of rocks, often resulting in a dramatic cliff.

Penitentes Catholic sect in nineteenth-century New Mexico; see p.157.

petroglyph Ancient rock-art image carved or pecked into stone.

pictograph Ancient rock-art image painted into stone.

Presidio Spanish term for a fortress built during the colonial period.

Pueblo Spanish word meaning "village;" applied to ancient Native American dwellings and also to modern Indian communities and peoples.

reef Word applied by early Anglo settlers to such vast natural barriers to their progress across the desert (usually created by monoclines) as Utah's Capitol Reef; see p.413.

reredos Painted altarpiece, as seen in Hispanic churches at Chimayó (see p.156) and elsewhere.

retablo Kind of Hispanic religious folk art, painted on tin or wood.

ristra Garland of chile peppers, sold as souvenirs in New Mexico.

santo In Hispanic folk art, an image or holy object.

Sinagua Ancient people of central Arizona.

sipapu In Pueblo religion, the hole through which humans reached this earth.

slickrock Pioneer term for smooth, undulating stretches of sandstone, as a rule only slick after rain.

syncline The opposite of an anticline, a syncline is a rock formation created by an underground collapse.

talus Fallen rock debris which accumulates to form slopes at the bases of cliffs and canyon walls.

viga A broad beam of ponderosa or fir, as used by the Ancestral Puebloans in roof construction, and prominent in adobe architecture today.

Small print and
Index

A Rough Guide to Rough Guides

Published in 1982, the first Rough Guide – to Greece – was a student scheme that became a publishing phenomenon. Mark Ellingham, a recent graduate in English from Bristol University, had been travelling in Greece the previous summer and couldn't find the right guidebook. With a small group of friends he wrote his own guide, combining a highly contemporary, journalistic style with a thoroughly practical approach to travellers' needs.

The immediate success of the book spawned a series that rapidly covered dozens of destinations. And, in addition to impecunious backpackers, Rough Guides soon acquired a much broader and older readership that relished the guides' wit and inquisitiveness as much as their enthusiastic, critical approach and value-for-money ethos.

These days, Rough Guides include recommendations from shoestring to luxury and cover more than 200 destinations around the globe, including almost every country in the Americas and Europe, more than half of Africa and most of Asia and Australasia. Our ever-growing team of authors and photographers is spread all over the world, particularly in Europe, the USA and Australia.

In the early 1990s, Rough Guides branched out of travel, with the publication of Rough Guides to World Music, Classical Music and the Internet. All three have become benchmark titles in their fields, spearheading the publication of a wide range of books under the Rough Guide name.

Including the travel series, Rough Guides now number more than 350 titles, covering: phrasebooks, waterproof maps, music guides from Opera to Heavy Metal, reference works as diverse as Conspiracy Theories and Shakespeare, and popular culture books from iPods to Poker. Rough Guides also produce a series of more than 120 World Music CDs in partnership with World Music Network.

Visit www.roughguides.com to see our latest publications.

Rough Guide travel images are available for commercial licensing at www.roughguidespictures.com

Rough Guide credits

Text editor: Lucy Cowie
Layout: Jessica Subramanian
Cartography: Swati Handoo
Picture editor: Harriet Mills
Production: Rebecca Short
Proofreader: Susannah Wight
Cover design: Chloë Roberts
Editorial: Ruth Blackmore, Andy Turner, Keith Drew, Edward Aves, Alice Park, Lucy White, Jo Kirby, James Smart, Natasha Foges, Róisín Cameron, Emma Traynor, Emma Gibbs, Kathryn Lane, Christina Valhouli, Monica Woods, Mani Ramaswamy, Harry Wilson, Helen Ochyra, Amanda Howard, Lara Kavanagh, Alison Roberts, Joe Staines, Peter Buckley, Matthew Milton, Tracy Hopkins, Ruth Tidball; **Delhi** Madhavi Singh, Karen D'Souza, Lubna Shaheen
Design & Pictures: **London** Scott Stickland, Dan May, Diana Jarvis, Mark Thomas, Chloë Roberts, Nicole Newman, Sarah Cummins, Emily Taylor; **Delhi** Umesh Aggarwal, Ajay Verma, Ankur Guha, Pradeep Thapliyal, Sachin Tanwar, Anita Singh, Nikhil Agarwal, Sachin Gupta
Production: Vicky Baldwin

Cartography: **London** Maxine Repath, Ed Wright, Katie Lloyd-Jones; **Delhi** Rajesh Chhibber, Ashutosh Bharti, Rajesh Mishra, Animesh Pathak, Jasbir Sandhu, Karobi Gogoi, Alakananda Bhattacharya, Deshpal Dabas
Online: **London** George Atwell, Faye Hellon, Jeanette Angell, Fergus Day, Justine Bright, Clare Bryson, Aine Fearon, Adrian Low, Ezgi Celebi, Amber Bloomfield; **Delhi** Amit Verma, Rahul Kumar, Narender Kumar, Ravi Yadav, Debojit Borah, Rakesh Kumar, Ganesh Sharma, Shisir Basumatari
Marketing & Publicity: **London** Liz Statham, Niki Hanmer, Louise Maher, Jess Carter, Vanessa Godden, Vivienne Watton, Anna Paynton, Rachel Sprackett, Libby Jellie, Laura Vipond, Vanessa McDonald; **New York** Katy Ball, Judi Powers, Nancy Lambert; **Delhi** Ragini Govind
Manager India: Punita Singh
Reference Director: Andrew Lockett
Operations Manager: Helen Phillips
PA to Publishing Director: Nicola Henderson
Publishing Director: Martin Dunford
Commercial Manager: Gino Magnotta
Managing Director: John Duhigg

Publishing information

This fifth edition published October 2009 by
Rough Guides Ltd,
80 Strand, London WC2R 0RL
14 Local Shopping Centre, Panchsheel Park, New Delhi 110017, India
Distributed by the Penguin Group
Penguin Books Ltd,
80 Strand, London WC2R 0RL
Penguin Group (USA)
375 Hudson Street, NY 10014, USA
Penguin Group (Australia)
250 Camberwell Road, Camberwell, Victoria 3124, Australia
Penguin Group (Canada)
195 Harry Walker Parkway N, Newmarket, ON, L3Y 7B3 Canada
Penguin Group (NZ)
67 Apollo Drive, Mairangi Bay, Auckland 1310, New Zealand
Cover concept by Peter Dyer.

Typeset in Bembo and Helvetica to an original design by Henry Iles.
Printed in Singapore
© Greg Ward 2009
No part of this book may be reproduced in any form without permission from the publisher except for the quotation of brief passages in reviews.
544pp includes index
A catalogue record for this book is available from the British Library
ISBN: 978-1-84836-187-4

The publishers and authors have done their best to ensure the accuracy and currency of all the information in **The Rough Guide to Southwest USA**, however, they can accept no responsibility for any loss, injury, or inconvenience sustained by any traveller as a result of information or advice contained in the guide.

1 3 5 7 9 8 6 4 2

Help us update

We've gone to a lot of effort to ensure that the fifth edition of **The Rough Guide to Southwest USA** is accurate and up-to-date. However, things change – places get "discovered", opening hours are notoriously fickle, restaurants and rooms raise prices or lower standards. If you feel we've got it wrong or left something out, we'd like to know, and if you can remember the address, the price, the hours, the phone number, so much the better.

Please send your comments with the subject line "**Rough Guide Southwest USA Update**" to ⓒmail@roughguides.com. We'll credit all contributions and send a copy of the next edition (or any other Rough Guide if you prefer) for the very best emails.

Have your questions answered and tell others about your trip at ⓦcommunity.roughguides.com

Acknowledgements

Greg Ward: Thanks to Sam Cook, as ever, for sharing it all, and especially for her boundless support and encouragement. Thanks too to Lucy Cowie at Rough Guides for all her input, and for shepherding me so painlessly through the editorial process, and to Kate Berens for her help. On the road, thanks especially to Steve Lewis in Santa Fe, Stephanie Heckathorne and Scott Dunn in Phoenix, and Marian Delay and Callie Tranter in Moab.

Readers' letters

Thanks to all the readers who have taken the time to write in with comments and suggestions (and apologies if we've inadvertently omitted or misspelt anyone's name):

Stuart and Pauline Ballard, Allison Baron, Nirmalla Barros, Sarah Boyd, Eileen Brooks, Jeff Ecker, Linda Hutjens, Jerry Muller, Nan Mutford, Jackey Phillips, Sarah Reynolds, Gwilym Shephard, Paul Symchych, John White, David Wolfenden.

SMALL PRINT

Photo credits

All photos by Greg Ward (with additional Las Vegas photos by Greg Roden) © Rough Guides except the following:

Cover
Main front picture: Grand Canyon and Colorado River © Momatiuk – Eastcott/Photolibrary.com

Introduction
p.8 Red chile peppers, Santa Fe © Greg Ward
p.10 Moccasins of a Zuni Pueblo Dancer, Gallup Inter-tribal Indian Ceremonial © North Wind Picture Archives/Photolibrary.com
p.10 Tucson city dome © Richard Paul/istockphoto
p.11 Views from Muley Point, Utah © Greg Ward
p.12 Skulls for sale, Santa Fe © Greg Ward

Things not to miss
02 Cataract Canyon, Canyonlands National Park © James Kerrick/Alamy
06 Albuquerque International Balloon Fiesta © Albuquerque International Balloon Fiesta/Marlon Long
09 La Fonda de Santa Fe © Greg Ward
12 Toroweap Point © National Parks Service
14 Zuni Pueblo Dancers, Gallup Inter-tribal Indian Ceremonial © North Wind Picture Archives/Photolibrary.com
17 Tombstone © Greg Ward
19 Durango & Silverton railroad © Robert Harding/Photolibrary.com
26 San Xavier del Bac © DK Images

28 "O", Cirque du Soleil © Tomasz Rossa/Cirque du Soleil

Pueblo peoples color section
Betatakin ruin, Navajo National Monument © Greg Ward
Ancestral Puebloan pottery, Millicent Rogers Museum © Greg Ward
Taos Pueblo © DK Images
Acoma Pueblo Dancer, Gallup Inter-Tribal Indian Ceremonial © Chuck Place/Alamy

Camera! Drive! Action! color section
Thelma and Louise © The Moviestore Collection
Easy Rider © The Moviestore Collection

Black and whites
p.56 Monument Valley © DK Images
p.63 The hike to Betatakin © Greg Ward
p.120 La Fonda de Santa Fe © Eric Swanson/La Fonda de Santa Fe
p.168 Hispanic Death Cart, Millicent Rogers Museum, Taos © Greg Ward
p.200 Billy the Kid © M L Pearson/Alamy
p.301 Verde Canyon Railroad © www.verdecanyonrr.com
p.388 Coral Pink Sand Dunes © istockphoto/Brian Hudson
p.458 Mountain biking, Slick Rock Bike Trail © Paul Morton/istockphoto.com

Index

Map entries are in color.

I

Q

R

S

W

Y

Z

Map symbols

maps are listed in the full index using colored text

-----	Chapter division boundary	⧫	General point of interest
-..-..	International border	@	Internet access
-. ..	State border	ⓘ	Tourist office
17	Interstate highway	✉	Post office
89	U.S. highway	⊞	Hospital/clinic
12	State highway	🅿	Parking
======	Dirt road/track	�	Viewpoint/overlook
}===={	Tunnel	◉	Accommodation
———	Railway	⛺	Campsite
------	Footpath	⌂	Lodge
....	Hiking trail	■	Pueblo
○——○	Tramway	∴	Ruin
———	Waterway	♀	Museum
≍	Bridge/pass	⊠-⊠	Gate
⋏⋏	Mountains	⚐	Ski area
▲	Peak	✈	Airport
⤳⤳	Gorge/canyon/cliffs	Ⓜ	Metro
⌂	Cave	▬	Building
⌒	Arch	⊞	Church
⚱	Butte	⊡	Cemetery
⚲	Waterfall	▨	Park/monument
≋	Rapids	◺	Indian reservation
⋔	Spring